Profess

DotNetN

Professional DotNetNuke® 5

Professional DotNetNuke® 5 Open Source Web Application Framework for ASP.NET

Shaun Walker
Brian Scarbeau
Darrell Hardy
Stan Schultes
Ryan Morgan

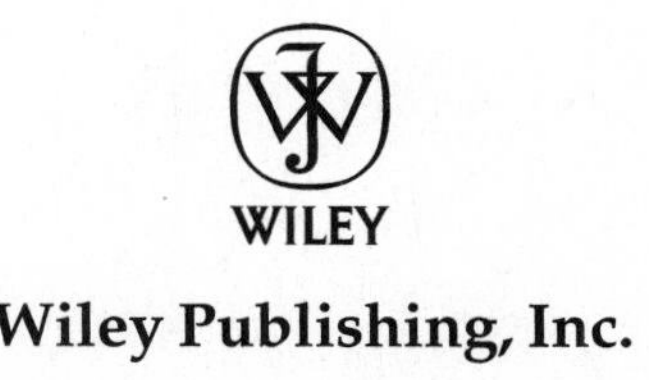

Wiley Publishing, Inc.

Professional DotNetNuke®5

Published by
Wiley Publishing, Inc.
10475 Crosspoint Boulevard
Indianapolis, IN 46256
www.wiley.com

Published by Wiley Publishing, Inc., Indianapolis, Indiana

Published simultaneously in Canada

ISBN: 978-0-470-43870-1

Manufactured in the United States of America

10 9 8 7 6 5 4 3 2 1

Library of Congress Cataloging-in-Publication Data is available from the publisher.

For general information on our other products and services please contact our Customer Care Department within the United States at (877) 762-2974, outside the United States at (317) 572-3993 or fax (317) 572-4002.

Wiley also publishes its books in a variety of electronic formats. Some content that appears in print may not be available in electronic books.

I would like to dedicate my part of this book to my parents, Sam and Virginia Hardy, my wife, Kathy Hardy, and my God, all of whom have had a major part of making me who I am and without whom my contribution to this book would not have been possible.

— Darrell Hardy

To my wonderful wife Laurie, who just smiles when I take on new projects when I'm already too busy. I'm a very lucky man! Also to my sons Tyler and Erik — both in college and making that often difficult transition to adulthood. Best of luck to you both in the coming years.

— Stan Schultes

Thank you to Jesus for saving me, my wife for being my strength, and my family and friends for always making me laugh.

— Ryan Morgan

About the Wrox DotNetNuke Series Editor

Shaun Walker (MVP, ASPInsider) is co-founder, Vice President of Engineering of DotNetNuke Corporation and chief architect of DotNetNuke. Shaun has 15 years of professional experience in architecting and implementing large-scale software solutions for private and public organizations. Shaun is the original creator and maintainer of DotNetNuke, a web application framework for ASP.NET which has spawned the largest and most successful Open Source community project on the Microsoft platform. Based on his significant community contributions he was recognized as a Microsoft Most Valuable Professional (MVP) in 2004 and an ASPInsider in 2005. He is a frequent speaker at User Groups in his local area and is a contributing author to the WROX Press books *Professional DotNetNuke 4 — Open Source Web Application Framework* and *Professional DotNetNuke ASP.NET Portals.*

About the Authors

Brian Scarbeau is a Microsoft MVP and a seasoned computer science trainer. He has his MBA and Certifications as a WebMaster and Network Instructor. He has spoken at various Code Camps about DotNetNuke® and more recently at the DotNetNuke Open Force 08 event in Orlando, FL. He has developed a DotNetNuke® curriculum and a series of webcasts for Microsoft Corporation. He was also selected by Microsoft Corporation to be part of a Faculty Advisory Board. He has traveled the United States and Canada conducting training seminars on .NET products. Presently, he is on the Board of Directors for the Computer Science Teacher's Association and he started the Orlando DotNetNuke® User Group. His blog is here: `http://geekswithblogs.net/bscarbeau`

Darrell Hardy has been designing and building data-driven applications for more than 20 years. Having spent several years working with a management consulting firm, he brings to the table not only technical expertise but also an understanding of the business side of the equation. His passion is for software that matches business processes and allows for improvements in the business process as well as the software. Currently Darrell is the Vice President of Hardy Consulting, Inc. (`http://www.hardyconsulting.com/`) and manages several domestic and international accounts. He enjoys speaking, teaching, problem solving, and helping people become problem solvers.

Stan Schultes is an Architect and Software Developer at a mid-size, high-tech manufacturing company, where he designs and builds engineering design automation systems. He has been building enterprise manufacturing software and systems for more than 25 years, and building Microsoft solutions since 1994. He has led application development teams in companies as diverse as a small startup to the Fortune 200. Stan is a Microsoft MVP in Visual Basic, a former columnist and Contributing Editor with *Visual Studio Magazine*, and has written for MSDN online. He is very active within the Microsoft developer community, and he runs or is involved in several developer groups. Stan is a prolific speaker at community events such as the Visual Studio 2008 and 2005 launch events, Day of Patterns & Practices, Code Camps, user groups, and DevDays. He has recorded nearly 20 MSDN webcasts, and is currently co-developing episodes of a developer seminar series that may end up on TV. He can be reached through his web site and blog at `http://www.VBNetExpert.com`. Stan resides in Sarasota, FL, with his family, and that's where he hangs out with his geeky friends, a bunch of beer lovers, and some fitness fanatics.

Ryan Morgan is managing partner and software architect at Arrow Consulting & Design in West Palm Beach, FL. At Arrow Consulting & Design, Ryan has designed, developed, and delivered projects for federal and local government clients, enterprise clients with global reach, and hundreds of small businesses throughout North America and Western Europe. Ryan has used his unique mix of marketing background and development expertise to help audiences learn DotNetNuke at Florida Code Camps, .NET User Groups, and webcasts at http://www.ArrowNuke.com. Ryan also writes a DotNetNuke consulting blog at http://www.DotNetNukeConsulting.Wordpress.com, a DotNetNuke skinning blog at http://www.dotnetnuke-skin.blogspot.com, and a development blog at http://www.ArrowNuke.com.

About the Technical Editors

Philip Beadle (MCAD, MVP) is a founding member of the DotNetNuke Core Team, a Microsoft Certified Application Developer, and is experienced in the development and commercial application of the DotNetNuke framework based on Microsoft's .NET technology. He has successfully developed and implemented sites for clients in Australia and overseas and was recently awarded the Microsoft Most Valuable Professional (MVP) award in ASP/ASP.NET. Philip is a regular contributor to online technical lists and communities and is a sought-after speaker at technology conferences and .NET User Groups such as the Victoria .Net Users Group (http://www.victoriadotnet.com.au/index.aspx?link_id=84). He recently completed the MSDN update tour for Australia and New Zealand and presented at Microsoft's Tech Ed 2005. Philip is employed as a Senior Consultant by Readify (http://readify.com.au/Default.aspx?tabid=1), which is a group of elite consultants, specializing in technical readiness, who help organizations evolve with emerging Microsoft technologies, keeping them a step ahead of their competitors.

Jon Henning is a senior consultant with Solution Partners Inc. (http://www.solpart.com), a Chicago-based consulting company specializing in Microsoft technologies. He is an MCSD who has been working with Visual Studio .NET since the PDC release. Though he has written several articles dealing with all aspects of programming, his current love is the development of rich client-side functionality. With the introduction of DotNetNuke v3, Jon initiated the development of the DotNetNuke ClientAPI, which enabled developers to write rich client-side cross-browser logic against a simple API. The use of this API can be found throughout DotNetNuke, including the DotNetNuke Suite of web controls found at http://webcontrols.dotnetnuke.com. More recently he has provided DotNetNuke AJAX Module templates that utilize both new functionality in the ClientAPI and the Microsoft AJAX Framework at http://www.codeplex.com/codeendeavortemplate. Jon resides in Aurora, IL, with his wife Holly, and two children, Kyle and Carter.

Charles Nurse (MVP) has been developing software for more than 25 years. He is currently Senior Architect for DotNetNuke Corporation and has been a DotNetNuke developer for more than 6 years, the last 4.5 years as a Trustee of the project. His primary role on the DotNetNuke Project is as a Core Developer. A native of Bristol, England, he obtained a Bachelor of Arts in Chemistry from Oxford University. In 1978, he moved to Canada to continue his studies at the University of British Columbia where he obtained a Ph.D. (also in chemistry), and where he met his wife Eileen. More recently (2003) he completed a Post Baccalaureate Certificate in Object Technology Programming at Simon Fraser University. In 2007 he was made a Microsoft ASP.NET MVP and in 2008 he was elected to be a member of the ASPInsiders group. He has spoken at a number of conferences (Software Developers Conference, DevConnections, DevTeach) and User Groups, and has acted as Technical Advisor for two DotNetNuke-related books. He has a blog at http://www.charlesnurse.com. He lives in Langley, BC, Canada with his wife and two adult children, both students at Simon Fraser University.

Will Strohl is an ASP.NET architect and developer based in the Orlando area. Having been in the web development field for more than 10 years, he began professionally in 2000. Currently, Will is the Technology Director for an exciting new online travel company called RezHub.com. He is also an active member and President of the Orlando DotNetNuke Users Group, and a member of the reformed DotNetNuke

Media Module Project Team. He regularly speaks at local events about DotNetNuke and the various ways it can be used and managed. Most recently, Will has been publishing DNN videos on JumptStartTV.

Lorraine Young (DNNangel) works as a freelance consultant and maintains a web site at `http://www.dnnangel.com`. She has extensive experience in developing user documentation, and provides training and support for DotNetNuke applications. She is the primary author of the Wiley Press *DotNetNuke for Dummies* book as well as a number of *DotNetNuke User Manuals*, which are available from the DotNetNuke Marketplace. She also created and maintains the free DotNetNuke Online Help resource. Lorraine is a founding member of the DotNetNuke Core Team and a member of the Help project team. She holds a Bachelor of Arts degree in Professional Writing and Literature and a Post Graduate degree in Orientation and Mobility for vision-impaired adults and children.

Credits

Development Editor
Christopher J. Rivera

Production Editor
Rebecca Coleman

Copy Editor
Kim Cofer

Editorial Manager
Mary Beth Wakefield

Production Manager
Tim Tate

Vice President and Executive Group Publisher
Richard Swadley

Vice President and Executive Publisher
Barry Pruett

Associate Publisher
Jim Minatel

Project Coordinator, Cover
Lynsey Stanford

Proofreader
Amy Morales, Word One New York

Indexer
Jack Lewis

Senior Technical Editor
Charles Nurse

Technical Editors
Philip Beadle
Jon Henning
Will Strohl
Lorraine Young

Acknowledgments

It has been a pleasure working with a dedicated team of professionals while putting together the chapters in this book. Many thanks to Charles Nurse from the DotNetNuke Core Team who answered all of our technical questions relating to this new version. A special thanks to the Orlando DotNetNuke President, Will Strohl, for his input. Thanks to the Wrox team of editors for their hard work of making each chapter better with their edits. Thanks to all who have contributed to make DotNetNuke the number one web portal that it is.

Finally, thanks to my wife Cathy for her patience, encouragement, and support.

— *Brian Scarbeau*

Contents

Introduction

DotNetNuke version 5 is a web application framework built utilizing ASP.NET and allowing for the easy creation of web sites. The system can be used as is or you can leverage the many capabilities of the platform to develop your own custom ASP.NET web applications. This book is aimed at people with development knowledge and those who are just interested in learning more about how DotNetNuke works.

Who This Book Is For

This book is for the nondeveloper or administrator who wants to dive into the exciting DotNetNuke framework. It is also for experienced ASP.NET developers who want to use DotNetNuke to build dynamic ASP.NET sites or create add-ins to DotNetNuke.

Experienced developers of ASP.NET and those who are knowledgeable about DotNetNuke may want to skip Chapters 1–6. These chapters provide an overview of DotNetNuke and its operations. Chapters 7–17 tackle DotNetNuke architecture and development. However, you'll gain valuable insight into how DotNetNuke works by reading the entire book from front to back.

What This Book Covers

The content of this book is logically divided into three sections. The first section explores the history of the project, demonstrates how to install DotNetNuke on the server, and explains how to manage and administer a DotNetNuke portal and the standard modules included out of the box. The second section explores how the application works through the DotNetNuke application architecture and its major Application Programming Interfaces (APIs), including the core application, member role, and client (AJAX) APIs. The final section of the book demonstrates how you can extend the portal framework by developing and distributing modules that plug into a DotNetNuke portal. This section also looks at how to localize your modules to languages besides English, and examines the flexible skinning capabilities of DotNetNuke and how you can create a unique look for your portal.

How This Book Is Structured

Chapter 1: An Inside Look at the Evolution of DotNetNuke. Learn the past, present, and future of DotNetNuke.

Chapter 2: Installing DotNetNuke. This chapter reviews the installation process of the available packages that come with DotNetNuke (DNN). DNN has simplified the installation process by including an automated installer. There are four packages to choose when you consider installing DotNetNuke. The Installation Package contains only the files needed for a runtime deployment to a web server. The Source

Package contains everything, including full application source code. The Starter Kit Package contains the files needed to configure a development environment in Visual Web Developer Express, which is a free tool for creating and working with ASP.NET web applications or Visual Studio 2005/2008. You can also use SQL Express for your database. All of these are free from Microsoft Corporation. The Upgrade Package contains only the files needed for an upgrade of an existing installation.

Chapter 3: Portal Overview. DotNetNuke portals contain four main organization elements that are examined in this chapter. They are parent/child portals, pages, panes, and containers.

Chapter 4: Portal Administration. This chapter covers in detail the role of an administrator using DotNetNuke as a web portal.

Chapter 5: Host Administration. The host has the main responsibility of controlling the installation of DotNetNuke, the creation of portals, the assignment of administrators, and the uploading of skins and modules. The host is a major player in the DotNetNuke world, and this chapter reviews the features of DotNetNuke important to the host.

Chapter 6: Modules. This chapter explores how to use the functionality available to portal administrators through modules. It explores the concept and use of modules in a DotNetNuke portal and covers managing modules' layouts and settings to control the display of modules on a page. The chapter also covers all of the core modules that are included with DotNetNuke and how to use them.

Chapter 7: DotNetNuke Architecture. This chapter explores the history, structure, and foundation of the DotNetNuke application. You will see how the design patterns and practices used, along with the key building blocks of the application, make DotNetNuke an extremely extensible application framework. Topics covered include DotNetNuke's extensive use of the Provider Pattern, application layers, security model, and general organization structure of the framework.

Chapter 8: Core DotNetNuke APIs. In this chapter, you discover many of the core APIs that provide the true power behind DotNetNuke. By leveraging these common APIs, you will be able to extend the DotNetNuke application framework in almost any direction by extending or replacing core functionality without touching the original source code base.

Chapter 9: Member Role. This chapter explains how and why DotNetNuke uses the Microsoft ASP.NET Membership Management Component. You see how DotNetNuke leverages the benefits of using the functionality provided by the MemberRole.dll without giving up existing additional functionality provided by the DotNetNuke framework. This understanding will help you to be able to integrate DotNetNuke into your existing membership structures by modifying or replacing the Membership, Profile, Roles, and Authentication providers.

Chapter 10: Client API. This chapter introduces the Client API. You learn that the Client API is a combination of both server-side and client-side code that work together to enable a simple and reliable interface for developers to provide a rich client-side experience. By leveraging the Client API, developers will be taking advantage of a structured set of solutions to common development challenges in providing rich client-side experiences. An additional benefit is that the Client API will also limit the learning curve for providing this type functionality.

Chapter 11: Localization. In this chapter, you learn to use the core localization API in the DotNetNuke framework. Developers will learn how to replace hard-coded text with dynamic strings using local resource files as a repository for language-specific text. The chapter also covers the new token replacement engine available to developers.

Chapter 12: Beginning Module Development. This chapter covers a wide variety of topics related to custom module development. The first section asks a few business questions related to module development, and continues with a discussion of custom module types, platform choices, and Visual Studio project types. The next section introduces module development, provides an overview of the sample WROX.Suggestion custom module, and walks through the configuration process for DotNetNuke and Visual Studio custom module development. It also outlines how to build a custom module from scratch using the DotNetNuke Starter Kit. The final section briefly discusses the DNN 5 module architecture and the direction the project is taking in the future.

Chapter 13: Developing Modules: the Database Layer. This chapter covers in detail all aspects of building your module's data layer, using the sample WROX.Suggestion module as an example. First, the physical database design is presented, detailing the table layouts and stored procedures. Next, the SQL Server data provider code is examined to see how a concrete (database specific) data layer implementation is created. Finally, a walkthrough of the data abstraction (database independent) layer finishes up the data layer discussion.

Chapter 14: Developing Modules: the Business Logic Layer. This chapter starts with the business object classes for the sample WROX.Suggestion module that store info as it moves between the application and database, including the optional IHydratable interface that you can implement to speed up data transfer operations. Next are the business controller classes, which are responsible for loading and managing the business object classes, including the optional ISearchable and IPortable interfaces that handle portal search and module import/export operations, respectively.

Chapter 15: Developing Modules: the Presentation Layer. This chapter covers the user controls that implement the WROX.Suggestion module user interface, including two View controls, the Settings control, and the module Edit control. At appropriate points in the chapter, a series of important topics are introduced including CSS styling, language localization and display string resources, user control base classes, the IActionable interface for defining menu commands, using module settings, and the reusable DotNetNuke user controls. Finally, a section on DNN Helper functions including error handling and navigation URLs rounds out the discussion of building your module's user interface.

Chapter 16: Skinning DotNetNuke. In this chapter, designers will learn how to use the DotNetNuke skinning engine to turn graphic designs into functional templates for DotNetNuke web sites. The examples focus on pure CSS layout techniques to create contemporary skins that use web standards to produce accessible and search engine optimized web sites. You also learn how to use features that are new in DotNetNuke 5 such as client-side widgets, Super Stylesheets, and the Yahoo! YUI CSS framework.

Chapter 17: Distribution. This chapter wraps up the development chapters with the new extensions model for distributing and installing add-ons for DotNetNuke. The new version of the framework introduces a unified model for all extensions to DotNetNuke, including skins, modules, libraries, authentication systems, and language packs. You learn about the new unified model for packaging extensions for distribution and explore the manifest file format for managing the packages.

Chapter 18: DotNetNuke's Commercial Evolution. This chapter looks briefly at the future of DotNetNuke and its impact on business.

What You Need to Use This Book

To install and test DotNetNuke you need any of Windows 2003/2008 Server, Windows Vista, or Windows XP (the latter two for development only). This book covers a basic install of DotNetNuke using a SQL Server database as the data provider. You must have access to SQL Server 2000/2005/2008 or the SQL Express Editions (development only) on the same machine or remotely over the network. To participate in the development chapters, you need Visual Studio 2008/2005 or the free Visual Web Developer 2008/2005. DotNetNuke 5 runs on the .NET Framework 2.0 and above.

DotNetNuke Corporation

Shaun Walker *see "About the Wrox DotNetNuke Series Editor."*

Nik Kalyani (MVP) is the Director of Products & Strategy, Co-Founder of DotNetNuke Corporation. Nik is a successful entrepreneur committed to the business of technology. His previous venture, Speerio, was built upon the valuable experience he gained developing and growing his prior two software companies. Nik is proficient in many areas of software development and strives to create the highest quality software. Nik is a marketing leader, user experience specialist, and evangelist. He blogs at TechBubble.

Joe Brinkman (MVP) is Technical Fellow, Co-Founder of DotNetNuke Corporation. With more than 25 years of experience in software development and network administration and a Computer Science degree from the United States Naval Academy, Joe brings a broad range of experience and expertise in a variety of software and hardware architectures. He has been actively involved with the DotNetNuke project since the early days of 2003, was a founding Core Team and Board of Directors member and co-authored two bestselling Wrox books on DotNetNuke. Joe has been a Microsoft MVP for ASP.NET for the past two years and during his off time likes making sawdust in his woodshop, chasing a little white ball around a golf course, or spending a quiet afternoon in a movie theater with his wife, Gloria.

Scott Willhite (MVP) is the Director of Community Relations, Co-Founder of DotNetNuke Corporation. His technology pedigree is distinguished, including Bachelor of Science in Computer Science and MBA with honors in Information Systems Management degrees from Baylor University. As former Senior Manager and Technical Architect for Andersen Consulting (now Accenture), acting CTO and VP of Technology for 10x Labs, and Program Director for Safeco's Office of the CIO, Scott has architected, developed systems, and managed organizations using technologies ranging from COBOL to Java and .NET, solving real-world business problems in industries from energy and banking to healthcare. He has co-authored two DotNetNuke books with Wrox Press and *DotNetNuke for Dummies* for Wiley. Scott is an active member of his local community, organizing business support through the West Seattle Junction Association, raising money for local charities and schools, and leading community groups for Mars Hill Church. He is a proud father of 12-year-old Kyle and loving husband to his inspiration, Allison.

Core Team Members & Trustees

Cathal Connolly (MCSD, MVP) is an independent consultant based in Belfast, Northern Ireland. He's worked a wide gamut of technologies from COBOL to Java to .NET. Cathal is a long-time member of the Core Team, and also serves as the Security Lead for the project.

Steve Fabian (MVP) (`http://www.Gooddogs.com`) has been designing and developing software solutions for 19 years. In addition to programming in more than a dozen different languages, Steve is proficient in graphics and web design and for the past few years has focused on user interface design, .NET development (both client and browser based), and most recently, DotNetNuke. Gooddogs.com provides both free and custom skins for the DotNetNuke community as well as the free Gooddogs Repository Module for DotNetNuke. Steve lives in New Jersey with his wife and his five dogs, Kahlua, Amaretto, Sambucca, Daiquiri, and Whiskey. In his extremely limited free time, Steve and his wife do volunteer work for BARKS, an animal rescue shelter in Byram, NJ.

Jon Henning *see "About the Technical Editors."*

Vicenç Masanas (MVP) is the principal at Disgrafic (`http://www.disgrafic.com`), a software consultancy company based in Banyoles, Spain, specializing in web development and design on the DotNetNuke platform. Vicenç has been a member of the DotNetNuke Core Team since 2003 where he serves as a core developer. He is also responsible for the Localization and Globalization efforts for the DotNetNuke platform. Vicenç is also the publisher of the dnnJungle web site (`http://www.dnnjungle.vmasanas.net`) where he provides community support for DotNetNuke, free modules, developer tools, and highly acclaimed templates for DotNetNuke development since DotNetNuke version 2.x.

Charles Nurse *see "About the Technical Editors."*

Chris Paterra is a Lead Architect for AppTheory (`http://www.apptheory.com`), located in Atlanta, GA. Since 2003 Chris has been actively involved with the DotNetNuke project as a founding Core Team member. In 2004, Chris officially released the Core Forum module as the first official DotNetNuke module project, which he still actively maintains. For his involvement in the community, Chris has been rewarded with a Microsoft MVP for ASP.NET since 2007. Chris has also written several magazine articles and is a contributing author to Wiley's *DotNetNuke for Dummies* as well as the Wrox Press book *Professional DotNetNuke 4 — Open Source Web Application Framework.*

Core Team Members

Bryan Andrews, Founder and President of AppTheory (est 2000), has worked in various capacities in Marketing and Technology and has been involved with internet related technologies since 1994. During his years at Cox Communications he served as Program Manager, Knowledge Management Services Group and headed a team that managed all external and internal web initiatives including Cox.com and CoxIntranet. He worked many years as CTO of Trend Influence (a sister division) before taking the role of President for AppTheory. Bryan is active in the open source development community and is a Core Team Member of the DotNetNuke open source project. He was a member of the AspElite (previously AspFriends/AspAces), and a moderator and member of the AspAdvice mentoring community. He also serves on the Tenet Healthcare/Atlanta Medical Center Institutional Review Board for Ethical Human Research.

Erik van Ballegoij (MVP) of Apollo Software (`http://www.apollo-software.nl`) holds a master's degree in economics, and started developing web applications in 1997. After having built a few custom CMS applications, he switched to DotNetNuke in 2004. In early 2005, he developed a few of the first multilingual solutions for DotNetNuke. Erik's responsibilities within the Core Team are Project Lead for the Announcement module, and Core Team sponsor for the Events, Chat, and Links modules. Furthermore, Erik is also board member of the Dutch DotNetNuke User Group, with more than 1500 members, one of the largest DNN User Groups, and is also an active member of the Dutch-based Software Development Network (SDN). In 2007 and 2008 he was awarded Microsoft MVP.

Philip Beadle *see "About the Technical Editors."*

Stefan Cullmann is the head of the IT department of a technical association, based in Berlin, Germany. He is a graduate engineer for medical physics with a fable for software development. Stefan wrote his first lines of Basic code on a Sinclair ZX81 in 1981. DotNetNuke has turned into his favorite tool for running public web sites over the past years. As requirements forced him to enhance the platform on his own, Stefan took the chance to join a project team. Today Stefan is engaged within the IFrame, XML, and UserDefinedTable projects. Stefan loves to use XML and XSL everywhere possible. He prefers code generation instead of rewriting and he often goes hunting bugs with passion.

Salar Golestanian specializes in Skinning and UI, working solely in the DotNetNuke environment. He is currently targeting clients wanting content management solutions, and has years of creative design experience. Salar is working on a number of projects based on the DotNetNuke platform. The links to various projects and showcases are available on salaro.com. Salar's background is in Internet technology using Microsoft tools. He has a Bachelor of Science and MPhil in Physics. He lives with his fiancée and daughter near London, UK.

Chris Hammond is the VP of Training Services with Engage Software in St. Louis, MO. Having worked with DNN since its inception, Chris has solidified his role within the community as a leading expert on the platform by presenting at conferences and user groups around the world and is a member of the INETA Speaker's Bureau. As a DotNetNuke Core Team member, Chris has been able to provide community support to users all across the globe. Chris founded the St. Louis DotNetNuke User Group. In the little free time he has, Chris participates in the Sports Car Club of America, including autocross and club racing, and he manages multiple community portals relating to those efforts. You can read more about Chris on his blog at `http://www.chrishammond.com`.

Sebastian Leupold (MVP) is responsible for overseeing the team's module release process and co-lead for the User Defined Table project. Additionally, Sebastian creates and maintains German language packs for the DotNetNuke framework and modules. He is co-founder of the German DotNetNuke User Group and the European Network of DotNetNuke Professionals. Sebastian is CEO of gamma concept, a solutions company specializing in developing database-driven software for PC and web, which is part of dnnWerk, a compound of leading DotNetNuke experts in Germany. After studying economics and business engineering at Karlsruhe University, Sebastian acquired professional experience in software applications for about 18 years and became Microsoft MVP in 2007.

Mauricio Márquez has managed the ITC department of the United Nations in Bolivia (UNDP) since 1998 and has been developing software since the age of 15. He studied information technology in university and became an enthusiastic developer upon graduation. Discovering DNN when it was still called IBuySpy Workshop, Mauricio has made DotNetNuke the standard platform for every new application in his department. He is the lead for the ever popular FCKeditor™ provider project and also hosts a site dedicated to DNN with some well-known, very useful, and free tools for localization and optimization in the DNN platform (`http://dnn.tiendaboliviana.com`). One of his projects is his own intranet where he included a large number of custom modules as well as new emerging technologies like AJAX. The main module for his intranet has now more than 500 .ascx files.

Shawn Mehaffie (MCAD) has 18 years of programming experience, and has worked with .NET (VB.NET, ASP.NET, and C#) since it was released. He was on a team that wrote a Payment Engine web service as part of the Microsoft .NET Blaze program. As a side job, Shawn owns his own company, PC Resources, LLC (`http://www.pcresourcesllc.com/`). Shawn has been a part of the DotNetNuke community since v1.0 and currently uses DotNetNuke to create web sites for his customers (non-profit organizations, churches, and small businesses). Shawn is the Testing Team Leader and he helps administer the issue tracking application. Shawn is excited about the positive contributions his team can have on future releases of DotNetNuke. Shawn lives in Blue Springs, Missouri with his lovely wife Josephine and their two sons (Austin and Tyler). Shawn supports a great mentoring ministry called "Saving Our Boys" by donating his time to maintain their web site (`http://www.savingourboys.net`). He also supports "Autism Speaks" (`http://www.autismspeaks.org/`), which helps spread the word about autism.

Andrew Nurse is in his final year of Computing Science at Simon Fraser University in Vancouver, Canada, and has done DotNetNuke development work for Perpetual Motion Interactive Systems, Inc. He has been programming since a young age thanks to the support and teaching of his father, Charles (who is also a Core Team member). Andrew has experience in VB.NET, C#, Java, and Microsoft SQL Server and has developed custom DNN modules for Data Reporting, Engineering Project Management, Software Test Case Management, and more. He is currently the Project Lead on the DotNetNuke Reports module. Andrew recently completed two internships at Microsoft, first on the Visual Studio team, and second on the ASP.NET team.

Leigh Pointer has spent more than a decade managing dynamic, complicated solutions for clients, providing guidance and understanding. His skills in user interaction design are goal directed, which enables him to keep the client and the user in focus and happy. When organizations ask him for help, he immediately starts working to clarify their goals, and then tailors an engagement to meet their needs. Leigh is a Core Team member of the DotNetNuke project, which he also consults on, and can manage the process from installation to go live, whether the solution is Internet or intranet. Leigh is constantly designing and developing new modules for DotNetNuke, giving even more added functionality to what is already in the box. He is also the founder of the Netherlands and European DNN user groups and worked closely with Microsoft to achieve this. His passion is the community and will assist in any way to make a new community happen.

Michael Washington (MVP) is a web site developer and an ASP.NET, C#, and Visual Basic programmer. He is has been named Microsoft MVP in ASP.NET for two straight years. He is a DotNetNuke Core Team member and has served for more than three years. Michael is the author of the module development chapter in *Building Websites with VB.NET and DotNetNuke 4* (Packt Publishing). He has authored more than 100 pages of tutorials on his site covering subjects such as Linq, Silverlight, WCF, and Web Services. One of the founding members of the Southern California DotNetNuke Users Group (`http://www.socaldug.org`), Michael is also the author of "The DotNetNuke 4 Module Development Guide" as well as numerous DotNetNuke modules. He has a son, Zachary, and resides in Los Angeles with his wife Valerie.

Lorraine Young *see "About the Technical Editors."*

Project Team Leaders

Antonio Chagoury is the CEO and Chief Software Architect of Inspector IT Inc (`http://www.inspectorit.com`), a .NET and DotNetNuke solutions provider based in the Washington, DC, Metro Area. As a member of the DotNetNuke Core Team and Project Lead of the Blog module as well as the Installer utility, he is an active contributor and supporter of DotNetNuke and Open Source. Antonio is the co-founder and President of the Capital DotNetNuke User Group (`http://www.capitaldug.org`), an effort intended to get DotNetNuke enthusiasts in one room once a month to discuss a wide range of topics as well as share ideas, knowledge, and experience on the platform. His technical specialties range from Enterprise Software Architecture and Engineering, Business Systems Integrations, SOA, and of course all development based on the .NET Framework. He considers DotNetNuke Software Development and Consulting, Web 2.0, Office 2.0, and Enterprise 2.0 his hobbies. Antonio has lived and travelled extensively in Europe, Africa, and the Middle East and settled in the Washington, DC, area in 1999. He speaks English, Italian, French, Spanish, Portuguese, and Arabic. He blogs (in English) regularly at `http://www.cto20.com`. Antonio is the author of Wrox's ''Building a Custom DotNetNuke Membership Provider'' (Wrox Blox).

Mitchel Sellers (MCITP, MCPD) is the CEO of IowaComputerGurus Inc, a Microsoft Certified Partner that specializes in solutions using the .NET and DotNetNuke development frameworks. As an active member in the development community you will often find Mitchel writing articles for various online and print resources including his personal blog (`http://www.mitchelsellers.com`), posting to one of many forums, or speaking at events such as user groups or conferences. Mitchel is the author of Wrox's *Professional DotNetNuke Module Programming* and is also the Project Lead for the Documents module project. Through IowaComputerGurus, Mitchel also offers many free DotNetNuke modules, all available via their site (`http://www.iowacomputergurus.com`). These well-refined and modules have been adopted by a large number of users across the DotNetNuke community and all receive regular updates to add new features. Mitchel lives in Des Moines, IA. For more information, please visit his personal site.

Kevin Schreiner is the Chief Software Architect for R2Integrated, a US-based digital marketing/advertising and technology firm with a broad focus of expertise. He is the key engineer behind popular DotNetNuke modules including GoMap, NukeDK, ListX, and Open Web Studio, the open source development platform. Within the DotNetNuke community he is the Project Lead for DotNetNuke Map.

Ernst Peter Tamminga has been active in the IT field for more than 20 years. He is CEO of XCESS expertise center b.v., a Microsoft Gold Certified Partner, specializing in custom IT solutions for mid-size companies. As a speaker at numerous Developers conferences, he combines experience in development with his role as business owner of a mid-size commercial IT service organization. Ernst Peter is Project Lead of the Events team.

Peter Donker completed his PhD in 1999 at the University of Technology in Delft, The Netherlands entitled ''SCAFFOLD: Structuring Communication in the Architectural Forum For Online Design,'' which examined the communication process during the design process and proposed ways to improve this using IT. After Delft he left for Enschede, where he worked for three years at the Telematica Instituut (`http://www.telin.nl`) to continue research in ICT and human collaboration. His focus was knowledge management. For personal reasons in 2002 he left for Switzerland. In late 2003 he ran into DotNetNuke while working on an intranet project. Realizing its potential, he started his own company Bring2mind (`http://www.bring2mind.net`), which now specializes in Document Management on the DNN framework.

Alex Shirley has a BSc Honours Degree in Business Information Systems and is a chartered member of the British Computer Society. Presently he helps a group of businesses build, implement, and maintain web sites/intranets using the DotNetNuke platform in London, United Kingdom. In addition, he improves business workflow/processes around technology-based solutions, and has a background as a Windows systems administrator and as ASP.NET developer/DBA. He can be contacted through `http://www.yourwebsitenow.net`. His primary role in the DotNetNuke project is to maintain and validate outstanding issues logged at `http://support.dotnetnuke.com`.

David Dyer works as a senior web developer for Cybreze Enterprises. David has been developing web applications for five years, and has been developing custom modules for DotNetNuke since version 2.

He has a bachelor's degree in Computer Science and is a Microsoft Certified Professional Web Developer. He is an active member in the Orlando DotNetNuke User Group.

Sanjay Mehrotra works as a Senior Developer and Consultant with Avanade, Inc. (`http://www.avanade.com`), a leading Microsoft Solutions Provider. He has been designing and developing software applications for more than nine years and has focused on a variety of Microsoft technologies including .NET and WPF. His current focus is in the Microsoft Dynamics space and he has been an active participant in the DotNetNuke community since its inception. Sanjay is also the author of the Oracle data provider for DotNetNuke (allows DotNetNuke to run using Oracle as the database instead of SQL Server). The data provider (AcuitiDP, `http://www.acuitisolutions.com`) has been available as a commercially supported software package right from the early days of DotNetNuke (version 2.1.2) and is continuously being updated as new versions of DotNetNuke are released. He lives in Phoenix, AZ, with his wife and son and has three huskies, which are a very important part of his family. He is an MCPD (Enterprise Applications) and holds a B.Sc. in Computer Systems/Business Management.

Stefan Kamphuis works as a Microsoft Solution Developer with Giraffe IT in The Netherlands. He started his career in IT with programming in COBOL, but turned to Microsoft's technology in 1999. He is a Microsoft MVP for ASP/ASP.NET. Stefan has been using DotNetNuke ever since the IBuySpy Workshop days and has been hooked to it ever since. He is the Team Leader for the Chat module in the DotNetNuke team. Besides that, he's a board member for the Dutch DNN User Group and is the Section Leader of the DotNetNuke Track within the largest Dutch software development community SDN, which co-hosts OpenForce Europe.

Brandon Haynes is CEO at Everysport.net Inc., which delivers enterprise resource planning, web-presence, e-commerce, and integration-related functionality to recreational facilities. It is his second successful corporate venture, the previous having been divested through private acquisition. He sits on the board of several organizations, and is a member of the DotNetNuke security team. A graduate of the University of Illinois at Urbana-Champaign — consistently ranked among the top-five computer-science programs worldwide — Brandon has a long history of intellectual curiosity and accomplishment. In addition to membership in Mensa International, he began college at the age of twelve and was (briefly) the youngest person to be enrolled at Washington University. With more than 20 years of experience in software development, Brandon feels old when forced to admit that he has built a black box, written TSRs, and developed several BBS doors. He is currently pursuing a graduate degree at Harvard University. Brandon's professional interests are currently focused on the nexus between intellectual property law, technology, and business. In his spare time he reads classic literature (pre-20th century and dystopian, please) and writes (mostly on his blog). He plays chess more often than poker, but enjoys both. He rarely writes about himself in the third person.

Timo Breumelhof leads the DotNetNuke Skinning Team. He has a degree in Design from Design Academy Eindhoven (the Netherlands) and has been designing and developing websites for 10 years, first in HTML/ASP and using DotNetNuke for the last 3 years. His company, "Timo-Design", offers a range of web related services and specializes in DotNetNuke custom skinning. He provides a free service to the community, HYPERLINK `www.searchdotnetnuke.com`, which uses Google to search for specific DotNetNuke information (forums and general info).

Conventions

To help you get the most from the text and keep track of what's happening, we've used a number of conventions throughout the book.

For styles in the text:

- We show keyboard strokes like this: Ctrl+A.
- We show file names, URLs, and code within the text like so: `persistence.properties`.
- We present blocks of code as follows:

```
We use a monofont type with no highlighting for most code examples.
```

Source Code

As you work through the examples in this book, you may choose either to type in all the code manually or to use the source code files that accompany the book. All of the source code used in this book is available for download at `http://www.wrox.com`. Once at the site, simply locate the book's title (either by using the Search box or by using one of the title lists) and click the Download Code link on the book's detail page to obtain all the source code for the book.

Because many books have similar titles, you may find it easiest to search by ISBN; this book's ISBN is 978-0-470-43870-1.

Once you download the code, just decompress it with your favorite compression tool. Alternatively, you can go to the main Wrox code download page at `http://www.wrox.com/dynamic/books/download.aspx` to see the code available for this book and all other Wrox books.

Errata

We make every effort to ensure that there are no errors in the text or in the code. However, no one is perfect, and mistakes do occur. If you find an error in one of our books, like a spelling mistake or faulty piece of code, we would be very grateful for your feedback. By sending in errata you may save another reader hours of frustration and at the same time you will be helping us provide even higher quality information.

To find the errata page for this book, go to `http://www.wrox.com` and locate the title using the Search box or one of the title lists. Then, on the book details page, click the Book Errata link. On this page you can view all errata that has been submitted for this book and posted by Wrox editors. A complete book list including links to each book's errata is also available at `http://www.wrox.com/misc-pages/booklist.shtml`.

If you don't spot "your" error on the Book Errata page, go to `http://www.wrox.com/contact/techsupport.shtml` and complete the form there to send us the error you have found. We'll check the information and, if appropriate, post a message to the book's errata page and fix the problem in subsequent editions of the book.

p2p.wrox.com

For author and peer discussion, join the P2P forums at `http://p2p.wrox.com`. The forums are a Web-based system for you to post messages relating to Wrox books and related technologies and interact with other readers and technology users. The forums offer a subscription feature to e-mail you topics of interest of your choosing when new posts are made to the forums. Wrox authors, editors, other industry experts, and your fellow readers are present on these forums.

At `http://p2p.wrox.com` you will find a number of different forums that will help you not only as you read this book, but also as you develop your own applications. To join the forums, just follow these steps:

1. Go to `http://p2p.wrox.com` and click the Register link.
2. Read the terms of use and click Agree.
3. Complete the required information to join as well as any optional information you wish to provide and click Submit.
4. You will receive an e-mail with information describing how to verify your account and complete the joining process.

You can read messages in the forums without joining P2P but in order to post your own messages, you must join.

Once you join, you can post new messages and respond to messages other users post. You can read messages at any time on the Web. If you would like to have new messages from a particular forum e-mailed to you, click the Subscribe to this Forum icon by the forum name in the forum listing.

For more information about how to use the Wrox P2P, be sure to read the P2P FAQs for answers to questions about how the forum software works as well as many common questions specific to P2P and Wrox books. To read the FAQs, click the FAQ link on any P2P page.

1

An Inside Look at the Evolution of DotNetNuke

By Shaun Walker

Project Creator and Chief Architect

As much as DotNetNuke is an open source software application written for the Microsoft ASP.NET platform, it is also a vibrant community with developers, end users, vendors, and volunteers — all working together collaboratively in a rich and diverse ecosystem. This chapter attempts to capture the essence of the project, expose its humble beginnings, provide insight into its evolution, and document its many achievements, but not shy away from some of the hard lessons learned in the process. The lifeblood of any community is its people; therefore, it is a distinct honor and privilege to be able to share some of the emotion and passion that has gone into the DotNetNuke project so that you may be able to establish a personal connection with the various stakeholders and perhaps precipitate your own decision to join this burgeoning ecosystem.

In 2001–2002, I was working for a medium-sized software consulting company that was providing outsourced software development services to a variety of large U.S. clients specializing primarily in e-Learning initiatives. The internal push was to achieve CMM 3.0 on a fairly aggressive schedule so that we could compete with the emerging outsourcing powerhouses from India and China. As a result there was an incredible amount of focus on process and procedure and somewhat less focus on the technical aspects of software engineering. Because the majority of the client base was interested in the J2EE platform, the company primarily hired resources with Java skills — leaving me with my legacy Microsoft background to assume more of an internal-development and project-management role. The process improvement exercise consumed a lot of time and energy for the company, attempting to better define roles and responsibilities and ensuring proper documentation throughout the project life cycle. Delving into CMM and the PMBOK were great educational benefits for me — skills that would prove to be invaluable in future endeavors. Ultimately the large U.S. clients decided to test the overseas outsourcing options anyway, which resulted in severe downsizing for the company. It was during these tumultuous times that I recognized the potential of the newly released .NET Framework (beta) and decided that I would need to take my own initiative to learn this exciting new platform to preserve my long-term employment outlook.

For a number of years, I had been maintaining an amateur hockey statistics application as a sideline hobby business. The client application was written in Visual Basic 6.0 with a Microsoft Access backend and I augmented it with a simplistic web publishing service using Active Server Pages 3.0 and SQL Server 7.0. However, better integration with the World Wide Web was quickly becoming the most highly requested enhancement, and I concluded that an exploration into ASP.NET was the best way to enhance the application, and at the same time acquire the skills necessary to adapt to the changing landscape. My preferred approach to learning new technologies is to experience them firsthand rather than through theory or traditional education. It was during a Microsoft Developer Days conference in Vancouver, British Columbia, in 2001 that I became aware of a reference application known as the IBuySpy Portal.

IBuySpy Portal

Realizing the educational value of sample applications, Microsoft built a number of source projects that were released with the .NET Framework 1.0 Beta to encourage developers to cut their teeth on the new platform. These projects included full source code and a liberal End User License Agreement (EULA), which provided nearly unrestricted usage. Microsoft co-developed the IBuySpy Portal with Vertigo Software and promoted it as a "best practice" example for building applications in the new ASP.NET environment. Despite its obvious shortcomings, the IBuySpy Portal had some strong similarities to both Microsoft Sharepoint as well as other open source portal applications on the Linux/Apache/mySQL/PHP (LAMP) platform. The portal allowed you to create a completely dynamic web site consisting of an unlimited number of virtual "tabs" (pages). Each page had a standard header and three content panes — a left pane, middle pane, and right pane (a standard layout for most portal sites). Within these panes, the administrator could dynamically inject "modules" — essentially mini-applications for managing specific types of web content. The IBuySpy Portal application shipped with six modules designed to cover the most common content types (announcements, links, images, discussions, html/text, and XML) as well as a number of modules for administrating the portal site. As an application framework, the IBuySpy Portal (see Figure 1-1) provided a mechanism for managing users, roles, permissions, tabs, and modules. With these basic services, the portal offered just enough to whet the appetite of many aspiring ASP.NET developers.

ASP.NET

The second critical item that Microsoft delivered at this point in time was a community forums page on the `www.asp.net` web site (see Figure 1-2). This forum provided a focal point for Microsoft developers to meet and collaborate on common issues in an open, moderated environment. Prior to the release of the forums on `www.asp.net`, there was a real void in terms of Microsoft community participation in the online or global sphere, especially when compared to the excellent community environments on other platforms.

One discussion forum on the `www.asp.net` site was dedicated to the discussion of the IBuySpy Portal application, and it soon became a hotbed for developers to discuss their enhancements, share source code enhancements, and debate IT politics. I became involved in this forum early on and gradually increased my community participation as my confidence in ASP.NET and the IBuySpy Portal application grew.

To appeal to the maximum number of community stakeholders, the IBuySpy Portal was available in a number of different source-code release packages. There were VB.NET and C#.NET language versions, each containing their own VS.NET and SDK variants. Although Microsoft was aggressively pushing the newly released C# language, I did not feel a compelling urge to abandon my familiar Visual Basic roots. In addition, my experience with classic ASP 3.0 allowed me to conclude that the new code-behind model in VS.NET was far superior to the inline model of the SDK. As luck would have it, I was able to get access to Visual Studio.NET through my employer. So as a result, I moved forward with the VB.NET/VS.NET version as my baseline framework. This decision would ultimately prove to be extremely important in terms of community acceptance, as I'll explain later.

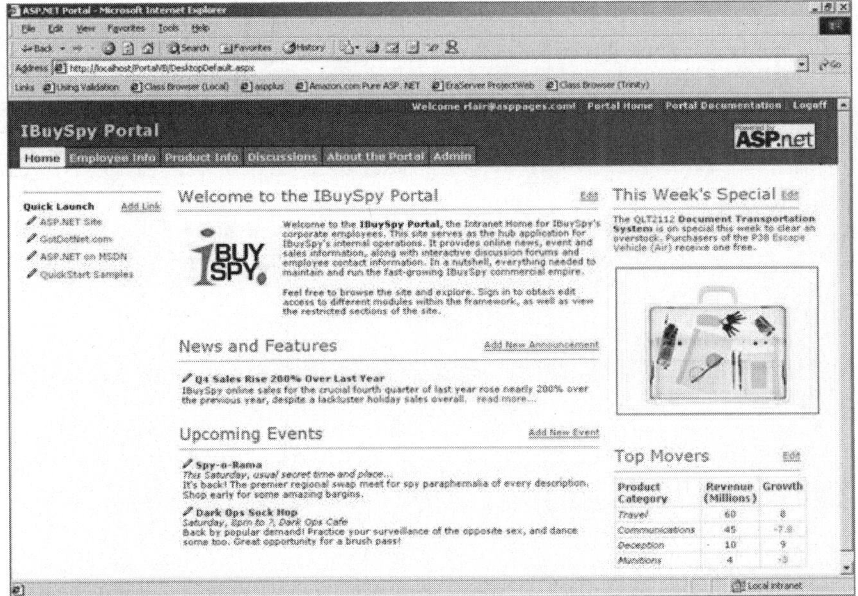

Figure 1-1

When I first started experimenting with the IBuySpy Portal application, I had some specific objectives in mind. To support amateur sports organizations, I had collected a comprehensive set of end-user requirements based on actual client feedback. However, after evaluating the IBuySpy Portal functionality, it quickly became apparent that some significant enhancements were necessary if I hoped to achieve my goals. My early development efforts, although certainly not elegant or perfectly architected, proved that the IBuySpy Portal framework was highly adaptable for building custom applications and could be successfully used as the foundation for my amateur sports hosting application.

The most significant enhancement I made to the IBuySpy Portal application during these early stages was a feature that is now referred to as "multi-portal" or "site virtualization." Effectively this was a fundamental requirement for my amateur sports hosting model. Organizations wanted to have a self-maintained web site, but they also wanted to retain their individual identity. A number of vendors emerged with semi-self-maintained web applications, but nearly all of them forced the organization to adopt the vendor's identity (that is, `www.vendor.com/clientname` rather than `www.clientname.com`). Although this may seem like a trivial distinction for some, it has some major effects in terms of brand recognition, site discovery, search engine ranking, and so on. The IBuySpy Portal application already partitioned its data by portal (site), and it had a field in the Portals database table named PortalAlias that was a perfect candidate for mapping a specific domain name to a portal. It was as if the original creators (Microsoft and Vertigo) considered this use case during development but did not have enough time to complete the implementation, so they simply left the "hook" exposed for future development. I immediately saw the potential of this concept and implemented some logic that allowed the application to serve up custom content based on domain name. Essentially, when a web request was received by the application, it would parse the domain name from the URL and perform a lookup on the PortalAlias field to determine the content that should be displayed. This site virtualization capability would ultimately become the "killer" feature that would allow the application to achieve immediate popularity as an open source project.

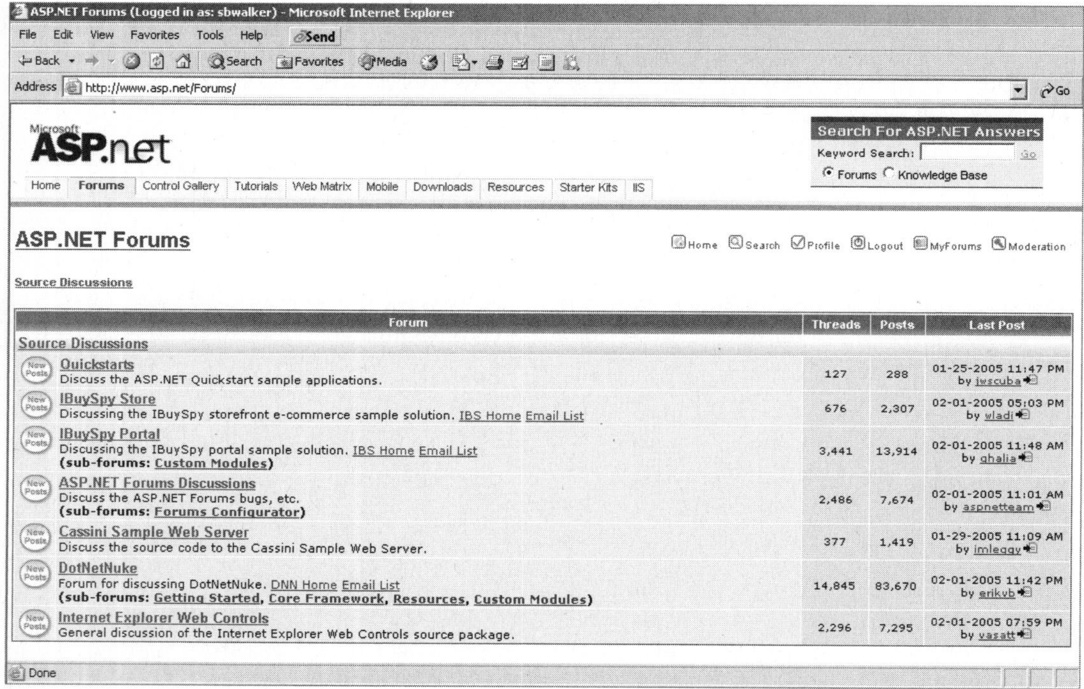

Figure 1-2

Over the next 8 to 10 months, I continued to enhance and refactor the IBuySpy Portal application as I created my own custom implementation (now code-named SportsManager.Net). I added numerous features to improve the somewhat limited portal administration and content management aspects. At one point, I enlisted the help of another developer, John Lucarino, and together we steadily improved the framework using whatever spare time we were able to invest. Unfortunately, because all of this was going on outside of regular work hours, there was little time that could be focused on building a viable commercial venture. So at the end of 2002, it soon became apparent that we did not have enough financial backing or a business model to take the amateur sports venture to the next level. This brought the commercial nature of the endeavor under scrutiny. If the commercial intentions were not going to succeed, I at least wanted to feel that my efforts were not in vain. This forced me to evaluate alternative non-commercial uses of the application. Coincidentally, I had released the source code for a number of minor application enhancements to the `www.asp.net` community forum during the year and I began to hypothesize that if I abandoned the amateur sports venture altogether, it was still possible that my efforts could benefit the larger ASP.NET community.

The fundamental problem with the IBuySpy Portal community was the fact that there was no central authority in charge of managing its growth. Although Microsoft and Vertigo developed the initial code base, there was no public commitment to maintain or enhance the product in any way. Basically the product was a static implementation, frozen in time, an evolutionary dead-end. However, the IBuySpy Portal EULA was extremely liberal, which meant that developers were free to enhance, license, and redistribute the source code in an unrestricted manner. This led to many developers creating their own customized versions of the application, sometimes sharing discrete patches with the general community, but more often keeping their enhancements private, revealing only their public-facing web sites for community recognition (one of the most popular threads at this time was titled "Show me your Portal"). In hindsight, I really don't understand what each developer was hoping to achieve by keeping his enhancements private. Most probably thought there was a commercial opportunity in building a portal application with a richer feature set than their competitor. Or perhaps individuals were hoping to establish an expert reputation based on their public-facing efforts. Either way, the problem was that this mindset was really not conducive to building a community but rather to fragmenting it — a standard trap that tends to consume many things on the Microsoft platform. The concept of sharing source code in an unrestricted manner was really a foreign concept, which is obviously why nobody thought to step forward with an organized open source plan.

I have to admit I had a limited knowledge of the open source philosophy at this point because all of my previous experience was in the Microsoft community — an area where "open source" was simply equated to the Linux operating system movement. However, there was chatter in the forums at various times regarding the organized sharing of source code, and there was obviously some interest in this area. The concept of incorporating the best enhancements into a rapidly evolving open source application made a lot of sense because it benefited the entire community and created a wealth of opportunities for everyone. Coincidentally, a few open source projects had recently emerged on the Microsoft platform to imitate some of the more successful open source projects in the LAMP community. In evaluating my amateur sports application, I soon realized that nearly all of my enhancements were generic enough that they could be applied to nearly any web site — they were not sports-related whatsoever. I concluded that I should release my full application source code to the ASP.NET community as a new open source project. So, as a matter of fact, the initial decision to open source what would eventually become DotNetNuke happened more out of frustration of not achieving my commercial goals rather than predicated philanthropic intentions.

IBuySpy Portal Forum

On December 24, 2002, I released the full open source application by creating a simple web site with a ZIP file for download. The lack of foresight of what this would become was extremely evident when you consider the casual nature of this original release. However, as luck would have it, I did do three things right. First, I thought I should leverage the "IBuySpy" brand in my own open source implementation so that it would be immediately obvious that the code base was a hybrid of the original IBuySpy Portal application, an application with widespread recognition in the Microsoft community. The name I chose was IBuySpy Workshop because it seemed to summarize the evolution of the original application — not to mention the fact that the IBSW abbreviation preferred by the community contained an abstract personal reference (SW are my initials). Ironically I did not even have the domain name resolution properly configured for `www.ibuyspyworkshop.com` when I released (the initial download links were based on an IP address, `http://65.174.86.217/ibuyspyworkshop`). The second thing I did right was to require people to register on my web site before they were able to download the source code. This allowed me to track the actual interest in the application at a more granular level than simply by the total number of downloads. Third, I publicized the availability of the application in the IBuySpy Portal Forum on `www.asp.net` (see Figure 1-3). This particular forum was extremely popular at this time; and as far as I know, nobody had ever released anything other than small code snippet enhancements for general consumption. The original post was made on Christmas Eve, December 24, 2002, which had excellent symbolism in terms of the application being a gift to the community.

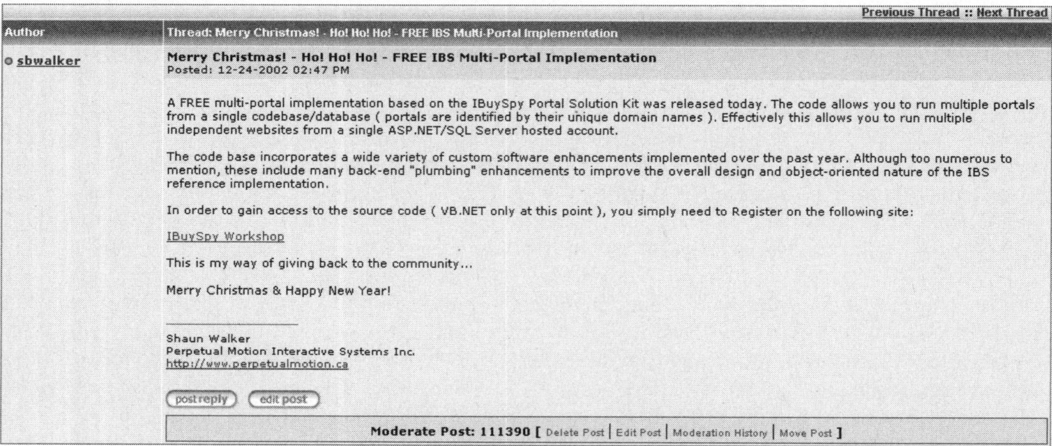

Figure 1-3

IBuySpy Workshop

The public release of the IBuySpy Workshop (see Figure 1-4) created such a surge in forum activity that it was all I could do to keep up with the feedback; especially because this all occurred during the Christmas holidays. I had a family vacation booked for the first two weeks of January, and I left for Mexico on January 2, 2003 (one week after the initial IBuySpy Workshop release). At the time, the timing of this family vacation seemed poor because the groundswell of interest in the IBuySpy Workshop seemed like it could really use my dedicated focus. However, in hindsight the timing could not have been better, because it proved that the community could support itself — a critical element in any open source project. When I returned home from vacation, I was amazed at the massive response the release achieved. The IBuySpy Portal Forum became dominated with posts about the IBuySpy Workshop and my Inbox was full of messages thanking me for my efforts and requesting me to provide support and enhancements. This certainly validated my decision to release the application as an open source project but also emphasized the fact that I had started a locomotive down the tracks and it was going to take some significant engineering to keep it on the rails.

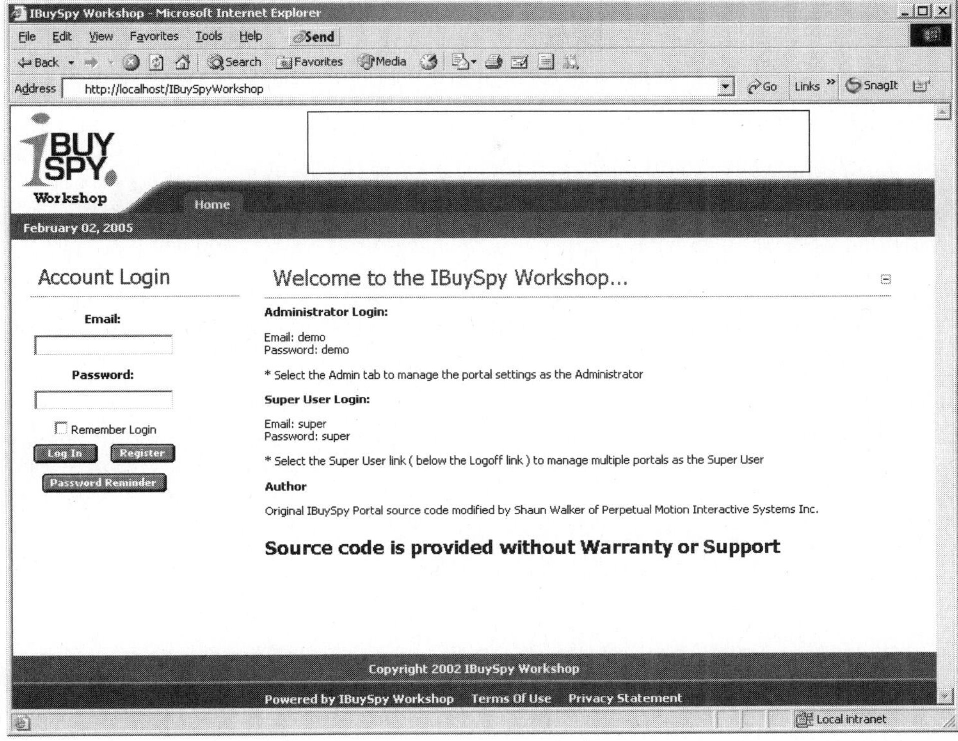

Figure 1-4

Over the next few months, I frantically attempted to incorporate all community suggestions into the application while at the same time keep up with the plethora of community support questions. Because I was working a day job that prevented effort on the open source project, most of my evenings were consumed with work on the IBuySpy Workshop, which definitely caused some strain on my marriage and family life. Four hours of sleep per night is not conducive to a healthy lifestyle but, like I said, the train was rolling and I had a feeling the project was destined for bigger things.

Supporting a user base through upgrades is fundamental in any software product. This is especially true in open source projects where the application can evolve quickly based on community feedback and technical advancements. The popular open source expression is that "no user should be left on an evolutionary dead-end." As luck would have it, I had designed a reliable upgrade mechanism in the original sports management application that I included in the IBuySpy Workshop code base. This feature enabled users of the application to easily migrate from one release version to the next — a critical factor in keeping the community engaged and committed to the evolution of the product.

In February 2003, the IBuySpy Portal Forum had become so congested with IBuySpy Workshop threads that it started to become difficult for the two communities to co-exist peacefully. At this point, I sent an email to the anonymous alias posted at the bottom of the forums page on the `www.asp.net` site with a request to create a dedicated forum for the IBuySpy Workshop. Because the product functionality and source code of the two applications diverged so significantly, my intent was to try and keep the forum posts for the two applications separated, providing both communities the means to support their membership. I certainly did not have high hopes that my email request was even going to be read — let alone granted. But to my surprise, I received a positive response from none other than Rob Howard (an ASP.NET icon), which proved to be a great introduction to a long-term partnership with Microsoft. Rob created the forum and even went a step further and added a link to the Source Download page of the `www.asp.net` site, an event that would ultimately drive a huge amount of traffic to the emerging IBuySpy Workshop community.

There are a number of reasons why the IBuySpy Workshop became so immediately popular when it was released in early 2003. The obvious reason is because the base application contained a huge number of enhancements over the IBuySpy Portal application, and people could immediately leverage them to build more powerful web sites. From a community perspective, the open source project provided a central management authority that was dedicated to the ongoing growth and support of the application framework, a factor that was definitely lacking in the original IBuySpy Portal community. This concept of open source on the Microsoft platform attracted many developers; some with pure philosophical intentions, and others who viewed the application as a vehicle to further their own revenue-generating interests. Yet another factor, which I think is often overlooked, relates to the programming language on which the project was based. With the release of the .NET Framework 1.0, Microsoft spent a lot of energy promoting the benefits of the new C# programming language. The C# language was intended to provide a migration path for C++ developers as well as a means to entice Java developers working on other platforms to switch. This left the Visual Basic and ASP 3.0 developer communities feeling neglected and somewhat unappreciated. The IBuySpy Workshop, with its core framework in VB.NET, provided an essential community ecosystem where legacy VB developers could interact, learn, and share.

Subscription Fiasco

In late February 2003, the lack of sleep, family priorities, and community demands finally came to a head and I decided that I should reach out for help. I contacted a former employer and mentor, Kent Alstad, with my dilemma and we spent a few lengthy telephone calls brainstorming possible outcomes. However, my personal stress level at the time and my urgency to change direction on the project ultimately caused me to move too fast and with more aggression than I should have. I announced that the IBuySpy Workshop would immediately become a subscription service where developers would need to pay a monthly fee to get access to the latest source code. From a personal perspective, the intent was to generate enough revenue that I could leave my day job and focus my full energy on the management of the open source project. And with 2000 registered users, a subscription service seemed like a viable model (see Figure 1-5).

However, the true philosophy of the open source model immediately came to light, and I had to face the wrath of a scorned community. Among other things, I was accused of misleading the community, lying about the open source nature of the project, and letting my personal greed cloud my vision. For every one supporter of my decision, there were 10 more who publicly crucified me as the evil incarnate. Luckily for me, Kent had a trusted work associate named Andy Baron, a senior consultant at MCW Technologies and a Microsoft Most Valuable Professional since 1995, who has incredible wisdom when it comes to the Microsoft development community. Andy helped me craft a public apology message (see Figure 1-6) that managed to appease the community and restore the IBuySpy Workshop to full open source status.

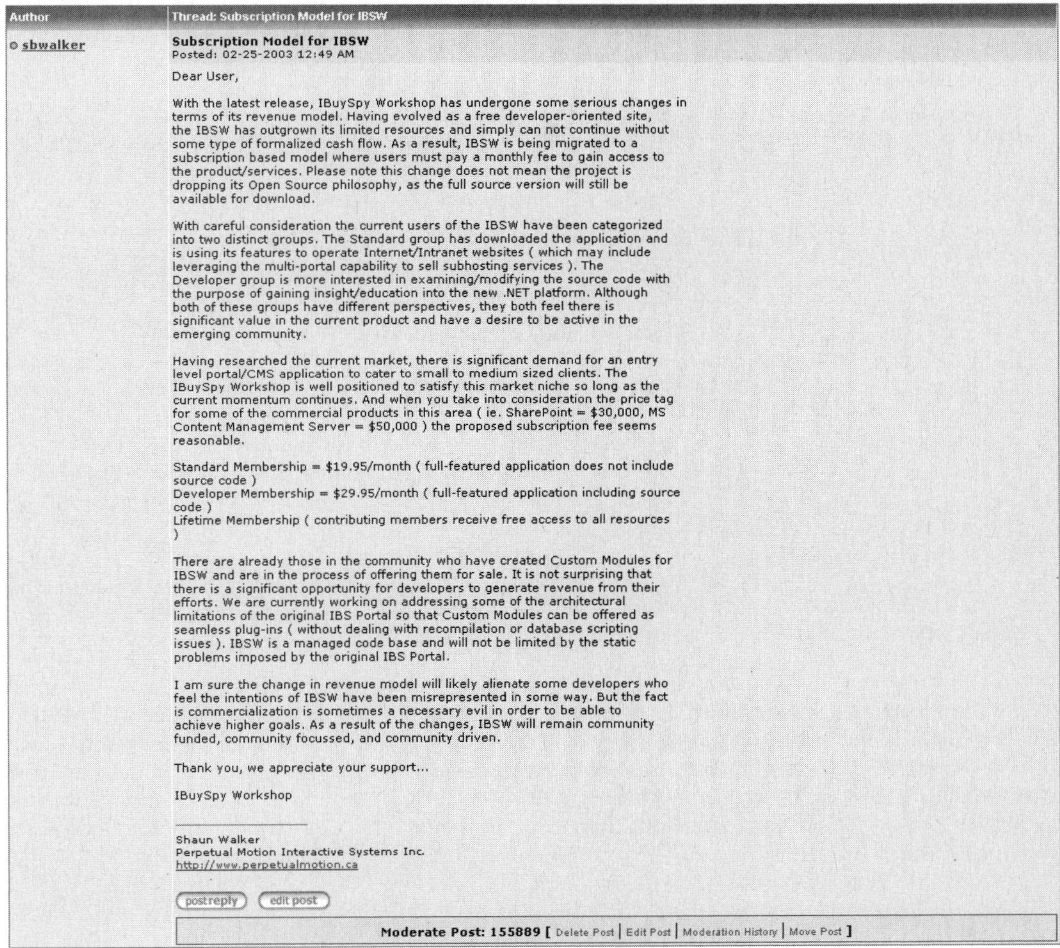

Author | Thread: Subscription Model for IBSW

sbwalker

Subscription Model for IBSW
Posted: 02-25-2003 12:49 AM

Dear User,

With the latest release, IBuySpy Workshop has undergone some serious changes in terms of its revenue model. Having evolved as a free developer-oriented site, the IBSW has outgrown its limited resources and simply can not continue without some type of formalized cash flow. As a result, IBSW is being migrated to a subscription based model where users must pay a monthly fee to gain access to the product/services. Please note this change does not mean the project is dropping its Open Source philosophy, as the full source version will still be available for download.

With careful consideration the current users of the IBSW have been categorized into two distinct groups. The Standard group has downloaded the application and is using its features to operate Internet/Intranet websites (which may include leveraging the multi-portal capability to sell subhosting services). The Developer group is more interested in examining/modifying the source code with the purpose of gaining insight/education into the new .NET platform. Although both of these groups have different perspectives, they both feel there is significant value in the current product and have a desire to be active in the emerging community.

Having researched the current market, there is significant demand for an entry level portal/CMS application to cater to small to medium sized clients. The IBuySpy Workshop is well positioned to satisfy this market niche so long as the current momentum continues. And when you take into consideration the price tag for some of the commercial products in this area (ie. SharePoint = $30,000, MS Content Management Server = $50,000) the proposed subscription fee seems reasonable.

Standard Membership = $19.95/month (full-featured application does not include source code)
Developer Membership = $29.95/month (full-featured application including source code)
Lifetime Membership (contributing members receive free access to all resources)

There are already those in the community who have created Custom Modules for IBSW and are in the process of offering them for sale. It is not surprising that there is a significant opportunity for developers to generate revenue from their efforts. We are currently working on addressing some of the architectural limitations of the original IBS Portal so that Custom Modules can be offered as seamless plug-ins (without dealing with recompilation or database scripting issues). IBSW is a managed code base and will not be limited by the static problems imposed by the original IBS Portal.

I am sure the change in revenue model will likely alienate some developers who feel the intentions of IBSW have been misrepresented in some way. But the fact is commercialization is sometimes a necessary evil in order to be able to achieve higher goals. As a result of the changes, IBSW will remain community funded, community focussed, and community driven.

Thank you, we appreciate your support...

IBuySpy Workshop

Shaun Walker
Perpetual Motion Interactive Systems Inc.
http://www.perpetualmotion.ca

post reply | edit post

Moderate Post: 155889 [Delete Post | Edit Post | Moderation History | Move Post]

Figure 1-5

Microsoft

Coincidentally, the political nightmare I created in the IBuySpy Workshop Forum with my subscription announcement resulted in some direct attention from the Microsoft ASP.NET product team (the maintainers of the `www.asp.net` site). Still trying to recover from the damage I incurred, I received an email from none other than Scott Guthrie (co-founder of the Microsoft ASP.NET Team), asking me to reexamine my decision on the subscription model and making suggestions on how the project could continue as a free, open source venture. It seemed that Microsoft was protective of its evolving community and did not want to see the progress in this area splinter and dissolve just as it seemed to be gaining momentum. Scott Guthrie made no promises at this point but he did open a direct dialogue that ultimately led to some fundamental discussions on sponsorship and collaboration. In fact, this initial email led to a number of telephone conversations and ultimately an invitation to Redmond to discuss the future of the IBuySpy Workshop.

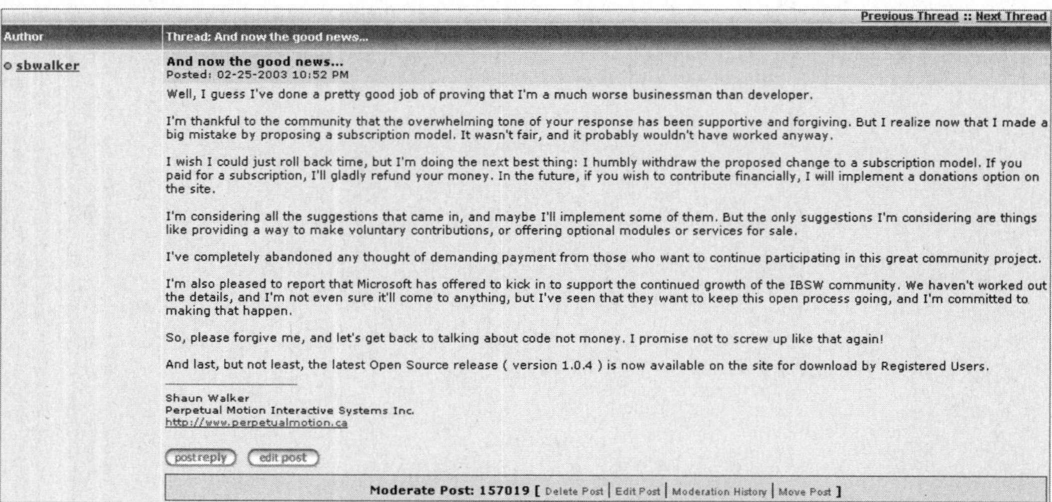
Previous Thread :: Next Thread

Author | Thread: And now the good news...

sbwalker

And now the good news...
Posted: 02-25-2003 10:52 PM

Well, I guess I've done a pretty good job of proving that I'm a much worse businessman than developer.

I'm thankful to the community that the overwhelming tone of your response has been supportive and forgiving. But I realize now that I made a big mistake by proposing a subscription model. It wasn't fair, and it probably wouldn't have worked anyway.

I wish I could just roll back time, but I'm doing the next best thing: I humbly withdraw the proposed change to a subscription model. If you paid for a subscription, I'll gladly refund your money. In the future, if you wish to contribute financially, I will implement a donations option on the site.

I'm considering all the suggestions that came in, and maybe I'll implement some of them. But the only suggestions I'm considering are things like providing a way to make voluntary contributions, or offering optional modules or services for sale.

I've completely abandoned any thought of demanding payment from those who want to continue participating in this great community project.

I'm also pleased to report that Microsoft has offered to kick in to support the continued growth of the IBSW community. We haven't worked out the details, and I'm not even sure it'll come to anything, but I've seen that they want to keep this open process going, and I'm committed to making that happen.

So, please forgive me, and let's get back to talking about code not money. I promise not to screw up like that again!

And last, but not least, the latest Open Source release (version 1.0.4) is now available on the site for download by Registered Users.

Shaun Walker
Perpetual Motion Interactive Systems Inc.
http://www.perpetualmotion.ca

post reply | edit post

Moderate Post: 157019 [Delete Post | Edit Post | Moderation History | Move Post]

Figure 1-6

I still remember the combination of nerves and excitement as I drove from my home in Abbotsford, British Columbia to Microsoft's head office in Redmond, Washington (about a three-hour trek). I really did not know what to expect, and I tried to strategize all possible angles. Essentially all of my planning turned out to be moot, because my meeting with Scott Guthrie turned out to be far more laid back and transparent than I could have ever imagined. Scott took me to his unassuming office and we spent the next three hours brainstorming ideas about how the IBuySpy Workshop fit into the current ASP.NET landscape. Much of this centered on the evolving vision of ASP.NET 2.0 — an area where I had little or no knowledge prior to the meeting (the Whidbey Alpha had not even been released at this point).

At the beginning of the meeting, Scott had me demonstrate the current version of the IBuySpy Workshop, explaining its key features and benefits. We also discussed the long-term goals of the project as well as my proposed roadmap for future enhancements. Scott's knowledge of both the technical and community aspects of the ASP.NET platform really amazed me — I guess that's why he is the undisputed "Father of ASP.NET." In hindsight, I can hardly believe my good fortune to have received three dedicated hours of his time to discuss the project — it really changed my "ivory tower" perception of Microsoft and forged a strong relationship for future collaboration.

Upon leaving Redmond, I had to stifle my excitement as I realized that, regardless of the direct interaction with Microsoft, I personally was still in the same situation as before the subscription model announcement. Because the subscription model failed to generate the much-needed revenue that would have

allowed me to devote 100% of my time to the project, I was forced to examine other possible alternatives. There were a number of suggestions from the community and the concept that seemed to have the most potential was related to web hosting.

In these early stages, there were few economical Microsoft Windows hosting options available that offered a SQL Server database — a fundamental requirement for running the IBuySpy Workshop application. Coincidentally, I had recently struck up a relationship with an individual from New Jersey who was active in the IBuySpy Workshop forums on `www.asp.net`. This individual had a solid background in web hosting and proposed a partnership whereby he would manage the web hosting infrastructure and I would continue to enhance the application and drive traffic to the business. Initially there were a lot of community members who signed up for this service — some because of the low-cost hosting option, others because they were looking for a way to support the open source project. It soon became obvious that the costs to build and support the infrastructure were consuming the majority of the revenue generated. And over time the amount of effort to support the growing client base became more intense. Eventually it came to a point where it was intimated that my contributions to the web hosting business were not substantial enough to justify the current partnership structure. I was informed that the partnership should be dissolved. This is where things got complicated because there was never any formal agreement signed by either party to initiate the partnership. Without documentation, it made the negotiation for a fair settlement difficult and resulted in some bad feelings on both sides. This was unfortunate because I think the relationship was formed with the best intentions but the demands of the business resulted in a poor outcome. Regardless, this ordeal was an important lesson I needed to learn: regardless of the open source nature of the project, it was imperative to have all contractually binding items properly documented.

DotNetNuke

One of the topics that Scott Guthrie and I discussed in our early conversations was the issue of product branding. IBuySpy Workshop achieved its early goals of providing a public reference to the IBuySpy Portal community. This resulted in an influx of ASP.NET developers who were familiar with the IBuySpy Portal application and were interested in this new open source concept. But as the code bases diverged, there was a need for a new project identity — a unique brand that would differentiate the community and provide the mechanism for building an internationally recognized ecosystem. Research of competing portal applications on other platforms revealed a strong tendency toward the "nuke" slogan.

The "nuke" slogan was originally coined by Francisco Burzi of PHP-Nuke fame (the oft-disputed pioneer of open source portal applications). Over the years, a variety of other projects adopted the slogan as well — so many that the term had obtained industry recognition in the portal-application genre. To my surprise, a WHOIS search revealed that `dotnetnuke.com`, `.net`, and `.org` were not registered and, in my opinion, seemed to be the perfect identity for the project. Again emphasizing the bare-bones resources under which the project was initiated, my credit card transaction to register the three domain names was denied, and I was only able to register `dotnetnuke.com` (in the long run an embarrassing and contentious issue as the `.net` and `.org` domain names were immediately registered by other individuals). Equally as spontaneous, I did an Internet search for images containing the word "nuke" and located a three-dimensional graphic of a circular gear with a nuclear symbol embossed on it. I contacted the owner of the site and was given permission to use the image (it was in fact, simply one of many public domain images they were using for a fictitious storefront demonstration). A new project identity was born — Version 1.0.5 of the IBuySpy Workshop was re-branded as DotNetNuke, which the community immediately abbreviated to DNN for simplicity (see Figure 1-7).

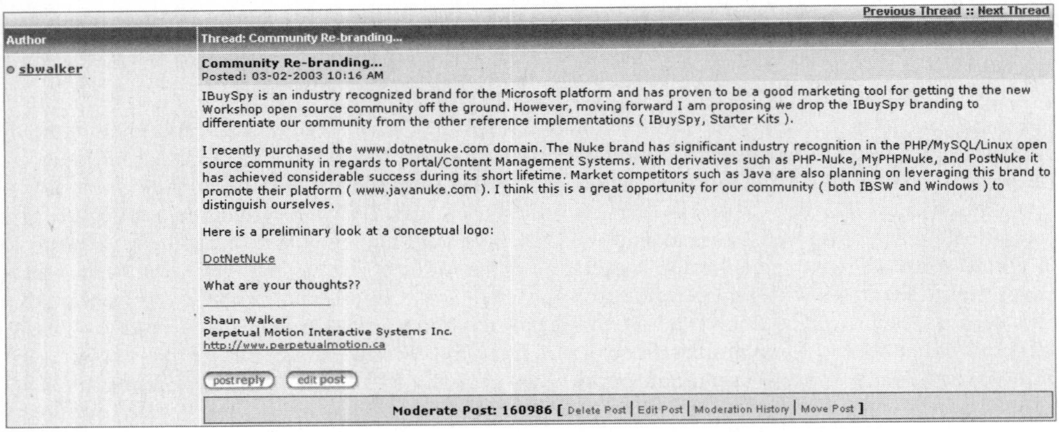

Previous Thread :: Next Thread

Author	Thread: Community Re-branding...
sbwalker	**Community Re-branding...** Posted: 03-02-2003 10:16 AM IBuySpy is an industry recognized brand for the Microsoft platform and has proven to be a good marketing tool for getting the the new Workshop open source community off the ground. However, moving forward I am proposing we drop the IBuySpy branding to differentiate our community from the other reference implementations (IBuySpy, Starter Kits). I recently purchased the www.dotnetnuke.com domain. The Nuke brand has significant industry recognition in the PHP/MySQL/Linux open source community in regards to Portal/Content Management Systems. With derivatives such as PHP-Nuke, MyPHPNuke, and PostNuke it has achieved considerable success during its short lifetime. Market competitors such as Java are also planning on leveraging this brand to promote their platform (www.javanuke.com). I think this is a great opportunity for our community (both IBSW and Windows) to distinguish ourselves. Here is a preliminary look at a conceptual logo: DotNetNuke What are your thoughts?? Shaun Walker Perpetual Motion Interactive Systems Inc. http://www.perpetualmotion.ca post reply edit post **Moderate Post: 160986** [Delete Post | Edit Post | Moderation History | Move Post]

Figure 1-7

Licensing

A secondary issue that was not addressed during the early stages of the project was licensing. The original IBuySpy Portal was released under a liberal Microsoft EULA license that allowed for unrestricted usage, modification, and distribution. However, the code base underwent such a major transformation that it could hardly be compared with its predecessor. Therefore, when the IBuySpy Workshop application was released, I did not include the original Microsoft EULA, nor did I include any copyright or license of my own. Essentially this meant that the application was in the public domain. This is certainly not the most accepted approach to an open source project and eventually some of the more legal-savvy community members brought the issue to a head. I was forced to take a hard look at open source licensing models to determine which license was most appropriate for the project.

In stark contrast to the spontaneous approach taken to finding a project identity, the licensing issue had much deeper ramifications. Had I not performed extensive research on this subject, I would have likely chosen a GPL license because it seemed to dominate the vast majority of open source projects in existence. However, digging beneath the surface, I quickly realized that the GPL did not seem to be a good candidate for my objectives of allowing DotNetNuke to be used in both commercial and non-commercial environments. Ultimately the selection of a license for an open source project is largely dependent upon your business model, your product architecture, and understanding who owns the intellectual property in your application. The combination of these factors prompted me to take a hard look at the open source licensing options available.

For those of you who have not researched open source software, you would be surprised at the major differences between the most popular open source licensing models. It is true that these licenses all meet the standards of the Open Source Definition, a set of guidelines managed by the Open Source Initiative (OSI) at `www.open-source.org`. These principles include the right to use open source software for any purpose, the right to make and distribute copies, the right to create and distribute derivative works, the right to access and use source code, and the right to combine open source and other software. With such fundamental rights shared between all open source licenses, it probably makes you wonder why there is need for more than one license at all. Well the reason is because each license has the ability to impose additional rights or restrictions on top of these base principles. The additional rights and restrictions have the effect of altering the license so that it meets the specific objectives of each project. Because it is generally bad practice to create brand new licenses (based on the fact that the existing licenses have gained industry acceptance as well as a proven track record), people generally gravitate toward either a GPL or BSD license.

The GPL (or GNU Public License) was created in 1989 by Richard Stallman, founder of the Free Software Foundation. The GPL is what is now known as a "copyleft" license, a term coined based on its controversial reciprocity clause. Essentially this clause stipulates that you are allowed to use the software on the condition that any derivative works that you create from it and distribute must be licensed to all under the same license. This is intended to ensure that the software and any enhancements to it remain in the public domain for everyone to share. Although this is a great humanitarian goal, it seriously restricts the use of the software in a commercial environment.

The BSD (or Berkeley Software Distribution) was created by the University of California and was designed to permit the free use, modification, and distribution of software without any return obligation on the part of the community. The BSD is essentially a "copyright" license, meaning that you are free to use the software on the condition that you retain the copyright notice in all copies or derivative works. The BSD is also known as an "academic" license because it provides the highest degree of intellectual property sharing.

Ultimately I settled on a standard BSD license for DotNetNuke; a license that allows the maximum licensing freedom in both commercial and non-commercial environments — with only minimal restrictions to preserve the copyright of the project. The change in license went widely unnoticed by the community because it did not impose any additional restrictions on usage or distribution. However, it was a fundamental milestone in establishing DotNetNuke as a true open source project:

```
DotNetNuke(r) - http://www.dotnetnuke.com
Copyright (c) 2002-2006
by Perpetual Motion Interactive Systems Inc. (http://www.perpetualmotion.ca)

Permission is hereby granted, free of charge, to any person obtaining a copy
of this software and associated documentation files (the "Software"), to deal
in the Software without restriction, including without limitation the rights
to use, copy, modify, merge, publish, distribute, sublicense, and/or sell
copies of the Software, and to permit persons to whom the Software is
furnished to do so, subject to the following conditions:

The above copyright notice and this permission notice shall be included in
all copies or substantial portions of the Software.

THE SOFTWARE IS PROVIDED "AS IS", WITHOUT WARRANTY OF ANY KIND, EXPRESS OR
IMPLIED, INCLUDING BUT NOT LIMITED TO THE WARRANTIES OF MERCHANTABILITY,
FITNESS FOR A PARTICULAR PURPOSE AND NONINFRINGEMENT. IN NO EVENT SHALL THE
AUTHORS OR COPYRIGHT HOLDERS BE LIABLE FOR ANY CLAIM, DAMAGES OR OTHER
LIABILITY, WHETHER IN AN ACTION OF CONTRACT, TORT OR OTHERWISE, ARISING FROM,
OUT OF OR IN CONNECTION WITH THE SOFTWARE OR THE USE OR OTHER DEALINGS IN THE
SOFTWARE.
```

Core Team

The next major milestone in the project's open source evolution occurred in the summer of 2003. Up until this point, I had been acting as the sole maintainer of the DotNetNuke code base, a task that was consuming 110% of my free time as I feverishly fixed bugs and enhanced the framework based on community feedback. Still I felt more like a bottleneck than a provider, in spite of the fact that I was churning out at least one significant release every month leading up to this point. The more active community members were becoming restless due to a lack of direct input into the progress of the project. In fact, a small faction of these members even went so far as to create their own hybrid or "fork" of the DotNetNuke code base that attempted to forge ahead and add features at a more aggressive pace than I was capable of on my own. These were challenging times from a political standpoint because I was eventually forced to confront all of these issues in a direct and public manner — flexing my "benevolent dictator" muscles for the first time — an act I was not the least bit comfortable performing. Luckily for me, I had a number of loyal and trustworthy community members who supported my position and ultimately provided the backing to form a strong and committed Core Team.

As a result of the single-threaded issues I mentioned earlier, most successful open source projects are comprised of a number of community volunteers who earn their positions of authority within the community based on their specific expertise or community support activities. This is known as a *meritocracy*, a term that means that an individual's influence is directly proportional to the ability that the individual demonstrates within the project. It's a well-observed fact that individuals with more experience and skills have less time to devote to volunteer activities; however, their minimal contributions prove to be incredibly valuable. Similarly, individuals with less experience may be able to invest more time but may only be capable of performing the more repetitive, menial tasks. Building a healthy balance of these two roles is exactly what is required in every successful open source project; and in fact, is one of the more challenging items to achieve from a management perspective.

The original DotNetNuke Core Team was selected based on their participation and dedication to the DotNetNuke project in the months leading up to the team's formation. In most cases this was solely based on an individual's public image and reputation established in the DotNetNuke Forum on the `www.asp.net` web site. And in fact, in these early stages, the online persona of each individual proved to be a good indicator of the specific skills they could bring to the project. Some members were highly skilled architects, others were seasoned developers, and others were better at discussing functionality from an end-user perspective and providing quality support to their community peers.

To establish some basic structure for the newly formed Core Team, I attempted to summarize some basic project guidelines. My initial efforts combined some of the best Extreme Programming (XP) rules with the principles of other successful open source projects. This became the basis of the DotNetNuke Manifest document:

- **Development is a team effort**: The whole is exponentially greater than the sum of its parts. Large-scale open source projects are only viable if a large enough community of highly skilled developers can be amassed to attack a problem. Treating your users as co-developers is your most effective option for rapid code improvement and effective debugging.
- **Build the right product before you build the product right**: Focus should be directed at understanding and implementing the high-level business requirements before attempting to construct the perfect technical architecture. Listen to your customers.
- **Incremental development**: Every software product has infinite growth potential if managed correctly. Functionality should be added in incremental units rather than attempting a monolithic implementation. Release often but with a level of quality that instills confidence.

- **Law of diminishing return**: The majority of the effort should be invested in implementing features that have the most benefit and widest general usage by the community.

DotNetNuke version 1.0.10 was the proving grounds for the original Core Team. The idea was to establish the infrastructure to support disconnected team development by working on a stabilization release of the current product. A lot of debate went into the selection of the appropriate source-control system because, ironically enough, many of the Core Team had never worked with a formal source control process in the past (a fact that certainly emphasized the varied professional background of the Core Team members). The debate centered on whether to use a CVS or VSS model.

CVS is a source-control system that is popular in the open source world that enables developers to work in an unrestricted manner on their local project files and handles any conflicts between versions when you attempt to commit your changes to the central repository. Visual SourceSafe (VSS) is a Microsoft source-control system that is supported by the Microsoft development tool suite, which requires developers to explicitly lock project files before making modifications to prevent version conflicts. Ultimately the familiarity with the Microsoft model won out and we decided to use the free WorkSpaces service on the GotDotNet web site (a new developer community site supported by Microsoft). GotDotNet also provided a simplistic Bug Tracker application that provided us with a means to manage the tracking of issues and enhancement requests. With these infrastructure components in place, we were able to focus on the stabilization of the application, correcting known defects and adding some minor usability enhancements. It was during this time that Scott Willhite stepped forward to assume a greater role of responsibility in the project; assisting in management activities, communication, prioritization, and scheduling.

A significant enhancement that was introduced in this stabilization release came from a third party who had contacted me with some specific enhancements they had implemented and wished to contribute. The University of Texas at El Paso had done extensive work making the DotNetNuke application compliant with the guidelines of the American Disabilities Association (ADA) and Section 508 of the United States Rehabilitation Act. The United States government made compliancy mandatory for most public organizations; therefore, this was a great enhancement for DotNetNuke because it allowed the application to be used in government, educational, and military scenarios. Bruce Hopkins became the Core Team owner of this item in these early stages, a role that required a great deal of patience as the rest of the team came to grips with the new concept.

Establishing and managing a team was no small challenge. On one hand, there were the technical challenges of allowing multiple team members, all in different geographic regions, to communicate and collaborate in a cost-effective, secure environment. Certainly this would have never been possible without the Internet and its vast array of online tools. On the other hand, there was the challenge of identifying different personality types and channeling them into areas where they would be most effective. Because there are limited financial motivators in the open source model, people must rely on more basic incentives to justify their volunteer efforts. Generally this leads to a paradigm where contributions to the project become the de facto channel for building a reputation within the community — a primary motivator in any meritocracy. As a result of working with the team, it soon became obvious that there were two extremes in this area: those who would selflessly sacrifice all of their free time (often to their own detriment) to the open source project, and those who would invest the minimal effort and expect the maximum reward. As the creator and maintainer of the project it was my duty to remain objective and put the interests of the community first. This often caused me to become frustrated with the behavior of specific individuals, but in nearly all cases these issues could be resolved without introducing any hard feelings on either side. This is true in all cases except one.

XXL Fork

Early in the project history, I was approached by an individual from Germany with a request to maintain a localized DotNetNuke site for the German community. I was certainly not naïve to the dangers of forking at this point and I told him that it would be fine so long as the site stayed consistent with the official source code base, which was under my jurisdiction. This was agreed upon and in the coming months I had periodic communication with this individual regarding his localization efforts. However as time wore on, he became critical of the manner in which the project was being managed, in particular the sole maintainer aspect, and began to voice his disapproval in the public forum. There was a group who believed that there should be greater degree of transparency in the project — that developers should be able to get access to the latest development source code at anytime, and that the maintenance of the application should be conducted by a team rather than an individual. He was able to convince a number of community members to collaborate with him on a modified version of DotNetNuke, a version that integrated a number of the more popular community enhancements available, and called it DotNetNuke XXL.

Now I have to admit that much of this occurred due to my own inability to respond quickly and form a Core Team. In addition, I was not providing adequate feedback to the community regarding my goals and objectives for the future of the project. The reality is that the background management tasks of creating the DotNetNuke Core Team and managing the myriad other issues had undermined my ability to deliver source code enhancements and support to the community. The combination of these factors resulted in an unpleasant situation, one that I should have mitigated sooner but was afraid to act upon due to the fragility of the newly formed community. And you also need to remember that the creator of the XXL variant had broken no license agreement by creating a fork — it was completely legal based on the freedom of the BSD open source license.

Eventually the issue came to a head when members of the XXL group began promoting their full-source-code hybrid in the DotNetNuke Forum. Essentially piggy-backing on the primary promotion channel for the DotNetNuke project, they were able to convince many people to switch to the XXL code base. This had some bad consequences for the DotNetNuke community. Mainly it threatened to splinter the emerging community on territorial boundaries — an event I wanted to avoid at all costs. This situation was the closest attempt of project hijacking that I can realistically imagine. The DotNetNuke XXL fork seemed to be fixated on becoming the official version of DotNetNuke and assuming control of the future project roadmap. The only saving grace was that I personally managed the DotNetNuke infrastructure and therefore had some influence over key aspects of the open source environment.

In searching for an effective mechanism to protect the integrity of the community and prevent the XXL fork from gaining momentum, some basic business fundamentals came into play. Any product or service is only as successful as its promotion or marketing channel. The DotNetNuke Forum on the `www.asp.net` web site was the primary communication hub to the DotNetNuke community. Therefore it was not difficult to realize that restricting discussion on XXL in the forum was the simplest method to mitigate its growth. In probably the most aggressive political move I have ever been forced to make, I introduced some bold changes to the DotNetNuke project. I established some guidelines for Core Team conduct that included, among other things, restrictions on promoting competing open source hybrids of the DotNetNuke application. I also posted some policies on the DotNetNuke Forum that emphasized that the forum was dedicated solely to the discussion of the official DotNetNuke application and that discussion of third-party commercial or open source products was strictly forbidden. This was an especially difficult decision to make from a moral standpoint as I was well aware that the DotNetNuke application had been introduced to the community via the IBuySpy Portal Forum. Nonetheless, the combination of these two announcements resulted in both the resignation of the XXL project leader from the Core Team as well as the end of discussion of the XXL fork in the DotNetNuke Forum. It is important to note that such a defensive move would not have been possible without the loyalty and support of the rest of the Core Team in terms of enforcing the guidelines.

The unfortunate side effect, one about which I had been cautioning members of the community for weeks, was that users who had upgraded to the XXL fork were effectively left on an evolutionary dead-end — a product version with no support mechanism or promise of future upgrades. This is because many of the XXL enhancements were never going to be integrated into the official DotNetNuke code base (either due to design limitations or inapplicability to the general public). This situation, as unpleasant as it may have been for those caught on the dead-end side of the equation, was a real educational experience for the community in general as they began to understand the longer-term and deeper implications of open source project philosophy. In general the community feedback was positive to the project changes, with only occasional flare-ups in the weeks following. In addition, the Core Team seemed to gel more as a result of these decisions because it provided some much-needed policies on conduct, loyalty, and dedication as well a concrete example of how inappropriate behavior would be penalized.

Trademarks

Emerging from the XXL dilemma, I realized that I needed to establish some legal protection for the long-term preservation of the project. Because standard copyright and the BSD license offered no real insurance from third-party threats, I began to explore intellectual property law in greater detail. After much research and legal advice, I decided that the best option was to apply for a trademark for the DotNetNuke name. Registering a trademark protects a project's name or logo, which is often a project's most valuable asset. After the trademark was approved it would mean that although an individual or company could still create a fork of the application, they legally could not refer to it by the DotNetNuke name. This appeared to be an important distinction so I proceeded with trademark registration in Canada (because this is the country in which Perpetual Motion Interactive Systems Inc. is incorporated).

I must admit the entire trademark approval process was quite an educational experience. Before you can register your trademark, you need to define a category and description of your wares and/or services. This can be challenging, although most trademark agencies now provide public access to their database where you can browse for similar items that have been approved in the past. You pay your processing fee when you submit the initial application, but the trademark agency has the right to reject your application for any number of reasons — whereby, you need to modify your application and submit it again. Each iteration can take a couple of months, so patience is indeed a requirement. After the trademark is accepted, it must be published in a public trademark journal for a specified amount of time, providing third parties the opportunity to contest the trademark before it is approved. If it makes it through this final stage, you can pay your registration fee for the trademark to become official. To emphasize the lengthy process involved, the DotNetNuke trademark was initially submitted on October 9, 2003, and was finally approved on November 15, 2004 (TMA625,364).

Sponsorship

In August 2003, I finally came to an agreement with Microsoft regarding a sponsorship proposal for the DotNetNuke project. In a nutshell, Microsoft wanted DotNetNuke to be enhanced in a number of key areas; the intent being to use the open source project as a means of demonstrating the strengths of the ASP.NET platform. Because these enhancements were completely congruent with the future goals of the project, there was little negative consequence from a technical perspective. In return for implementing the enhancements, Microsoft would provide a number of sponsorship benefits to the project including web hosting for the `www.dotnetnuke.com` web site, weekly meetings with an ASP.NET Team representative (Rob Howard), continued promotion via the `www.asp.net` web site, and more direct access to Microsoft resources for mentoring and guidance. It took five months for this sponsorship proposal to come together, which demonstrates the patience and perseverance required to collaborate with such an influential partner as Microsoft. Nonetheless, this was potentially a one-time offer and at such a critical stage in the project evolution, it seemed too important to ignore.

An interesting perception that most people have in the IT industry is that Microsoft is morally against the entire open source phenomenon. In my opinion, this is far from the truth — and the reality is so much more simplistic. Like any other business that is trying to enhance its market position, Microsoft is merely concerned about competition. This is nothing new. In the past, Microsoft faced competitive challenges from many sources — companies, individuals, and governments. However, the current environment makes it much more emotional and newsworthy to suggest that Microsoft is pitted against a grassroots community movement rather than a business or legal concern. So in my opinion, it is merely a coincidence that the only real competition facing Microsoft at this point is coming from the open source development community. And there is no doubt it will take some time and effort for Microsoft to adapt to the changing landscape. But the chances are probably high that Microsoft will eventually embrace open source to some degree to remain competitive.

When it comes to DotNetNuke, many people probably question why Microsoft would be interested in assisting an open source project where it receives no direct benefit. And it may be perplexing why Microsoft would sponsor a product that competes to some degree with several of its own commercial applications. But you do not have to look much further than the obvious indirect benefits to see why this relationship has tremendous value. First and foremost, at this point the DotNetNuke application is only designed for use on the Microsoft platform. This means that to use DotNetNuke, you must have valid licenses for a number of Microsoft infrastructure components (Windows operating system, database server, and so on). So this provides the financial value. In addition, DotNetNuke promotes the benefits of the .NET Framework and encourages developers to migrate to this new development platform. This provides the educational value. Finally, it cultivates an active and passionate community — a network of loyal supporters who are motivated to leverage and promote Microsoft technology on an international scale. This provides the marketing value.

Enhancements

In September 2003, with the assistance of the newly formed Core Team, we embarked on an ambitious mission to implement the enhancements suggested by Microsoft. The problem at this point was that in addition to the Microsoft enhancements, there were some critical community enhancements, which I ultimately perceived as an even higher priority if the project should hope to grow to the next level. So the scope of the enhancement project began to snowball, and estimated release dates began to slip. The quality of the release code was also considered to be so crucial a factor that early beta packages were not deemed worthy of distribution. Ultimately, the code base evolved so much that there was little question the next release would need to be labeled version 2.0. During this phase of internal development, some members of the Core Team did an outstanding job of supporting the 1.x community and generating excitement about the next major release. This was critical in keeping the DotNetNuke community engaged and committed to the evolving project.

A number of excellent community enhancements for the DotNetNuke 1.0 platform also emerged during this stage. This sparked an active third-party reseller and support community, establishing yet another essential factor in any largely successful open source project. Unfortunately, at this point the underlying architecture of the DotNetNuke application was not particularly extensible, which made the third-party enhancements susceptible to upgrade complications and somewhat challenging to integrate for end users. As a Core Team, we recognized this limitation and focused on full modularity as a guiding principle for all future enhancements.

Modularity is an architecture principle that basically involves the creation of well-defined interfaces for the purpose of extending an application. The goal of any framework should be to provide interfaces in all areas that are likely to require customization based on business requirements or personalization based on individuality. DotNetNuke provides extensibility in the area of modules, skins, templates, data providers, and localization. And DotNetNuke typically goes one step beyond defining the basic interface: it actually provides the full spectrum of related resource services including creation, packaging, distribution, and installation. With all of these services available, it makes it extremely easy for developers to build and share application extensions with other members of the community.

One of the benefits of working on an open source project is the fact that there is a high priority placed on creating the optimal solution or architecture. I think it was Bill Gates who promoted the concept of "magical software" and it is certainly a key aspiration in many open source projects. This goal often results in more preliminary analysis and design that tends to elongate the schedule but also results in a more extensible and adaptable architecture. This differs from traditional application development that often suffers from time and budget constraints, resulting in shortcuts, poor design decisions, and delivery of functionality before it is validated. Another related benefit is that the developers of open source software also represent a portion of its overall user community, meaning they actually "eat their own dog food" so to speak. This is really critical when it comes to understanding the business requirements under which the application needs to operate. Far too often you find commercial vendors who build their software in a virtual vacuum, never experiencing the fundamental application use cases in a real-world environment.

One of the challenges in allowing the Core Team to work together on the DotNetNuke application was the lack of high-quality infrastructure tools. Probably the most fundamental elements from a software development standpoint were the need for a reliable source-code-control system and issue-management system. Because the project had little to no financial resources to draw upon, we were forced to use whatever free services were available in the open source community. And although some of these services are leveraged successfully by other open source projects, the performance, management, and disaster recovery aspects are sorely lacking. This led to a decision to approach some of the more successful commercial vendors in these areas with requests for pro-bono software licenses. Surprisingly, these vendors were more than happy to assist the DotNetNuke open source project — in exchange for some minimal sponsorship recognition. This model has ultimately been carried on in other project areas to acquire the professional infrastructure, development tools, and services necessary to support our growing organization.

As we worked through the enhancements for the DotNetNuke 2.0 project, a number of Core Team members gained considerable respect within the project based on their high level of commitment, unselfish behavior, and expert development skills. Joe Brinkman, Dan Caron, Scott McCulloch, and Geert Veenstra sacrificed a lot of personal time and energy to improve the DotNetNuke open source project. And the important thing to realize is that they did so because they wanted to help others and make a difference, not because of self-serving agendas or premeditated expectations. The satisfaction of working with other highly talented individuals in an open, collaborative environment is reward enough for some developers. And it is this particular aspect of open source development that continues to confound and amaze people as time goes on.

In October 2003, there was a Microsoft Professional Developers Conference (PDC) in Los Angeles, California. The PDC is the premier software development spectacle for the Microsoft platform; an event that occurs only every two years. About a month prior to the event Cory Isakson, a developer on the Rainbow Portal open source project, contacted me, saying that "Open Source Portals" had been nominated as a category for a "Birds of Feather" session at the event. I posted the details in the DotNetNuke Forum and soon the item had collected enough community votes that it was approved as an official BOF session. This provided a great opportunity to meet with DotNetNuke enthusiasts and critics from all over the globe. It also provided a great networking opportunity to chat with the most influential commercial software vendors in the .NET development space (contacts made with SourceGear and MaximumASP at this event proved to be important to DotNetNuke, as time would tell).

Security Flaw

In January 2004, another interesting dilemma presented itself. I received an email from an external party, a web application security specialist who claimed to have discovered a severe vulnerability in the DotNetNuke application (version 1.0). Upon further research, I confirmed that the security hole was indeed valid and immediately called an emergency meeting of the more trusted Core Team members to determine the most appropriate course of action. At this point, we were fully focused on the DotNetNuke 2.0 development project but also realized that it was our responsibility to serve and protect the growing DotNetNuke 1.0 community. From a technical perspective, the patch for the vulnerability proved to be a simple code modification.

The more challenging problem was related to communicating the details of the security issue to the community. On the one hand we needed the community to understand the severity of the issue so that they would be motivated to patch their applications. On the other hand, we did not want to cause widespread alarm, which could lead to a public perception that DotNetNuke was an insecure platform. Exposing too many details of the vulnerability would be an open invitation for hackers to try and exploit DotNetNuke web sites, but revealing too few details would downplay the severity. And the fact that the project is open source meant that the magnitude of the problem was amplified. Traditional software products have the benefit of tracking and identifying users through restrictive licensing policies. Open source projects have licenses that allow for free redistribution, which means the maintainer of the project has no way to track the actual usage of the application and no way to directly contact all community members who are affected.

The whole situation really put security issues into perspective for me. It's one thing to be an outsider, expressing your opinions on how a software vendor should or should not react to critical security issues in their products. It's quite another thing to be an insider, stuck in the vicious dilemma between divulging too much or too little information, knowing full well that both options have the potential to put your customers at even greater risk. Ultimately, we created a new release version and issued a general security alert that was sent directly to all registered users of the DotNetNuke application by email and posted in the DotNetNuke Forum on `www.asp.net`:

```
Subject: DotNetNuke Security Alert

Yesterday we became aware of a security vulnerability in DotNetNuke.

It is the immediate recommendation of the DotNetNuke Core Team that all
users of DotNetNuke based systems download and install this security patch
as soon as possible. As part of our standard security policy, no further
```

```
detailed information regarding the nature of the exploit will be provided to
the general public.

This email provides the steps to immediately fix existing sites and mitigate
the potential for a malicious attack.

Who is vulnerable?

-- Any version of DotNetNuke from version 1.0.6 to 1.0.10d

What is the vulnerability?

A malicious user can anonymously download files from the server. This is not
the same download security issue that has been well documented in the past
whereby an anonymous user can gain access to files in the /Portals directory
if they know the exact URL. This particular exploit bypasses the file
security mechanism of the IIS server completely and allows a malicious user
to download files with protected mappings (ie. *.aspx).

The vulnerability specifically *does not* enable the following actions:

-- A hacker *cannot* take over the server (e.g. it does not allow hacker
code to be executed on the server)

How to fix the vulnerability?

For Users:

{ Instructions on where to download the latest release and how to install }

For Developers:

{ Instructions with actual source code snippets for developers who had
diverged from the official DotNetNuke code base and were therefore unable to
apply a general release patch }

Please note that this public service announcement demonstrates the
professional responsibility of the Core Team to treat all possible security
exploits as serious and respond in a timely and decisive manner.

We sincerely apologize for the inconvenience that this has caused.

Thank you, we appreciate your support...

DotNetNuke - The Web of the Future
```

The security dilemma brings to light another often misunderstood paradigm when it comes to open source projects. Most open source projects have a license that explicitly states that there is no support or warranty of any kind for users of the application. And while this may be true from a purely legal standpoint, it does not mean that the maintainer of the open source application can ignore the needs of the community when issues arise. The fact is, if the maintainer did not accept responsibility for the application, the users would quickly lose trust and the community would dissolve. This implicit trust relationship is what all successful open source communities are based upon. So in reality, the open source license acts as little more than a waiver of direct liability for the maintainer. The DotNetNuke project certainly conforms to this model because we take on the responsibility to ensure that all users of the application are never left on an evolutionary dead-end and security issues are always dealt with in a professional and expedient manner.

DotNetNuke 2.0

After six months of development, including a full month of public beta releases and community feedback, DotNetNuke 2.0 was released on March 23, 2004. This release was significant because it occurred at VS Live! in San Francisco, California — a large-scale software development event sponsored by Microsoft and Fawcette publications. Due to our strong working relationship with Microsoft, I was invited to attend official press briefings conducted by the ASP.NET Team. Essentially, this involved up to eight private sessions with the leading press agencies (Fawcette, PC Magazine, Computer Wire, Ziff Davis, and so on) where I was able to summarize the DotNetNuke project, show them a short demonstration, and answer their specific questions. The event proved to be spectacularly successful and resulted in a surge of new traffic to the community (now totaling more than 40,000 registered users).

DotNetNuke 2.0 was a hit. We had successfully delivered a high-quality release that encapsulated the majority of the most requested product enhancements from the community. And we had done so in a manner that allowed for clean customization and extensibility. In particular, the skinning solution in DotNetNuke 2.0 achieved widespread critical acclaim.

In DotNetNuke 1.X, the user interface of the application allowed for little personalization — essentially all DNN sites looked much the same, a negative restriction considering the highly creative environment of the World Wide Web. DotNetNuke 2.0 removed this restriction and opened up the application to a whole new group of stakeholders: web designers. As the popularity of portal applications had increased in recent years, the ability for web designers to create rich, graphical user interfaces had diminished significantly. This is because the majority of portal applications were based on platforms that did not allow for clear separation between form and function, or were architected by developers who had little understanding of the creative needs of web designers. DotNetNuke 2.0 focused on this problem and implemented a solution where the portal environment and creative design process could be developed independently and then combined to produce a stunningly harmonious end-user experience. The process was not complicated and did not require the use of custom tools or methodologies. It did not take long before we began to see DotNetNuke sites with richly creative and highly graphical layouts emerge — proving the effectiveness of the solution and creating a "Can you top this?" community mentality for innovative portal designs.

DotNetNuke (DNN) Web Site

To demonstrate the effectiveness of the skinning solution, I commissioned a local web design company, Circle Graphics, to create a compelling design for the `www.dotnetnuke.com` web site (see Figure 1-8). As an open source project, I felt that I could get away with an unorthodox, somewhat aggressive site design and I was impressed by some of Circle Graphics' futuristic, industrial concepts I had seen.

It turned out that the designer who had created these visuals had since moved on but was willing to take on a small contract as a personal favor to the owner. He created a skin that included some stunning 3-D imagery including the now infamous "nuke-gear" logo, circuit board, and plenty of twisted metallic pipes and containers. The integration with the application worked flawlessly and the community was wildly impressed with the stunning result. Coincidentally, the designer of the DotNetNuke skin, Anson

Vogt, has since gone on to bigger and better things, working with rapper Eminem as the Art Director for 3-D animation on the critically acclaimed Mosh video.

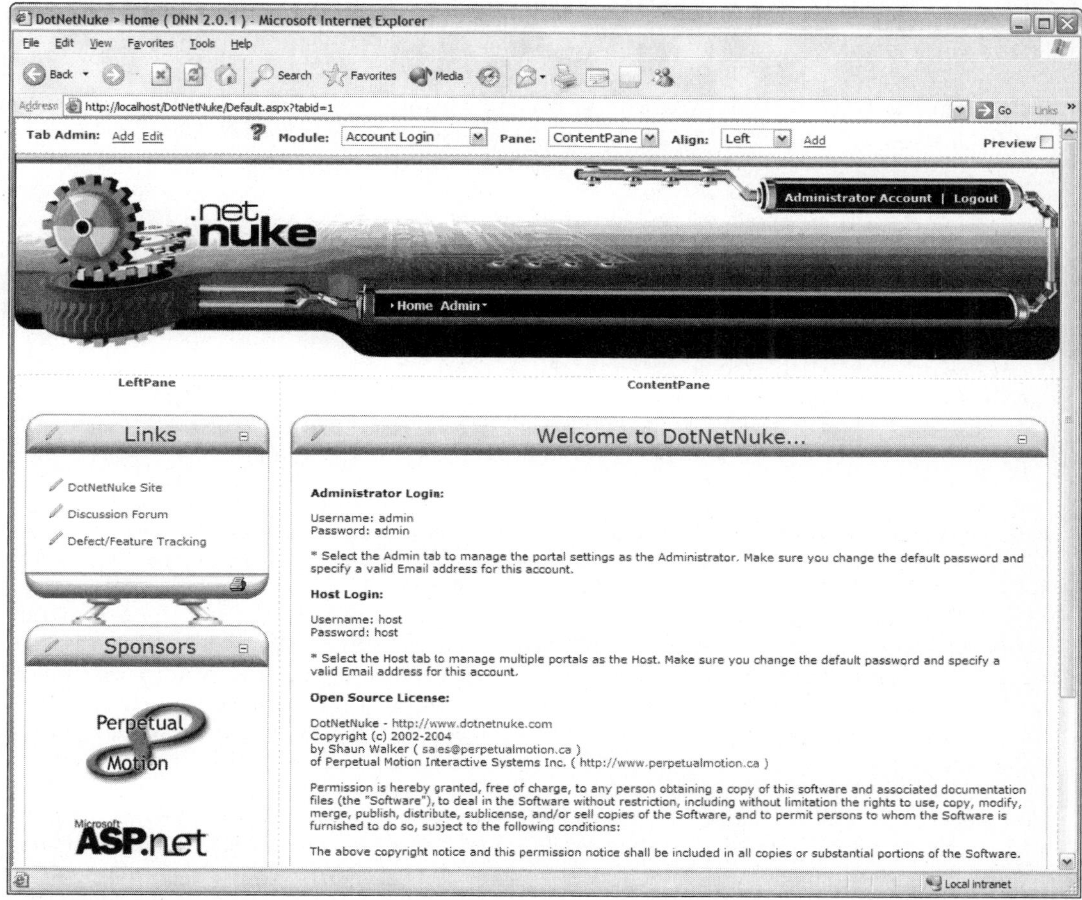

Figure 1-8

Provider Model

One of the large-scale enhancements that Microsoft insisted on for DotNetNuke 2.0 also proved to be popular. The Data Access Layer in DotNetNuke had been re-architected using an abstract factory model that effectively allowed it to interface with any number of relational databases. Microsoft coined the term "provider model" and emphasized it as a key component in the future ASP.NET 2.0 framework. Therefore, getting a reference implementation of this pattern in use in ASP.NET 1.x had plenty of positive educational benefits for Microsoft and DotNetNuke developers. DotNetNuke 2.0 included both a fully functional SQL Server and MS Access version, and the community soon stepped forward with mySQL and Oracle implementations as well. Again the extensibility benefits of good architecture were extremely obvious and demonstrated the direction we planned to pursue in all future product development.

Upon review of the DotNetNuke 2.0 code base, it was obvious that the application bore little resemblance to the original IBuySpy Portal application. This was a good thing because it raised the bar significantly in terms of n-tiered, object-oriented, enterprise-level software development. However, it was also bad in some ways because it alienated some of the early DotNetNuke enthusiasts who were in fact "hobby programmers," using the application more as a learning tool than a professional product. This is an interesting paradigm to observe in many open source projects. In the early stages, the developer community drives the feature set and extensibility requirements that, in turn, results in a much higher level of sophistication in terms of system architecture and design. However, as time goes on, this can sometimes result in the application surpassing the technical capabilities of some of its early adopters. DotNetNuke had ballooned from 15,000 lines of managed code to 46,000 lines of managed code in a little more than six months. The project was getting large enough that it required some serious effort to understand its organizational structure, dependencies, and development patterns.

Open Source Philosophy

When researching the open source phenomenon, there are a few fundamental details that are often ignored in favor of positive marketing rhetoric. I would like to take the opportunity to bring some of these to the surface because they provide some additional insight into some of the issues we face in the DotNetNuke project.

The first myth surrounds the belief that open source projects basically have an unlimited resource pool at their immediate disposal. Although this may be true from a purely theoretical perspective, the reality is that you still require a dedicated management structure to ensure that all of the resources are channeled in an efficient and productive manner. An army of developers without some type of central management authority will never consistently produce a cohesive application; and more likely, their efforts will result in total chaos. As much as the concept is often despised by hard-core programmers, dedicated management is absolutely necessary to set expectations and goals, ensure product quality, mitigate risk, recognize critical dependencies, manage scope, and assume ultimate responsibility. You will find no successful open source project that does not have an efficient and highly respected management team.

Also with regards to the unlimited resourcing myth, there are in fact few resources who become involved in an open source project that possess the level of competency and communication skills required to earn a highly trusted position in the meritocracy. More often, the resources who get involved are capable of handling more consumer-oriented tasks such as testing, support, and minor defect corrections. This is not to say that these resources do not play a critical role in the success of the project — every focused ounce of volunteer effort certainly helps sustain the health of the project. But my point is that there is usually a relatively small group on most open source projects who are responsible for the larger-scale architectural enhancements.

Yet another myth is related to the belief that anyone can make a direct and immediate impact on an open source project. Although this may be true to some degree, you generally need to build a trusted reputation within the community before you are granted any type of privilege. And there are few individuals who are ever awarded direct write access to the source code repository. Anyone has the ability to submit a patch or enhancement suggestion; however, there's no guarantee that it will be added to the open source project code base. In fact, all submissions are rigorously peer-reviewed by trusted resources, and only when they have passed all validation criteria are they introduced to the source code repository. In addition, although a specific submission may appear to be quite useful when judged in isolation, there may be higher-level issues to consider in terms of upgrade support (a situation that can lead to submitter frustration if the issues are not fully explained). From a control standpoint, this is not much different than source control management on a traditional software project. However, the open source model does significantly alter this paradigm in that everyone is able to review the source code. As a result, the sheer volume of patches submitted to this process can be massive.

There are also some interesting interpretations of open source philosophy that occasionally result in differences of opinion and, in the worst cases, all-out community revolts. This generally occurs because the guidelines for open source are quite non-explicit and subjective. One particularly hot topic that relates to DotNetNuke is source code access.

Some open source projects provide anonymous read-only access to the development source code base at all times. This full transparency is appreciated by developers who want to stay abreast of the latest development efforts — even if they are not trusted members of the inner project team. These developers accept the fact that the development code may be in various stages of stability on any given day, yet they appreciate the direct access to critical fixes or enhancements. Although this model does promote more active external peer review, it can often lead to a number of serious problems. If developers decide to use pre-release code in a production environment, they may find themselves maintaining an insecure or unstable application. This can lead to a situation in which the community is expected to support many hybrid variants rather than a consistent baseline application. Another possible issue is that a developer who succumbs to personal motivations may be inclined to incorporate some of the development enhancements into the current production version and release it as a new application version. Although the open source license may allow this, it seriously affects the ability of the official project maintainer to support the community. It is the responsibility of the project maintainer to always ensure a managed migration path from one version to the next. This model can only be supported if people are forced to use the official baseline releases offered by the project maintainer. Without these constants to build from, upgrades become a manual effort and many users are left on evolutionary dead-ends. For these reasons, DotNetNuke chooses to restrict anonymous read access to the development source code repository. Instead, we choose to issue periodic point releases that allow us to provide a consistent upgrade mechanism as the project evolves.

Stabilization

Following the success of DotNetNuke 2.0, we focused on improving the stability and quality of the application. Many production issues were discovered after the release that we would have never anticipated during internal testing. As an application becomes more extensible, people find ingenious new ways to apply it, which often produces unexpected results. We also integrated some key Roadmap enhancements that were developed in isolation by Core Team members. These enhancements were actually quite advanced because they added a whole new level of professional features to the DotNetNuke code base, transforming it into a viable enterprise application framework.

It was during this time that Dan Caron single-handedly made a significant impact on the project. Based on his experience with other enterprise applications, he proceeded to add integrated exception handling and event logging to DotNetNuke. This provided stability and "auditability" — two major factors in most professional software products. He also added a complex, multi-threaded scheduler to the application. The scheduler was not just a simple hard-coded implementation like I had seen in other ASP.NET projects, but rather it was fully configurable via an administrative user interface. This powerful new feature could be used to run background housekeeping jobs as well as long-running tasks. With this in place, the extensibility of the application improved yet again.

Third-Party Components

An interesting concern that came to our attention at this time was related to our dependence on external components. To provide the most powerful application, we had leveraged a number of rich third-party controls for their expert functionality. Because each of these controls was available under its own open source license, they seemed to be a good fit for the DotNetNuke project. But the fact is there are some major risks to consider. Some open source licenses are viral in nature and have the potential to alter the license of the application they are combined with. In addition, there is nothing that prevents third parties from changing their licensing policy at any time. If this situation occurs, then it is possible that all users of the application who reference the control could be in violation of the new license terms. That's a fairly significant issue and certainly not something that can be taken lightly. Based on this knowledge, we quickly came up with a strategy that was aimed at minimizing our dependency on third-party components. We constructed a policy whereby we would always focus on building the functionality ourselves before considering an external control. And in the cases where a component was too elaborate to replicate, we would use a provider model, much like we had in the database layer, to abstract the application from the control in such a way that it would allow for a plug-in replacement. This strategy protects the community from external license changes and also provides some additional extensibility for the application.

With the great publicity on the `www.asp.net` web site following VS Live! and the consistent release of powerful new enhancements, the spring of 2004 brought a lot of traffic to the `dotnetnuke.com` community web site. At this point, the site was poorly organized and sparse on content due to a lack of dedicated effort. Patrick Santry had been on the Core Team since its inception and his experience with building web sites for the ASP.NET community became valuable at this time. We managed to make some fairly major changes to improve the site, but I soon realized that a dedicated resource would be required to accomplish all of our goals. Without the funding to secure such a resource, many of the plans had to unfortunately be shelved.

Core Team Reorganization

The summer of 2004 was a restructuring period for DotNetNuke. Thirty new community members were nominated for Core Team inclusion and the Core Team itself underwent a reorganization of sorts. The team was divided into an Inner Team and an Outer Team. The Inner Team designation was reserved for those original Core Team individuals who had demonstrated the most loyalty, commitment, and value to the project over the past year. The Outer Team represented individuals who had earned recognition for their community efforts and were given the opportunity to work toward Inner Team status. Among other privileges, write access to the source code repository is the pinnacle of achievement in any source code project, and members of both teams were awarded this distinction to varying degrees.

In addition to the restructuring, a set of Core Team guidelines was established that helped formalize the expectations for team members. Prior to the creation of these guidelines, it was difficult to isolate non-performers because there were no objective criteria by which they could be judged. In addition to the new recruits, a number of inactive members from the original team were retired, mostly to demonstrate that Core Team inclusion was a privilege, not a right. The restructuring process also brought to light several deficiencies in the management of intellectual property and confidentiality among team members. As a result, all team members were required to sign a retroactive non-disclosure agreement as well as an intellectual property contribution agreement. All of the items exemplified the fact that the project had graduated from its "hobby" roots to a professional open source project.

Microsoft Membership API

During these formative stages, I was once again approached by Microsoft with an opportunity to showcase some specific ASP.NET features. Specifically, a Membership API had been developed by Microsoft for Whidbey (ASP.NET 2.0), and they were planning on creating a backported version for ASP.NET 1.1 that we could leverage in DotNetNuke. This time the benefits were not so immediately obvious and required some thorough analysis. This is because DotNetNuke already had more functionality in these areas than the new Microsoft API could deliver. So to integrate the Microsoft components without losing any features, we would need to wrap the Microsoft API and augment it with our own business logic. Before embarking on such an invasive enhancement, we needed to understand the clear business benefit provided.

Well, you can never discount Microsoft's potential to impact the industry. Therefore being one of the first to integrate and support the new Whidbey APIs would certainly be a positive move. In recent months there had been numerous community questions regarding the applicability of DotNetNuke with the early Whidbey Beta releases now in active circulation. Early integration of such a core component from Whidbey would surely appease this group of critics. From a technology perspective, the Microsoft industry had long been awaiting an API to converge upon in this particular area, making application interoperability possible and providing best practice due diligence in the area of user and security information. Integrating the Microsoft API would allow DotNetNuke to "play nicely" with other ASP.NET applications — a key factor in some of the larger-scale extensibility we were hoping to achieve. Last, but not least, it would further our positive relationship with Microsoft — a factor that was not lost on most as the key contributor to the DotNetNuke project's growth and success.

The reorganization of the Core Team also resulted in the formation of a small group of highly trusted project resources that, for lack of a better term, we named the Board of Directors. The members included Scott Willhite, Dan Caron, Joe Brinkman, Patrick Santry, and me. The purpose of this group was to oversee the long-term strategic direction of the project. This included discussion on confidential issues pertaining to partners, competitors, and revenue. In August 2004, we scheduled our first general meeting for Philadelphia, Pennsylvania. With all members in attendance, we made some excellent progress on defining action items for the coming months. This was also a great opportunity to finally meet in person some of the individuals with whom we had only experienced Internet contact in the past. With the first day of meetings behind us, the second day was dedicated to sightseeing in the historic city of Philadelphia. The parallels between the freedom symbolized by the Liberty Bell and the software freedom of open source were not lost on any of us that day.

Returning from Philadelphia, I knew that I had some significant deliverables on my plate. We began the Microsoft Membership API integration project with high expectations of completion within three months. But as before, there were a number of high-priority community enhancements that had been promised prior to the Microsoft initiative, and as a result the scope snowballed. Scope management is an extremely difficult task when you have such an active and vocal community.

"Breaking" Changes

The snowball effect soon revealed that the next major release would need to be labeled version 3.0. This is mostly because of "breaking" changes: modifications to the DotNetNuke core application that changed the primary interfaces to the point that plug-ins from the previous version 2.0 release would not integrate without at least some minimal changes. The catalyst for this was due to changes in the Membership API from Microsoft, but this only led to a decision of "If you are forced to break compatibility, introduce all of your breaking changes in one breaking release." The fact is there was a lot of baggage preserved from the IBuySpy Portal that we were restricted from removing due to legacy support considerations. DotNetNuke 3.0 provided the opportunity to reexamine the entire project from a higher level and make some of the fundamental changes we had been delaying for years in some cases. This included the removal of a lot of dead code and deprecated methods as well as a full namespace reorganization that finally accurately broke the project API into logical components.

DotNetNuke 3.0 also demonstrated another technical concept that would both enrich the functionality of the application framework as well as improve the extensibility without the threat of breaking binary compatibility. Up until version 3.0, the service architecture for DotNetNuke was completely uni-directional. Custom modules could consume the resources and services offered by the core DotNetNuke framework but not vice versa. So although the application managed the secure presentation of custom modules within the portal environment, it could not get access to the custom module content information. Optional interfaces enable custom modules to provide plug-in implementations for defined core portal functions. They also provide a simple mechanism for the core framework to call into third-party modules, providing a bi-directional communication channel so that modules could finally offer resources and services to the core (see Figure 1-9).

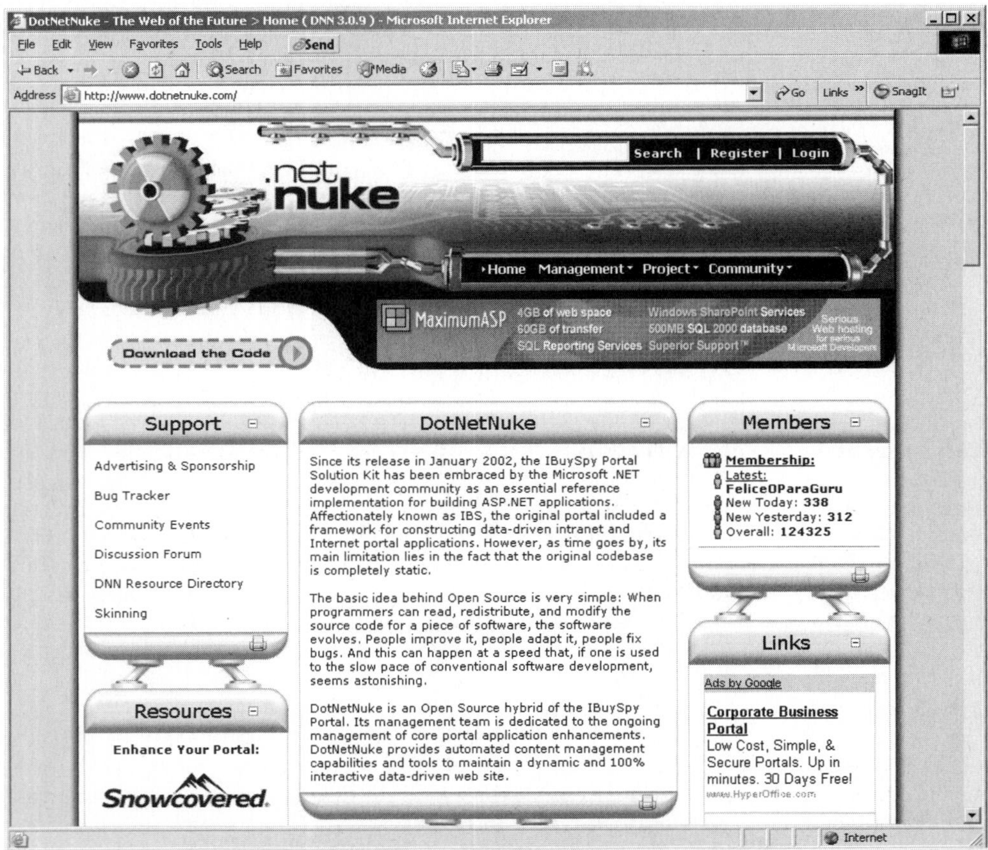

Figure 1-9

Web Hosters

Along with its many technological advances, DotNetNuke 3.0 was also being groomed for use by entirely new stakeholders: Web Hosters. For a number of years, the popularity of Linux hosting has been growing at a far greater pace than Windows hosting. The instability arguments of early Microsoft web servers were beginning to lose their weight as Microsoft released more resilient and higher-quality server operating systems. Windows Server 2003 had finally shed its clunky Windows NT 4.0 roots and was a true force to be reckoned with. Aside from the obvious economic licensing reasons, there was another clear reason why Hosters were still favoring Linux over Windows for their clients: the availability of end-user applications.

The Linux platform had long been blessed with a plethora of open source applications running on the Apache web server, built with languages such as PHP, Perl, and Python, and leveraging open source databases such as mySQL. (The combination of these technologies is commonly referred to as LAMP.) The Windows platform was really lacking in this area and was desperately in need of applications to fill this void.

For DotNetNuke to take advantage of this opportunity, it needed a usability overhaul to transform it from a niche developer–oriented framework to a polished end-user product. This included a usability enhancement from both the portal administration as well as the web host perspectives. Since Rob Howard left Microsoft in June 2004, my primary Microsoft contact was Shawn Nandi. Shawn did a great job of drawing upon his usability background at Microsoft to come up with suggestions to improve the DotNetNuke end-user experience. Portal administrators received a multi-lingual user interface with both field-level and module-level help. Enhanced management functions were added in key locations to improve the intuitive nature of the application. Web Hosters received a customizable installation mechanism. In addition, the application underwent a security review to enable it to run in a Medium Trust — Code Access Security (CAS) environment. The end result was a powerful open source, web-application framework that could compete with the open source products on other platforms and offer Web Hosters a viable Windows alternative for their clients.

DotNetNuke 3.0

Much of the integration work on the Membership API and usability improvements were fueled by a much larger hosting initiative that Microsoft was preparing to unleash in May 2005. This initiative included a comprehensive program aimed at increasing awareness for Windows-based hosting solutions on an international level. Based on its strength as a framework for building consumer web sites, Microsoft invited DotNetNuke to participate in the program as long as it could meet a defined set of technical criteria, including Membership API integration, Medium Trust CAS compliance, localization, and usability improvements. Nearly all of the enhancements were already identified on the product roadmap, so the opportunity to be included in the hosting program was really a win-win proposition for the project and the community. In addition, we believed that the benefit of participating in such a large-scale initiative would be enormous in terms of lending credibility to the DotNetNuke product, introducing the project to influential new stakeholders, and helping to build brand equity.

Core Team members made significant contributions during the development of DotNetNuke 3.0. Scott McCulloch, with the assistance of Jeremy White, implemented a full-featured URL rewriting component that allowed DotNetNuke to use standard URLs. Vicenc Masanas was instrumental in working on localization, templating, and stabilization tasks. Joe Brinkman implemented search-engine architecture, enabling content indexing across all modules in a portal instance. Jon Henning introduced a Client API library, enabling powerful client-side behavior in DotNetNuke modules. Perhaps the greatest code contributions were made by Charles Nurse. Realizing the massive amount of work that would be required to deliver the enhancements for the hosting program (and knowing that using only volunteer efforts would not hit the schedule deadlines), I hired the first full-time DotNetNuke contract resource. Charles was immediately put to work abstracting all of the core modules into independent private assemblies. At the same time, he reorganized entry fields in all application user interfaces and added full localization capabilities, including field-level online help.

The concept of localization was one the most commonly requested enhancements for the DotNetNuke application. Localization actually has multiple meanings when it comes to software applications because there is a distinct difference between static and dynamic content. Static content is information that is delivered as part of the core application typically implemented by developers. Dynamic content is information that is provided by users of the application and is typically entered by knowledge workers or webmasters. In DotNetNuke 3.0, we delivered full static localization for all administrative interfaces. This meant that all labels, messages, and help text could be translated and displayed in different languages based on the preference of the user. Developing a scalable architecture in this area turned out to be a challenging task because the solutions offered by Microsoft as part of the ASP.NET 1.x framework were better suited for desktop applications and had serious deficiencies and limitations for web applications. Instead, we decided to target the ASP.NET 2.0 localization architecture, which better addressed the web scenario. However, due to the specific business requirements of DotNetNuke, we soon realized that we were going to have to take some liberties with the proposed ASP.NET 2.0 localization architecture to enable us to achieve our goals for runtime updatability and scalability in a shared hosting environment. In the end, we were able to deliver a powerful solution that satisfied our business needs and provided forward compatibility to the upcoming ASP.NET 2.0 release.

The optional interface architectural model described earlier reaped rewards in DotNetNuke 3.0 in a number of key application areas. Registration of module actions in earlier versions of DotNetNuke was always less than optimal because they were dependent on page life-cycle events that were difficult to manage in a variety of scenarios. Optional interfaces finally provided a clean mechanism for the core framework to programmatically call into modules and retrieve their module actions. Other new features based on optional interfaces included content indexing, import, and export. In each of these cases, the core framework could rely on modules to provide content in a specific format that then allowed the core framework to provide advanced portal services.

After multiple beta releases (some of which were deemed not fit for public consumption), DotNetNuke 3.0 was officially released on March 12, 2005. Although there were breaking changes between DotNetNuke 2.0 and DotNetNuke 3.0, a number of modules were immediately available for DotNetNuke 3.0 due to the success of a pilot program named "30 for 3.0." This program was the shrewd strategy of Scott Willhite, and allowed a serious group of commercial module developers to have early access to beta releases of the DotNetNuke 3.0 product, enabling them to deal with any compatibility issues before the core framework became publicly available. Aside from the obvious benefits of having "applications" immediately available for the new platform, this program also provided some excellent business intelligence. It proved one of Scott's earlier assumptions that the vocal forums community represented only a small portion of the overall DotNetNuke user community. It also exposed the fact that DotNetNuke had found its way into Fortune 500 companies, military applications, government web sites, international software vendors, and a variety of other high-profile installations.

DotNetNuke 3.0 was released with two supported languages: English and German. Delivering two complete language packs adhered to one of our newer philosophies of always attempting to provide multiple functional examples to prove the effectiveness of a particular extensibility model. Before long, community members began submitting new language packs in their native dialects that were posted on the `dotnetnuke.com` site for download. The total number of supported language packs soon surpassed 30. This resulted in incredible growth and adoption for the DotNetNuke framework on an international basis.

Release Schedule

A common open source concept is referred to as "release early, release often." The justification is that the sooner you release, the sooner the open source community can validate the functionality, and the sooner you get feedback — good and bad — which helps improve the overall product. This concept is often combined with a "public daily build" paradigm, where continuous integration is used to automatically build, package, and publish a new application version every day. These concepts make a lot of sense for single-purpose applications; that is, applications that have closed APIs and have no external dependencies. But plug-in framework applications such as DotNetNuke possess a different set of requirements, many of which are not complementary with the "release early, release often" model.

Consider the case of any entity that has developed plug-in resources for the DotNetNuke framework. These could include modules, language packs, skins, or providers. Every time a new core version is released, each of these resources needs to be validated to ensure that it functions correctly. In many cases, this involves extensive testing, packaging a new version of the specific resource, publishing compatibility information, updating related documentation, communicating availability and/or issues to users, servicing compatibility support requests, updating commercial product listings, and so on. You must also consider the issues for the resource consumer. Consumers need to feel confident in the acquisition and installation of application resources. They are not keen on analyzing complicated compatibility matrices to manage their investment. And resellers such as Hosters represent an even larger superset of application consumers. The effort involved to perform application upgrades becomes more complicated and costly as the release frequency increases. This is clearly a case where "release early, release often" can lead to issues for framework consumers and suppliers.

For these reasons, DotNetNuke has always tried to follow a fairly well-structured release cycle. This has resulted in fewer major public releases but a much higher quality, more stable, core application. In general, it has enabled DotNetNuke resource suppliers and consumers to participate in a functional product ecosystem. However, as the number of serious platform adopters increased, so did the demands for better core-release communication.

DotNetNuke Projects

One of the goals of the DotNetNuke 3.0 product release that had tremendous value for the community at large was the abstraction of the modules that were traditionally bundled with the core framework. The core modules were neglected in favor of adding more functionality to the core framework services. This resulted in a set of modules that demonstrated limited functionality and were not evolving at the same pace as the rest of the project. The abstraction of the modules from the core framework led to the formation of the DotNetNuke Projects program: a new organizational concept modeled after the Apache Foundation that allowed many complementary open source projects to thrive within the DotNetNuke ecosystem. From a technical perspective, the modules were abstracted in a manner that conformed to our extensibility model for building "private assembly" modules and allowed each module to be managed as its own independent project. The benefit was that each module could form its own team of developers, with its own roadmap for enhancements, and its own release schedule. As a governing entity, DotNetNuke would provide infrastructure services such as a source code repository, issue tracker, project home page, and email services for the project as well as a highly visible and respected distribution and marketing channel.

Obviously there are tradeoffs that need to be accepted when decomposing a monolithic system into its constituent components, but the overall benefits of this approach reaped substantial rewards for the project. For one thing, it provided a new opportunity for developer participation — basically providing a sandbox where developers could demonstrate their skills and passion for the DotNetNuke project. This helped promote the "meritocracy" model and aided in our Core Team recruitment efforts. The community benefited through the availability of powerful, free, open source components that were licensed under the standard DotNetNuke BSD license. It also allowed the modules to evolve much more rapidly and with more focus than they ever received as part of the monolithic DotNetNuke application. Abstracting the core set of modules was a good start; however, the platform was lacking some other essential modules — modules that were well integrated and provided the common functionality required by most consumer web sites. These items included a discussion forum, blog, and photo gallery.

Early in the DotNetNuke 3.0 life cycle, there were discussions with a high-profile third-party software development company that was actively developing an integrated suite of components with forum, blog, and gallery functionality. Although early indications seemed to be positive regarding collaboration, they unfortunately did not comprehend the opportunity of working with the DotNetNuke community and ultimately decided to instead focus their efforts on constructing their own proprietary solution. Because this decision was not communicated to us until late in the DotNetNuke 3.0 development cycle, it meant that we had to scramble to find a suitable alternative. Luckily, two of our own Core Team members — Tam Tram Minh of TTT Corporation and Bryan Andrews of AppTheory — had been collaborating on a comparable set of modules and had already been offering them for free download to the DotNetNuke community. Discussions with them led to the creation of three powerful new DotNetNuke Projects: the DotNetNuke Forums, Blog, and Gallery.

Integrating third-party modules is not without its share of challenges. An "incubation" period is required to make the module conform to the official DotNetNuke project standards. An official marketing name must be defined for the project and all references to the old module name need to be updated. This includes namespaces, folder names, filenames, code comments, database object names, release package metadata, and documentation. To allow legacy users of the contributed module to be able to migrate to the new DotNetNuke project, a robust upgrade mechanism must be created. The module also needs to be reviewed to ensure that it does not contain any security flaws or serious defects that could affect the general community. From an infrastructure perspective, the code needs to be uploaded to a dedicated source code repository, an issue tracker project must be created, and a project home page complete with discussion forum and blog needs to be created on `dotnetnuke.com`. These tasks represent the technical integration issues that need to be addressed; but an item of even greater importance for third-party modules is management of the associated intellectual property.

Intellectual Property

There are two main contributing factors when it comes to intellectual property: copyright and licensing. The copyright holder is the person who owns the rights to the intellectual property. Normally this is the creator; however, copyright can also be transferred to other individuals or companies. The copyright holder has the right to decide how his intellectual property can be used by others. When it comes to software, these usage details are generally published as a license agreement. License agreements can vary a great deal depending on the environment, but they generally resemble a standard legal contract, explicitly outlining the rights and responsibilities of each party. The copyright holder also has the right to change the license for the intellectual property at their discretion. It is this scenario that requires the most due diligence when dealing with third-party contributions.

Anybody who contributes source code to the DotNetNuke project must submit a signed Contributor License Agreement. This document ensures that the individual has the right to contribute intellectual property to the project without any type of encumbrance. It also transfers copyright for any contributed intellectual property to the project. This is important because DotNetNuke needs to be able to ensure all of its intellectual property is licensed consistently throughout the entire application. It protects the community from a situation where an individual copyright holder could change the license restrictions for a specific piece of intellectual property, forcing the entire community into a reactive situation (a situation we have already seen multiple times in the still nascent Microsoft open source community).

In the case of third-party modules that are fully functional applications with an existing and active user base, the intellectual property rights are owned by the external party. Under this scenario, we cannot adopt the intellectual property into the DotNetNuke project because it would mean that we would have no control over its licensing. Even if the contributor agreed to license the intellectual property under a complementary BSD open source license, the original copyright holder would still have the ability to change the license at any time in the future, which would put all users of the module in jeopardy. To mitigate this risk, we require that DotNetNuke must have sufficient rights to the intellectual property so that the community is adequately protected. However, we do not feel it would be fair to force a contributor to release all of the rights to their own intellectual property. Therefore, we have a Software Grant Agreement — a contract that provides both parties with full copyright to the specified intellectual property. Essentially this means that the intellectual property has been split into two independent versions. The contributor owns one version and is allowed to license it or modify it as they see fit. DotNetNuke owns the other version and licenses it under the standard DotNetNuke BSD License for distribution and enhancement. The end result is a win-win situation for both parties as well as the community.

Marketing

The success of any serious initiative must begin with the formulation of specific goals and the ability to measure progress as you work toward those goals. In terms of measuring the growth of the DotNetNuke project, we had traditionally monitored the total number of registered users on the `dotnetnuke.com` web site, the number of new users per month, and the number of downloads per month. These metrics revealed some definite trends but were rather myopic in terms of providing a relative comparison to other open source or commercial products. As a result, we looked for some other indicators that we could use to measure our overall market impact.

Alexa is a free service provided by Amazon that can be used to judge the popularity of an Internet web site. Popularity is an interesting metric because traffic distribution on the Internet conforms to a 90/10 rule: 10% of web sites account for 90% of the overall traffic, and 90% of web sites share the other 10%. This logarithmic scale means that it gets progressively more difficult to make substantial gains in your Alexa ranking as your web site popularity increases. Although the Alexa ranking is not a conventional progress indicator, we decided to use it as one of our key performance indicators (KPIs) in determining the impact of our marketing efforts. The `dotnetnuke.com` web site had an Alexa ranking of 19,000 in April 2005.

SourceForge is the world's largest development and download repository of open source code and applications. Early in its project history, DotNetNuke had established a presence on SourceForge.Net (`http://sourceforge.net/projects/dnn` as shown in Figure 1-10) and continued to leverage its mirrored download infrastructure and bandwidth for hosting all project release packages. Because SourceForge.Net contained listings for all of largest and most successful open source projects in existence, it also provided a variety of comparison and ranking statistics that could be used to judge activity and popularity. This seemed to be another good KPI to measure our impact in the open source realm. In April 2005, the DotNetNuke project had an overall project ranking of 1,271.

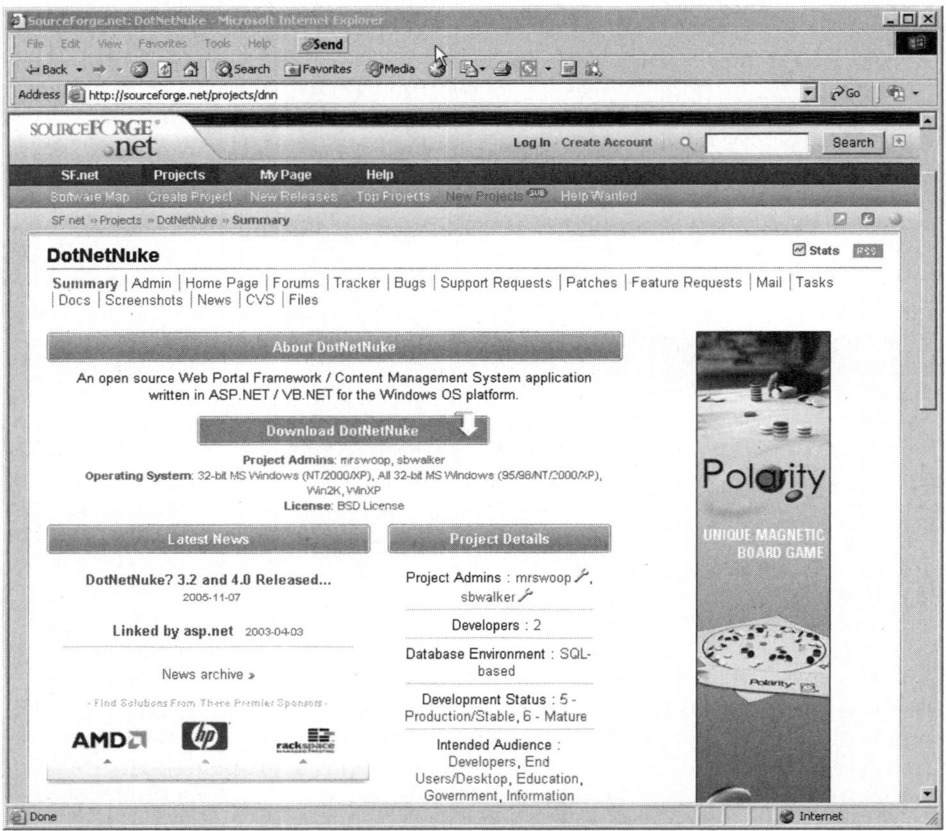

Figure 1-10

One of the items that had been neglected over the life of the project was the `dotnetnuke.com` web site. It had long been a goal to build this asset into a content-rich communication hub for the DotNetNuke community. Patrick Santry made some early progress in this area but recently found his volunteer time diminishing due to personal and family commitments. Because a web site is largely an extension of product marketing (another function that had long been ignored) the `dotnetnuke.com` web site suffered from sparse content, poor organization, and inconsistent focus. After the release of DotNetNuke 3.0, a significant effort was invested in improving all aspects of the web site. Much of the initial improvements came as a result of evaluating web sites of other open source projects. After extensive deliberation, we decided to organize the site information into three functional areas: user-oriented information, community collaboration, and developer information. New "sticky" content areas were added for project news and community events. The Home Page was completely revamped to provide summary marketing information and project metrics.

In March 2005, another significant milestone occurred in DotNetNuke history. Dan Egan, a passionate DotNetNuke community member, wrote a book for PackT Publishing entitled *Building Websites with VB.NET and DotNetNuke 3.0*. This was the first book published about DotNetNuke and was essential in proving the demand for the product, paving the way for future DotNetNuke books from a variety of other publishers. In addition, a handful of Core Team members, including me, were also collaborating on a book for WROX Press during this time frame, but the demands of getting the DotNetNuke 3.0 product ready for release forced us to slip the publication date. Regardless, any technical content that makes it to mass publication through traditional channels lends an incredible amount of credibility and equity to the project or technology for which it is written. In addition, books can have a positive marketing impact; especially if they reach wide circulation through online retailers and brick-and-mortar bookstores.

In May of 2005, Core Team member Jim Duffy was successful in securing a DotNetNuke session on DotNetRocks!, an Internet radio talk show hosted by Carl Franklin and Richard Campbell. This was our second appearance on the show (the first being in August of 2004), and it was a lot of fun to talk about DotNetNuke in such a relaxed and open atmosphere. The show focused on the recent DotNetNuke 3.0 release and proved to be great way to promote some of the incredible new application features. It is hard to estimate the impact of the appearance on the DotNetRocks! show, but it certainly made me a firm believer in the benefits of podcasting as a powerful broad distribution marketing medium.

Microsoft Hosting Program

Throughout the month of May 2005, Microsoft launched the aforementioned Hosting program. The purpose of the program was to encourage shared hosting providers to take advantage of Windows technology to grow their hosting businesses. The primary benefit of this program was the Service Provider License Agreement (SPLA), which allowed hosting companies to avoid large capital expenditures and pay their licensing fees based on actual usage. This lowered the barrier of entry in terms of cost and provided a risk-free model to test the demand for services. In addition to the SPLA, Microsoft recognized the value of end-user applications and included substantial promotion of DotNetNuke in the hosting seminars encompassing thirty cities around the globe. I was fortunate enough to attend the first seminar in Redmond, Washington, which provided an excellent opportunity to network with the Microsoft Hosting Evangelists, a group of hard-working individuals who were dedicated to the growth of Windows web hosting on an international basis. At the beginning of June, I was also privileged to attend a WSHA seminar in Amsterdam, Netherlands. The invitation was extended by Microsoft Europe, which was especially interested in the localization capabilities of the DotNetNuke application. This trip gave me a deeper understanding of the localization challenges of the international community and also provided me the opportunity to meet Geert Veenstra and Leigh Pointer — two Core Team members who actively participated in and evangelized DotNetNuke since its creation.

Although the Microsoft Hosting program did not reap any direct financial rewards for DotNetNuke, it provided a number of powerful benefits. It exposed the application to an influential group of organizations: large-scale web hosting companies that dominate the shared hosting market in terms of customer base and annual revenues. Companies such as GoDaddy, Pipex, and 1and1 began offering DotNetNuke as part of their Windows hosting plans. The hosting program also caught the attention of the largest hosting control panel vendors. Companies such as SW-Soft (Plesk), WebHostAutomation (Helm), and Ensim added integrated installation support for the DotNetNuke application within their control panel applications. All of these strategic partnerships exposed DotNetNuke to a much larger consumer audience and would not have been possible had it not been for the Microsoft Hosting program.

Collaboration with web hosts also resulted in new application features that were added to satisfy some of their specific business requirements. The ability for DotNetNuke to run in a web farm environment was one such feature that really addressed the application scalability questions beyond a single web server configuration. Dan Caron stepped up yet again to champion these enhancements, producing an architecture with two different caching providers to satisfy the widest array of use cases. Charles Nurse also completed the abstraction of all modules into isolated components that could be optionally installed and uninstalled from the core framework. This change provided additional flexibility for Web Hosters in terms of being able to customize their offering for clients.

Infrastructure

One of the benefits of the original sponsorship agreement with Microsoft was a free shared hosting account on the servers managed by the ASP.NET team at OrcsWeb. This arrangement served us well in the early stages but the fact that we had extremely limited access (that is, FTP) to the account and absolutely no control over the associated infrastructure services eventually created some challenges for the project. In addition, we had long been leveraging services from PortalWebHosting for back office items such as DNS, source control, issue tracking, and email, but a recent change in ownership created some friction in regards to legacy promises and agreements. Approaching premium hosting provider MaximumASP in the fall of 2004, we were able to secure a generous formal sponsorship agreement that paved the way for a more centralized and professionally managed project infrastructure.

Initially, MaximumASP provided us with two dedicated servers and a Virtual Private Server (VPS) account on a shared server. One of the dedicated servers was configured as a SQL Server database server and the other as a back office server. The VPS account was provisioned as a web account for our public web site. This configuration served us well initially, but the rapid growth of membership and the lack of control over the web server soon forced us to look for other options. Further discussions with MaximumASP resulted in the allocation of a dedicated web server for our public web site. The combination of a dedicated web server and a dedicated database server proved flexible enough to handle our full web site requirements. It was not until we added discussion forums to our site and pushed our traffic past 4 million page views a month that we felt the need to consider a web farm configuration.

The physical abstraction of the core application into a more modular organization had a direct impact on our back office project infrastructure. Rather than simply managing a single source code repository and issue tracking database, we now had to deal with many Project sandboxes — each with their own membership and security considerations. In addition, establishing effective communication channels for different stakeholder groups was critical for managing the project. This is one of the reasons why the DotNetNuke Forums Project played such a significant role in the evolution of the DotNetNuke projects. It allowed for a variety of discussion forums to be created, some public and some private, providing focused communication channels for project members.

During 2005, Scott Willhite also made some huge contributions to the project in terms of infrastructure management. In a project of this size with so many active participants, there is an incredible amount of administrative work that goes on behind-the-scenes to keep the project moving forward. As most people know, administrative tasks are largely unappreciated and only seem to get attention when there is a problem. Scott does his best to keep the endless stream of infrastructure tasks flowing; receiving little or no recognition for his efforts, but playing an instrumental role in the success of the DotNetNuke project.

Branding

One of the things that became obvious during the writing of *Professional DotNetNuke ASP.NET Portals* (Wiley Publishing, Inc.) was that our branding message was not clear. Although our trademark and domain name reflected "DotNetNuke," our logo contained an abbreviated terminology of "`.netnuke.`" This led to confusion for authors of the book as well as the publisher in terms of what was the correct product branding. As I mentioned earlier in this chapter, the initial branding was constructed with little or no foresight; therefore, it came as no surprise that a major overhaul was necessary.

Initial conversations within the Core Team offered some interesting and sometimes surprising opinions on the DotNetNuke brand. When discussion came to a stalemate, the topic was raised in the public forums that resulted in a similar scenario. Some folks considered the "nuke" term to be too offensive, unprofessional, or shocking to be used as a serious brand name. Others placed a significant metaphorical value in the current logo, which contained a gear embossed with a nuclear symbol. Some preferred a transition to the "DNN" acronym that was often used as a shorthand reference in various communication channels. Further debate ensued over the category we occupied (portal, content management system, framework, and so on) and the clear marketing message we wished to convey.

As the project founder, I had my own opinions on the brand positioning and ultimately decided to resort to an authoritarian model rather that a committee model so that we could make a decision and move forward. From my perspective, when it comes to technology companies, there is a lot of acceptance for non-traditional brand names (consider Google, Yahoo!, Go Daddy, and so on). In addition, due to the press coverage of the Microsoft Hosting program, the DotNetNuke name achieved a significant amount of exposure; therefore, a complete change in brand would impose a serious setback in terms of brand acceptance and market reach. Taking into consideration the valued perspectives of the Core Team and community, I felt there should be a way to provide a win-win solution for everyone.

I first tried working with a local design company (the same company that produced the DotNetNuke 2.0 site skin), and although they had a real talent for brand identity services, there were no concepts produced that really grabbed my attention or satisfied my goals for the project. Perhaps I was being overly critical in my judgment of various designs, but I knew that I absolutely did not want to settle for a concept unless I thought it met 100% of my criteria. Although Nik Kalyani had been on the Core Team for eight months and had even expressed a serious interest in the marketing activities of the project, it was not until the re-branding exercise where his talents were truly exemplified.

Nik and I started an offline dialog where we quickly established some complementary goals, at least at a conceptual level. The basic decision was that we wanted to retain the full "DotNetNuke" brand name and strengthen rather than dilute its brand emphasis. We also wanted to reduce or eliminate the negative imagery associated with the nuclear warning symbol in the current logo. Although the abbreviated form of the word "nuke" tended to evoke a negative response from the general population (relating it to bombs and radiation), the expanded form of "nuclear" and "nucleus" had a much more positive response (related to science, energy, and power). The word "nucleus" also had some complementary terms associated with it such as "core," "kernel," and so on that worked well with the open source project philosophy. The trick was to find a way to emphasize one aspect over another.

Nik spent countless hours designing alternative logo concepts. From a typeface perspective, he suggested using the Neuropol font, and I really liked the fact that it had a strong technical overtone but not so much that it could not be used effectively in other mainstream media applications. To achieve a uniform appearance for the typeface, we decided to use all capital letters — even though the standard format for the brand name in regular print would continue to be mixed case. Nik included a unique customization for the "E" and the "T" letters that resulted in a distinctive, yet professional styling for the word-mark contained within the logo.

Creating the graphical element for the logo was a much bigger challenge because we were looking for a radically new design that exemplified so many diverse project attributes. To summarize some of the more important criteria, we were looking for something simple yet distinctive, with at least some elements that provided a visual reference to the old logo for continuity. It needed to be scalable and adaptable to a wide range of media (both digital and print) and cost-effective to reproduce. And perhaps the most subjective item I promoted was that the logo should be stylish — with my acceptance criteria being, "Would my wife permit me to wear clothing embossed with the logo when we went out in public together?" Nik created more than 40 unique logo concepts before arriving at a design that seemed to catch the full essence of what we were trying to accomplish (see Figure 1-11). After working at this for so long and dealing with the discouragement and frustration, it was a euphoric moment to discover the proverbial "love at first sight."

Figure 1-11

It is amazing how many diverse concepts can be represented in a single image. The saying "a picture is worth a thousand words" is cliché, but in this case, it certainly summarized the final product. The new logo had the basic shape of a nuclear atom. The nucleus of the atom was shaped like a gear to retain its heritage to the previous project logo. The logo was two basic colors — red and black (using shades of grey to achieve a 3-D effect) — making it much more adaptable and simple to reproduce in a wide variety of media formats than the previous logo (which used shadows and gradients for 3-D effects). The gear had twelve teeth (a number considered to be lucky in many cultures). The intersection of the three revolving electron trails (referred to as the "triad") could still be subtly viewed as a nuclear symbol reference. With some creative inference, they could also be viewed as the three-letter project acronym: DNN. Later, someone on the Core Team mentioned that the triad bore some resemblance to the Perpetual Motion Interactive Systems Inc. "infinity" logo — a reference I had never formally recognized but something that I am sure played a subliminal role in my selection.

In terms of brand acceptance, we realized there may be significant community backlash related to the new creative brand, especially from companies who were currently leveraging the existing DotNetNuke branding in their marketing materials. Therefore we were pleasantly surprised at the overwhelming positive feedback we received regarding the new brand identity. Our goal was to roll out the brand in progressive stages with the DotNetNuke 3.1 product release representing the official brand launch to the general community.

With the creative elements out of the way, it was time to finalize the rest of the branding process. Because DotNetNuke serves many different stakeholder groups, it was difficult to come up with a product category that was focused but not too limiting in scope. From a marketing perspective, the board agonized over the optimal brand message. "Content management" was a powerful industry buzzword, but if you compared the capabilities of DotNetNuke in this area with other enterprise software offerings, it became obvious that it would be some time before we could be considered a market leader. The term "portal" had been so overused in recent years that it became severely diluted and lost its clarity as an effective marketing message. Conversely, the emerging term "framework" began to surface more regularly and was starting to gain industry acceptance with both developers and management groups as a powerful software development category. Because DotNetNuke's architectural principles were predicated on simplicity and extensibility, the framework category seemed to be a natural fit. The next step involved clarifying the type of framework. DotNetNuke was primarily designed for use in a web environment and its breadth of features made it well-suited for building advanced data-driven Internet applications. The resulting "web application framework" was an emerging industry category in which DotNetNuke could take an immediate leadership role. Where applicable, we could also leverage our "open source" classification to emphasize our community philosophy and values.

One of the toughest parts of any re-branding exercise involves updating all existing brand references to reflect the new identity. In DotNetNuke's case, this affected the content and design of the `dotnetnuke.com` web site, the marketing references in the DotNetNuke release package, and all technical and user documentation. Compared to the time it took to construct the new logo, the time it took Nik Kalyani to create a new site design was minimal (which is truly amazing considering the amount of time and effort that typically goes into a custom site design). I had long been a fan of Nik's minimalist style, which emphasized clean presentation, lightweight graphics, and plenty of whitespace. Nik's expert grasp of the DotNetNuke skinning architecture enabled him to create a combination of skins and containers that were applied in a matter of minutes to completely transform the entire web site. The new site design was creative yet professional and eliminated the "cartoonish" criticisms of the previous site design (see Figure 1-12). Nik also created our first professional document templates that would provide consistency and emphasis of our branding elements within our technical and user documentation.

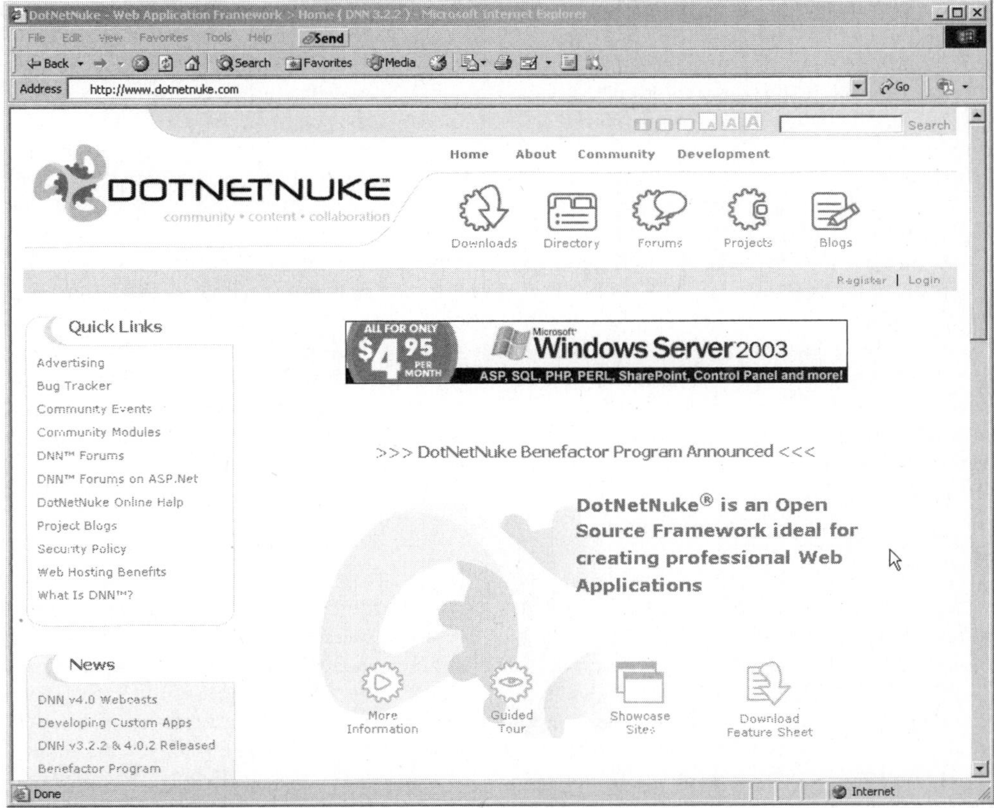

Figure 1-12

Tech Ed

At the beginning of June, there was a massive Microsoft technology conference, Tech Ed, in Orlando, Florida. Based on a generous invitation from the International .NET Association (INETA), Scott Willhite and I were provided with an opportunity to attend the event as their special guests. The timing was perfect because *Professional DotNetNuke ASP.NET Portals* was officially released at this event, as was the new project branding. Joe Brinkman and Dan Caron were able to attend some aspects of the book launch festivities, and we managed to jam a substantial amount of marketing activities into the five-day event. We had a dedicated Birds of Feather session, two community focus sessions at the INETA booth, a guest appearance at an INETA User Group workshop related to building effective web sites (where we learned 90% of .NET user groups were already using DotNetNuke), and a number of book signings scheduled by WROX Press at the Tech Ed bookstore. The DotNetNuke book was the top-selling developer book at the Tech Ed bookstore for the event — a fact that emphasized the growing popularity of the project. We also distributed official DotNetNuke T-shirts that showcased the new project branding, a popular item amid all the typical free swag provided at these events.

Seizing the opportunity of having the majority of the DotNetNuke Board of Directors together in one place, we had our second official board meeting — an all-day session in the conference room of our hotel in Orlando. On the agenda was a serious discussion related to Core Team reorganization and key project roles. For quite some time, we had realized that the current flat organizational structure was somewhat dysfunctional and that we ultimately needed more dedicated management resources to accomplish our goals. However, to support these resources, we needed a sufficient financial model. Discussion focused on the pros and cons of various revenue opportunities, their revenue potential, and their perceived effect on the community ecosystem. We also talked about what it would take for the current Board members to commit to full-time dedicated roles in the organization and the associated financial and security implications. A lot of really deep discussion ensued, which gave us a much better mental picture of the challenges that lay ahead if we truly wanted to take the project to the next level.

Following the publication of *Professional DotNetNuke ASP.NET Portals*, there was a bit of a media frenzy around the relationship between Microsoft and the open source phenomenon. Some of my personal opinions and quotes from the book found their way into an article published on CNET (one of the leading mainstream news sites), resulting in a lot of additional exposure for the project. It was interesting to see the power of the media at work, where a reference in a highly visible and trusted journalism channel can lead to broad distribution of a particular message (much like a stone in a pond leads to a concentric series of expanding ripples). For the most part, large companies are the most successful at leveraging these medial channels, but special-interest organizations also have the opportunity to make a significant impression.

Credibility

Although DotNetNuke had experienced a healthy growth rate through its open source philosophy, it had largely done so by appealing to the needs of grass-roots developers. Although these stakeholders represent an integral part of the high-tech marketplace, there is another group that is far more influential in terms of market impact. The so-called "decision-makers" represent the management interests in serious enterprise-level business organizations. For DotNetNuke to make the transition from a developer-oriented open source project to a serious enterprise software contender, it needed to appeal to the decision-maker mentality.

Where developers think in terms of short-term technical decisions (that is, "What tool can I use to get this job done as quickly as possible so that I can impress my boss?"), decision-makers think in terms of long-term business decisions. They are interested in the future support of a platform or product. They consider solutions in terms of "investments," "security," and how much "risk" is associated with adopting a particular technology as part of their company infrastructure. And regardless of the technical superiority of a software solution, the adoption criteria always come down to basic trust and consumer confidence. So the challenge for an open source project like DotNetNuke is establishing the necessary level of credibility to be taken seriously.

In the commercial world, customers get a sense of confidence based on the fact that they have paid licensing fees to a vendor that generally provides them with a certain level of future support. Obviously nothing is guaranteed, but this financial model provides both parties with a sense of security and responsibility. Another thing that the financial model affords is the ability to market the product through traditional channels — channels that "decision-makers" tend to monitor on a regular basis.

In the open source world, there are no licensing fees, which helps contribute to the lower cost of ownership but also leaves the investment/security aspect somewhat lacking. If you look at Linux, for example, you will notice that the broad industry buy-in for the operating system did not occur until after some serious market vendors (Sun and IBM) pledged their support. As soon as this happened, many medium-large companies began to take Linux more seriously. And this was not because Linux received any product improvements through these relationships, but rather because it reduced its risk perception in the general marketplace. And without traditional licensing fees, open source products generally do not have the budget to leverage traditional marketing channels and must instead rely on grassroots and viral marketing techniques.

So let's consider some of the ways in which an open source product can improve its credibility and reduce its risk perception for decision-makers. Clearly one way is that it can align itself with large, respected vendors who lend credibility (that is, "If vendor X thinks its good, then so do we."). Another way is to have mainstream books, magazines, and mass media distributors publish information about the product, contributing to the overall community knowledge base and providing recognition. Yet another option is to identify reference implementations that exemplify the best qualities of the product and impress people with their performance, elegance, or extensibility. Another way is to demonstrate a proven track record and history for supporting the community, especially through platform transitions where the likelihood of project failure is high. The overall size of the community ecosystem, including the open source participants, consumers, and third-party service providers, is another critical aspect in demonstrating credibility.

DotNetNuke definitely made some significant advancements in credibility in 2005. The strong working relationship with Microsoft reaped rewards with the Hosting program. The publication of *Professional DotNetNuke ASP.NET Portals* by Wiley Publishing, Inc. and *Building Websites with VB.NET and DotNetNuke 3.0* by PackT Press provided some excellent recognition through traditional publishing channels. Articles and references in mainstream magazines such as *Visual Studio Magazine*, *ASP.NET Pro*, *CoDe Magazine*, and *.NET Developers Journal* also provided some great benefits. The showcase on `dotnetnuke.com` contained many diverse reference implementations and we had proven through three years of product upgrades that we were committed to supporting the community. The membership and download metrics continued to grow exponentially, as did the number of independent software vendors (ISVs) providing products or services within the DotNetNuke ecosystem.

Trademark Policy

Unfortunately, an unexpected issue arose in the summer of 2005 that immediately put the project into crisis mode. Based on some invalid assumptions, a software consultant from Australia recommended that their client register a trademark for the DotNetNuke name in Australia. Aside from the obvious ethical implications, the immediate reaction was that this move was based on ulterior motives that could potentially hold the entire Australian DotNetNuke community hostage. Further communication revealed that the Australian company had concerns over the official trademark registered in Canada; specifically in regards to the fact it was embedded within the application source code and binaries, and that their business investment could be compromised if restrictions were ever put on trademark usage. Ultimately this whole situation revealed a number of critical issues when it comes to trademarks. First, the holder of the trademark must publish a policy that clearly defines the allowable usage of the mark under a wide range of use cases. Second, the trademark holder must make every attempt to enforce the policy so that the mark does not become a common term and lose its value as a protected asset. Third, a trademark must be registered in every jurisdiction where it intends to be used.

To satisfy the first requirement, I firmly believe in the philosophy of "standing on the shoulders of giants." Research revealed that Mozilla had recently gone through a similar project challenge, so we decided to use their recently published trademark policy as a template for our own. The political ramifications of introducing the policy at this point seemed controversial, but absolutely necessary if we intended to protect our brand. After extensive research, review, and legal advice, we finally announced the trademark policy in conjunction with the logo guidelines in July 2005. The overall community feedback was quite positive, because the policy made every effort to emphasize our open source roots and strong community ideals.

To satisfy the second requirement, all marketing materials were updated to reflect the trademark policy guidelines, and many community sites made changes to bring their use of the trademark into compliance. We also obtained legal advice on the creation of a Trademark License Agreement to be used in situations where third parties required the right to use the DotNetNuke trademarks for specific business purposes.

The third requirement was somewhat more challenging to deal with because it had substantial financial implications. The cost to register an individual trademark in a specific jurisdiction (country) can cost anywhere from $2000.00 to $5000.00. As an organization, we simply do not have the financial means to support such a large expenditure. So instead of considering all jurisdictions, we decided to focus on those jurisdictions that had a large project following. These included the United States, Canada, Australia, Japan, and the European Union. This whole experience gave me a much deeper understanding of the financial commitment required by large multinational companies who wish to protect their brand around the world.

ASP.NET 2.0

In July 2005, we recognized that we had approximately four months to prepare for the launch of Microsoft's next-generation software development platform. ASP.NET 2.0 had been under development for three years and had finally reached the point where it was ready for public release. Aside from reading the standard marketing propaganda in the various trade magazines catering to the Windows platform, I had not done significant research into the specific challenges DotNetNuke faced as a product related to this platform upgrade. And, as is usually the case, we quickly found out it was going to be some of the unpublicized platform changes that were going to cause us the most difficulty.

Based on early community feedback for the ASP.NET 1.0 release, Microsoft decided to completely overhaul the way web projects operated, including substantial changes to the underlying compilation model. Because DotNetNuke's advanced modular architecture strayed so far from the traditional monolithic ASP.NET application model, these platform changes had a significant impact on the project. Our solid working relationship with Microsoft reaped benefits in that we were able to engage in some focused dialog and onsite meetings in Redmond with the Microsoft Product Managers who understood the nuances of the new ASP.NET 2.0 platform better than anyone. Scott Guthrie, Simon Calvert, Omar Khan, and a number of other key Microsoft resources got personally involved in assisting us to find a suitable migration path.

I have to admit I was a vocal critic during these early discussions, because I could not understand the business cases that precipitated some of the major architectural changes. But after working closely with the Microsoft Product Managers, I began to warm up to the benefits of the new model and started to envision how we could leverage its capabilities to expose some powerful new options to the DotNetNuke community. But before we could focus on these new options, our most critical requirement was that we could not have breaking changes in the DotNetNuke framework in our ASP.NET 2.0 release. The main business criteria driving this requirement was the fact we had just had a major release with significant breaking changes in March 2005, and we could not risk an all-out community revolt (or product fork) based on compatibility issues.

Research and discussion proceeded throughout the months of July and August as we worked with Microsoft to find an optimal solution. Feedback from the community seemed to be mixed. People who were victims of the Microsoft propaganda machine seemed to think that the release of ASP.NET 2.0 would signal the end of DotNetNuke, because it promised to deliver so many overlapping application features. Other people who had adopted DotNetNuke as part of their business infrastructure expressed apprehension and fear regarding ASP.NET 2.0, based on their past experience that a significant platform upgrade usually resulted in a costly migration effort. Surprisingly, out of all the feedback collected, it appeared that nobody was making a serious attempt to perform the upgrade on their own, and that they were waiting for us to provide a migration path (as we had always done in the past). This element of trust was not lost on me, and I did my best to blog on a regular basis to provide public communication of our progress.

Reorganization

Throughout the summer and fall of 2005 there was ongoing discussion related to Core Team reorganization. Based on the guidelines that had been created when individuals were invited to join the team in the summer of 2004, there was clearly a group of members who had not lived up to their commitments. The list of responsibilities included staying involved in Core Team business through the private discussion forum; participating in weekly Core Team chats; contributing bug fixes, enhancements, or documentation to the core product; and being active in community support channels. There were many legitimate reasons, both personal and business-related, which led to inactivity for team members. However, the unfortunate side effect is that it led to a community perception that based on the total number of Core Team members, we were underachieving in terms of our capabilities as a whole. The Core Team reorganization meant that a number of team members needed to be retired to make way for some new members who had earned the right to participate based on their community accomplishments over the past year. The project had never had to deal with a situation like this in the past, and it's safe to say that as software developers, we are much more adept at solving technical problems than human-resources issues. So the dilemma was how to break the news to the inactive members in a professional and courteous manner that still respected their past accomplishments and left the door open for future participation. It was Scott Willhite who demonstrated the most experience and wisdom in this area, as we worked on establishing effective human resources processes for the organization.

Since the original formation of the Core Team, all members had received equal rights in terms of project participation. This included not only communication channels but also permissions to the product source code repository. This model worked well when the team was small and all members were on equal footing in terms of their technical abilities. However, it proved to be a challenge when the team grew in size and members were added with varying technical backgrounds. DotNetNuke had grown into a mission-critical web application framework that many businesses now relied on for rock solid performance and reliability. We could no longer accept the risk of inexperienced team members checking in code that could compromise the stability of the application. As a result, we needed to re-factor our project roles to reflect the new project requirements.

A common theme that helped drive the re-factoring of the project roles was accountability. In the past, we had witnessed the fact that without accountability, an individual would not exhibit the same level of commitment, dedication, or passion for the project. As a result, it was important to provide Core Team members with areas of accountability where their contributions would be highly visible and easily recognized by the general public. This public aspect provided them with a much greater benefit in terms of visibility in the community, but it also made them a target for criticism if they were inactive because they were personally responsible for specific areas of the project.

Using the Apache Foundation as a meritocracy reference, we made some significant changes to the organizational model of the project. The old "Inner Team" designation was abolished in favor of a new "Core Team Trustee" role. Scott Willhite came up with this new name based on the desire for industry-accepted terminology and the fact that this innermost project role assumed the highest level of trust from a development perspective. Core Team Trustees had multiple years of experience on the project, had successfully demonstrated their technical aptitude, and as a result were granted write access to the core repository. The old "Outer Team" designation was simplified to "Core Team Member" — a role that was able to participate in all Core Team communication channels, but was only provided read access to the source code repository. In addition, we added a role for the DotNetNuke Projects of "Project Team Lead." This role was responsible for managing the project infrastructure and communicating project status to the Core Team.

Microsoft Conferences

The month of September 2005 began with the Professional Developer Conference (PDC) in Los Angeles, California. Based on a kind gesture from Microsoft, a large number of Core Team members were provided with free registration for the event in exchange for analysis of key ASP.NET 2.0 features that could be used in the DotNetNuke framework. Scott Willhite, Dan Caron, Nik Kalyani, Jon Henning, John Mitchell, Charles Nurse, and I were all able to attend the event, bringing together in one place the largest group of Core Team members ever. It was an excellent opportunity to get to know one another and we spent a lot of time hanging out together, exploring the exhibitor area, hosting a Birds of Feather session, visiting Universal Studios, and attending a variety of conference sessions.

The DotNetNuke Board, with the recent inclusion of Nik Kalyani, also took the opportunity to have some serious meetings regarding the progress of the revenue opportunities discussed at Tech Ed. The summer had not been productive in getting any programs launched other than Advertising and Sponsorship, and Nik took a lead role in attempting to clarify both our marketing and financial initiatives for the next 12 months. Specific board members were assigned to each major opportunity, and projections were presented and discussed in terms of assumptions, benefits, and execution tasks. We had a lot of work ahead of us, including a major platform transition, now firmly scheduled for November 7, 2005.

Later in September, Microsoft hosted a three-day summit for its Most Valuable Professional (MVP) community members. Based on public achievements, a number of DotNetNuke Core Team members earned this award of distinction in 2005. Bruce Hopkins (Georgia, USA), Phil Beadle (Australia), Cathal

Connelly (Ireland), Jim Duffy (USA), and I (Canada) were all able to attend the private summit in Redmond, Washington. The summit provided the opportunity to get to know these Core Team members on a more personal level, including their appetite for social festivities. I was also able to spend some time with a number of prominent ASP.NET personalities and DotNetNuke evangelists whom I greatly respected in terms of their contributions to the community. In addition, there was also a large representation of Microsoft employees at the MVP summit that resulted in some excellent networking opportunities and offline discussions. Steve Balmer's keynote address provided some valuable insight into the roadmap for Microsoft's products and revealed areas where DotNetNuke could focus its efforts to strengthen its market position in the coming year.

Directly following the MVP summit, I had the privilege of attending my first ASPInsiders summit as well. The ASPInsiders represent a group of well-respected industry leaders in the Microsoft ASP.NET community. I had recently been inducted as an official member and appreciated the opportunity to be included in such an elite group of professionals. Perhaps the most important benefit of being an ASPInsider was that it provided representation for the DotNetNuke development community and validation of our extensive contributions to the industry. Due to its small focused membership, the ASPInsiders summit had a personal and direct interaction with Microsoft employees, allowing its members to provide feedback on a number of exciting new technologies. The networking opportunity was incredible, and the intricate dynamics of the various personalities and companies represented was especially interesting.

DotNetNuke 4.0

Throughout the months of September and October, Charles Nurse was instrumental in working on the migration to the ASP.NET 2.0 platform. He invested a massive amount of time researching compatibility issues, creating various proof of concepts, and communicating regularly with Microsoft. He actually pursued two different agendas simultaneously: the upgrade of DotNetNuke 3.0 to ASP.NET 2.0 from a runtime perspective, and the creation of a new web project model for DotNetNuke 4.0 that provided a development strategy for the future.

To support the community, we concluded that we would need to support two parallel code bases for an undetermined period of time: DotNetNuke 3.x (ASP.NET 1.1) and DotNetNuke 4.0 (ASP.NET 2.0). Obviously, a more optimal solution would have been a single code base that worked on both platforms; however, this simply was not possible based on the platform compilation changes in ASP.NET 2.0. In addition, we did not know what to expect in terms of the adoption rate for the new Microsoft platform. Therefore, it seemed natural that we focus on developing for both ASP.NET 1.1 and 2.0 in the short term. An unfortunate side effect of this model involved a general recommendation to develop to the lowest common denominator (that is, not leverage ASP.NET 2.0-specific technology) and synchronizing all fixes and enhancements across the two code bases.

One of the greatest achievements in the platform migration was that we were able to fully satisfy our business requirement for no breaking changes. DotNetNuke modules and skins developed on ASP.NET 1.1 could be installed directly into the ASP.NET 2.0 environment without any changes whatsoever. This had massive benefits for the commercial DotNetNuke ecosystem because vendors could continue developing their modules as a single code base on the ASP.NET 1.1 platform but offer their packaged products for sale in both channels.

The only item that remained outstanding right up until the week before the November 7th launch was how to develop DotNetNuke 4.0 modules on the ASP.NET 2.0 platform. The new dynamic compilation model in ASP.NET 2.0 created some challenges for many of our runtime extensibility features, especially where they relied on object instantiation through reflection. As is often the case with technical problems, the answer is out there — it's just a matter of finding the right person to ask. As luck would have it, a Microsoft developer (Ting-Hao Yang) who was copied on some of the communication between our team and the Microsoft ASP.NET Product Manager group finally responded with details on a new ASP.NET 2.0 framework method that ultimately solved all of our remaining reflection issues. In the end, all that was required was a change to a single method in the DotNetNuke 4.0 core framework (to use BuildManager.GetType).

One of the benefits of the new ASP.NET 2.0 platform was that Microsoft had put a lot of focus on making the technology more accessible to the general developer community. A key deliverable in this strategy was the release of an entire suite of free "Express" tools. Included in the Express line was a tool named "Visual Web Developer" that provided a functional Integrated Development Environment (IDE) for ASP.NET 2.0. Leveraging the benefits of this powerful new tool, we created a DotNetNuke 4.0 Starter Kit that enabled a developer to configure a fully functional development environment within minutes. This had significant implications on the DotNetNuke development community because it lowered the barrier of entry and now made it possible for any aspiring software developer, from beginner to advanced, to be instantly productive with the DotNetNuke web application framework. Combine this with the free SQL Server 2005 Express database engine and you have a zero cost development environment. Visual Web Developer could not be used to develop server controls or class libraries; however, the fact that the DotNetNuke extensibility architecture was based on user controls made it a perfect fit.

Not wanting to neglect the existing DotNetNuke 3.0 community by focusing solely on ASP.NET 2.0 migration, we decided to integrate a few powerful new features that had long been requested by the general community. Core Team member Tam Tran Minh had been developing an Active Directory integration component for a number of years and agreed to contribute it as a fully supported core framework component. Additionally, Jon Henning had been busy working on a full-featured JavaScript API that would allow developers to leverage powerful client-side behavior in their modules. This included a new menu control, the DNN Menu, and an implementation of the popular Asynchronous JavaScript for XML (or AJAX) technology. AJAX technology had become one of the hottest new trends for web development, and it is important to note that DotNetNuke included a powerful AJAX library well before the announcement of ATLAS by Microsoft. The combination of these features offered benefits to both platform consumers and application developers, and further strengthened our core platform offering.

The official Microsoft launch date for ASP.NET 2.0 was set for November 7, 2005. We knew if we could release DotNetNuke 4.0 to coincide with this event, we would be able to ride the huge marketing wave created by Microsoft. Because we had always advocated "releasing software when it is ready," this hard deadline imposed some serious challenges on our meager project resources. Aside from the obvious technical deliverables, we had communication and marketing deliverables that also needed to roll out in unison. Nik Kalyani and Bill Walker showed their ability to pull things together on a tight schedule, and we launched our first monthly newsletter to the entire DotNetNuke registered user base (now 200,000 registered users) on November 7. The response was overwhelmingly positive as the significance of the achievement began to sink in. In the month of November, we recorded 165,000 downloads, far eclipsing any previous monthly download total in the history of the project.

An interesting aspect to consider in the ASP.NET 2.0 migration was that we delivered a fully managed upgrade to users of the DotNetNuke web application framework. Anyone who has ever attempted a major platform upgrade on their own should recognize the incredible value of this accomplishment. We had effectively eliminated a budget line item of considerable cost and effort from thousands of IT departments and business entities around the world. Compare this to scenarios where companies create their own custom ASP.NET 1.1 applications. In these cases, each company would need to invest significant resources and funding to work out their own web application migration strategy. Or compare this to another scenario where you adopt another web application framework, commercial or open source, which had not even considered the upgrade challenges posed by ASP.NET 2.0 and were going to force you to postpone your upgrade until it fit their own release schedule. In either case, the decision to adopt DotNetNuke as part of an organization's business infrastructure had certainly paid dividends worthy of the attention of any business decision-maker.

Immediately following the DotNetNuke 4.0 release, we focused on stabilization issues that were exposed through testing by a larger community audience. Another area that received dedicated focus was the Module Item Template feature of the DotNetNuke 4.0 Starter Kit. Through research and persistence, we were able to construct a DotNetNuke Module Template that could automatically create all of the development resources required to build a fully functional module in DotNetNuke 4.0. It even had some parameterization capabilities so that the template could be customized at runtime to meet the needs of the developer. I wrote an article describing the Starter Kit and Module Template and posted it on the public forums on `www.asp.net`. The article proved to be popular, with nearly 30,000 views recorded in the six weeks following its publication. It turned out that the changes in ASP.NET 2.0 resulted in some decent productivity benefits for module developers, further improving the capabilities of the DotNetNuke framework.

An interesting event occurred in December 2005, well after the official launch of ASP.NET 2.0. Based largely on the feedback that we provided Microsoft during our product migration efforts, Microsoft announced some add-ons for Visual Studio 2005 that added back ASP.NET 1.1 development support through Web Application Projects as well as compilation and merge support through Web Deployment Projects. Based on its superior architecture and incredible popularity, DotNetNuke was able to unite a significant portion of the Microsoft developer community and create a much stronger voice and more compelling argument in favor of specific platform features than would have ever been possible for individual developers. Besides the fact that these add-ons provided some critical options for web application developers, it was really gratifying to see that our direct feedback could have such an immediate and influential effect on the industry.

Slashdotted

In October 2005, I wrote a blog titled "No Respect for Windows Open Source." The blog was a political rant based on the fact that because DotNetNuke did not run on a fully open source stack of software components (that is, Linux/Apache/MySQL/PHP or LAMP), it did not get any respect from the general open source community. Further, it argued that all open source projects regardless of platform should be judged solely on the validity of their open source license and ideals. The blog was picked up by Slashdot, the largest independent news site for information technology, and resulted in a lot of exposure for the project (see Figure 1-13). The posting on Slashdot generated more than 500 comments, each with their unique perspective on the Windows open source paradigm.

In October, we were approached by *.NET Developers Journal* (*.NETDJ*) to do a series of articles on the DotNetNuke project. This was an excellent opportunity to showcase various aspects of the project in a mainstream magazine. A number of Core Team members were identified as potential authors and the first article in a series of six was published in the November edition of *.NETDJ*. Forging relationships with publishers is a great way to raise the profile of the project and open doors for future opportunities. In this case, working with SYS-CON (the publisher of *.NETDJ*) reaped rewards in terms of being approved as a featured speaker in the upcoming SYS-CON Enterprise Open Source conference in June 2006.

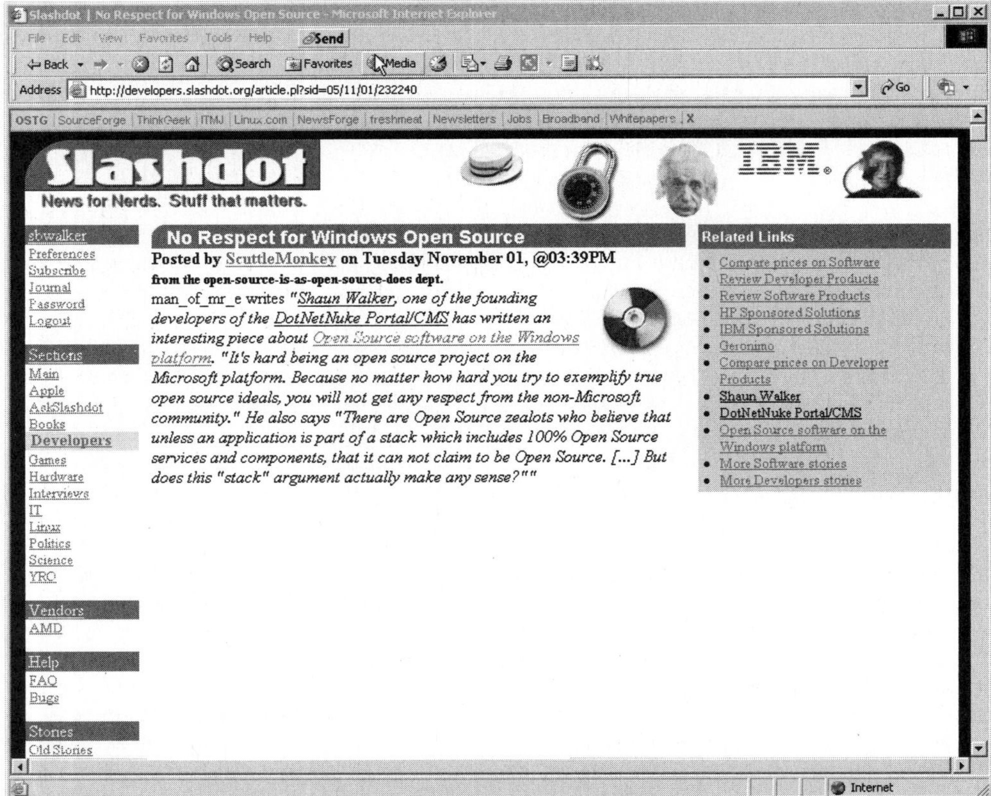

Figure 1-13

By the end of 2005, the `dotnetnuke.com` web site had achieved an impressive Alexa ranking of 6,741 and our SourceForge.Net ranking had climbed to #75 (out of all the open source projects in the world). We were consistently getting 15,000 new registered users per month and our project downloads averaged 120,000 per month. The `dotnetnuke.com` site was now serving 4.5 million page views per month, and every indication was pointing to even more improvement in 2006.

Benefactor Program

As much as there is a romantic notion regarding a distributed group of purely volunteer resources working together in their free time to produce an enterprise-level software product, it does not represent reality. To effectively manage all of the aspects of a professional software product, dedicated management is an absolute requirement. This does not just entail the standard project management principles for software development, but also the legal and marketing aspects of managing a high-profile technology asset. Since the project inception, I had been able to commit 100% of my time to the project only because there was a sufficient stream of project revenue to support my needs. And throughout the life of the project, a number of team members had been financially compensated for various deliverables so that we could meet obligations and scheduled deadlines. The financial resources came from a variety of sources, including third-party sponsorship, advertising, and custom consulting opportunities. Unfortunately, the revenue streams were not sizable or stable in terms of securing multiple resources for long-term engagements. Essentially, we were trying to operate a product company without any direct product revenue. And with the constant growth of the project, the demands were increasing rather than decreasing, putting even more pressure on the minimal set of project resources.

Back in July 2005, I concluded that without a dedicated sales effort, the `dotnetnuke.com` web site was never going to reach its full potential as a revenue-generating asset. (We had published ad rates on the site months earlier and had not received many serious inquiries.) I decided it was time to more actively cultivate our advertising and sponsorship revenue streams and that it was going to require spending some money to make money. Armed with a huge number of industry contacts collected at Tech Ed, I hired a full-time resource to actively manage the advertising and sponsorship program. Due to major content improvements made in the previous four months, the `dotnetnuke.com` web site became a targeted channel for the Microsoft development community. By simplifying the advertising rate sheet and employing traditional sales techniques, we were successfully able to grow this revenue stream in a relatively short time frame.

In the fall of 2005, while driving home from a business trip, I spent some dedicated time immersing myself in the revenue model dilemma. Over the years, I did a lot of research on business models for open source projects, and the big question was, "How do you sustain an open source organization while still adhering to its open source ideals?" There were obviously a number of companies that had demonstrated their ability to succeed in this area by employing a variety of financial options; however, I was keenly aware that each model had its own set of disadvantages.

One of the other recurring themes I kept thinking about is "who we serve." In a traditional business model, you serve your customers — but this generally assumes that some money is changing hands. For DotNetNuke, I would like to think that our open source community is who we serve — but because they are essentially using the product for free, it becomes challenging when other stakeholders step forward with financial support. Examining each of the more popular open source revenue models based on this theme proved to be a useful exercise.

The Pure Volunteer option has no revenue model. As a result, it has no resource cost — but at the same time it has no accountability, responsibility, or dedicated management. It could be argued that although it is supposed to serve the open source community, it really does not because there are no motivating factors driving the development and support.

The Dual License model has become popular in recent years because it allows for an open source version as well as a commercial version of the same product. This is only possible if the project owner has clear ownership of the copyright for the code. The commercial version provides traditional licensing revenue that helps sustain dedicated management and developer resources, resulting in improved accountability. Unfortunately, it tends to lead to a number of conflict-of-interest scenarios within the ecosystem. For one thing, there is a constant problem of deciding which features belong in the open source version of the product and which in the commercial version. The commercial license often eliminates many of the advantages that are fundamental to a customer choosing an open source solution. Extensibility options are sometimes throttled as the company attempts to control the financial ecosystem around the product. And the company is often forced to show favoritism through support and marketing channels to its paying commercial customers over the organic open source community.

The Sponsorship model involves utilizing a revenue stream from one or more third-party funding sources. Although this revenue model results in funding for dedicated management, it often compromises the project ideals as the sponsor attempts to exert their influence over the project roadmap and marketing goals. It also results in a revenue stream that is variable, creating challenges in terms of cash-flow requirements. In addition, the project needs to be extremely diligent regarding the ownership of the intellectual property so as not to put itself in a situation where the third party could sue the project for copyright infringement or affect the open source project licensing.

The Professional Services model is based on a concept where the platform maintainer does a significant amount of custom consulting for a third-party client. The revenue from the custom consulting is used to fund the dedicated management for the open source product. Unfortunately, this model tends to consume a high level of resources to qualify leads, formulate contracts, manage accounts, obtain signoff, and keep the pipeline full of revenue opportunities. The revenue stream is variable, affecting cash flow, and key project resources are often required to focus on specific client requirements rather than supporting and improving the open source product.

The Charitable Donations model is popular in the traditional open source world because it involves voluntary community financial support of the project. The problem is that it does not generate a consistent, sustainable revenue stream, which means it is unable to secure dedicated management resources. In addition, there is a tendency for community members to assume that other members are making financial donations, when in reality the project is receiving no financial contributions from anyone.

The Vertical Application model leverages the open source product to create a highly specialized, commercial, vertical market application. The vertical market application typically generates revenue through as application service provider (ASP) revenue model, which contributes funding back to the open source project. The challenge is that it requires focused management and marketing in the vertical market, complete with domain challenges, competition, legal considerations, and political constraints. The open source application also tends to cater the product roadmap to the needs of the vertical market application, resulting in a less robust application framework.

Because each of the common revenue models seem to have their own set of issues, it made me brainstorm what I would consider to be an optimal open source revenue model. The main criterion is that the project should serve the open source community ("by the people, for the people"). It should be objective and open, avoiding conflict of interest and adhering to open source ideals. Finally, the revenue stream must be consistent and sustainable, capable of sustaining multiple dedicated resources.

An interesting economics philosophy that Scott Willhite turned me on to was the concept of the "abundance mentality." In terms of business value, an "abundance mentality" refers to an attitude of growth. Essentially, it means that the overall size of the ecosystem becomes larger as the number of opportunities within the ecosystem increases. By working together with various stakeholders in the ecosystem, all members of the collective group benefit through a greater abundance of revenue-generating opportunities. The opposite of the "abundance mentality" is the "scarcity mentality," where participants consider the size of the ecosystem to be constrained and the goal is to capture as much of the market share as possible (choking out the smaller competitors in the process). DotNetNuke's extensible architecture and open source philosophy constantly pushes the envelope in terms of creating new business opportunities within the community. It was another principle that needed to be adhered to in our quest for a suitable revenue model.

With all of these ideas swirling in my head, I concluded that a Membership Subscription concept would be an effective revenue model for advancing our goals. It would mean that the open source project was funded by the community. It would also mean that the project was accountable and responsible to the community. Through the creation of new benefits, we would be able to provide more opportunities for community members to participate in the project ecosystem. From a public perspective, it would provide a defined method for any supporter, big or small, to contribute to the project. And we would not need to compromise any of our open source ideals. Membership would be available by subscription that would create on ongoing, consistent revenue stream.

The DotNetNuke Benefactor Program (see Figure 1-14) was officially launched in December 2005. Nik Kalyani came up with the marketing term "benefactor" because it clearly communicated the financial support goal of the program. The program had four levels of participation to cater to the needs of various stakeholders in the community, from individual developers to enterprise business organizations. The initial set of benefits was targeted to each program level and the administrative aspects of the program were automated as much as possible to provide a seamless user experience. The overall response to the program was positive and paved the way for future revenue opportunities.

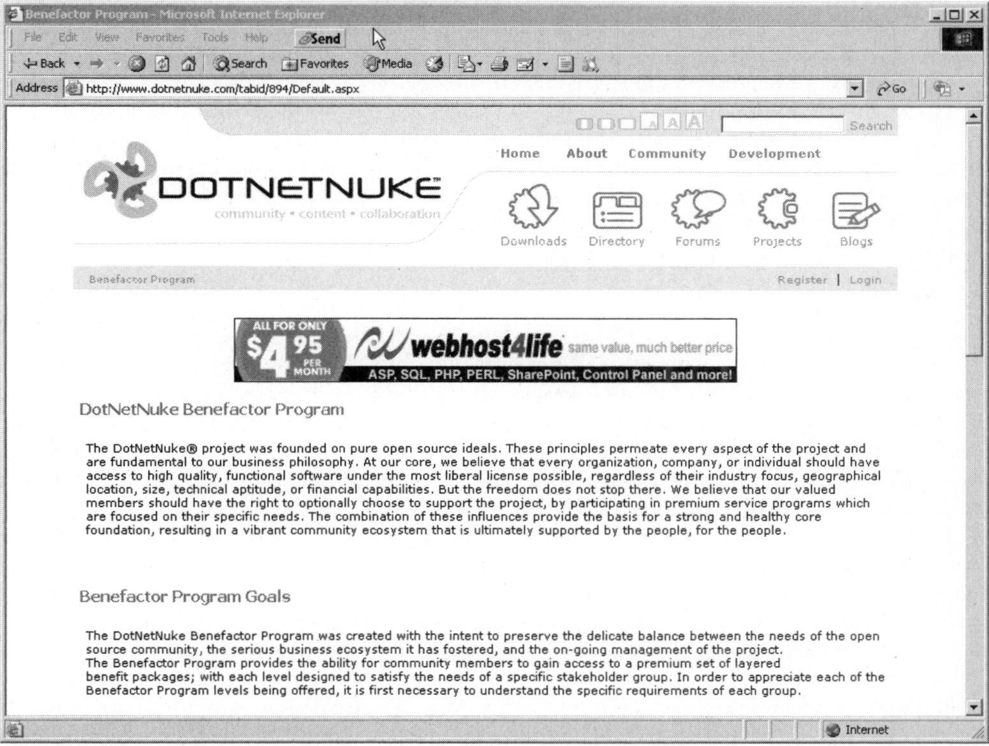

Figure 1-14

Opportunists

In the fall of 2005, DotNetNuke was starting to gain considerable momentum. The open source community was growing and the commercial ecosystem was becoming stronger and more diverse. DotNetNuke was being used in more enterprise deployments than ever before, and the brand was beginning to become more recognized and respected in the industry. A huge opportunity began to emerge, and this caught the attention of a number of serial entrepreneurs who were eager to capitalize on it.

One entrepreneur in particular was especially aggressive in the manner in which he approached the DotNetNuke community. With significant exits under his belt from a number of previous business ventures, he had the connections and proven track record of being able to take an emerging opportunity to market. Without prior introduction, he called me on the telephone one afternoon, and we had a casual conversation about the state of the DotNetNuke project and some of the areas in which we were planning on offering professional services to the community. Later, at his request, we had a face-to-face meeting in Seattle near Pikes Place Market, where he told me some of his own business ideas and informed me that he would like to contribute to the financial health of the project so that it could achieve even greater growth. Offers such as this do not come without strings attached, so I warily kept my distance as I tried to learn more about his philosophy and values to determine if they were in alignment with the project.

Much to my surprise in March 2006, a press release was issued that announced that his company had raised $1.75 million in seed venture capital based on a concept of providing an "economic platform" for developers leveraging the DotNetNuke framework. Clearly some of this so-called "economic platform" overlapped the professional services that we ourselves had begun to provide, and as result the situation became complicated. At their insistence, a business meeting was scheduled in April at the Westin Towers in Seattle where some of their high-level business goals were presented to Scott Willhite and myself. Clearly the goal of the meeting was to convince us to make a commitment to formulating a deeper partnership. However, the meeting offered few tangible details on how our organizations were going to work together, other than the fact they wanted us to continue focusing on the technology while they focused on commerce.

It takes more than a few meetings or conversations to establish the trust required to form a business partnership, and as a result we really did not feel comfortable moving forward at this juncture. The fact is, the DotNetNuke Board had been working very hard on the project for a number of years, and it was not clear to me how the members of our team were going to be included in the venture. In addition, some of the stories the entrepreneur had shared in an attempt to demonstrate his past business prowess had actually left an unpleasant taste in my mouth, as they appeared to not be aligned with the community ideals on which the DotNetNuke project was founded. When they realized that their open wallet was not going to result in open arms, I believe they were genuinely surprised and disappointed. However, this simply echoed the fact that they did not understand or share our same philosophies or values. We advised them that they should first become contributing citizens to the community, establish a positive reputation, and then we could consider cultivating a deeper relationship. They agreed to act on this advice and so began a rather tenuous relationship in the months following.

I do think it is important to give credit where it is due. This serial entrepreneur saw the potential in DotNetNuke and was effective in painting a large vision for the project. He had some very solid business ideas that were based on his real-world experience in monetizing other technology platforms and industries. He was a skilled speaker, a tenacious salesman, buzz-word compliant, and knowledgeable on most of the *hot* technology and globalization concepts promoted through books such as *The World is Flat*, *The Tipping Point*, and *The Long Tail*. Like any good student, I absorbed as much of his wisdom as I could, and it really precipitated a change in my perspective from always looking at the project from a technical viewpoint to focusing more on the business model and broader ecosystem benefits.

The most important thing I realized from this experience was what a tremendous opportunity DotNetNuke represented, and that we had reached a critical inflection point — if we did not take steps on our own to take the project to a higher level, somebody else would do it without our participation. Scott

Willhite's wisdom and experience were instrumental throughout this process in terms of keeping us focused on the primary goals:

1. Building the DotNetNuke economy to its fullest potential (globally)
2. Preserving the cultural roots of DotNetNuke and its universal accessibility (that is, free/open source/empowering)
3. Rewarding those who have contributed (and continue to contribute) to its success

Yin and Yang

In June 2006 I attended my first non-Microsoft technology conference, SYS-CON Enterprise Open Source in New York. I had been selected as a speaker, and my session focused on open source software on the Microsoft platform. Going in, I thought this was going to be hostile territory, but I soon realized that the "enterprise" focus resulted in the conference being technology-agnostic for the most part. The big news at the conference was that Marc Fleury, who was scheduled to do the keynote, was unable to attend because his company JBOSS has been acquired by RedHat. SugarCRM, who had already completed a Series C round of financing, was a major sponsor of the event, and I spent a fair amount of time talking to its founders, recognizing the many similarities that existed between our platforms. Overall the conference was a good experience and gave me a better sense of open source commercialization — especially in regards to high-tech startups and venture financing.

In the summer of 2006 we had our third annual Board meeting and one of most significant themes at the meeting was the concept of "balance." In the past, we had always taken what we thought was an objective stance on the separation between the open source project and its commercial ecosystem. Because we were the stewards of the core project, we tried to avoid anything that could lead to potential conflict-of-interest scenarios. Generally this involved focusing on the open source community and avoiding direct interaction with commercial stakeholders. Interestingly, the commercial ecosystem seemed to thrive almost in spite of the fact that we were trying to ignore it. Gradually, we came to the realization that there were actually two very powerful influences in the project and that both were essential to its long-term stability — the "yin" and "yang" of DotNetNuke. These complementary forces needed to be embraced in order to preserve the delicate balance within the project and ensure its future.

Up until this point the DotNetNuke Board had been serving the project in an unofficial capacity for a number of years, dealing with the various management tasks as best it could. Other than myself, the other members of the Board were either self-employed entrepreneurs or were employed by other companies, which made it difficult to function as a cohesive team. Dan Caron had stepped down from the Board in December 2005 due to the time commitment and amount of strain it was putting on his family. This left Scott Willhite, Joe Brinkman, Nik Kalyani, and myself remaining as Board members. As the months went by it became apparent that the project needed a different corporate structure and a full-time management team, but in order to support such an organization financially, it needed an adequate revenue base. And because the current services revenue was not scalable or predictable, it left little choice but to pursue alternative funding sources.

A New Company

It so happened that Scott Willhite had a good friend named Blair Garrou. Blair was managing director at DFJ Mercury, a seed and early-stage venture capital fund based in Houston, Texas. We had a conference call with Blair, and he indicated that although the DotNetNuke opportunity was not the right fit for his firm, he told us he would make some introductions.

The first introduction he made was to Mark Radcliffe, a Partner with DLA Piper who operates out of its Palo Alto office in California. Mark specializes in strategic intellectual property advice, private financing, corporate partnering, software licensing, and copyright and trademark matters. In the open source software realm, he is one of the most widely recognized and respected attorneys. After an initial meeting with Mark, we signed an engagement letter where DLA Piper agreed to defer billing for its services up to a certain threshold in exchange for a warrant to purchase stock in the company when it reached specific trigger conditions. DLA Piper was going to help us form an open source company that could better manage the needs of the DotNetNuke community and provide a solid business foundation for future growth.

DotNetNuke Corporation was formed September 21, 2006. Rather than coming up with a brand new company name, we took the simpler approach, which had the benefit of providing a direct link between the open source project and the company. The purpose of the new company was to assume a stewardship role and provide infrastructure, management, and support to the open source project as part of its regular operations. The previous Board members, Scott Willhite, Joe Brinkman, and Nik Kalyani, all came aboard as official co-founders in the new entity. A commitment was made to transfer all of the existing intellectual property from Perpetual Motion Interactive Systems Inc. to DotNetNuke Corporation. A public press release was issued and great care was taken to educate the community about the structural change to the project. Although there was some initial concern raised in regards to the "Corporation" branding, the community was overwhelmingly receptive to the change, and the transition created no serious disruption to the ecosystem. At this time the number of registered users on the `dotnetnuke.com` website (see Figure 1-15) was 335,000 members, and 2 million downloads had been recorded all-time.

DotNetNuke's first challenge was constructing a business plan that would provide the foundation enough to sustain the project long term. The Benefactor program had been successful in providing members of the ecosystem with an opportunity to support the project and receive some additional benefits. Unfortunately, the number of participants in the program was not enough to generate sufficient revenue. In addition, we realized that the benefits being offered did not meet the needs of all community members. Specifically, there was a group of serious users of the platform who were in need of more professional support services, which were not offered through the program.

The week following the public announcement of the formation of DotNetNuke Corporation came news of another DotNetNuke event. The company that had its eyes set on creating an "economic platform" for DotNetNuke was hosting a private mini-conference in Las Vegas, Nevada. They had approached the majority of commercial vendors in the DotNetNuke ecosystem and had offered to pay for their expenses to attend the event. This turned out to be a self-serving effort, as the main goal was to demonstrate and collect feedback in regards to module licensing opportunities. Ironically, even though the entire event was predicated on modular software leveraging the DotNetNuke platform, DotNetNuke Corporation had not been invited. This sent a clear message that we were not working together and the unfortunate side effect was that the commercial vendors were caught in the middle. This would prove to be a challenging situation in the coming months, as much time and effort was spent on cultivating relationships and preserving the integrity of the ecosystem.

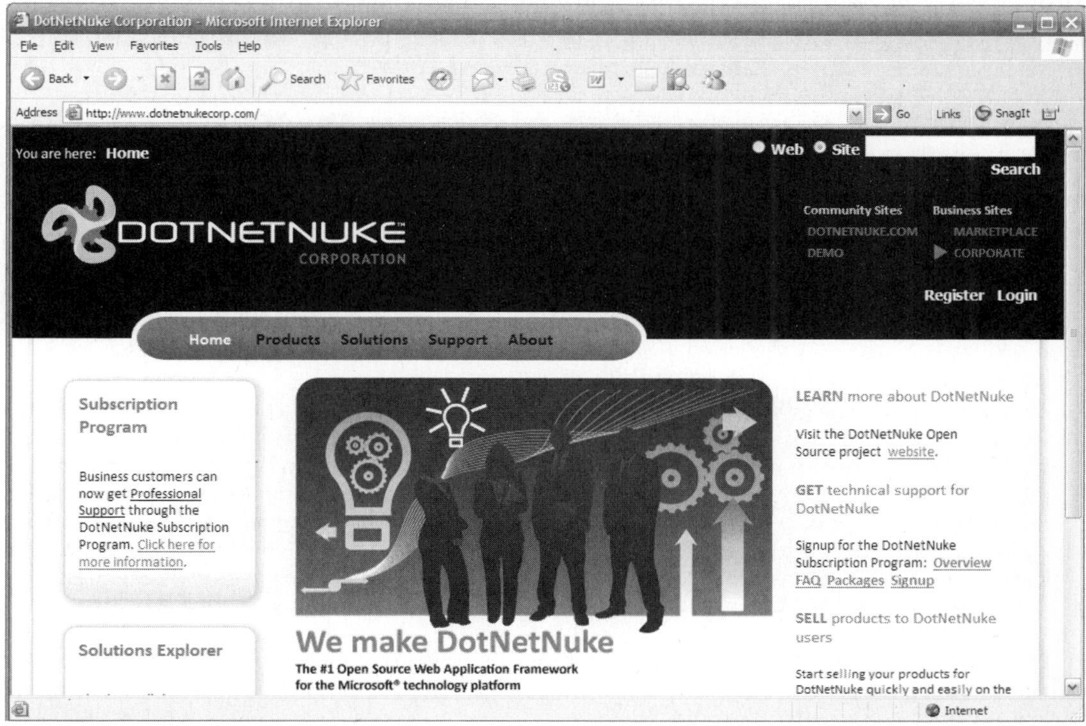

Figure 1-15

Larry Augustin

As part of his high-profile practice in the Bay Area, Mark Radcliffe had access to an enviable list of influential personal contacts in the software and venture financing industry. One of the first individuals he introduced us to in the fall of 2006 was Larry Augustin. Larry Augustin is an angel investor and advisor to early stage technology companies. A member of the group that coined the term "Open Source," he has written and spoken extensively on the topic worldwide. In 1993 he founded VA Linux (now SourceForge, NASDAQ:LNUX), where he led the company through an IPO in 1999 and served as CEO until August 2002. He currently serves on the Boards of Directors of a number of commercial open source companies including Compiere, Fonality, Hyperic, Medsphere, Pentaho, SugarCRM, and XenSource.

I flew down to San Francisco in November 2006 and met with Larry at DLA Piper's offices in Palo Alto. We had a great conversation about the DotNetNuke community, the commercial ecosystem for extensions, and open source business models. Given Larry's background in enterprise Linux, I was initially curious as to why he would be interested in an open source project on the Microsoft platform. However, I soon realized that as a veteran entrepreneur, Larry was interested in any software ecosystem where open source was being leveraged as a disruptive business advantage. Larry had relationships with the majority of top-tier venture capital firms in Silicon Valley, and specifically with the general partners who were receptive to open source business models. This initial meeting provided the foundation for a mutually beneficial and productive relationship between Larry and DotNetNuke.

Performance

Based on the feedback from hosting providers participating in the Microsoft Windows Shared Hosting Accelerator program, scalability and performance became a high priority in the fall of 2006. After many discussions, Microsoft actually allocated one of its experts on ASP.NET and Windows Server performance to work with us on optimizing the DotNetNuke application for the shared hosting environment. Charles Nurse spent a week in Redmond working side-by-side with this expert in the Patterns & Practices testing lab to learn how to effectively simulate load and performance test the application.

The scalability of the DotNetNuke application improved dramatically over this time frame, and the end result was released as DotNetNuke 4.4 in November 2006 to an overwhelmingly appreciative community. From this point forward, we had a regression baseline that could be used to compare new versions of the product in order to determine if performance had been degraded by new enhancements to the platform. As part of this process we also learned that there were very few developers in the Microsoft ecosystem who truly understood the ASP.NET/IIS/Windows Server dependencies or constraints from a performance perspective. We shared a lot of great knowledge with the general Microsoft developer community and DotNetNuke's reputation as an enterprise web platform was bolstered.

In December 2006, more than a year after ASP.NET 2.0 was released, we made the decision to sunset the DotNetNuke 3.x product. DotNetNuke 3.x was based on ASP.NET 1.1, and we had seen interest in this legacy platform drop off to the point where it no longer made sense to continue actively maintaining a parallel code base. Determining how and when to drop support for legacy versions of the Microsoft platform would continue to be a difficult challenge on an ongoing basis for the DotNetNuke project.

DotNetNuke Marketplace

The extensibility model in DotNetNuke had spawned a very active commercial ecosystem. By the end of 2006, hundreds of commercial modules and skins were available for the DotNetNuke platform. In addition, many companies were providing business services exclusively to the DotNetNuke market. This dynamic ecosystem was helping propel the growth of the project, but it was not without its share of issues.

Early in the project's history, a third party created a reseller environment that allowed developers and designers to sell their DotNetNuke products to consumers. This made it extremely easy for anyone, from a hobbyist developer to a serious independent software vendor, to get involved in the DotNetNuke commercial ecosystem. In the early stages, the existence of an established business environment for commercial components was critical to the growth of the project and adoption by business users. However, one of the most common types of feedback that we overheard related to this environment was about the questionable quality of third-party products and services.

Based on the reseller environment's low barrier of entry, the quality of commercial DotNetNuke components was extremely inconsistent. Some vendors were providing high-quality components, with professional support and explicit licensing terms. Others were essentially providing basic HTML scripts at a minimal fee with no support or licensing considerations. The combination of these polar opposites posed issues in terms of our goals to promote DotNetNuke as a professional framework. Effectively, the existing reseller environment was promoting a "Buyer Beware" mentality that was not complementary with our goals for taking the project to a higher level of business acceptance. In fact, some of the more serious independent software vendors told us that in order for them to get involved in the ecosystem, a more professional reseller channel would need to be made available.

To deal with the quality issue, we believed that a product review service could solve a number of problems. Although a comprehensive product review could provide great value, it would not be cost effective to perform, and therefore the review criteria would need to focus on some of the more fundamental product attributes such as whether the product installs and uninstalls properly. Although minimalist, such a review program would still provide value to the ecosystem. First, it would provide consumers with confidence that the product they are purchasing is fully functional. It also would provide educational guidance to software vendors in terms of project standards and expectations.

We had approached the current reseller a number of times in the past with hopes that we could form a business partnership. The main benefit was if the reseller became a contributing citizen of the DotNetNuke community, we could work together to elevate the ecosystem to a higher level. It would also provide us with critical business intelligence related to the usage of the product. For us to effectively manage the product roadmap, it was becoming increasingly more important that we get in touch with our entire user community. The discussion forums represented a small but vocal group of community members who offered feedback, but there was a much larger group of users with whom we had absolutely no contact. Unfortunately, the reseller was not interested in working with us in this capacity, which left us with a single alternative: establishing our own reseller channel.

Combining the concepts of the review program with a reseller channel seemed to be a great way to satisfy a variety of project goals. Initially our reseller channel would only sell components that passed our review program. This would improve the overall perception of quality and confidence in the community and provide a new revenue stream to help us secure more dedicated project resources.

The development process of the reseller channel took longer than expected. In reviewing the requirements we recognized that there were no products with e-commerce functionality within the DotNetNuke ecosystem that could satisfy our needs. Therefore, we had to look elsewhere, and we were pleased to work out an agreement with AspDotNetStoreFront, an established product vendor providing a robust e-commerce solution to the Microsoft market. AspDotNetStoreFront was even interested in migrating a version of its software to the DotNetNuke platform, so we forged an agreement with them in hope of establishing a long-term business relationship.

The DotNetNuke Marketplace was launched in January 2007 (see Figure 1-16). Similar to `dotnetnuke.com` it took a minimalist approach to the web site design. And one of the design goals was to ensure a consistent, professional user experience, as we felt it would be a good differentiator from the other reseller site. The number of products available grew slowly as awareness of the Marketplace grew in the vendor community, and product reviews were completed.

It did not take long before we learned a variety of valuable lessons. First, we had underestimated the first-mover advantage that the incumbent reseller had in our ecosystem. Without an incentive there was no motivating factor to encourage vendors to list their products in our marketplace. Without products, there was also no incentive for consumers to browse our marketplace and make purchases. The review program that we had assumed would be a great benefit actually became a barrier to entry, as we discovered that most vendors were not keen on paying a fee, no matter how minimal, to have their product reviewed. In hindsight this made perfect sense, because unless consumers are specifically demanding reviewed products, there is no motivation for vendors to invest in the program. In addition, our initial process for listing products was cumbersome, especially in comparison to the incumbent reseller. This resulted in some hesitation on the part of vendors to list their products and keep them regularly updated.

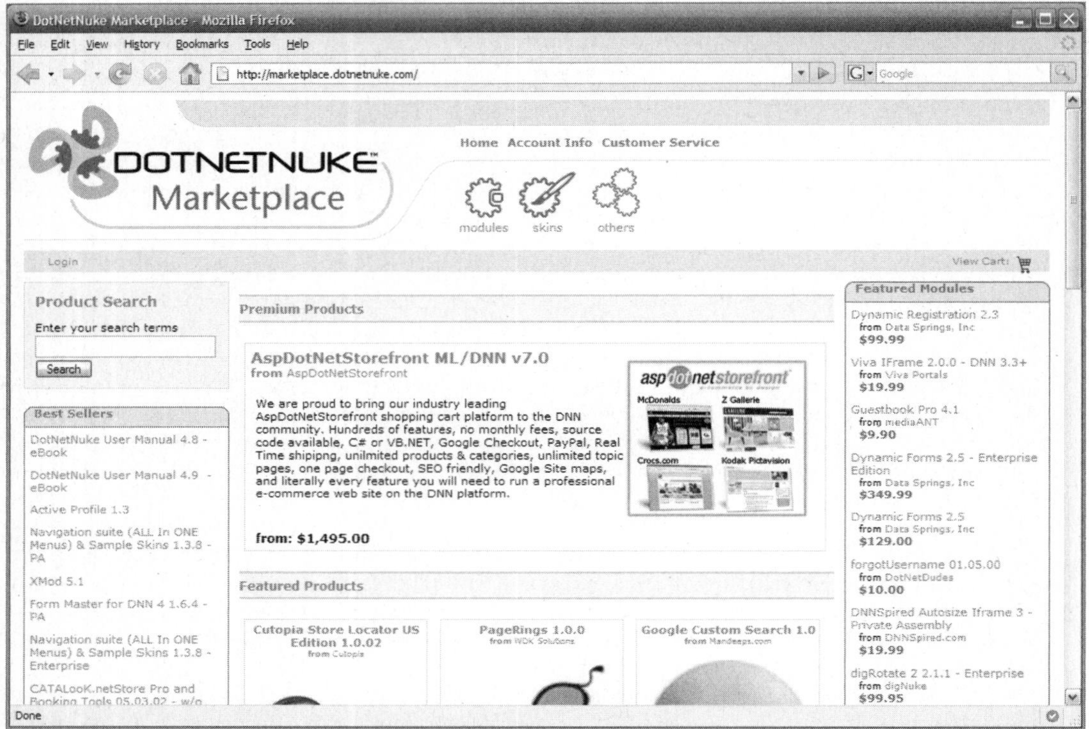

Figure 1-16

Another mistake we made was to maintain too much parity with the incumbent reseller in terms of the features and business model. In order to be truly competitive, we needed to introduce some disruptive concepts and differentiate ourselves. As we learned these valuable lessons we adapted the Marketplace and slowly began to garner a greater inventory of products and consumer traffic, but still continued to lag behind the incumbent reseller. The most significant problem we faced was in regards to resources. Without startup capital there was not enough revenue to allow for dedicated management of the Marketplace and as a result it did not get the attention it deserved or required to achieve momentum. Considering the strategic value of this area, it goes without saying that more time and effort must be invested for it to achieve its true potential.

Free Module Promotion

Without a working relationship with DotNetNuke Corporation, the funded entity that had promised to create an "economic platform" for DotNetNuke was aggressively trying to establish a foothold in the e-commerce portion of the ecosystem throughout the latter half of 2006. In July of 2006 they had provided

us with a proposal where they would pay us a royalty if we made them the exclusive e-commerce partner for the DotNetNuke ecosystem. However, based on the fact we were already establishing our own reseller marketplace coupled with the fact that we did not see eye-to-eye on many business practices, we told them that we did not wish to move forward with this opportunity.

In December 2006, with participation from a number of commercial module vendors, they launched a promotion where a variety of the most popular modules were offered as a free subscription package for one year to DotNetNuke users. The package was mainly offered through hosting providers and community sites, and was ultimately an attempt to build a large user base and validate their proprietary software licensing solution. Although the concept of a recurring revenue stream for commercial module vendors seemed attractive, it did not take long before a few critical problems came to the surface; the most significant being the fact that commercial module vendors found themselves providing support services to users who had not paid for their products. This was not a viable model and within a few months, the majority of the module vendors pulled out of the promotion.

In April 2007 the company announced that it had received another $5 million in venture capital funding and was expanding its vision to include commercial software outside the DotNetNuke ecosystem. We did not hear from them again, and by 2008 their focus appeared to have shifted away from software licensing and DotNetNuke as they worked on developing a web site that provided product reviewers with tools to critique technology-based products and consumers the ability to browse the reviews.

Conferences

The first unofficial DotNetNuke conference occurred in May 2006 in Papendal, The Netherlands. It was hosted by the Software Developer Network (SDN), which had recently added DotNetNuke as an officially recognized technology in its user group organization (based largely on the fact that Core Team member Leigh Pointer had successfully built a DotNetNuke user group of more than 300 members in The Netherlands). I was offered an all-expenses-paid trip to come and speak at the event, which I gratefully accepted. The DotNetNuke track ran in parallel with the other Software Developer Conference (SDC) tracks and featured sessions by Core Team member Vicenc Masanas as well as other DotNetNuke experts from the Dutch community.

In October 2006, David Walker from Tulsa, Oklahoma organized the first of what was to become an annual community technology event, which he named Tulsa TechFest. It was an ambitious conference, free to attendees, and funded by sponsors with many parallel tracks and notable speakers. Because he was a fan of the DotNetNuke platform, David reserved a track for DotNetNuke and invited me to come and speak. I had the honor of doing my first-ever conference keynote at this event, and it was a great experience to meet a number of Core Team members for the first time (John Mitchell, Chris Hammond, and Shawn Mehaffie) as well as a number of Microsoft MVPs in person.

Based on the rapid growth of the DotNetNuke ecosystem, by the end of 2006 we thought the community was ready for an official DotNetNuke conference event. Conferences involve a significant amount of time, effort, and expertise to manage, so we recognized that our best approach would be to partner with an established conference organizer and potentially co-locate with an existing technology event. Initially we approached SYS-CON Media but after a couple months of trying to work through contract logistics, we realized that some chemistry was missing from the relationship and that we would be better off looking for a different partner.

We approached a variety of other conference organizers and quickly learned that the majority of them were either already at capacity or were not willing to take a risk on a DotNetNuke conference event. Rather frustrated, we were at the point of giving up on the conference idea entirely when Joe Brinkman made contact with Shirley Brothers from DevConnections.

DevConnections is one of the longest-running independent developer conferences focused on Microsoft technology and a perfect fit for the DotNetNuke platform. It turned out that Brian Goldfarb and Scott Guthrie from Microsoft had put in a good word for us with Shirley, and she was willing to entertain a DotNetNuke event that would be co-located with DevConnections at Mandalay Bay in Las Vegas in the fall of 2007. Working through the contract details with Shirley was a positive experience, and we ultimately agreed on two DotNetNuke conference tracks: one for developers and the other for designers and administrators.

One of the most significant benefits of co-locating with DevConnections was the fact that attendees were not restricted to only DotNetNuke sessions but were free to take advantage of any DevConnections content being presented in any track including ASP.NET, Visual Studio, and SQL Server. Nik Kalyani came up with a DotNetNuke conference brand of ''OpenForce'' and Joe Brinkman took ownership of managing the conference logistics and spent considerable time in the months leading up to the event recruiting speakers, managing interactions with DevConnections, scheduling sessions, and leading marketing activities.

Based on the agreement struck with DevConnections, in the summer of 2007 we decided to approach the Software Developer Network in The Netherlands with a proposal of more officially partnering for their next SDC event, by using the ''OpenForce' brand and assisting with marketing activities. An agreement was reached to provide two dedicated DotNetNuke tracks at the SDC event, and our first official European conference was scheduled for September 2007.

Microsoft Valuable Professionals

As the size and influence of the DotNetNuke ecosystem had grown, so had the visibility of its participants in the Microsoft community. Microsoft had a program called the Microsoft Valuable Professional (or MVP) program, which was designed to recognize individuals who made significant community contributions. Between the years 2005 and 2007, nearly 20 DotNetNuke Core Team members achieved this level of distinction.

In the spring of 2007 Microsoft held a global summit in Redmond for all MVPs worldwide, and this provided an excellent opportunity for our team to get together face-to-face. Because the majority of interaction between our geographically dispersed team occurs online, it was great way to get to know one another and socialize. We booked a conference room at our temp office at Two Union Square and had team meetings during the week. We also treated the team to a group dinner at an Italian restaurant in downtown Seattle where the beer (micro-brew of course) and conversation flowed freely.

Fundraising

By the spring of 2007, DotNetNuke Corporation had prepared a business plan and was ready to present it to potential investors. Rather than leveraging friends and family, or even angel investors, we decided that professional or institutional investors should be our primary target. Nik Kalyani's past experience with fundraising was valuable in this process, and we felt confident that the product adoption and size of the community would be significant assets for our pitch.

Our relationship with Larry Augustin proved to be very valuable at this point, as he had many connections on Sand Hill Road. Larry was instrumental in setting up meetings for us with many of the top-tier venture firms in Silicon Valley. We met with Sequoia Capital, Accel Partners, Azure Capital, O'Reilly Alpha Tech Ventures, New Enterprise Associates, and Draper Fisher Jurvetson (DFJ).

Unfortunately, none of the firms we met with was interested in committing to DotNetNuke at this time. In a number of cases we had repeat meetings with the same VC, progressing from an initial meeting with an associate, to a general partner, and then to an all partners Monday meeting. In general the meetings were always positive; the VCs were courteous, thoughtful, and more than willing to provide advice on how we should capitalize on the opportunity. However, the most common piece of feedback was that we had not yet demonstrated a financial model that would create a ''large company'' opportunity. When VCs say ''large company'' they mean a company that can potentially reach a valuation of $100 million dollars in five years. The frustrating part was that if we had already proven the financial model, there would be no need for investment capital at all. Other feedback included a preference for us to have a presence in the Bay Area because VCs prefer to have their portfolio companies nearby. And there was also some question about level of business leadership experience in the company. All of these items would need to be addressed one way or another in order for us to be successful in our fundraising efforts.

Awards and Accolades

The summer of 2007 was significant for DotNetNuke as the project received some recognition from a number of notable third parties. *Visual Studio Magazine* selected DotNetNuke as its Editor's Choice Winner for 2007 (see Figure 1-17), an award that had previously been given to Microsoft SharePoint in 2006. A month later, Info-Tech, an independent research group, selected DotNetNuke as a Leader in its Decision Diamond for Web Content Management for the small enterprise. The Info-Tech Decision Diamond award recognizes vendors that provide products and services of outstanding quality, with a strong enterprise strategy and high levels of customer satisfaction and retention. Both of these awards were unexpected and highly appreciated.

Figure 1-17

Later in the summer, we issued a release of DotNetNuke that contained support for the new OpenID authentication system. Because we were one of the first open source projects to implement OpenID, we received a cash award bounty of $5000. Dick Hardt, CEO of SXIP and a legend in the open source Perl community based on his tenure at ActiveState, was able to gain us passes to OSCON in Portland, Oregon where the bounty award was presented. Other recipients of the bounty included Drupal and Plone.

Based on the publicity provided by the OpenID bounty, we were contacted by Microsoft with a proposal to integrate Windows LiveID support into the platform. This seemed to be good fit, as many developers in the Microsoft world have become comfortable with the LiveID single-sign-on system. Integration also provided a sponsorship opportunity with the Microsoft Live team, a relationship that would reap rewards in the future.

DotNetNuke OpenForce 07

In September 2007 we had our first official DotNetNuke conference in Papendal. The conference was branded DotNetNuke OpenForce Europe and had 80 registered attendees, each paying about €700. The conference attracted users from the United Kingdom, Ireland, France, Belgium, Spain, Portugal, Switzerland, Germany, Italy, Austria, Sweden, Norway, Denmark, and even from as far away as South Africa and Aruba. Joe Brinkman, Charles Nurse, and I attended the event from DotNetNuke Corporation and a number of Core Team members and Project Leads led sessions as well. The conference was a great success and established a solid working relationship with the Software Development Network for future events.

In November 2007, we had our first official North American DotNetNuke conference, co-located as planned with DevConnections at the Mandalay Bay Hotel and Casino in Las Vegas, Nevada. The conference managed to attract 225 registered attendees at $1500 and had two dedicated tracks spanning three days. Two vendors from the DotNetNuke ecosystem, ActiveModules and R2Integrated, opted to become exhibitors in the DevConnections exhibit hall. The visibility that the project received at this event was incredible, as the DotNetNuke logo was displayed on all conference marketing materials alongside Microsoft products such as ASP.NET, Visual Studio, and SQL Server. Carl Franklin and Richard Campbell from the DotNetRocks! podcast helped host the final panel discussion for DotNetNuke Corporation, and at the conclusion the Core Team members in attendance finally got some of the public recognition they so generously deserved.

One of the ideas we had for OpenForce was to allow other Microsoft platform open source projects to participate at the event, and we were successful in attracting a number of distinguished guests including Scott Hanselman, Phil Haack, and Rob Connery. The ironic thing that happened, however, is that in the months leading up to the conference, each of these guests announced that they had accepted employment offers with Microsoft to work on the new ASP.NET MVC team. So when the conference finally arrived, we had an open source panel discussion, but the independent nature of it had definitely lost some of its impact. Regardless, we were still pleased to have been able to provide visibility and insight into a variety of open source projects on the Microsoft platform.

At the keynote for OpenForce North America we announced "Cambrian" as the new marketing codename for DotNetNuke 5.0. Nik Kalyani had come up with the name in reference to the "Cambrian Explosion," a period in the earth's evolution where there was a dramatic increase in more complex life forms. We announced a roadmap, which included the major features we were planning on implementing in the coming year as well as a tentative release schedule. We also mentioned that we were actively pursuing funding opportunities and shared some details on the current business model for

DotNetNuke Corporation. Overall, this conference had a very strong business influence and demonstrated the momentum the project had achieved in professional and enterprise environments.

SLA Program

Initially mentioned at OpenForce North America and later rolled out publicly in January 2008, the DotNetNuke SLA Program was a professional support offering available on an annual subscription basis by DotNetNuke Corporation. The program was introduced in response to community demand for professional support services for the DotNetNuke product and DotNetNuke Corporation offered a Bronze and Silver level to cater to the needs of different customers. The fact that open source projects make their source code available to everybody does not make everybody an expert. The fact that the open source software is offered for free doesn't mean that commercial services are irrelevant. In fact, open source software requires a dependable commercial ecosystem and a reputable vendor that stands behind its software and provides consumer confidence.

The SLA Program was successful in engaging a variety of large customers who were using DotNetNuke in mission-critical deployments. For a long time we had relied solely on users communicating their issues through online channels and as the software became more complex, it became increasingly more difficult to reproduce issues occurring in the wild. The information received through diagnosing customer problems directly in enterprise environments was essential in identifying and solving deficiencies in the software and building a higher quality product. At this point it definitely became obvious that a healthy balance between open source users and professional customers was the optimal mix to create a powerful platform. With the introduction of the program, the legacy Benefactor Program was phased out with some customers migrating to the new Sponsorship program, which provided visibility and marketing benefits, while others moved to the SLA Program.

Although the program was successful we also learned some unanticipated valuable lessons. First, because the only benefit being offered through the program was technical support, there was no incentive to purchase a subscription unless you were experiencing a problem and were in need of immediate assistance. Because the DotNetNuke software was so mature and stable, many companies had no immediate support requirement; therefore, the lack of a sales trigger significantly reduced our opportunity to engage with customers in a meaningful way. Second, we discovered that the vendors within our own ecosystem became our largest source of competition. As soon as we announced our SLA offering, a number of vendors published their own copycat SLA offerings at a lower price, undercutting our program and, in at least one instance, making an attempt to discredit the reputation of DotNetNuke Corporation. Obviously, these vendors had no way to support the DotNetNuke product itself as they had no ability to affect changes in the source code, but it did not stop them from getting some traction; albeit at the expense of the platform.

More Fundraising

In the fall of 2007 we had reorganized the management team and appointed Nik Kalyani as CEO. The changes were made in order to better reflect the roles we were playing in the organization and address some internal issues regarding vision and business leadership. We all agreed that Nik should focus his time and effort almost exclusively on fundraising, and he even volunteered to move himself and his family to California as he felt that we would have a better probability of getting funded if we had a person "on the ground" in the Bay Area. Due to a number of personal reasons, Nik had to delay his move until January 2008, but once there, it became obvious that his presence in Silicon Valley was definitely going to reap rewards for the company.

Following the success of the conferences, we made contact with a number of VCs (mostly via introductions from Larry Augustin). Firms we met with included Azure Capital and Benchmark Capital, both of whom allowed us to present to all of their General Partners at an all-partners meeting. Although our pitch was much more refined by this time, we still had difficulty getting the VCs to believe in the revenue potential of the opportunity. One of the specific pieces of feedback was in regards to the "exit" potential. In a tech market where very few IPOs were occurring, the focus shifts to merger and acquisition (M&A) outcomes, and the VCs wanted to know who specifically would be interested in acquiring DotNetNuke in the future. This is obviously a hypothetical question, as nobody has a crystal ball, but we were still expected to have some solid defensible answers.

Another piece of feedback we received was that a "platform" was too broad of a category and was not focused enough to reveal a distinct monetization strategy. This led us to consider a more focused approach, and out of frustration we actually tried pitching an Enterprise 2.0 social networking application at one point to gauge the interest in it versus our platform approach. This was likely an unwise decision as the VC we pitched to was already familiar with our previous messaging, and to shift gears so abruptly left them questioning the focus of our management team. Ultimately we reverted back to the platform approach for future VC interactions, as regardless of the allergic reaction that some folks had, it was more closely aligned and fundamental to the success of the project to date.

In January 2008 a couple of significant events occurred. Larry Augustin ran into an experienced CEO named Navin Nagiah at a software conference. Navin was currently employed by Cignex, a successful systems integrator for open source content management systems including Alfresco, LifeRay, and Plone. Navin was looking for a startup opportunity with large potential, and Larry mentioned that he may want to take a look at DotNetNuke. Larry made the introductions via email and Nik followed up. In the same month, we received an anonymous solicitation through our web site from Hummer Winblad Venture Partners, a respected VC from San Francisco. This was the first time a VC had come to us (rather than vice versa) and Nik worked very hard to close a deal with Hummer Winblad, doing many presentations and staying constantly engaged in the coming months.

When you get to the point of VCs wanting to call business references, you know you are getting close to a term sheet. Hummer Winblad asked if they could contact some of our references, and we supplied them with a number of enterprise customers and partners. This process was drawn out over a number of weeks, and we were even lucky enough to even get some notable folks from Microsoft to speak with them about the DotNetNuke opportunity. In the end Hummer Winblad could not get past their opinion that Microsoft's traditional low pricing model makes it difficult for a company on the Microsoft platform to get larger enterprise sales deals. They indicated that greater sales potential was available on the J2EE platform, and it is these basic business principles, not the open source angle, which results in fewer investments in Microsoft platform vendors.

CodePlex

For a long time we had been looking for an organized way to allow community members to share their open source offerings with the community. Taking on the burden of managing the infrastructure for adhoc projects was not something DotNetNuke Corporation could provide, as deliberately managing our own DNN Projects had become enough of a challenge on their own.

In 2006 Microsoft had launched a new developer community site to replace the ill-fated GotDotNet. The new site was called CodePlex, and it provided a robust set of tools (based on the Microsoft Team Foundation Server architecture) that developers could use to manage their open source projects. The site was not solely available to Microsoft platform developers, but because of its close association to Microsoft, it soon developed into the go-to place for Microsoft platform open source projects. It provided some nice marketing capabilities, which provided projects with visibility and accessibility within the Microsoft ecosystem. And the fact that some teams from Microsoft Corporation were using CodePlex to manage and distribute their own out-of-band releases meant that there was commitment from the company to ensure the site was regularly maintained and innovated (a fundamental failing of its predecessor GotDotNet).

In late 2007 we approached Microsoft with a collaboration proposal where we offered to push our community members to CodePlex for managing its DotNetNuke open source projects. In exchange, CodePlex would contribute the infrastructure and also provide the DotNetNuke projects with some unique visibility to differentiate them from the other ASP.NET projects on the site. We worked closely with CodePlex team member Jonathan Wanagel on the integration and in February 2008, the DotNetNuke Forge was announced.

In April 2008 there was another Microsoft Global MVP Summit in Seattle, which provided a great opportunity for the team to get together. We also leveraged the opportunity to invite a group of the more prominent vendors in the DotNetNuke ecosystem to participate in an information-gathering meeting to determine the most important attributes for a successful Partner program. Attendees included AppTheory, Seablick Consulting, T-Worx, Adcuent, Cybreze, Inspector-IT, R2Integrated, and DataSprings. Navin Nagiah attended the event to gain some familiarity and insight into the various players in the DotNetNuke community. And Jeff Loomans, a general partner from Sierra Ventures a venture capital firm from Silicon Valley, flew up to Seattle to meet with us as well and discuss the DotNetNuke opportunity.

Security Issues

In the early spring of 2008 the project experienced a number of security issues which required our immediate attention as well as strategic management to ensure the reputation of the project was not tarnished. When it comes to security vulnerabilities in software it is not always the technical issues which are the primary challenge but rather the motivations of the parties involved which play a significant role in defining an appropriate solution.

The first security issue was reported to us by Will Morgenweck of ActiveModules, a well known and respected vendor in our ecosystem. He indicated that his own site had been compromised and he sent us his IIS logs in order to help us identify the problem. However, deep analysis of the logs and the application source code in the area targeted did not reveal the vulnerability. Without the ability to replicate the problem it would be impossible to fix; therefore, we had to try to get to the bottom of it. When the third party had compromised Will's system, they had used a login account which provided some clue about their identity. I decided to take a chance and reach out to the them via email; however I was not confident that I would receive any response. Luckily they did respond and over the coming weeks I was able to establish a relationship through a series of email conversations.

It turned out we were dealing with a 22 year old Iranian student named Morteza Kermani who was a member of the DotNetNuke Iran User Group. He indicated that he had not meant to cause any harm and would be willing to help us solve the problem. He explained the actions he had taken to bypass the security mechanisms and this provided us with the detail we needed to replicate the problem locally. It turned out that he was relying on an undocumented behavior within the .NET Framework which

DotNetNuke had not taken into consideration. Basically, if a person specified a trailing period for a filename, the .NET Framework would not throw an Invalid Filename error, but would instead strip the trailing period from the filename and then create the file on the disk. This vulnerability allowed Morteza to bypass DotNetNuke's file extension security, upload a shell script to the server, and then browse to it directly from a web browser, where he could then navigate the server file system. Now I would personally consider this .NET Framework behavior to be a bug; however, since we have no control over the underlying bits, we had to implement our own security mechanisms to prevent this type of exploit in the future. The patch was made available as soon as we successfully validated our solution, and very few sites were affected.

The second security issue occurred in May and was much less severe in terms of the potential damage to the users system; however, it was much worse in terms of public visibility. A group from Iran calling themselves the ISCN or Iran Security Center Networks had discovered a vulnerability in the third party FCKEditor rich text editor control which allowed an anonymous user to upload a file to a public website. The DotNetNuke file upload mechanism did have preventive code in place to prevent them from uploading malicious files; therefore, in most instances they simply uploaded a basic text file named ISCN.txt which contained the following text:

```
!!! Persian Gulf For Ever !!!
Owned By : Magic-Boy , Imm02tal , Mormoroth
Contact Us : ISCN1td@GMail.coM
ISCN Team
!!! Persian Gulf For Ever !!!
```

Although the text file did not represent a threat to a users site, the ISCN group also posted links to every system they were able to successfully compromise on a security site called Zone-H. As the list grew, we knew we had to move very quickly to issue a patch or else the reputation of the project as a secure platform would be affected. Tomotoshi Sugishita of the DotNetNuke Japan User Group and Mitchell Sellers were both extremely helpful in identifying and resolving the vulnerability.

The third security issue was discovered by a Hosting provider within our ecosystem. In this case, the vulnerability was again not severe; however, it was the actions taken by the Hosting provider which resulted in some serious problems. Rather than reporting the problem to our security alias and working with us to create a patch for the community, the Hosting provider decided the security vulnerability represented a revenue opportunity for their business. They quickly created a "patch" support service which users could purchase to have the security problem immediately resolved on their site. And then they issued a public press release on PRWEB announcing the existence of the vulnerability. This unprofessional behavior was not well received within the DotNetNuke developer community and there was considerable backlash. Ultimately the Hosting provider did finally submit the problem to us and we were able to analyze its impact. In this case, the problem was related to manual invoking the install wizard which could cause problems for some installations, as not all installation tasks are designed to be re-executable. We were able to successfully resolve the problem almost immediately and issue a new general release.

IP Disputes

In April 2008 I received an unsolicited phone call from a person in San Francisco indicating that he owned the `dnn.com` domain name and was wondering if we were interesting in acquiring it. Interestingly, the `dnn.com` domain name had previously been owned by media titan Knight Ridder Digital, and I had spoken to one of their attorneys in 2005 to determine if they were willing to part with the domain name, but was told that they wished to retain it. Somehow in early 2008, a domain name trader had managed to acquire the name from Knight Ridder, and they had decided to contact us because a vendor in the DotNetNuke ecosystem had expressed an interest in purchasing the name but had notified them that there may be trademark implications. Events transpired very quickly in the coming week, as the domain name trader tried to create a bidding war between ourselves and the vendor. Ultimately the price was too high, and we had to resort to legal means to try and acquire the domain name.

ICANN has a formal process known as the Uniform Domain-Name Dispute-Resolution Policy (UDRP). This policy is designed for situations that involve trademark-based domain-name disputes, typically where a complainant wishes to acquire the domain name rights for one of their trademarks. Based on the fact that we owned a trademark for the term "DNN," coupled with the fact that the domain name trader had approached us and tried to extort a significant sum of money, led us to believe that we had a strong UDRP case. We hired an IP attorney and filed the necessary motions with ICANN.

The UDRP process is rather rigid, and what we discovered is that it tends to favor the domain name owner. It is up to the trademark holder to present a strong case in accordance with the UDRP criteria in order to try and convince a panel of judges that they should be the rightful owner to the domain in question. Demonstrating ownership of a trademark is fairly straightforward; however, demonstrating that an owner of a domain name is using it or plans to use it in bad faith to disparage your trademark is not easy. And this is not a legal proceeding; the decision is final — there is no provision for appeals.

In our situation, the domain name trader made a case that he was planning on using the domain name to create a web site for "Domain Name Network" and had not had sufficient time to complete its construction. This seemed a bit far-fetched, given how eager he had been to try and sell the domain name to multiple parties. Unfortunately, the UDRP panel accepted this story and allowed the domain name trader to retain ownership. Within a week of the decision he sold the domain name to the "Domain News Network" for an undisclosed sum of money. We were highly disappointed with the outcome and also learned a valuable lesson about the weaknesses of the legal system.

Compounding our legal issues (and consuming our financial resources), in the summer of 2008 we received a notice from the United States Patent and Trademark Office (USPTO) informing us that a third party had filed a Notice of Opposition to our most recent application for the "DotNetNuke" trademark, as well as a Petition for Cancellation to the previously registered "DotNetNuke" trademark. The notices were filed by a vendor within our own ecosystem, and the basis of the complaints was that the DotNetNuke name was generic, and "used in the computer industry to reference open source web content management systems." This argument was flattering but far from reality, as DotNetNuke had clearly not reached the level of ubiquity where the term was being used in a generic way to describe various open source content management systems. In fact DotNetNuke had never even been marketed as a CMS, but rather as a web application framework. Regardless of the frivolous nature of the dispute, as trademark owners we were required to defend ourselves or risk losing ownership of the mark entirely. The irony of this whole situation is that the freedoms we had provided to the community in regards to the use of our trademarks were now being used as a weapon by an individual against the community itself.

So again, we were forced into a complicated legal proceeding; a proceeding where the USPTO defined a schedule for submissions and disclosures that would take 13 months from start to finish. The only alternative to following the complete USPTO process was to come to a settlement agreement, and this was the solution recommended by our attorney. Through direct discussion with the vendor we realized that the biggest problem leading up to the legal filing was a lack of communication and understanding on the goals and motivations of each party. The vendor had built a business and was afraid of how changes in the trademark policy could potentially affect their livelihood. From our perspective this appeared rather paranoid, as this vendor was only one of many organizations that were conducting business in the DotNetNuke ecosystem, and we understood that ensuring the viability and longevity of all of these entities was definitely vital to the success of the project. Regardless, we were able to successfully structure an agreement that dealt with their concerns and allowed us to avoid a lengthy and costly legal process.

Term Sheets

Throughout the late spring and summer of 2008, Nik Kalyani worked closely with Navin Nagiah to get him up to speed on the DotNetNuke ecosystem. Navin had already given his notice at Cignex, and he was eager to join the team; however, from a cashflow perspective, we were not able to accommodate his needs. We constructed an agreement where he would act as a business advisor to the company and commit 100% of his time to fundraising. In exchange we agreed that he would come aboard as CEO post-funding.

Navin had worked in the Bay Area for quite some time and had his own network of trusted business advisors and associates that he was able to leverage for VC introductions. Navin got to work immediately, setting up meetings with investors and pitching the DotNetNuke opportunity. In the late spring and summer of 2008, Navin made contact with many reputable firms including Sigma Partners, El Dorado Ventures, Charles River Ventures, SAP Ventures, Walden International, Emergence Capital, Matrix Partners, Trinity Ventures, and Menlo Ventures. In most cases Nik accompanied Navin for the in-person meetings, and I participated via conference call. Sometimes we were dismissed after an introductory conversation, and in other cases we did presentations in all-partner meetings. By this time our pitch was becoming very clear and consistent. But although the interest among these firms was high, there was still something holding them back from taking the next step. The biggest issue still seemed to be a lack of confidence in whether an open source company could reach critical mass on the Microsoft platform. And although we could provide metrics and indicators to help mitigate this risk, it ultimately came down to a gut reaction that left the VCs feeling uneasy.

By mid summer of 2008, we had reduced our list of seriously interested firms down to three: Onset Ventures, August Capital, and Highland Capital Partners. In the case of Onset we had met with them repeated times, with our introductory session occurring through Navin back in February of 2008. Onset had been a great firm to work with through the process, as its team had provided a great deal of advice and guidance that helped us clarify our message as well as our market opportunity. Our interactions with August Capital were through general partner Vivek Mehra, whom we found to be very direct and insightful, and the fact that one of August Capital's co-founders, David Marquardt, had been on the Microsoft board of directors since 1981 was a definite plus. Navin flew out to Boston to meet with Highland and had a productive meeting, but because it was an East Coast firm, it made follow-up communications and in-person meetings with the partnership a bit more challenging. Although each of these firms showed significant interest, had met with us repeatedly, and had spoken to our business references; none of them were making a funding decision. We felt that we needed a catalyst of some sort to bring the process to a climax. That catalyst came in a most unlikely form.

At the MVP Global Summit in the spring I had promised Oliver Nguyen that I would do a DotNetNuke presentation at his BAY.NET User Group the next time he had an opening for a speaker. The user group meeting was scheduled for August 27, and it provided a great opportunity to give the investors some real-world exposure to the DotNetNuke project and community. The event attracted about 50 members and general partners from August Capital, Onset Ventures, and Highland Capital were all in attendance. This was one of the most nerve-wracking presentations I have ever done, and I was very relieved to be able to pull it off without a hitch. Nik Kalyani provided me with support during the Q&A section and Oliver Nguyen and the BAY.NET User Group leadership were great hosts of the event. It turned out that this meeting created some unintended consequences. Two of the investors decided to pull the trigger, and we received two competing term sheets. And thus began the real education when it comes to venture capital funding.

All things being equal, the term sheets we received were similar in a number of ways. The pre-money valuation (the current value of the company) and the investment amount offered was identical, as was the amount of equity in the company the investors were demanding for themselves and the portion of equity they wanted to carve out for an Options pool. Both term sheets were also based on syndicated deals, where the investor needed another VC partner to come aboard to complete the deal. This is how a VC reduces risk in an early stage investment, but it definitely added a dilemma for us, as signing a term sheet with only a 50% commitment does not guarantee that you will find a partner for the other 50%. Items that differed in the term sheets were that one firm was offering funding in "tranches," basically meaning that the investment amount would be provided in multiple installment payments when specific milestones had been reached. This "tranched" approach coincided with their opinion that we were missing some key business leadership in the company, which meant that we would immediately have to perform an executive search to bring in a heavy hitter. And where one term sheet had a "no shop" clause preventing us from shopping around for better terms, the other term sheet had no restriction in this area.

After much deliberation (and day and night conference calls) we decided to accept the term sheet from August Capital near midnight on September 2, 2008 (the other term sheet was scheduled to explode on September 3). The reasons for this decision were that we felt most comfortable with the style and approach of Vivek Mehra, the general partner on the deal, the reputation and pedigree of August Capital would ensure higher quality advice and strategic opportunities, the chemistry of the current management team could be maintained, and we could focus immediately on executing the business plan rather than performing an executive search, and given the uncertainty of the global economy we wanted to get the entire investment amount into our bank account in one lump sum. In addition, this term sheet did not have a no shop clause and would have provided some flexibility if things went sideways.

Although we had accepted a term sheet, it did not mean we had completed the funding process. We still needed to find a partner to join August Capital on the deal. Our earlier relationship with Sierra Ventures from the Global MVP Summit became advantageous at this point, because based on its previous interest in the opportunity, coupled with our signed term sheet with August Capital, Sierra invited us to an all-partners meeting in the morning on Monday, September 8. At the conclusion of the meeting they asked us to stick around and within half an hour we received confirmation that they wanted to become the syndicate partner on the deal. The next decision we had regarded which partner from Sierra would manage the investment, as we had previously engaged with two members of their team, Jeff Loomans and Tim Guleri. We went out for a celebratory dinner with August Capital and Sierra Ventures the next evening, and afterwards, based on Tim's more extensive open source experience with SourceFire, we concluded that he would be the better candidate.

After signing the final version of the term sheet on September 11, we moved on to the due diligence stage. Due diligence involves the disclosure of every legal contract or agreement that has a bearing on the company's assets or liabilities. Essentially the investors are acquiring partial ownership of the company and need to ensure that everything is in order from a financial and legal perspective. Because of the maturity and complexity of the DotNetNuke open source project, the due diligence process in our situation was more complicated than average. We needed to dig up executed copies of all Contributor License Agreements, Software Grants, Non-Disclosure Agreements, third-party consulting contracts, sponsorship agreements, advertising agreements, independent contractor agreements, trademark registrations, domain registrations, financial records, tax returns, incorporation documents, and so on. At one point I realized that I had spent three full weeks doing nothing but collecting paperwork, signing it, faxing it to our attorney, and then couriering the physical documents.

DotNetNuke OpenForce 08

As is customary for the month of June every year, Microsoft was hosting the Tech-Ed conference in Orlando, Florida. However for the first time in 2008, Microsoft decided to split the Developer and IT Pro tracks into two consecutive weeks. This left the convention center empty over the weekend between the two weeks, and Microsoft graciously made the space available to community groups.

A couple of eager members from the DotNetNuke community in Florida, Brian Scarbeau and Michael Webb, convinced Joe Healy from Microsoft that DotNetNuke could leverage a room for its own developer event. With the assistance of DotNetNuke Corporation and especially from advertising manager Bill Walker, OpenForce Connect became a reality. A large contingent of vendors from the DotNetNuke ecosystem stepped forward to sponsor the event, and a variety of prizes were donated to be distributed among attendees. Overall the mini-conference was a great success, and the thing I found most interesting was the fact that many attendees had travelled long distances to attend OpenForce Connect, even though they had no intentions of attending Tech-Ed.

In October 2008 we had our second annual DotNetNuke OpenForce Europe conference in The Netherlands. Co-located with the SDC, this time the event was moved to Noordwijkerhout, which is located near Amsterdam. The overall attendance to this conference was down slightly from the previous year, but this was not surprising given the current state of the global economy. We had two tracks spanning two days, and the conference once again provided a great opportunity to network with members of the European community.

November 10–14 we had our second annual DotNetNuke OpenForce North America conference (see Figure 1-18), once again co-located with DevConnections at Mandalay Bay in Las Vegas, Nevada. We had two tracks spanning three days, and we added a DotNetNuke training day as well that was hosted by our official training partner, Engage Software. Overall attendance to the conference was down, but the number of vendors who participated in the exhibitor area increased dramatically. In addition to DotNetNuke Corporation, there was representation from Active Modules, Data Springs, IowaComputerGurus, Seablick Consulting, R2Integrated, AppTheory, Engage Software, `iHOSTASP.net`, and PowerDNN. This participation definitely increased the visibility and impact of DotNetNuke at the conference over the previous year, as I overheard more than one conference attendee proclaim "DotNetNuke is everywhere this year!"

Bill Walker worked closely with Will Morgenweck to schedule a community event one evening where attendees of OpenForce could get together and socialize in a casual setting, and people would be eligible for prizes donated by vendors. With more than $80,000 in prizes up for grabs, it actually convinced a number of DevConnections conference attendees to switch their registration to the OpenForce track so they could attend the community night. In addition to the community night, R2Integrated also created a social networking site at `dnnconnections.com`, which transmitted live podcasts, news, and interviews from the conference so that the community could feel more connected.

We had hoped to make a funding announcement at the conference so that it would have the greatest impact; however, the due diligence took longer than expected, and we missed our window by a couple weeks. Although we could not mention the imminent investment, we did take the opportunity to make another major announcement during the keynote.

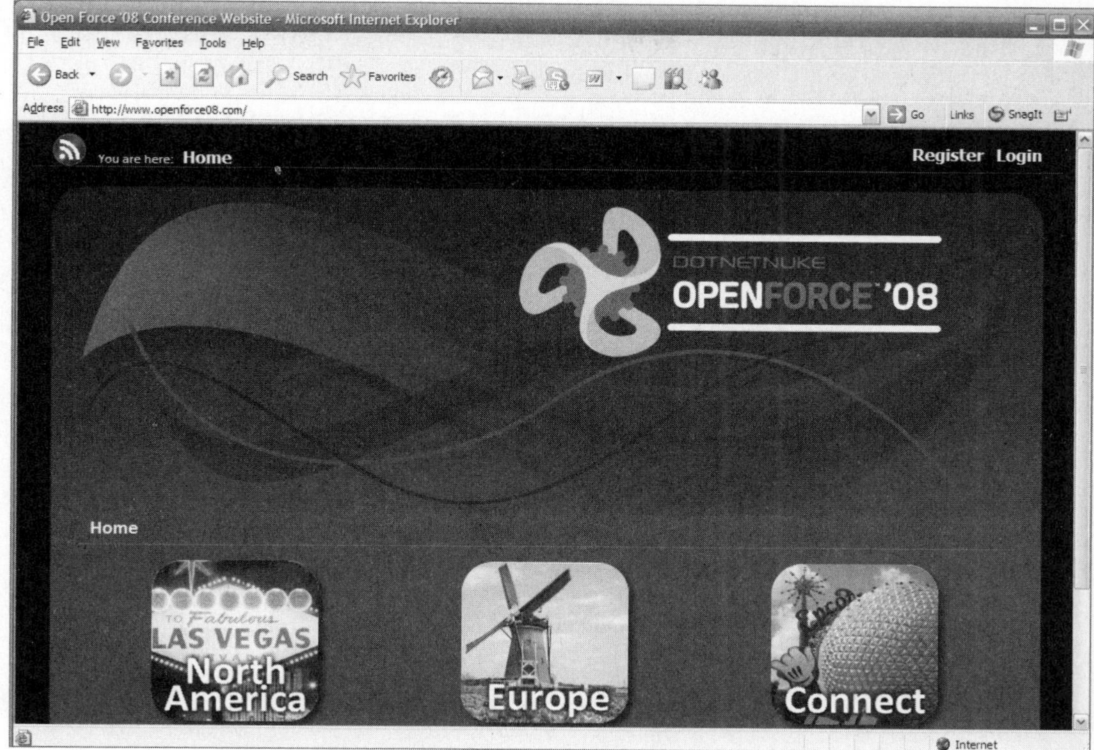

Figure 1-18

DotNetNuke Professional

As we worked through our business plan, we had looked at a variety of business models that other open source companies were using to successfully balance the requirements of commerce and community. In almost all cases, companies were making a commercial version of their open source product available under a yearly subscription model. In many cases this did not mean that the licensing of the commercial product was any different than that of the free product; it was still open source and provided the same freedoms to users. However, the commercial version did provide access to expert technical support and value-added network services that simplified and optimized the development and maintenance of the product. In fact, serious business users of the DotNetNuke platform had been demanding this for quite some time. In some ways, it was simply a repackaging of our existing SLA program, but in others it was a completely new strategy and direction for the project.

DotNetNuke Professional Edition was announced at the OpenForce North America conference and was promised to be available in Q1 2009. It would be based on the mature DotNetNuke 4.9 code base and would include the essential modules for building a robust site. In keeping with the spirit of the open source development model, the core elements of the commercial distribution would be licensed under the current BSD open source license, and we promised to work continually to provide new innovation and increased value in the free, open source core product.

Series A Announcement

The due diligence ended up taking 10 weeks to complete (it usually takes 4–6 weeks), but also served a useful purpose in terms of getting all of the legal artifacts within the company in order. Aside from the internal due diligence there was also the funding documentation itself as well as the related filings to provide preferred shares to the investors. Our legal team at DLA Piper worked very hard to ensure that all bases were covered, and we successfully closed the deal. The actual funding hit our bank account on November 20, 2008, and we made our public Series A announcement on November 25, 2008 (see Figure 1-19).

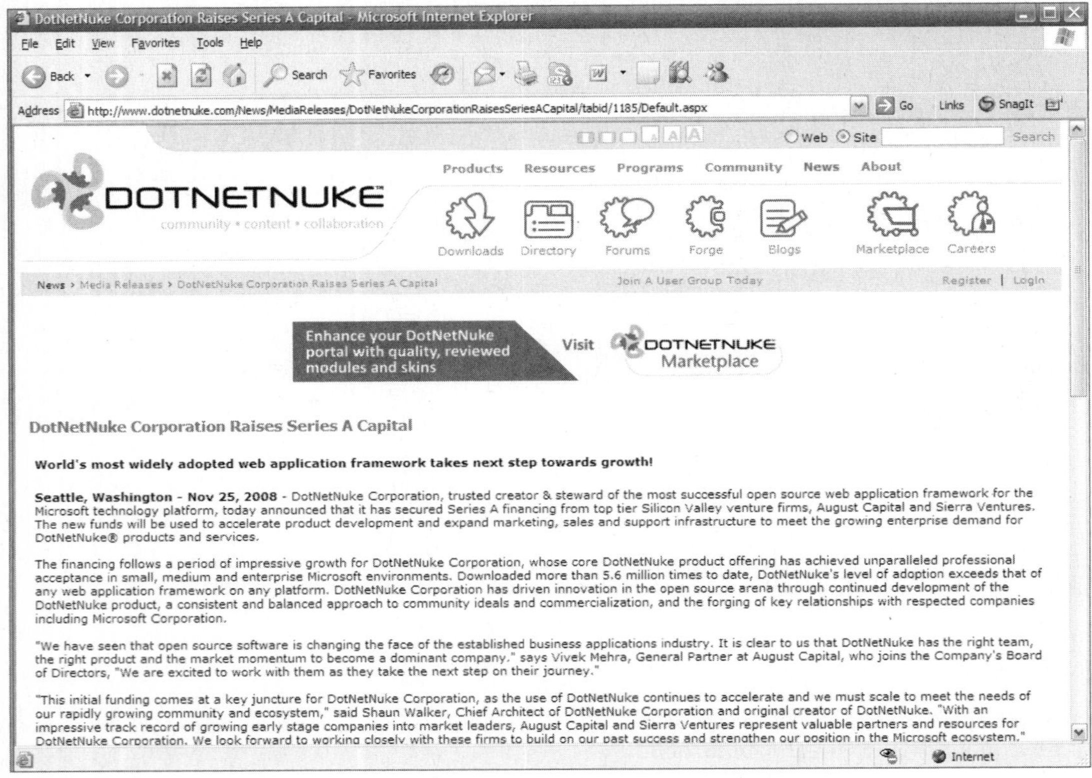

Figure 1-19

The following week, we announced that Navin Nagiah was officially joining the company as CEO. It had been a long journey for Navin, as he had originally been introduced to us in January 2008 and had worked full-time with us for four months without any compensation as we tried to close our round of funding. Navin had certainly demonstrated his commitment and faith in the opportunity, and we were glad to have him come aboard. There was a lot of work to be done on an aggressive schedule, but we finally felt like we had all the pieces of the puzzle in place to start the next step of our journey.

The new Board of Directors consisted of Navin, myself, Vivek Mehra from August Capital, and Tim Guleri from Sierra Ventures. We needed one more external party to join the Board of Directors, and Larry

Augustin was the obvious candidate. Because Larry was already involved in so many other high-profile, funded open source companies, it took some arm twisting to convince him to come aboard. But ultimately he agreed to join the team and a public press release soon followed.

DotNetNuke 5.0

After the initial announcement of "Cambrian" at OpenForce North America 07, not much news had been shared with the community about its ongoing development. Our roadmap slipped behind schedule due to our focus on fundraising, and we made a number of releases to the 4.x product to deal with some security issues and improve the overall stability of the application based on insight gained through the SLA Program.

Meanwhile, Charles Nurse continued to work diligently on DotNetNuke 5.0, and by the summer of 2008 we had a reached a point where we believed we were code complete on all of the major enhancements that had been introduced to the platform in this iteration. We had not tackled all of the features promised in the Cambrian roadmap, but we had implemented a lot of fundamental changes that would be essential to delivering future functionality.

DotNetNuke 5.0 may not appear to be a significant release on the surface, but once you dig a little deeper you quickly realize that there are a ton of major enhancements. The entire packaging format for extensions has been overhauled, security has been improved through Deny permissions and other refactoring, performance has been optimized with a brand new data caching pattern, the administrative area has been opened up to allow for complete flexibility, page creation and management has been streamlined, the skinning engine received some designer-friendly new concepts, and the overall stability and quality of the application was maintained.

Keeping with tradition, DotNetNuke 5.0 was publicly released on December 24, 2008, six years from the date I originally released the IBuySpy Workshop. In 2009, DotNetNuke 5.0 will continue to evolve in accordance to the product roadmap, receiving highly requested features such as social networking, workflow/versioning, content localization, and an updated web user interface.

Summary

DotNetNuke is an evolving open source web platform. The organic community ecosystem that has grown up around DotNetNuke is vibrant and dynamic, providing the essential environment for long-term growth and prosperity. You will always be able to get the latest high-quality release, including full source code, from `http://www.dotnetnuke.com`.

2

Installing DotNetNuke Version 5

This chapter reviews the installation processes of the available packages that come with DotNetNuke. The installation process has been simplified with the automated installer, and you have four packages to choose from when you consider installing DotNetNuke.

The Install Package contains only the files needed for a runtime deployment to a web server. The Source Package contains everything, including full application source code. The Starter Kit Package contains the files needed to configure a development environment in Visual Web Developer Express, which is a free tool for creating and working with ASP.NET web applications or Visual Studio 2005/2008 applications. You can also use SQL Express for your database. All of these are free from Microsoft Corporation.

The Upgrade Package contains only the files needed for an upgrade of an existing installation. Your previous edition for the upgrade should be v4.x.

Which package is good for your application? Select the Source Package if you are a web developer and need to customize the DotNetNuke web application framework. Select the Install Package if you want to deploy a live site to a web server with minimum required files. The Upgrade Package would be used to upgrade an existing installation to a newer version.

To get these downloads, you need to go to `www.dotnetnuke.com`, register on the site, and click the Download icon located on the top of the page.

What You Need to Install DNN 5

Table 2-1 shows the requirements for installing DNN5.

Table 2-1: Prerequisites

Software	Description
Web Server	Microsoft Internet Information Server 5 or greater contained in Windows 2000 Server, Windows XP Professional, Windows Vista, and Windows 2003 Server
Microsoft .NET Runtime	ASP.NET 2.0 or higher
Database	Microsoft SQL Server 2000 or greater
Development	Optional: The starter kit requires the use of Visual Web Environment; Developer or Visual Studio 2005 and SQL Express Edition

To install DotNetNuke 5, follow these steps:

1. Download the appropriate software for your needs.
2. Unzip the package.
3. Create a database in SQL Server.
4. Create a database login.
5. Set file permissions.
6. Configure IIS (Internet Information Server).
7. Install.

Step 1: Download the Software

Navigate your web browser to `www.dotnetnuke.com`, which is the official DotNetNuke web site, as shown in Figure 2-1. You will be required to register on the site and then click the Download icon and select the appropriate package for your needs.

Step 2: Unzip the Package

Extract the entire contents of the zip file to your chosen installation directory. On a local intranet, you can place your web site anywhere (for example, `c:\websites\dotnetnuke`). On a remote hosting server, you will need to upload the files to your web site following the procedures provided by your hosting provider.

To extract a zip file, you can use either the built-in zip functionality of Windows or a third-party compression tool, such as WinZip, which you can obtain from `www.winzip.com`.

Step 3: Create a Database in SQL Server 2005

If you are using a remote host, your hosting provider most likely has configured a SQL Server database for you and can provide instructions on connecting to the database.

Figure 2-1

Open SQL Server Management Studio, right-click Database, and select New Database as shown in Figure 2-2.

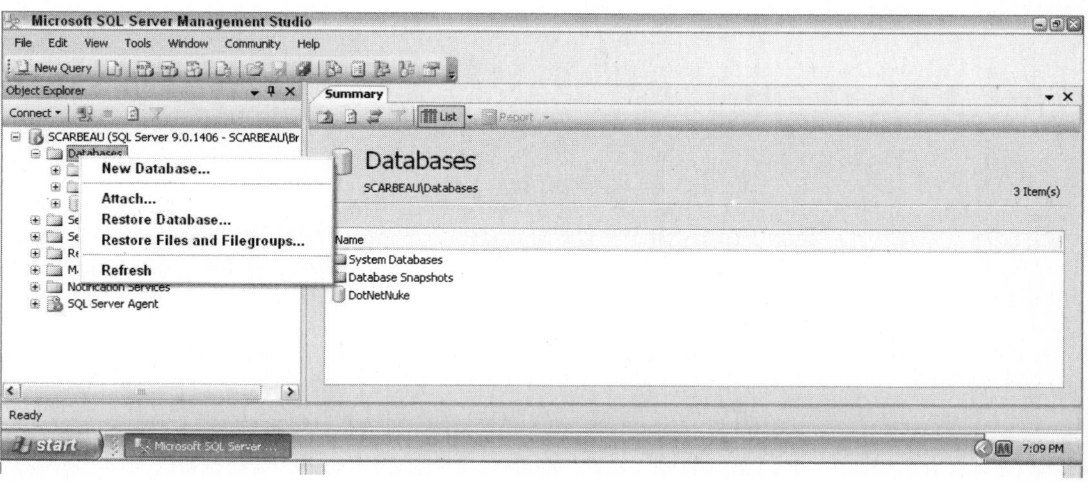

Figure 2-2

Name the database DotNetNuke, and click OK as shown in Figure 2-3.

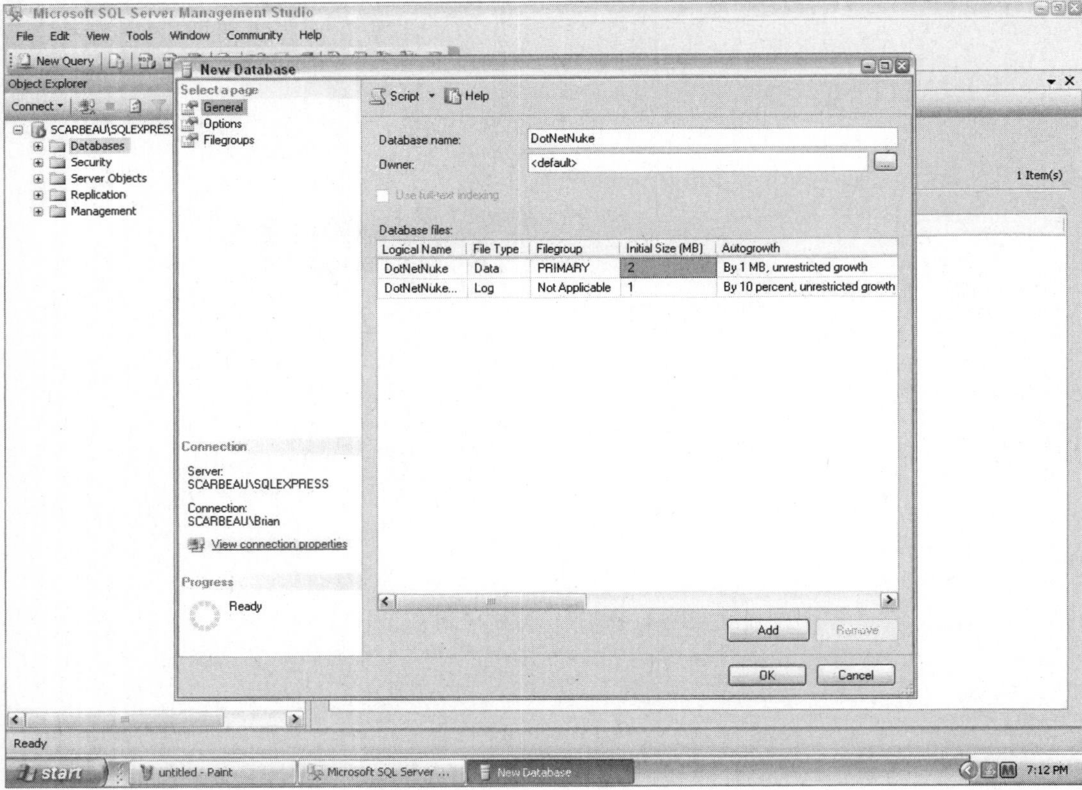

Figure 2-3

Step 4: Create a Database Login

You have two options when creating a user account to access your newly created database:

1. **Windows Security:** Uses the account under which your application is running to access the database. (This is the more secure option, but is not supported in all environments, particularly in shared hosting.)
2. **SQL Server Security:** Uses a username along with a password to access the database.

Right-click the Security folder and select New Login as shown in Figure 2-4.

This book uses Windows Authentication, which is the default selection in this example as shown in Figure 2-5.

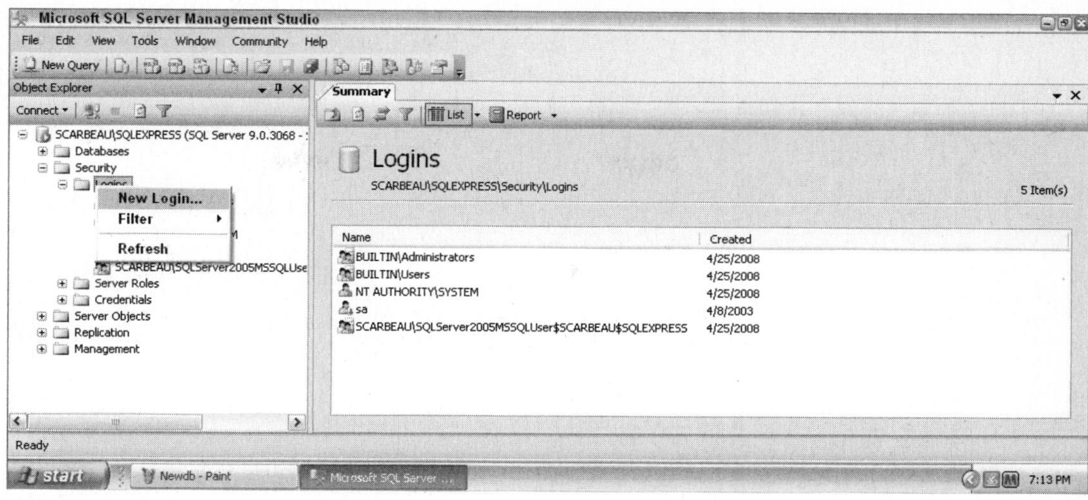

Figure 2-4

Figure 2-5

Click Search to find the user account. Now, click Advanced; see Figure 2-6.

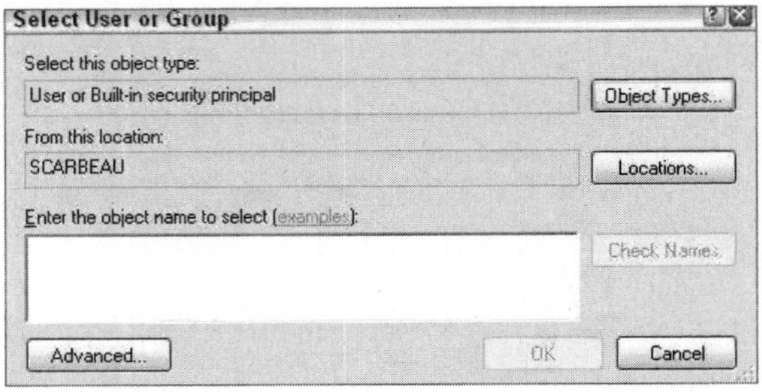

Figure 2-6

Click Find Now as shown in Figure 2-7, and scroll down to add the user that you want to select. Select the user and click OK, and then click OK again.

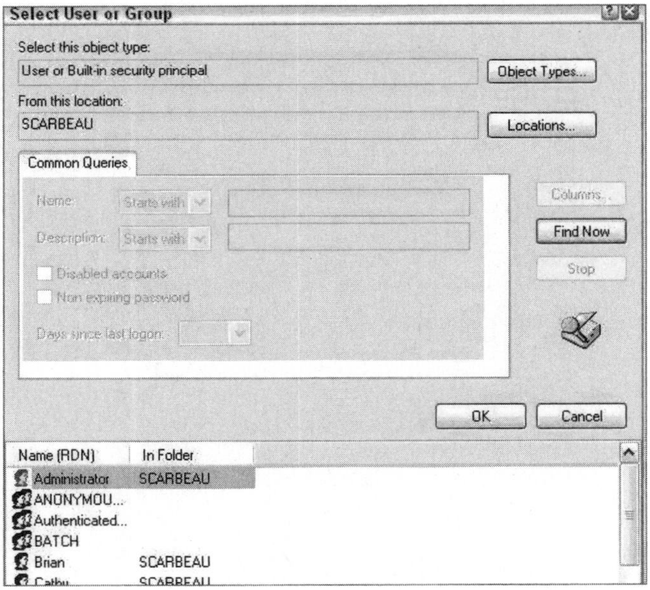

Figure 2-7

Now that your database user has been selected, you need to select the DotNetNuke database from the Default Database drop-down list, and select English from the Default Language drop-down list. See Figure 2-8.

Now select User Mapping from the selections on the left. See Figure 2-9. Select the DotNetNuke database and select db_owner, and then click OK.

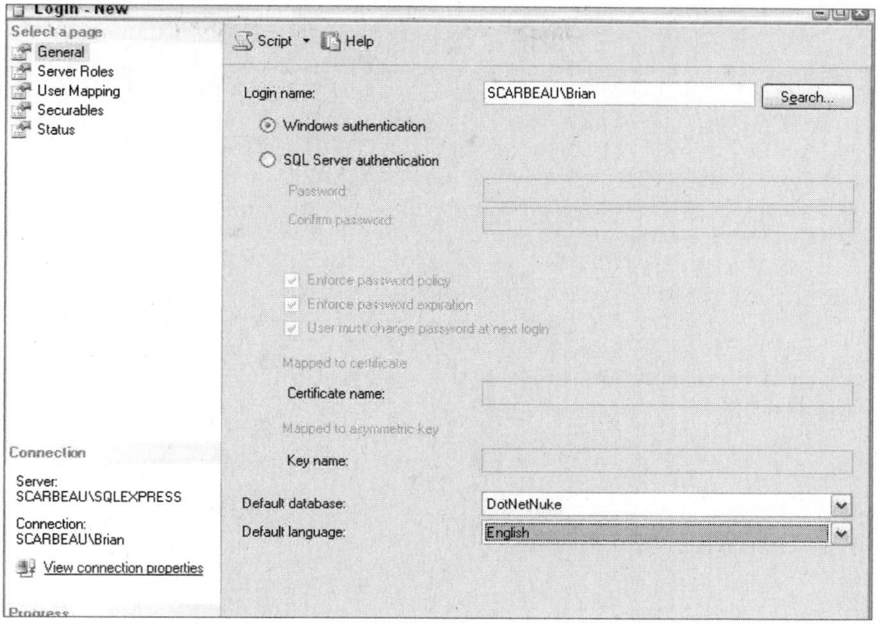

Figure 2-8

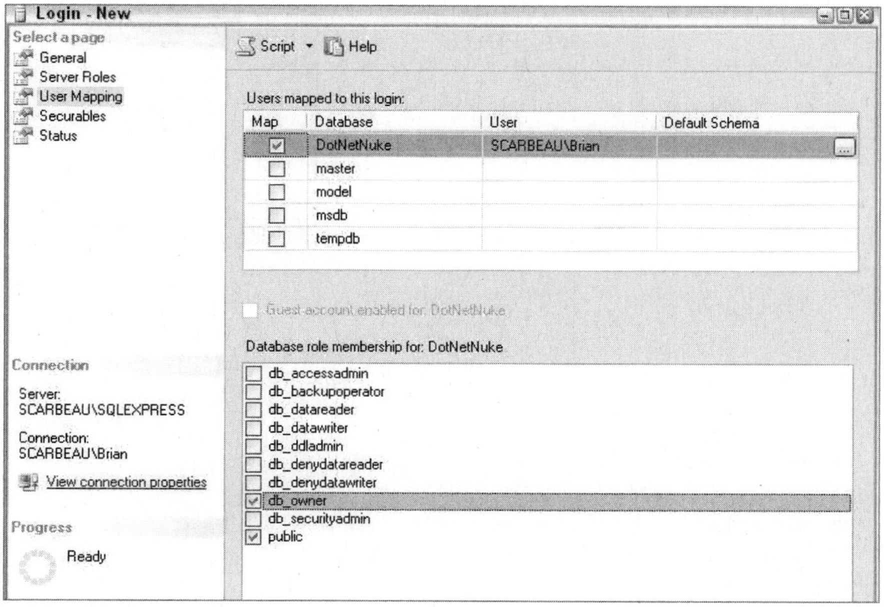

Figure 2-9

Step 5: Set File Permissions

In order to use IIS, you need to set file permissions on the folder in which you plan to install DotNetNuke. In your case, use c:\dotnetnuke. The example here uses Microsoft Windows Vista. Right-click over the c:\dotnetnuke folder, scroll down to Properties, and click that. Click the Security tab as shown in Figure 2-10.

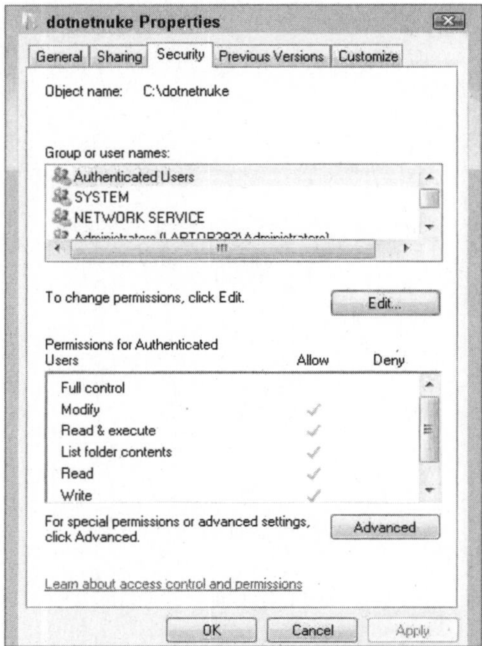

Figure 2-10

Click, Edit, Add, Advanced, Find Now. Scroll down to NETWORK SERVICE and click OK twice. Highlight NETWORK SERVICE and click Full Control. Click OK, OK, OK.

The NETWORK SERVICE account is the one that the site will run under by default.

See Figure 2-11.

Step 6: Configure IIS (Internet Information Server)

The next step is to create a web site pointing at the DotNetNuke installation files. Follow these steps to complete that task in Windows Vista.

Click the Start icon, type `inetmgr` in the Start Search box, and press your Enter key. Click Continue. IIS is now loaded. See Figure 2-12.

Click Sites, right-click over Default Web Site, and scroll down to Add Application as shown in Figure 2-13.

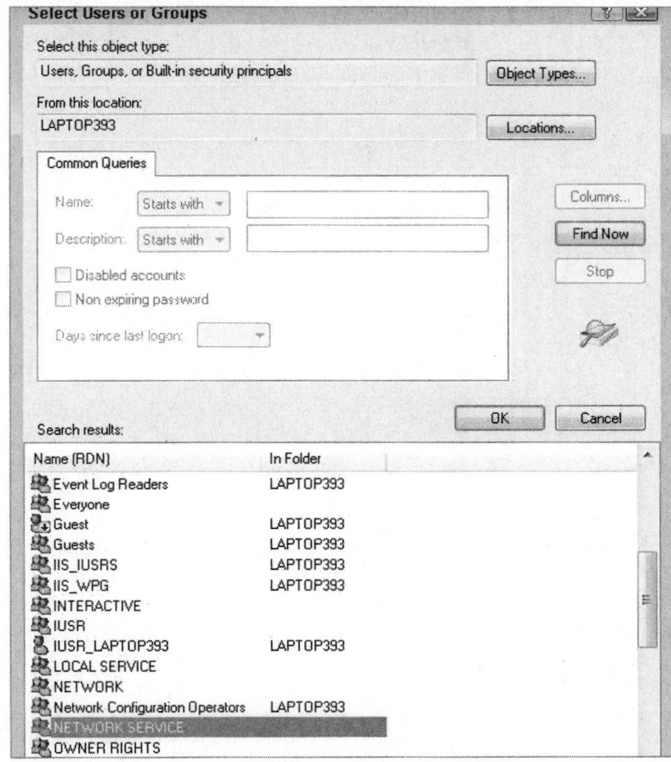

Figure 2-11

Type the name of the folder path into the Physical Path textbox, type DotNetNuke under Alias, and select Classic .NET AppPool under Application Pool. Now select the physical path to the DotNetNuke location. See Figure 2-14.

Step 7: Perform the Installation

Open Internet Explorer and key in `http://localhost/dotnetnuke/default.aspx`. See Figure 2-15.

You have three options available to select. The first is called Custom, and this installation method provides you with the ability to customize your DotNetNuke installation completely. Select this option if you want to control which optional components get installed. Next is the Typical installation, which makes some typical choices for you during the installation. Finally, there is the Auto installation, which bypasses the wizard completely and uses the legacy Auto-Install procedure.

Select Auto and click Next.

The installation files will be created. Scroll down and click Click Here To Access Your Portal.

Congratulations! Your site has been created, and you're ready to explore the power of DotNetNuke. Your site should look like Figure 2-16.

Figure 2-12

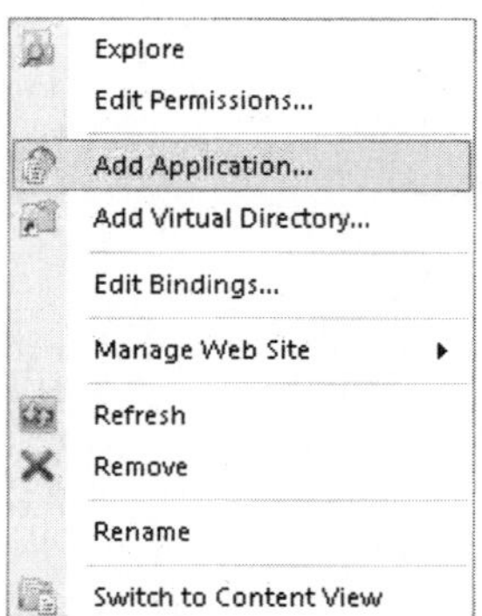

Figure 2-13

Add Application
Site name: Default Web Site
Path: /
Alias:
dotnetnuke
Example: sales
Application pool:
Classic .NET AppPool
Select...
Physical path:
c:\dotnetnuke
Pass-through authentication
Connect as...
Test Settings...
OK
Cancel

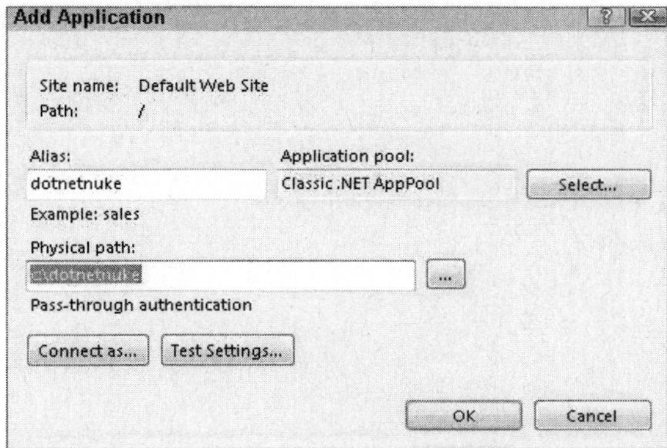

Figure 2-14

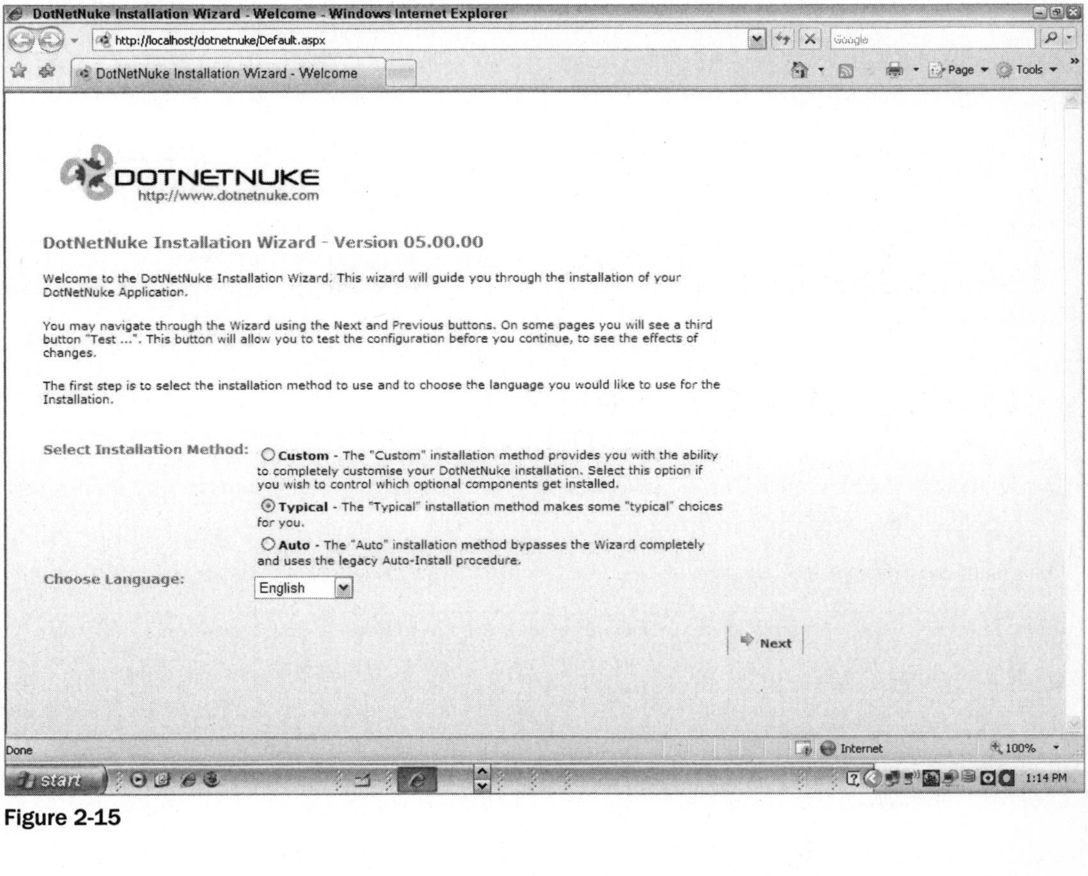

DotNetNuke Installation Wizard - Welcome - Windows Internet Explorer
http://localhost/dotnetnuke/Default.aspx
DotNetNuke Installation Wizard - Welcome
DOTNETNUKE
http://www.dotnetnuke.com
DotNetNuke Installation Wizard - Version 05.00.00
Welcome to the DotNetNuke Installation Wizard. This wizard will guide you through the installation of your DotNetNuke Application.
You may navigate through the Wizard using the Next and Previous buttons. On some pages you will see a third button "Test ...". This button will allow you to test the configuration before you continue, to see the effects of changes.
The first step is to select the installation method to use and to choose the language you would like to use for the Installation.
Select Installation Method:
Custom - The "Custom" installation method provides you with the ability to completely customise your DotNetNuke installation. Select this option if you wish to control which optional components get installed.
Typical - The "Typical" installation method makes some "typical" choices for you.
Auto - The "Auto" installation method bypasses the Wizard completely and uses the legacy Auto-Install procedure.
Choose Language:
English
Next
Done
Internet
100%
start
1:14 PM

Figure 2-15

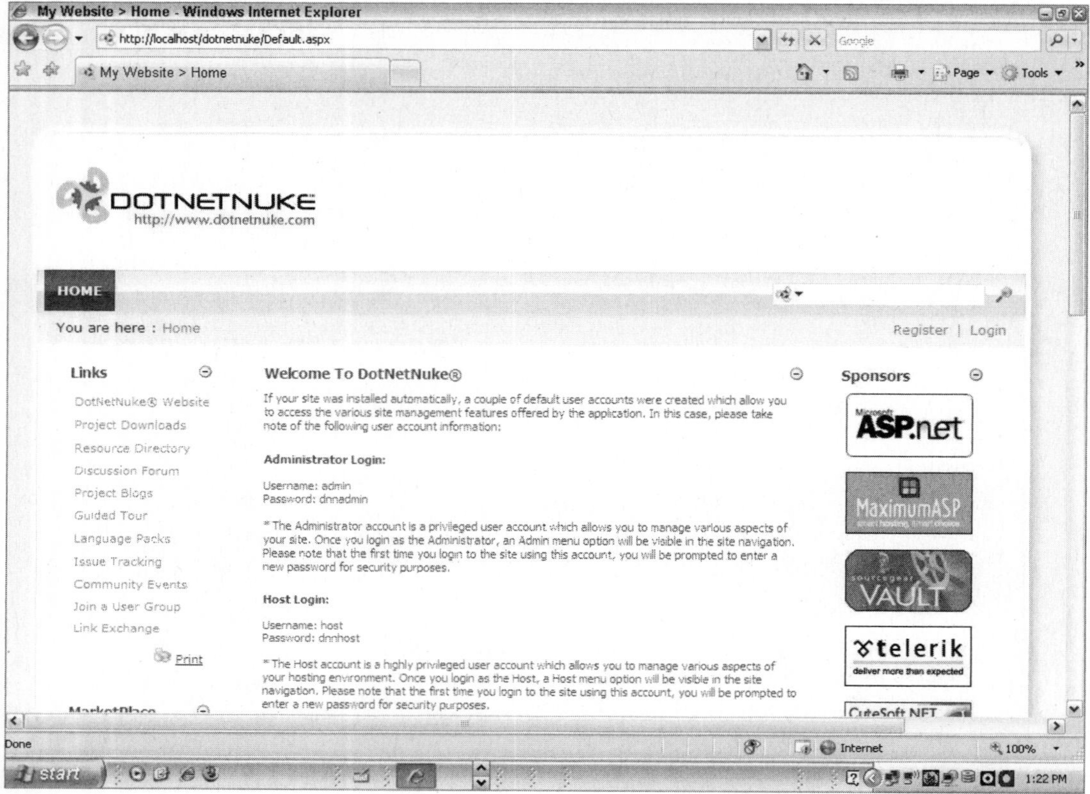

Figure 2-16

Installing the Starter Kit

You would use the Starter Kit installation when you want to use Visual Web Developer or Visual Studio while you are working with DotNetNuke. Visual Web Developer includes its own web server, so you don't need to work with IIS if you choose this installation.

To install the Starter Kit Package, you need to download that package from the dotnetnuke.com site.

Save that `.vsi` file on your desktop and double-click the file to open it. See Figure 2-17.

Click Next. You'll receive the error message shown in Figure 2-18.

Click Yes to continue and then click Finish.

You will see a screen like that shown in Figure 2-19; click Close.

Open Microsoft Visual Web Developer. Click File, New, Website. On the New Web Site dialog box under My Templates, select DotNetNuke Web Application Framework. Browse to the location of your installation, C:\dotnetnuke, and click OK. See Figure 2-20.

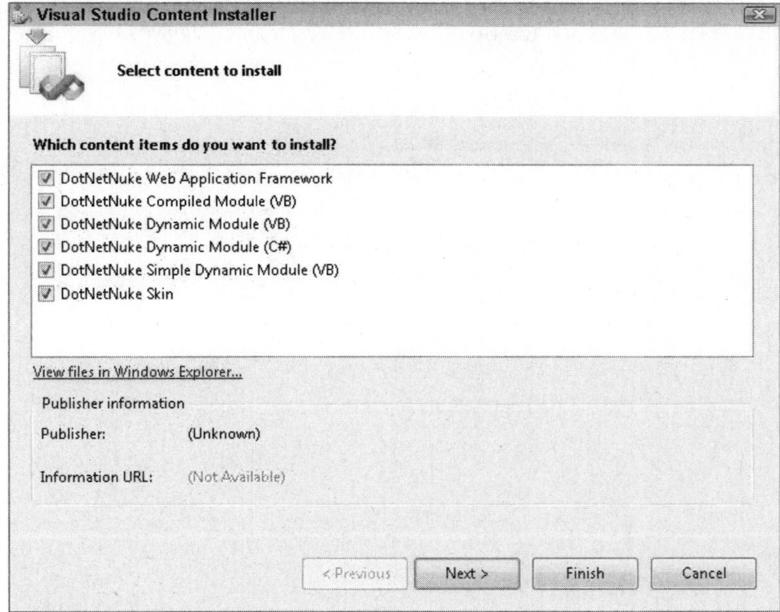

Figure 2-17

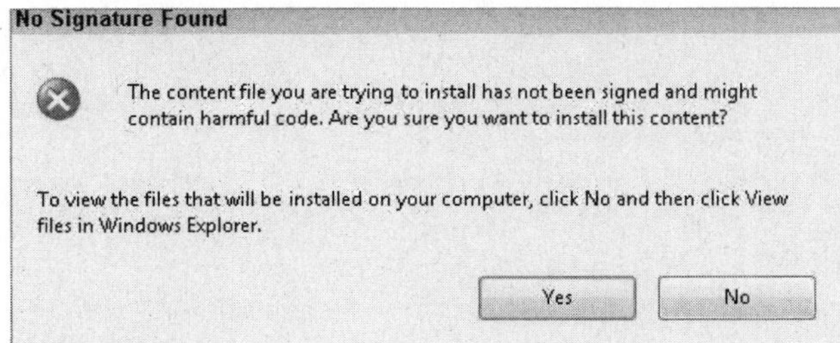

Figure 2-18

You should see a screen similar to Figure 2-21. Now, press the Ctrl F5 key to build and start the site.

Your next screen should look like Figure 2-22. Select Auto and click Next.

The Auto installation bypasses the wizard and uses the legacy Auto-Install procedure.

The installation files will be created on the next screen. Scroll down and click Click Here To Access Your Portal. You will also see the local web server load on your taskbar.

You should see your site like in Figure 2-16. You will need to open your site in Visual Web Developer and then right-click over the Default.aspx file which is located on the right in the Solutions Explorer pane, and select view in Browser option, if you close out of Visual Web Developer.

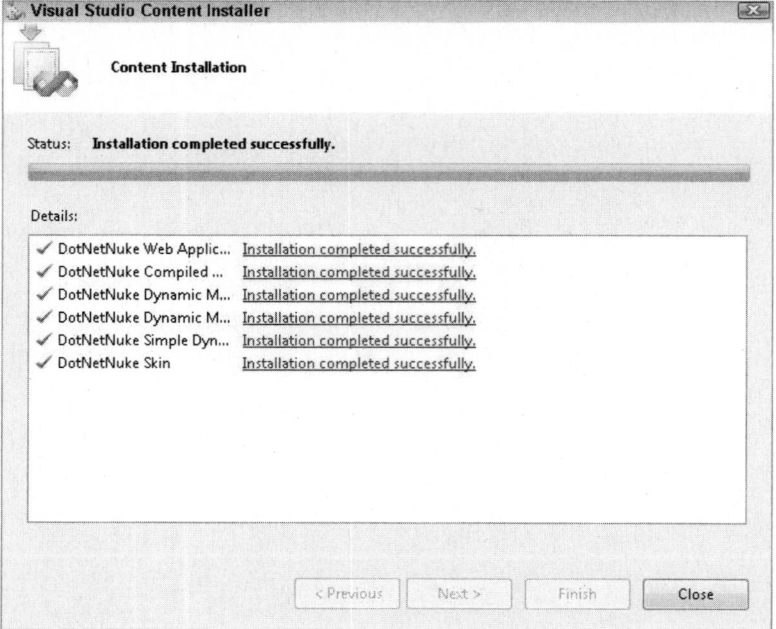

Figure 2-19

Figure 2-20

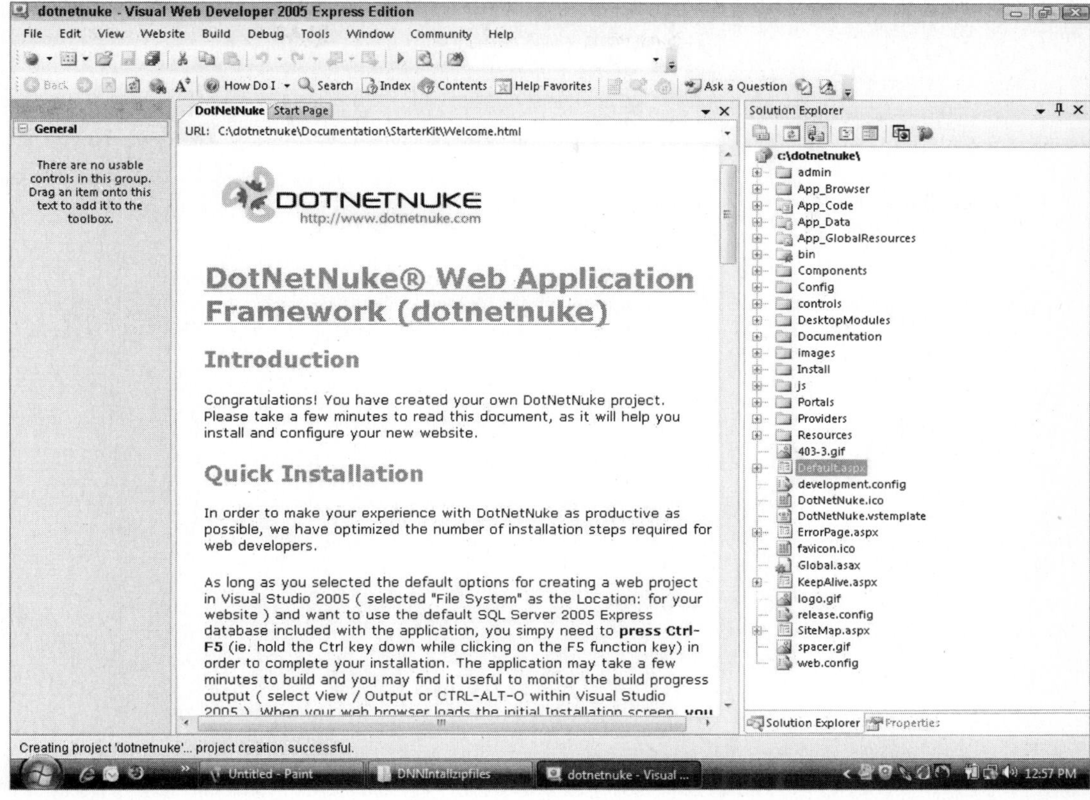

Figure 2-21

Upgrading to DotNetNuke 5

The upgrade process for DotNetNuke is very similar to the installation procedure. It contains an automated process with fewer steps because the infrastructure is already in place. This section focuses on the upgrade from a DotNetNuke 4.x site to a DotNetNuke 5 site.

Back up your site. We recommend that you back up all of your site files along with your database files. At a minimum, you must back up your web.config file.

Download the software. As described earlier in this chapter, go to the dotnetnuke.com site, register, log in, and go to the download section to download the Upgrade Package. This package contains only the files needed for an upgrade of an existing installation.

Unzip the package over the existing DotNetNuke folder for your site. Overwrite any files when you unzip the package.

Load your site with the site URL. You will see files being installed with an Upgrade Status Report and then an Upgrade Complete. Scroll down and click the link that says Click Here to Access Portal. Click that to access your upgraded site.

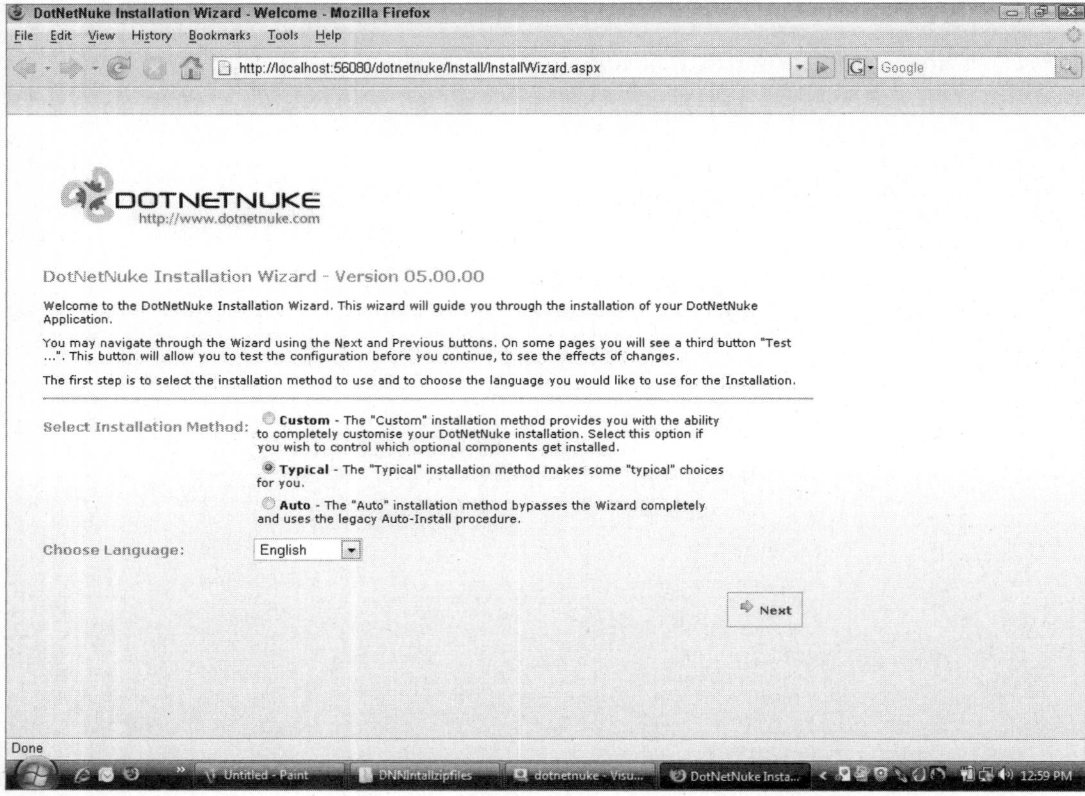

Figure 2-22

Common Installation Issues

The DotNetNuke Core Team has provided screens to assist in diagnosing installation problems. Common problems are:

- Invalid Connection String, which means that the web.config file did not understand the database information that is required upon installation. Check to make sure you placed the connection string in both settings in the web.config file and make sure you save the file.
- Insufficient File Permissions, when you have not granted the correct access to the root folder. Make sure that you review the instructions for setting file permissions earlier in this chapter.

Finally, DotNetNuke has a large community of users. Go to the dotnetnuke.com site and search the forum for any errors you might have. You may find a solution right away from the forum. If not, post your error in the forum and within a short period of time, someone will give you an answer to try to help you.

Summary

DotNetNuke has several installation packages to choose from:

- The Source Package contains everything, including full application source code.
- The Starter Kit Package contains only the files needed to configure a development environment in Visual Web Developer Express or Visual Studio 2005.
- The Install Package contains only the files needed for a runtime deployment to a web server.
- The Upgrade Package contains only the files needed for an upgrade of an existing installation (does not include module packages).

This chapter guided you through all the necessary steps to install DotNetNuke.

3

Portal Overview

One of the many advantages of using DotNetNuke is that you can create one installation but have as many child portals as you want. According to Wikipedia, a "web portal is a site that provides a single function via a web page or site. Web portals often function as a point of access to information on the World Wide Web." DotNetNuke has been a successful web portal for global companies running web sites on the Internet, intranet, and extranet as well.

DotNetNuke provides the opportunity to have a portal administrator who is called the host, and as many child portals as needed. Also, additional host accounts can be created for users using the Host Accounts feature. This will give them the same privileges as the host. The URL for the host is `http://www.yourdomainname.com`. A child portal URL would be `http://www.yourdomainname.com/newsite`. An administrator is assigned to those sites, and that administrator is called an admin for that site.

As the portal administrator, you may set up hundreds of various web sites on the same portal. To accomplish this task, a child portal is created under the parent (discussed later in this chapter). At runtime, the application will determine the proper content to display based on the PortalID of the portal accessed. This is one of the powerful features of DotNetNuke and has contributed to the rapid growth of the application.

Portal Organization Elements

DotNetNuke portals contain four main organization elements that are examined in this chapter. They are parent/child portals, pages, panes, and containers.

Parent/Child Portals

DotNetNuke creates a physical directory and file that enables IIS to recognize the portal. Child portals make sense within a single domain, and run under that domain.

If you click Host, Portals, you'll see the parent web site and any child web sites that have been created. Figure 3-1 lists an example. Only child portals can be deleted with the delete icon.

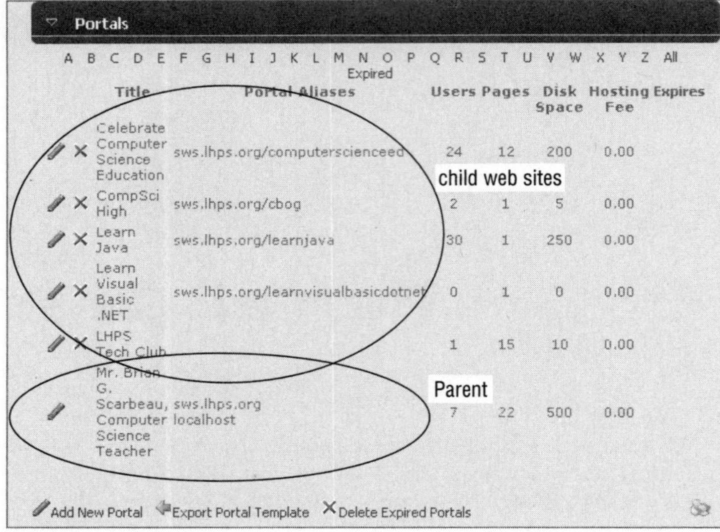

Title	Portal Aliases	Users	Pages	Disk Space	Hosting Fee	Expires
Celebrate Computer Science Education	sws.lhps.org/computerscienceed	24	12	200	0.00	
CompSci High	sws.lhps.org/cbog	2	1	5	0.00	
Learn Java	sws.lhps.org/learnjava	30	1	250	0.00	
Learn Visual Basic .NET	sws.lhps.org/learnvisualbasicdotnet	0	1	0	0.00	
LHPS Tech Club		1	15	10	0.00	
Mr. Brian G. Scarbeau, Computer Science Teacher	sws.lhps.org localhost	7	22	500	0.00	

Figure 3-1

When you click Add New Portal, you'll see the screen shown in Figure 3-2.

Portal Setup

Portal Type: Parent Child

Portal Alias:

Home Directory: Portals/[PortalID]

Customize

Title:

Description:

Keywords:

Template: None Specified

Security Settings

Username:

First Name:

Last Name:

Email:

Password:

Confirm:

Create Portal Cancel

Figure 3-2

The radio button selection under Portal Alias is what you would select for setting up a parent or child portal. As you can see in Figure 3-1, portal aliases are created when creating a child portal. To set up a parent portal, you need to create an additional web site in your IIS Manager with host headers in your domain name. Then, create a DNS record to point to the IP address of your web server. Information on how to perform these tasks is outside the scope of this book, so please refer to your IIS and DNS help files for the steps. You can find specific details on setting up a new portal in Chapter 5, "Host Administration," which covers the host functions of DotNetNuke.

Pages

A DotNetNuke page is the same as a static HTML page. What goes on the page is up to the person designing the site. Several modules are discussed later in this chapter that you can place on pages. You might see the term "tabs" as referring to pages in DotNetNuke because that's what pages were called in legacy versions of DotNetNuke. In fact, when you click Admin, Pages, you will see the title Tabs listed, and not Pages.

You can place a new page on your site in two ways. The easiest way is for you to first maximize the Show Control Panel icon, which is located at the top right of your first page. See Figure 3-3.

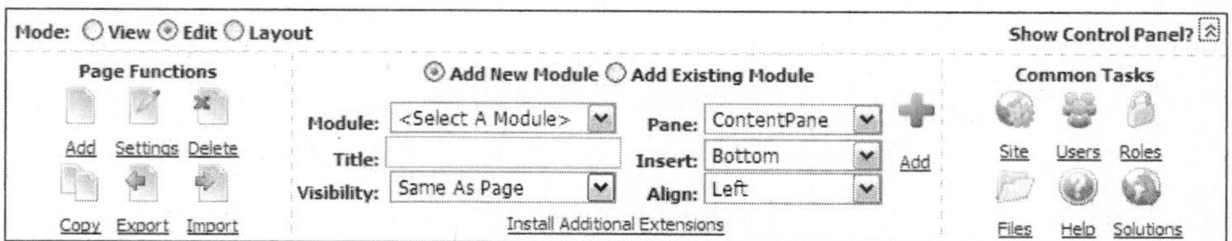

Figure 3-3

On the left side are the six Page Functions that you can select. These are described in Table 3-1.

Table 3-1: Page Functions

Function	Description
Add	You add a page to your site with this option. When you click the icon, you will see the page management control where you can define properties, such as page name, title, keywords, or permissions.
Settings	Click this icon when you need to modify page settings.
Delete	Click this icon to delete a page. (Note: even though the page has been deleted, the Admin can go to Admin, Recycle Bin to retrieve that page.) See Figure 3-4. This feature is discussed in more detail in Chapter 5.
Copy	Click this icon to copy a page. All modules that are located on the page will be copied.
Import/Export	You can only Export or Import pages using the Page Functions that are in the Show Control Panel. You can export a page into a templates folder and then import the page when you need the page. See Figure 3-5.

Figure 3-4 shows an example of the Recycle Bin wherein you can restore deleted pages or modules to pages. An example of a page export is shown in Figure 3-5.

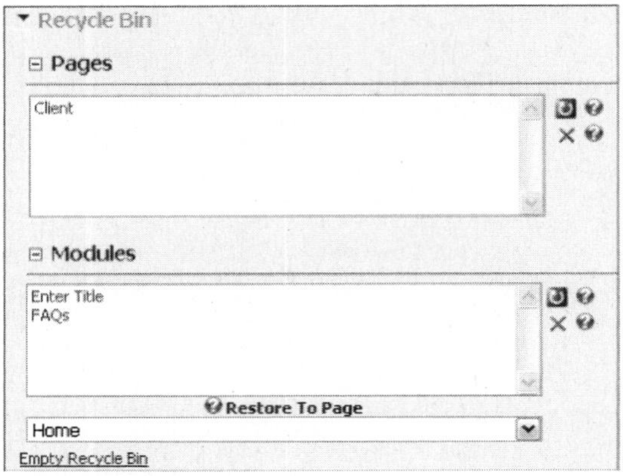

Figure 3-4

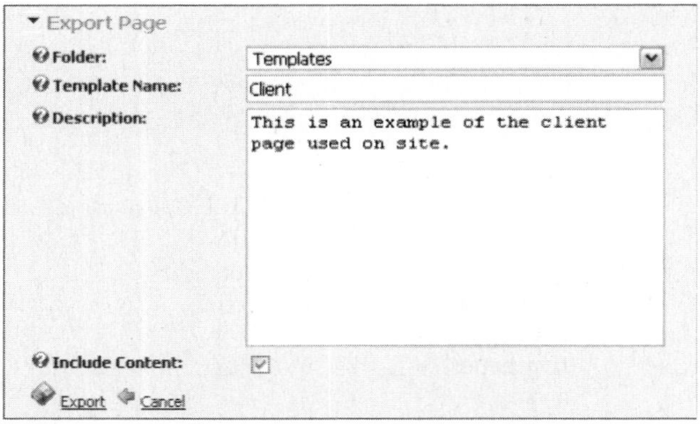

Figure 3-5

Child pages can be created as well. Child pages would be located under a parent page. You would select a parent page in the settings if you wanted to create a new child page. Select None if you don't want that option from the drop-down list. See Figure 3-6 for Page Management Settings.

Figure 3-6 shows an example of new page added to a portal.

Notice the question mark images in the figure. These images expand when you click them. They provide additional information to speed your learning.

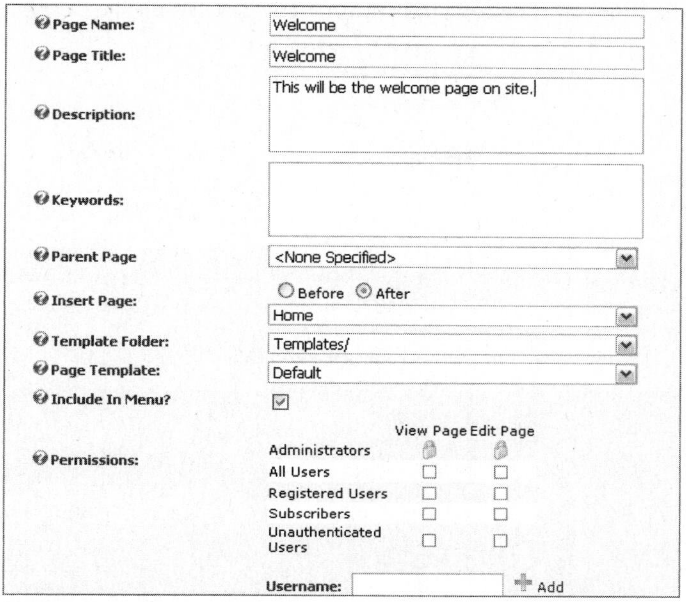

Page Name: Welcome
Page Title: Welcome
Description: This will be the welcome page on site.
Keywords:
Parent Page: <None Specified>
Insert Page: Before After
Home
Template Folder: Templates/
Page Template: Default
Include In Menu?
Permissions: View Page Edit Page
Administrators
All Users
Registered Users
Subscribers
Unauthenticated Users
Username: Add

Figure 3-6

Panes

Panes are the areas that are defined in your skin in which you can place modules to display on your pages. You can view your panes by clicking on Layout, which is located aside of Mode on the top left of your page.

Skin developers will determine how many panes you can have using that particular skin. For example, the default skin called MinimalExtropy has three panes: the Content Pane, the Left Pane, and the Right Pane. The DNN-Blue skin has five panes: Top Pane, Left Pane, Content Pane, Right Pane, and Bottom Pane. See Figure 3-7 for an example.

If a pane is not found, DotNetNuke places the module in the Content Pane area. Skins determine where modules appear on pages.

Skins

A skin is a collection of designs that are used to change the look and feel of a DotNetNuke site. You can have a different skin for each web site that you create. Or, you can have a separate skin for each of your pages if you want. In addition, you can have a separate skin for the Admin and Host Settings as well. To install additional skins, go to the home page, click Show Control Panel, and click Install Additional Extensions. Scroll down to Available Skins and select Install Selected Extensions. After your selection, you can go to Host, Settings and select the skin that you want; then click Update. You'll learn in later chapters how to upload a skin.

Figure 3-7

Figure 3-8 gives an example of the MinimalExtropy skin.

Containers

A container decorates a module used on a page. Changes made to a container will only be applied to that module for which the change is being made. Skin developers also design containers to match their skin. For example, the MinimalExtropy skin has three containers called title_blue, title_grey, and title_red that you can use. You can install additional containers using the same steps as installing a skin, but scroll down to Available Containers and select one that looks good with your skin. Click Install Selected Extensions and then go to Host, Settings and select the Container and click Update.

To change the Links module container, you would first click the down arrow and then select Settings. See Figure 3-9.

Scroll down to Page Settings, click the plus sign to expand the settings and, under Basic Settings, select Module Container and click in the box to see the installed containers that you can use. The default selection on the radio button is set at Host to view containers and you can click Site to view containers that are available only to this portal site. See Figure 3-10.

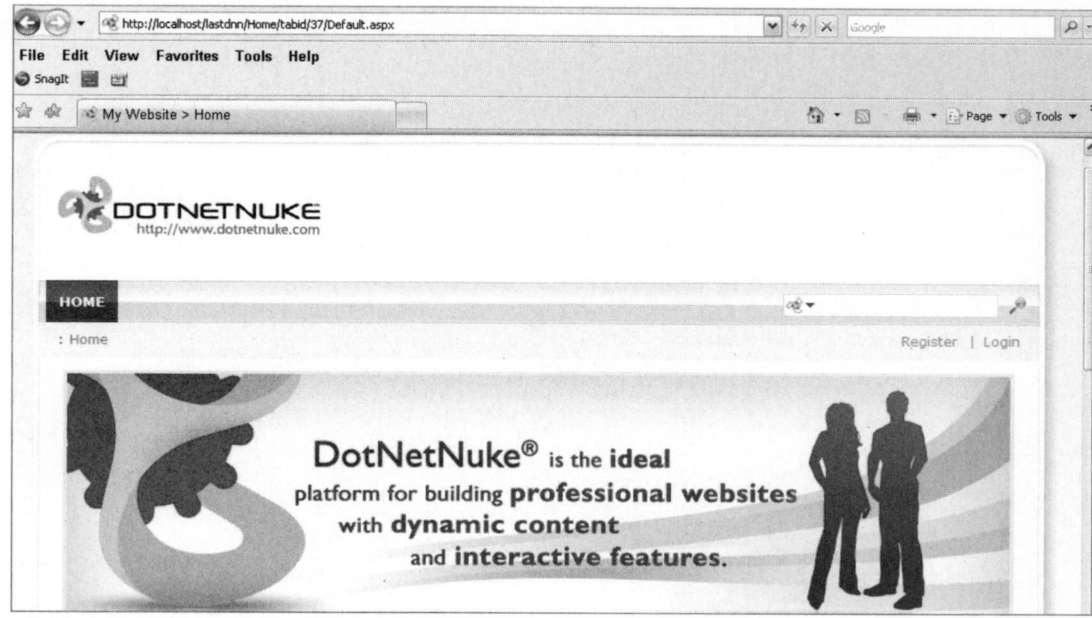

Figure 3-8

Figure 3-9

DNN Blue- Text Header- Color Background was selected. Figure 3-11 displays the changed container.

Modules

A module gives your page functionality. There are core modules that come with the installation of DotNetNuke. There are also third-party modules that are either free or can be purchased (at DotNetNuke Marketplace or the Snowcovered.com web site). Chapter 6, ''Modules,'' covers modules in more detail.

As a host user, you can view the installed modules by going to Host and then Module Definitions.

Table 3-2 reviews the default modules.

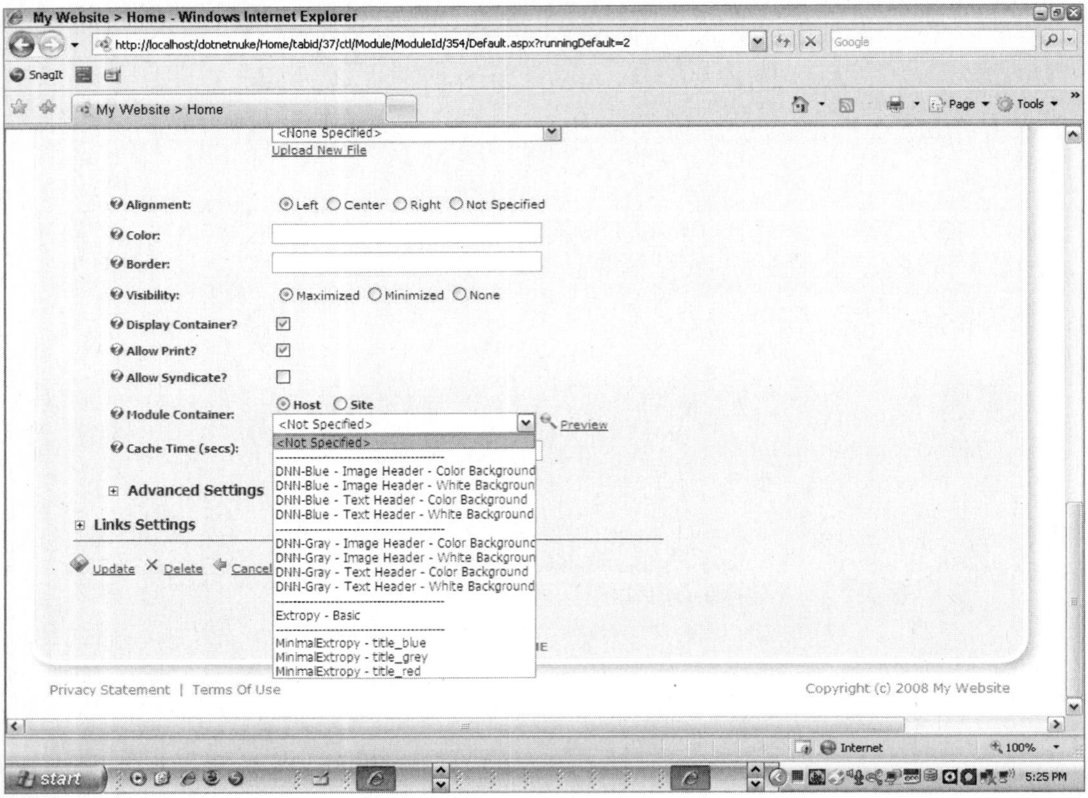

Figure 3-10

Figure 3-11

Table 3-2: Core Modules

Name	Description
Authentication	Allows you to manage authentication settings for sites using Windows Authentication.
Banners	Banner advertising is managed through the Vendors module in the Admin tab. You can select the number of banners to display as well as the banner type.
Feed Explorer	Allows users to browse RSS feeds using a tabbed user interface.
File Manager	Administrators can manage the files stored in their upload directory. This module allows you to upload new files, download files, delete files, and synchronize your upload directory. It also provides information on the amount of disk space used and available.
Google Adsense	Allows you to create Google Adsense ads on your site.
Host Settings	The Super User can manage the configuration settings that apply to the entire site.
Links	This module renders a list of hyperlinks. The Links module includes an edit page, which allows authorized users to edit the Links data stored in the SQL database.
Lists	Allows you to edit common lists.
Log Viewer	Allows you to view log entries for portal events.
MarketShare	The DotNetNuke MarketShare affiliate program provides you with the ability to generate 10% commission on gross product sales through direct referrals to the DotNetNuke Marketplace.
Newsletters	Administrators can send bulk email to all users belonging to a particular Role.
Portal Aliases	Allows you to view portal aliases.
Portals	The Super User can manage the various parent and child portals within the site. This module allows you to add a new portal, modify an existing portal, and delete a portal.
Recycle Bin	The Recycle Bin provides an interface for restoring or permanently deleting tabs and modules.
Scheduler	Allows you to schedule tasks to be run at specified intervals.
Search Admin	The Search Administrator provides the ability to manage search settings.

Continued

Table 3-2: Core Modules *(continued)*

Name	Description
Search Input	The Search Input module allows searches to be submitted by users, and requires the Search Results module in order to display the results.
Search Results	The Search Results module displays search results.
Security	Administrators can manage the security roles defined for their portal. The module allows you to add new security roles, modify existing security roles, delete security roles, and manage the users assigned to security roles.
Site Log	Administrators can view the details of visitors using their portal. A variety of reports are available to display information regarding site usage, membership, and volumes.
Site Wizard	The Administrator can use this user-friendly wizard to set up the common features of the portal/site.
SQL	The Super User can execute SQL statements against the database.
Tabs	Administrators can manage the tabs within the portal. This module allows you to create a new tab, modify an existing tab, delete tabs, change the tab order, and change the hierarchical tab level.
Text/HTML	This module renders a block of HTML or Text content. The Text/HTML module allows authorized users to edit the content either inline or in a separate administration page. The content is stored in the database. According to module settings, tokens can be used that get replaced during display.
Vendors	Administrators can manage the vendors and banners associated with the portal. This module allows you to add a new vendor, modify an existing vendor, and delete a vendor.

To place a module on a page, you simply select a module from the drop-down list on the Control Panel and place it on the appropriate pane, insert it at the top or bottom, align the module, give it a title, and click Add. See Figure 3-12.

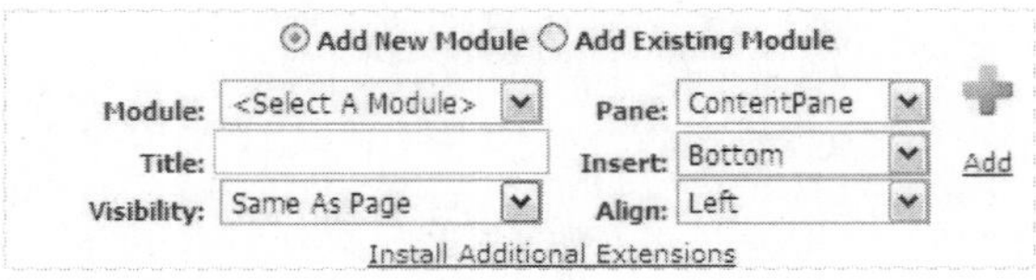

Figure 3-12

Modules that have not been installed can be found by clicking Install Additional Extensions. Only the host can install additional modules. See Figure 3-12.

Figure 3-13 lists all available modules. Select the modules that you want to use, scroll down to the bottom of the page, and click Install Selected Extensions.

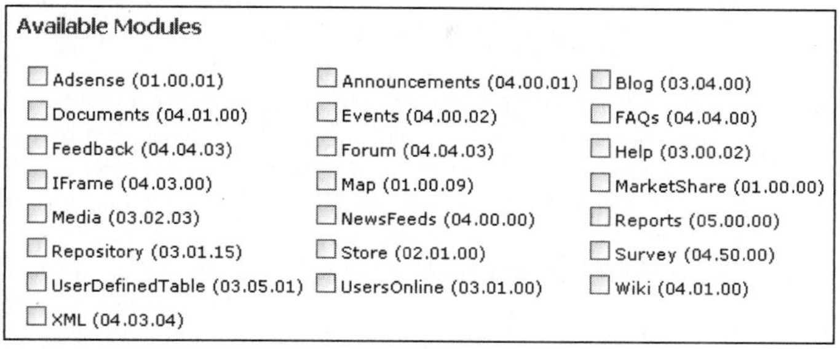

Available Modules

☐ Adsense (01.00.01)	☐ Announcements (04.00.01)	☐ Blog (03.04.00)
☐ Documents (04.01.00)	☐ Events (04.00.02)	☐ FAQs (04.04.00)
☐ Feedback (04.04.03)	☐ Forum (04.04.03)	☐ Help (03.00.02)
☐ IFrame (04.03.00)	☐ Map (01.00.09)	☐ MarketShare (01.00.00)
☐ Media (03.02.03)	☐ NewsFeeds (04.00.00)	☐ Reports (05.00.00)
☐ Repository (03.01.15)	☐ Store (02.01.00)	☐ Survey (04.50.00)
☐ UserDefinedTable (03.05.01)	☐ UsersOnline (03.01.00)	☐ Wiki (04.01.00)
☐ XML (04.03.04)		

Figure 3-13

Table 3-3 gives a description of what various modules can do.

Because DotNetNuke is an open source web portal written in Visual Basic.NET, modular developers have made several modifications to these modules. Some of these changes are given out for free and some can be purchased. See the Resources section for more information.

User Roles

One of the unique aspects of working with DotNetNuke is that you can assign roles to users or a group of users. This allows an administrator of a site to give full responsibility of the content of a web page to a user or a group of users, or the administrator can give only certain modules user role permissions to edit that module. The administrator can also give certain users page permissions that allow them to view certain pages or edit pages.

You need to create the security role under Admin, Security Roles. To assign a role to a page, go to the page settings and scroll down to Permissions; then assign permissions to the security role that you want. You can assign View Page or Edit Page permissions as seen in Figure 3-14.

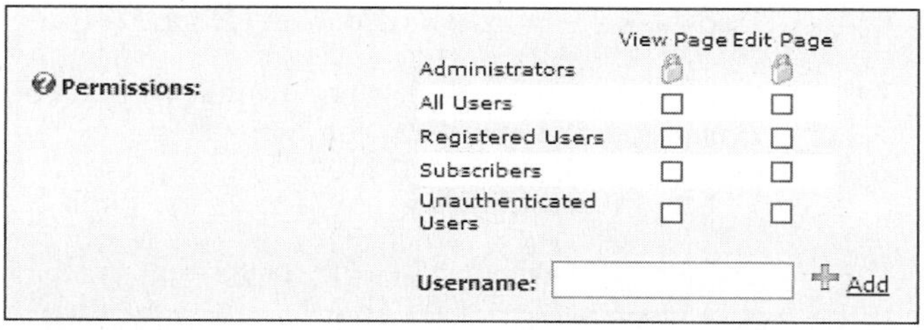

Permissions:

	View Page	Edit Page
Administrators		
All Users	☐	☐
Registered Users	☐	☐
Subscribers	☐	☐
Unauthenticated Users	☐	☐

Username: Add

Figure 3-14

Table 3-3: Available Modules

Name	Description
Announcements	This module renders a list of announcements. Each announcement includes title, text, and a "read more" link.
Blog	Blog module for DNN 3.x and 4.x.
Documents	This module renders a list of documents, including links to browse or download the document. The Documents module includes an edit page, which allows authorized users to edit the information about the documents (for example, a friendly title) stored in the SQL database.
Events	This module renders single and recurring events and includes Master and Sub Calendars with Event Rollup, TimeZone Adjustment, Event Enrollment, and Event Notification.
FAQs	FAQs allow you to manage a list of Frequently Asked Questions and their corresponding answers.
Feedback	Feedback allows visitors to send messages to the Administrator of the portal.
Forum	The core forum module for DotNetNuke.
Help	The Help module renders tutorials in a structured manner and allows for easy navigation of the tutorials.
IFrame	The HTML iframe creates an inline frame that contains another document, which can be located on your or any other site.
Media	This module renders Media files. The module looks at the file extension and creates the correct tag block to render the media in the browser.
News Feeds (RSS)	News Feed allows you to consume syndicated news feeds in Rich Site Summary (RSS) format.
Reports	This module displays a report based on the results of a SQL Query. The display is controlled by selecting one of many Visualizers to display the data, ranging from a Grid to an HTML Template and even more!
Repository	A file/object repository module that includes skinning and community features like comments and user ratings.
Store	Ecommerce module to create an online store.
Survey	Survey allows you to create custom surveys to obtain public feedback.

Continued

Table 3-3: Available Modules *(continued)*

Name	Description
User Defined Table	The User Defined Table module allows editors to create a custom data table for managing tabular information with individually defined fields (columns). Users can be allowed (by security roles) to add, edit, or delete their own or all users' data. Besides default grid rendering, data display can be optionally formatted using XSL stylesheets.
UsersOnline	UsersOnline allows you to see who is online in your portal, and see membership counts.
Wiki	An entire Wiki site in a single module.
XML/XSL	This module queries XML Data from a file or an http request, transforms the XML data using an XSL transformation, and returns the result back to the user.

For modules, you select Settings for the module you want to allow a role to edit, and then scroll down to Permissions to assign the role that you want. It will look like Figure 3-14.

By default, five roles are already defined: Administrators, All Users, Registered Users, Subscribers, and Unauthenticated Users. The Administrator gets full access to the page. The All Users role is for anyone viewing your web site. The Registered User is for only those users who you want to view certain pages or modules. All registered users are subscribers. Subscribers can remove themselves from the portal registration. Unauthenticated users would see pages or modules if this role were selected. Chapter 4, "Portal Administration," has additional information about roles.

Summary

This chapter introduced a DotNetNuke portal and parent and child pages. In addition, this chapter introduced pages and panes, and, briefly, skins and containers in a web portal. A complete list of all the modules with a brief description was given. Finally, user roles were covered. Future chapters discuss these concepts in more detail.

4

Portal Administration

Chapter 3 taught you the concept of a portal. This chapter covers in detail the role of an administrator using DotNetNuke as a web portal. It is best to use a real-world application of building a new portal, so this portal will be created for the Red Sox Little League team.

Who Is the Portal Administrator?

By default, when a host creates a portal in DotNetNuke, a new user is also created. There is one primary Portal Administrator, which is the one created when the site is created. The Administrator security role can be assigned to additional users that are registered on the site if needed.

Later in this chapter, you learn how to give the administrator role to another person. Because there is only one main Portal Administrator, and it's that person's email address that will appear in the "from: address" for all email sent by the portal and as the default address for the Feedback module.

Where Do I Begin?

David Viscott says, "If you could get up the courage to begin, you have the courage to succeed."

Follow these steps to build the Red Sox Little League portal:

1. Navigate to your web site. If you are working on your local computer and using a localhost, you should have created a folder with your DotNetNuke files. Name your folder redsox and navigate to that folder: `http://localhost/redsox`.
2. Click the login link located in the upper right-hand corner of the page.
3. Log in to your portal using the Portal Administrator User Name, which is **`Admin`**, and Password, which is **`dnnadmin`**. You will immediately be asked to change the password. Key in the current password, **`dnnadmin`**, and then key in a new password and click Change Password. See Figure 4-1.

Figure 4-1

After you log in, you will get a screen that looks like Figure 4-2.

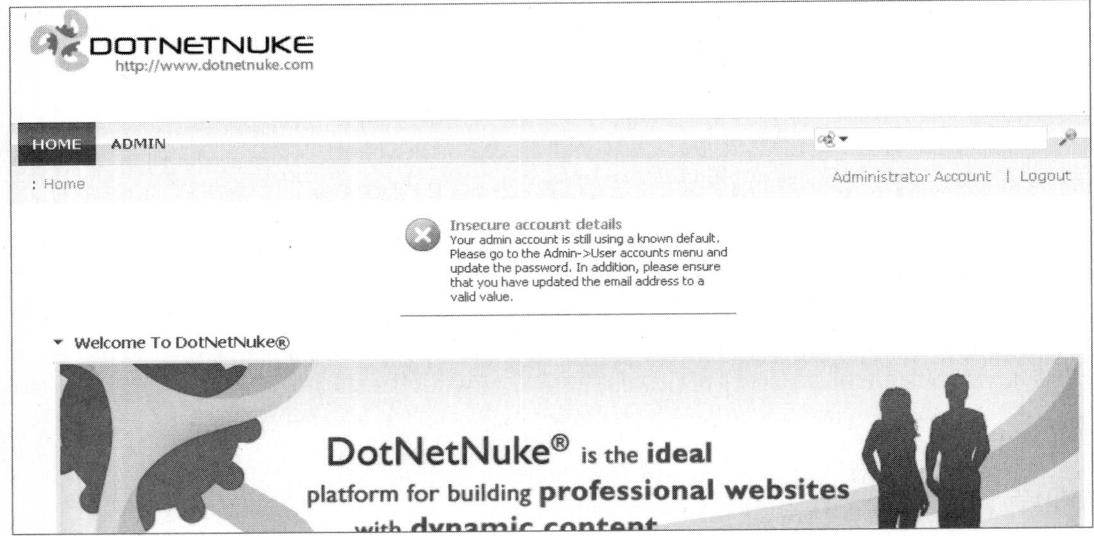

Figure 4-2

You will get an Insecure Account Details message to update the password and email address. Click Administrator Account on the top right. Change the email address to your own email address. Click Manage Password. Enter your current password and then enter a new password, and enter the new password again to confirm and click Change Password.

The Control Panel

The Control Panel contains many shortcuts for frequently used tasks, but it needs to be expanded before you can use the commands. Click the icon to the right of Show Control Panel to expand it. You have Page Functions, Adding Modules, and Common Task commands to use. See Figure 4-3.

Figure 4-3

The quickest and easiest way to create a web site using DotNetNuke is to use the Site Wizard to create your site. The Site Wizard allows Administrators to choose a template that is provided by default or one that is provided by the host and then select a skin and container. Finally, you can add site details as well.

The Site Wizard

To access the Site Wizard, hover your mouse over Admin on the menu and scroll down to Site Wizard.

The Site Configuration Wizard provides an Administrator with a user-friendly way to set up the more common features of a portal. You can step through the wizard using the Next/Back buttons at the bottom of the wizard page. Once enough detail has been collected to complete the wizard, the Finish button will be enabled.

Figure 4-4 displays the Site Configuration Wizard. Click Next.

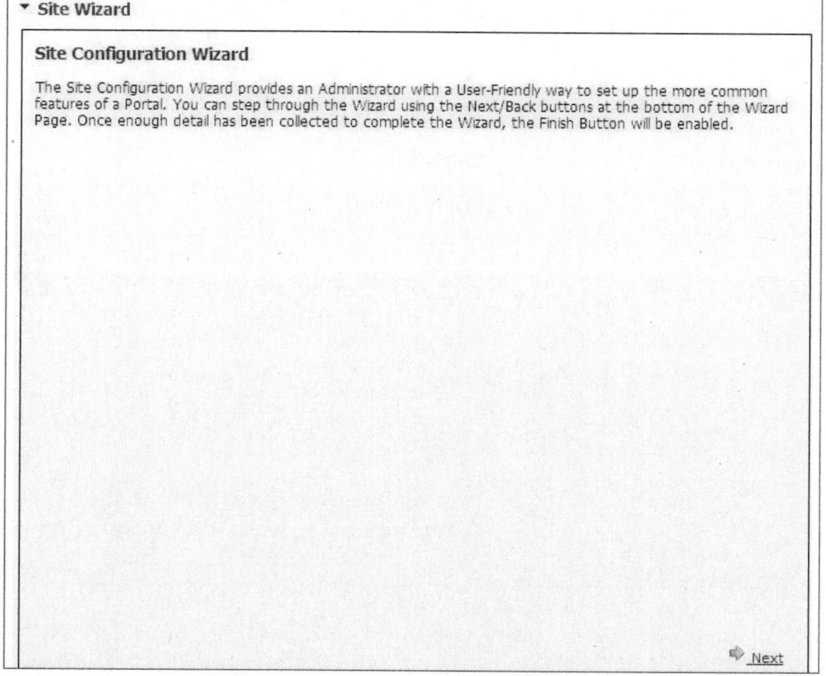

Figure 4-4

Step 1: **Select a Template**

The following steps lead you through using the site wizard. The available template is called DotNetNuke. Select that template by clicking Build Your Site from a Template (below).

Click DotNetNuke. See Figure 4-5.

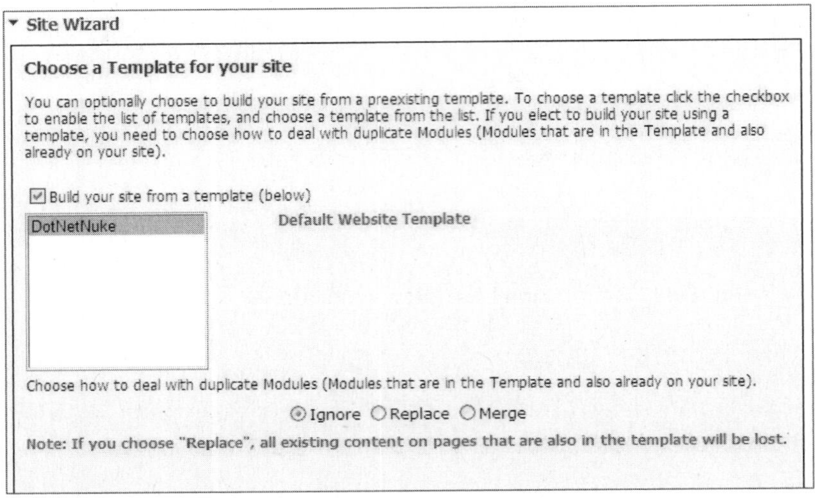

Figure 4-5

Before you proceed, you need to understand how to deal with duplicate modules. These are modules that are in the template and already on an existing site if you had one available. Because this is a new site, leave the default at Ignore. Table 4-1 explains the options.

Table 4-1: Dealing with Duplicate Modules

Option	Description
Ignore	If a module of the same name and type as the one in the template already exists, the module in the template is ignored.
Replace	If a module of the same name and type as the one in the template already exists, it is replaced by the definition in the template.
Merge	If a module of the same name and type as the one in the template already exists, the content is appended to the existing module content.

Make your selection based on your needs. Click Next to move on to Step 2.

Step 2: **Select a Skin for Your Site**

DotNetNuke provides several skins by default to use. A skin changes the look of your site. See Figure 4-6.

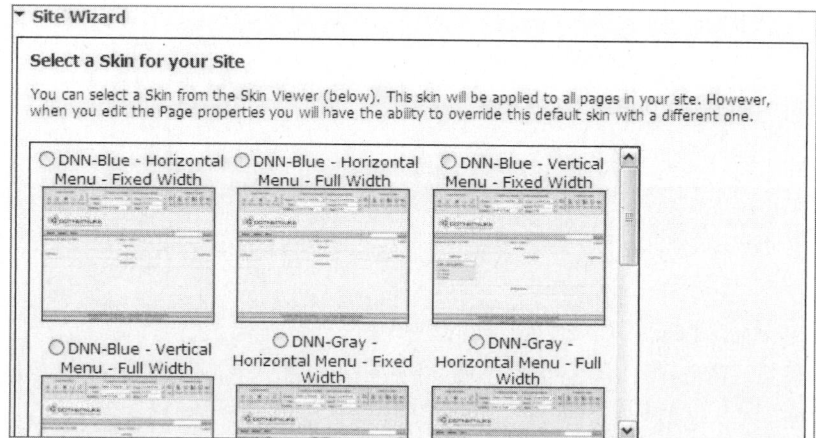

Figure 4-6

Make sure you scroll down to see all of the default skins. Select the one that you like by clicking the radio button. You can click the thumbnail graphic to see a preview. Your host will upload the skins that you want to use if you don't find one here that you like. There are also several professional skins that you can purchase or get for free.

Chapter 16, "Skinning DotNetNuke," includes detailed information on how to create and package your own skins. Click Next to continue.

Step 3: **Select a Default Container for Your Site**

The next step is to select the default container for your site. The containers in Figure 4-7 have been packaged with the appropriate skin. Containers are the graphics that dress up a module that is located on your page. A good rule of thumb is to select a container that you want to use with all of your modules. The skin or container that you select can be changed. In fact, you can have a separate skin on any page that you want. The same goes for having a different container for each of your modules.

If you want to see all the containers from other skin packages, click Show All Containers. All of the containers listed in Figure 4-7 are associated with the DNN-Blue skin.

After you select your container, click Next.

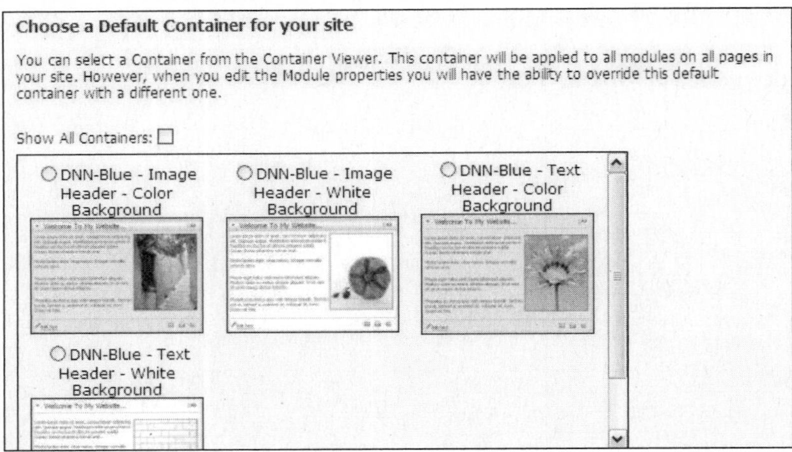

Figure 4-7

Step 4: **Add Site Details**

This step allows you to identify your web site with a name, description, keywords for search engines, and add a logo. See Figure 4-8.

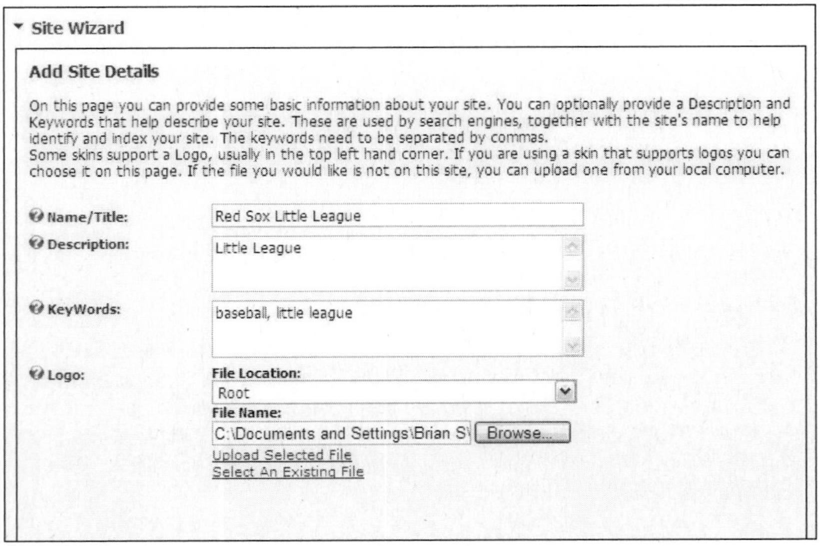

Site Wizard

Add Site Details

On this page you can provide some basic information about your site. You can optionally provide a Description and Keywords that help describe your site. These are used by search engines, together with the site's name to help identify and index your site. The keywords need to be separated by commas.
Some skins support a Logo, usually in the top left hand corner. If you are using a skin that supports logos you can choose it on this page. If the file you would like is not on this site, you can upload one from your local computer.

Name/Title: Red Sox Little League

Description: Little League

KeyWords: baseball, little league

Logo: **File Location:** Root
File Name: C:\Documents and Settings\Brian S\ Browse...
Upload Selected File
Select An Existing File

Figure 4-8

To upload a logo, click Upload New File, browse to the location of your logo graphic file, and then click Upload Selected File. Table 4-2 lists each field and describes how its value affects your portal.

Table 4-2: Site Details

Field	Description
Name/Title	Used in several places in the portal operation. You will see this in your title bar at the top of your web browser.
Description	The default value to populate the HTML META tag for Description in each page of your site. This information is important to search engines.
Keywords	Keywords are also used as a default value to populate HTML META tag for KEYWORDS in each page of your site. This information improves search engine placement. Separate each keyword with a comma.

Once you are finished, click Finish.

You will get a message that your site has been completed. See Figure 4-9.

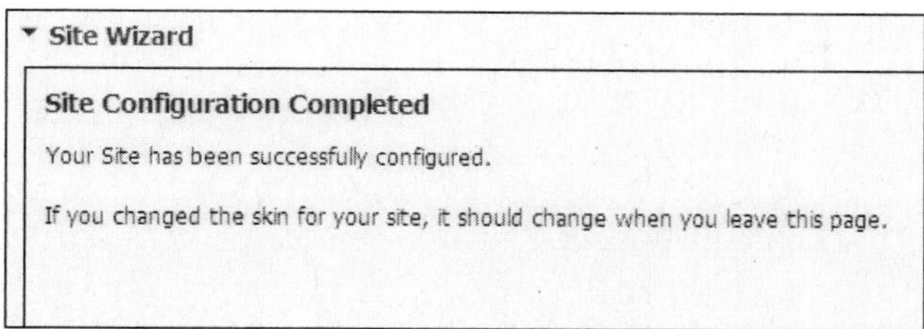

Figure 4-9

Click Home to view your newly created site. See Figure 4-10.

Configuring Your Portal

The next step to building your web site would be to start deleting modules from the default first page and add new pages to your site. Before you do that, you need to learn more about admin settings.

The Portal Administrator has access to a wealth of configuration options that can customize the look, content, and behavior of the site. This section covers many of those admin settings.

Site Settings

Mouse over the Admin page and select the Site Settings page. This page contains expandable and collapsible categories of configuration options. No changes will be made to any options until the Update link is clicked at the bottom of the page.

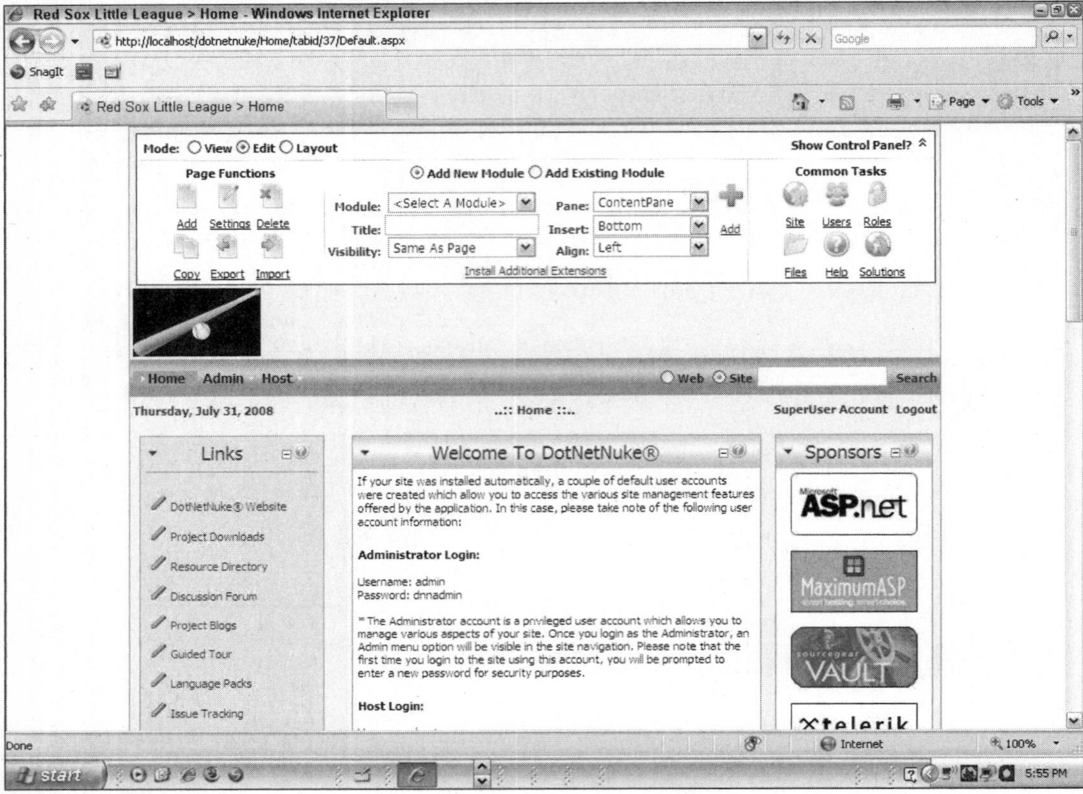

Figure 4-10

Basic Settings

The following three settings fall into the basic category.

Site Details

Most of the settings that you see on the page look familiar because you added some of the settings when you worked with the Site Wizard. There are two items here that you did not see. One is the GUID, which is a unique identifier that can be used to identify your portal. Copyright is also new and you can add a company name, if you want, at this location. Certain skins that you use might not show this information because the person who created the skin did not include the skin token that is needed to display the copyright information. Skin tokens are discussed in Chapter 16.

Site Marketing

At this location, you can submit your site to different search engines. Google is the default, but you can click the drop-down button to select Yahoo and Microsoft as well. Click Submit after you select the search engine.

For Google, you can also submit your Site Map URL to get better search optimization for your site. Click Submit, and you'll be taken to Google's site where you can register and get a Google Webmaster Tools account and verify your site ownership. Once verified, you can select the General Web Sitemap option on the Google Sitemaps tab, and then paste the Site Map Url displayed.

When you sign up with Google Webmaster Tools, you will need to verify your site ownership. Choose the Upload an HTML File method from the Google Verification screen, enter the filename that is displayed in the Verification textbox, and click Create. Return to Google and select the Verify button.

Banners is displayed next and is set at None. This setting is for Banner Advertising, which is discussed later in this chapter.

Appearance

If you expand on the Appearance settings you should see Figure 4-11.

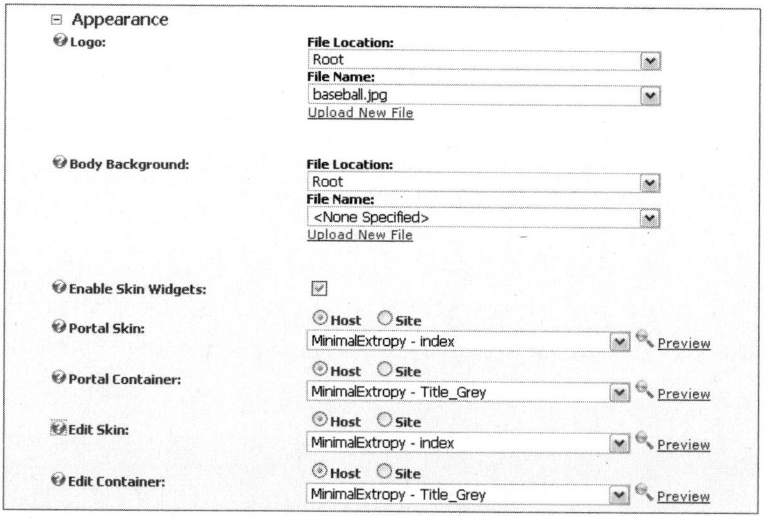

Figure 4-11

Review these options in Table 4-3.

The Preview link provides the opportunity to see what the skin or container will look like before your selection is made. Close the window when you are done previewing the skin, and remember to click Update to finalize the selections made.

Advanced Settings

The following settings fall into the advanced category.

Security Settings

Portal registration is discussed in this section. There are several selections to consider when you have a web site with registration. You can select None to have no registration enabled on your portal. If you select Private, the owner of the portal needs to authorize that registration and give permission. The registrant will get an email to complete the registration to the site. The Public selection allows anyone to register and a welcome email is sent to the registrant. Finally, the Verified selection generates a verification code via email for the registrant to key in upon returning to your site to login.

Table 4-3: Appearance Settings

Setting	Description
Body Background	This selection is used in the HTML body of every page to render a tiled background image. If selected, the skin may behind the image, making the skin useless. If you don't intend on having a body background, it is best to leave this as None Specified.
Enable Skin Widgets	You want to keep this selected so that you can view widgets in your site. A client-side widget is a mini application that is run in JavaScript and adds Web 2.0-style interactivity and DOM manipulation to DotNetNuke skins.
Portal Skin	The selected skin will be applied to all pages in the web site.
Portal Container	The selected container will be applied to all modules on pages in the web site.
Edit Skin	You can select a different skin package here and it will show up only when you are in the edit mode.
Edit Container	You can select a different container package here and it will show up only when you are in the edit mode.

See Figure 4-12.

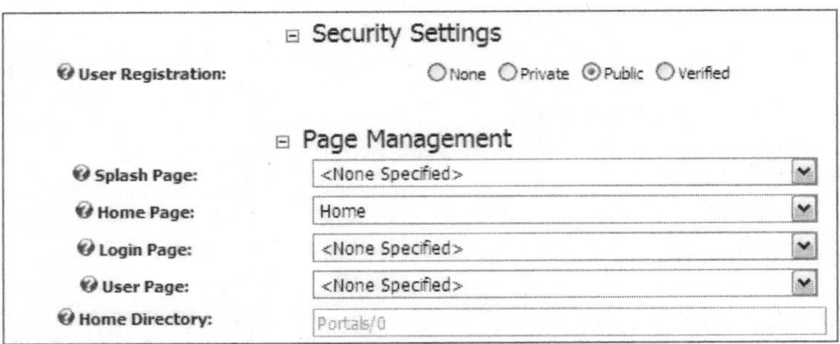

Figure 4-12

Page Management

These settings allow you the ability to customize pages. See Figure 4-13.

There is a drop-down of pages listed beside each category for you to use and select the appropriate page. None Specified is listed as the default. Table 4-4 explains the settings.

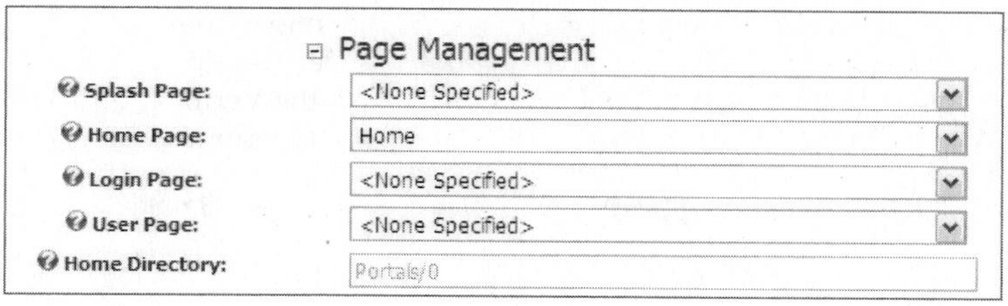

Page Management

Splash Page: <None Specified>
Home Page: Home
Login Page: <None Specified>
User Page: <None Specified>
Home Directory: Portals/0

Figure 4-13

Table 4-4: Page Management Settings

Setting	Description
Splash Page	By default, when a visitor comes to your site via your URL, the home page is displayed. If a Splash Page is selected, the visitor will see that page instead of the home page.
Home Page	The default page that gets loaded first. If there is no Home Page, the first page in navigation order is used.
Login Page	You can select any page to be your login page. You create the page and then place the Account Login module on that page. At this location you would select the new page you created and click Update.
User Page	This displays a user's registration information and preferences, provides for password changes, and manage profile. You can see this by clicking the Registration button or by clicking the user's name after they log in. The default User Page is provided for your convenience and has skinning limitations like the Login page.
Home Directory	This identifies the path of your portal files. The directory created by the Host and represents a location relative to the web site root (for example http://www.dotnetnuke.com/Portals/1).

Payment

The Payment Settings (see Figure 4-14) have been preserved from earlier versions of DotNetNuke for legacy support purposes. Only the PayPal option is supported using the POST method to emulate PayPal's Buy Now button functionality. You need to have an account with PayPal to use this. Currently, these settings come into play when public roles are defined with fees or when online portal signup is permitted. They are not used in any of the several eCommerce store or payment components available through third-party providers or in the free DotNetNuke store module. These settings may be deprecated in a future version in favor of a more robust eCommerce API.

The Red Sox Little League team will offer at least one premium content area for subscription; you would need sign up for a PayPal account and use it to process payments for these services.

Figure 4-14

Usability Settings

These settings allow the Administrator to choose who can view the Edit/View Mode section of the Control Panel by either restricting it to Page Editors only, or by setting it to be visible to both Page Editors and Module Editors. See Figure 4-15.

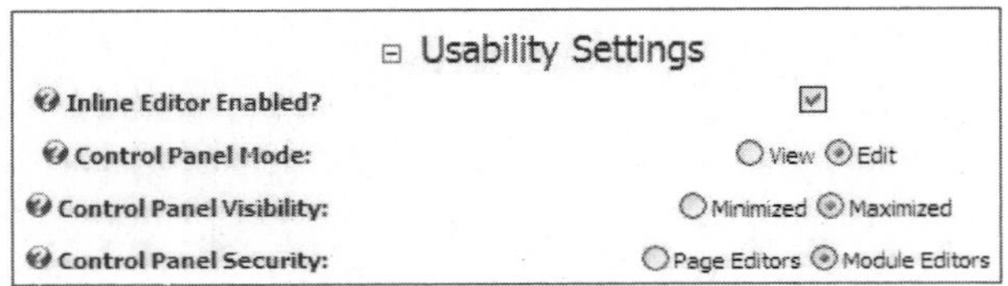

Figure 4-15

Other Settings

This setting is for selecting the primary Administrator of the site, default language, and portal time zone. See Figure 4-16.

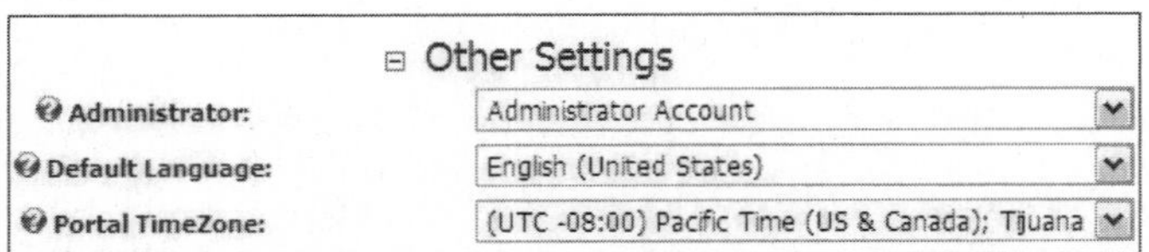

Figure 4-16

Stylesheet Editor

DotNetNuke supports Cascading Style Sheets so that skin and container designers, as well as module developers, have a means to customize components they provide. This file is named portal.css and is located in the home directory. The editor enables you to change the CSS styles to your liking. See Figure 4-17.

If you want to restore the original default stylesheet, you can click the Restore Default Style Sheet link.

DotNetNuke deliberately makes the portal.css file the last cascading order so that a Portal Administrator can quickly and easily update styles for a given site. If a skin designer adds a stylesheet reference or inline styles directly to a skin, the cascading order will be broken. A properly designed skin allows DotNetNuke to inject the skin's CSS file into the proper cascading order without an explicit reference.

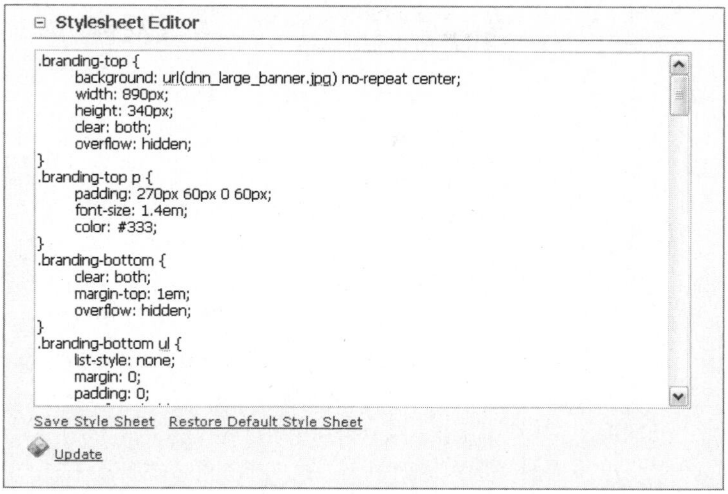

⊟ Stylesheet Editor

```
.branding-top {
	background: url(dnn_large_banner.jpg) no-repeat center;
	width: 890px;
	height: 340px;
	clear: both;
	overflow: hidden;
}
.branding-top p {
	padding: 270px 60px 0 60px;
	font-size: 1.4em;
	color: #333;
}
.branding-bottom {
	clear: both;
	margin-top: 1em;
	overflow: hidden;
}
.branding-bottom ul {
	list-style: none;
	margin: 0;
	padding: 0;
```

Save Style Sheet Restore Default Style Sheet

Update

Figure 4-17

Pages

There are two ways to add a new page. One is to click Add under the Page Functions in the Control Panel. The other way is to click Admin, Pages and click Add New Page at the bottom of the screen. Always click the Update link when you're finished. Add some pages to the Red Sox Little League Team. The first page that you'll add is called Coach's Corner. See Figure 4-18.

Table 4-5 reviews the Basic Settings of a page.

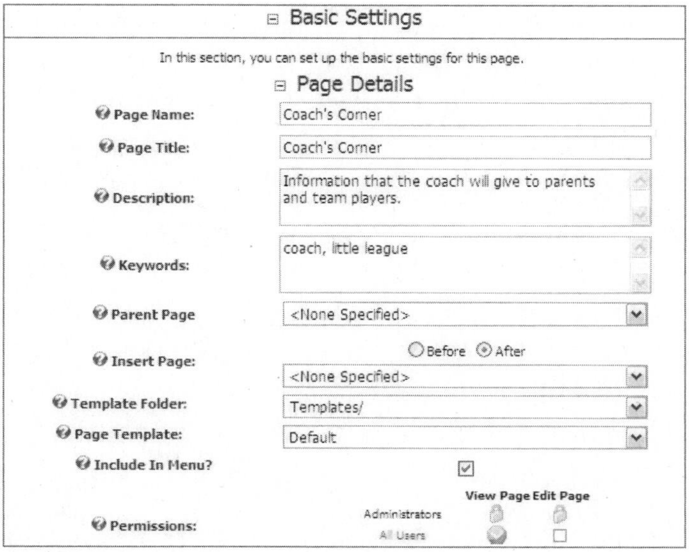

⊟ Basic Settings

In this section, you can set up the basic settings for this page.

⊟ Page Details

Page Name: Coach's Corner

Page Title: Coach's Corner

Description: Information that the coach will give to parents and team players.

Keywords: coach, little league

Parent Page: <None Specified>

Insert Page: Before / After (selected) <None Specified>

Template Folder: Templates/

Page Template: Default

Include In Menu? ☑

Permissions:

	View Page	Edit Page
Administrators		
All Users		☐

Figure 4-18

Table 4-5: Add New Page — Basic Settings

Setting	Description
Page Name	This name appears in text in the menu item where pages are listed.
Page Title	This appears on the title bar in the user browser. This name is also used in search engine listings.
Description	A relevant description about the page should be included.
Keywords	Unique keywords about the page will help its ranking with search engines.
Parent Page	Select this if you want this page to be a child page. A child page will go under the Parent Page in the menu order.
Insert Page	Select the page that you would like this page to be inserted before or after, or optionally add the page to the end of the current level.
Template Folder	If you are using a template, you would select the folder here.
Page Template	If you are using a template, you would select a page template that you would like to use to create this page.
Include In Menu	You have the choice of whether or not to include the page in the main navigation menu. If a page is not included in the menu, you can still link to the page based on its URL. This feature is selected by default.
Permissions	You want to make sure that All Users is selected to ensure everyone can view that page. Security Roles are discussed in this chapter. Once a role is created you can select Permissions for only that role to view or edit pages. You can even have just a user name permission for a page.

Click All Users to view the page. All users would be anyone viewing your site. Registered users are those who have registered to your site and have logged in.

When creating a page, you have the option to copy modules from another page. Select the page that you want to copy and then select the modules that you would like to have on your new page. In addition, specify if you want to create a new module (without content), a copy of the module (with content), or a reference to an existing module (shared content).

See Figure 4-19.

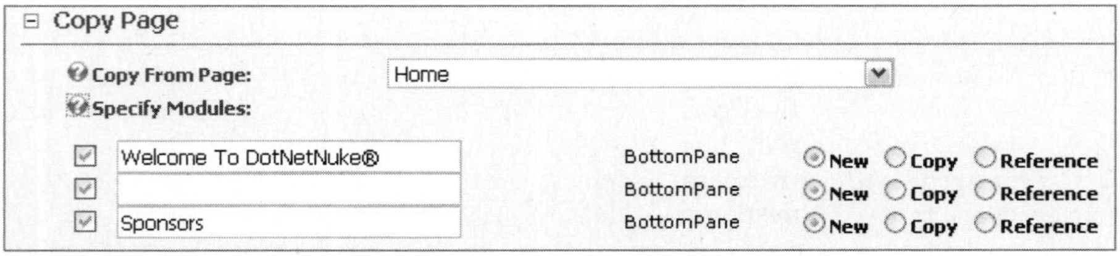

Figure 4-19

Table 4-6 explains the fields in the advanced settings area.

Table 4-6: Add New Page — Advanced Settings

Setting	Description
Appearance Icon	Identifies an image that will be displayed beside the page name in the menu. 16x16 images look best.
Page Skin	The selected skin will be applied only to this page. This will be different than the portal skin.
Page Container	The selected container will be applied to all modules on this page. This will be different than portal containers.
Disabled	If the page is disabled, it is not available to users of the site. You can use this option to suppress content that you might wish to show at a later time.
Refresh Interval (seconds)	Enter the interval to wait between automatic page refreshes. Enter 60 for 1 minute or leave blank to disable.
Page Header Tags	Enter any META tags that should be rendered in the Head tag of the HTML for this page.
Other Settings	
Secure	Specify whether or not this page should be forced to use a secure connection (SSL). This option will only be enabled if the administrator has enabled SSL in the site settings.
Start Date	Select the start date for displaying the page.
End Date	Select the end date for displaying the page.
Link Url	If you would like this page to behave as a navigation link to another source such as an URL, Page, or File on your site, you can select it here. This is optional.

Changing Navigational Structure

Under Admin, Pages, you can change the navigational structure of your site. For example, if you want the new Coach's Corner page to go after the Home page, you can move that page up. You highlight the page and then move it to the order that you want it in. You can move your page up to the top of the current level, move it up in the current level, move it down in the current level, move it to the bottom of the current level, move it up one hierarchical level, or move it down one hierarchical level. Hover your mouse over the question mark beside each arrow to see what the move will be. Finally, you can edit or delete pages at this location as well. Those commands are found under Actions. See Figure 4-20.

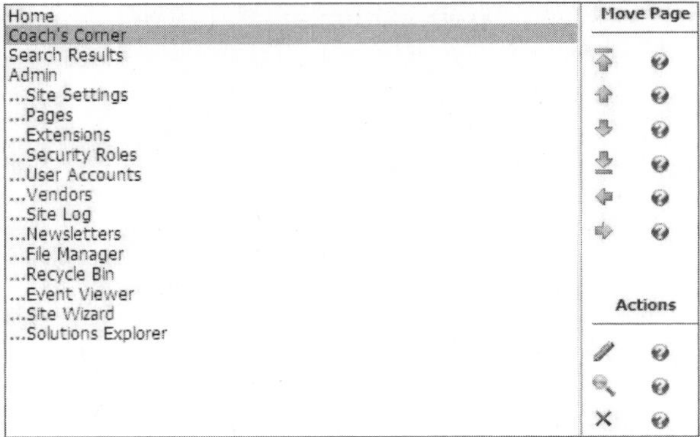

Figure 4-20

Extensions

Extensions are new to this version of DotNetNuke. According to Core Team member Charles Nurse, "The idea behind 'Extensions' is that there should be a one-stop shop for any DNN Extension. Under the covers some changes have been made so that all extensions whether Modules, Skins, Languages, SkinObjects have some common behaviours — mainly related to installation/uninstallation. There is a new top-level object in the API (Package) and all package types (extension types) will be installed using a Universal (Extensible) Installer. In 5.0 the original Pages will remain for each extension type (Languages, Module Definitions, Skins) but a new page Extensions is introduced. All four cases, the original pages and the new ones, use the same 'Extensions' module, which is customized by Module Settings for the legacy pages."

See Figure 4-21.

Extensions

Select Extension Type: Not Specified

Not Specified
Authentication System
Container
Module
Skin

Name		Version	Upgrade?
Default Authenticati		1.0.0	
Minimal Extropy Conta	the Default Container for DotNetNuke.	1.0.0	
Default Language		1.0.0	
Announcements	This module renders a list of announcements. Each announcement includes title, text and a "read more" link.	3.4.0	
Authentication	Allows you to manage authentication settings for sites using Windows Authentication.	1.0.0	
Banners	Banner advertising is managed through the Vendors module in the Admin tab. You can select the number of banners to display as well as the banner type.	1.0.0	
Blog	Blog Module for DNN 3.X and 4.x	3.3.1	

Figure 4-21

From Select Extension Type, you can select to filter installed extensions by either Authentication System, Container, Module, or Skin. Administrators can manage skins at this location. Click the icon for Manage Skins at the bottom right of the page. You can get a preview of the skin and container that has been uploaded for you to use by the host administrator. Simply select the skin or container that you want to preview, and if you like it, click Apply. Skins are covered in more detail in Chapter 16.

Security Roles

Under Admin, Security Roles are the default security roles. See Figure 4-22.

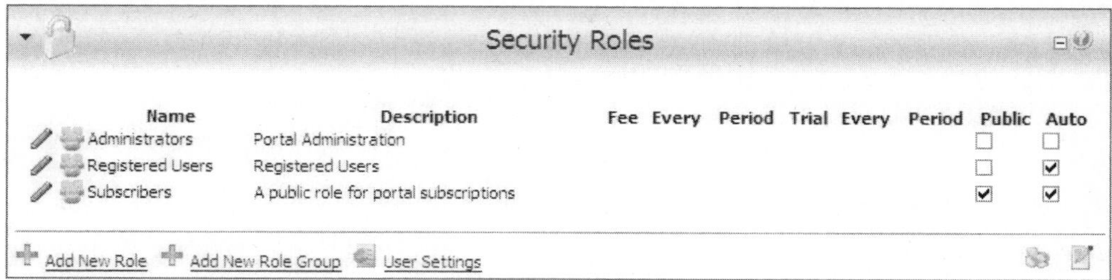

Figure 4-22

A role is a group of users with the same purpose, so for the Red Sox Little League team site you can have a Parent Role, Coaches Role, and Player Role. Each of these roles will have different responsibilities. For example, the coach will have the responsibility to put content on the Text/HTML module on the Coach's page. He or she is the only one that can do this with the role that they have been assigned. DotNetNuke includes three default Security Roles:

- **Administrator**: This role permits full access to add, delete, and edit all pages and modules. This role also gives full access to the Admin pages.
- **Registered Users**: Users must be logged in to the site to gain access to pages and modules restricted to this role. All users are automatically added to the Registered Users security role, unless the Authorized check box is unchecked.
- **Subscribers**: All Registered Users are automatically added to this role upon registration. (This role is set as Auto Assignment.) Authenticated users can unsubscribe and re-subscribe to this role under Membership Services on the Security module. The Administrator can choose to delete this role, or change its settings as required.

Administrators or users with those rights can assign different security roles for viewing and editing pages and modules. For example, the coach of the Red Sox wants to add information in the Text/HTML module on that page. First, add the coach as a user and then as a coach with that security level.

Creating a New Role

Click Users on the Control Panel, click Add New User, and then fill in this information: See Figure 4-23.

Use any password for Coach. Now, make a Security Role and then add Coach Jones to that role. Go to Admin, Security Roles. Click Add New Role and fill in the Role Name and Description as seen in Figure 4-24. You can also go to the Control Panel and under Common Tasks, select Roles. See Figure 4-24.

Now that the role has been created, you need to add Coach Jones to that role. Click Users from the Control Panel and beside Coach Jones you'll see a pencil icon, which is the edit icon in DotNetNuke. Click that. Click Manage Roles for Users and from the drop-down list, select Coach and click Add Role to User. See Figure 4-25.

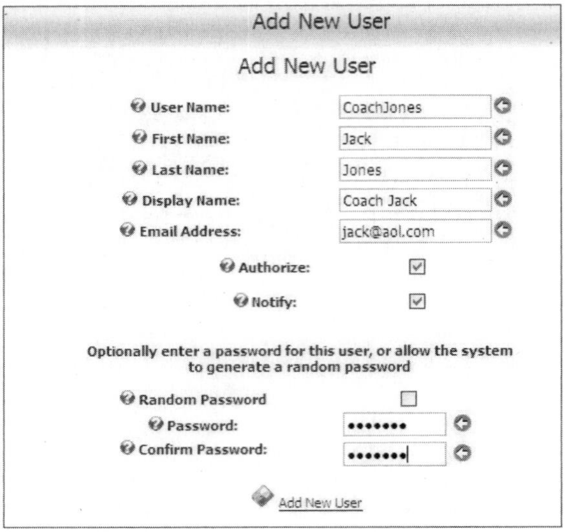

Add New User

Add New User

User Name: CoachJones
First Name: Jack
Last Name: Jones
Display Name: Coach Jack
Email Address: jack@aol.com
Authorize:
Notify:

Optionally enter a password for this user, or allow the system to generate a random password

Random Password
Password:
Confirm Password:

Add New User

Figure 4-23

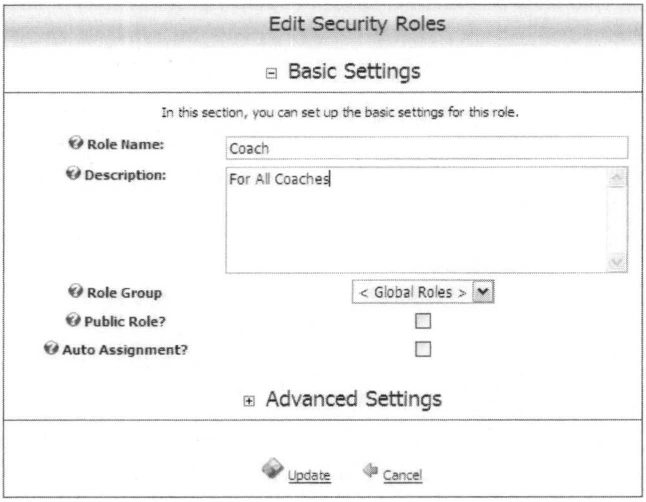

Edit Security Roles

Basic Settings

In this section, you can set up the basic settings for this role.

Role Name: Coach
Description: For All Coaches
Role Group: < Global Roles >
Public Role?
Auto Assignment?

Advanced Settings

Update Cancel

Figure 4-24

Now you will see that the user Coach has the security role called Coach. See how to use this role. Go to the Coach's Corner page. Add a Text/HTML module on that page and place it in the Content Pane. From the Control Panel, click <Select A Module>, scroll down to and select Text/HTML, and click Add. See Figure 4-26.

On the left side of the module, click the down arrow icon and click Settings. See Figure 4-27.

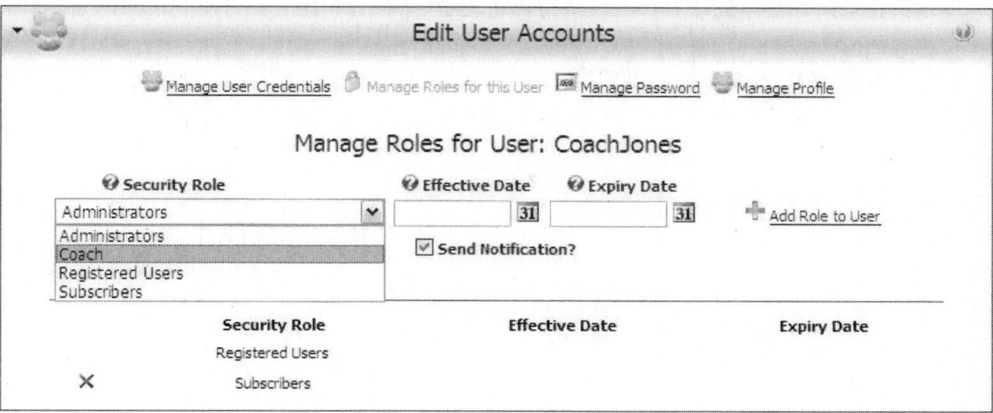

Figure 4-25

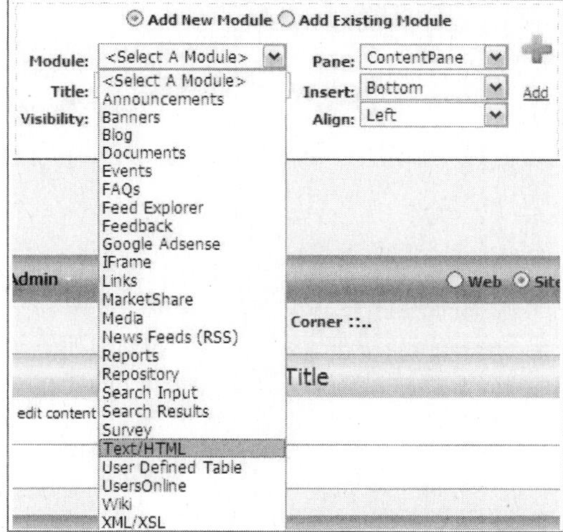

Figure 4-26

Change the Module Title and click Edit Module under Permissions beside Coach. See Figure 4-28.

Now, when Coach logs into the web site, he can edit the content of the Text/HTML module located on this page. If the Portal Administrator adds more content modules to that page, Coach would not have permission to modify those modules, just the Text/HTML module.

Security Role — Advanced Setting

The Red Sox Little League would like to raise money with their web portal. They are going to have a page that will be full of game photos, and parents can pay a fee for the rights to that page to download any picture that they want. First, go to the Admin, Site Settings, and under Payment Settings, make sure PayPal is selected for the Payment Processor for this option.

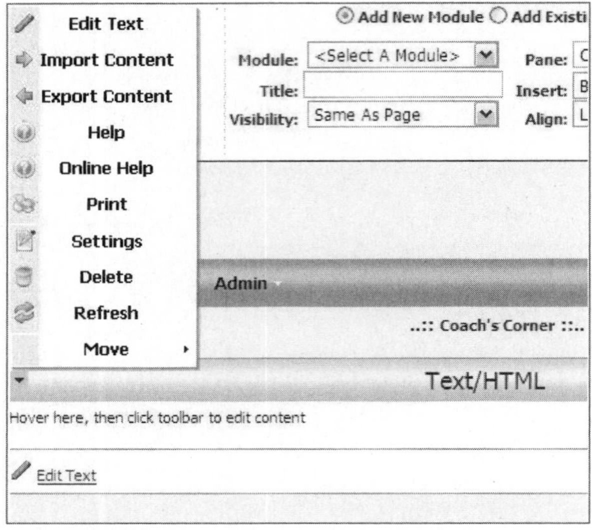

Figure 4-27

Module Title: Tips from Coach

Permissions:

	View Module	Edit Module
Administrators		
All Users		☐
Coach		✓
Registered Users		☐
Subscribers		☐
Unauthenticated Users		☐

Figure 4-28

Next, you need to create a security role called Gallery. Go to Admin, Security Roles, Add a New Role, call it Gallery Subscribers, and then click Advanced Setting. The team will charge each parent a monthly fee of $25.00, so you can key that in. See Figure 4-29.

Create a new Gallery Page, and then go to Page Settings and change the permissions for the Gallery Subscribers to view the page. See Figure 4-30. You'll assign that role to parents as they are added to your portal. The parents will pay the fee for this privilege through PayPal.

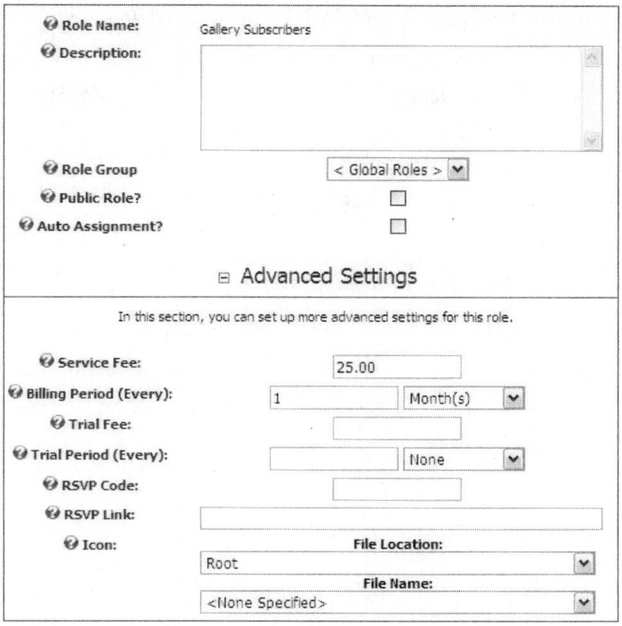

Role Name: Gallery Subscribers
Description:
Role Group < Global Roles >
Public Role?
Auto Assignment?

Advanced Settings

In this section, you can set up more advanced settings for this role.

Service Fee: 25.00
Billing Period (Every): 1 Month(s)
Trial Fee:
Trial Period (Every): None
RSVP Code:
RSVP Link:
Icon: File Location: Root
File Name: <None Specified>

Figure 4-29

Page Details

Page Name: Gallery
Page Title: Gallery
Description:
Keywords:
Parent Page <None Specified>
Insert Page: Before After <None Specified>
Template Folder: Templates/
Page Template: Default
Include In Menu?
Permissions: View Page Edit Page
Administrators
All Users
Coach
Gallery Subscribers

Figure 4-30

Public Roles and Membership Services

Public roles are available to users from the Member Services area of their Manage Profile page. See Figure 4-31.

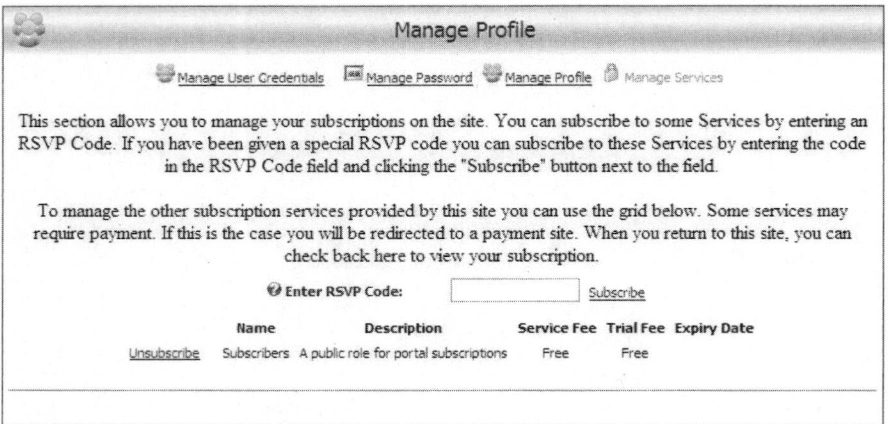

Figure 4-31

Delegating Authority or Assigning Privileges

Roles that are not public must be assigned to users, as with the coach of the Little League team. See Figure 4-32.

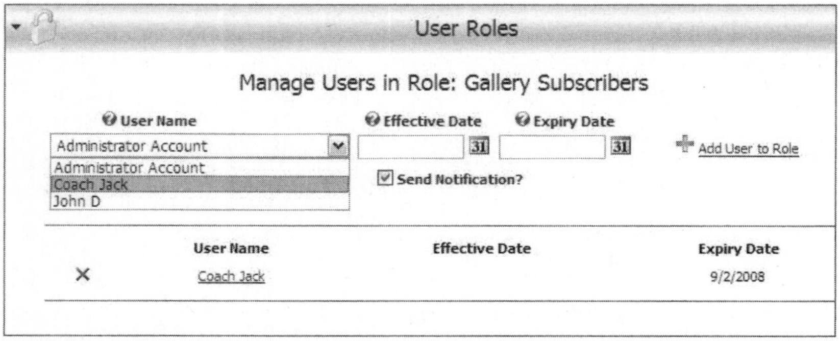

Figure 4-32

An expiry date can be specified like in the Gallery Subscribers role. All users assigned to the role appear in the list. You can click the red x to delete that user from the role. The next section reviews User Accounts. You can get access to this by Admin, User Accounts or clicking Users in the Control Panel. See Figure 4-33.

Here you can search for users on your portal, add new users, delete unauthorized users, manage profile properties, and view user settings. Create a new parent for the Red Sox Little League team. Go to Admin, User Accounts. Enter the information in Figure 4-34, `teammom` as the password, and click Add New User.

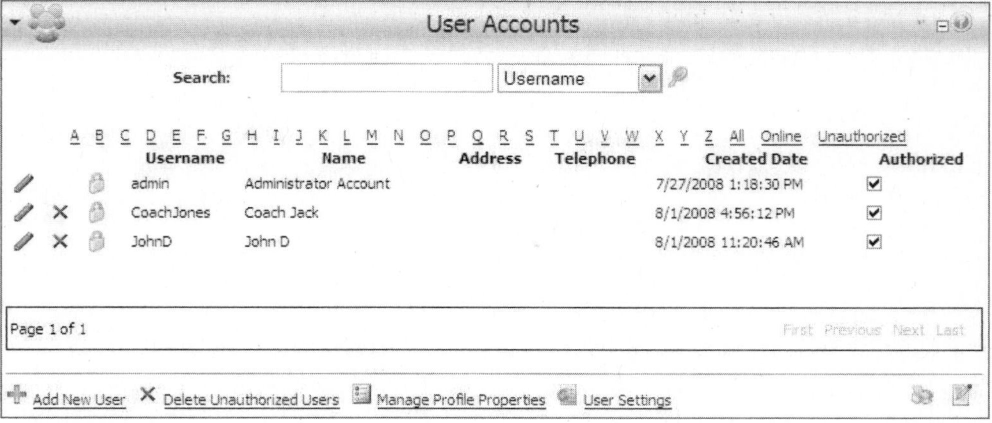

Figure 4-33

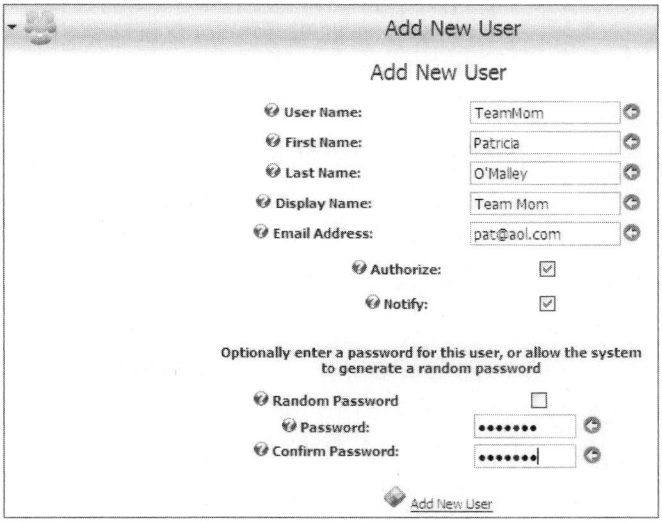

Add New User

Add New User

User Name: TeamMom
First Name: Patricia
Last Name: O'Malley
Display Name: Team Mom
Email Address: pat@aol.com
Authorize:
Notify:

Optionally enter a password for this user, or allow the system to generate a random password

Random Password
Password: •••••••
Confirm Password: •••••••

Add New User

Figure 4-34

An unauthorized user is a user who registered on your site and is unknown to you; you don't want that user to get access to your portal. Any users listed can be deleted by clicking the red x beside their name.

Manage Profile Properties is where you can change the order of the profile fields, and whether they are Required or Visible on this screen. Click the Apply Changes button to save any changes you make. To edit other properties of each profile property, click the pencil icon in the first column of the grid. See Figure 4-35.

Administrators can choose which fields they want to require the user to input to register on the site by simply selecting Required. You can delete any fields that you don't want, and you can customize and add a new profile property, if you want.

Edit	Del	Dn	Up	Name	Category	DataType	Length	Default Value	Validation Expression	Required	Visible
										☐	☑
	✕			Prefix	Name	Text	50			☐	☑
				FirstName	Name	Text	50			☑	☑
	✕			MiddleName	Name	Text	50			☐	☑
				LastName	Name	Text	50			☑	☑
	✕			Suffix	Name	Text	50			☐	☑
	✕			Unit	Address	Text	50			☐	☑
	✕			Street	Address	Text	50			☑	☑
	✕			City	Address	Text	50			☑	☑
	✕			Region	Address	Region	0			☑	☑
	✕			Country	Address	Country	0			☑	☑
	✕			PostalCode	Address	Text	50			☑	☑
	✕			Telephone	Contact Info	Text	50			☐	☑
	✕			Cell	Contact Info	Text	50			☐	☑
	✕			Fax	Contact Info	Text	50			☐	☑
	✕			Website	Contact Info	Text	50			☐	☑
	✕			IM	Contact Info	Text	50			☐	☑

Figure 4-35

Vendors

Using vendors would be a great way for the Red Sox Little League team to get sponsors to support the team and to charge the sponsors for space on the web portal. To create a vendor, go to Admin, Vendors and click Add New Vendor. The first vendor will be Harry Hardware Inc., and you can fill out the appropriate information, as shown in Figure 4-36. Use your email address so you don't get any errors. Click Update when finished.

Banner Advertising

When you are finished, go to Admin, Vendors, and edit the new vendor by clicking the pencil icon. See Figure 4-37.

Scroll down to Banner Advertising and expand that area by clicking the +. Click Add New Banner. There are several ways to advertise vendors on your site. You can use a graphic and select that or just use text. You'll use text for this demonstration. Key the following:

- Banner Name: `Harry's Hardware, Inc.`
- Banner Type: `Text`

Scroll down to CPM/Cost: 0.05 CPM is the cost for 1000 impressions.

Select a Start Date. Click Update.

Figure 4-36

Name	Address	Telephone	Fax	Email	Authorized	Banners
Harry Hardware Inc.	4602 Buildmore St., Orlando, Florida, United States, 32811	4072823456	4072823456	Harry@hardware.com	☑	0

Figure 4-37

Now, create a new page and call it Sponsors. Go to that page, and add the Banners module to that page. Click Banner Options, and copy what is on Figure 4-38. Remember to click Update when you finish.

Edit Banner

Banner Source: ○ Host ⦿ Site
Banner Type: Text
Banner Group:
Banner Count: 1
Orientation: ⦿ Vertical ○ Horizontal
Border Width: 0
Border Color:
Cell Padding: 4
Row Height:
Column Width:

Update Cancel

Figure 4-38

Now, you'll see the link on your Sponsor page to Harry's Hardware Inc. See Figure 4-39.

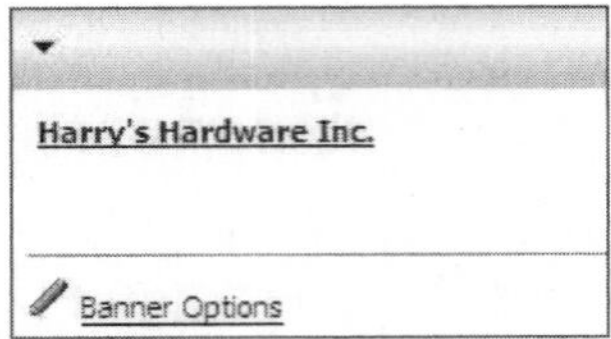

Figure 4-39

If you needed to edit the banner settings, go to Admin, Vendors, click the pencil icon, scroll down to Banner Advertising and click the +.

Now, click the pencil icon aside of the banner that you created. Table 4-7 reviews the different options.

Table 4-7: Edit Banner Settings

Settings	Description
Banner Name	Identifies the banner in lists, and is used as the ALT text for graphic banners and as hyperlinked text on text banners.
Banner Type	Of the available banner types, only two really impact how the banner fields are used. When you place banners on your site with the Banners module, you select the type of banner it should display. Choosing Banner, MicroButton, Button, Block, and Skyscraper provides logical groupings of banners that fall into common width and height formats. There are no actual rules, but these groupings help to organize banners so that you don't wind up displaying wide banners in button-sized locations in your skin. Text and Script types are special cases. If you choose a Text banner, you can mimic the look of Google Adsense. Choosing a Script banner allows free-form HTML in the text box, which is helpful for a number of generated links for things like Amazon products.
Banner Group	Further aids in the ad-hoc grouping of banners. For example, DotNetNuke.com displays rotating button banners for its sponsors. To keep sponsor buttons separate from other banners, each has Sponsor in its Banner Group field. Likewise, the Banner Options for the module specifies Sponsor in its Banner Group. Because this field is ad-hoc, there is no real way to track how or where it is used. You have to keep up with that on your own. But it does provide for all the logical separation you should ever need.

Continued

Table 4-7: *(continued)*

Settings	Description
Image	Specifies whether your image (if applicable) is to be rendered from a file on your site or from a remote URL.
Text/Script	The text in this field is handled differently depending on the Banner Type previously selected. For most banner types, just leave this field blank. For type Text, the value appears as simple text (unlinked) below the hyperlinked Banner Name field. For the Script Type, this field can contain raw HTML supporting a variety of link types and formats.
URL	If this value is populated, it is used instead of the URL associated with the vendor. You can use this URL to point to specific pages in a vendor's site or to configure extra query string parameters. This field also displays as hyperlinked text on banners of the Text type.
CPM/Cost	Provides a convenient place to record this information in the context of the banner.
Impressions	If specified, this value is one of the criteria used to determine whether a banner should be shown. To limit a banner's display based on the number of impressions, this field removes it from rotation after the value has been reached.
Start Date	You can set up banners in advance to begin displaying at a future date.
End Date	Together with Start Date, you can create banners to run for specific date durations for events, special deals, holidays, and so on.
Criteria	Specifies how the Impressions and Date constraints should be enforced. If they are enforced independently of one another (OR), a banner ceases to display outside of its date constraint or even within its date constraint if the number of impressions has been reached. If they are enforced jointly (AND), all criteria must be true for the banner to cease display. The AND option helps address a lack of throttling control. On a busy site with few banners in rotation, a given number of impressions can be used up quickly and so displayed over a brief time period. By jointly evaluating the criteria, a more equitable rotation is achieved by providing for additional banner impressions during the time period.

You can advise vendors of the status of a banner by clicking the Email Status To Vendor button at the bottom of the Edit Banner page. This sends an email to the address specified in the Vendor details, which relays the banner field information (text, costs, and constraints) and performance (view and click-through counts).

Vendors as Affiliates

You can ask your vendors to link to you and set up the vendor as an affiliate. You can even track your vendor's click-through performance to your site. You can add a vendor as just an affiliate when you add the vendor via Admin, Vendor. Add the vendor and expand the Affiliate Referrals. See Figure 4-40.

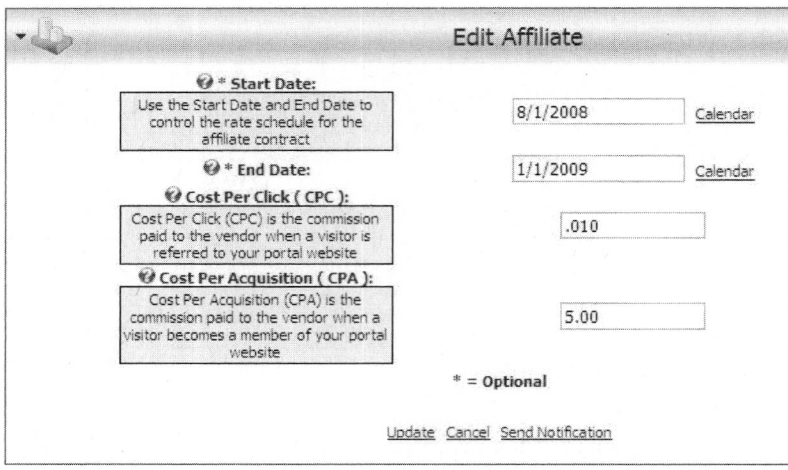

Figure 4-40

The CPC information for affiliate referrals is summarized in the Edit Vendor List, just as click-through is for banners; however, the CPA information is currently unused. You can specify multiple affiliate relationships under a single vendor to provide for tracking during discrete time periods.

Site Log

Under Admin, Site Log, Administrators can get twelve different reports to track users that visit your site. Each report provides different information and they are explained next.

The Site Log is a text-based report how users come to your site. Your Host needs to set up your portal for you to get access to this feature. Login as Host, go to Portals, Edit Portals, Advanced Settings, Host Settings and enter **365** at Site Log History (Days). Click Update. See Figure 4-41.

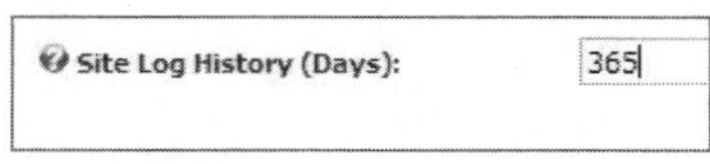

Figure 4-41

Now you can go to Admin, Site Log. See Figure 4-42.

There are several Report Types to select. Table 4-8 reviews each option.

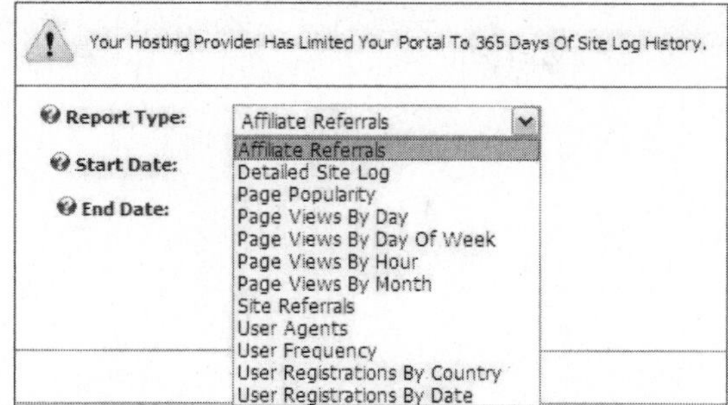

Figure 4-42

Table 4-8: Site Log Report Types

Type	Description
Affiliate Referrals	Tracks referrals from vendors who are defined as affiliates. By using their affiliate ID numbers in links to your site, you can capture how productive those affiliate links are.
Detailed Site Log	Includes all users and displays date and time, username, referrer, user agent, user host address, and page name.
Page Popularity	Displays the total number of visits to the pages on your site in the period specified.
Page Views By	This series of reports provides a summary of the number of visitors (anonymous) and users (logged in) that accessed your site in the intervals specified (Day, Day of Week, Hour, Month).
Site Referrals	Summary list of web pages (including search engines) that users have clicked to lead them to your site.
User Details	This series of reports provides a summary of the number of page visits recorded according to the characteristic specified (Agents, Frequency, Registrations by Country, and Registrations by Date). The Report by Frequency can be interesting because it identifies your most frequent visitors in any given period.

Figure 4-43 shows a live site with Site Referrals listing for a month's time.

Newsletters

DotNetNuke provides a great way to communicate with all of your users with an email newsletter. You can select user groups via security roles for each newsletter you want to send out. For example, you may want to send out a newsletter only to Coach and Parents. See Figure 4-44.

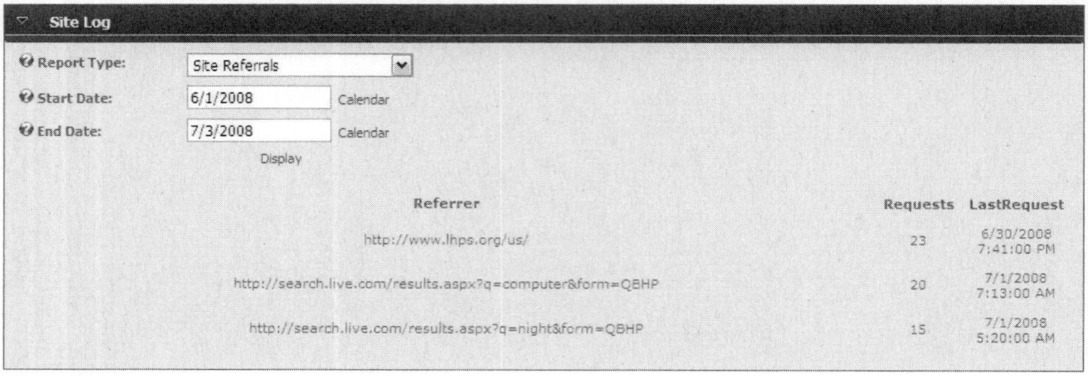

Site Log

Report Type: Site Referrals

Start Date: 6/1/2008 Calendar

End Date: 7/3/2008 Calendar

Display

Referrer	Requests	LastRequest
http://www.lhps.org/us/	23	6/30/2008 7:41:00 PM
http://search.live.com/results.aspx?q=computer&form=QBHP	20	7/1/2008 7:13:00 AM
http://search.live.com/results.aspx?q=night&form=QBHP	15	7/1/2008 5:20:00 AM

Figure 4-43

Newsletters

Basic Settings

In this section, you can set up required sender and recipients, as well as subject for your message.

Addressees

User Role(s):

- Administrators
- Coach
- Gallery Subscribers
- Parents
- Registered Users
- Subscribers

Additional Emails:

From:

Reply To:

Subject:

Figure 4-44

You can then type your message below in the Message area. In addition, there are Advanced Settings where you can attach a file and choose priority settings. The Send method allows you to personalize your email. You can also select send actions to be Synchronous or Asynchronous. Use Asynchronous if you have a large list of users. DotNetNuke batches email addresses into groups in the background, so you never actually try to send an email with thousands of BCC recipients. Finally, you can customize a newsletter by deselecting tokens and then keying a person's name in the newsletter. This option takes the default tokens out of your newsletter. See Figure 4-45.

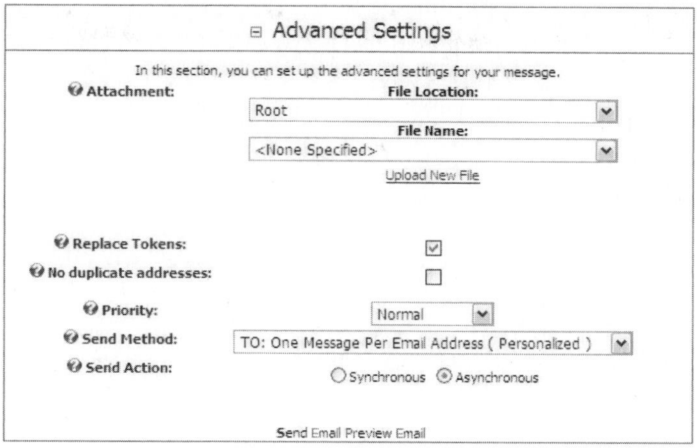

⊟ Advanced Settings

In this section, you can set up the advanced settings for your message.

Attachment: File Location: Root

File Name: <None Specified>

Upload New File

Replace Tokens: ☑

No duplicate addresses: ☐

Priority: Normal

Send Method: TO: One Message Per Email Address (Personalized)

Send Action: ○ Synchronous ⦿ Asynchronous

Send Email Preview Email

Figure 4-45

File Manager

Admin, File Manager allows the Administrator to upload files like documents or images to the portal. The Portal Administrator can even assign security roles to folders so that parent photographers can upload pictures to the Red Sox Little League portal. Only the host has permissions to change file extensions that are allowed using DotNetNuke. For example, if you wanted to upload an mp3 file you would get an error. The host needs to change the settings and add .mp3 so you can upload that file. Go to Admin File Manager, key in **Pictures** to the left of Add Folder, and then click the Add Folder icon. Now you'll see the folder Pictures once you click the + to expand the portal folders. See Figure 4-46.

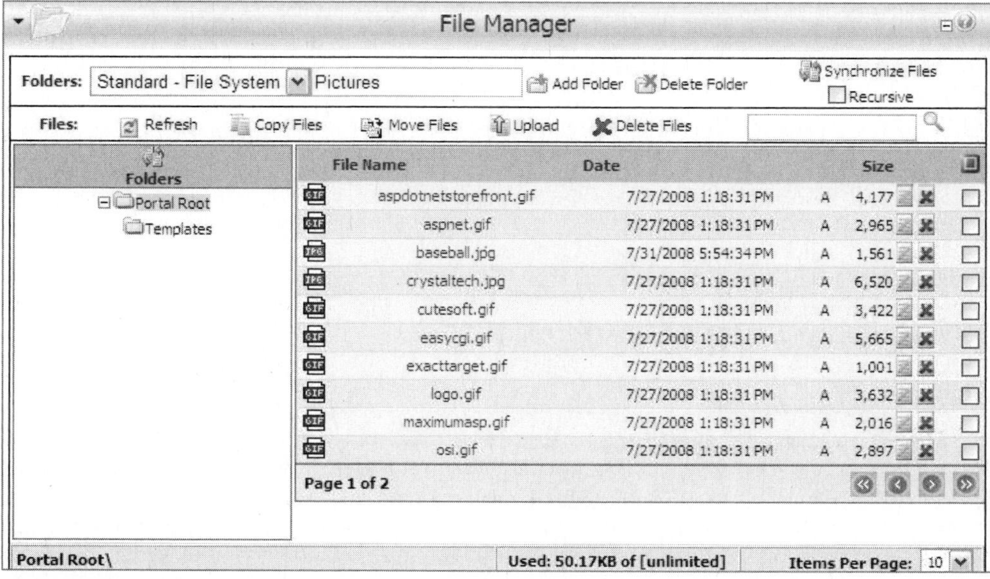

Figure 4-46

Now, scroll down to Folder Security Settings. Scroll down to Parents, and click View Folder and Write to Folder. This allows any user in the Parent security role to upload images to the Pictures folder. See Figure 4-47.

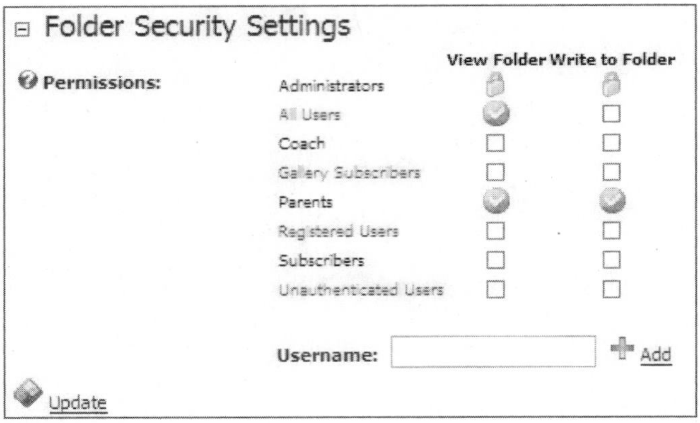

Figure 4-47

Uploading Files

Uploading a file to a DotNetNuke portal is a simple task. Basically, all you have to do is decide what folder you want the file to go in. Are you going to put the file in the Portal Root folder or do you need to create a new folder for those files you want to upload?

Simply click the Upload link and then the Browse button, locate the file you want to upload, and click Upload File. You can select the folder to upload to from the drop-down list. There's also a check box for Decompress Zip Files, which helps out with bandwidth. This feature is optional and will open a zipped file into a folder. Properties of the .NET Framework HttpPostedFileClass dictate the size limits for uploading files. DotNetNuke sets these properties in the default web.config file as follows:

```
<httpRuntime useFullyQualifiedRedirectUrl="true"
maxRequestLength="8192" requestLengthDiskThreshold="8192" />
```

Administrators have the permission to add the File Manager module on a page and only give permissions to a user or a group of users to upload files. For example, only photographers of the Red Sox site will be given permission to upload graphic image files to the site.

FTP with File Manager

The File Manager provides a convenient way to move files through the interface. For bulk operations, however, you may prefer to use FTP to transfer files (if permitted by your Host). If files are added to your site through any means other than the file upload interface, you need to click the Synchronize Files button. That command instructs DotNetNuke to iterate through the portal root and resolve for any files and folders that may be added or missing. Your Host may have enabled a scheduled job to perform this synchronization for you on a periodic basis, but if you do it yourself, you'll see those files in your drop-down lists immediately. Do not delete files outside of File Manager. Using the File Manager ensures that database references are updated appropriately throughout the application where file references are made (in other modules, for example).

Recycle Bin

The Recycle Bin acts like the Recycle Bin that you have with the Windows operating system. If you delete a page or a module and want to restore it, you can go to the Recycle Bin to do that. See Figure 4-48.

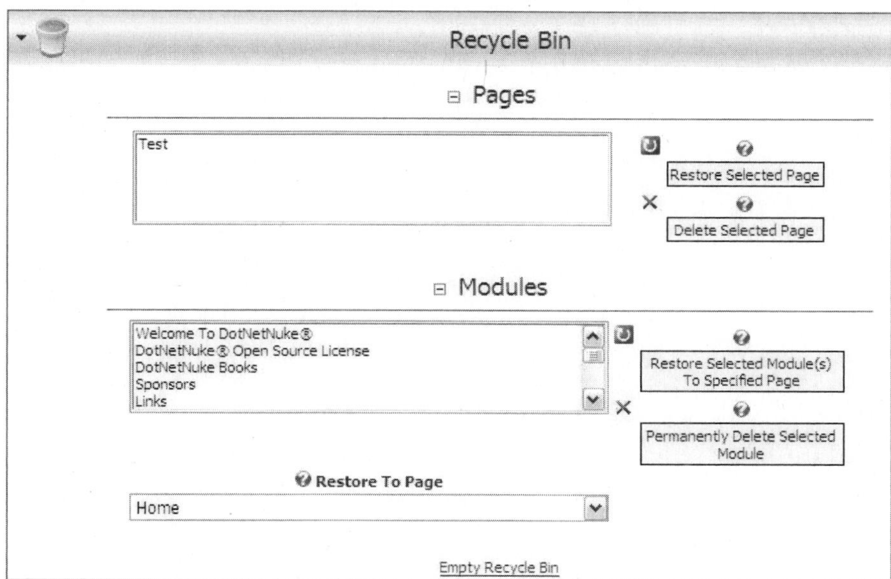

Figure 4-48

In Figure 4-48, you can see the pages and modules that have been deleted. You simply select the page or module that you would like to restore and click the icon to restore the page or module back to the portal.

The act of deleting a page or module doesn't really delete anything because it merely sets a flag that DotNetNuke understands internally as deleted and ignores it in the general interface. Developers can see this implementation by looking at the database fields Tab.IsDeleted and Modules.IsDeleted.

Recycling Modules

When modules are deleted, they lose their association to a specific page. So when they are restored, you must select a target page for them to appear on. Currently, a restored module has the same view and edit permissions that it did originally. However, this may not be what you have in mind if you are restoring a module that has been in the Recycle Bin for a while. In fact, because there is no convenient way to look at a module that is in the bin, you might be just restoring one to see what it was. The best way to do this is to restore modules to a page that is not visible to your users (a starting page). Then you can check it out for yourself and change whatever settings are necessary before moving it to its final (visible) home.

Portal Cleaning Up

When working with a portal for a long period of time, you'll get lots of pages and modules collected in the Recycle Bin. Periodically, it is good to empty out the bin by clicking Empty Recycle Bin.

Event Viewer

Portal Administrators can go to Admin, Event Viewer to view any type of activity that gets logged in the database on the portal. Exception errors are color coded in different categories to make it easier to locate errors. See Figure 4-49.

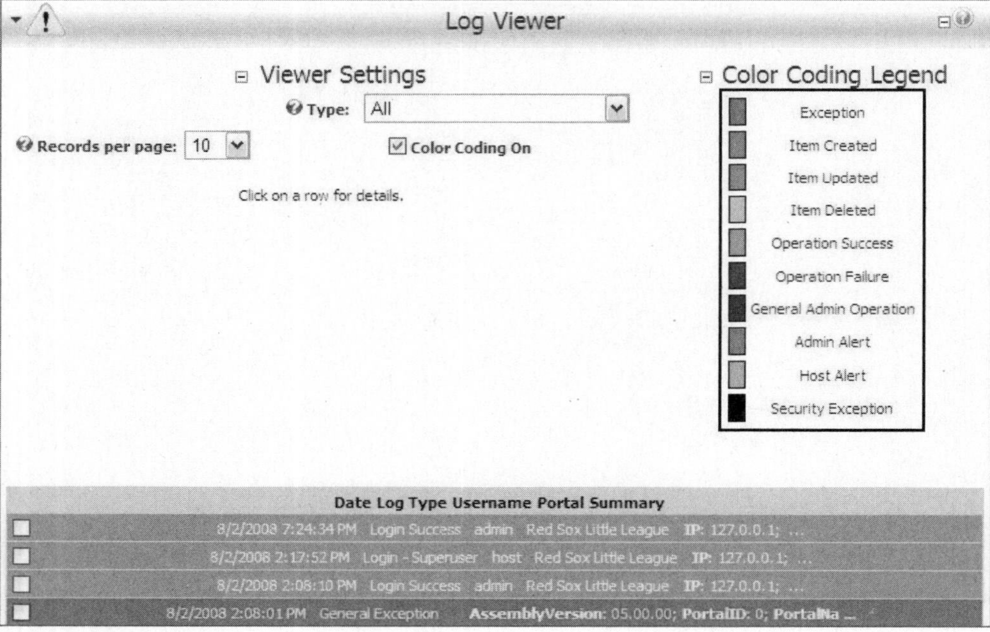

Figure 4-49

You can even click the drop-down list beside Type and only show events that you want to see. Figure 4-50.

Finally, a Portal Administrator can email the exceptions to anyone if the errors need further viewing by a Host Administrator or DotNetNuke consultant. See Figure 4-51.

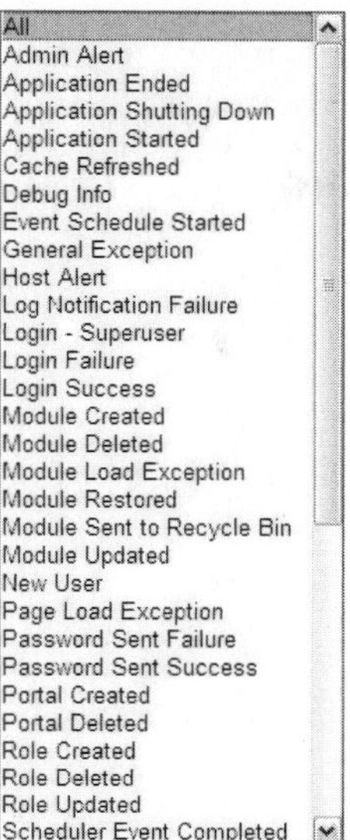
All
Admin Alert
Application Ended
Application Shutting Down
Application Started
Cache Refreshed
Debug Info
Event Schedule Started
General Exception
Host Alert
Log Notification Failure
Login - Superuser
Login Failure
Login Success
Module Created
Module Deleted
Module Load Exception
Module Restored
Module Sent to Recycle Bin
Module Updated
New User
Page Load Exception
Password Sent Failure
Password Sent Success
Portal Created
Portal Deleted
Role Created
Role Deleted
Role Updated
Scheduler Event Completed

Figure 4-50

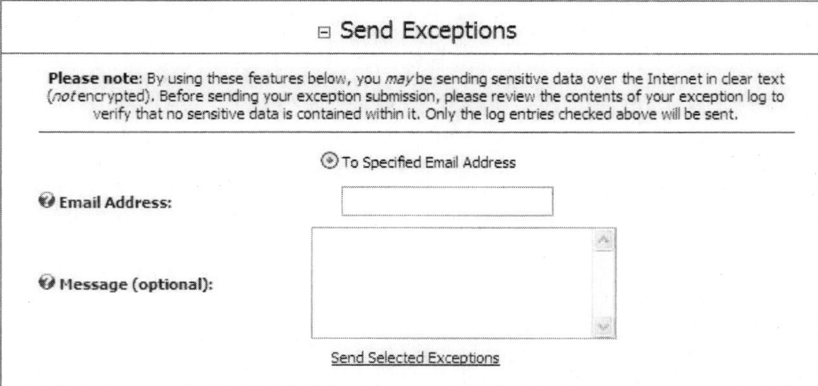

Figure 4-51

Site Wizard

The Admin, Site Wizard was used at the beginning of this chapter to create the Red Sox Little League web site. You walk through a series of screens and select your skin, container, add site details, and then click Finish. After, you add pages, security roles, and modules to build your site.

Solutions Explorer

The Admin, Solutions Explorer is a convenient way of finding information about DotNetNuke products such as skins or modules. There are tabs set up for DotNetNuke Providers, Utility, Core, and Component but there is no content on that site yet. There is also an About tab waiting for content. See Figure 4-52.

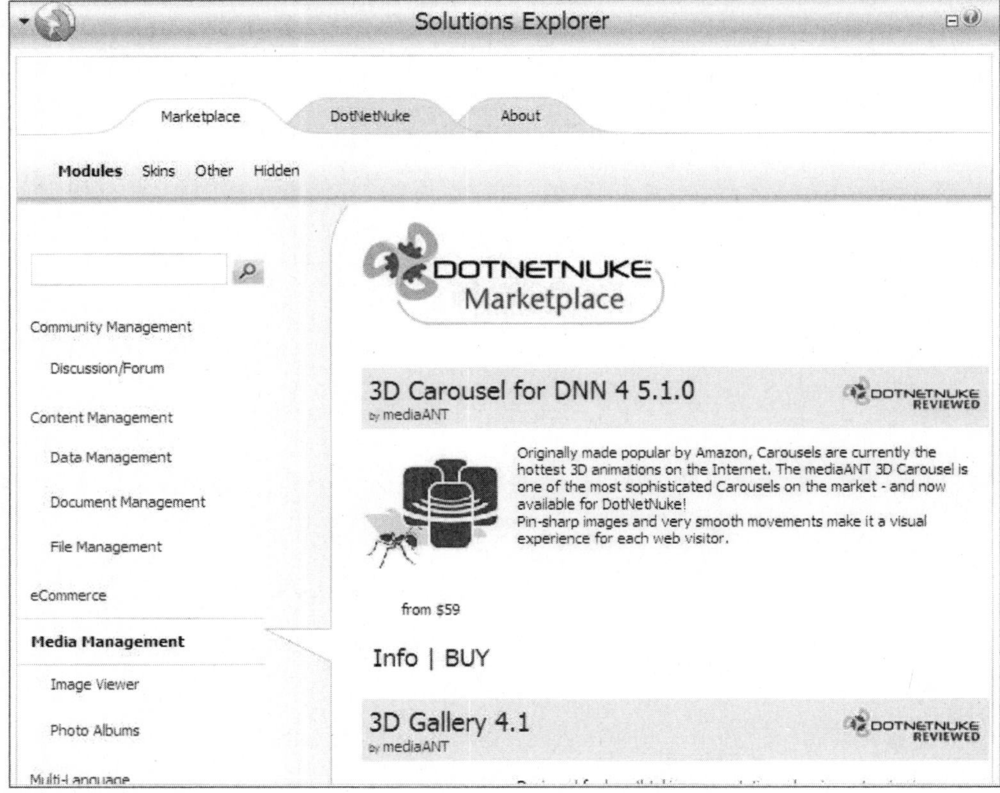

Figure 4-52

What's New

Under Admin/What's New, you'll find a new setting which gives you a summary of the major features for this DotNetNuke release. See Figure 4-53. You can view Major Highlights, Security Fixes, Updated Modules/Providers, along with a link to the official change log.

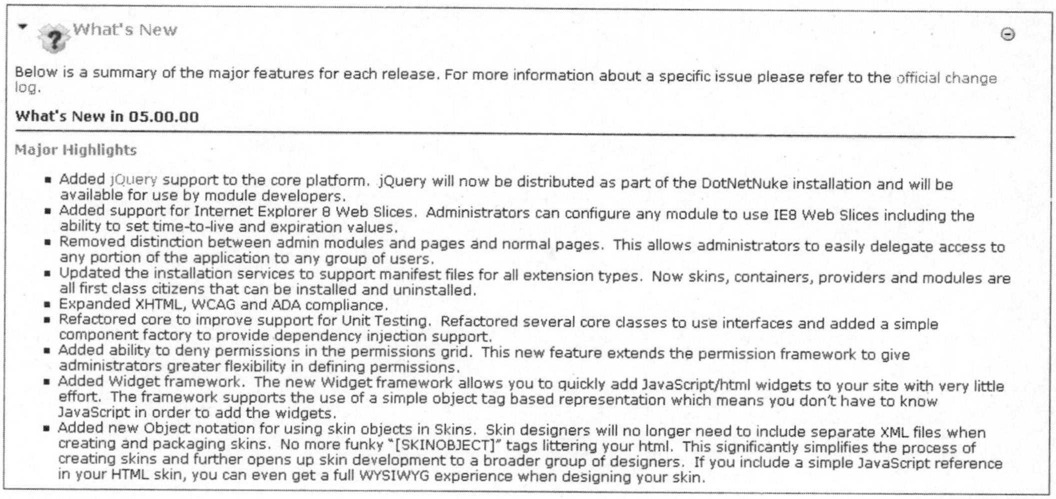

What's New

Below is a summary of the major features for each release. For more information about a specific issue please refer to the official change log.

What's New in 05.00.00

Major Highlights

- Added jQuery support to the core platform. jQuery will now be distributed as part of the DotNetNuke installation and will be available for use by module developers.
- Added support for Internet Explorer 8 Web Slices. Administrators can configure any module to use IE8 Web Slices including the ability to set time-to-live and expiration values.
- Removed distinction between admin modules and pages and normal pages. This allows administrators to easily delegate access to any portion of the application to any group of users.
- Updated the installation services to support manifest files for all extension types. Now skins, containers, providers and modules are all first class citizens that can be installed and uninstalled.
- Expanded XHTML, WCAG and ADA compliance.
- Refactored core to improve support for Unit Testing. Refactored several core classes to use interfaces and added a simple component factory to provide dependency injection support.
- Added ability to deny permissions in the permissions grid. This new feature extends the permission framework to give administrators greater flexibility in defining permissions.
- Added Widget framework. The new Widget framework allows you to quickly add JavaScript/html widgets to your site with very little effort. The framework supports the use of a simple object tag based representation which means you don't have to know JavaScript in order to add the widgets.
- Added new Object notation for using skin objects in Skins. Skin designers will no longer need to include separate XML files when creating and packaging skins. No more funky "[SKINOBJECT]" tags littering your html. This significantly simplifies the process of creating skins and further opens up skin development to a broader group of designers. If you include a simple JavaScript reference in your HTML skin, you can even get a full WYSIWYG experience when designing your skin.

Figure 4-53

Summary

This chapter covered many of the settings that are in Admin to give you an overview of what responsibilities the Portal Administrator has. The chapter started with building a web site for the Red Sox Little League team with the Site Wizard.

Key features included the following:

- Control Panel
- Site Wizard

You were able to configure your portal with the following settings:

- Site Settings
- Security Roles
- Pages
- Skins
- Containers
- File Manager

You also learned how to manage elements of your portal such as the following:

- User Accounts
- Vendors
- Newsletters
- Site Log
- Recycle Bin
- Events Viewer

Now you are capable of creating your own portal and working with the many features of DotNetNuke.

5

Host Administration

Chapter 4 gave you a good overview of the role a DotNetNuke administrator has when working with a web portal. This chapter reviews the role of the "Boss" of the web portal, the host.

The host has the main responsibility of controlling the installation of DotNetNuke, the creation of portals, the assignment of administrators, the uploading of skins and modules, and of course all the headaches of all those jobs. Kidding aside, the host is a major player in the DotNetNuke world, and this chapter reviews the features of DotNetNuke that are important to the host.

Defining the Host

The host, or host administrator (the terms are interchangeable), has the distinction of being the SuperUser, and has an account with that name as well. By default the SuperUser Account gets privileges that no other account gets by default. In addition to host account settings, this account has all of the admin settings privileges discussed in the preceding chapter. Also, the host can log in to any portal in your DotNetNuke setup.

The host has responsibilities to make sure that DotNetNuke is running correctly on the web hosting environment. All administrators must communicate with the host if there are any problems with their web sites.

Where to Start?

First and foremost, it is important for the host to create another SuperUser account so that no one will try to hack into your web site using the default setup. Simply click the SuperUser Account name on the top right-hand side of your portal. See Figure 5-1.

Figure 5-1

Change the information required under Manage Profile. Key your name for First Name, Last Name, Display Name, and Email Address and click Update. See Figure 5-2.

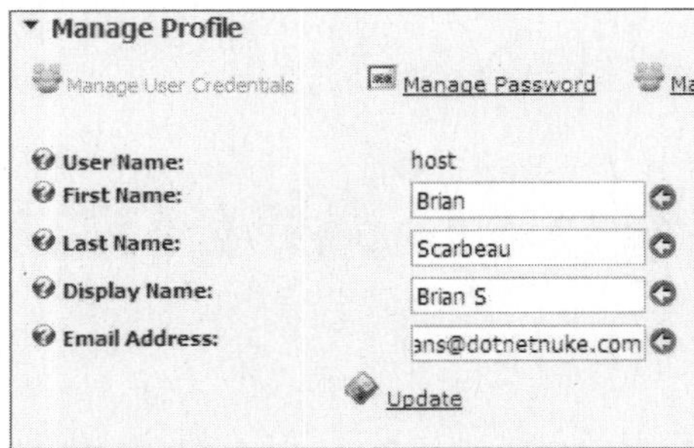

Figure 5-2

Now, click Manage Password. Key in the Current Password, `dnnhost`, and then change the password under New Password and Confirm Password. See Figure 5-3.

KEEP THIS PASSWORD IN A SAFE PLACE.

Figure 5-3

Installing Additional Modules

If you click Show Control Panel and then click <Select A Module>, you'll see the selection of modules that are pre-installed with DotNetNuke. You can install additional modules by clicking the Install Additional Extension link in the Control Panel. You can also view new skins and containers. Simply select the module that you want to install by clicking the check box, and then click Install Selected Extensions.

Working with Host Settings

There are thirteen settings that the host needs to know in order to manage the installed portals with DotNetNuke. See Figure 5-4. The host administrator works with these settings at various life cycles of the portal. For example, some settings are required at installation time, some for routine operations, and some for maintenance, reporting, and troubleshooting. The host settings consist of two categories: Basic and Advanced.

Figure 5-4

Host Settings: Basic

The Basic settings consist of settings for Configuration; Host Details, Appearance; and Payment Settings. Table 5-1 reviews the read-only fields in Site Configuration.

Host Details

These settings consist of Host Portal, Host Title, Host URL, Host Email, Default Doctype, and Enable Remember Me on Login Controls. Table 5-2 reviews each setting.

Table 5-1: Host Basic Settings — Configuration Fields

Field	Description
DotNetNuke Version	This is the DotNetNuke application version you are running.
Check for Upgrades	This option, enabled by default, will check to see whether there are any upgrades available.
Data Provider	This lists the provider name, which is identified as the default data provider in the web.config file.
.NET Framework	This information, specified through IIS, is the version of the .NET CLS that DotNetNuke is running under.
ASP.NET Identity	This identifies the Windows user account in which the application is running.
Host Name	This is the name of the site.
Permissions	This setting displays the code access permissions available in the hosting environment.
Relative Path	This identifies the relative location of the application in relation to the root of the site.
Physical Path	This is the physical location of the site root on the server.
Server Time	This is the current date and time for the web server.
Web Farm Enabled	This indicates whether the site is running a web farm configuration.
GUID	This is the globally unique identifier that can be used to identify this application.

Table 5-2: Host Details Settings

Setting	Description
Host Portal	This is the default portal.
Host Title	This is the name of your Hosting Account.
Host URL	This is the URL of your Host.
Host Email	This is the support email of the Hosting Account.
Default Doctype	This is the skin doctype for web pages.
Enable Remember Me on Login Controls	This sets the Remember Me check box on login controls.

Creating the Appearance

The options set in this area deal with creating the appearance of your host. See Figure 5-5. Table 5-3 reviews these settings.

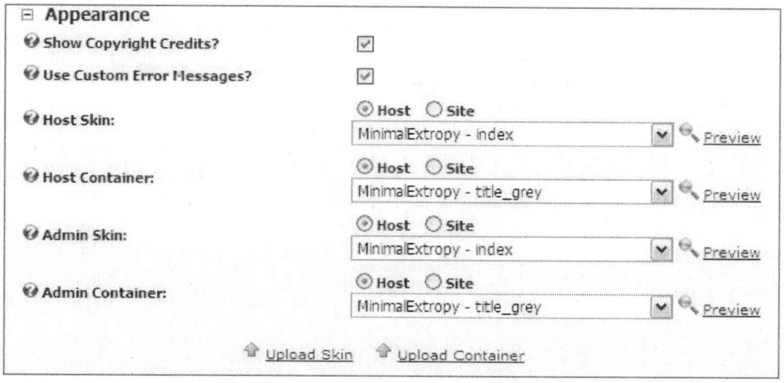

Figure 5-5

Table 5-3: Host Appearance Settings

Setting	Description
Show Copyright Credits	This will show the DotNetNuke copyright credits at the bottom of your web portal. Uncheck it if you don't want spiders to locate your site as a DotNetNuke site.
Use Custom Error Messages	This option by default enables DotNetNuke to show error messages vs. ASP.NET error messages, which are not user friendly.
Host Skin	The Host Skin appears on all pages of the Host. You can select skins that are pre-loaded on a DotNetNuke installation, or you can upload a skin to the portal.
Host Container	The Host Container appears on all pages of the Host. You can select a container that is pre-loaded on a DotNetNuke installation, or you can upload a container to the portal to use instead.
Edit Skin	The selected skin will be applied to all edit mode pages on your sites.
Edit Container	The selected container will be applied to all edit mode pages on your sites.

Host Payment Settings

You learned in Chapter 4 that you could use PayPal with DotNetNuke to collect payment. Table 5-4 reviews the options for these settings.

Table 5-4: Payment Settings

Setting	Description
Payment Processor	PayPal is the only provider, at this time.
Processor UserId	Enter the UserId for the payment processor.
Processor Password	Enter the password for the payment processor.
Hosting Fee	This is the monthly fee you would charge for hosting a portal.
Hosting Currency	You can select the currency from the drop-down list. U.S. Dollars is the default setting.
Hosting Space (MB)	Place a value here for the amount of disk space you want to allot your new portals.
Page Quota	You can specify a maximum number of pages per portal.
User Quota	You can specify a maximum number of users per portal.
Demo Period	If anonymous Demo Signup is enabled, the expiry date for a new portal is set in days.
Anonymous Demo Signup	This is a legacy feature and its use is highly discouraged. If this option is disabled, only the Host Administrator can create a new portal.

Disk space is very valuable when you install DotNetNuke and plan to have several portals with hundreds of users. Enforcing file upload protects you from extensive file uploading by users. By default, all file uploads should be performed with File Manager.

Host Settings Advanced

There are several settings here, which include Friendly URL Settings, Request Filter Settings, Proxy Settings, SMTP Server Settings, Performance Settings, Compression Settings, and Other Settings. Table 5-5 reviews these settings.

Table 5-5: Advanced Settings

Setting	Description
Friendly URL Settings	This is checked by default to allow search engine friendly URLs. You have the option of adding a new rule if needed.
Request Filter Settings	This allows you to add rules requests using server variables. Once enabled, you can add a rule. See Figure 5-6.

Continued

Table 5-5: *(continued)*

Setting	Description
	There is a convenient link to Microsoft's Library site for IIS Server Variables. **WARNING**: Adding an incorrect request filter rule may prevent you or your customers from being able to access your DotNetNuke web site, and may require you to edit the DotNetNuke.config file to remove the incorrectly configured rule.
Proxy Settings	Some custom modules may require you to change proxy settings. Here you enter the proxy server address, port, proxy username, password, and web request timeout.
SMTP Settings	Here you enter the SMTP server address. You can also specify an alternative port by adding a colon and the port number. You select the SMTP Authentication and SMTP Enable SSL. There is a convenient test link that will test the connection as well. See Figure 5-7. If the test is successful, a message, "Email sent Successfully," will be displayed.
Performance Settings	You can select several performance settings options at this location. Page State Persistence can be either set at Page, which is the default, or in cache memory. Module Caching can be set at memory, which provides the most flexibility and is the highest performance method; however, it also consumes the most system resources. Disk Caching is set at default is the least expensive on resources, but does not offer any flexibility. For Performance Settings, there are four options to choose: No Caching, which is not recommended. Light Caching, which is cached every 30 seconds. Moderate Caching, which is cached every minute. Heavy Caching, which is cached every 2 minutes. There is also a link to Clear Cache.
Authenticated Cacheabilty	This feature sets the cache control HTTP header value for authenticated users. There are six settings. Some modules run better under certain settings, as determined by the developer. Some modular developers may require a different setting for their module than the default settings. The developers will give you the appropriate setting change for their module. Leave this alone if the module doesn't need the feature.
ServerAndNoCache	This is set up by default and is most secure. NoCache gives no cache option to the client, and is cached at the server. Private is cacheable only on the client and not the proxy. If set to Public, this allows both client and proxy to share the cache. ServerAndPrivate settings do not allow proxy servers and are not allowed to cache the response.

Continued

Table 5-5: *(continued)*

Setting	Description
Compression Settings	Compression is a simple, effective way to save bandwidth and speed up your site. The default is No Compression, but you have a choice of using Deflate or GZip Compression.
Use Whitespace Filter	You can select this item to remove excess whitespace from the response sent to the client. This will result in smaller download (10%-15%), but it will make the html less readable.
Other Compression Settings	Excluded Paths allows you to exclude pages or resources from being compressed.
Whitespace Filter	This setting will strip whitespace from your generated page content following the Regular Expression specified in the Whitespace Filter option under Compression Settings.

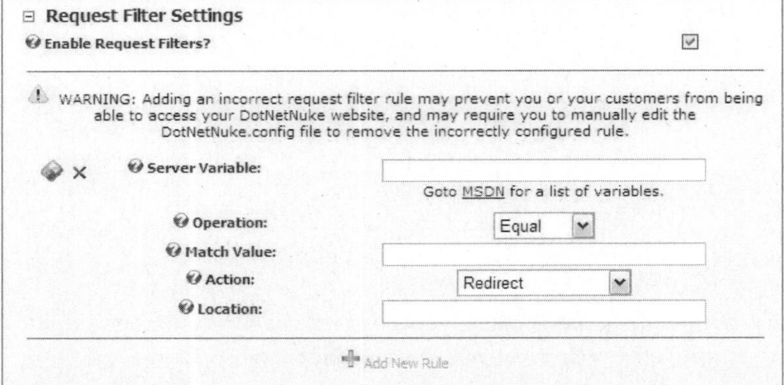

Figure 5-6

Figure 5-7

Other Settings

This area includes many host settings that could not be categorized. A word of caution needs to be placed here regarding changing a setting that might disable your portal. Be careful before you click Update with these settings. See Figure 5-8. Table 5-6 reviews these options.

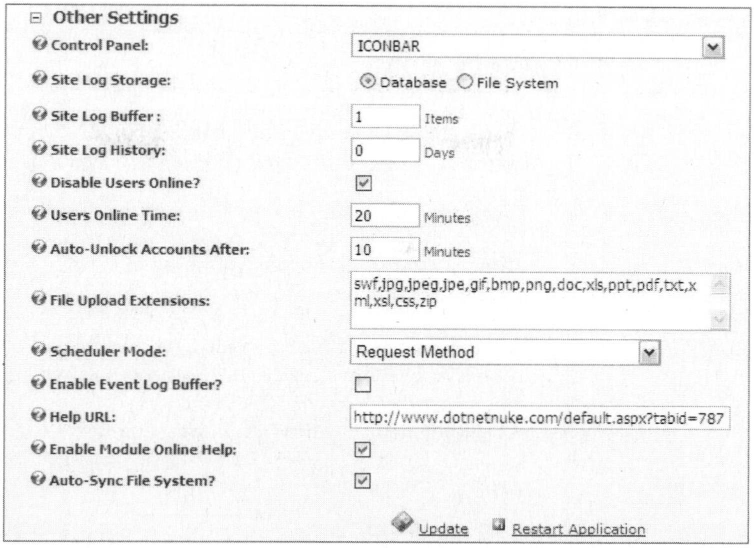

Other Settings

Control Panel:	ICONBAR
Site Log Storage:	Database / File System
Site Log Buffer :	1 Items
Site Log History:	0 Days
Disable Users Online?	☑
Users Online Time:	20 Minutes
Auto-Unlock Accounts After:	10 Minutes
File Upload Extensions:	swf,jpg,jpeg,jpe,gif,bmp,png,doc,xls,ppt,pdf,txt,xml,xsl,css,zip
Scheduler Mode:	Request Method
Enable Event Log Buffer?	☐
Help URL:	http://www.dotnetnuke.com/default.aspx?tabid=787
Enable Module Online Help:	☑
Auto-Sync File System?	☑

Update Restart Application

Figure 5-8

jQuery

jQuery is a lightweight JavaScript library that emphasizes interaction between JavaScript and HTML. According to Joe Brinkman, co-founder and the Chief Technology Officer of DotNetNuke Corp., Microsoft Corporation will include jQuery in the next version of Visual Studio.

> Starting in DotNetNuke 5.0, we will fully support jQuery in the base DotNetNuke platform. Over the next several releases, we will begin migrating our existing libraries to delegate as much work as possible to jQuery. There are still many areas where the ClientAPI and Widget framework provide needed functionality that is not available in jQuery or ASP.Net AJAX, but there is a lot of code which can now be greatly simplified.
>
> When you login as Host in DNN 5, you will have access to jQuery settings on the Host Settings screen. Using these settings allows you to configure the jQuery library which will be used in the framework. By default, DNN 5 will use the minified version of jQuery that is served from the DotNetNuke resources directory. This configuration provides good performance while also minimizing external dependencies. For those looking to maximize their performance, we have included support for using a hosted version of jQuery. The default hosted jQuery version will be the minified version hosted on Google. By using a hosted version of the library, you increase the likelihood that the user will already have a cached version of the library. This also allows hosts to specify which version of the jQuery library they wish to use. This allows hosts to have greater control over their environment. Just remember that the core and some third party modules may have version dependencies so you should be careful about pointing to older versions of the scripts.

This support makes it easy for developers to add jQuery to their modules and know that it will already be available on the server. We have not yet decided on whether to also include jQuery UI support, but I suspect that it will also be made available once we figure out which specific UI features to support (the whole UI library is over 200K and definitely too much for most sites).

Table 5-6: Other Settings

Settings	Description
Control Panel	This setting is used for page administration. ICONBAR gives you the Common Tasks and Wizard. CLASSIC is a legacy view of pages.
Site Log Storage	This item selects the storage location for the site log.
Site Log Buffer	Here you enter the number of items in the site log buffer. This item gets sent to the database after being collected in the buffer.
Site Log History	You have the option of choosing the number of days that you want to keep activity in the site log. Some experts recommend that you should set this to 0, which disables the site log and prevents a potentially critical filling of database tables.
Disable Users Online	Users Online is disabled by default for performance reasons.
Users Online Time	Enter the length of the user's online buffer. The default is 20 minutes.
Auto-Unlock Accounts After	After an account is locked out due to unsuccessful login attempts, it can be automatically unlocked with a successful authentication after a certain period has elapsed. Enter the number of minutes to wait until the account can be unlocked. A 0 will disable this feature. 10 minutes is set by default.
File Upload Extensions	Here you will see a list of default file extensions allowed to upload to your DotNetNuke portal. You will go here to enter new file extensions that you want allowed uploaded to your portal.
Scheduler Mode	The default method is Request Method. This executes tasks when HTTP Requests are made. The Timer Method maintains a separate thread to execute scheduled tasks while the worker process is still alive.
Enable Event Log Buffer	Selecting this option will cause log entries to be logged to memory and then purged regularly to the data store. Deselecting will cause log entries to be written immediately.
Help URL	This is the URL for the Online Help you will be providing. If you leave the entry blank, no help is provided for the Admin/Host areas of DotNetNuke.
Enable Module Online Help	You can enable or disable the Online Help Action Menu for Modules. If enabled, you will need to provide the Help URL for the module in the Module Definitions, although this may have been provided by the developer of the module.
Auto-Sync File System	Check this box to synchronize the file system automatically.

Table 5-7: jQuery Settings

Installed jQuery Version	Lists the version of jQuery installed.
Use jQuery Debug Version	If checked, the standard jQuery script file is used. If unchecked, a smaller version is used that significantly reduces the size of the JavaScript file but decreases readability of the JavaScript.
Use Hosted jQuery Version	If checked, the associated URL will be used for the jQuery file. If unchecked, local copies of the file will be used.
Hosted jQuery URL	This is the full URL for the jQuery script. By default, this is set to the latest jQuery smaller script hosted on Google CDN servers for optimum performance.

With jQuery we have tried to provide a mechanism that only loads the jQuery library when absolutely necessary. If none of the modules or skin-objects on a page require jQuery, then it won't be included in the page. If your module wants to use jQuery, then you must include a long, complicated block of code that looks like this:

```
DotNetNuke.Framework.jQuery.RequestRegistration()
```

Joe Brinkman blogs about the use of jQuery and DotNetNuke. His blog reviews why jQuery was selected to be part of DotNetNuke and how jQuery will be used for Pane Previews.

> During the rendering phase of the page lifecycle, the framework will determine if anyone has requested jQuery and will add the appropriate jQuery reference to the page header section. This ensures that jQuery is loaded on the page before any other scripts which might use it.
>
> **NOTE:** The framework will not remember who requested the jQuery service after a postback, so make sure to call RequestRegistration for each page request.
>
> Because DotNetNuke 5.0 will include both Asp.Net AJAX support and jQuery support, you should read up on potential problems and conflicts that can occur if you are not careful.

You can stay current and learn more about jQuery and DotNetNuke at Joe's blog: `http://blog.theaccidentalgreek.com`.

Host Portals

The Host Portal settings allow you to add a new portal, export a portal template, and delete expired portals.

Add a new portal for the Chicago White Sox Little League team. See Figure 5-9. This is going to be a child portal, so click the radio button for that option. The portal alias will be `localhost/dotnetnuke/chicagowhitesox`.

Title: Chicago White Sox Little League

Description: little league team

Keywords: little league baseball

Template: DotNetNuke

Portal Type: ○ Parent ◉ Child

Portal Alias: localhost/dotnetnuke/chichagowhitesox

Home Directory: Portals/[PortalID]

Customize

Title: Chicago White Sox Little League

Description: little league team

Keywords: little league baseball

Template: DotNetNuke

Default Website Template

⊟ Security Settings

Username: CoachJack

First Name: Jack

Last Name: Jones

Email: J@aol.com

Password: •••••••

Confirm: •••••••

Create Portal Cancel

Figure 5-9

Coach Jack Jones will be the owner of this portal, so, under Security Settings, key in his Username, First Name, Last Name, Email address, Password, and Confirm.

Now click Create Portal.

When a new child portal is created, a physical directory is also created in the root of the web site with the child portal's name. A page called subhost.aspx is copied into the directory as the default.aspx. That's how DotNetNuke can implement addressing the child portal by the alias name.

Why are child portals created? With a single registered domain name, you can create an infinite number of portals. The most popular reason is the capability to emulate a single sign-on solution where credentials appear to be shared between portals. This is common with intranets where departments can be child portals.

Portal Templates

You were introduced to portal templates in the previous chapter when you created a site using the Site Wizard. You had the opportunity to import a portal template. Re-creating a portal saves time and effort if you like the pages and modules on the portal. Figure 5-10 creates the template.

If you go back to Admin, Site Wizard, you'll be able to see the newly created Little League template that can be selected for every new site. See Figure 5-11.

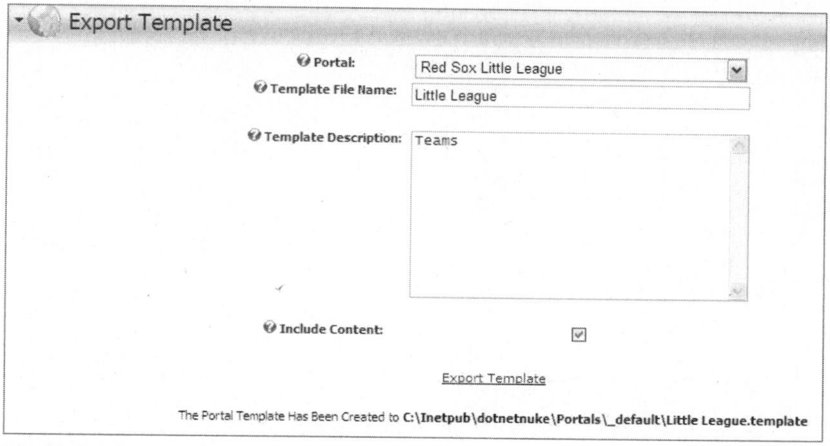

Figure 5-10

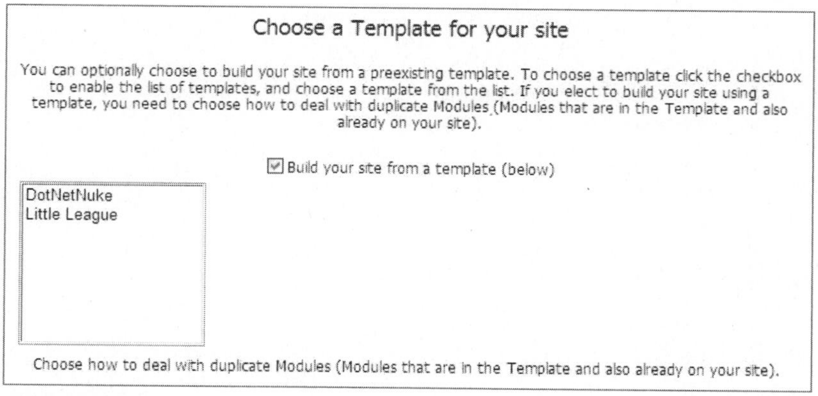

Figure 5-11

Expired Portals

As part of routine housekeeping, the host should make sure that any unused portals are deleted. Go to Host, Portals and click Delete Expired Portals to remove portals that are on the hard disk but have expired.

Host Module Definition

The Host Module Definitions page will display all of the installed modules that you have available to use on pages in your portal. The Name, Description, Version, and Upgrade are listed for each module you have installed on your portal. You can edit or delete existing modules here or add new modules as well. See Figure 5-12.

If you click the pencil next to the module name, it will take you to Edit Extensions page. See Figure 5-13.

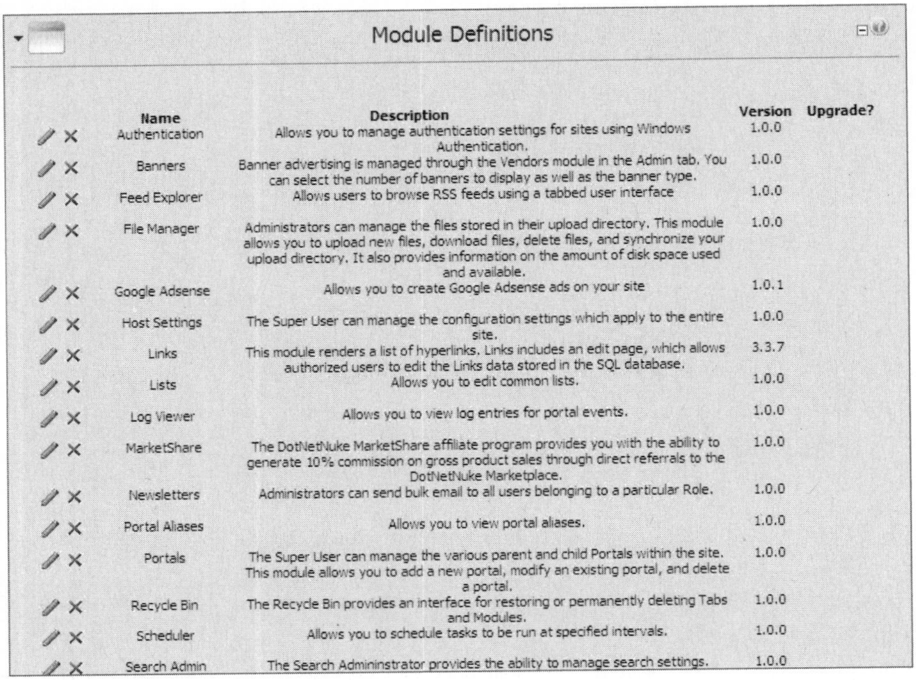

Module Definitions

	Name	Description	Version	Upgrade?
	Authentication	Allows you to manage authentication settings for sites using Windows Authentication.	1.0.0	
	Banners	Banner advertising is managed through the Vendors module in the Admin tab. You can select the number of banners to display as well as the banner type.	1.0.0	
	Feed Explorer	Allows users to browse RSS feeds using a tabbed user interface	1.0.0	
	File Manager	Administrators can manage the files stored in their upload directory. This module allows you to upload new files, download files, delete files, and synchronize your upload directory. It also provides information on the amount of disk space used and available.	1.0.0	
	Google Adsense	Allows you to create Google Adsense ads on your site	1.0.1	
	Host Settings	The Super User can manage the configuration settings which apply to the entire site.	1.0.0	
	Links	This module renders a list of hyperlinks. Links includes an edit page, which allows authorized users to edit the Links data stored in the SQL database.	3.3.7	
	Lists	Allows you to edit common lists.	1.0.0	
	Log Viewer	Allows you to view log entries for portal events.	1.0.0	
	MarketShare	The DotNetNuke MarketShare affiliate program provides you with the ability to generate 10% commission on gross product sales through direct referrals to the DotNetNuke Marketplace.	1.0.0	
	Newsletters	Administrators can send bulk email to all users belonging to a particular Role.	1.0.0	
	Portal Aliases	Allows you to view portal aliases.	1.0.0	
	Portals	The Super User can manage the various parent and child Portals within the site. This module allows you to add a new portal, modify an existing portal, and delete a portal.	1.0.0	
	Recycle Bin	The Recycle Bin provides an interface for restoring or permanently deleting Tabs and Modules.	1.0.0	
	Scheduler	Allows you to schedule tasks to be run at specified intervals.	1.0.0	
	Search Admin	The Search Admininstrator provides the ability to manage search settings.	1.0.0	

Figure 5-12

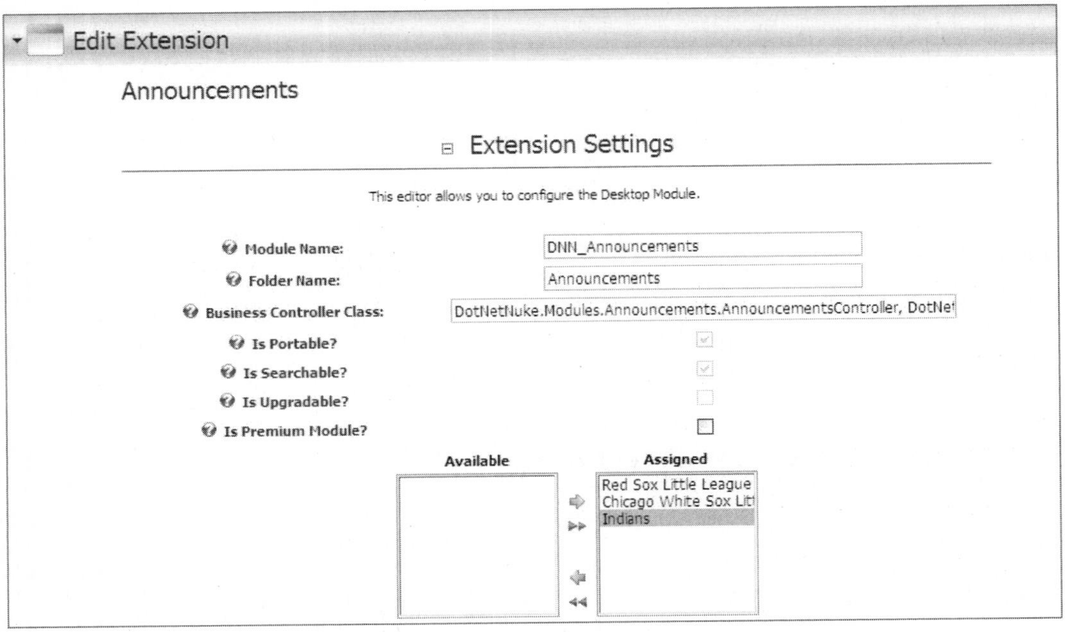

Edit Extension

Announcements

Extension Settings

This editor allows you to configure the Desktop Module.

Module Name: DNN_Announcements

Folder Name: Announcements

Business Controller Class: DotNetNuke.Modules.Announcements.AnnouncementsController, DotNet

Is Portable?

Is Searchable?

Is Upgradable?

Is Premium Module?

Available

Assigned

Red Sox Little League

Chicago White Sox Lit

Indians

Figure 5-13

The top half of the settings allow you to view the Module Name, Folder Name, and Business Controller Class, to see whether the module is Portable, Searchable, Upgradable, and Premium Module.

If the module is a premium module, that module can be assigned to specific portals.

The settings located in the middle allow you to view the Definition for the module, the Friendly Name, Default Cache Time, and the Module Controls for the module. See Figure 5-14.

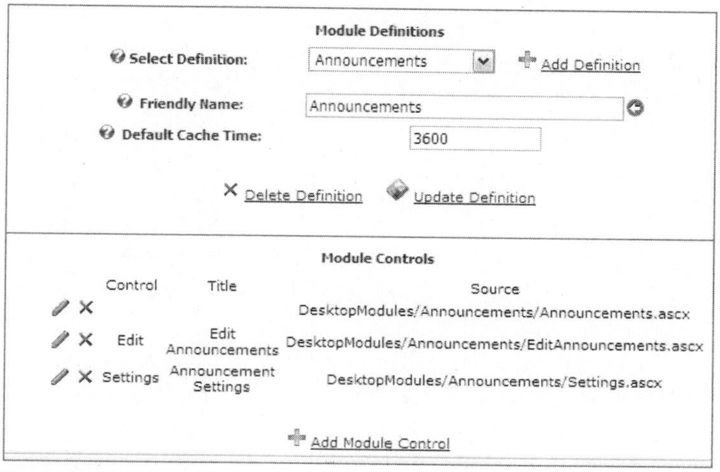

Figure 5-14

A module can have any number of definitions. A definition directly matches to a single component of a module. For this reason, most modules have one definition; they only add one component to the page. The Announcement module has only one component, and it is called Announcements, as shown in Figure 5-14.

Some modules may add many components to a page, with each component providing different functionality but part of a logical group. For example, a blogging module might contain a calendar, a list of blog entries, and a search module. These would be configured as three different definitions, but would still belong to the same Module Name.

You can add definitions by typing their name and clicking Add Definition. See Figure 5-14. You can also delete a definition at this location.

Each definition may have a number of controls associated with it. The controls directly map to ASP.NET user controls and each is marked with a name known as a key, which allows DotNetNuke to determine which control to load at runtime.

The Announcement module has several controls: one to view the announcement, one to edit the announcement, and one for announcement settings.

The Add Control section allows you to add new controls, edit an existing control by clicking the pencil icon, or delete a control by clicking the "X."

Module Package Settings

The Package Settings give you information about the module that you have installed on a DotNetNuke portal. See Figure 5-15. You see the Name of your module, Friendly Name, Description, Version, License, Release Notes, Owner, Organization, URL, and Email Address. Here you can also Update Module, UnInstall Extension, Create Package, or Cancel. These are covered in later chapters on module development.

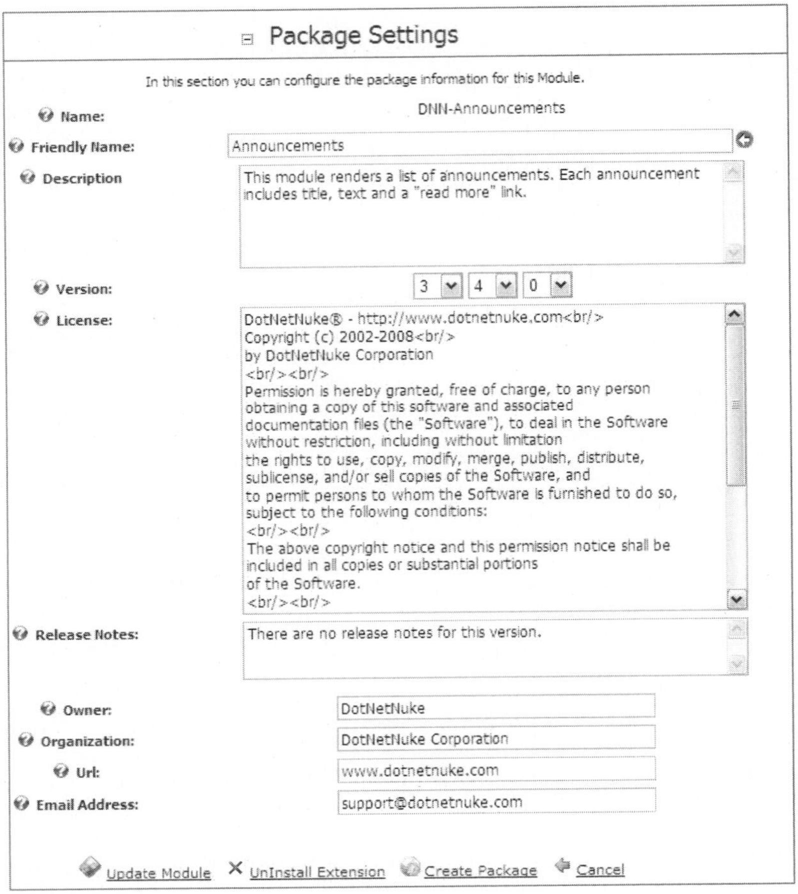

Package Settings

In this section you can configure the package information for this Module.

Name: DNN-Announcements

Friendly Name: Announcements

Description: This module renders a list of announcements. Each announcement includes title, text and a "read more" link.

Version: 3 4 0

License: DotNetNuke® - http://www.dotnetnuke.com
Copyright (c) 2002-2008
by DotNetNuke Corporation

Permission is hereby granted, free of charge, to any person obtaining a copy of this software and associated documentation files (the "Software"), to deal in the Software without restriction, including without limitation the rights to use, copy, modify, merge, publish, distribute, sublicense, and/or sell copies of the Software, and to permit persons to whom the Software is furnished to do so, subject to the following conditions:

The above copyright notice and this permission notice shall be included in all copies or substantial portions of the Software.

Release Notes: There are no release notes for this version.

Owner: DotNetNuke

Organization: DotNetNuke Corporation

Url: www.dotnetnuke.com

Email Address: support@dotnetnuke.com

Update Module   UnInstall Extension   Create Package   Cancel

Figure 5-15

Installing a New Module

There are several ways to install new modules to your DotNetNuke portal. One way is to perform an automated install, which can be accomplished in three areas, Host, Module Definition or Host Extensions. The other way is manually adding the module definition, which is covered in Chapter 17, "Distribution."

Performing an automated install involves uploading a zip file containing the module (often referred to as a "module package" or "module install"). These zip files are generally available from independent developers and companies that create them.

It is worth noting that DotNetNuke is an open source portal and many developers have modified the existing DotNetNuke modules or have created their own modules and have given back to the community by giving away these modules for free. Some developers charge for their work and you can find these modules at the DotNetNuke Marketplace or on Snowcovered.com.

Before you purchase a module, make sure that that module is going to work in your environment, and get references from users who have purchased the module.

On the DotNetNuke site, log in and go to the Supplementary Downloads section to view additional modules that you can use on your site.

The core framework bundles a number of components that are packaged separately (for example, modules) but that are not part of the DotNetNuke Projects program. These downloads are provided for your convenience. The DotNetNuke Projects (New Releases) are shown in Figure 5-16.

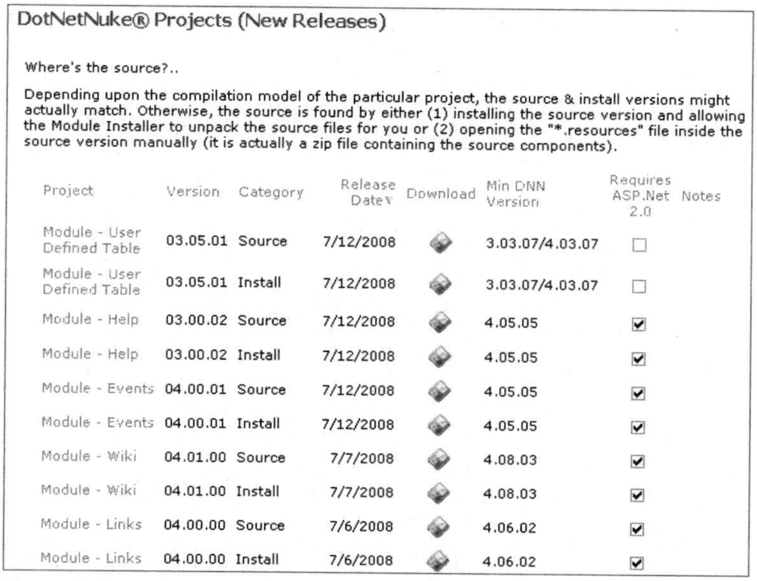

DotNetNuke® Projects (New Releases)

Where's the source?..

Depending upon the compilation model of the particular project, the source & install versions might actually match. Otherwise, the source is found by either (1) installing the source version and allowing the Module Installer to unpack the source files for you or (2) opening the "*.resources" file inside the source version manually (it is actually a zip file containing the source components).

Project	Version	Category	Release Date	Download	Min DNN Version	Requires ASP.Net 2.0	Notes
Module - User Defined Table	03.05.01	Source	7/12/2008		3.03.07/4.03.07	☐	
Module - User Defined Table	03.05.01	Install	7/12/2008		3.03.07/4.03.07	☐	
Module - Help	03.00.02	Source	7/12/2008		4.05.05	☑	
Module - Help	03.00.02	Install	7/12/2008		4.05.05	☑	
Module - Events	04.00.01	Source	7/12/2008		4.05.05	☑	
Module - Events	04.00.01	Install	7/12/2008		4.05.05	☑	
Module - Wiki	04.01.00	Source	7/7/2008		4.08.03	☑	
Module - Wiki	04.01.00	Install	7/7/2008		4.08.03	☑	
Module - Links	04.00.00	Source	7/6/2008		4.06.02	☑	
Module - Links	04.00.00	Install	7/6/2008		4.06.02	☑	

Figure 5-16

To install a new module, click Install Module at the bottom of the page under Host, Module Definition. Now, select the zip file of the module you want to use. See Figure 5-17.

Click Next to view the Package Information of the module. Here you will see the Name of the module, Type, Friendly Name, Description, Version, Owner, Organization, URL, and Email Address. See Figure 5-18.

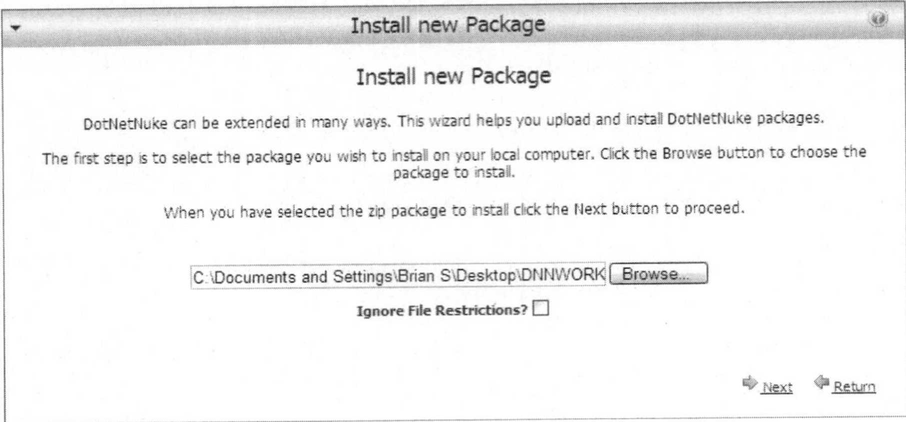

Figure 5-17

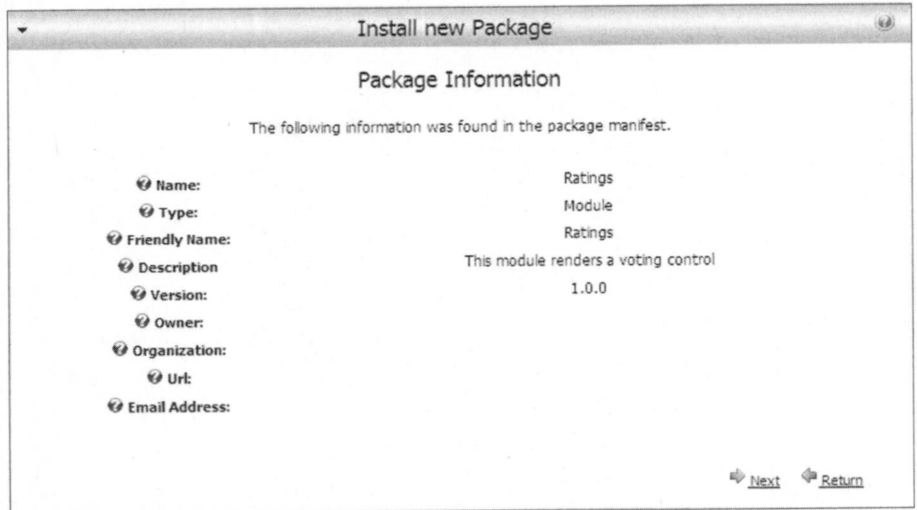

Figure 5-18

Click Next to review any Release Notes and click Next again to see the License and accept the terms, if any, for that module. Click Next to see the package install. See Figure 5-19.

Always scroll down to ensure that the module was properly installed. Now, click Return. You will be able to see your new module in the Module Definition and you can now place that module on any page.

If you have modules that you are not using, you can delete them by clicking the ''X.''

Package Installation Report

See below for the results of the package installation

StartJob	Starting Installation
Info	Starting Installation - Ratings
Info	Starting Installation - Script
Info	Begin Sql execution
Info	Folder Created - C:\Inetpub\dotnetnuke\DesktopModules\BTBRatings\
Info	Created - 01.00.00.SqlDataProvider
Info	Executing 01.00.00.SqlDataProvider
Info	Start Sql execution: 01.00.00.SqlDataProvider file
Info	End Sql execution: 01.00.00.SqlDataProvider file
Info	Created - Uninstall.SqlDataProvider
Info	Finished Sql execution
Info	Component installed successfully - Script
Info	Starting Installation - Module
Info	Module registered successfully - Ratings
Info	Component installed successfully - Module
Info	Starting Installation - Assembly
Info	Assembly registered - bin\BiteTheBullet.DNN.Modules.BTBRating.dll
Info	Created - bin\BiteTheBullet.DNN.Modules.BTBRating.dll
Info	Assembly registered - bin\BiteTheBullet.DNN.Modules.BTBRating.SqlDataProvider.dll
Info	Created - bin\BiteTheBullet.DNN.Modules.BTBRating.SqlDataProvider.dll
Info	Component installed successfully - Assembly

Figure 5-19

Host File Manager

The Host, File Manager is very similar to Admin, File Manager except for the location of the files, which would be the Host Root for the host location. You can Add or Delete Folders at this location along with Move Files, Copy Files, Upload Files, or Delete Files. You would upload skins and containers under Host, Skins or Host Extensions and upload modules under Host, Module Definition or Host Extensions. See Figure 5-20.

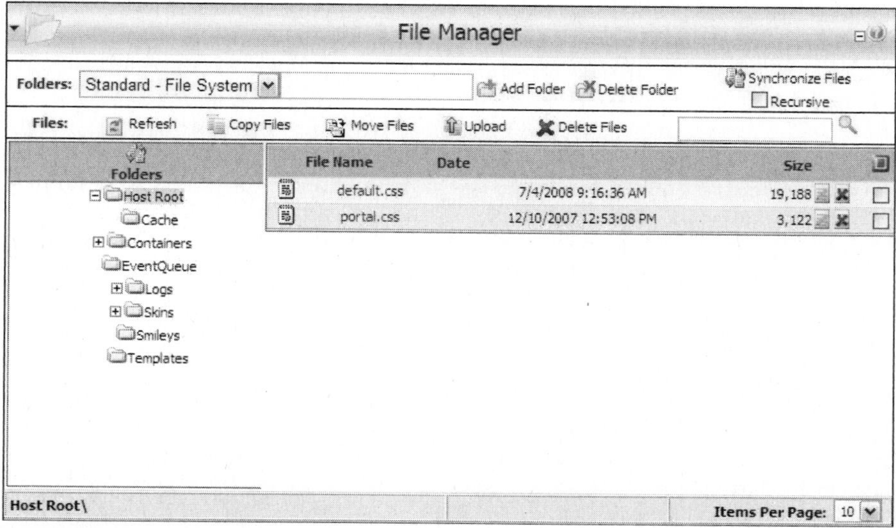

Figure 5-20

Host Vendors

Just like the vendor list that was created with Admin, Vendors, the Host can create its own vendors list for banner ads. The big difference is that with the Admin, Vendors list, each portal administrator can manage the vendors list within their own portal.

If you have the need to manage vendors for all your portals with your DotNetNuke installation, you would create them under this option. One benefit of creating this list under Host is that you can choose to display banners under Host or Site.

Host SQL

The Host SQL page (see Figure 5-21) is a great utility built into your portal. Here you can process simple queries and return results in a tabular format. You can execute compound SQL queries and update queries when you select the Run As Script check box.

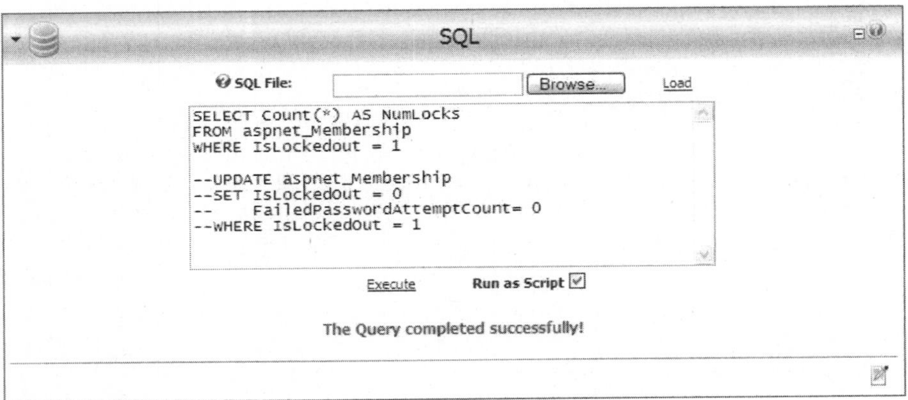

Figure 5-21

Figure 5-21 illustrates a couple of handy queries for managing user accounts locked out by the Member-Role Provider due to invalid password attempts. Although this can be accomplished on a user basis on each portal's User Page (or by waiting 10 minutes), the query method can unlock all users in all portals with one query and is a convenient example.

Host Schedule

Here you can see the services of batch processing of DotNetNuke tasks whereby the Scheduler lists each particular job along with information about whether that job is Enabled, the Frequency, Retry Time Lapse, and Next Start. See Figure 5-22.

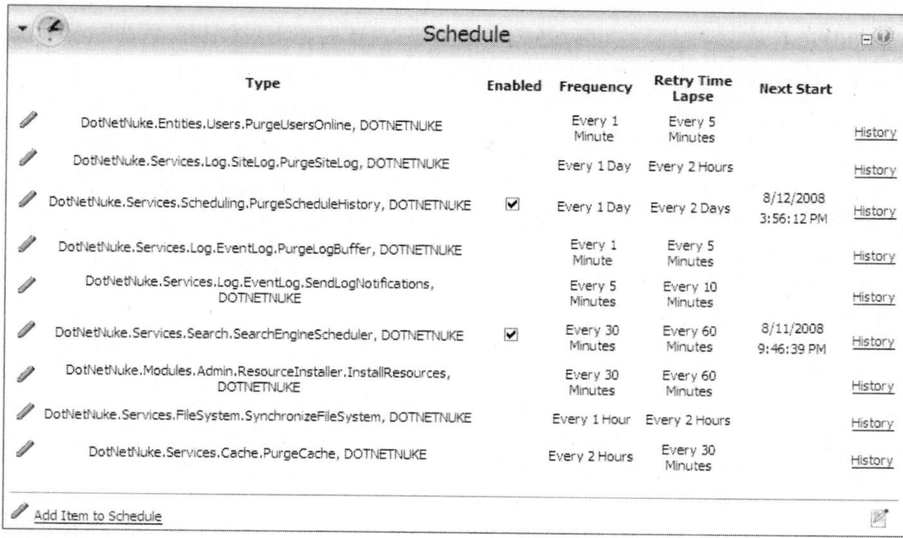

Schedule

Type	Enabled	Frequency	Retry Time Lapse	Next Start	
DotNetNuke.Entities.Users.PurgeUsersOnline, DOTNETNUKE		Every 1 Minute	Every 5 Minutes		History
DotNetNuke.Services.Log.SiteLog.PurgeSiteLog, DOTNETNUKE		Every 1 Day	Every 2 Hours		History
DotNetNuke.Services.Scheduling.PurgeScheduleHistory, DOTNETNUKE	☑	Every 1 Day	Every 2 Days	8/12/2008 3:56:12 PM	History
DotNetNuke.Services.Log.EventLog.PurgeLogBuffer, DOTNETNUKE		Every 1 Minute	Every 5 Minutes		History
DotNetNuke.Services.Log.EventLog.SendLogNotifications, DOTNETNUKE		Every 5 Minutes	Every 10 Minutes		History
DotNetNuke.Services.Search.SearchEngineScheduler, DOTNETNUKE	☑	Every 30 Minutes	Every 60 Minutes	8/11/2008 9:46:39 PM	History
DotNetNuke.Modules.Admin.ResourceInstaller.InstallResources, DOTNETNUKE		Every 30 Minutes	Every 60 Minutes		History
DotNetNuke.Services.FileSystem.SynchronizeFileSystem, DOTNETNUKE		Every 1 Hour	Every 2 Hours		History
DotNetNuke.Services.Cache.PurgeCache, DOTNETNUKE		Every 2 Hours	Every 30 Minutes		History

Add Item to Schedule

Figure 5-22

You can view the history of any of the jobs. See Figure 5-23.

Description	Duration (seconds)	Succeeded	Start/End/Next Start
DotNetNuke.Services.Search.SearchEngineScheduler, DOTNETNUKE Completed re-indexing content	1.13	True	S: 8/12/2008 3:48:39 PM E: 8/12/2008 3:48:40 PM N: 8/12/2008 4:18:39 PM
DotNetNuke.Services.Search.SearchEngineScheduler, DOTNETNUKE Completed re-indexing content	0.71	True	S: 8/11/2008 9:16:39 PM E: 8/11/2008 9:16:40 PM N: 8/11/2008 9:46:39 PM
DotNetNuke.Services.Search.SearchEngineScheduler, DOTNETNUKE Completed re-indexing content	4.173	True	S: 8/11/2008 8:43:12 PM E: 8/11/2008 8:43:16 PM N: 8/11/2008 9:13:12 PM
DotNetNuke.Services.Search.SearchEngineScheduler, DOTNETNUKE Completed re-indexing content	13.59	True	S: 8/11/2008 7:55:04 PM E: 8/11/2008 7:55:18 PM N: 8/11/2008 8:25:04 PM
DotNetNuke.Services.Search.SearchEngineScheduler, DOTNETNUKE Completed re-indexing content	1.1	True	S: 8/11/2008 6:12:28 PM E: 8/11/2008 6:12:29 PM N: 8/11/2008 6:42:28 PM
DotNetNuke.Services.Search.SearchEngineScheduler, DOTNETNUKE Completed re-indexing content	3.974	True	S: 8/11/2008 5:12:51 PM E: 8/11/2008 5:12:55 PM N: 8/11/2008 5:42:51 PM
DotNetNuke.Services.Search.SearchEngineScheduler, DOTNETNUKE Completed re-indexing content	0.6	True	S: 8/11/2008 4:26:53 PM E: 8/11/2008 4:26:54 PM N: 8/11/2008 4:56:53 PM
DotNetNuke.Services.Search.SearchEngineScheduler, DOTNETNUKE Completed re-indexing content	11.087	True	S: 8/11/2008 3:56:12 PM E: 8/11/2008 3:56:24 PM N: 8/11/2008 4:26:12 PM

Figure 5-23

Schedule Item Details

Click the pencil icon to edit any item; that opens the Edit Schedule page. See Figure 5-24.

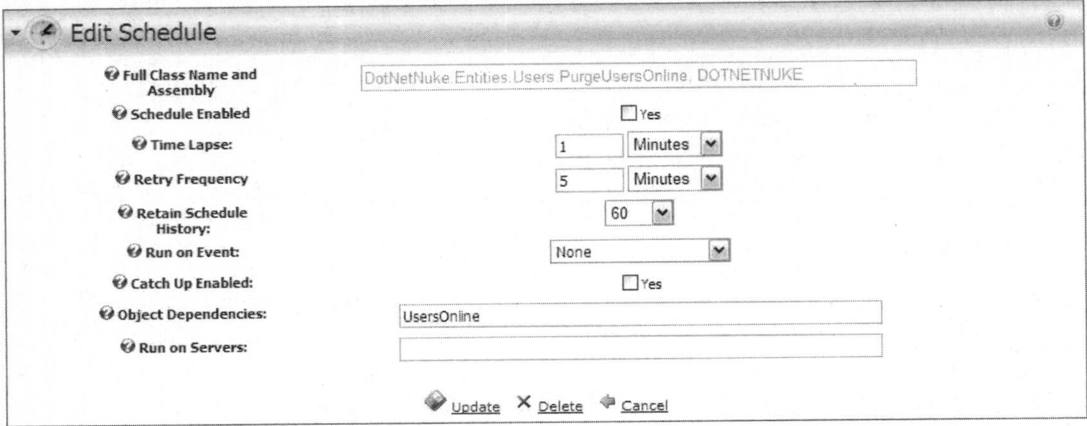

Figure 5-24

Table 5-8 reviews each of the schedule item settings in detail. Setting changes take effect immediately.

Schedule Status

You can view the schedule status by clicking the down arrow icon beside the clock image. See Figure 5-25.

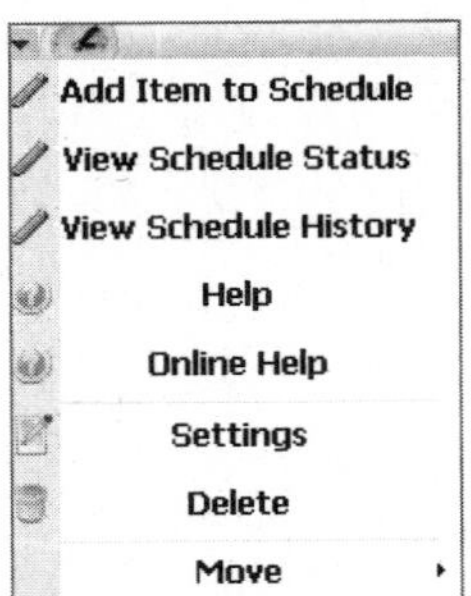

Figure 5-25

The Schedule Status page shows a detailed view of the current state of the Scheduler and running or pending jobs. See Figure 5-26.

There are two display areas on this page: Items Processing and Items In Queue. If you refresh while watching the Time Remaining run down to 0 for a specific item, you may catch it actually in execution, which is when it displays the Items In Processing area.

Command buttons at the top of the page enable you to Stop/Start the Scheduler if necessary. This suspends the execution of the jobs although the timers continue to run. Note that these buttons are not enabled if the Scheduler is running under the Request Method.

Table 5-8: Edit Schedule Settings

Setting	Description
Full Class Name and Assembly	This is the full class name followed by the assembly name. Example: `DotNetNuke.Entities.Users.PurgeUsersOnline`, DOTNETNUKE Installing a component (or module) may actually create a Scheduler item for you rather than relying on you to create it yourself. Read the instructions carefully for any modules or components you install.
Schedule Enabled	This will enable or disable the schedule item.
Time Lapse	This will set the frequency for running the item by minutes.
Retry Frequency	This will set the retry frequency for running the item by minutes.
Retain Schedule History	Each time a scheduled item is run, its success/fail status and a number of other useful information items are logged. You can set the most recent schedule history rows. Sixty is set by default.
Run on Event	You have the option to run on an event rather than a schedule. Select Application Start to run this event when the web application starts. Note: events run on APPLICATION_END may not run reliably on some hosts.
Catch Up Enabled	When this feature is activated, if the web server ever goes out of service, then when the web server comes back into service, this event will run once for each frequency that was missed during that downtime.
Object Dependencies	When the Scheduler Mode is set to the Timer Method in the Host Settings, it executes as a multithreaded process. This requires some method of protection against possible deadlock conditions for simultaneously running threads. This field provides for the specification of one or more comma-separated string values that serve as semaphores to avoid deadlock. For example, if one scheduled item performs a select on the Users table, and another item performs a massive update on the Users table, you might want to prevent these two items from running at the same time. So both items should have an object dependency on the same string value (for example "LockUsersTable"). The dependency suppresses the start of any other items until the currently running item has finished.
Run on Servers	When you're running a web farm environment, it may be necessary to limit the instances of any given scheduled process. If this comma-delimited field is empty, a server runs the process only if it finds a match on its server name. Using this method, a web farm can be configured to prevent multiple web servers from attempting the same database operation at the same time. Redundancy can be preserved by configuring the same processes to run on different servers on complementary schedules.

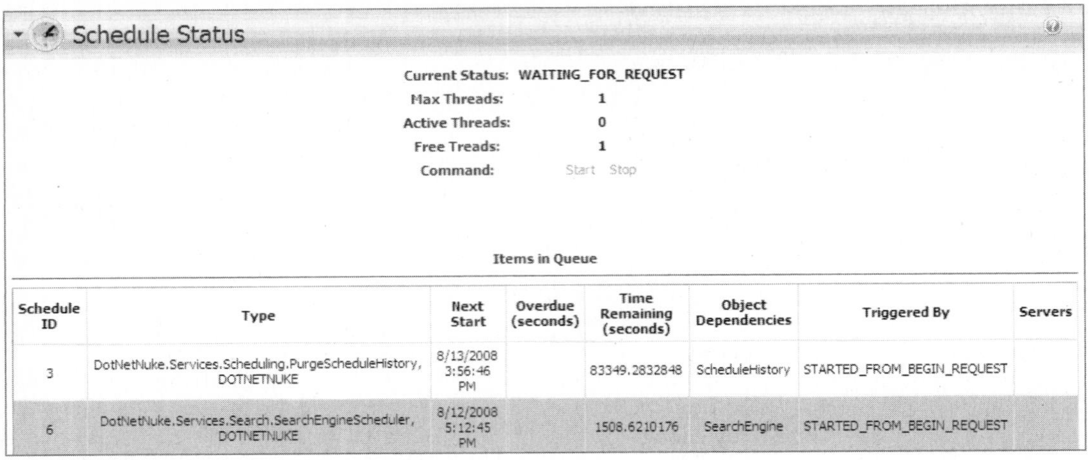

Schedule Status

Current Status: WAITING_FOR_REQUEST
Max Threads: 1
Active Threads: 0
Free Treads: 1
Command: Start Stop

Items in Queue

Schedule ID	Type	Next Start	Overdue (seconds)	Time Remaining (seconds)	Object Dependencies	Triggered By	Servers
3	DotNetNuke.Services.Scheduling.PurgeScheduleHistory, DOTNETNUKE	8/13/2008 3:56:46 PM		83349.2832848	ScheduleHistory	STARTED_FROM_BEGIN_REQUEST	
6	DotNetNuke.Services.Search.SearchEngineScheduler, DOTNETNUKE	8/12/2008 5:12:45 PM		1508.6210176	SearchEngine	STARTED_FROM_BEGIN_REQUEST	

Figure 5-26

Configuration

The Scheduler has a couple of useful settings that can be manipulated in the application's web.config file. To locate these settings, look for the section that resembles the following code. The effects of these settings are summarized in Table 5-9.

```
<scheduling defaultProvider="DNNScheduler">
      <providers>
        <clear />
        <add name="DNNScheduler"
type="DotNetNuke.Services.Scheduling.DNNScheduling.DNNScheduler,
                                        DotNetNuke.DNNScheduler"

providerPath="~\Providers\SchedulingProviders\DNNScheduler\"
                                        debug="false" maxThreads="1" />
      </providers>
    </scheduling>
```

Table 5-9: Schedule Provider Configuration Settings

Settings	Description
Debug	When this is set to "true," a lot of log file entries are generated that help in debugging Scheduler-related development (that is, developing your own Scheduler items). Debugging multithreaded applications is always a challenge. This is one setting that can help you figure out why a particular task is or is not being run.
maxThreads	This specifies the maximum number of threads to use for the Scheduler (when in Timer Method); -1 is the default value, which means "leave it up to the Scheduler to figure out." If you specify a value greater than 0, the Scheduler uses that number as the maximum number of thread pools.

Considerations

One limitation of the Timer Method mode of the Scheduler is that it cannot run 24/7 without help from an external program, the ASP.NET worker process. This is a constraint of ASP.NET, not of DotNetNuke. The web site's worker process periodically recycles according to settings in IIS or machine.config. Some hosts may have settings that recycle the worker process every 30 minutes, which is forced, whereas others may have more complicated settings, such as recycling the worker processes after 3000 web site hits, or after 20 minutes of inactivity. It is this recycling of the worker process that shuts down the Scheduler until the worker process is started again (by someone hitting the web site, which in turn starts up the worker process, starting up the Scheduler as well).

This functionality is actually a major benefit to web applications as a whole in a hosted environment, because it keeps runaway applications from taking the server down, but it isn't without drawbacks.

The bottom line is that the Scheduler will run 24/7 in the Timer Method mode as long as someone is visiting your web site frequently enough to keep the worker process active. It is during periods of inactivity that the worker process could possibly shut down. It is for this reason that you should carefully plan the types of tasks you schedule. Make sure that they are not time critical; that is, they don't have to run "every night at midnight" and so on. A more suitable task is one that runs "once per day" or "once every few minutes," and doesn't mind if it's not run during periods of inactivity.

The Request Method does not have the same dependency on the ASP.NET worker process; however, it is entirely dependent upon the timing of visitors to your web site. During periods of inactivity on your web site, scheduled jobs do not run.

Host Languages

One of the reasons why DotNetNuke has been so successful around the world has been the fact that the Core Team implemented a localization framework to allow for different languages, time zones, currencies, and express times and dates.

DotNetNuke includes a multi-language localization feature that allows administrators to translate their projects and portals into any language. With an international group of hosts and developers working with DotNetNuke, native support is always close at hand. You can find several language packs located on the dotnetnuke.com site.

Hover your mouse over the down arrow icon beside the word Languages to view the commands. The commands are Install Language Pack, Create Language Pack, Time Zone Editor, and Resource Verifier.

Installing a New Language Pack

Click Install New Language Pack.

Browse to the downloaded zip file and click Add. Click Upload New File. You should now see a log with the details of the import. Click the Return link at the bottom of the log and you should now see your installed package. If you click the pencil icon for the Default Language (see Figure 5-27) it will take you to the Extension Settings.

This editor allows you to configure the language pack. You can set the name of the pack as well as a fallback language to use if the resource is not available in this pack. To edit the language files in this pack, click the Edit Language Files button to take you to the Language Editor module. See Figure 5-28.

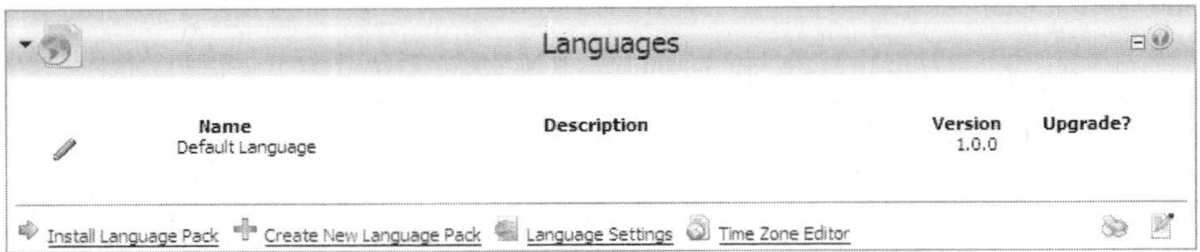

Figure 5-27

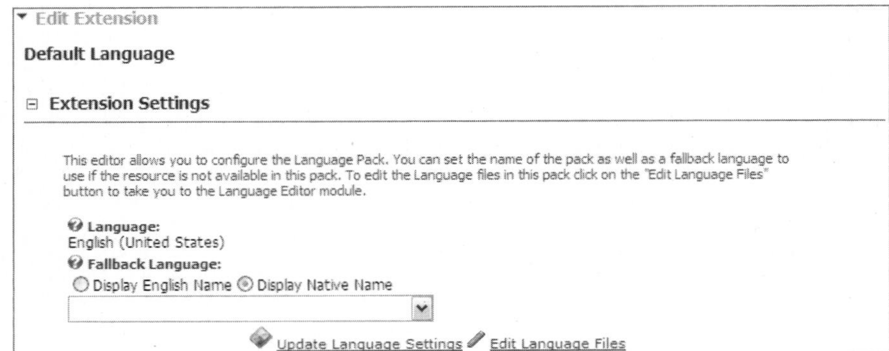

Figure 5-28

You can edit the language files by clicking the link. You are now in the Language Editor. If the Portal Administrator edits a resource file, it will override all resources loaded from the default resource file. Even if the Host subsequently makes changes to the same set of resource strings, these changes will not be reflected in the portal, which has its own copy of the original resources. See Figure 5-29.

You can personalize your email welcome to your new portal registrants. The tokens used to edit are covered in more detail in Chapter 11, "Localization."

Globalization

Globalizing an application requires more than just having content appear in a specific language. Another aspect of globalizing an application requires that the application understand the time zone of the current user. If the server logs show that a critical event happened at 1:00 AM, what does that really mean? If you are in Germany and the web server is in Texas, what time did the event happen? To solve this problem, DotNetNuke stores all time in Universal Time Coordinated (UTC) format. Each user can associate a TimeZone with his or her profile. This setting is used to localize the time for the current user. See Figure 5-30.

You can view the Language Settings by clicking on the link. See Figure 5-31.

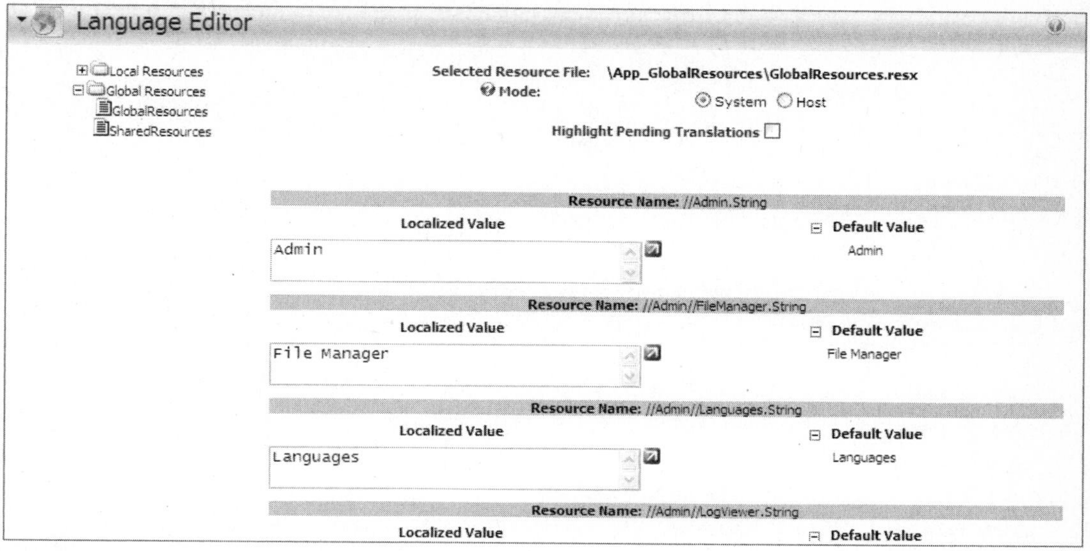

Language Editor

Local Resources
Global Resources
GlobalResources
SharedResources

Selected Resource File: \App_GlobalResources\GlobalResources.resx
Mode: System Host
Highlight Pending Translations

Resource Name: //Admin.String
Localized Value: Admin
Default Value: Admin

Resource Name: //Admin//FileManager.String
Localized Value: File Manager
Default Value: File Manager

Resource Name: //Admin//Languages.String
Localized Value: Languages
Default Value: Languages

Resource Name: //Admin//LogViewer.String
Localized Value
Default Value

Figure 5-29

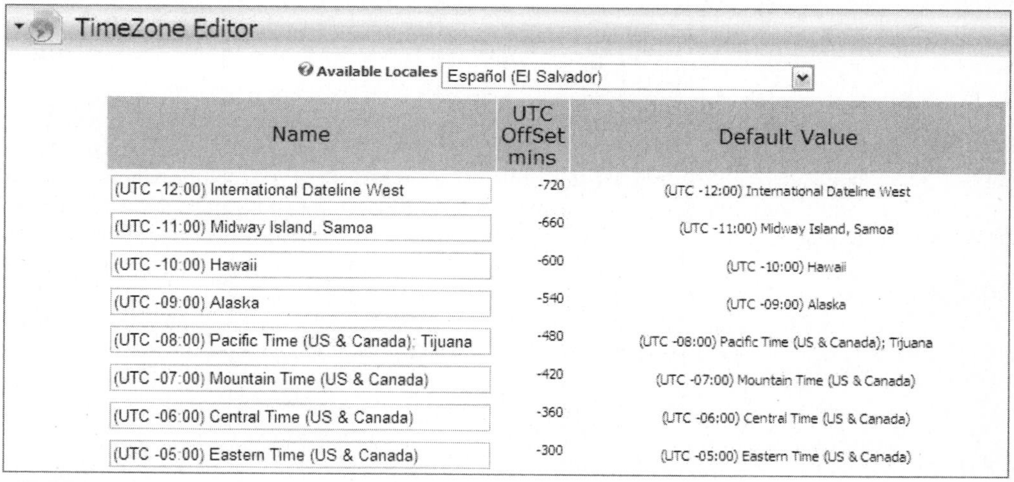

TimeZone Editor

Available Locales: Español (El Salvador)

Name	UTC OffSet mins	Default Value
(UTC -12:00) International Dateline West	-720	(UTC -12:00) International Dateline West
(UTC -11:00) Midway Island, Samoa	-660	(UTC -11:00) Midway Island, Samoa
(UTC -10:00) Hawaii	-600	(UTC -10:00) Hawaii
(UTC -09:00) Alaska	-540	(UTC -09:00) Alaska
(UTC -08:00) Pacific Time (US & Canada); Tijuana	-480	(UTC -08:00) Pacific Time (US & Canada); Tijuana
(UTC -07:00) Mountain Time (US & Canada)	-420	(UTC -07:00) Mountain Time (US & Canada)
(UTC -06:00) Central Time (US & Canada)	-360	(UTC -06:00) Central Time (US & Canada)
(UTC -05:00) Eastern Time (US & Canada)	-300	(UTC -05:00) Eastern Time (US & Canada)

Figure 5-30

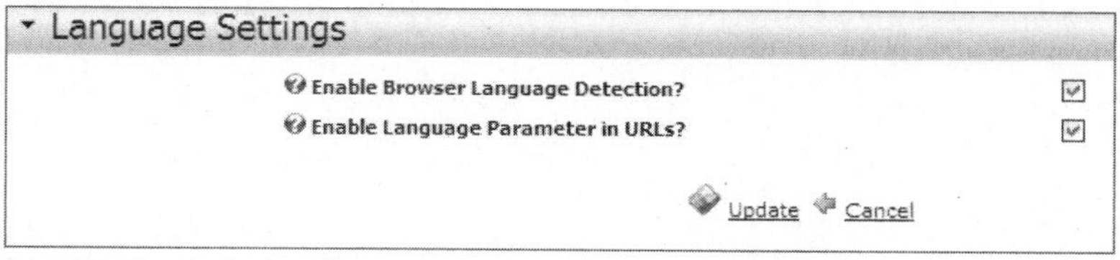

Language Settings

Enable Browser Language Detection?
Enable Language Parameter in URLs?

Update Cancel

Figure 5-31

The Resource File Verifier allows you to compare any new language pack installed to the default language, which is English United States. After you verify the files, you'll be able to view any missing resource files and any missing or obsolete entries.

Finally, you can create a language pack at Host, Languages. See Figure 5-32.

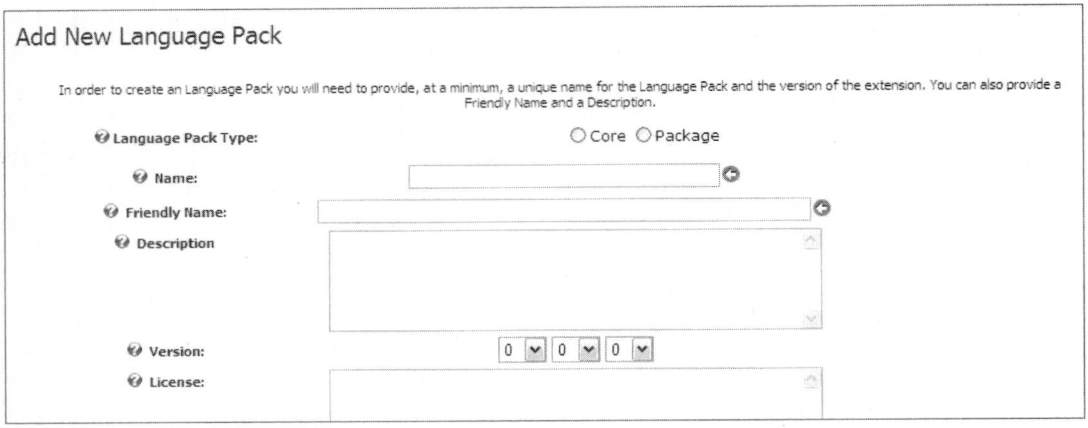

Add New Language Pack

In order to create an Language Pack you will need to provide, at a minimum, a unique name for the Language Pack and the version of the extension. You can also provide a Friendly Name and a Description.

Language Pack Type: Core Package

Name:

Friendly Name:

Description

Version: 0 0 0

License:

Figure 5-32

Host Search Admin

This Search Admin allows the Portal Administrator to change some of the default setting of the search engine for the DotNetNuke web portal. You can change the Maximum and Minimum word length, which helps to prevent you from indexing unreasonable terms. If you deselect Include Common Words, the search engine won't bother indexing words that exist in the Search Common Words database table. That table has the capability to create common word entries for each locale (for Multilanguage customization), although only the English language common words are included by default. You can choose to Include Numbers or to ignore them when content is indexed.

Finally, the changes that are made in Search Admin make changes to your entire portal. See Figure 5-33.

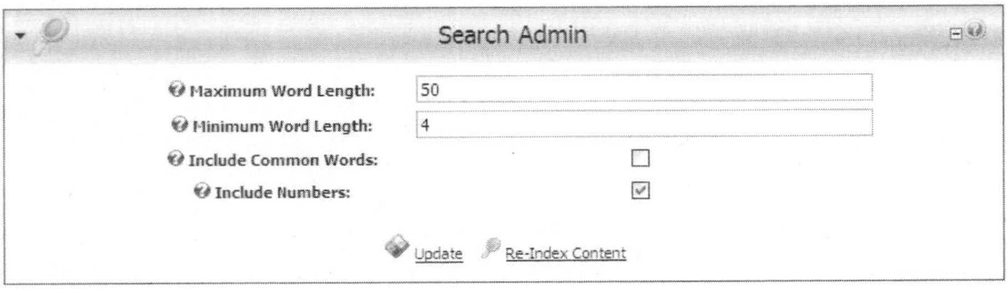

Search Admin

Maximum Word Length: 50

Minimum Word Length: 4

Include Common Words:

Include Numbers:

Update Re-Index Content

Figure 5-33

Host Lists

This setting enables the Portal Administration to manage the content of lists. There are several lists, such as Country, Currency, Data Type, Frequency, Processor, and Site Log Reports. See Figure 5-34.

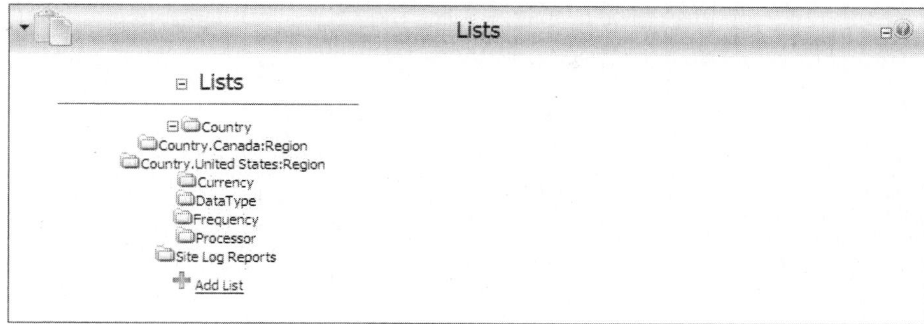

Figure 5-34

To add to the list, you simply click + Add List. You can add to the Country List by keying Region for List Name and then select Country from the drop-down list. The Parent Entry will be Country:Mexico for this example and the Entry Text and Entry Value will be Mexico City. Click Save. See Figure 5-35.

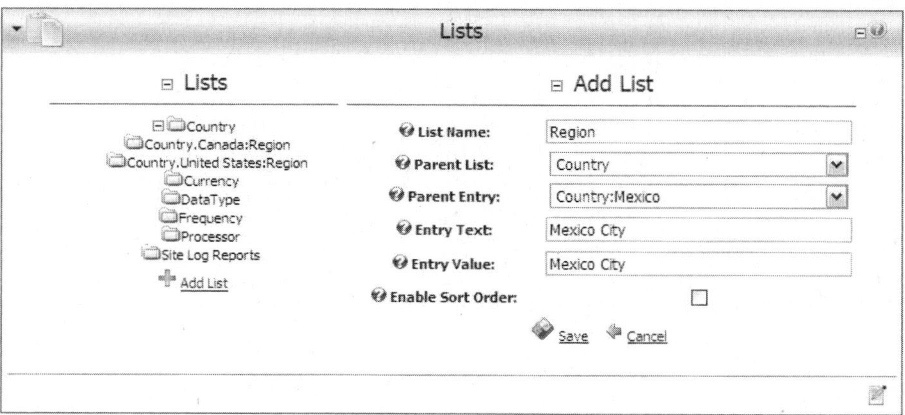

Figure 5-35

Now you will be able to see the new entry for the Country list called Country.Mexico.Region. See Figure 5-36.

Deleting or editing some of the default lists may result in an error. For example, if you remove an entry from the Site Log Reports list, it would prevent the Portal Administrators from ever running that report on their portal. In addition, adding to the list may cause errors.

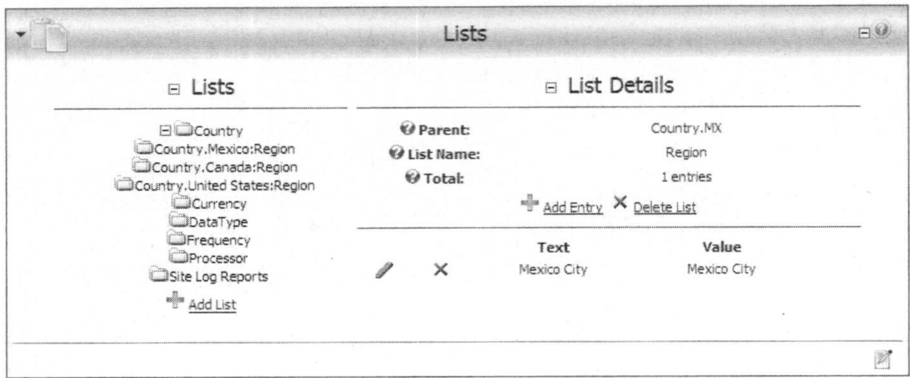

Figure 5-36

Host SuperUser Accounts

Here you can add a new host account to your DotNetNuke web portal or manage existing users. See Figure 5-37.

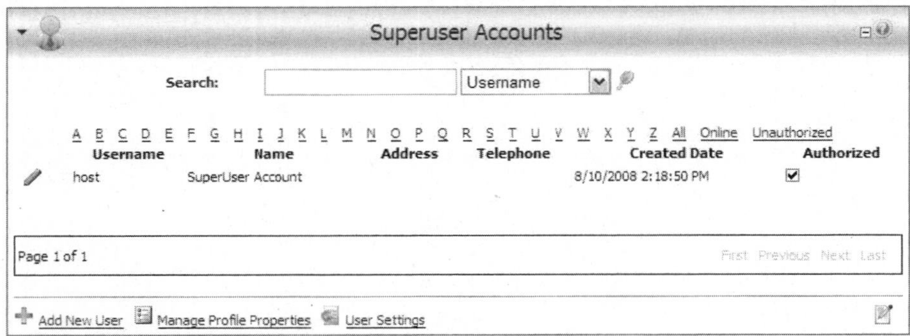

Figure 5-37

To add a new user, click + Add New User. You will be taken to the Add New User page, shown in Figure 5-38, where you will enter the User Name, First Name, Last Name, Display Name, and Email Address. If you don't want to email the person, you can deselect the Notify check box, but you need to Authorize that user to be a SuperUser Host user. Now enter a password, confirm the password, and click Add New User.

You can also Manage Profile Properties. See Figure 5-39. You can make changes to what information from the user that you want. This feature is also located under Admin, User Accounts.

You can delete fields, rearrange them, and add new fields as well.

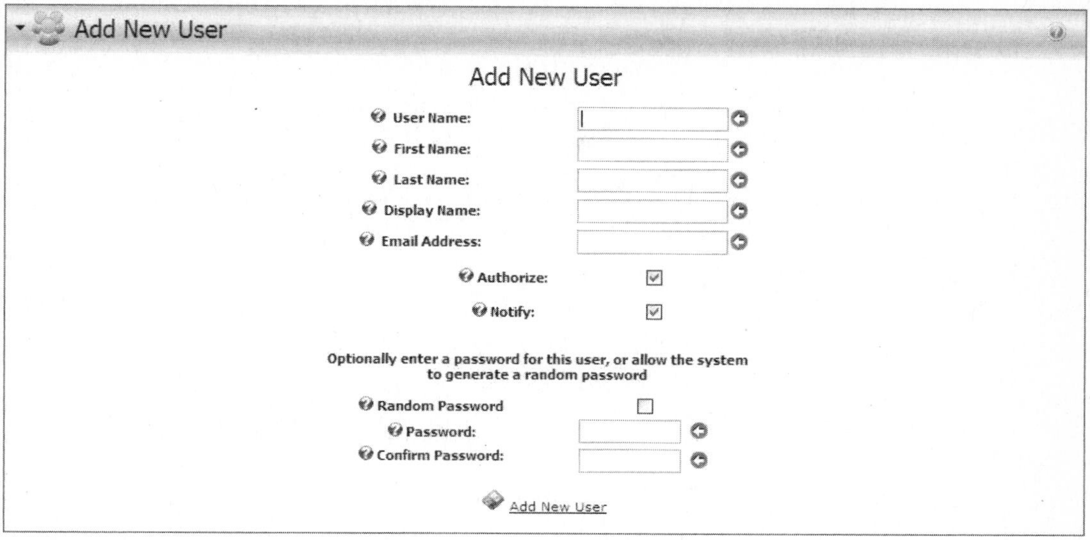

Figure 5-38

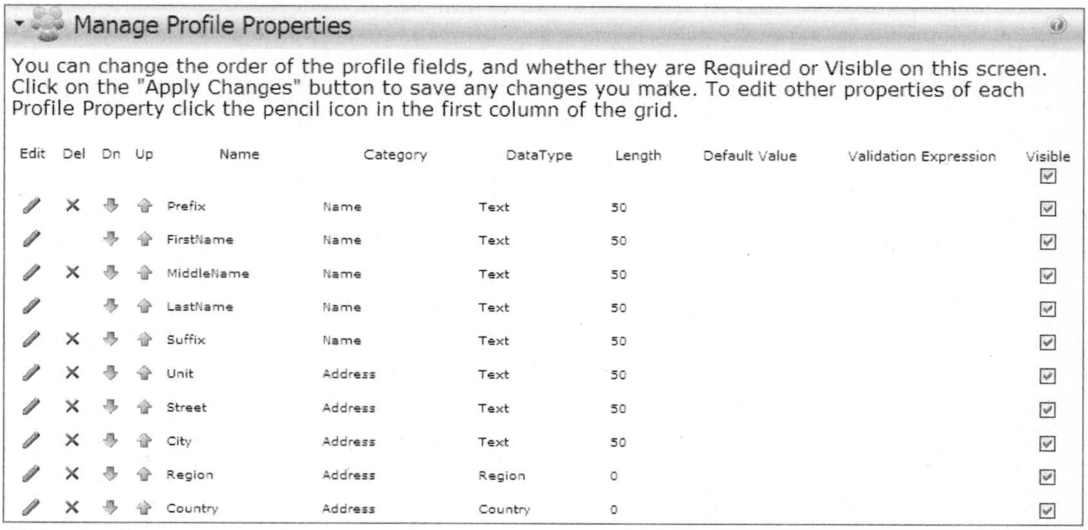

Edit	Del	Dn	Up	Name	Category	DataType	Length	Default Value	Validation Expression	Visible
				Prefix	Name	Text	50			
				FirstName	Name	Text	50			
				MiddleName	Name	Text	50			
				LastName	Name	Text	50			
				Suffix	Name	Text	50			
				Unit	Address	Text	50			
				Street	Address	Text	50			
				City	Address	Text	50			
				Region	Address	Region	0			
				Country	Address	Country	0			

Figure 5-39

You change User Settings like with Admin, User Accounts. There are three sections on the User Settings page. In the Member Provider Settings (Figure 5-40) section, you can review the membership provider's settings. Some providers may allow you to edit the settings. The default provider based on the ASP.NET MemberRole requires you to edit the web.config file, so the settings cannot be updated here.

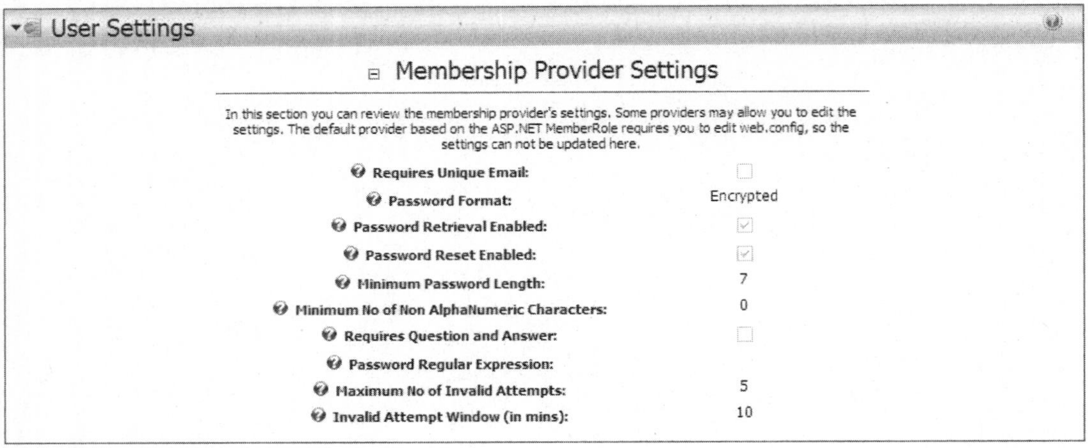

User Settings

Membership Provider Settings

In this section you can review the membership provider's settings. Some providers may allow you to edit the settings. The default provider based on the ASP.NET MemberRole requires you to edit web.config, so the settings can not be updated here.

Requires Unique Email:	☐
Password Format:	Encrypted
Password Retrieval Enabled:	☑
Password Reset Enabled:	☑
Minimum Password Length:	7
Minimum No of Non AlphaNumeric Characters:	0
Requires Question and Answer:	☐
Password Regular Expression:	
Maximum No of Invalid Attempts:	5
Invalid Attempt Window (in mins):	10

Figure 5-40

The next section is the Password Aging Settings. See Figure 5-41. You can set up Password aging settings here for number of days for Password Expiry and Password Expiry Reminder.

Password Aging Settings

You can set up Password aging settings in this section.

Password Expiry (in days):	0
Password Expiry Reminder (in days):	7

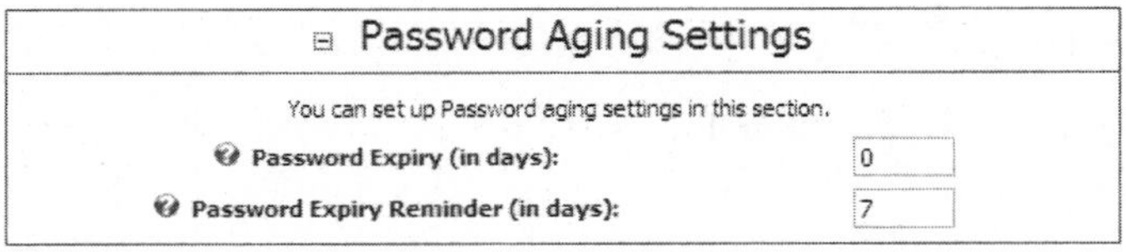

Figure 5-41

The last section is for User Account Settings. See Figure 5-42. A number of settings here can be changed depending on how you want to view the host account.

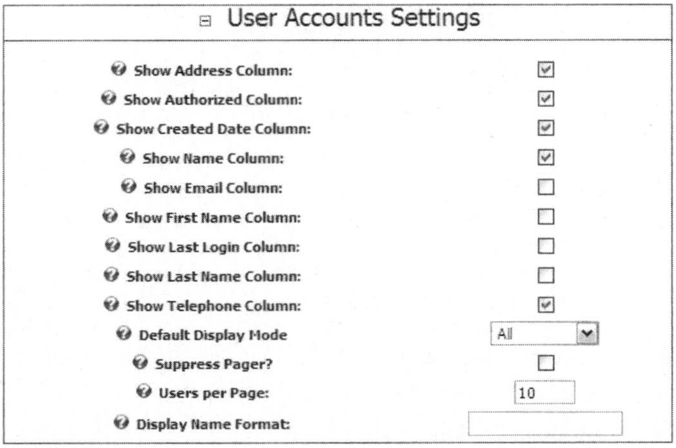

User Accounts Settings

Show Address Column:	☑
Show Authorized Column:	☑
Show Created Date Column:	☑
Show Name Column:	☑
Show Email Column:	☐
Show First Name Column:	☐
Show Last Login Column:	☐
Show Last Name Column:	☐
Show Telephone Column:	☑
Default Display Mode	All
Suppress Pager?	☐
Users per Page:	10
Display Name Format:	

Figure 5-42

For example, by default the Show Address, Authorized, Created Date, and Show Name Column are selected. See Figure 5-43.

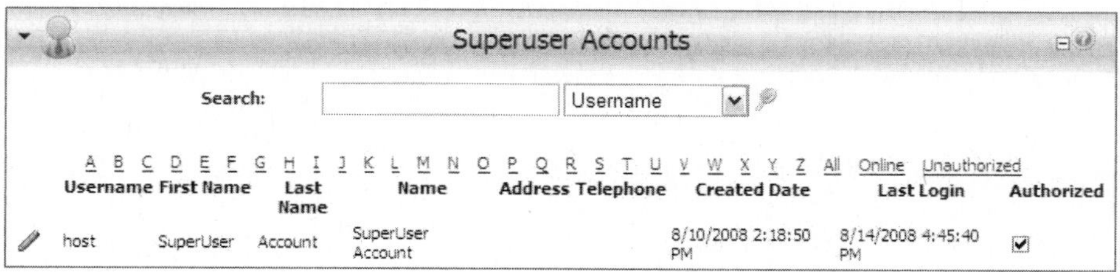

Figure 5-43

You have the control to show more information if you want by selecting the check boxes. You can change the Default Display Mode and show more users per page as well. If you don't want to number the first page, you can click Suppress Pager. For the Display Name Format, you can specify a format for the user's display name. The format can include tokens for dynamic substitution suck as [FIRSTNAME] [LASTNAME]. If a display name format is specified, the display name will no longer be editable through the user interface.

Host Skins

There are many options at this location for you to make regarding the skins and containers for your site. Chapter 16, "Skinning DotNetNuke," covers the topic of skinning in much more detail. This section only does an overview. See Figure 5-44.

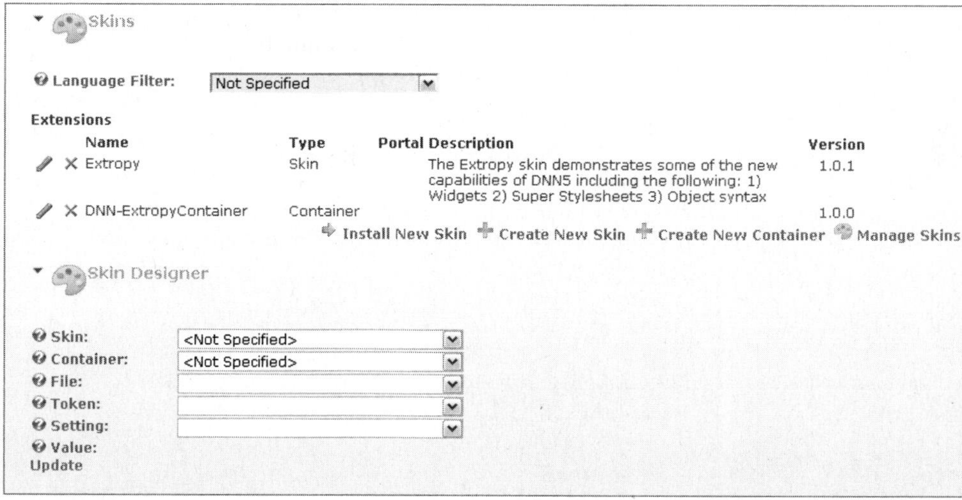

Figure 5-44

First, you can see the list of default skins that are installed on your portal. You can click Manage Skins to get a thumbnail view of these skins and containers. See Figure 5-45.

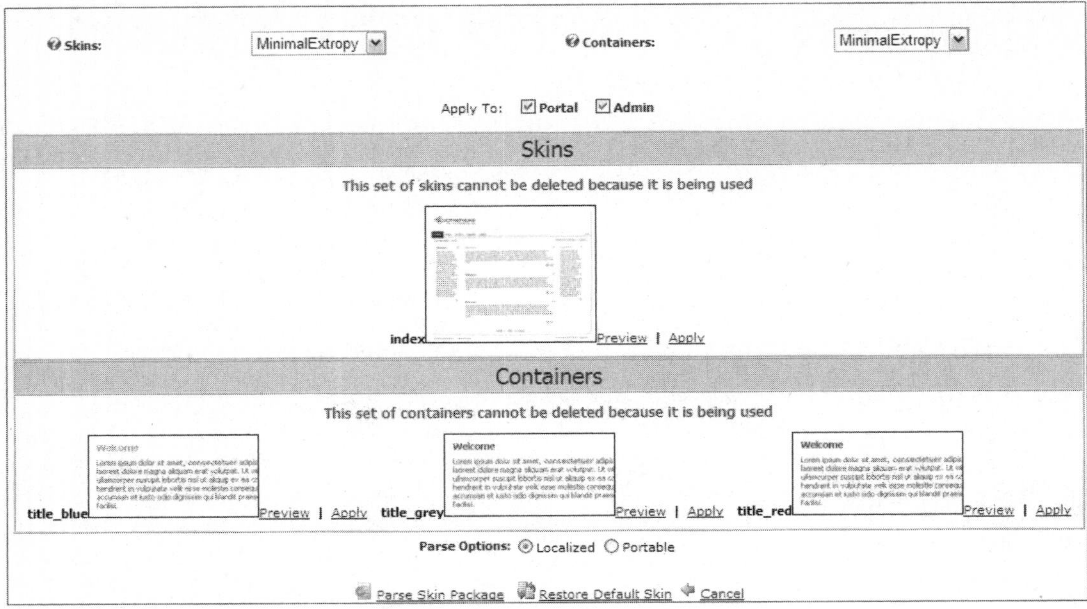

Figure 5-45

You can select a new skin and container from the drop-down list and preview both and then click Apply To Portal or Admin. Your Admin pages can have a different skin by simply selecting the skin from the drop-down list and clicking Apply To Admin.

If you modify an existing skin, you can parse the skin with the Parse Skin Package link. You can select Localized for the parse, which will include the full path, or Portable, which does not include the full path.

Finally, you can restore the default skin at this location.

Create New Skin

In order to create a skin you will need to provide, at a minimum, a unique name for the skin and the version of the skin. You can also provide a Friendly Name, Description, Version, License, Release Notes, Owner, Organization, URL, and Email address.

See Figure 5-46.

After the skin is created, it will be listed with all the other skins. See Figure 5-47.

Install New Skin

DotNetNuke can be extended in many ways. This wizard helps you upload and install DotNetNuke packages. The first step is to select the package you wish to install on your local computer. This is covered in full detail in Chapter 16 Skinning DotNetNuke.

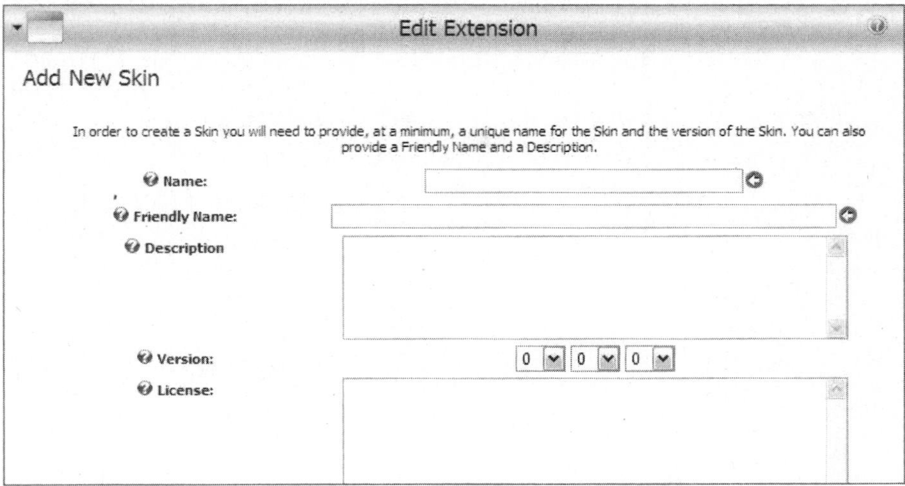

Figure 5-46

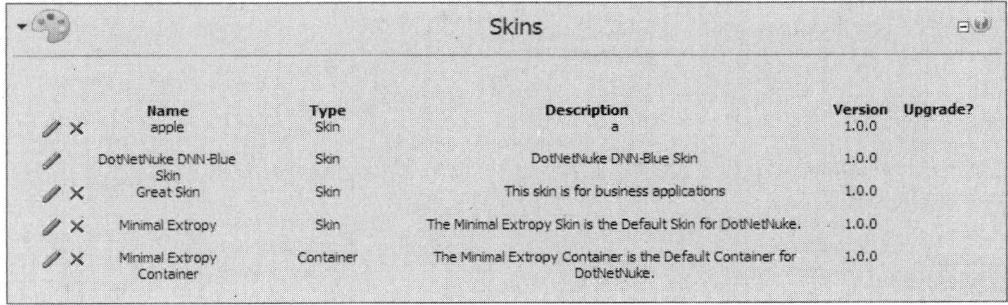

Figure 5-47

Finally, the Skin Designer enables you to set the value for a specific skin or container token and setting.

Host Extensions

Just like what you saw with Admin Extensions, the Host Extensions give a similar view with more to see. By default, you see the Authentication System, Container, Core Language Pack, Extension Language Pack, Library, Module, Provider, and Skin and Skin Objects.

If you only want to see a specific extension type, you can select that type from the drop-down list. See Figure 5-48.

Authentication SystemDotNetNuke allows you to have Windows Live and Open ID authentication systems. This allows your users to log in to your portal with their existing username and password. See Figure 5-49.

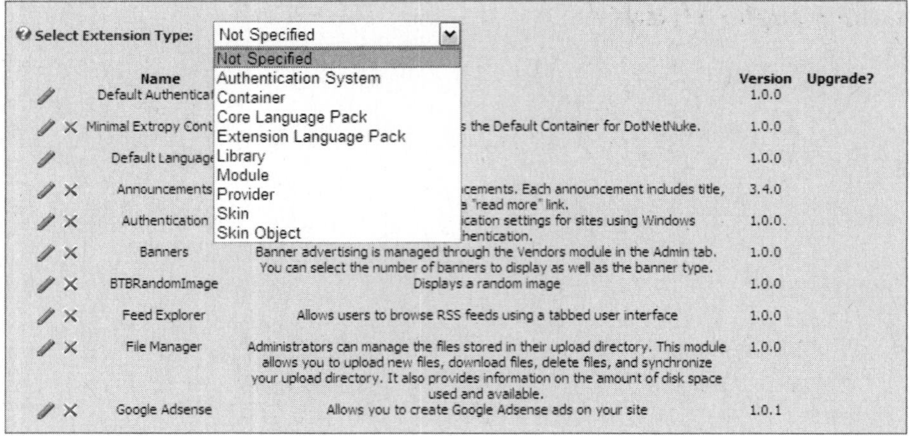

Figure 5-48

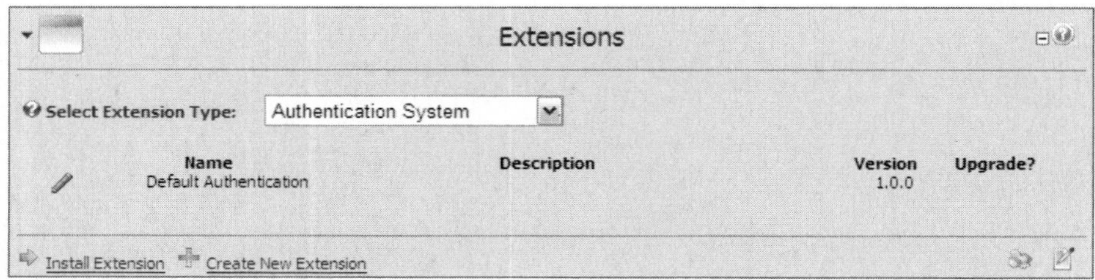

Figure 5-49

Container

Any containers that you have installed can be viewed at this location. Any legacy containers can be viewed at Host, Skins, Manage Skins. See Figure 5-50.

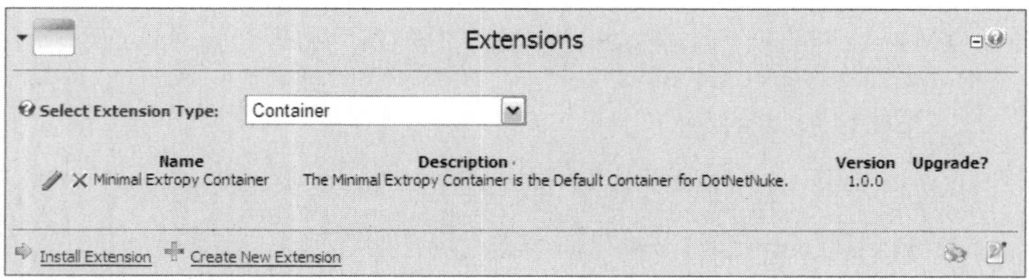

Figure 5-50

Core Language Pack

Here you will see the language packs that have been installed on your portal. You can search the DotNetNuke site for more language packs to install on your portal. See Figure 5-51.

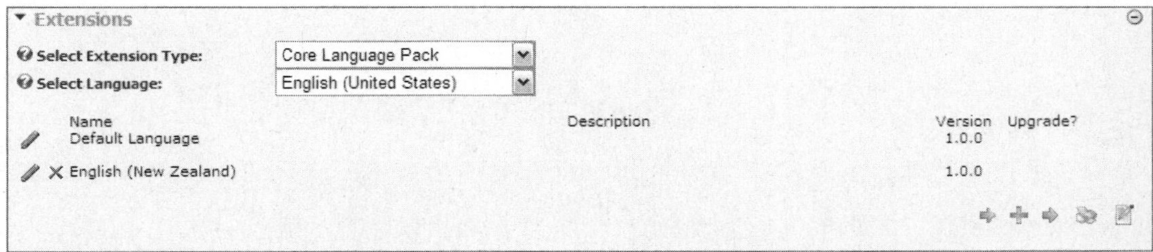

Figure 5-51

Extension Language Pack

At this location, you can use the Install Extension Wizard, Create New Extension, or Batch Install Extensions. See Figure 5-52.

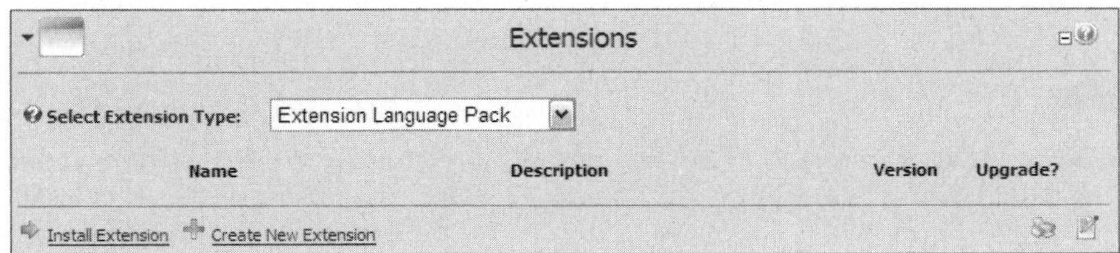

Figure 5-52

Library

A Library package type would be an assembly that might be shared by other extensions. For example, a set of controls compiled into an assembly might be used by multiple modules. These could now be separately installed and managed. See Figure 5-53.

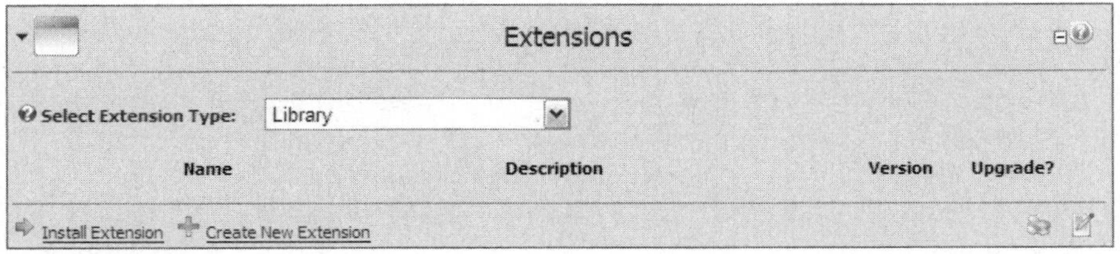

Figure 5-53

Module

A list of all installed modules are listed with their description. See Figure 5-54.

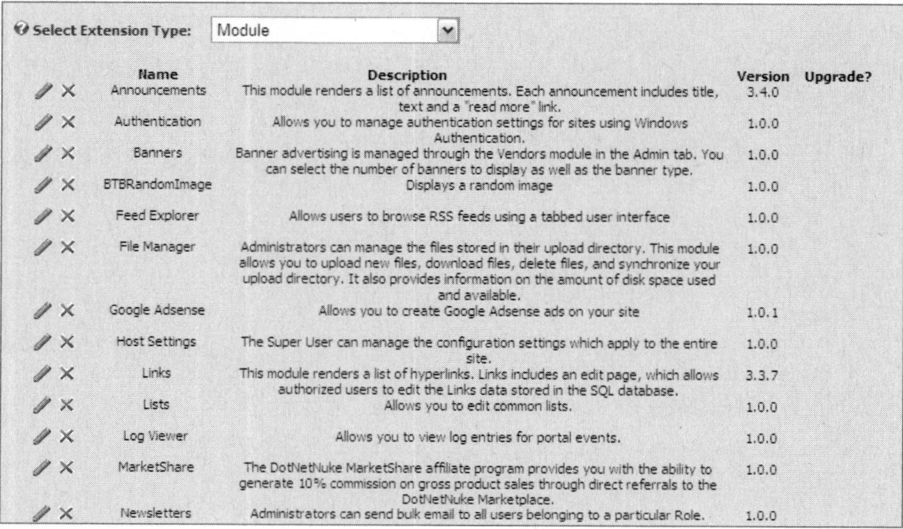

Figure 5-54

Provider

A provider is a contract between an API and the business logic that establishes the functionality that the implementation of the API must provide. You can view the installed providers here. See Figure 5-55.

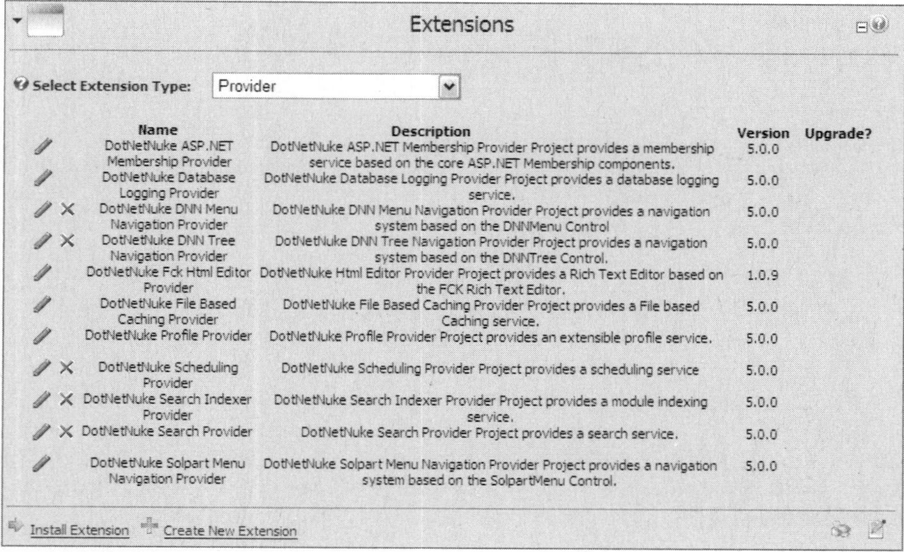

Figure 5-55

Skin

All installed skins are listed here. Skins are covered in more detail in Chapter 16. See Figure 5-56.

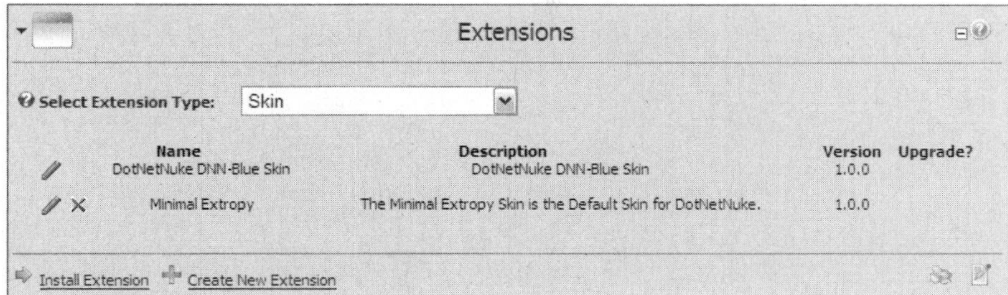

Figure 5-56

Skin Object

All skin objects used in skinning are listed at this location. See Figure 5-57.

Select Extension Type: Skin Object

Name	Description	Version	Upgrade?
ACTIONBUTTON		1.0.0	
ACTIONS		1.0.0	
BANNER		1.0.0	
BREADCRUMB		1.0.0	
COPYRIGHT		1.0.0	
CURRENTDATE		1.0.0	
DOTNETNUKE		1.0.0	
DROPDOWNACTIONS		1.0.0	
HELP		1.0.0	
HOSTNAME		1.0.0	
ICON		1.0.0	
LANGUAGE		1.0.0	
LINKACTIONS		1.0.0	

Figure 5-57

DotNetNuke Release 4.91 and 5.0 has a new feature under Host, Dashboard. See Figure 5-58. Information about your setup is given in several different categories. Under Web Server, there is information about your server setup. Database Server provides Server Information along with Database Backup History and Database Files. Host gives full detail of Host Settings. Portals gives information about the Name of the Site, GUID, Pages, Roles and Users. Modules will list the module name, version, and used instances. Finally, under Skins are the installed skins. All of this information can be exported as an XML file.

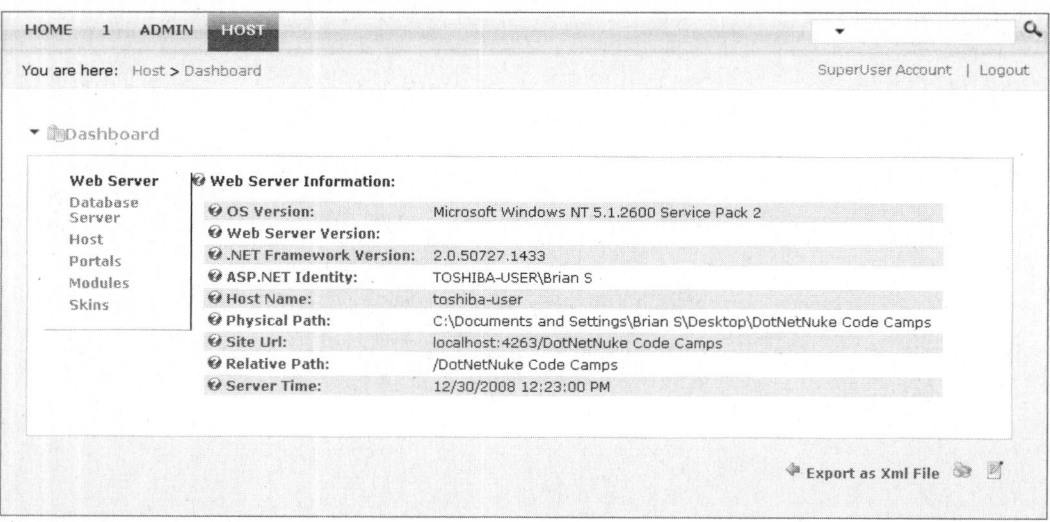

Figure 5-58

Summary

The chapter covered all responsibilities that the host has when being in charge of a DotNetNuke portal. The following topics were covered:

- Host Settings
- Portals
- Module Definition
- File Manager
- Vendors
- SQL
- Schedule
- Languages
- Search Admin
- Lists
- Hosts Accounts
- Skins
- Extensions
- Dashboard

6

Modules

Often, when a user who is familiar with web design uses DotNetNuke for the first time, the modular nature of the functionality can be confusing. Traditionally, web sites are composed of pages of HTML content with functionality built into each page. In this scenario, the modular unit of functionality is the page. The flexibility, and arguably the popularity, of DotNetNuke is in the ability to create dynamic and sometimes complex web sites without being a programmer. The learning curve is overcome once a user realizes that all content on a page is displayed through modules. Even static HTML is displayed through a module.

In Chapter 4, "Portal Administration," you learned to add a page to your portal and manage the settings of your page for different effects. This chapter builds upon what you learned about host, portal, and page administration by introducing you to the building blocks of DotNetNuke web sites: modules. You learn the general concept of a module and explore the options for managing modules. This chapter gives an introduction to the core modules in DotNetNuke and points Portal Administrators to resources for open source and third-party modules.

DotNetNuke Modules

A module is a reusable, pluggable piece of functionality used to display content or interactive functionality. This definition is similar to a traditional ASP.NET page, except that there can be multiple instances of a module type on a page. ASP.NET developers will relate modules to an ASCX user control because they are familiar with reusing functionality with self-contained markup and code. DotNetNuke provides a number of modules packaged with the base installation of DotNetNuke for adding and managing content types like Text/HTML, Vendor Banners, Links, Community Forums, and more. A DotNetNuke page has regions where content (modules) can be added, called *panes*. Panes can contain multiple instances of a module. Figure 6-1 is the homepage from the standard installation of DotNetNuke. The page has five regions: `TopPane`, `LeftPane`, `ContentPane`, `RightPane`, and `BottomPane`. The pane named `BottomPane` contains three Text/HTML modules to display content on the page.

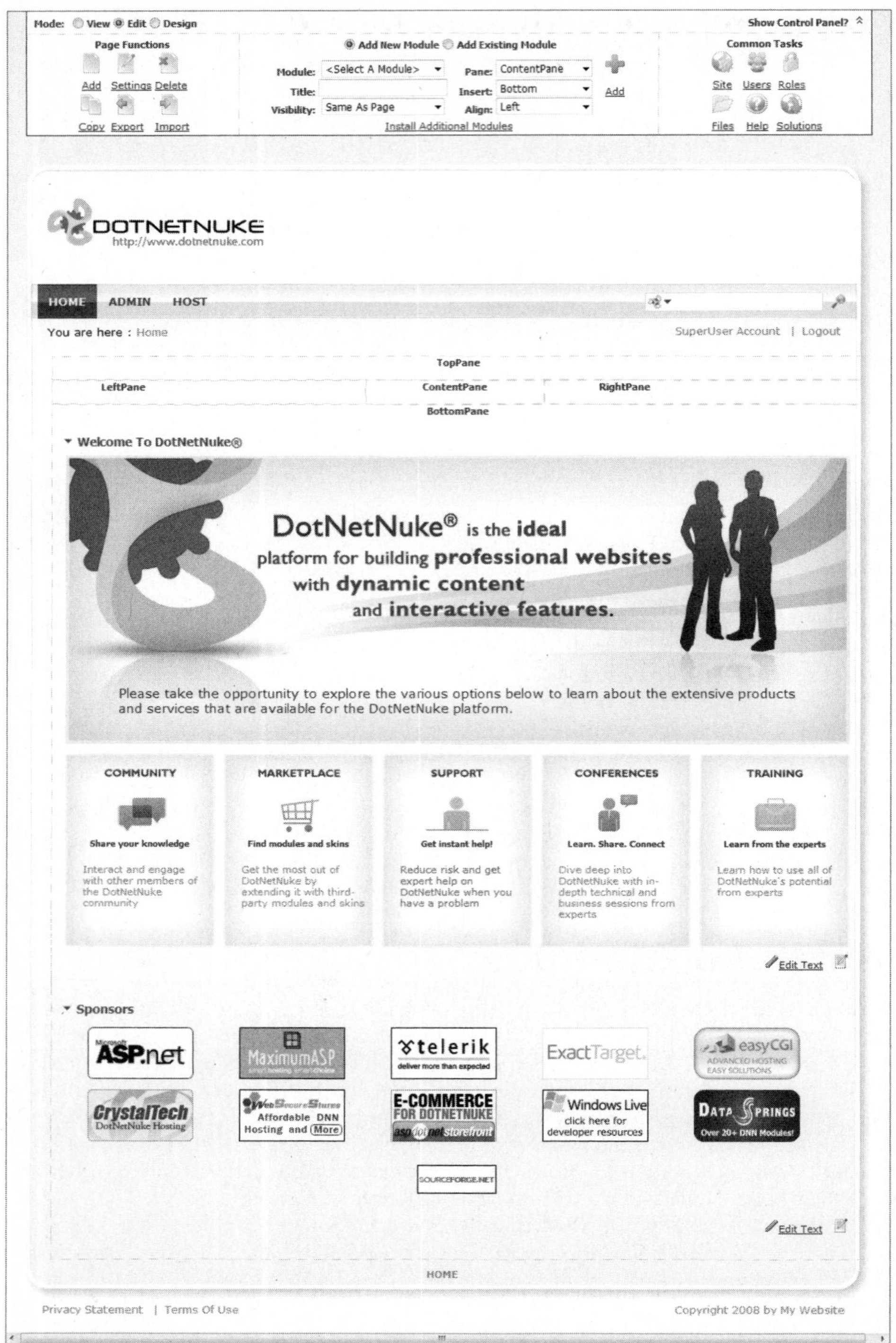
Mode: View Edit Design
Show Control Panel?
Page Functions
Add Settings Delete
Copy Export Import
Add New Module Add Existing Module
Module: <Select A Module>
Title:
Visibility: Same As Page
Pane: ContentPane
Insert: Bottom
Align: Left
Add
Install Additional Modules
Common Tasks
Site Users Roles
Files Help Solutions
DOTNETNUKE
http://www.dotnetnuke.com
HOME ADMIN HOST
You are here : Home
SuperUser Account | Logout
TopPane
LeftPane
ContentPane
RightPane
BottomPane
Welcome To DotNetNuke®
DotNetNuke® is the ideal platform for building professional websites with dynamic content and interactive features.
Please take the opportunity to explore the various options below to learn about the extensive products and services that are available for the DotNetNuke platform.
COMMUNITY
Share your knowledge
Interact and engage with other members of the DotNetNuke community
MARKETPLACE
Find modules and skins
Get the most out of DotNetNuke by extending it with third-party modules and skins
SUPPORT
Get instant help!
Reduce risk and get expert help on DotNetNuke when you have a problem
CONFERENCES
Learn. Share. Connect
Dive deep into DotNetNuke with in-depth technical and business sessions from experts
TRAINING
Learn from the experts
Learn how to use all of DotNetNuke's potential from experts
Edit Text
Sponsors
ASP.net
MaximumASP
telerik
deliver more than expected
ExactTarget.
easyCGI
ADVANCED HOSTING EASY SOLUTIONS
CrystalTech
DotNetNuke Hosting
WebSecureStores
Affordable DNN Hosting and (More)
E-COMMERCE FOR DOTNETNUKE
aspdotnetstorefront
Windows Live
click here for developer resources
DATA SPRINGS
Over 20+ DNN Modules!
SOURCEFORGE.NET
Edit Text
HOME
Privacy Statement | Terms Of Use
Copyright 2008 by My Website

Figure 6-1

Adding and Managing Modules on Pages

All of the modules that are installed in an installation of DotNetNuke are available to add to each page using the Control Panel. Hosts, Portal Administrators, and users with the appropriate security privileges use the Control Panel to add any of the available modules to a page's panes (see Figure 6-2).

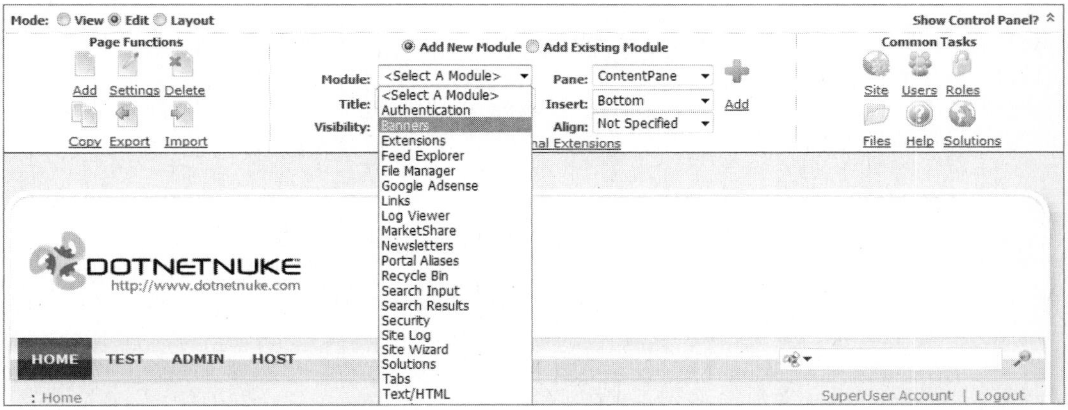

Figure 6-2

The *add module* section of the Control Panel has two ways to add a module to a page. The default mode of operation is Add New Module, as shown in Figure 6-2. To add a new module, select the desired module from the Module drop-down list, specify the pane to inject the module into, specify a title for the desired module, and then choose the alignment for the text within the module. Click the Add button to inject the module into the current page.

The other mode of operation is Add Existing Module, as shown in Figure 6-3. This mode enables you to add the same instance of a module that appears on another page. This means that any updates done to the module will automatically appear in both locations no matter on which page the update was performed. To add an existing module, select the desired page from the drop-down list, specify the pane to inject the module into, select the module (populated from the page selected) you want to add to the current page, and then choose the alignment for the text within the module. Click the Add button to inject the module into the current page.

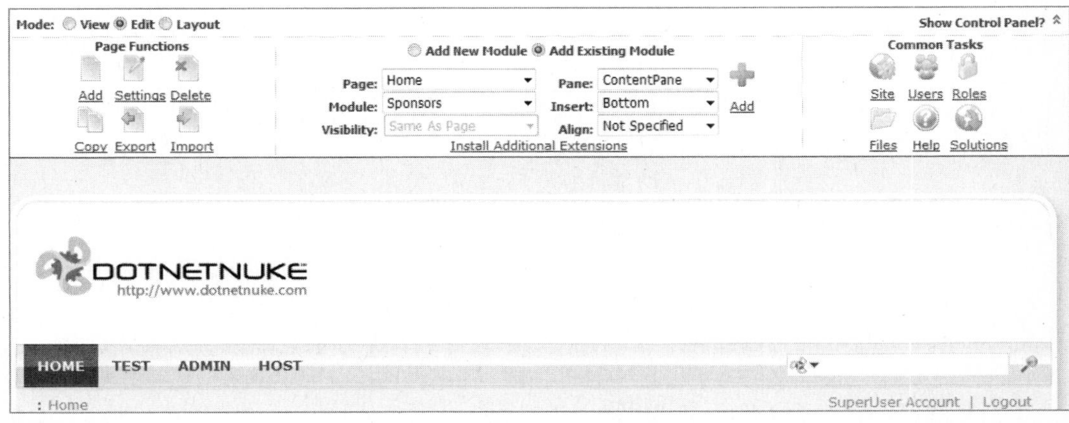

Figure 6-3

Module Layout

DotNetNuke offers a rich management interface for web site administrators. Once a module is on a page, the web site administrators can move modules from one pane to another using the options in the hover menu or with drag and drop. To drag and drop a module, use the Control Panel to switch from View or Edit mode to Layout mode. To start dragging a module, click and hold the left mouse button over the module title until it appears to pop out of place. To place the module, use the blue hints to drag the module up and down so that the module is ordered within the pane the way you like and release the left mouse button (Figure 6-4).

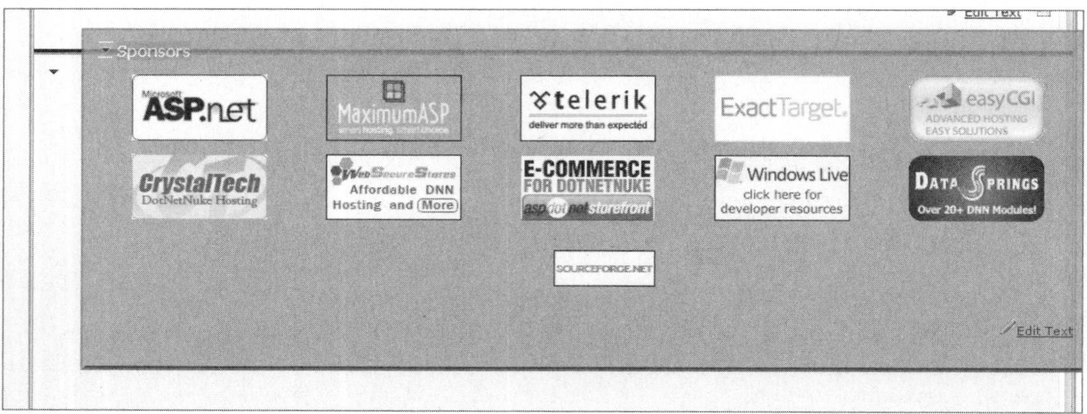

Figure 6-4

Make sure you wait until the module pops out of place before you move your mouse. If you move your mouse too quickly during drag and drop, the mouse can get ahead of where the module is and make the feature ineffective.

In addition to drag and drop, modules also have a hover menu that gives options to manage modules. The Move submenu gives the ability to move the module up or down within a pane that contains other modules and the ability to move the module to another pane on the same page (Figure 6-5).

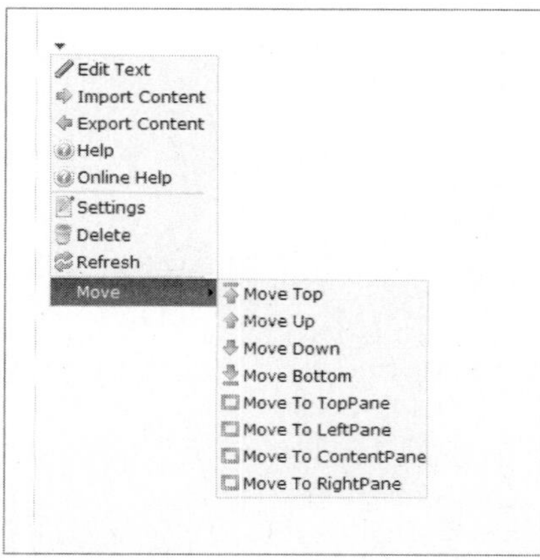

Figure 6-5

Module Settings

Beyond layout on a page, several other settings control the behavior and appearance of a module. DotNetNuke provides the means to manage display and security options that are common to all modules through the *settings* interface. To manage the settings for a module, use the Settings link in the hover menu or click the settings icon at the bottom of the module (Figure 6-6).

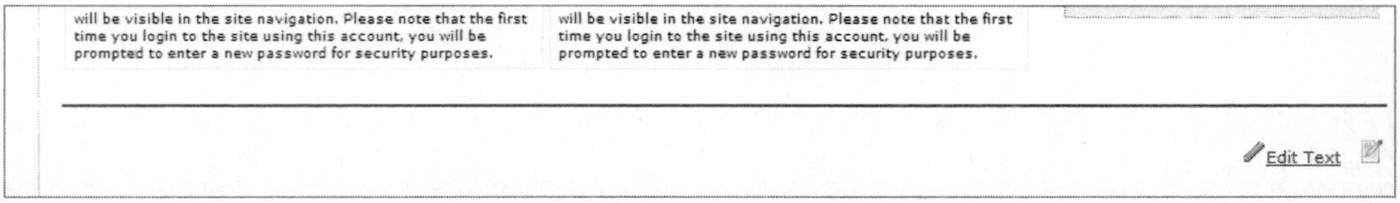

Figure 6-6

Basic Settings

The Basic Settings section controls the title and security options for a module. In most modules, there are two types of permissions: View and Edit. Using role-based or user-specific security, administrators can control which users have access to the page. In previous versions of DotNetNuke, administrators only had the ability to grant or not to grant access to a resource or functionality. Now in DotNetNuke version 5, administrators can deny a specific user or role permission to View or Edit a module. Use the following example as a template for how to implement this functionality in your modules:

1. Create a new user with the username *test* and the password of *password* through the Admin, User Accounts page.
2. Add a Text/HTML module to a page.
3. Navigate to the settings management interface for the module by clicking the Settings link in the hover menu.
4. Uncheck the Inherit View Permissions from Page check box.
5. Check the box next to All Users under the View column to allow all authenticated and unauthenticated users to see this module.
6. Type the username of the user you created in step 1 into the Username textbox and click the Add link.
7. Click the green check mark to change to the red X icon (Figure 6-7).
8. Click the Update link to save the changes for the module.
9. Log out and navigate to the page with your test module — confirm that the module is viewable when you are unauthenticated.
10. Log in with the test user to confirm that the user cannot see the module.

By adding the user to the permissions grid, you were able to override the View permissions by using the new Deny permission with the multi-state check box in DotNetNuke 5. Tables 6-1 and 6-2 show how to manage modules using the options in the Basic Settings and the Basic Setting's Advanced Features options.

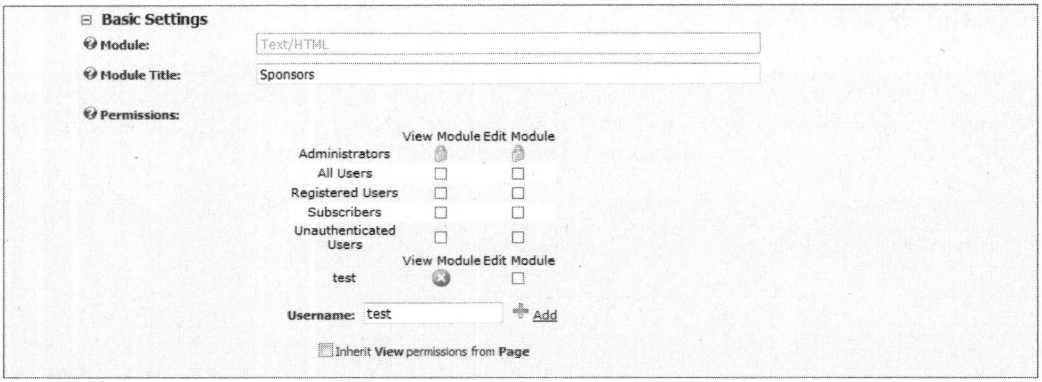

Figure 6-7

Table 6-1: Basic Settings Features

Option	Description
Module Title	Controls the title of the module
Permissions	Controls which users or groups of users have permission to access a module

Table 6-2: Basic Settings Section's ⇨ Advanced Features Options

Option	Description
Display Module on All Pages	Controls whether the module should be added by default to all new and existing pages
Header	Adds text directly above the content area of a module (max 2000 chars)
Footer	Adds text directly below the content area of a module (max 2000 chars)
Start Date	Controls when the module should automatically begin to display to users that do not have edit permissions for the module
End Date	Controls when the module should automatically stop displaying to users that do not have edit permissions for the module

Page Settings

The Page Settings section allows users to control display options for a specific instance of a module on a page. For modules that are added from another page or are displayed on every page, this group of settings allows for overriding the settings from the original module for the specific page on which the settings are edited. The following table explains the Page Settings section of the module management on the Settings interface for a module:

Table 6-3: Page Settings

Option	Description
Icon	Controls the icon displayed for containers that implement the icon token. For more information on the icon token see chapter 16,"Skinning DotNetNuke."
Alignment	Controls the alignment of a module's contents.
Color	Controls the background color to be applied to a module's contents.
Border	Controls the width of the border around the module's contents.
Visibility	Controls the default behavior of the min/max container control.
Allow Print	Controls the display of the print icon for each module.
Allow Syndicate	Controls the setting to allow RSS feeds to be generated for modules that implement the ISearchable interface.
Module Container	Allows users with edit permissions to choose the container for the module. If left to the default, the module will display the parent page's or site default container.
Cache Time	Controls how often a module's cached contents should be regenerated.

For modules that display dynamic content and Text/HTML modules that use the token system, you need to set the cache time to 0 to disable module caching. Adding caching to a module that has interactive functionality can break your module's ability to function.

Module-Specific Settings

Many modules require additional configuration or provide additional options to control the display or behavior of a module through module-specific settings. For example, the Text/HTML module implements the Token Replacement Engine discussed in Chapter 11, "Localization." Because this requires additional overhead to render each page, the Text/HTML module requires module editors to turn on the Token Replacement Engine. Rather than create an entirely new interface for managing this simple setting, the Text/HTML module uses DotNetNuke's module-specific settings section to inject its own settings into the settings management interface (Figure 6-8).

Table 6-4: Page Setting's Advanced Settings Section

Option	Description
Set as Default Settings	Instructs DotNetNuke to use the display settings in the current module for *all future* modules
Apply to All Modules	Applies the current display settings to *all existing* modules
Move to Page	Moves the module from the current page to the page selected in the drop-down

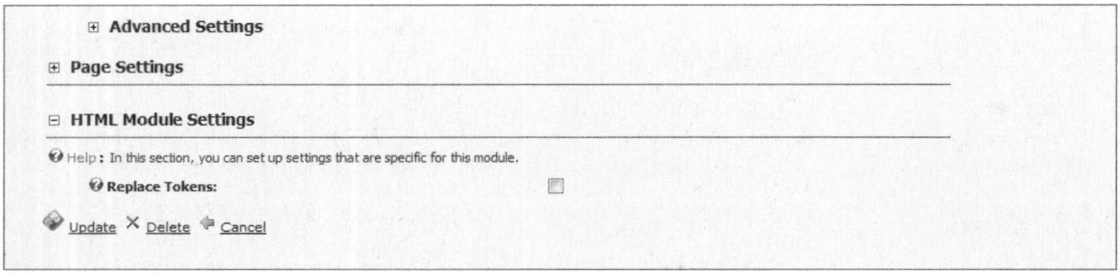

Figure 6-8

Using Modules to Display Content

In DotNetNuke 5, there has been a significant change in the way administration pages and modules are handled. In previous versions, there was a designation within the database to mark a page or module as an "admin page" or an "admin module." This flag kept users of any security level from being able to manage these pages and use or manage the modules in any way outside of the preset format. Although the database field is still there and is still in use for modules that should never be accessed by non-host-level users like the SQL module, the admin modules are no longer marked with this flag. This change makes administration of the admin section of the web site more flexible for host- and administrator-level users, but may leave long-time DotNetNuke portal administrators asking, "Where did all of these new modules come from?" See the following list of the modules that are no longer hidden from portal administrators. For more information on using the administration modules, see Chapter 4, "Portal Administration."

- Extensions
- Feed Explorer
- File Manager
- Log Viewer
- Marketshare
- Newsletters
- Portal Aliases
- Recycle Bin

- Security
- Site Log
- Site Wizard
- Solutions
- Tabs
- Vendors

Host administrators that prefer to hide these modules from their portal administrators can mark them as premium or manually update the `IsAdmin` *field of the* `DesktopModules` *table for the appropriate module directly in the database. For more information on using the premium setting for modules, see Chapter 5, "Host Administration."*

User Content Modules

At the time of writing, DotNetNuke comes with twenty user content modules pre-installed. Fourteen of those twenty standard modules are used for portal administration and are listed in the previous section. The other six modules are designed to display public content. This section explores those six modules.

Text/HTML

For most web sites, Text/HTML will be the module that portal administrators use most. The Text/HTML module is the building block to create static HTML content on DotNetNuke web sites. The Text/HTML module comes with an inline editor for quick edits to content on a page (Figure 6-9). To enter inline editing mode, hover over the content in the Text/HTML module and click the pencil icon that appears at the top-left of your content. When finished with editing, click the disc icon to save or the X icon to cancel.

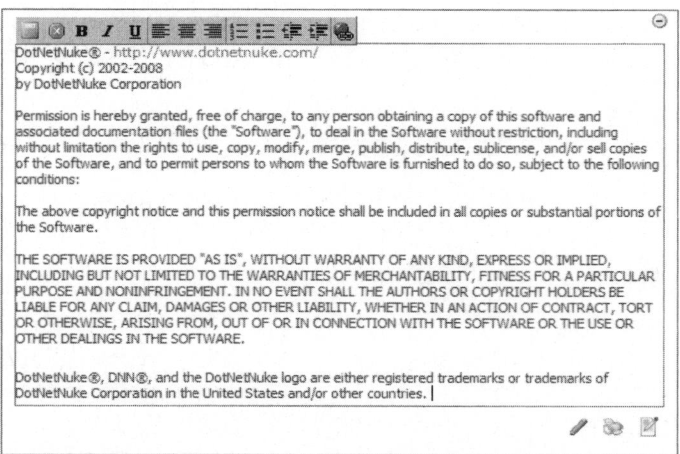

Figure 6-9

For advanced editing, users can click the Edit Text link from the hover menu to go into a WYSIWYG mode using the FCK Editor. Using the FCK Editor, administrators can place HTML-formatted content, images, or Flash. The editor is integrated with DotNetNuke in a way that allows portal managers the functionality to create links to pages within the portal (Figure 6-10) and browse galleries of images that are uploaded into the portal (Figure 6-11) to insert images into your web site's content.

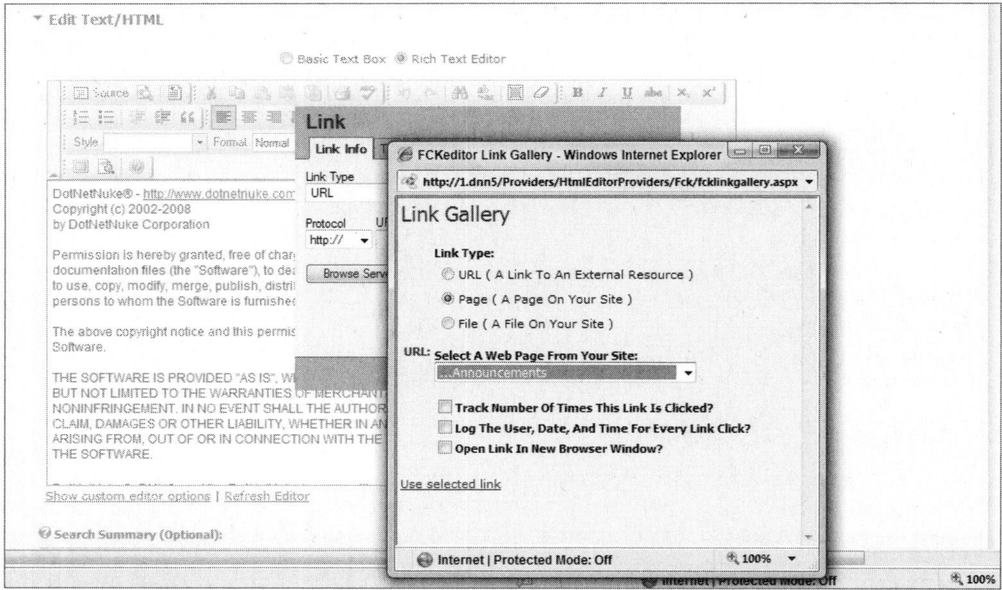

Figure 6-10

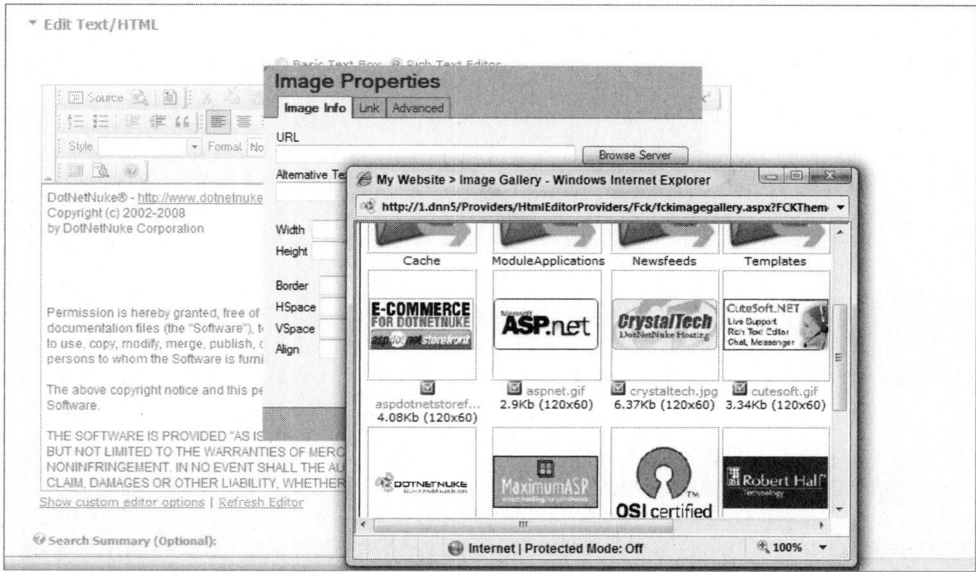

Figure 6-11

The Text/HTML edit mode also has a Search Summary area. The DotNetNuke search functions are capable of indexing all the content in this module. The type of content entered in this module may become quite large, so the Core Team felt it would be useful to allow a mechanism for the module administrator to add a summary of the content for the search engine to use. This accomplishes two functions: It enables you to provide the gist of the content that will be displayed to users when they search for similar content, and it helps with the performance of the search engine because there is no need to index all the content that may appear in this type of module.

A relatively new feature to the Text/HTML module is the ability to use the token replacement engine. By using the token replacement engine, portal content managers can create personalized and dynamic content as described in Chapter 11. To enable token replacement for a module, edit the settings for the Text/HTML module. First, disable module caching by setting the cache time to 0; then, check the box next to Replace Tokens in the HTML Module Settings section. The following code snippet shows a few example tokens and how they are rendered with the token replacement engine enabled:

```
Welcome [User:DisplayName],
Check out the daily specials for [Date:Now|MM-dd-yyy] to all users from
[Profile:City], [Profile:Region]!
Welcome Ryan Morgan,
Check out the daily specials for 09-18-2008 to all users from West Palm Beach,
Florida!
```

Banners

The Banners module provides a method of offering advertisements in the DotNetNuke application. Administering this module is a little different from any of the other base modules because this module works in conjunction with the Vendors module, which is an administrator-only module. Banners can be controlled from the Host level or Portal level, and the Host account controls this behavior.

Probably the first thing you will notice when you add this module to a page is that you see only a Banner Options action and not an Add New Action option, like some of the other modules display. This is because the banners will need to be added from either the Admin Vendors page or from the Host Vendors page. This is one of the functions that makes DotNetNuke a viable host platform, because you can offer free or inexpensive portals for your users and then recuperate your hosting costs by offering advertising on the individual portals in your DotNetNuke installation.

The previous two chapters discussed the Host and Admin functions and covered exactly how to add them. For now, assume you have already added a vendor and are ready to display a banner advertisement for that vendor. After you add the module to a page, click the Banner Options action. You are presented with the Edit Banner window, as shown in Figure 6-12.

As you can see, there is no option to add a banner to this control. That action is handled in the respective Vendors module by the Host or Portal Administrator, and this module is the mechanism you use to display those settings to the user. For a full description of managing the Vendor functions in DotNetNuke, refer to Chapters 4 and 5. Table 6-5 describes the Edit Banner options.

After you have set up your vendor accounts on the vendor pages, you will be able to earn revenue from your DotNetNuke installation. As you saw, there is really no direct editing of content from this module. This is a design decision, so you can let other roles in your installation handle these remedial types of tasks while you control your revenue generation from the higher accounts.

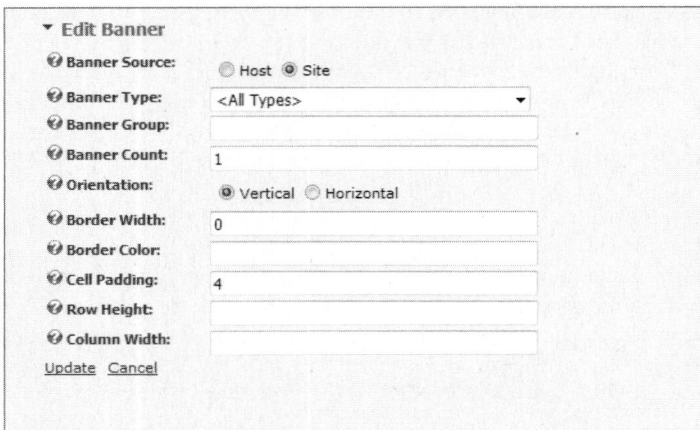

Figure 6-12

Table 6-5: Edit Banner Options

Option	Description
Banner Source	Selecting one of these radio buttons enables you to specify whether the vendor banners shown in this module should originate from the host or from the portal.
Banner Type	The type of banner that should be shown in this module. Banner types include Banner, MicroButton, Button, Block, Skyscraper, Text, and Script. Selecting a specific type means the vendor must have that type assigned to its account or the module won't show that vendor's advertisements.
Banner Group	Enables you to associate a group of banners in the administrator vendor's module, such as the Site Banner group. Entering the banner group here enables you to group the same types of banners.
Banner Count	Defines the number of times a banner will display to the users.
Orientation	Enables you to display the banner either vertically or horizontally. The type of banner you chose usually dictates which option you should select.
Border Width	Defines the width of the border.
Border Color	Sets the border color.
Cell Padding	Sets the space between the banners and the border.
Row Height	Sets a row height for your banner.
Column Width	Sets a column width for your banner.

Google Adsense

Google Adsense is a free service from Google that allows web site owners to display text or graphical advertisements from Google's popular Adwords service. Like the Banners module, the Google Adsense module creates a way for web site owners to offer free or low-cost web sites by having a simple way to generate revenue. Setting up Adsense for your web site is easy once you have your Adsense ID. Table 6-6 explains the settings available for displaying Adsense on a page.

Table 6-6: Adsense Setup Configuration

Option	Description
Adsense ID	Your Google Adsense ID.
Format	Controls the layout of the ads to fit the design of the page.
Channel ID	Optionally allows you to enter the Channel ID to control certain settings controlled through your Adsense account.
Border Color	Controls the border color around the add area.
Title Color	Controls the color of the title.
Background Color	Controls the color of the background in the add area.
Text Color	Controls the color of the text in the add area.
URL Color	Controls the color of URLs in the add area.

Links

The Links module is likely one of the most used modules in DotNetNuke installations, perhaps second only to the Text/HTML module. As its name suggests, this module enables you to add links to allow users to navigate to other areas of your site or to remote web sites. In the new version, the abilities to add links directly to files and to view user profiles have been added. There are a few unique settings with which you need to be familiar. Figure 6-13 shows the Module Settings pane for the Links Settings.

You have several options for controlling the behavior and view of the Links module. The Control Type radio buttons enable you to define whether the link list displays as a drop-down list or a normal, data-bound list. You also have the option of controlling the orientation of the list with the List Display Format option. Display Info Link enables you to show users a short description of the web page to which the link navigates, which is useful because it allows some additional keywords to be associated with the link. Two new options are Wrap Links, which provides the ability to disallow wrapping for the text in a link, and Display Icon, which allows for an icon to be displayed next to each link. For this example, just accept the defaults in the Link Settings and move on to adding your link, as shown in Figure 6-14.

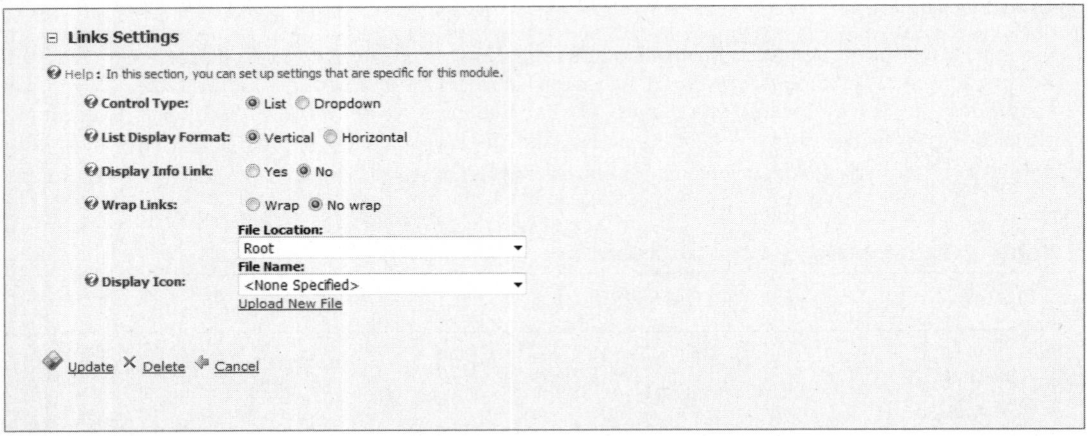

Figure 6-13

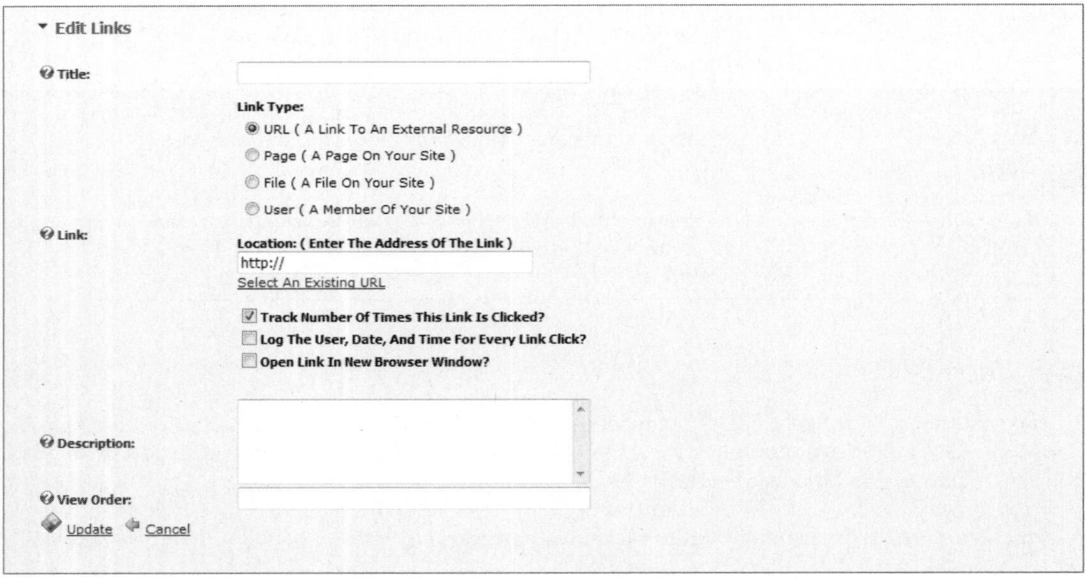

Figure 6-14

The text you enter in the Title field is what users will see as the link. As with other modules, the Link Settings offer options for linking to an external resource, a page on your site, or an internal file in your module, and the audit controls let you track your visitors' behavior. The Description field contains the text you would enter if you selected the Display Info Link option in Figure 6-13. The View Order option enables you to specify the order in which your links are displayed.

Links that point to user profiles will only show profile properties that the selected user has set to be public through his or her profile manager. Links to users that do not have any public properties will display a message as shown in Figure 6-15.

View Profile
This user has elected to hide his/her profile.

Figure 6-15

Links to files and users are generated in a way that obscures information that could lead to secure information being displayed, like the file location or a user id. Instead, the Links module uses an encrypted key to deliver the file or user profile after DotNetNuke's security has confirmed that the content delivery is authorized. This also allows the tracking system to keep track of activity for the specified link when Track Number of Times This Link is Clicked is checked in the settings for a link.

If you are using the Links module to link to a page on your web site, consider the search engine optimization implications before you turn on link count tracking. With link count tracking enabled for a page link, the link must pass through linkclick.aspx with parameters passed into the URL to instruct DotNetNuke how to redirect the page. If you have many of these links throughout the site, search engines may see this as duplicate content, and it may result in lower-ranking pages in your web site.

Search Input

Search Input allows users to add the search input to a page and allows users to enter a word or phrase to search on through all module content that has been indexed by the DotNetNuke search engine. Figure 6-16 shows the settings specific to the module.

Search Input Settings

Help: In this section, you can set up settings that are specific for this module.

Search Results Module: Search Results

Show Go Image: ☑

Show Search Image: ☑

Update ✕ Delete Cancel

Figure 6-16

Search Results

The Search Results module is the core module that handles displaying results from the DotNetNuke search engine. A default installation of DotNetNuke includes a Search Results page with this module already placed. Most Portal Administrators will never need to use this module. Settings for the Search Results module are listed in Table 6-7.

Table 6-7: Search Results Settings

Option	Description
Maximum Search Results	Controls the maximum number of results to return.
Results Per Page	Controls the maximum number of search items to be shown per page of search results.
Maximum Title Length	Controls how many characters of the module title should be displayed. (The title is pulled from the module whose indexed content is returned in the search results. The default option is to not truncate the module title.)
Maximum Description Length	Controls how much of the description should be displayed before truncating the search result's description.
Show Description	Controls whether to show the description in the search results.

DotNetNuke Project Modules

The DotNetNuke Core Team made the decision not to install all modules automatically into an installation when it is first created. The decision was made after feedback from the community that DotNetNuke came pre-installed with too many modules that not all installations need, and this caused extra work to remove those modules after an installation. DotNetNuke now comes with all of the Project modules and certain Sub-Project modules in the file system and ready to be installed, but only after they are manually installed by the Host user.

To pick and choose which modules to install into your application and to install multiple included modules at once, go to the Host, Extensions page and choose the Batch Install Extensions (Figure 6-17).

Announcements

The Announcements module enables portal managers to manage a list of announcements or upcoming events with a title, image, description, and a date range of when the announcement should be displayed. The Announcements module has been extended to allow display templates using the tokens in Table 6-8. This module will serve you well for a quick way to add upcoming events and announcements to your portal, but if you need more control over the fields that are available and how the announcement is displayed, try the Forms & Lists module (formerly User Defined Table) discussed later in this chapter.

Blog

The Blog module allows portal managers to add an online journal or weblog to their DotNetNuke web site. The DotNetNuke Blog is tied to a specific user on a portal. That means that you can have multiple blogs on a web site by logging in as a different user and creating new blogs. Once you have created a blog with a specific user, you will need to continue to authenticate as that user anytime you want to add, edit, or delete entries to your blog. Beyond that nuance, the Blog module is very intuitive to set up and use. Just remember that you cannot create all blogs from the Admin or Host accounts as you can with most other content types.

Figure 6-17

To set up your blog, add the Blog module to a page. It will add five modules at once and it will be up to you to arrange them and give them more user-friendly titles after that. The first thing that you will want to do is to set the permissions to hide the New_Blog module from all users that you do not want to have access to create and manage a blog. Once you have arranged the Blog modules on the page the way you want, log in with the user that you want to be associated with the blog for your web site and click the Create Blog link. Follow the instructions for each section to set up your blog and then you will be able to add blog entries. Figure 6-18 shows a common layout for the blog modules.

Table 6-8: Announcement Template Tokens

Token	Result
[CREATEDBYUSER]	The display name of the user that created the Announcement.
[CREATEDDATE]	The announcement creation date, in localized long date form.
[DESCRIPTION]	The announcement description.
[IMAGESOURCE]	The announcement image as defined in the announcement.
[MODULEID]	The ID of the current module.
[MORE]	The localized "read more..." text.
[NEWWINDOW]	Used to open a link in a new window.
[PUBLISHDATE]	The announcement's publish date, in localized long date form.
[TITLE]	The announcement title field.
[URL]	The announcement's URL field.
[VIEWORDER]	The announcement's view order field.

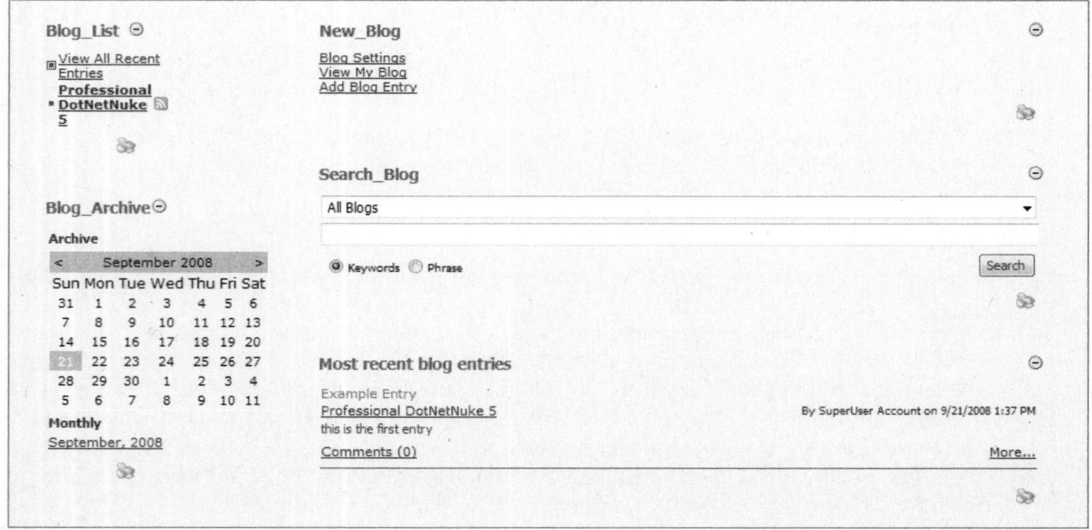

Figure 6-18

Documents

The Documents module enables you to upload files to your portal and offer those files to your users for download. This is a fairly useful module because you will likely need to offer examples or additional information in the form of Word documents or other types of files to your users. The types of files you can use with this module are controlled by the file type settings under the Host Settings page. By default, DotNetNuke allows the following extensions:

- .jpg
- .jpeg
- .jpe
- .gif
- .bmp
- .png
- .doc
- .xls
- .ppt
- .pdf
- .txt
- .xml
- .xsl
- .css
- .zip

If you require additional file types not allowed by default, you will need to add the extension under the Host Settings page in the File Upload Extensions field. If you are going to allow your users to upload files, you should be careful as to the types of files allowed because users may introduce viruses or other undesirable files into your portal file system. The application offers no default protection in this area, so diligence is needed to protect the integrity of the system.

Figure 6-19 shows the interface you use to add new documents to this module. As in other areas of the application, the files you make available through this module will reside in your portal's default file directory.

Enter the title, description, category, and link for your module. You may notice that the Link section appears similar to the Link control in the Announcements module. This is another example of the object-oriented nature of DotNetNuke, which reuses code wherever possible to enable a simpler user interface and to promote best programming practices. The only difference between the two is that the Announcements module enables you to select a page in your portal as one of the links. Because it should never be necessary to offer a page for download, this option is not included in the Documents module. Like the Announcements module, the Documents module enables you to track your users' actions to determine the content they are most interested in receiving. The Category field offers you the ability to group the files in the module logically. This category will be displayed as part of the Documents module so that users understand the type of file they are about to download or view. By default, the document is associated with the user uploading the file. Administrators have the ability to click the Change Owner link to choose a different registered user from the portal. The Sort Index field allows administrators to add an integer value to serve as the default sort.

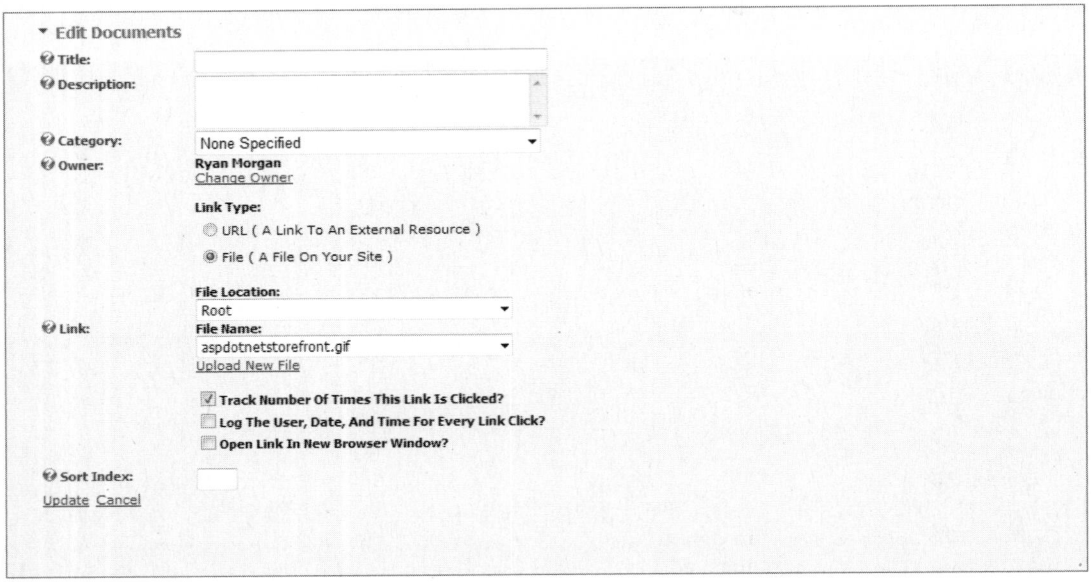

Figure 6-19

The newest version of the Documents module adds new display and behavior settings accessible through the settings interface (Figure 6-20). Portal managers are now able to control which columns in the document grid are shown and the order in which they are displayed. A custom sort can also be applied, sorting on multiple fields by selecting the fields to sort by and clicking Add Sort Order to the sort conditions list. The Show Title Link check box allows control over whether to render the title as a URL or as plain text. The final new feature creates a way to change the category textbox to a drop-down pulling the values from a list in the Host administration. Installing the module does not create this list for you, so you'll need to create a new list named Document Categories and add the entries there. To create a new list, use the Lists page in the Host menu. There is a drawback to this implementation in that there is not a way to create multiple lists in an installation or a portal.

Events

The Events module allows portal managers to add a calendar to their web site. The default configuration works as you would expect by displaying a calendar. Editors can add events using the Add Event option in the hover menu. It also provides a download in the details view for an event to download the event as an iCal appointment to be saved in the user's local calendar like Microsoft Outlook or Entourage. Figure 6-21 shows a basic Events module calendar with sample events for one of the dates.

Users with more advanced needs for enrollment, paid enrollment with PayPal, user-submitted events, and sub-calendars can explore the additional options for the Events module by editing the module-specific settings. All of the specific settings have great help tips associated with them, so Table 6-9 gives an overview and the use of each extended feature rather than an explanation of each setting.

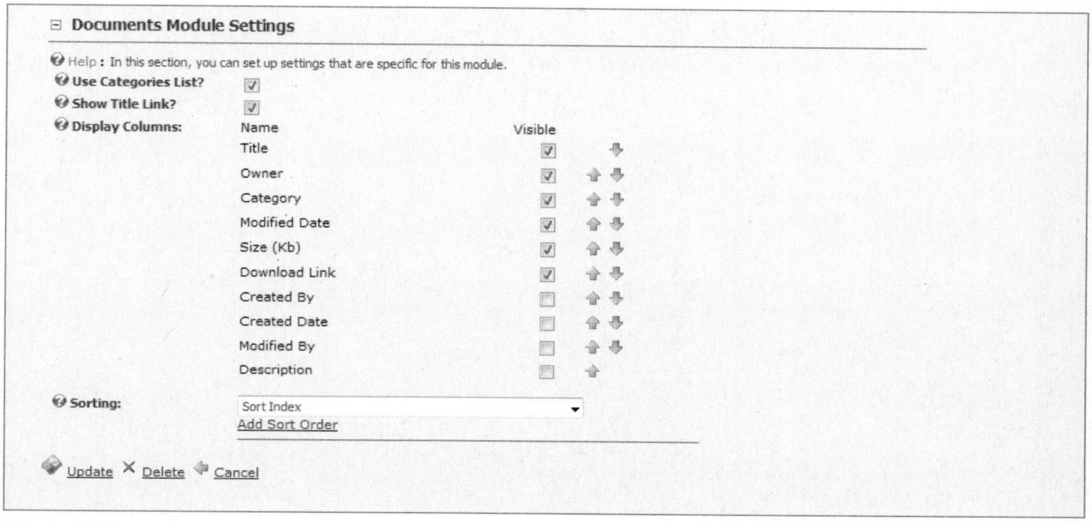

Figure 6-20

Using CSS stylesheets, you can define themes to be set in the settings of the Events module. To add a new theme to the Events settings, add a folder to the `\DesktopModules\events\themes` folder with your theme name and stylesheet, and it will automatically become available. For consistency and ease of management, many developers will choose to keep the styles that define the layout of the Events module within the skin's CSS files. For more information on creating skins for DotNetNuke, see Chapter 16.

FAQs

You can use the FAQs (Frequently Asked Questions) module to answer questions users may have about your web site or products. It is one of the simpler modules in DotNetNuke, but it's also one of the more powerful ones because it can save you hours of replying to emails. The interface for adding a new FAQ is quite simple and warrants little discussion. Basically, you enter a question for which you want to provide an answer, enter the answer, and optionally choose a category with which to associate the question. The module enables you to use the Rich Text editor to format your questions and answers in a way that is easy for your users to understand and to convey the intended message. Figure 6-22 shows the interface for the FAQs module's Edit functions.

The newest version of the FAQs module has added a couple of new features. First, there is a new interface for managing categories that are associated with a FAQ. To manage categories for a module instance, go to the Manage Categories link in the hover menu for the module. The manage categories screen allows you to manage a list of categories that can be associated with FAQs. More impressively, there is now the ability to manage the template used to render the questions and answers as HTML in the module. See Table 6-10 for a list of the settings available to control the display and behavior of the FAQs module.

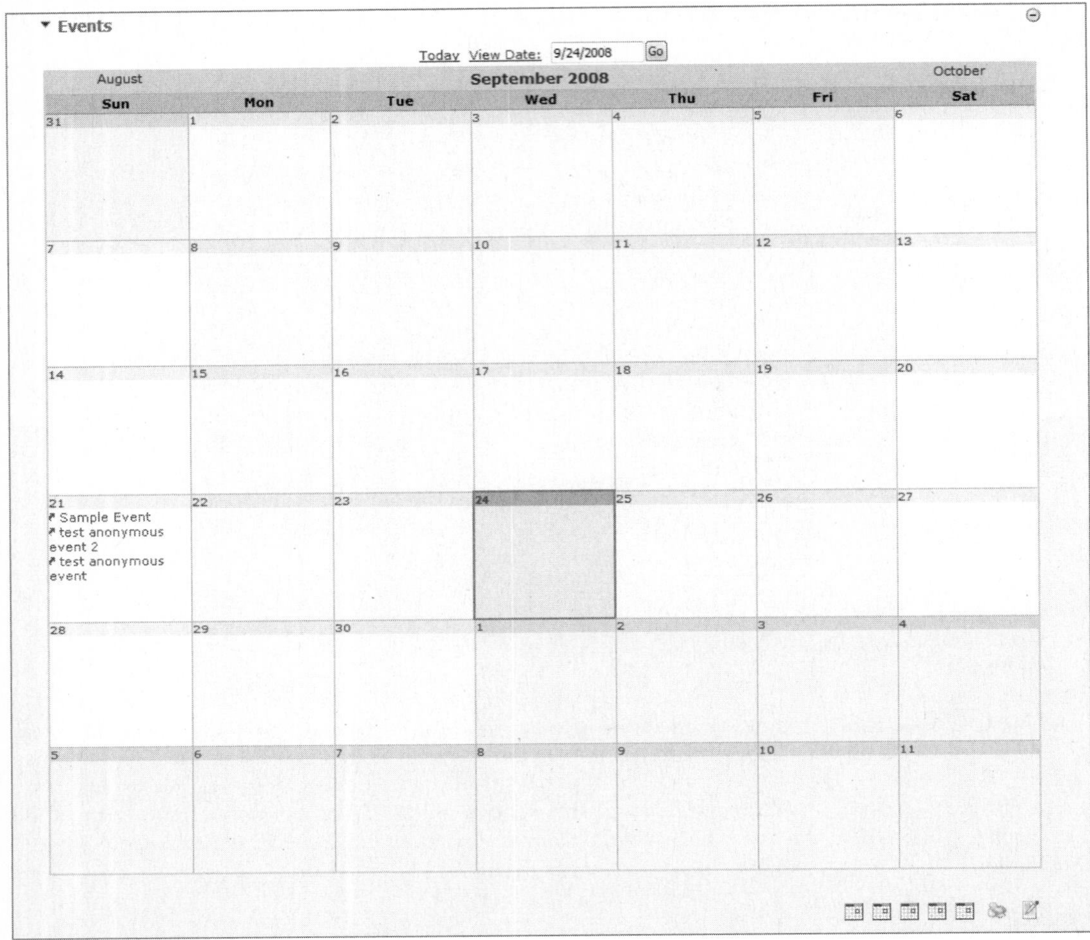

Figure 6-21

Feedback

The Feedback module offers you a mechanism for allowing users to contact you without exposing your email address to the many spam bots that regularly scan the Internet. The module does not have an Add function like the other modules because the purpose of the module does not require that functionality. Basically, users are adding feedback when they send you emails. The module contains some settings to control its display to users and to specify the address to which the emails are sent. The newest version adds a few features to make the module more useful, including the ability to add CAPTCHA to prevent automation scripts from abusing the form. There are also new settings to control drop-downs to ask for the subject and category of the feedback being submitted. You can also choose to publish and display feedback to the public using the Feedback Comments Viewer.

Table 6-9: Events Module Advanced Features

Option	Description
Enrollment	This feature allows user to enroll or RSVP to an event that they will attend. Additionally, managers can set whether an event is a paid event and requires payment to have a valid enrollment. PayPal is the only supported payment option.
Moderation	This feature controls the ability to approve each user-submitted event and user-submitted enrollment. Users or groups of users with Edit permissions for the module are able to add events.
Sub-Calendars	This feature allows portal managers to display events associated with another calendar. If your organization has multiple calendars, you can create one master calendar that displays all events by adding them as sub-calendars.

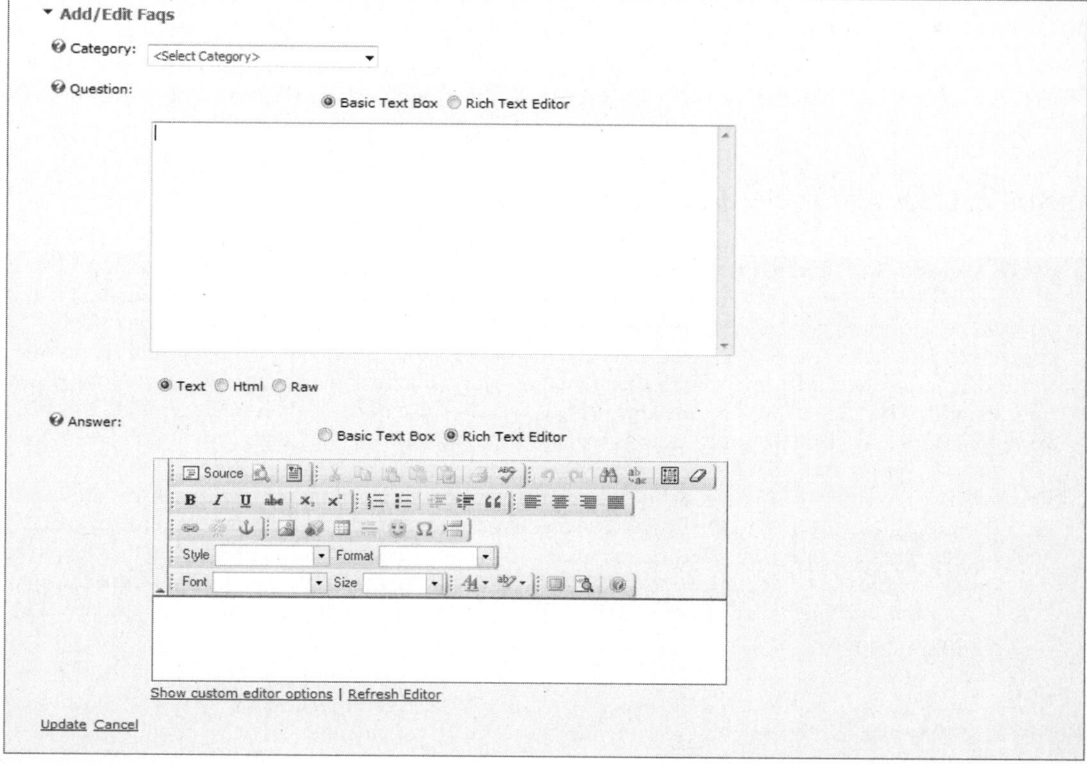

Figure 6-22

Table 6-10: FAQs Settings

Option	Description
Default Sorting	Controls how the entries should be sorted.
Enable AJAX	Controls whether to use the ASP.NET AJAX Update Panel to intercept and handle server postbacks.
Question Template	Controls the HTML used to render a question.
Answer Template	Controls the HTML used to render an answer.
Loading Template	Controls the HTML used to render the notification that the answer is loading after a user clicks the question. This setting is only applicable to FAQs that enable AJAX.

One thing to be aware of is that this module relies on the mail server settings on the Host Settings page to function properly. Ensure that you have successfully added your mail server and tested the settings before attempting to utilize this module's functionality.

Forms & Lists (Formerly User Defined Table)

Forms and Lists is the newest release of the module formerly named User Defined Table. This module is easily the most flexible core module in DotNetNuke. Using Forms and Lists, portal managers can create dynamically generated and formatted lists of data and with a definable form to collect the data from users with the appropriate permissions. Forms and Lists could be used for any purpose from a simple list of contacts in an organization, to a searchable catalog of products. The newest version of this module adds the ability to create public forms with the same flexibility, enabling portal managers to more efficiently interact with web site visitors. Forms and Lists also makes use of the Token Replacement Engine, giving administrators even greater opportunities for personalization in display data.

The first display when you add the module to your page is an interface for applying any pre-built configuration templates in the `\DesktopModules\userdefinedtable\ModuleApplications` or `\Portals\[CurrentPortalId]\ModuleApplications` folder. You can select one of the pre-built templates or bypass this screen and create a custom form from scratch by choosing the Forms & Lists Configuration option in the hover menu. Whichever option you use, configuration is required to define the columns that drive the data that is collected in a form and consequently available for display.

Columns and Data Types

Adding and editing columns in the module configuration is the best way to begin to understand the features available through Forms & Lists. To begin, choose the Forms & Lists Configuration option in the hover menu. The section at the top controls the column definitions for display and behavior. Adding a new column inserts a new editable row directly into the column grid. The inline editing for the grid controls the basic attributes like Title and Type, and whether the column is required, visible, or searchable.

When in add or edit mode for a column, an advanced column options area displays below (Figure 6-23). Table 6-11 explains the options available for column data types and how to use them.

Though most columns are relatively self-explanatory, the Calculated and Look-Up columns are the more advanced columns and may require more explanation. The Calculated column works by supplying a formula into the Advanced Column Options section. To use a column value in the calculation, wrap the column name in brackets. For example, to create a column that calculates the percentage score on a test, you would create an integer column named Correct Answers. Then, assuming a total possible score of 50, add a Calculated Column named Score with the following formula in the expression field: `([Correct Answers]/50) * 100`. Whenever a score is entered into the Correct Answers column, the Score column will automatically calculate the percentage of correct answers. The Look-Up column adds the ability to display meta information for file and user data types using the Token Replacement engine. For example, to display the email address of the user that created a record as a column, add a Look-Up column and set the Source Column setting to Created By and the Token Text setting to `[User:Email]`. Table 6-12 shows all tokens available in the Token Text field. For an example of how to use the URL tokens, apply the File List application configuration to a Forms & Lists module.

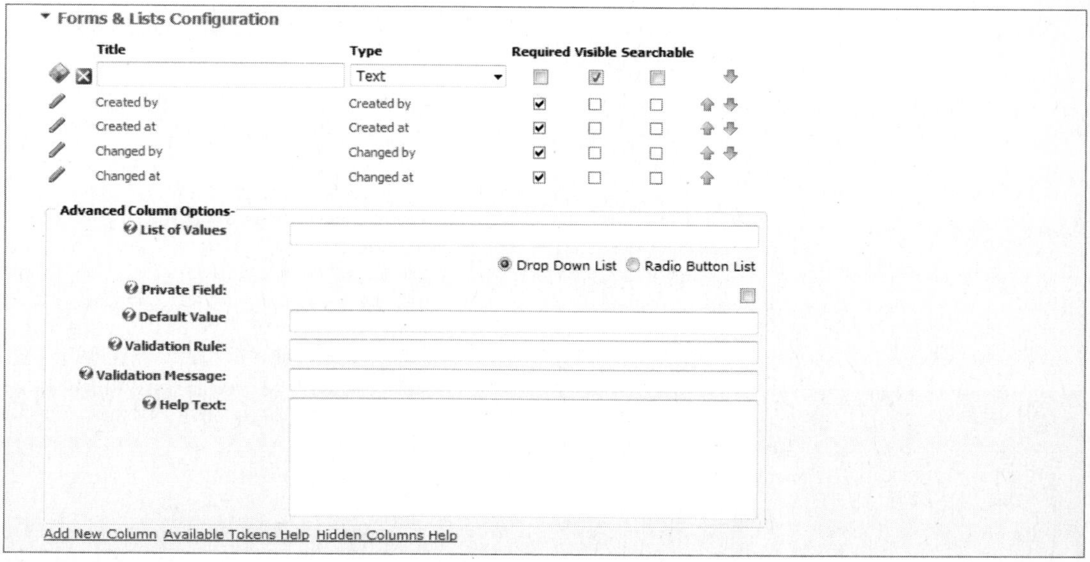

Figure 6-23

For more information on the formatting and using conditional logic in tokens, see Chapter 11.

Adding Records Using Forms

Forms & Lists will either collect data from an editor and display the results to public users, or collect data from public users and display the results to editors. The Application Mode setting on the Forms & Lists Configuration screen controls whether the module should be used as a form or a display (list) module. When in List mode, users with add and edit permissions are able to use the Add button to insert new records for display (Figure 6-24). When in Form mode, the default view is the Add New Record interface for users with permission to add new records (Figure 6-25).

Table 6-11: Column Data Types

Option	Description
Text	Used for text information collected through a textbox, drop-down list, or radio button list.
Calculated Column	Used to display calculated data based upon formulas supplied in the advanced settings for the column. Useful for calculating values based upon other fields in the row of data.
Currency	Formats and rounds numerical values as currency with two decimal places using the currency symbol supplied the advanced settings for the column and the current culture settings for the user.
Date	Displays a date value. In the form this column will display the DotNetNuke calendar for choosing a date.
Date and Time	Displays a date and time value. In the form this column will display the DotNetNuke calendar for choosing a date and have a second textbox to collect a time value.
Decimal	Displays a decimal value formatted according to the advanced settings for the column.
Download	Uses the DotNetNuke URL control to allow the form editor to select a file from the portal to display a download link to.
Email	Formats an email with a mailto link that has the email address obscured using JavaScript to make the email address less likely to be harvested by spam spiders.
Image	Displays an image using dynamic server-side resizing to generate a thumbnail according the image size field in the column settings configuration section.
Integer	Collects and displays a whole number.
Link to User's Profile	Collects a username and displays a link to that user's profile.
Look-Up	Provides access to meta data for the following user-based and file-based columns: CreatedBy, ChangedBy, UserLink, Downloads, and URLs.
Rich Text (HTML)	Collects HTML and displays the decoded HTML inline.
Separator	Used on the forms to group fields into sections with a label and horizontal rule.
Time	Collects and displays a time value.
True/False	Uses a check box to collect a value of true or false.
URL	Collects a page, file, or external URL using the DotNetNuke URL control.

Table 6-12: Available Token Fields

Token	Description
[Portal:Currency]	Currency String
[Portal:Description]	Portal Description
[Portal:Email]	Portal Admin Email
[Portal:FooterText]	Portal Copyright Text
[Portal:HomeDirectory]	Portal (relative) Path of Home Directory
[Portal:LogoFile]	Portal Path to Logo file
[Portal:PortalName]	Portal Name
[Portal:PortalAlias]	Portal URL
[Portal:Time-ZoneOffset]	Difference in minutes between Portal default time and UTC
[User:DisplayName]	User's Display Name
[User:Email]	User's Email Address
[User:FirstName]	User's First Name
[User:FullName]	[deprecated]
[User:LastName]	User's Last Name
[User:Username]	User's Login User Name
[Membership: Approved]	Is User Approved?
[Membership: CreatedDate]	User Signup Date
[Membership:IsOnline]	Is User Currently Online?
[Profile:<Property>]	Use any default or custom Property defined for user profiles as listed in the Profile Property Definition section of Manage User Accounts. Please use non-localized Property titles only.
[Tab:Description]	Page Description Text for Search Engine
[Tab:EndDate]	Page Display Until Date

Continued

Table 6-12: *(continued)*

Token	Description
[Tab:FullUrl]	Page Full URL
[Tab:IconFile]	Page Relative Path to Icon file
[Tab:KeyWords]	Page Keywords for Search Engine
[Tab:PageHeadText]	Page Header Text
[Tab:StartDate]	Page Display from Date
[Tab:TabName]	Page Name
[Tab:TabPath]	Page Relative Path
[Tab:Title]	Page Title (Window Title)
[Tab:URL]	Page URL
[Module:Description]	Module Definition Description
[Module:EndDate]	Module Display Until Date
[Module:Footer]	Module Footer Text
[Module:FriendlyName]	Module Definition Name
[Module:Header]	Module Header Text
[Module:HelpUrl]	Module Help URL
[Module:IconFile]	Module Path to Icon File
[Module:ModuleTitle]	Module Title
[Module:PaneName]	Module Name of Pane where UDT resides
[Module:StartDate]	Module Display from Date
[DateTime:Now]	Current Date and Time
[Ticks:Now]	CPU Tick Count for Current Second
[Ticks:Today]	CPU Tick Count since Midnight
[Ticks:TicksPerDay]	CPU Ticks per Day (for calculations)
[File:Name]	Name of File
[File:Folder]	Folder of file

Continued

Table 6-12: *(continued)*

Token	Description
[File:Path]	Complete path to file
[File:Size]	Size of file in Bytes
[File:SizeMb]	Size of file in Mega Bytes
[File:Clicks]	Number of Downloads
[File:Extension]	Extension of file

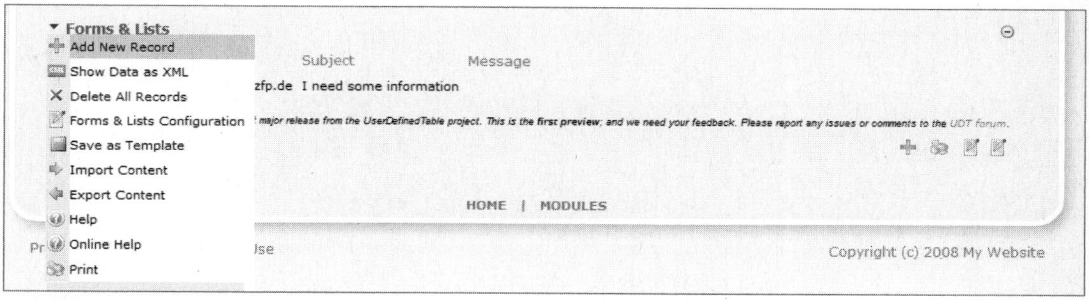

Figure 6-24

Figure 6-25

Applying Security Permissions and Module-Specific Settings

Forms & Lists extends the DotNetNuke permissions grid in the settings interface to give portal managers more control over the features to which users and groups of users have access (Figure 6-26). Remember that even if the module is in the Form application mode, you will still need to grant users access explicitly to submit records with the form. Table 6-13 explains the permissions in the permissions grid.

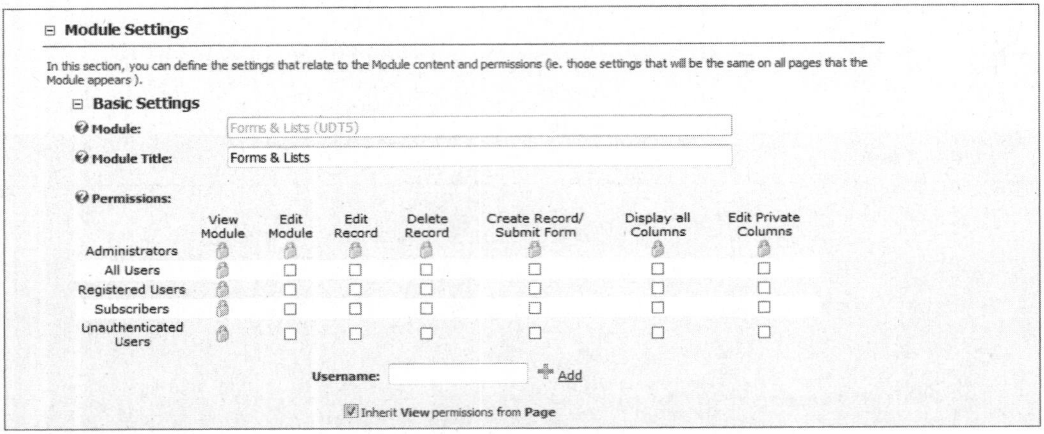

Figure 6-26

Table 6-13: Forms & Lists Permissions

Option	Description
View Module	Standard permission to control whether the module is to be displayed
Edit Module	Standard permission to control which users can edit module content and control module settings
Edit Record	Controls which users may edit existing records
Delete Record	Controls which users may delete existing records
Create Record/Submit Form	Controls which users may add new records in List application mode, and which users may submit the form in Form application mode
Display All Columns	Controls which users are able to see hidden columns
Edit Private Columns	Controls which users are able to edit and submit values for fields defined by columns marked as private

Forms & Lists Display Options

Forms & Lists' true power is in how flexible the display engine is for lists of data. The List Rendering Options section on the configuration screen allows portal managers to enable advanced features like sorting, paging, searching, and filtering by column values. Figure 6-27 shows the options in the Rendering Options section.

List rendering options

Rendering Method: Default Grid Table / XSLT using built-in stylesheets / XSLT using self made stylesheets

Sorting options

Sort Column: Not Specified

Sort Direction: Ascending

Paging: <no paging>

Search & Filter options

Filter statement:

Available Tokens Help Hidden Columns Help

Show Search Box:

Simple Search:

Show no records until Search:

Search URL paths:

Top Count:

Grid Table Settings

CSS Classes: "Normal UDT_Table"

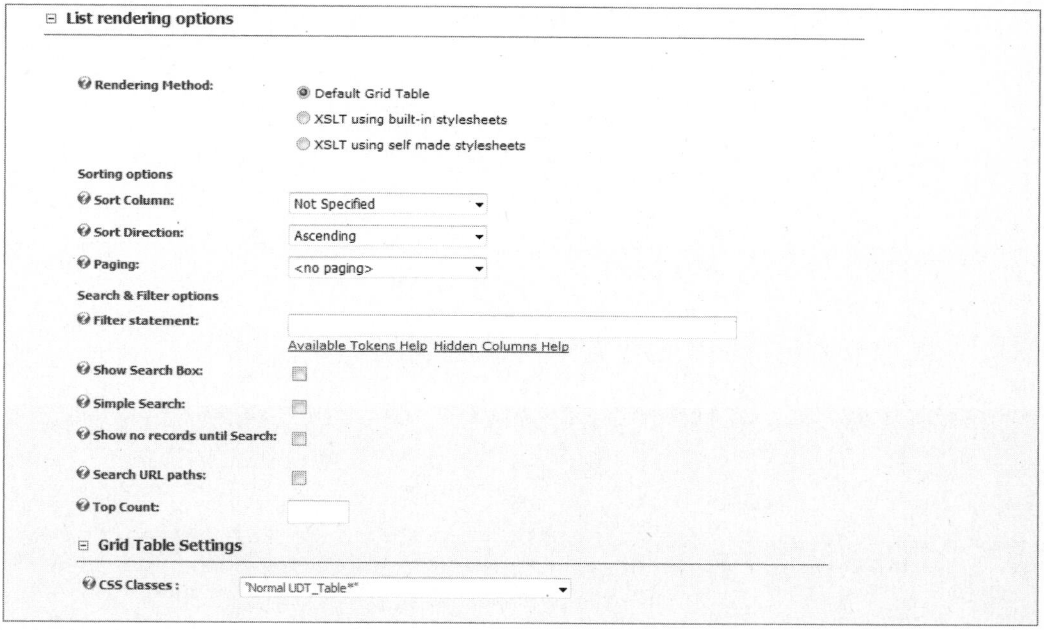

Figure 6-27

Beyond the basic grid, portal managers can have complete control over how their data is displayed using XSL stylesheets. Forms & Lists comes with five pre-built XSL stylesheets to offer additional options for display without needing to create a custom stylesheet. Users that need a master/detail view for their display should try the advancedtable.xsl. If you need to create your own layout, you won't even need to know how to create XSL stylesheets because there is a built-in XSLT Generator and Editor. On the Forms & Lists Configuration screen, select XSLT Using Self Made Stylesheets and click the Generate New link to go to the editor. The XSLT Generator and Editor, shown in Figure 6-28, has an interactive builder to design the layout in HTML and then convert it to XSL. Format your list by selecting fields or tokens from the Available Fields and Context drop-down, and then clicking the Insert link. Use the text area to format the list how you would want it to display in HTML, select your configuration options from the Options section, and click the Generate from HTML Template button. After the XSL stylesheet has been generated from the HTML template, make any manual changes in the script text area, supply a name for the stylesheet, then click Save File and Return.

Users familiar with XSL that want to create, test, and debug their stylesheets in an editor outside of DotNetNuke can get access to the XML source for the list by choosing the Show Data as XML option in the hover menu.

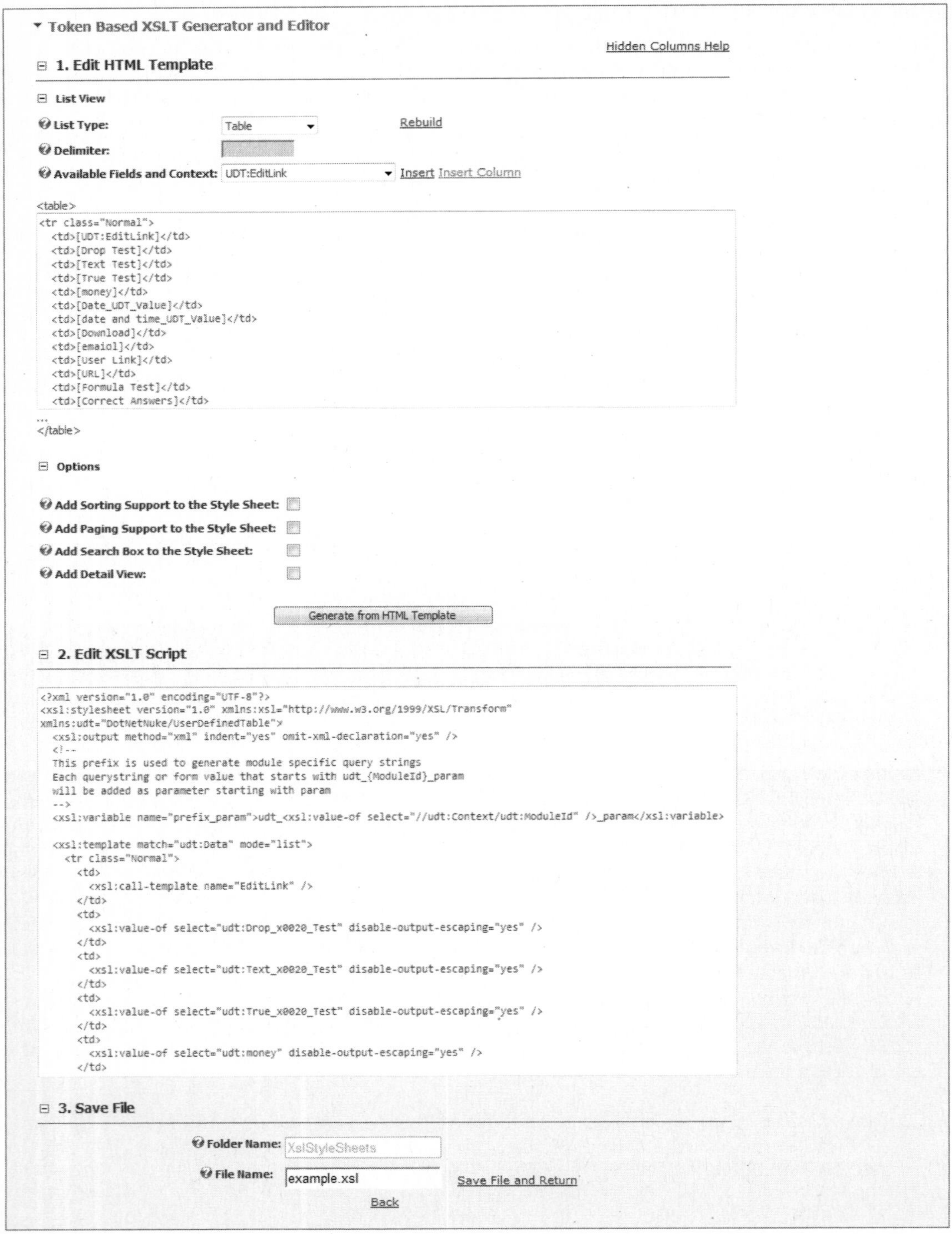

Token Based XSLT Generator and Editor
Hidden Columns Help
1. Edit HTML Template
List View
List Type: Table Rebuild
Delimiter:
Available Fields and Context: UDT:EditLink Insert Insert Column
<table>
<tr class="Normal">
<td>[UDT:EditLink]</td>
<td>[Drop Test]</td>
<td>[Text Test]</td>
<td>[True Test]</td>
<td>[money]</td>
<td>[Date_UDT_Value]</td>
<td>[date and time_UDT_Value]</td>
<td>[Download]</td>
<td>[emaiol]</td>
<td>[User Link]</td>
<td>[URL]</td>
<td>[Formula Test]</td>
<td>[Correct Answers]</td>
...
</table>
Options
Add Sorting Support to the Style Sheet:
Add Paging Support to the Style Sheet:
Add Search Box to the Style Sheet:
Add Detail View:
Generate from HTML Template
2. Edit XSLT Script
<?xml version="1.0" encoding="UTF-8"?>
<xsl:stylesheet version="1.0" xmlns:xsl="http://www.w3.org/1999/XSL/Transform"
xmlns:udt="DotNetNuke/UserDefinedTable">
<xsl:output method="xml" indent="yes" omit-xml-declaration="yes" />
<!--
This prefix is used to generate module specific query strings
Each querystring or form value that starts with udt_{ModuleId}_param
will be added as parameter starting with param
-->
<xsl:variable name="prefix_param">udt_<xsl:value-of select="//udt:Context/udt:ModuleId" />_param</xsl:variable>
<xsl:template match="udt:Data" mode="list">
<tr class="Normal">
<td>
<xsl:call-template name="EditLink" />
</td>
<td>
<xsl:value-of select="udt:Drop_x0020_Test" disable-output-escaping="yes" />
</td>
<td>
<xsl:value-of select="udt:Text_x0020_Test" disable-output-escaping="yes" />
</td>
<td>
<xsl:value-of select="udt:True_x0020_Test" disable-output-escaping="yes" />
</td>
<td>
<xsl:value-of select="udt:money" disable-output-escaping="yes" />
</td>
3. Save File
Folder Name: XslStyleSheets
File Name: example.xsl Save File and Return
Back

Figure 6-28

Portable Formats for Transferring Layouts and Data

The Configuration Templates feature in Forms & Lists allows you to save a configuration as a layout file. This makes it simple to distribute a layout, column, and data structure as a single file, making it easy to share across multiple instances in a portal or even to share with other users in a public forum. For forms and lists that contain data, you can alternatively use the Import or Export options in the hover menu to transfer the layout with all of the data stored within the list.

IFrame

The IFrame module enables you to display web pages from other web sites in your portal. When you set the page, the module should display and add an IFrame tag to your page and load the remote site into the frame. One of the main uses for this module mentioned in the DotNetNuke forums is to utilize legacy applications that were created with ASP or some other dynamic language that must still be used for some functionality. This enables companies to take advantage of the benefits of DotNetNuke while still using other functionality of previous applications. This usually is a short-term fix; as companies become more familiar with DotNetNuke module development, they can convert their legacy applications to fully compliant DotNetNuke modules to take advantage of full integration with DotNetNuke roles and user control functions. Table 6-14 describes the options available.

Media

The Media module is the replacement for the Image module. The Media module displays a single image or Flash movie. To control the image or movie options, choose Edit Media Options from the hover menu. The options to control how the Media module displays content are listed in Table 6-15.

News Feeds (RSS)

The News Feeds (RSS) module enables you to consume RSS content from another resource and display it to your users. Many web sites offer syndicated feeds that you can consume and from which you can display relevant content for your portal, some of which are free and some of which require a fee to use. With the News Feeds (RSS) module, you can use both types of feeds and display the information according to your feed stylesheet.

The newest version of the News Feeds (RSS) module allows you to have multiple RSS sources in a single module. This allows the module to act as a true aggregator and combine feeds from multiple sources always to be sure that new items are available for view. To manage the feeds, choose the Edit News Feeds option from the hover menu. All display options are now part of the module-specific settings. Expand the News Module Settings section of the settings interface to manage the XSL stylesheet to use with the feed, number of items to display, and cache options (Figure 6-29).

Survey

The Survey module supplies the popular functionality of creating web site visitor participation questions that people can vote on and compare their answers to other users'. To set up a survey, choose the Add Survey option from the hover menu, and enter your question text and available options. See Figure 6-30 for an example of a survey.

Users Online

The Users Online module displays statistics on membership and a snapshot of how many users are currently online. By default, the mechanism to monitor the number of users currently online is disabled because of the overhead associated with keeping track of which users are currently on the web site. To enable Users Online tracking, go to the Host Settings page under the Host menu and uncheck the Disable Users Online check box under Advanced Settings, Other Settings. Control the Users Online Time to increase or decrease the frequency at which the stats should be updated to balance performance with accuracy. A higher number is less accurate, but requires less load on the application. Figure 6-31 shows an active Users Online module.

Table 6-14: Edit IFrame Options

Option	Description
Source	The location of the web page you want to display in your module.
Width and Height	Determines the size of the IFrame and should be adjusted to fit the page you need to display. The fields can be entered either as pixels or as a percentage, depending on your needs.
Auto Height	Automatically stretches the height according to the content of the frame, but only works if the document inside the IFrame belongs to the same domain.
Scrolling	Determines whether the IFrame adds scrollbars for the frame. This is important if the target web page is larger than you can show in your portal without impeding the display or omitting certain content of the target page. The auto setting usually is the best choice because the module will determine whether the bars are needed based on the dimensions of the target page.
Border	Defines whether a border will appear around the target page.
Allow Transparency	Adds the allowtransparency=true to the IFrame. In order for this work, the inner document must also have the appropriate CSS transparency style applied.
Name	Use this to set the name for JavaScript and HTML links to be able to control the IFrame location.
Tool Tip	Text to display when users hover their mouse over the IFrame.
Onload (JavaScript)	This gives administrators only the ability to supply JavaScript to attach to the onload event of the IFrame and is often used for resizing.
QueryString Parameters	Allows for dynamic and context-based parameters to be supplied to IFrames through the querystring. This is useful for companies that need to connect user-based external functionality where a unique user identifier needs to be supplied.

Table 6-15: Media Display Options

Option	Description
Media Alignment	Controls how the media should layout within the content's space.
Media	Controls the file to be served through the Media module.
Alternate Text	Sets the text set in the `alt` attribute to be displayed for images.
Width	Controls the width of the media to be displayed.
Height	Controls the height of the media to be displayed.
Link	For images, makes the image link to a value specified in a module.

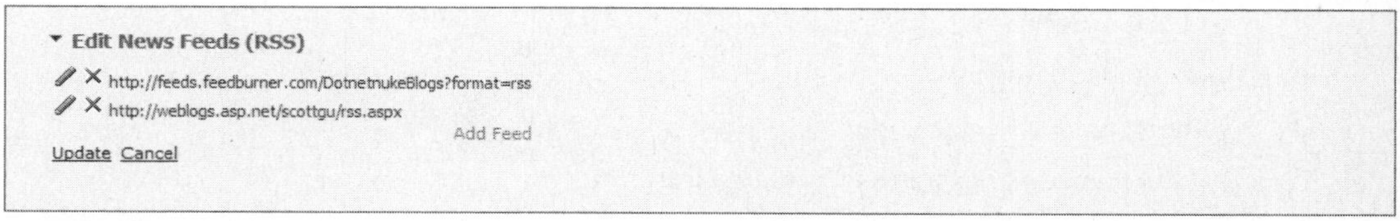

Figure 6-29

Figure 6-30

Figure 6-31

XML/XSL

The XML/XSL module allows binding to a remote or local XML or RSS data source and applying a custom XSL stylesheet to format the results. The newest version also enables portal managers to use information about the current user, portal, or installation to send as querystring parameters to the XML feed and as XSL parameters into the XSL stylesheet.

The XML module is best explained with an example. Use the following steps to create a personalized weather feed from Yahoo for the current user:

- Use Notepad to create a new text document with the text the example below and save it as weather.xsl.
- Add the XML/XSL module to a page.
- Choose the Edit XML/XSL Options from the hover menu.
- Set the URL to `http://weather.yahooapis.com/forecastrss`.
- Add two Querystring Parameters.
- Name: u, Static Value: f
- Name: p, User's Postal Code
- Upload the weather.xsl file you created in step 1.
- Add an XSL Parameter named DisplayName and select User's Display Name for the value.
- After your settings match Figure 6-32, save your settings.

```
<?xml version="1.0" encoding="UTF-8" ?>
<xsl:stylesheet version="1.0" xmlns:xsl="http://www.w3.org/1999/XSL/Transform">
<xsl:template match="/">
<xsl:apply-templates select="/rss/channel/item"/>
</xsl:template>
<xsl:param name="DisplayName"/>
<xsl:template match="item">
<div id="{guid}">
Personalized Weather for <xsl:value-of select="$DisplayName" disable-output-
escaping="yes"/><br/>
<xsl:value-of select="description" disable-output-escaping="yes"/>
</div>
</xsl:template>
</xsl:stylesheet>
```

Sub-Project Modules

To meet the growing needs of the community, a number of sub-projects have been formed to further extend the initial modules bundled within DotNetNuke. These projects are managed separately from the core project and are typically released in shorter time frames. If you have these modules installed in your application, make sure to check the Module Definitions page in your Host menu to check if a newer version is available. Popular sub-projects include the following:

- Forum
- Help

- Reports
- Repository
- Store
- Wiki
- Chat
- Gallery
- Map

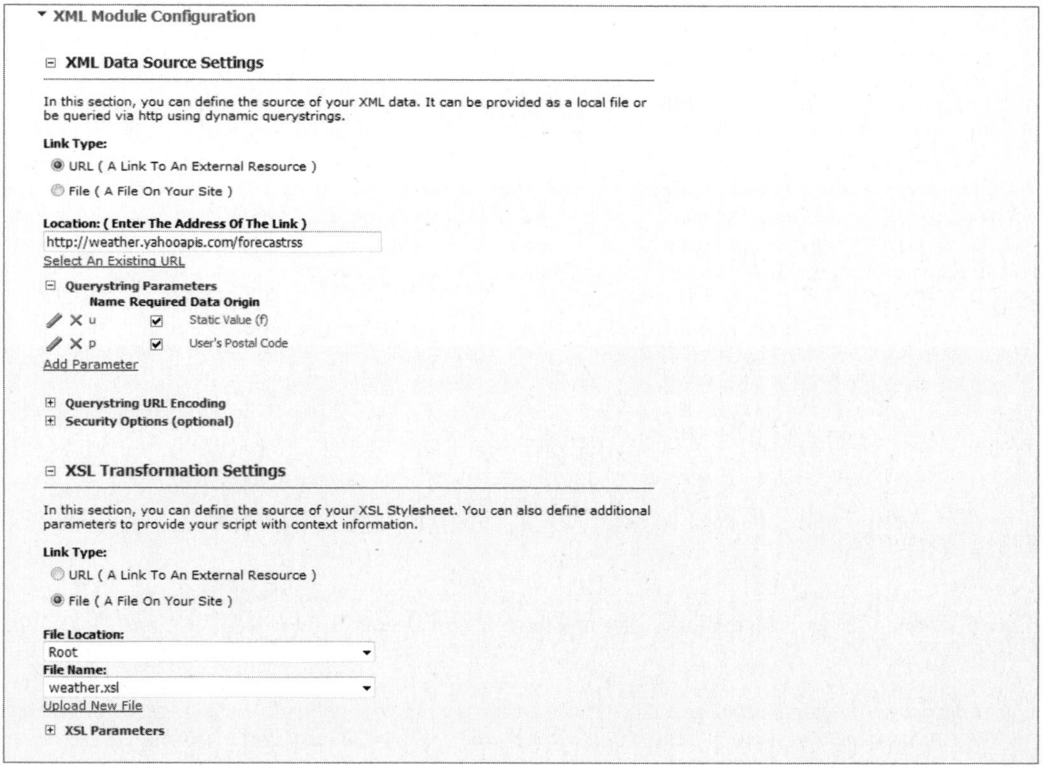

Figure 6-32

You can download these modules or find out more information about them at `http://www.dotnetnuke.com/DotNetNukeProjects/tabid/824/Default.aspx`.

Commercial and Open-Source Third-Party Modules

One of the most attractive aspects of the DotNetNuke community over other open source CMS platforms is the thriving third-party market. `SnowCovered.com` led the way in the beginning to give a place for commercial module and skin developers to sell their goods to the community. As the platform and community has grown, one of the complaints of the market was that there were too many low-cost, low-quality modules available, and it made it more difficult for web site owners to know which modules were safe to install. One of the ways that the DotNetNuke Core Team has tried to help the brand has been to establish the DotNetNuke MarketPlace at `http://MarketPlace.DotNetNuke.com`. The DotNetNuke MarketPlace has the advantage over other web sites that sell DotNetNuke modules in that many developers participate in the Code Review program by having their code reviewed by the DotNetNuke Core Team. DotNetNuke promotes the service by giving vendors that sell reviewed modules prime placement in the catalog and a logo to place on their product details page to differentiate the quality. Modules sold on MarketPlace tend to be a little more expensive, but generally come with better support and higher quality. Also, proceeds go to fund DotNetNuke Corporation, which funds certain initiatives and keeps the Core Team working on DotNetNuke.

Before you rush out and purchase and install every module, though, understand that adding modules to your installation does add overhead to you application. Installing third-party modules with dependencies on the DotNetNuke core can also have the added maintenance of making sure that they are compatible with the newest releases before you can upgrade to take advantage of new features or to address urgent security releases. There are some great modules and developers in the market creating features that make it easier to market, manage, and sell products and create communities on your DotNetNuke web site; just make sure that installing a module is worth the maintenance required to keep a module before you install.

In addition to the commercial market, DotNetNuke Forge was created in 2008 to establish a place where module developers that want to share their pet projects and open source add-ons for DotNetNuke can make them available through DotNetNuke.com and Microsoft's CodePlex web site. In the first months since its creation, Forge has produced a handful of very useful utilities that developers thought were too valuable to keep to themselves. Check it out at `http://www.dotnetnuke.com/tabid/824/default.aspx`.

Summary

This chapter explored how to use modules to display content on your DotNetNuke portals. You should now understand how to manage the settings that control security and display options for DotNetNuke modules.

This chapter also took an in-depth look at the DotNetNuke core modules and reviewed the management of those modules from a site administrator's perspective. It also examined management from a page perspective and examined the various controls, such as the hover menu, that are included within a module.

For a list of some of the authors' favorite free and commercial modules, see Appendix A, "Resources."

7

DotNetNuke Architecture

The architecture of DotNetNuke has evolved from a simple rewrite of the IBuySpy Portal into a best-practice example of enterprise-level design patterns and coding standards that can be applied in the real world. This chapter explains the components of the architecture behind DotNetNuke and how they work together to form an enterprise-worthy web application framework.

Before tackling the architectural overview, however, you should understand some key technologies that DotNetNuke employs.

Technologies Used

DotNetNuke was originally derived from the IBuySpy Portal Starter Kit. IBuySpy was written in VB.NET and showcased some interesting development concepts of the "new" ASP.NET platform. If you look under the hood of DotNetNuke today, it doesn't even resemble IBuySpy. We've taken the basic principles of dynamic content from IBuySpy and applied many best-practice design patterns and coding standards that have evolved as the .NET Framework has grown.

DotNetNuke uses several key technologies in its supported architecture:

- An operating system that supports ASP.NET (that is, Windows 2000 with SP4, Windows 2003 Server, Windows XP with SP3, Vista, and so on)
- The ASP.NET framework (Early versions of DotNetNuke ran on the then current version of ASP.NET. DotNetNuke versions 4 and 5 require the ASP.NET 2.0 or later framework for both runtime and development.)
- Visual Basic .NET (C# or any other CLR-compliant language can be used to write extensions to the platform.)
- Web forms
- Microsoft Internet Information Services (or any web server capable of supporting ASP.NET such as the built-in web server in VWD Express and so on)

- ADO.NET
- Microsoft SQL Server 2000, Microsoft SQL Server 2005 (Express, Standard, or Enterprise), or Microsoft SQL Server 2008 (Express, Standard or Enterprise)

In addition, DotNetNuke showcases several key design patterns and concepts that differentiate it from many other web application frameworks and provides a foundation that demonstrates and encourages best-practice programming:

- Provider Model
- Inversion of Control (New in DotNetNuke 5.0)
- Custom Business Objects and Controllers
- Centralized Custom Business Object Hydration
- Membership, Roles, and Profile Providers using ASP.NET 2.0 API
- Localization framework that mirrors the ASP.NET 2.0 implementation

Provider Model

The Provider Model is a design pattern that is used in the DotNetNuke architecture to allow core functionality to be replaced without modifying core code. The introduction of the Provider Model started with Microsoft in its need to provide a simple, extensible API in .NET. The Provider Model was formalized in ASP.NET 2.0 as a best-practice design pattern. The purpose of the Provider Model is to provide a well-documented, easy-to-understand API that has the benefits of simplicity and the power of extensibility.

To provide both simplicity and extensibility, the API is separated from the implementation of the API. A provider is a contract between an API and the business logic that establishes the functionality that the implementation of the API must provide. When a method in the API is called, it is the implementation of the API that fulfills the request. Simply put, the API doesn't care how the job is done, as long as it is done. If there is one useful concept garnered from this section, let it be this oversimplification of the purpose of the Provider Model: **Build things so they do not depend on the details of other things**.

This fundamental design concept was recognized well before the Provider Model came to fruition, but it truly speaks to what the Provider Model brings to developers. The API in the Provider Model does not depend on the details of the implementation of the API. Therefore, the implementation of the API can be changed easily, and the API itself is unaffected due to the abstraction.

Provider Model Usage

Several areas in DotNetNuke use the Provider Model:

- Data Provider
- Membership Provider
- Profile Provider
- Roles Provider

- Navigation Provider
- Caching Provider
- Authentication Provider
- Scheduling Provider
- Logging Provider
- HTML Editor Provider
- Search Provider
- Friendly URL Provider

The first implementation of the Provider Model in DotNetNuke was the Data Provider. DotNetNuke originally supported only Microsoft SQL Server. The core of the portal was tightly coupled with the data tier. There were many requests from the community to extend DotNetNuke to support other data stores. We needed a way to support a diverse array of data stores while maintaining a simple Data Access Layer and allowing for extensibility. That is when the concept of the Provider Model was first introduced into DotNetNuke.

Figure 7-1 shows that the Data Provider API is not dependent on a tightly coupled implementation of the API. Instead, the Data Provider API doesn't even know what kind of data store is being used until you configure an XML setting in the web.config file. Other than the settings in web.config, the only other requirement of the Data Provider API is that the implementation of the API must fulfill its contract by providing the necessary functionality defined in the base class. For example, all methods marked with `MustOverride` in the Data Provider API must be overridden in the implementation of the API.

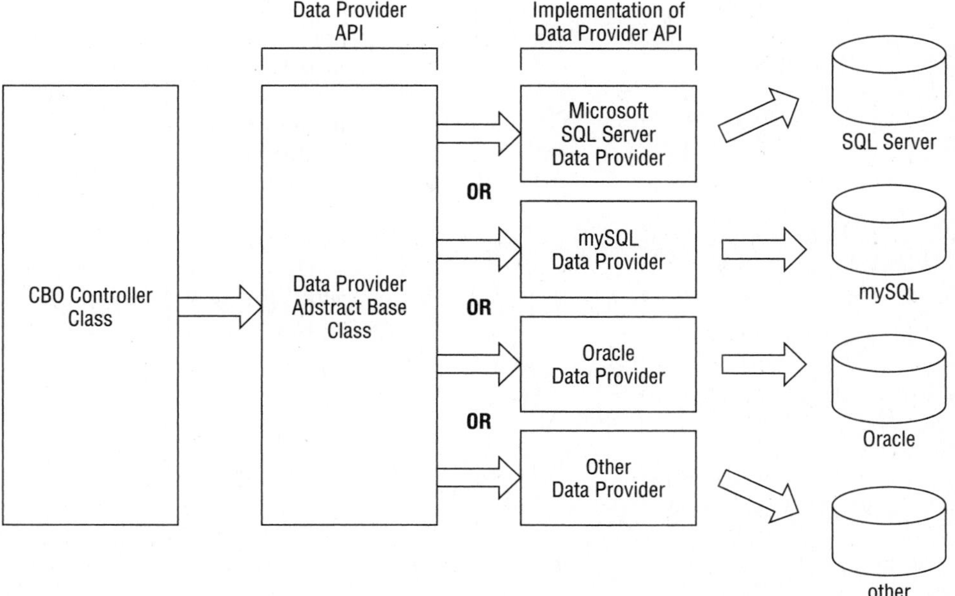

Figure 7-1

Provider Configuration

The Provider API has to be configured to work with the implementation of the API. The API needs to be configured to know which type and assembly to use for the implementation of the API. As mentioned in the previous section, this is handled in the web.config file.

The configuration settings are in XML in the web.config file. There is no standard for naming conventions or the structure of the configuration settings in the Provider Model in general. Nevertheless, DotNetNuke has followed a consistent pattern in each Provider Model API and the associated configuration settings.

Each API may have different requirements for configuration settings. For example, the Data Provider API needs a connection string defined in its configuration settings. The XML Logging Provider needs its log configuration file location defined in its configuration settings. So each API has configuration settings that are specific to it.

The DotNetNuke core providers store the Provider Model API configuration settings in web.config under the /configuration/dotnetnuke node. When a Provider Model API is first instantiated, it collects these settings, which enable it to use the specified implementation of the API. The configuration settings are then cached so that in subsequent requests, the configuration settings are retrieved more quickly. The following code shows a section of the web.config file that contains the Data Provider API's configuration settings:

```
<data defaultProvider="SqlDataProvider">
      <providers>
            <clear />
            <add name="SqlDataProvider"
            type="DotNetNuke.Data.SqlDataProvider, DotNetNuke.SqlDataProvider"
            connectionStringName="SiteSqlServer"
            upgradeConnectionString=""
            providerPath="~\Providers\DataProviders\SqlDataProvider\"
            objectQualifier=""
            templateFile="DotNetNuke_template.mdf"
            databaseOwner="dbo" />
      </providers>
</data>
```

New to DotNetNuke 5.0 is the ability to instantiate a provider without having to configure it in the web.config file. This is accomplished via the implementation of an Inversion of Control design pattern.

The Provider Model has brought great value to DotNetNuke in the way that it allows for functionality to be replaced without modifying the core code. In DotNetNuke, as in most open-source applications, the core code should not be modified by its consumers if at all possible. The Provider Model helps enforce this fundamental standard of open-source application development. It also provides a new level of abstraction between the Data Access Layer and the data store.

Custom Business Objects

A Custom Business Object (CBO) is essentially a blueprint, or representation, of an object that is important to the application. In DotNetNuke, an example of a CBO is an instance of the

DotNetNuke.Services.Vendors.AffiliateInfo class in Library/Services/Vendors/AffiliateInfo.vb. An instance of this class contains information about a single affiliate as shown in the following code:

```
Public Class AffiliateInfo
Private _AffiliateId As Integer
Private _VendorId As Integer
Private _StartDate As Date
Private _EndDate As Date
Private _CPC As Double
Private _Clicks As Integer
Private _CPCTotal As Double
Private _CPA As Double
Private _Acquisitions As Integer
Private _CPATotal As Double

Public Sub New()
End Sub

Public Property AffiliateId() As Integer
Get
Return _AffiliateId
End Get
Set(ByVal Value As Integer)
_AffiliateId = Value
End Set
End Property
Public Property VendorId() As Integer
Get
Return _VendorId
End Get
Set(ByVal Value As Integer)
_VendorId = Value
End Set
End Property
Public Property StartDate() As Date
Get
Return _StartDate
End Get
Set(ByVal Value As Date)
_StartDate = Value
End Set
End Property
Public Property EndDate() As Date
Get
Return _EndDate
End Get
Set(ByVal Value As Date)
_EndDate = Value
End Set
End Property
Public Property CPC() As Double
Get
Return _CPC
```

```
End Get
Set(ByVal Value As Double)
_CPC = Value
End Set
End Property
Public Property Clicks() As Integer
Get
Return _Clicks
End Get
Set(ByVal Value As Integer)
_Clicks = Value
End Set
End Property
Public Property CPCTotal() As Double
Get
Return _CPCTotal
End Get
Set(ByVal Value As Double)
_CPCTotal = Value
End Set
End Property
Public Property CPA() As Double
Get
Return _CPA
End Get
Set(ByVal Value As Double)
_CPA = Value
End Set
End Property
Public Property Acquisitions() As Integer
Get
Return _Acquisitions
End Get
Set(ByVal Value As Integer)
_Acquisitions = Value
End Set
End Property
Public Property CPATotal() As Double
Get
Return _CPATotal
End Get
Set(ByVal Value As Double)
_CPATotal = Value
End Set
End Property
End Class
```

The AffiliateInfo class has no methods, only properties. This is an important distinction to recognize — CBOs only have properties. The methods to manage the CBO are in a CBO Controller class specific to the CBO. A CBO Controller class contains the business logic necessary to work with its associated CBO class. For example, there is an AffiliateController class in Library/Services/Vendors/AffiliateController.vb that contains business logic for the AffiliateInfo CBO. The AffiliateInfo data is stored in the database. Therefore, the AffiliateController class contains the logic necessary to hydrate the AffiliateInfo object (or a collection of AffiliateInfo objects) with data retrieved from the database.

CBO Hydrator

One powerful core service is the CBO Hydrator, which is located in the CBO class in Library/Common/Utilities/CBO.vb. It is a collection of methods that provide a centralized means of hydrating a CBO or a collection of CBOs.

Figure 7-2 shows how a CBO Controller class makes a call to the CBO Hydrator by sending in an open DataReader and the type of object to fill. Depending on the method called within the CBO Hydrator, it returns either a single hydrated object or a collection of hydrated objects. When the CBO Hydrator fills an object's properties, it discovers the properties of the CBO using reflection. Then it caches the properties that it has discovered, so that the next time an object of the same type is hydrated, the properties won't need to be discovered. Instead, they can be pulled from the cache. In version 4.6.0 of DotNetNuke the IHydratable Interface was introduced as an additional way to avoid using reflection.

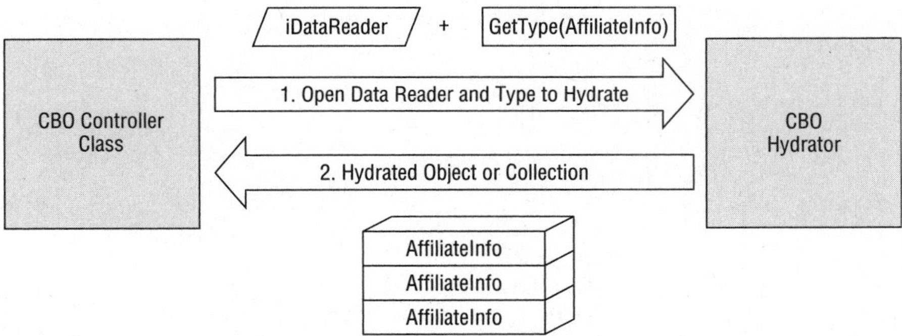

Figure 7-2

To hydrate a collection of CBOs, use the `DotNetNuke.Common.Utilities.CBO.FillCollection` method. The method accepts an `IDataReader` and a type as input parameters. It returns an ArrayList of objects of the type specified in the `objType` parameter. For example, the code-behind for the Portals module ($AppRoot/DesktopModules/Admin/Portals/Portals.ascx.vb) needs a collection of PortalInfo objects so it can display a list of Portals in the portal module's rendered output. The code-behind calls `DotNetNuke.Entities.Portals.PortalController.GetPortalsByName()` to get an ArrayList of PortalInfo objects. That ArrayList is filled by the `DotNetNuke.Common.Utilities.CBO.FillCollection` method, which converts an iDataReader object (from a database query) into a collection of hydrated PortalInfo objects. Here's the `DotNetNuke.Common.Utilities.CBO.FillCollection` method signature:

```
Public Shared Function FillCollection(ByVal dr As IDataReader, ByVal objType As _
System.Type) As System.Collections.ArrayList
```

To hydrate a single CBO rather than a collection, use the `CBO.FillObject` method. It accepts the same input parameters, but returns a single object. For example, in the code-behind for the Site Settings module ($AppRoot/DesktopModules/Admin/Portals/SiteSettings.ascx.vb), the control needs a PortalInfo object to display the portal settings in the module's rendered output. The code-behind gets the PortalInfo object from a call to `DotNetNuke.Entities.Portals.PortalController.GetPortal`. The `GetPortal` method first checks the cache and if the requested data is not there calls `DotNetNuke.Entities.Portals .GetPortalCallback`, which uses the `DotNetNuke.Common.Utilities.CBO.FillObject` method to convert an iDataReader object (from a database query) into a hydrated PortalInfo object. Following is the method signature for `DotNetNuke.Common.Utilities.CBO.FillObject`:

```
Public Shared Function FillObject(ByVal dr As IDataReader, ByVal _
objType As Type) As Object
```

There is also an overload of the FillObject method that uses Generics with the following signature used in DotNetNuke 5 as shown here:

```
Public Shared Function FillObject(Of TObject)(ByVal dr As _ System.Data.IDataReader)
As TObject
```

Using the CBO Hydrator

The AffiliateController shown in the following code is an example of a CBO Controller that utilizes the CBO Hydrator:

```
Public Class AffiliateController
   Public Function GetAffiliates(ByVal VendorId As Integer) As ArrayList
      Return CBO.FillCollection(DataProvider.Instance().GetAffiliates(VendorId), _
      GetType(AffiliateInfo))
   End Function
   Public Function GetAffiliate(ByVal AffiliateId As Integer, ByVal VendorId As _
   Integer,Byval PortalID as integer) As AffiliateInfo
      Return CType(CBO.FillObject(DataProvider.Instance().GetAffiliate( _
      AffiliateId,VendorId,PortalID), GetType(AffiliateInfo)), AffiliateInfo)
   End Function
   Public Sub DeleteAffiliate(ByVal AffiliateId As Integer)
      DataProvider.Instance().DeleteAffiliate(AffiliateId)
   End Sub
   Public Sub AddAffiliate(ByVal objAffiliate As AffiliateInfo)
      DataProvider.Instance().AddAffiliate(objAffiliate.VendorId, _
      objAffiliate.StartDate, objAffiliate.EndDate, objAffiliate.CPC, _
      objAffiliate.CPA)
   End Sub
   Public Sub UpdateAffiliate(ByVal objAffiliate As AffiliateInfo)
      DataProvider.Instance().UpdateAffiliate(objAffiliate.AffiliateId, _
      objAffiliate.StartDate, objAffiliate.EndDate, objAffiliate.CPC, _
      objAffiliate.CPA)
   End Sub
   Public Sub UpdateAffiliateStats(ByVal AffiliateId As Integer, _
   ByVal Clicks As Integer, ByVal Acquisitions As Integer)
      DataProvider.Instance().UpdateAffiliateStats(AffiliateId, Clicks, _
      Acquisitions)
   End Sub
End Class
```

Using the CBO Hydrator significantly reduces the amount of code needed to fill an object or collection of objects. Without using the CBO Hydrator, you would have to code at least one line per CBO property to fill that object with the contents of a DataReader. The following code is an example of filling a single AffilateInfo object without using the CBO Hydrator:

```
Dim dr As IDataReader
Try
    dr = DataProvider.Instance().GetAffiliate(AffiliateId, VendorId, PortalID)
    Dim f As New AffiliateInfo
    f.AffiliateId = Convert.ToInt32 (dr("AffiliateId"))
    f.VendorId = Convert.ToInt32 (dr("VendorId"))
    f.ToInt32 = Convert.ToInt32(dr("ToInt32"))
    f.EndDate = Convert.ToString(dr("EndDate"))
    f.CPC = Convert.ToString(dr("CPC"))
    f.Clicks = Convert.ToInt32(dr("Clicks"))
    f.CPCTotal = Convert.ToInt32(dr("CPCTotal"))
    f.CPA = Convert.ToInt32(dr("CPA"))
    f.Acquisitions = Convert.ToInt32(dr("Acquisitions"))
    f.CPATotal = Convert.ToInt32(dr("CPATotal"))

    Return f
Finally
    If Not dr Is Nothing Then
        dr.Close()
    End If
End Try
```

Instead of writing all of that code, the CBO Hydrator can be used to greatly simplify things. The following code does the same thing as the preceding code, except it uses the CBO Hydrator:

```
Return CType(CBO.FillObject(DataProvider.Instance().GetAffiliate(AffiliateId,
VendorId, PortalID), GetType(Services.Vendors.AffiliateInfo)), AffiliateInfo)
```

Custom Business Objects are used throughout DotNetNuke to create a truly object-oriented design. The objects provide for type safety and enhance performance by allowing code to work with disconnected collections and objects rather than coding directly against DataReaders, DataTables, or DataSets. Use the CBO Hydrator whenever possible to reduce the amount of coding and to enhance the maintainability of the application.

The exception is if your CBO is having performance issues. In that case you will want to create a custom hydrator via the IHydratable Interface.

Architectural Overview

The DotNetNuke architecture permits the application tiers to be distributed across two servers, the web server and the database server, as shown in Figure 7-3. The web server contains the Presentation, Business Logic, and Data Access Layers. The database server contains the Data Layer.

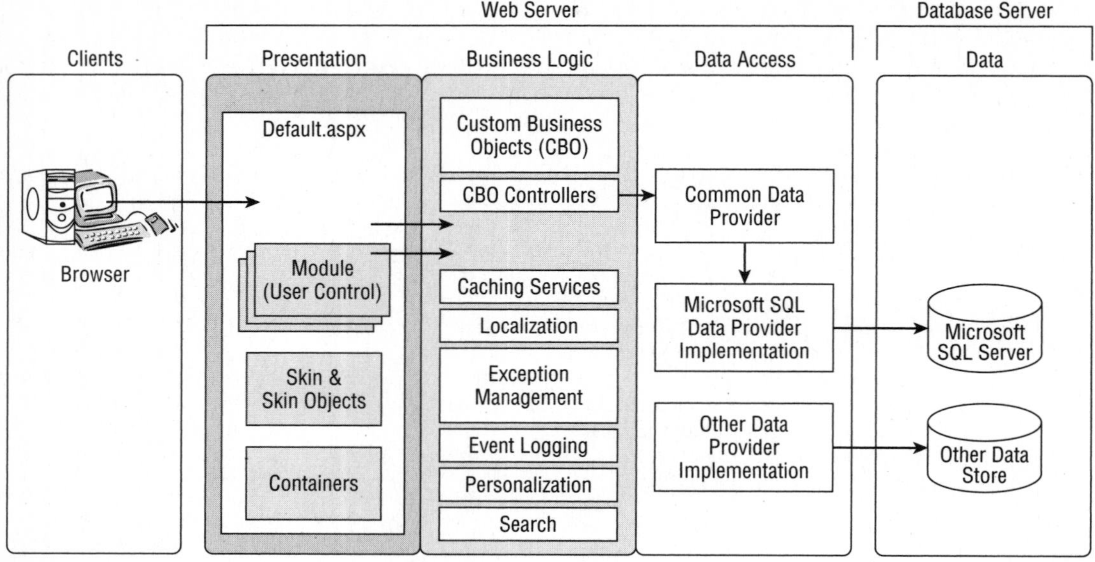

Figure 7-3

Presentation Layer

The Presentation Layer provides an interface for clients to access the portal application. This layer consists of the following elements:

- **Web forms**: The primary web form is Default.aspx. This page is the entry point to the application. It is responsible for dynamically loading the other elements of the Presentation Layer. Default.aspx is in the root installation directory.
- **Skins**: The Default.aspx web form loads the skin for the page based on the settings for each page and portal. The base Skin class is in the DotNetNuke.UI.Skins namespace. If you have installed the source code, you can find the base Skin class in the /Library/UI/Skins/Skin.vb file.
- **Panes**: New in DotNetNuke 5 is the Pane class. A Skin can contain multiple content-panes, which will form a collection of pane objects based on the design and settings for each skin, page, and portal. The base Pane class is located in the DotNetNuke.UI.Skins namespace. If you have installed the source code, you can find the base Pane class in the /Library/UI/Skins/Pane.vb file.
- **Containers**: The Pane object loads the container for each module based on the settings for each module, page, and portal. The base container class is located in the DotNetNuke.UI.Containers namespace. If you have installed the source code, you can find the base Container class in the /Library/UI./Containers/Container.vb file.
- **Module user controls**: Modules will have at least a single user control that is the user interface for the module. These user controls are loaded by a container object based on the settings for each module, page, and portal. The module user controls are in .ascx files in /DesktopModules/[module name].
- **Client-side scripts**: There are several client-side JavaScript files that are used by the core user-interface framework. For example, the /DotNetNuke/js/dnn.controls.dnnmenu.js script

file is used by the DNNMenu control. Custom modules can include and reference JavaScript files as well. Client-side JavaScript files that are used by the core are in the /js folder. Some skins may use client-side JavaScript, in which case the scripts are in the skin's installation directory. Any client-side scripts used by modules are located under the module's installation directory.

When visiting a DotNetNuke portal, the web form that loads the portal page is Default.aspx. The code-behind for this page ($AppRoot/Default.aspx.vb) loads the selected skin for the active page. The skin is a user control that must inherit from the DotNetNuke.UI.Skins.Skin base class. In previous versions of DotNetNuke, the Skin class was where most of the action happened. In DotNetNuke 5, the Skin is the start of the hierarchy for the Presentation Layer.

First, the Skin object creates a Pane object for each of the content-panes in the skin and places them in a collection of panes. Second, the Skin object iterates through all of the modules that are associated with the portal page. The skin then passes each module off to the appropriate Pane object. If more than one module is assigned to a given pane, the pane will have a collection of modules.

Next, each Pane object will determine what Container is assigned to each module. The Pane object then instantiates a Container object for each module and passes the module to the appropriate Container object.

In previous versions the Container provided a visual boundary that separated one module from another, and provided an action menu to allow access to the module administration. In DotNetNuke 5 the Container object also has the responsibility of ''injecting'' the module onto the page. A container class can be assigned to affect all modules within the entire portal, or a single module.

Next, the Container object determines whether the module implements the DotNetNuke.Entities.Modules.iActionable interface. If it does, the Container object discovers the actions that the module has defined and adds them to the container accordingly.

The Skin, Container, and module can all add references to style sheets to the rendered page. Each one looks for a css file in their specific installation directory. If the file exists, the object adds an `HtmlGenericControl` to the page to reference the style sheet.

All of this starts within the Skin class in the `Init` event as shown in Figure 7-4. The final rendering of the contents of a module is handled within each module's event lifecycle.

Finally, the code-behind ($AppRoot/Default.aspx.vb) renders the appropriate style-sheet links based on the configuration of the portal and its skin. See Chapter 16, ''Skinning DotNetNuke,'' for more details on style sheets and the order in which they are loaded.

Business Logic Layer

The Business Logic Layer provides the business logic for all core portal activity. This layer exposes many services to core and third-party modules. These services include:

- Localization
- Caching
- Exception management
- Event logging

- Personalization
- Search
- Installation and upgrades
- Membership, roles, and profile
- Security permissions

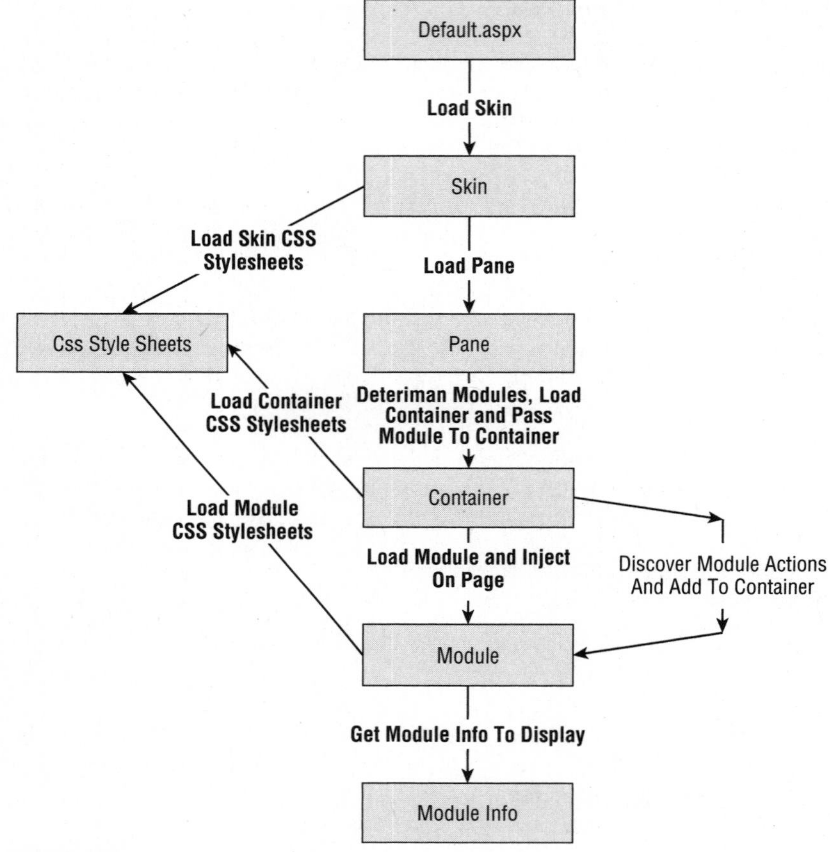

Figure 7-4

The Business Logic Layer is also home to Custom Business Objects (CBOs), whose fundamental purpose is to store information about an object.

Data Access Layer

The Data Access Layer provides data services to the Business Logic Layer. It allows for data to flow to and from a data store.

As described earlier in this chapter, the Data Access Layer uses the Provider Model to enable DotNetNuke to support a wide array of data stores. The Data Access Layer consists of two elements:

1. **Data Provider API**: An abstract base class that establishes the contract that the implementation of the API must fulfill.
2. **Implementation of Data Provider API**: A class that inherits from the Data Provider API class and fulfills the contract by overriding the necessary members and methods.

The core DotNetNuke release provides a Microsoft SQL Server implementation of the Data Provider API.

Beginning with the CBO Controller class, the following code snippets show how the Data Provider API works with the Implementation of the Data Provider API. The following code shows how the IDataReader that is sent into `CBO.FillObject` is a call to `DataProvider.Instance().GetAffiliate (AffiliateId, VendorId, PortalID)`:

```
Public Function GetAffiliate(ByVal AffiliateId As Integer, ByVal VendorId As _
Integer,Byval PortalID as integer) As AffiliateInfo
   Return CType(CBO.FillObject(DataProvider.Instance().GetAffiliate( _
   AffiliateId,VendorId,PortalID), GetType(AffiliateInfo)), AffiliateInfo)
End Function
```

Figure 7-5 breaks down each of the elements in this method call.

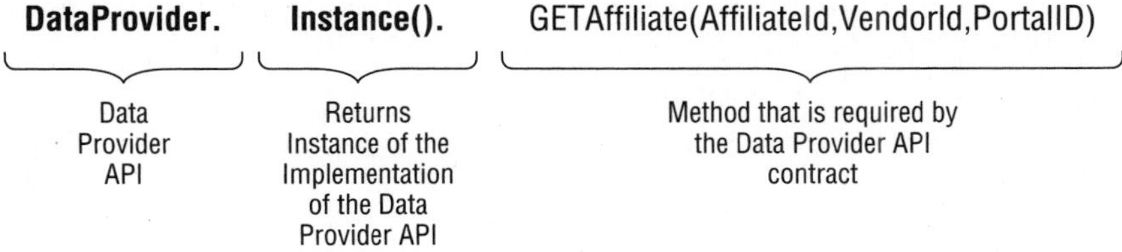

Figure 7-5

The `Instance()` method returns an instance of the implementation of the Data Provider API, and therefore executes the method in the provider itself. The `GetAffiliate` method called in the preceding listing is an abstract method that is detailed here:

```
Public MustOverride Function GetAffiliate(ByVal AffiliateId As Integer, _
ByVal VendorId As Integer, ByVal PortalID As Integer) As IDataReader
```

This method is part of the contract between the API and the implementation of the API. It is overridden in the implementation of the API as shown here:

```
Public Overrides Function GetAffiliate(ByVal AffiliateId As Integer, _
ByVal VendorId As Integer, ByVal PortalId As Integer) As IDataReader
   Return CType(SqlHelper.ExecuteReader(ConnectionString, DatabaseOwner _
   & ObjectQualifier & "GetAffiliate", AffiliateId, VendorId, _
   GetNull(PortalId)), IDataReader)
End Function
```

The preceding code shows a reference to the SqlHelper class, which is part of the Microsoft Data Access Application Block. DotNetNuke uses the Data Access Application Block to improve performance and reduce the amount of custom code required for data access. The Data Access Application Block is a .NET component that works with ADO.NET to call stored procedures and execute SQL commands on Microsoft SQL Server.

Data Layer

The Data Layer provides data to the Data Access Layer. The data store used in the Data Layer must be supported by the implementation of the Data Provider API to fulfill the data requests.

Because the DotNetNuke Data Provider Model is so extensible, several Data Providers are available, including core-released Data Providers and third-party providers such as Microsoft SQL Server, Firebird, MySQL, and Oracle providers. The core DotNetNuke release provides a Microsoft SQL Server implementation of the Data Provider API (which includes support for Microsoft SQL Server 2008 Express).

Installation Scripts

Included in the implementation of the API is a collection of scripts that creates the database in the Data Layer during the installation process. These scripts collectively create the database tables, stored procedures, and data necessary to run DotNetNuke. The installation scripts are run only during a new installation and are run from the `DotNetNuke.Services.Upgrade.Upgrade.InstallDNN` method. The scripts are as follows:

- **DotNetNuke.SetUp.SqlDataProvider**: Prepares the database for the installation by dropping some key tables.
- **DotNetNuke.Schema.SqlDataProvider**: Installs the tables and stored procedures.
- **DotNetNuke.Data.SqlDataProvider**: Fills the tables with data.

Upgrade Scripts

For subsequent upgrades performed after the initial installation, a collection of scripts that modify the schema or data during the upgrade process is run from the `DotNetNuke.Services.Upgrade.Upgrade.UpgradeDNN` method. There is one script per baseline version of DotNetNuke. A baseline version is a working version of DotNetNuke that represents some internal milestone. For example, after the Core Team integrates a major new feature, such as the Member Role Provider, the code is tested, compiled, and zipped for distribution among the Core Team. This doesn't necessarily mean that there is one script per released version of DotNetNuke — behind the scenes, there may be several baseline versions before a formal public release.

The file-naming convention includes the version of the script followed by the SqlDataProvider extension. The extension must be the same name as found in the DefaultProvider attribute of the Data Provider's configuration settings in the web.config file. For example, the filename for the upgrade script for upgrading from baseline version 4.0.2 to 4.0.3 is 04.00.03.SqlDataProvider.

When the DotNetNuke application is upgraded to another version, these scripts are executed in logical order according to the version number. Only the scripts with a version number that is less than or equal to the value of the constant `DotNetNuke.Common.Globals.glbAppVersion` are run. This constant is defined in the /Library/Common/Globals.vb file.

Script Syntax

The scripts are written in SQL, but there are two important non-SQL tags used in them: {databaseOwner} and {objectQualifier}. Both of these tags represent a programmatically replaceable element of the script. The first example code in this chapter showed the configuration settings for the Microsoft SQL Server Data Provider implementation that included two XML attributes named databaseOwner and objectQualifier. The databaseOwner attribute defines the database owner to append to data objects in the scripts. The objectQualifier attribute defines a string to prefix the data objects within the scripts.

For example, the following code shows how the GetSearchSettings stored procedure is created in the 03.00.04.SqlDataProvider script:

```
CREATE PROCEDURE {databaseOwner}{objectQualifier}GetSearchSettings
   @ModuleID int
AS
SELECT     tm.ModuleID,
           settings.SettingName,
           settings.SettingValue
FROM       {objectQualifier}Tabs searchTabs INNER JOIN
           {objectQualifier}TabModules searchTabModules
                     ON searchTabs.TabID = searchTabModules.TabID INNER JOIN
           {objectQualifier}Portals p
                     ON searchTabs.PortalID = p.PortalID INNER JOIN
           {objectQualifier}Tabs t
                     ON p.PortalID = t.PortalID INNER JOIN
           {objectQualifier}TabModules tm
                     ON t.TabID = tm.TabID INNER JOIN
           {objectQualifier}ModuleSettings settings

                     ON searchTabModules.ModuleID = settings.ModuleID
WHERE      searchTabs.TabName = N'Search Admin'
AND        tm.ModuleID = @ModuleID
GO
```

This code looks like SQL with the addition of the two non-SQL tags. The first line creates a new stored procedure:

```
CREATE PROCEDURE {databaseOwner}{objectQualifier}GetSearchSettings
```

It is created in the context of the databaseOwner defined in web.config, and the name of the stored procedure is prefixed with the objectQualifier value from web.config.

If in web.config the databaseOwner is set to dbo and the objectQualifier is set to DNN, the preceding line would be programmatically converted to

```
CREATE PROCEDURE dbo.DNN_GetSearchSettings
```

The objectQualifier attribute is useful when you want to maintain multiple instances of DotNetNuke in the same database. For example, you could have a single web server with ten DotNetNuke installations on it, each using the same database. You would not want these ten installations using the same data tables. The objectQualifier attribute adds the flexibility for you to store data from multiple DotNetNuke installations in the same database.

Security Model

In early DotNetNuke releases, the framework offered only a single security solution; the forms-based security that was included with the core release. That security worked well, but it limited the capability to implement DotNetNuke in a way that tightly integrates with other security mechanisms. Third-party developers provided enhancements that allow Windows authentication to be used, and DotNetNuke 4.0 supported Windows authentication directly in the core release. DotNetNuke 5.0 comes with five optional authentication providers: Forms (the default), Active Directory, Cardspace, LiveID, and OpenID.

Examining how security works in ASP.NET 2.0 will help you understand the challenges that the Core Team faced in implementing the Membership API, as well as the finer details of how security works in DotNetNuke today.

Security in ASP.NET 2.0

In ASP.NET 1.x, the native authentication and authorization services relied on external data stores or configuration in the web.config file. For example, in ASP.NET 1.1, an application can provide forms-based authentication. This requires the developer to create a login form and associated controls to acquire, validate, and manage user credentials. After authentication, authorization is provided through XML configurations in the web.config file.

In ASP.NET 2.0, the introduction of several new security enhancements expands on these services in three distinct ways:

1. **Login and user controls**: A new suite of login and user controls provides plenty of functionality out-of-the-box, reducing the need for each application to provide its own login and user controls. For example, it is easy to generate a set of pages for registering a new user, allowing an existing user to log in, and even handling forgotten passwords by simply placing the appropriate controls on a page and setting a few properties.
2. **User management**: ASP.NET 2.0 provides a configuration interface for each application that allows for easy management of the application. One feature of the configuration interface is the capability to manage security for the application. For example, you can easily create a new user and a new role and then add the user to the role, all within the ASP.NET 2.0 native configuration interface. As an alternative, security can be managed by writing a custom management tool to access the same functionality programmatically.
3. **Membership Provider**: This new provider is the conduit between the Presentation Layer (specifically the login/user controls and the configuration interface) and the persistence mechanism. It encapsulates all of the data access code required to manage users and roles.

Together these three components reduce the amount of code that is required to provide authentication and authorization services and persist the data to a data store.

DotNetNuke and ASP.NET 2.0

To build an application that fully supports authentication in ASP.NET 2.0, the Membership Provider has to be integrated into the application. There are several benefits to using this provider in an application. First, it can reduce the amount of code that is written to bring these services to the application. This is true as long as the business requirements fall within the functionality that the default Membership Provider supplies. Second, implementing the Membership Provider promotes developer and consumer confidence because Microsoft has taken on the responsibility of ensuring that its provider follows optimal security standards and has been subjected to rigorous threat modeling and penetration testing.

When the Membership/Roles Provider was first introduced in DotNetNuke 3.0, it leveraged a backported version of this component created by Microsoft because ASP.NET 2.0 had not yet been released. That version conformed to the same API found in ASP.NET 2.0, except that it ran in ASP.NET 1.1. This was a great addition to DotNetNuke for many reasons, but one key benefit is that it allowed DotNetNuke to conform to several ASP.NET 2.0 specifications even before ASP.NET 2.0 was released. DotNetNuke versions 4.0 and 5.0 use the ASP.NET 2.0 Membership/Role Provider.

Security in DotNetNuke 4.0

Security in DotNetNuke 4.0 was implemented with quite a bit of forward thinking. It combines the best features of prior versions of DotNetNuke with the features of the ASP.NET 2.0 Membership Provider. The result is an extensible security model that aligns DotNetNuke closely with best-practice security models in ASP.NET 2.0.

Portals and Applications

DotNetNuke supports running many portals from a single DotNetNuke installation. Each portal has its own users and roles that are not shared with other portals. A portal is identified by a unique key: the PortalID.

Because the default Membership Provider implementation is a generic solution, it does not natively support the concept of having multiple portals, each with its own users and roles. The default implementation was designed in a way that supports only a single portal site in a DotNetNuke installation. The Membership Provider refers to the DotNetNuke installation as an application, and without customization, that application can support only a single set of users and roles (a single portal instance).

To overcome this limitation, a wrapper was needed for the Membership Provider's SQL data providers. This customization allows application virtualization support. The end result is that the Membership Provider, as implemented in DotNetNuke, can support multiple applications (multiple portal instances in a single DotNetNuke installation).

Data Model for Membership

To achieve the full benefit from the Membership Provider, it is important to recognize that user information can be externalized from DotNetNuke and held in a data store that is independent of the main data store. For instance, DotNetNuke may use Microsoft SQL Server as its database to store content and system settings, but the Membership Provider may use Windows authentication, LDAP, or another mechanism to handle authentication and authorization. Because security can be externalized using the Provider Model, it was important to ensure that the implementation of the Membership Provider didn't customize any code or database tables used by the provider. Those data tables had to be independent from the other core DotNetNuke tables. We could not enforce referential integrity between DotNetNuke data and the Membership Provider data, nor could we use cascade deletes or other data level synchronization methods — all of the magic had to happen in the business layer.

One challenge in implementing the Membership Provider was dealing with the fields that DotNetNuke internally supports but that the Membership Provider does not support. Ideally, the Core Team would have completely replaced the DotNetNuke authentication and authorization tables with the tables used by the Membership Provider. Unfortunately, the team could not achieve this goal because the authentication and authorization tables in DotNetNuke were already tied to so many existing and necessary features of the application. For instance, the DotNetNuke Users table has a UserID column, which holds a unique identifier for each user. This UserID is used in nearly all core and third-party modules. The most significant problem with UserID was that it doesn't exist in the Membership Provider. Instead, the Membership Provider uses the Username as the unique key for a user within an application. We needed a way to maintain the UserID to preserve the DotNetNuke functionality that depended on it. This is just one example of an attribute that cannot be handled by Microsoft's default Membership Provider.

Ultimately, we decided that we would need to maintain satellite tables to support the DotNetNuke attributes that could not be managed by the Membership Provider. The goal was to maintain enough information in the DotNetNuke tables so that functionality was not lost, and offload whatever data we could to the Membership Provider tables. The end result is a data model that mirrors the Membership Provider data tables as shown in Figure 7-6.

Notice that none of the tables on top in Figure 7-6 has a database relationship to the any of the tables on the bottom. The lines connecting them simply show their relationship in theory, not an actual relationship in the database.

Because the data for portals, profiles, users, and roles are stored in multiple unrelated tables, the business layer is responsible for aggregating the data. For example, you cannot get a complete representation of a user without collecting data from both the aspnet_Users table (from the Membership Provider) and the Users table (native DotNetNuke table).

In addition to aggregation, data in the tables used by the Membership Provider and the native DotNetNuke tables must be automatically synchronized. Earlier in this chapter, you learned that the Membership Provider supports a wide array of data stores, and in ASP.NET 2.0, the data in those data stores can be managed through a common application configuration utility. If a user is added through that utility, the user is not added to the native DotNetNuke tables. Also, if your Membership Provider uses an LDAP implementation, for example, a user could be added to LDAP but would not be added to the native DotNetNuke tables. That's why synchronization services between the two data structures are provided. DotNetNuke 5.0 fully leverages features of the ASP.NET 2.0 Membership API. Atypical of applications built on new platform releases, DotNetNuke 5.0 provides a tested and proven solution on the ASP.NET 2.0 framework based on the backported component utilized in DotNetNuke 3.0. These features bring demonstrated flexibility and extensibility to the security framework.

Namespace Overview

DotNetNuke 5.0 is a moderately large framework, but it is organized as a coherent set of namespaces and class locations to facilitate ease-of-use for the developer. Figure 7-7 shows the second-level namespaces that fall under the root DotNetNuke namespace.

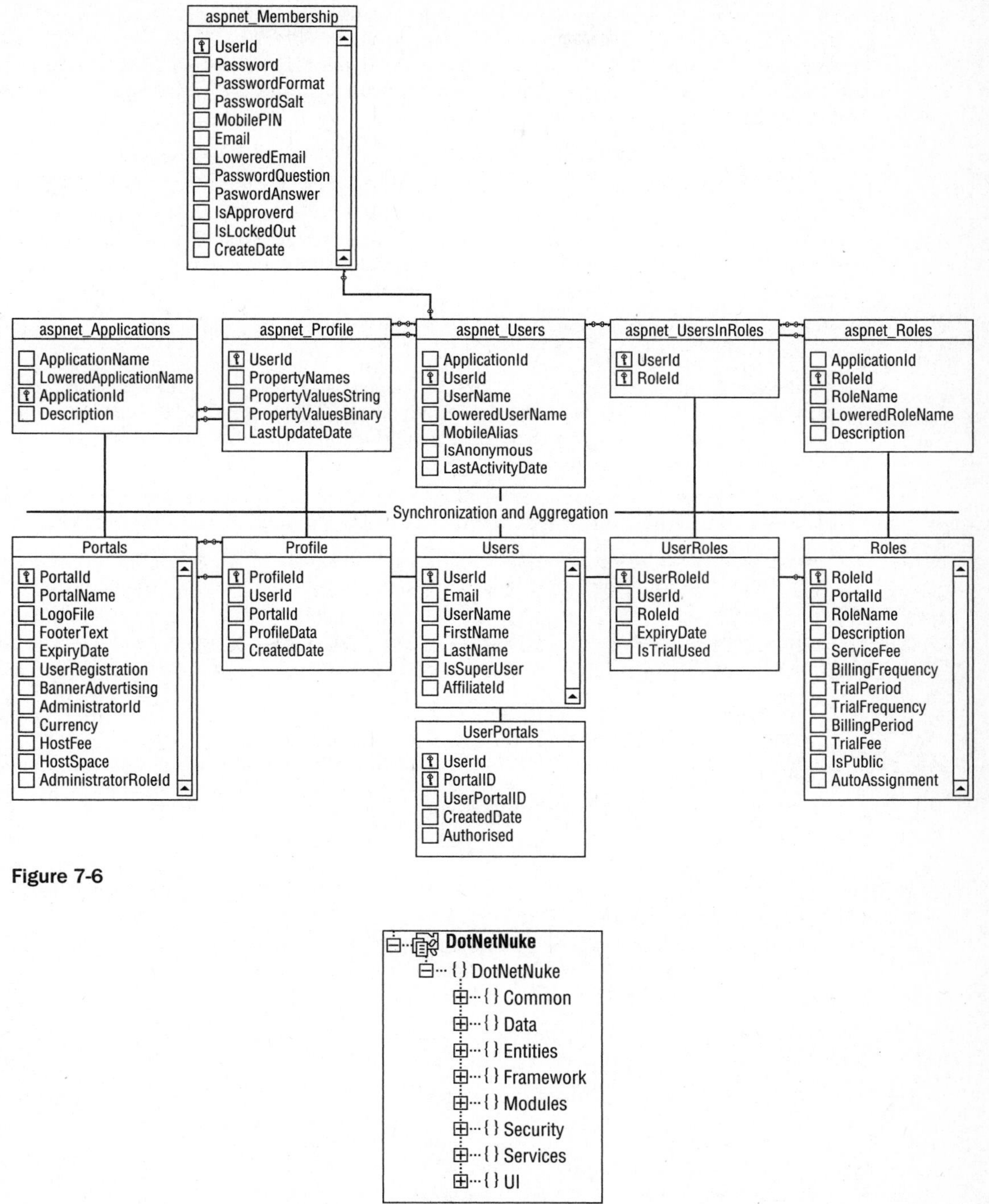

Figure 7-6

Figure 7-7

Here are brief descriptions of these namespaces.

- **DotNetNuke.Common**: Used for all classes used throughout the entire DotNetNuke application. For example, the global constants that are used throughout the application are found in the DotNetNuke.Common.Globals class.
- **DotNetNuke.Data**: Used for any classes relating to the Data Access Layer. For example, the DataProvider base class for the Data Provider API is in the DotNetNuke.Data namespace.
- **DotNetNuke.Entities**: Used for the classes that represent and manage the five entities that make a portal. They are Host, Portals, Tabs, Users, and Modules. The Modules namespace that falls under DotNetNuke.Entities is home to the functionality behind managing modules. The actual modules themselves have their own second-level namespace: DotNetNuke.Modules.
- **DotNetNuke.Framework**: Home to several base classes and other utilities used by the DotNetNuke application.
- **DotNetNuke.Modules**: Used for organizing portal modules. There is a child namespace in the core named DotNetNuke.Modules.Admin where the classes for all of the core admin modules reside. For example, the Host Settings module is found in the DotNetNuke.Modules .Admin.Host.HostSettingsModule class.
- **DotNetNuke.Security**: Used for authorization and authentication classes. This includes tab permissions, module permissions, folder permissions, roles, and other portal security classes.
- **DotNetNuke.Services**: Used for any services the core provides for modules. In this namespace, the child namespaces for exception management, localization, personalization, search, and several others reside.
- **DotNetNuke.UI**: Used for any user interface classes. For example, the Skin and Container classes are found in DotNetNuke.UI.Skins.Skin and DotNetNuke.UI.Containers.Container, respectively.

Summary

This chapter covered the architecture of the DotNetNuke application. Here are key points to understand about the architecture:

- The Provider Model design pattern enhanced DotNetNuke with greater extensibility without having to make core changes to realize that extensibility.
- The use of Custom Business Objects along with the CBO Hydrator created a foundation for developers to code using best-practice standards that enable them to build more maintainable modules and providers that perform well.
- The Membership Provider in DotNetNuke created an extensible security model that showcases an API that mirrors the API found in ASP.NET 2.0.
- The namespace model is organized in a logical hierarchy that makes it easy to find the classes used most often.

In the next chapter, you explore the core DotNetNuke APIs and discover many of the powerful services that the DotNetNuke core application provides developers.

8

Core DotNetNuke APIs

DotNetNuke provides significant capability straight out of the box. Just install and go. Sometimes, however, you may need to extend the base framework. DotNetNuke provides a variety of integration points — from HTTP modules to providers to custom modules. To take full advantage of the framework, it is important to understand some of the base services and APIs provided by DotNetNuke.

This chapter examines some of the core services provided by DotNetNuke. You can use these services from within your own code. Because most of the core services are built using the Provider design pattern, it's also possible to swap out the base functionality. If you need your events logged to a custom database or the Windows Event Logs, just create your own provider.

The second part of this chapter covers several HTTP modules that are installed with DotNetNuke. They provide features like Friendly URLs, Exception Management, and Users Online. Many of the providers installed with DotNetNuke use HTTP modules to hook into the request-processing pipeline. By examining the code used in the core HTTP modules, you can build your own custom extensions and use them in DotNetNuke as well as other ASP.NET applications.

The final section examines some of the core interfaces that you can implement in your own modules. These interfaces simplify the process of adding common features to your module, whether it is the module menu, searches, importing and exporting, or even custom upgrade logic. By using these interfaces in your modules, you can provide some of the same features you see in the core DotNetNuke modules with very little coding effort.

Event Logging

The Logging Provider in DotNetNuke provides a very configurable and extensible set of logging services. It is designed to handle a wide array of logging needs including exception logging, event auditing, and security logging. As you may have gathered from its name, the Logging Provider uses the Provider Model design pattern. This allows the default DB Logging Provider to be replaced with another logging mechanism without having to make changes to the core code. This section covers the ways you can use the Logging Provider to log events in custom modules.

Before you dive into the details of how to use the Logging Provider API, it is important to understand some concepts and terminology that will be used in this section:

- **Log classification** — There are two different types of log classifications in the Logging Provider. The first is the *event log* classification. This encapsulates all log entries related to some type of event within DotNetNuke. For example, you can configure the Logging Provider to write a log entry when a login attempt fails. This would be considered an event log entry. The second log classification is the *exception* log classification. You can configure the Logging Provider to log exceptions and stack traces when exceptions are thrown within DotNetNuke. These two classifications are distinct only because they have different needs in terms of what type of information they log.
- **Log type** — A *log type* defines the type of event that creates the log entry. For example, an event log type is `LOGIN_FAILURE`. The Logging Provider can react differently for each log type. You can configure the Logging Provider to enable or disable logging for each of the log types. Depending on the Logging Provider, you can configure it to log each log type to a different file or to send email notifications upon creating new log entries for that log type.
- **Log type configuration** — The Logging Provider is configured via a module that is accessible from the Event Viewer screen (the Edit Log Settings Module Action). This enables you to configure each log type to be handled differently by the Logging Provider.

The API

The Logging Provider functionality lives in the DotNetNuke.Services.Log.EventLog namespace. In this namespace, you will find the classes that comprise the Logging Provider API. These are described in Table 8-1.

The Controller Classes

The controller classes, EventLogController and ExceptionLogController, are the two that bring the most functionality to custom modules. Many of the other classes are used in concert with the controllers.

EventLogController

The EventLogController provides the methods necessary to log significant system events. This class is located in the DotNetNuke.Library in the Services/Log/EventLog/EventLogController.vb file. The class also defines the EventLogType enumeration that lists each log type that is handled by the EventLogController as shown here:

```
Public Enum EventLogType
        USER_CREATED
        USER_DELETED
        LOGIN_SUPERUSER
        LOGIN_SUCCESS
        LOGIN_FAILURE
        LOGIN_USERLOCKEDOUT
        LOGIN_USERNOTAPPROVED
        CACHE_REFRESHED
```

```
            PASSWORD_SENT_SUCCESS
            PASSWORD_SENT_FAILURE
            LOG_NOTIFICATION_FAILURE
            PORTAL_CREATED
            PORTAL_DELETED
            TAB_CREATED
            TAB_UPDATED
            TAB_DELETED
            TAB_SENT_TO_RECYCLE_BIN
            TAB_RESTORED
            USER_ROLE_CREATED
            USER_ROLE_DELETED
            ROLE_CREATED
            ROLE_UPDATED
            ROLE_DELETED
            MODULE_CREATED
            MODULE_UPDATED
            MODULE_DELETED
            MODULE_SENT_TO_RECYCLE_BIN
            MODULE_RESTORED
            SCHEDULER_EVENT_STARTED
            SCHEDULER_EVENT_PROGRESSING
            SCHEDULER_EVENT_COMPLETED
            APPLICATION_START
            APPLICATION_END
            APPLICATION_SHUTTING_DOWN
            SCHEDULER_STARTED
            SCHEDULER_SHUTTING_DOWN
            SCHEDULER_STOPPED
            ADMIN_ALERT
            HOST_ALERT
            CACHE_ERROR
        End Enum
```

The `EventLogController.AddLog()` method has several method overloads that enable a developer to log just about any values derived from an object or its properties. Following are descriptions of these overloaded methods, along with brief explanations of their parameters:

- The primary AddLog method is ultimately used by all of the other AddLog overloads and accepts a single LogInfo object. This method provides easy access to the base logging method in inherited LogController class:

  ```
  Public Overloads Sub AddLog(ByVal objEventLogInfo As LogInfo)
  ```

- To log the property names and values of a Custom Business Object, use the following method:

  ```
  Public Overloads Sub AddLog(ByVal objCBO As Object, ByVal _PortalSettings As _
  PortalSettings, ByVal UserID As Integer, ByVal UserName As String, ByVal _
  objLogType As Services.Log.EventLog.EventLogController.EventLogType)
  ```

Parameter	Type	Description
objCBO	Object	Custom Business Object.
_PortalSettings	PortalSettings	Current PortalSettings object.
UserID	Integer	UserID of the authenticated user of the request.
UserName	String	UserName of the authenticated user of the request.
objLogType	EventLogType	Event log type.

Table 8-1: Logging Provider Classes

Class	Description
EventLogController	Provides the methods necessary to write log entries with the event log classification. It inherits from LogController.
ExceptionLogController	Provides the methods necessary to write log entries with the exception log classification. It inherits from LogController.
LogController	Provides the methods that interact with the Logging Provider — the basic methods for adding, deleting, and getting log entries.
LogDetailInfo	Holds a single key/value pair of information from a log entry.
LoggingProvider	Provides the bridge to the implementation of the Logging Provider.
LogInfo	Container for the information that goes into a log entry.
LogInfoArray	Holds an array of LogInfo objects.
LogProperties	Holds an array of LogDetailInfo objects.
LogTypeConfigInfo	Container for the configuration data relating to how logs of a specific log type are to be handled.
LogTypeInfo	Container for the log type information.
PurgeLogBuffer	Scheduler task that can be executed regularly if Log Buffering is enabled.
SendLogNotifications	Scheduler task that can be executed regularly if any log type is configured to send email notifications.

- To add a log entry that has no custom properties, use the following method:

```
Public Overloads Sub AddLog(ByVal _PortalSettings As PortalSettings, _
ByVal UserID As Integer, ByVal objLogType As _
Services.Log.EventLog.EventLogController.EventLogType)
```

- This is useful if you simply need to log that an event has occurred, but you have no requirement to log any further details about the event.

Parameter	Type	Description
`_PortalSettings`	PortalSettings	Current PortalSettings object.
`UserID`	Integer	UserID of the authenticated user of the request.
`objLogType`	EventLogType	Event log type.

- To add a log entry that has a single property name and value, use the following method:

```
Public Overloads Sub AddLog(ByVal PropertyName As String, ByVal _
PropertyValue As String, ByVal _PortalSettings As PortalSettings, ByVal _
UserID As Integer, ByVal objLogType As _
Services.Log.EventLog.EventLogController.EventLogType)
```

Parameter	Type	Description
`PropertyName`	String	Name of the property to log.
`PropertyValue`	String	Value of the property to log.
`_PortalSettings`	PortalSettings	Current PortalSettings object.
`UserID`	Integer	UserID of the authenticated user of the request.
`objLogType`	EventLogType	Event log type.

- To add a log entry that has a single property name and value and the LogType is not defined in a core enumeration, use the following method:

```
Public Overloads Sub AddLog(ByVal PropertyName As String, ByVal _ PropertyValue
As String, ByVal _PortalSettings As PortalSettings, ByVal _ UserID As Integer,
ByVal LogType As String)
```

- This is useful for custom modules that define their own log types.

Parameter	Type	Description
`PropertyName`	String	Name of the property to log.
`PropertyValue`	String	Value of the property to log.
`_PortalSettings`	PortalSettings	Current PortalSettings object.
`UserID`	Integer	UserID of the authenticated user of the request.
`LogType`	String	Event log type string.

- To add a log entry that has multiple property names and values, use the following method. To use this method, you must send into it a LogProperties object that is composed of a collection of LogDetailInfo objects.

```
Public Overloads Sub AddLog(ByVal objProperties As LogProperties, ByVal _
_PortalSettings As PortalSettings, ByVal UserID As Integer, ByVal _
LogTypeKey As String, ByVal BypassBuffering As Boolean)
```

Parameter	Type	Description
objProperties	LogProperties	A collection of LogDetailInfo objects.
_PortalSettings	PortalSettings	Current PortalSettings object.
UserID	Integer	UserID of the authenticated user of the request.
LogTypeKey	String	Event log type.
BypassBuffering	Boolean	Specifies whether to write directly to the log (true) or to use log buffering (false) if log buffering is enabled.

The following code examples show how to use the two most common overloaded methods for `EventLogController.AddLog()`. To exemplify the flexibility of this method, the first example illustrates how you can send in a Custom Business Object and automatically log its property values:

```
Private Sub TestUserInfoLog()
   Dim objUserInfo As New UserInfo
   objUserInfo.FirstName = "John"
   objUserInfo.LastName = "Doe"
   objUserInfo.UserID = 6
   objUserInfo.Username = "jdoe"
   Dim objEventLog As New Services.Log.EventLog.EventLogController _
   objEventLog.AddLog(objUserInfo, PortalSettings, UserID, _
   UserInfo.Username, _
   Services.Log.EventLog.EventLogController.EventLogType.USER_CREATED)
End Sub
```

The resulting log entry, written by the XML Logging Provider for this example, includes each property name and value in the objUserInfo object, as shown in the `<properties/>` XML element in the following example:

```
<logs>
      <log LogGUID="92ca39e4-a135-475a-8c0c-7e4949c359b7" LogFileID="b86359bb-e984-
4483-891b-26a2b95bf9bd"
            LogTypeKey="USER_CREATED" LogUserID="-1" LogUserName="" LogPortalID="0"
LogPortalName="DotNetNuke"
```

```
            LogCreateDate="2005-02-04T14:33:46.9318672-05:00"
LogCreateDateNum="20050204143346931"
            LogServerName="DNNTEST">
            <properties>
                  <property>
                        <name>UserID</name>
                        <value>6</value>

                  </property>
                  <property>
                        <name>FirstName</name>
                        <value>John</value>
                  </property>
                  <property>
                        <name>LastName</name>
                        <value>Doe</value>
                  </property>
                  <property>
                        <name>UserName</name>
                        <value>jdoe</value>
                  </property>
            </properties>
      </log>
</logs>
```

If you are using the default DB LoggingProvider, this same information is stored in the EventLog table. The properties element is saved in the LogProperties column as an XML fragment. This format is similar to the properties node for the corresponding XML log version.

```
<ArrayOfAnyType
      xmlns:xsd="http://www.w3.org/2001/XMLSchema"
      xmlns:xsi="http://www.w3.org/2001/XMLSchema-instance">
      <anyType xsi:type="LogDetailInfo">
            <name>UserID</name>
            <value>4</value>
      </anyType>
      <anyType xsi:type="LogDetailInfo">
            <name>FirstName</name>
            <value>Darrell</value>
      </anyType>
      <anyType xsi:type="LogDetailInfo">
            <name>LastName</name>
            <value>Hardy</value>
      </anyType>
      <anyType xsi:type="LogDetailInfo">
            <name>UserName</name>
            <value>tuser2</value>
      </anyType>
      <anyType xsi:type="LogDetailInfo">
            <name>Email</name>
            <value>Darrell@HardyConsulting.com</value>
      </anyType>
</ArrayOfAnyType>
```

This example logs each of the properties of a Custom Business Object. There are other overloaded `EventLogController.AddLog()` methods available if you need to log less information or information that isn't stored in a Custom Business Object. The following example shows how you can use `EventLogController.AddLog()` to add a single key/value pair to the log:

```
Private Sub TestCreateRole()

   Dim objRoleController As New RoleController
   Dim objRoleInfo As New RoleInfo

   'create and add the new role
   objRoleInfo.RoleName = "Newsletter Subscribers"
   objRoleInfo.PortalID = 5
   objRoleController.AddRole(objRoleInfo)

   'log the event
   Dim objEventLog As New Services.Log.EventLog.EventLogController
   objEventLog.AddLog("Role", objRoleInfo.RoleName, PortalSettings, _
   UserId, objEventLog.EventLogType.USER_ROLE_CREATED)

End Sub
```

In this case, the key `Role` and the value `Newsletter Subscribers` will be logged. The resulting log entry written by the default XML Logging Provider for this example is shown in the `<properties/>` XML element in the following XML listing:

```
<logs>
      <log LogGUID="2145856a-1e4a-4974-86f6-da1f0ae5dcca" LogFileID="b86359bb-e984-
4483-891b-26a2b95bf9bd"
            LogTypeKey="ROLE_CREATED" LogUserID="1" LogUserName="host"
LogPortalID="0" LogPortalName="DotNetNuke"
            LogCreateDate="2005-02-04T22:00:22.0413424-05:00"
LogCreateDateNum="20050204220022041"
            LogServerName="DNNTEST">
            <properties>
                  <property>
                        <name>RoleName</name>
                        <value>Newsletter Subscribers</value>
                  </property>
            </properties>
      </log>
</logs>
```

ExceptionLogController

The ExceptionLogController exposes the methods necessary for adding information about exceptions to the log. This controller class also defines six exception types in the ExceptionLogType enumeration: `GENERAL_EXCEPTION`, `MODULE_LOAD_EXCEPTION`, `PAGE_LOAD_EXCEPTION`, `SCHEDULER_EXCEPTION`, `SECURITY_EXCEPTION`, and `SEARCH_INDEXER_EXCEPTION`. By defining different log types for exceptions, the configuration of the Logging Provider can treat each exception log type differently regarding how and if the exceptions get logged.

The next section covers exceptions in more detail. For now, the focus is on how to log the exceptions. The `ExceptionLogController.AddLog()` method has three overloaded methods that enable you to pass in various types of exceptions. The first method enables you to send in a System.Exception or any exception that inherits System.Exception:

```
Public Sub test()
    Try
        If 1 = 1 Then
            Throw New Exception("Oh no, an exception!")
        End If
    Catch exc As Exception
        Dim objExceptionLog As New _
            Services.Log.EventLog.ExceptionLogController
        objExceptionLog.AddLog(exc)
        'a shortcut to this is simply "LogException(exc)"
    End Try
End Sub
```

In this case, the properties of the System.Exception will be logged along with a collection of properties that are specific to the request. For instance, it will log the filename, line, and column number in which the exception occurred if it is available. The default XML Logging Provider would create the following entry for this example:

```
<logs>
      <log LogGUID="39c72059-bcd1-42ca-8886-002363d1c9dc"
           LogFileID="6b780a60-cf46-4588-8a76-75ae9c577277"
           LogTypeKey="GENERAL_EXCEPTION" LogUserID="-1"
           LogUserName="" LogPortalID="-1" LogPortalName=""
           LogCreateDate="2005-02-04T23:25:44.6873456-05:00"
           LogCreateDateNum="20081204232544687"
           LogServerName="DNNTEST">
            <properties>
                  <property>
                        <name>AssemblyVersion</name>
                        <value>05.00.00</value>
                  </property>
                  <property>
                        <name>Method</name>
                        <value>DotNetNuke.Framework.CDefault.test</value>
                  </property>
                  <property>
                        <name>FileName</name>
                        <value>c:\public\dotnetnuke\Default.aspx.vb</value>
                  </property>
                  <property>
                        <name>FileLineNumber</name>
                        <value>481</value>
                  </property>
                  <property>
                        <name>FileColumnNumber</name>
                        <value>21</value>

                  </property>
                  <property>
                        <name>PortalID</name>
                        <value>0</value>
```

```
</property>
<property>
      <name>PortalName</name>
      <value>DotNetNuke</value>
</property>
<property>
      <name>UserID</name>
      <value>-1</value>
</property>
<property>
      <name>UserName</name>
      <value />
</property>
<property>
      <name>ActiveTabID</name>
      <value>36</value>
</property>
<property>
      <name>ActiveTabName</name>
      <value>Home</value>
</property>
<property>
      <name>AbsoluteURL</name>
      <value>/DotNetNuke/Default.aspx</value>
</property>
<property>
      <name>AbsoluteURLReferrer</name>
      <value />
</property>
<property>
      <name>ExceptionGUID</name>
      <value>128455d6-064a-4222-993f-b54fd302e21e</value>
</property>
<property>
      <name>DefaultDataProvider</name>
      <value>DotNetNuke.Data.SqlDataProvider,
           DotNetNuke.SqlDataProvider</value>
</property>
<property>
      <name>InnerException</name>
      <value>Oh no, an exception!</value>
</property>
<property>
      <name>Message</name>
      <value>Oh no, an exception!</value>
</property>
<property>
      <name>StackTrace</name>
      <value>at DotNetNuke.Framework.CDefault.test() in
              c:\public\dotnetnuke\Default.aspx.vb:line 481</value>
</property>
<property>
      <name>Source</name>
      <value>DotNetNuke</value>
</property>
```

```
            </properties>
        </log>
    </logs>
```

Notice that the code does not tell you the portal module from which the exception was thrown. This is because a general exception was thrown (System.Exception). If a ModuleLoadException is thrown, more details about the portal module that throws the exception will be logged.

Exception Handling

The Exception Handling API in DotNetNuke provides a framework for handling exceptions uniformly and elegantly. Exception handling primarily uses four methods, most of which have several overloaded methods. Through these methods, developers can gracefully handle exceptions, log the exception trace and context, and display a user-friendly message to the end user.

The Exception Handling API

The Exception Handling API lives under the DotNetNuke.Services.Exceptions namespace. Table 8-2 lists the classes that constitute the Exception Handling API.

Table 8-2: Exception Handling Classes

Class	Description
BasePortalException	Inherits from System.Exception and contains many other properties specific to the portal application.
ErrorContainer	Generates formatting for the error message that will be displayed in the web browser.
ExceptionInfo	Stores information from the stack trace.
Exceptions	Contains most of the methods that are used in custom modules. It contains the methods necessary to process each type of portal exception.
ModuleLoadException	An exception type for exceptions thrown within portal modules. It inherits from BasePortalException.
PageLoadException	An exception type for exceptions thrown within pages.
SchedulerException	An exception type for exceptions thrown within the Scheduling Provider. It also inherits from BasePortalException.
SearchException	An exception type for exceptions thrown within the search engine. It also inherits from BasePortalException.
SecurityExceptions	An exception type for security exceptions. It also inherits from BasePortalException.

The Exceptions Class

Although there are many classes in the exception handling namespace, the primary class that module developers deal with regularly is the Exceptions class. This class contains all of the methods necessary to gracefully handle exceptions in DotNetNuke. The most widely used method for exception handling is `DotNetNuke.Services.Exceptions.ProcessModuleLoadException()`.

ProcessModuleLoadException Method

The `ProcessModuleLoadException` method serves two primary functions: to log the exceptions that are thrown from within a module to the Logging Provider, and to display a friendly error message in place of the module that threw the exception. The friendly error message is displayed only if the host option Use Custom Error Messages is enabled on the Host Settings page (see Chapter 5, "Host Administration").

`ProcessModuleLoadException` has six overloaded methods:

1. To process an exception that occurs in a portal module, use the following method. If the Custom Error Messages option has been enabled in Host Settings, this method will also handle displaying a user-friendly error message to the client browser:

```
Public Sub ProcessModuleLoadException(ByVal ctrlModule As _
Entities.Modules.PortalModuleBase, ByVal exc As Exception)
```

Parameter	Type	Description
`ctrlModule`	PortalModuleBase	Portal module object.
`exc`	Exception	Exception that was thrown.

2. This method is the same as the previous, although it provides the capability to suppress the error message from being displayed on the client browser:

```
Public Sub ProcessModuleLoadException(ByVal ctrlModule As _
Entities.Modules.PortalModuleBase, ByVal exc As Exception, ByVal _
DisplayErrorMessage As Boolean)
```

Parameter	Type	Description
`ctrlModule`	PortalModuleBase	Portal module object.
`exc`	Exception	Exception that was thrown.
`DisplayErrorMessage`	Boolean	Indicates whether the portal should render an error message to the client browser.

3. This overload adds the capability to provide a custom friendly message to the client browser. You should also use the following overloaded method if you are handling exceptions in a control that isn't directly in a portal module. For instance, if your portal module uses a server

control, you can use this method to handle exceptions within that server control. It displays a friendly error message if custom error messages are enabled.

```
Public Sub ProcessModuleLoadException(ByVal FriendlyMessage As String, _
ByVal UserCtrl As Control, ByVal exc As Exception)
```

Parameter	Type	Description
FriendlyMessage	String	Friendly message to display to the client browser.
UserCtrl	Control	The control. It can be anything that inherits from System.Web.UI.Control.
exc	Exception	Exception that was thrown.

4. This is the same as the previous method; however, it adds the capability to specify whether to display an error message to the client browser (the Host Settings option to Use Custom Error Messages takes precedence over this value).

```
Public Sub ProcessModuleLoadException(ByVal FriendlyMessage As String, _
ByVal ctrlModule As Control, ByVal exc As Exception, _
ByVal DisplayErrorMessage As Boolean)
```

Parameter	Type	Description
FriendlyMessage	String	Friendly message to display to the client browser.
ctrlModule	Control	The control. It can be anything that inherits from System.Web.UI.Control.
exc	Exception	Exception that was thrown.
DisplayErrorMessage	Boolean	Indicates whether the portal should render an error message to the client browser.

5. This is a simple method that has only two parameters. It displays a generic error message to the client browser if custom error messages are enabled.

```
Public Sub ProcessModuleLoadException(ByVal UserCtrl As Control, _
ByVal exc As Exception)
```

Parameter	Type	Description
UserCtrl	Control	The control. It can be anything that inherits from System.Web.UI.Control.
exc	Exception	Exception that was thrown.

6. This is the same as the previous method except it provides the capability to suppress the error message that is displayed in the client browser (the Host Settings option to Use Custom Error Messages takes precedence over this value).

```
Public Sub ProcessModuleLoadException(ByVal UserCtrl As Control, _
ByVal exc As Exception, ByVal DisplayErrorMessage As Boolean)
```

Parameter	Type	Description
`UserCtrl`	Control	The control. It can be anything that inherits from System.Web.UI.Control.
`exc`	Exception	Exception that was thrown.
`DisplayErrorMessage`	Boolean	Indicates whether the portal should render an error message to the client browser.

ProcessPageLoadException Method

Similar to the `ProcessModuleLoadException` method, the `ProcessPageLoadException` method serves two primary functions: to log the exceptions thrown from outside of a module to the Logging Provider, and to display a friendly error message on the page. The friendly error message will only be displayed if the host option Use Custom Error Messages is enabled on the Host Settings page (see Chapter 5).

`ProcessPageLoadException` has two overloaded methods:

1. To process an exception that occurs in an ASPX file or in logic outside of a portal module, use the following overloaded method. If the Use Custom Error Messages option has been enabled in Host Settings, this method also handles displaying a user-friendly error message to the client browser.

```
Public Sub ProcessPageLoadException(ByVal exc As Exception)
```

Parameter	Type	Description
`exc`	Exception	Exception that was thrown.

2. This is the same as the previous method; however, you must send in the URL parameter to redirect the request after logging the exception.

```
Public Sub ProcessPageLoadException(ByVal exc As Exception, _
ByVal URL As String)
```

Parameter	Type	Description
`exc`	Exception	Exception that was thrown.
`URL`	String	URL to redirect the request to.

LogException Method

The `LogException` method is used for adding exceptions to the log. It does not handle displaying any type of friendly message to the user. Instead, it simply logs the error without notifying the client browser of a problem. `LogException` has five overloaded methods:

1. To log an exception thrown from a module, use the following overloaded method:

```
Public Sub LogException(ByVal exc As ModuleLoadException)
```

Parameter	Type	Description
`exc`	ModuleLoadException	Exception that was thrown.

2. To log an exception thrown from a page or other logic outside of a module, use the following overloaded method:

```
Public Sub LogException(ByVal exc As PageLoadException)
```

Parameter	Type	Description
`exc`	PageLoadException	Exception that was thrown.

3. To log an exception thrown from within a Scheduling Provider Task, use the following overloaded method:

```
Public Sub LogException(ByVal exc As SchedulerException)
```

Parameter	Type	Description
`Exc`	SchedulerException	Exception that was thrown.

4. To log a security exception, use the following overloaded method:

```
Public Sub LogException(ByVal exc As SecurityException)
```

Parameter	Type	Description
`exc`	SecurityException	Exception that was thrown.

5. If you need to log an exception of another type, use the following overloaded method:

```
Public Sub LogException(ByVal exc As Exception)
```

Parameter	Type	Description
exc	Exception	Exception that was thrown.

ProcessSchedulerException Method

The `ProcessSchedulerException` method is used to log exceptions thrown from within a scheduled task. It simply logs the error.

To log an exception thrown from a scheduled task, use the following overloaded method:

```
Public Sub ProcessSchedulerException(ByVal exc As Exception)
```

Parameter	Type	Description
exc	Exception	Exception that was thrown.

The Exception Handling API abstracts developers from the complexity of logging exceptions and presenting error messages gracefully. It provides several powerful methods that handle all of the logic involved in working with the Logging Provider and the presentation layer. The next section covers the various interfaces that module developers can take advantage of to bring more core features to life in their modules.

Scheduler

The Scheduler in DotNetNuke is a mechanism that enables developers to schedule tasks to run at defined intervals. It is implemented using the Provider pattern; therefore, it can easily be replaced without modifying core code. Creating a scheduled task is a fairly simple process. First, though, it's important to understand which types of tasks are suitable for the Scheduler.

Because the Scheduler is run under the context of the web application, it is prone to the same types of application recycles as a web application. In a web-hosting environment, it is a common practice to conserve resources by recycling the worker process for a site periodically. When this happens, the Scheduler stops running. Therefore, the tasks run by the Scheduler do not run 24 hours a day, 7 days a week. They are executed according to a defined schedule, but they can only be triggered when the worker process is alive. For this reason, you cannot specify that a task should run every night at midnight. It is not possible in the web environment to meet this type of use case. Instead, you can specify how often a task is run by defining the execution frequency for each task. The execution frequency is defined as every *x* minutes/hours/days.

To create a scheduled task, you must create a class that inherits from DotNetNuke.Services .Scheduling.SchedulerClient. This class must provide a constructor and a `DoWork` method. An example of a scheduled task is shown in the following code. This sample scheduled task will move all event log files to a folder named with the current date. By configuring this scheduled task to run once per day, the log files will be automatically archived daily, which keeps the log file sizes manageable.

```
Public Class ArchiveEventLog
    Inherits DotNetNuke.Services.Scheduling.SchedulerClient
    Public Sub New(ByVal objScheduleHistoryItem As _
        DotNetNuke.Services.Scheduling.ScheduleHistoryItem)
        MyBase.new()
        Me.ScheduleHistoryItem = objScheduleHistoryItem    'REQUIRED
    End Sub
    Public Overrides Sub DoWork()
        Try
            'notification that the event is progressing
            'this is optional
            Me.Progressing()    'OPTIONAL
            'get the directory that logs are written to
            Dim LogDirectory As String
            LogDirectory = Common.Globals.HostMapPath + "Logs\"

            'create a folder with today's date
            Dim FolderName As String
            FolderName = LogDirectory + Now.Month.ToString + "-" + _
                Now.Day.ToString + "-" + Now.Year.ToString + "\"
            If Not IO.Directory.Exists(FolderName) Then
                IO.Directory.CreateDirectory(FolderName)
            End If

            'get the files in the log directory
            Dim s As String()
            s = IO.Directory.GetFiles(LogDirectory)
            'loop through the files
            Dim i As Integer
            For i = 0 To s.Length - 1
                Dim OldFileInfo As New IO.FileInfo(s(i))
                'move all files to the new folder except the file
                'used to store pending log notifications
                If OldFileInfo.Name <> _
                    "PendingLogNotifications.xml.resources" Then
                    Dim NewFileName As String
                    NewFileName = FolderName + OldFileInfo.Name
                    'check to see if the new file already exists
                    If IO.File.Exists(NewFileName) Then
                        Dim errMessage As String
                        errMessage = "An error occurred archiving " + _
                            "log file to " + _
                            NewFileName + ".  The file already exists."
                        LogException(New _
                            BasePortalException(errMessage))
                    Else
                        IO.File.Move(OldFileInfo.FullName, NewFileName)
                        Me.ScheduleHistoryItem.AddLogNote("Moved " + _
                            OldFileInfo.FullName + _
                                " to " + FolderName + _
                                OldFileInfo.Name + ".")      'OPTIONAL
                    End If
                End If
            Next
```

```
            Me.ScheduleHistoryItem.Succeeded = True     'REQUIRED

        Catch exc As Exception     'REQUIRED

            Me.ScheduleHistoryItem.Succeeded = False    'REQUIRED

            Me.ScheduleHistoryItem.AddLogNote(String.Format( _
                "Archiving log files failed.", _
                exc.ToString))     'OPTIONAL

            'notification that we have errored
            Me.Errored(exc)     'REQUIRED

            'log the exception
            LogException(exc)     'OPTIONAL
        End Try
    End Sub
End Class
```

After the class has been compiled into the bin directory, the task can be scheduled from the Scheduling module under the Host page (see Chapter 6, "Modules," for details). Please note the lines marked as REQUIRED in the preceding listing. It is important to include each of these lines of code in your constructor. These collectively ensure that both the exception handling and the schedule management are handled uniformly throughout all scheduled tasks.

HTTP Modules

ASP.NET provides a number of options for extending the path that data takes between client and server (known as the HTTP Pipeline). A popular method to extend the pipeline is through the use of custom components known as HTTP modules. An HTTP module enables you to add pre- and post-processing to each HTTP request coming into your application.

DotNetNuke implements a number of HTTP modules to extend the pipeline. They include features such as URL Rewriting, Exception Management, Users Online, Profile, Anonymous Identification, Role Management, DotNetNuke Membership, and Personalization.

Originally, a lot of the HTTP modules were implemented inside the core application (`global.asax.vb`). There were a number of reasons why the functionally was moved to HTTP modules:

- Administrators can optionally enable or disable an HTTP module.
- Developers can replace or modify HTTP modules without altering the core application.
- Provides templates for extending the HTTP Pipeline.

HTTP Modules 101

This section further examines the concepts of HTTP modules so you'll know when and where to implement them. To comprehend how HTTP modules work, it's necessary to understand the HTTP Pipeline and how ASP.NET processes incoming requests. Figure 8-1 shows the HTTP Pipeline.

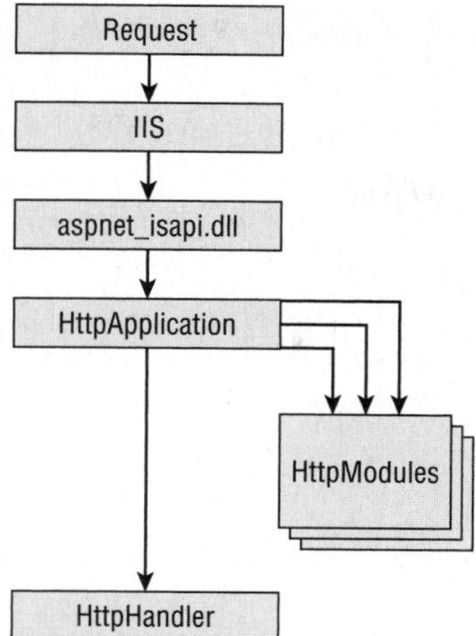

Figure 8-1

When a request is first made, it passes through a number of stages before it is actually handled by your application. The first participant in the pipeline is Microsoft Internet Information Server (IIS); its job is to route ASP.NET requests to the ASP.NET runtime. When an ASPX file is requested (or any other ASP.NET file), IIS forwards the request to the ASP.NET runtime (via an ISAPI extension).

Now that the request has been received by ASP.NET, it must pass through an instance of HttpApplication. The HttpApplication object handles application-wide methods, data, and events. It is also responsible for pushing the request through one or more HTTP module objects. The ASP.NET runtime determines which modules to load by examining the configuration files located at either machine level (`machine.config`) or application level (`web.config`). The following XML fragment shows the HTTP Modules Configuration Section `<httpModules>` of the web.config file:

```
<httpModules>
  <add name="Compression"
        type="DotNetNuke.HttpModules.Compression.CompressionModule,
              DotNetNuke.HttpModules" />
  <add name="RequestFilter"
        type="DotNetNuke.HttpModules.RequestFilter.RequestFilterModule,
              DotNetNuke.HttpModules" />
  <add name="UrlRewrite"
        type="DotNetNuke.HttpModules.UrlRewriteModule,
              DotNetNuke.HttpModules" />
  <add name="Exception"
        type="DotNetNuke.HttpModules.Exceptions.ExceptionModule,
              DotNetNuke.HttpModules" />
  <add name="UsersOnline"
        type="DotNetNuke.HttpModules.UsersOnline.UsersOnlineModule,
              DotNetNuke.HttpModules" />
  <add name="DNNMembership"
        type="DotNetNuke.HttpModules.Membership.MembershipModule,
              DotNetNuke.HttpModules" />
  <add name="Personalization"
```

```
            type="DotNetNuke.HttpModules.Personalization.PersonalizationModule,
            DotNetNuke.HttpModules" />
    <add name="ScriptModule"
            type="System.Web.Handlers.ScriptModule,System.Web.Extensions,
                Version=1.0.61025.0, Culture=neutral,
                PublicKeyToken=31bf3856ad364e35" />
</httpModules>
```

To invoke each HTTP module, the `Init` method of each module is invoked. At the end of each request, the `Dispose` method is invoked to enable each HTTP module to clean up its resources. In fact, those two methods form the interface (IHttpModule) each module must implement. Here is the actual IHttpModule interface code:

```
Public Interface IHttpModule
    Sub Init(ByVal context As HttpApplication)
    Sub Dispose()
End Interface
```

During the `Init` event, each module may subscribe to a number of events raised by the HttpApplication object. Table 8-3 shows the events that are raised before the application executes. The events are listed in the order in which they occur.

Table 8-3: HTTP Module Events (Before the Application Executes)

Event	Description
`BeginRequest`	Signals a new request; guaranteed to be raised on each request.
`AuthenticateRequest`	Signals that the request is ready to be authenticated; used by the Security module.
`AuthorizeRequest`	Signals that the request is ready to be authorized; used by the Security module.
`ResolveRequestCache`	Used by the Output Cache module to short-circuit the processing of requests that have been cached.
`AcquireRequestState`	Signals that the per-request state should be obtained.
`PreRequestHandlerExecute`	Signals that the request handler is about to execute. This is the last event you can participate in before the HTTP handler for this request is called.

Table 8-4 shows the events that are raised after an application has returned. The events are listed in the order in which they occur.

In addition, there are three per-request events that can be raised in a nondeterministic order. They are described in Table 8-5.

Table 8-4: HTTP Module Events (After the Application Has Returned)

Event	Description
`PostRequestHandlerExecute`	Signals that the HTTP handler has completed processing the request.
`ReleaseRequestState`	Signals that the request state should be stored because the application is finished with the request.
`UpdateRequestCache`	Signals that code processing is complete and the file is ready to be added to the ASP.NET cache.
`EndRequest`	Signals that all processing has finished for the request. This is the last event called when the application ends.

Table 8-5: HTTP Module Events (Nondeterministic)

Event	Description
`PreSendRequestHeaders`	Signals that HTTP headers are about to be sent to the client. This provides an opportunity to add, remove, or modify the headers before they are sent.
`PreSendRequestContent`	Signals that content is about to be sent to the client. This provides an opportunity to modify the content before it is sent.
`Error`	Signals an unhandled exception.

After the request has been pushed through the HTTP modules configured for your application, the HTTP handler responsible for the requested file's extension (.ASPX) handles the processing of that file. If you are familiar with ASP.NET development, you'll be familiar with the handler for an ASPX page — System.Web.UI.Page. The HTTP handler then handles the life cycle of the page-level request raising events such as `Page_Init`, `Page_Load`, and so on.

DotNetNuke HTTP Modules

As stated earlier, DotNetNuke (like ASP.NET) comes with a number of HTTP modules. These modules enable developers to customize the HTTP Pipeline to provide additional functionality on each request. In this section, you explore several DotNetNuke HTTP modules, and examine their purpose and possibilities for extension.

URL Rewriter

The URL rewriter is an HTTP module that provides a mechanism for mapping virtual resource names to physical resource names at runtime — in other words, it provides a URL that is friendly. The term "friendly" has two aspects. One is to make the URL search-engine friendly, which is solved with the default implementation.

Most search engines ignore URL parameters, and because DotNetNuke relies on URL parameters to navigate to portal pages, the older application is not search-engine friendly. To index your site effectively, you need a parameterless mechanism for constructing URLs that search engines will process.

If you browse to a DotNetNuke site that is version 3.0 or greater, you may notice different URLs from earlier versions. Traditionally, a DotNetNuke URL looks something like the following:

```
http://www.dotnetnuke.com/default.aspx?tabid=622
```

With friendly URLs enabled, the preceding URL might look like this:

```
http://www.dotnetnuke.com/RoadMap/FriendlyURLs/tabid/622/default.aspx
```

URL rewriter is invoked during the HTTP Pipeline's processing of a request and can optionally subscribe to application-wide events. The particular event of interest for this module is `BeginRequest`. This event enables you to modify the URL before the Page HTTP handler is invoked and make it believe the URL requested was that of the old non-friendly format.

The transformation process occurs through the use of regular expressions defined in SiteUrls.config in the root of your DotNetNuke installation. This file contains a number of expressions to `LookFor` and with corresponding URLs to `SendTo`. The following XML snippet shows the default SiteUrls .config file:

```
<?xml version="1.0" encoding="utf-8" ?>
<RewriterConfig>
<Rules>
      <RewriterRule>
            <LookFor>.*/TabId/(\d+)(.*)/Logoff.aspx</LookFor>
            <SendTo>~/Admin/Security/Logoff.aspx?tabid=$1</SendTo>
      </RewriterRule>
      <RewriterRule>
            <LookFor>.*/TabId/(\d+)(.*)/rss.aspx</LookFor>
            <SendTo>~/rss.aspx?TabId=$1</SendTo>
      </RewriterRule>
      <RewriterRule>
            <LookFor>[^?]*/TabId/(\d+)(.*)</LookFor>
            <SendTo>~/Default.aspx?TabId=$1</SendTo>
      </RewriterRule>
</Rules>
</RewriterConfig>
```

The rules defined in this configuration file cover the default login and logoff page. You could potentially add any number of additional rules, and even hardcode some extra rules in there. For example, if you wanted to hardcode a link, such as `http://www.dotnetnuke.com/FriendlyUrl.aspx`, and have it map to another URL elsewhere, your entry might look like the following:

```
<?xml version="1.0" encoding="utf-8" ?>
<RewriterConfig>
<Rules>
```

```
        <RewriterRule>
              <LookFor>.*/FriendlyUrl.aspx</LookFor>
              <SendTo>~/default.aspx?tabid=622</SendTo>
        </RewriterRule>

        <RewriterRule>
              <LookFor>.*/TabId/(\d+)(.*)/Logoff.aspx</LookFor>
              <SendTo>~/Admin/Security/Logoff.aspx?tabid=$1</SendTo>
        </RewriterRule>
        <RewriterRule>
              <LookFor>.*/TabId/(\d+)(.*)/rss.aspx</LookFor>
              <SendTo>~/rss.aspx?TabId=$1</SendTo>
        </RewriterRule>
        <RewriterRule>
              <LookFor>[^?]*/TabId/(\d+)(.*)</LookFor>
              <SendTo>~/Default.aspx?TabId=$1</SendTo>
        </RewriterRule>
  </Rules>
  </RewriterConfig>
```

The preceding URL scheme is an excellent implementation for your own applications as well, particularly those with fixed pages. Unfortunately DotNetNuke has potentially any number of pages, so the team added some functionality that would transform any number of query string parameters.

Take a look at the default scheme for URL rewriting. You can see from the friendly URL shown earlier (`http://www.dotnetnuke.com/RoadMap/FriendlyURLs/tabid/622/default.aspx`) that the requirement is met; that is, the URL would have no parameters. URLs generally adhere to the following pattern:

- `http://www.dotnetnuke.com/` – The site Host URL.
- `RoadMap/Friendly URLs/` — The breadcrumb path back to the home page.
- `tabid/622/` — The query string from the original URL transformed (?tabid=622).
- `default.aspx` — The standard web page for DotNetNuke.

The advantage of this scheme is that it requires no database lookups for the transformation, just raw regular expression processing that is typically quite fast.

For some situations, the breadcrumb path may not be desired. In those cases, simply modify the web.config `friendlyUrl` provider setting to turn off the feature. To turn it off, change the `includePageName` value shown in the following example from "`true`" to "`false`":

```
<friendlyUrl defaultProvider="DNNFriendlyUrl">
    <providers>
        <clear />
        <add name="DNNFriendlyUrl"
        type="DotNetNuke.Services.Url.FriendlyUrl.DNNFriendlyUrlProvider,

        DotNetNuke.HttpModules.UrlRewrite" includePageName="true"

        regexMatch="[^a-zA-Z0-9 _-]" />
    </providers>
</friendlyUrl>
```

Earlier in this chapter, it was mentioned that there are two aspects of friendly URLs; so far, only one (search-engine friendly) has been discussed. The second aspect, known as human-friendly URLs, can sometimes impact performance.

A URL that is human friendly is easily remembered or able to be worked out by a human. For example, if you had a login to `http://www.dotnetnuke.com` and you wanted to visit your profile page without navigating to it, you might expect the URL to be `http://www.dotnetnuke.com/profile/dhardy.aspx`.

That URL could easily be remembered, but would require additional processing on the request for two reasons:

1. The URL contains no TabID. That would have to be looked up.
2. The URL contains no UserID. A lookup on dhardy is needed to find the corresponding UserID.

For these reasons, this approach was not universally chosen. Human-friendly URLs like the preceding example can be implemented by hardcoding the TabID and any other necessary parameters in the rewriter rules.

DotNetNuke 5.0 does include a general human-friendly option as part of the friendly URL engine. To use the human-friendly URLs, a change must be made to the web.config file. In the dotnetnuke section, the attribute urlFormat="HumanFriendly" must be added to the friendlyUrl module handler. The following code snippet shows the correct section and the change that must be made to the web.config file:

```
<dotnetnuke>
 ...
 <friendlyUrl defaultProvider="DNNFriendlyUrl">
  <providers>
    <clear />
    <add name="DNNFriendlyUrl"
            type="DotNetNuke.Services.Url.FriendlyUrl.DNNFriendlyUrlProvider,
                  DotNetNuke.HttpModules" includePageName="true"
                  regexMatch="[^a-zA-Z0-9 _-]" urlFormat="HumanFriendly"
                  urlFormat="HumanFriendly"/>
  </providers>
 </friendlyUrl> ...  </dotnetnuke>
```

Using the friendly URL example,

```
http://www.dotnetnuke.com/RoadMap/FriendlyURLs/tabid/622/default.aspx
```

would look like

```
http://www.dotnetnuke.com/RoadMap/FriendlyURLs.aspx
```

with the urlFormat set to HumanFriendly.

So far, how incoming requests are interpreted has been explained, but how outgoing links are transformed into the friendly URL scheme have not. A number of options have been explored on how to transform the outgoing links, but the best option was to implement a provider-based component that would transform a given link into the chosen scheme. Figure 8-2 shows the URL rewriter architecture.

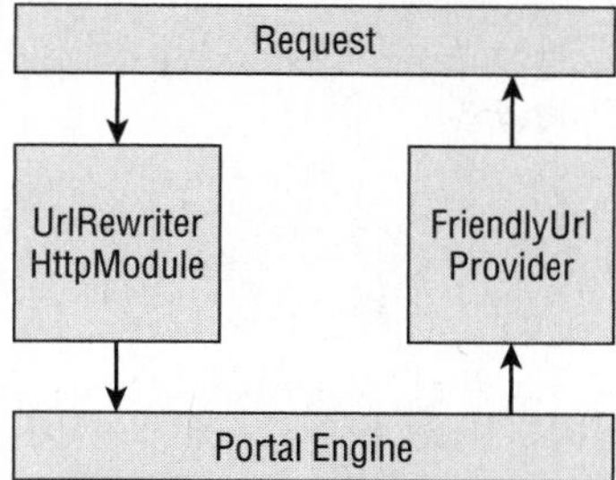

Figure 8-2

Luckily, DotNetNuke already had used two shortcut methods for building links within the application (`NavigateUrl` and `EditUrl`). It was relatively simple to place a call to the provider from each of these methods, effectively upgrading the site to the new URL format instantly.

This approach also tightly coupled the HTTP module with the provider, which is why you can find them in the same assembly (DotNetNuke.HttpModules.UrlRewrite.dll).

You can see from the architecture that it is quite plausible for you to write your own URL rewriting scheme. If you have different URL requirements, you could create a new provider to format outgoing URLs, and a new HTTP module to interpret the incoming requests.

Writing a new provider involves supplying new implementations of the methods in the FriendlyUrl-Provider base class. The following code shows the methods that must be overridden in your concrete implementation:

```
Public MustOverride Function FriendlyUrl(ByVal objtab as TabInfo, _
    ByVal path As String) As String
Public MustOverride Function FriendlyUrl(ByVal objtab as TabInfo, _
    ByVal path As String, ByVal pageName As String) As String
Public MustOverride Function FriendlyUrl(ByVal objtab as TabInfo, _
    ByVal path As String, ByVal pageName As String, _
    ByVal settings As PortalSettings) As String
Public MustOverride Function FriendlyUrl(ByVal objtab as TabInfo, _
    ByVal path As String, ByVal pageName As String, ByVal portalAlias As String) _
    As String
```

As you can see, there are only four methods to implement so that you can write your URLs in your desired format. The most important part is to come up with a scheme and to find an efficient, reliable means of interpretation by your HTTP module. After you have written your provider, you can make an additional entry in the providers section of web.config. Make sure to set the `defaultProvider` attribute as shown here:

```
<friendlyUrl defaultProvider="CustomFriendlyUrl">
  <providers>
    <clear />
    <add name="DNNFriendlyUrl"
      type="DotNetNuke.Services.Url.FriendlyUrl.DNNFriendlyUrlProvider,
      DotNetNuke.HttpModules.UrlRewrite" includePageName="true"
      regexMatch="[^a-zA-Z0-9 _-]"/>
```

```
        <add name="CustomFriendlyUrl"
            type="CompanyName.FriendlyUrlProvider, CompanyName.FriendlyUrlProvider" />
        </providers>
    </friendlyUrl>
```

Exception Management

The Exception Management HTTP module subscribes to the error event raised by the HttpApplication object. Any time an error occurs within DotNetNuke, the error event is called. During the processing of this event, the last error to have occurred is captured and sent to the exception logging class, which calls the Logging Provider that handles the writing of that exception to a data store (the default is the DB Logging Provider).

Users Online

Users Online was implemented during version 2 of DotNetNuke. It allows other modules to interrogate the application's data store for information regarding who is online, expressed as registered users and anonymous users. Previously it had been a custom add-on and was session-based. Before the addition of the functionality to the core (like many add-ons incorporated into the core), research was undertaken to investigate the best way to handle not only registered users, but also anonymous users.

The module subscribes to the `AuthorizeRequest` event. This event is the first chance an HTTP module has to examine details about the user performing the request. The HTTP module examines the request, determines whether the user is anonymous or authenticated, and stores the request in cache. Anonymous users are also given a temporary cookie so they are not counted twice in the future. A scheduled job from the Scheduler executes every minute on a background thread, pulling the relevant details out of cache and updating them in the database. It also clears up any old records. The records are stored within two tables: AnonymousUsers and UsersOnline.

The HTTP module is a good module to disable (comment out of web.config) if you do not need this information within your portal. Alternatively, you can just disable it in Host Settings.

DNNMembership

The DNNMembership HTTP module performs tasks around the security of a user. It stores role information about a user in an HTTP cookie so the same information does not have to be requested again and performs security checks for users switching portals.

There is no real need to extend this module because it is critical to DotNetNuke's operation.

Personalization

The Personalization HTTP module is very similar to the Microsoft-provided Profile HTTP module, and in fact, was based on the same concept, just integrated much earlier. It loads a user's personalized information into a serialized XML object at the beginning of the request, and saves it at the end of the request.

If you are interested in storing personalized information about a user, see the personalization classes (described in Table 8-6) under /Library/Services/Personalization/.

Table 8-6: Personalization Classes

Class	Purpose
Personalization	The primary API for using the personalization system. It encapsulates the few DotNetNuke business rules for using the personalization system.
PersonalizationController	Represents a low-level API that converts personalization database references into business objects.
PersonalizationInfo	The data transfer object that represents the data in a programming friendly object.

Module Interfaces

Modules represent a discrete set of functionality that can extend the portal framework. In past versions of DotNetNuke, module interactions with the portal were primarily limited to making method calls into the core portal APIs. Though this one-way interaction provides some capability to use portal services and methods within the module, it limits the capability of the portal to provide more advanced services.

To provide two-way interactions with modules, the portal needs to have a mechanism to make method calls into the module. There are several distinct mechanisms for allowing a program to call methods on an arbitrary set of code, where the module code is unknown at the time the portal is being developed. Three of these "calling" mechanisms are used within DotNetNuke:

1. Inheritance
2. Delegates
3. Interfaces

As discussed previously, every module inherits from the PortalModuleBase class (located in the /Library/Entities/Modules directory). This base class provides a common set of methods and properties that can be used by the module as well as the portal to control the behavior of each module instance. Because the module must inherit from this class, the portal has a set of known methods that it can use to control the module. The portal could extend the base class to add methods to handle new services. One downside to this approach is that there is not an easy mechanism for determining whether a subclass implements custom logic for a specific method or property. Because of this restriction, inheritance is generally limited to providing services that are needed or required for every subclass.

A second method for interacting with the modules involves the use of delegates. A delegate is essentially a pointer to a method that has a specific set of parameters and return type. Delegates are useful when a service can be implemented with a single method call and are the underlying mechanism behind VB.NET's event handling. DotNetNuke uses delegates to implement callback methods for the Module Action menu action event. Although delegates are very useful in some situations, they are more difficult to implement and understand than alternative methods.

The third calling mechanism used by DotNetNuke is the use of interfaces. An interface defines a set of methods, events, and properties without providing any implementation details for these elements. Any class that implements an interface is responsible for providing the specific logic for each method, event, and property defined in the interface. Interfaces are especially useful for defining optional services that a module may implement. The portal can detect if a class implements a specific interface and can then call any of the methods, events, or properties defined in the interface.

Starting in version 3.0, DotNetNuke significantly extended its use of module interfaces. DotNetNuke 5.0 has nine main interfaces that are intended for use by modules:

1. IActionable
2. IPortable
3. IUpgradeable
4. IModuleCommunicator
5. IModuleListener
6. ISearchable
7. IModuleControl
8. ISkinControl
9. IActionControl

IActionable

Every module has a menu that contains several possible action items for activities like editing module settings, module movement, and viewing help. These menu items are called Module Actions. The module menu can be extended with your own custom actions. When your module inherits from the PortalModuleBase class, it receives a default set of actions, which are defined by the portal to handle common editing functions. Your module can extend these actions by implementing the IActionable interface.

Interface

As shown in the following code snippet, the IActionable interface consists of a single method that returns a collection of Module Actions. The `ModuleActions` property is used when DotNetNuke renders the module.

```
Namespace DotNetNuke.Entities.Modules
  Public Interface IActionable
    ReadOnly Property ModuleActions() As Actions.ModuleActionCollection
  End Interface
End Namespace
```

The following code shows an example usage as implemented in the Announcements module. The first two lines tell the compiler that this method implements the `ModuleAction` method of the IActionable interface. It is a read-only method, so you only need to provide a `Get` function. The first step is to create a new collection to hold the custom actions. Then you use the collection's `Add` method to create a new action item in the collection. Finally, you return the new collection.

```
Public ReadOnly Property ModuleActions() As ModuleActionCollection _
  Implements IActionable.ModuleActions
  Get
    Dim Actions As New ModuleActionCollection

    Actions.Add(GetNextActionID, _
                Localization.GetString(ModuleActionType.AddContent, _
                                       LocalResourceFile), _
                ModuleActionType.AddContent, _
                "", _
                "", _
                EditUrl(), _
                False, _
                Security.SecurityAccessLevel.Edit, _
                True, _
                False)

    Return Actions
  End Get
End Property
```

This is a simple example that demonstrates the basic steps to follow for your own custom module menus. DotNetNuke provides extensive control over each Module Action.

ModuleAction API

To take full advantage of the power provided by Module Actions and the IActionable interface, you need to examine the classes, properties, and methods that make up the Module Action API.

Table 8-7 lists the classes that comprise the Module Action API.

The ModuleAction class is the heart of the API. Tables 8-8 and 8-9 show the properties and methods available in the ModuleAction class. Each item in the Module Action menu is represented by a single ModuleAction instance.

DotNetNuke includes several standard Module Actions that are provided by the PortalModuleBase class or that are used by several of the core modules. ModuleActionTypes can also be used to access localized strings for the `ModuleAction.Title` property. This helps promote a consistent user interface for both core and third-party modules. These ModuleActionType constants can be seen it the following class:

```
Public Class ModuleActionType
  Public Const AddContent As String = "AddContent.Action"
  Public Const EditContent As String = "EditContent.Action"
  Public Const ContentOptions As String = "ContentOptions.Action"
  Public Const SyndicateModule As String = "SyndicateModule.Action"
  Public Const ImportModule As String = "ImportModule.Action"
  Public Const ExportModule As String = "ExportModule.Action"
  Public Const OnlineHelp As String = "OnlineHelp.Action"
  Public Const ModuleHelp As String = "ModuleHelp.Action"
  Public Const PrintModule As String = "PrintModule.Action"
  Public Const ModuleSettings As String = "ModuleSettings.Action"
  Public Const DeleteModule As String = "DeleteModule.Action"
  Public Const ClearCache As String = "ClearCache.Action"
```

```
    Public Const MoveTop As String = "MoveTop.Action"
    Public Const MoveUp As String = "MoveUp.Action"
    Public Const MoveDown As String = "MoveDown.Action"
    Public Const MoveBottom As String = "MoveBottom.Action"
    Public Const MovePane As String = "MovePane.Action"
    Public Const MoveRoot As String = "MoveRoot.Action"
  End Class
```

Table 8-7: Module Action Classes

Class	Description
ModuleAction	Defines a specific function for a given module. Each module can define one or more actions that the portal will present to the user. Each module container can define the skin object used to render the Module Actions.
ModuleActionType	Defines a set of constants used for distinguishing common action types.
ModuleActionCollection	A collection of Module Actions.
ModuleActionEventListener	Holds callback information when a module registers for Action events.
ActionEventArgs	Passes data during the click event that is fired when a Module Action is selected by the user.
ActionEventHandler	A delegate that defines the method signature required for responding to the Action event.
ActionBase	Creates ModuleAction skin objects. The core framework includes three different implementations: SolPartActions.ascx, DropDownActions.ascx, and LinkActions.ascx.

DotNetNuke provides standard behavior for the following ModuleActionTypes: `ModuleHelp`, `OnlineHelp`, `ModuleSettings`, `DeleteModule`, `PrintModule`, `ClearCache`, `MovePane`, `MoveTop`, `MoveUp`, `MoveDown`, and `MoveBottom`. All ModuleActionTypes in this subset will ignore the `UseActionEvent` and `NewWindow` properties. The ModuleActionTypes can be further subdivided into three groups:

1. **Basic redirection** — The ModuleActionTypes that perform simple redirection and cause the user to navigate to the URL identified in the URL property: ModuleHelp, OnlineHelp, ModuleSettings, and PrintModule.
2. **Module movement** — The ModuleActionTypes that change the order or location of modules on the current page: MovePane, MoveTop, MoveUp, MoveDown, and MoveBottom.
3. **Custom logic** — The ModuleActionTypes with custom business logic that use core portal APIs to perform standard module-related actions: DeleteModule and ClearCache.

DotNetNuke uses a custom collection class for working with Module Actions. The ModuleActionCollection inherits from .Net System.Collections.CollectionBase class and provides a strongly

Table 8-8: ModuleAction Properties

Property	Type	Description
`Actions`	Module Action Collection	Contains the collection of Module Action items that can be used to form hierarchical menu structures. Every skin object that inherits from ActionBase may choose how to render the menu based on the capability to support hierarchical items. For example, the default SolpartActions skin object supports submenus, whereas the DropDownActions skin object only supports a flat menu structure.
`Id`	Integer	Every Module Action for a given module instance must contain a unique `Id`. The PortalModuleBase class defines the `GetNextActionId` method, which can be used to generate unique Module Action IDs.
`Command Name`	String	Distinguishes which Module Action triggered an action event. DotNetNuke includes 19 standard `ModuleActionTypes` that provide access to standard functionality. Custom Module Actions can use their own string to identify commands recognized by the module.
`Command Argument`	String	Provides additional information during action event processing. For example, the DotNetNuke core uses `CommandArgument` to pass the `Module ID` for common commands like `DeleteModule.Action`.
`Title`	String	Sets the text that is displayed in the Module Action menu.
`Icon`	String	Name of the Icon file to use for the Module Action item.
`Url`	String	When set, this property allows a menu item to redirect the user to another web page.
`Client Script`	String	JavaScript to run during the `menuClick` event in the browser. If the `ClientScript` property is present, it is called prior to the postback occurring. If the `ClientScript` returns `false`, the postback is canceled.
`UseAction Event`	Boolean	Causes the portal to raise an Action Event on the server and notify any registered event listeners. If `UseActionEvent` is `false`, the portal handles the event, but does not raise the event back to any event listeners. The following CommandNames prevent the Action Event from firing: `ModuleHelp`, `OnlineHelp`, `ModuleSettings`, `DeleteModule`, `PrintModule`, `ClearCache`, `MovePane`, `MoveTop`, `MoveUp`, `MoveDown`, and `MoveBottom`.
`Secure`	Security Access Level	Determines the required security level of the user. If the current user does not have the necessary permissions, the Module Action is not displayed.
`Visible`	Boolean	If set to `false`, the Module Action will not be displayed. This property enables you to control the visibility of a Module Action based on custom business logic.
`NewWindow`	Boolean	Forces an action to open the associated URL in a new window. This property is not used if `UseActionEvent` is `true` or if the following CommandNames are used: `ModuleHelp`, `Online Help`, `ModuleSettings`, or `PrintModule`.

Table 8-9: ModuleAction Method

Method	Return Type	Description
`HasChildren`	Boolean	Returns `True` if the `ModuleAction.Actions` property has any items (`Actions.Count` > `0`).

typed collection class. That minimizes the possibility of typecasting errors that can occur when using generic collection classes such as ArrayList.

Most module developers only need to worry about creating the ModuleActionCollection to implement the IActionable interface. The two primary methods for adding ModuleActions to the collection are illustrated in the following code. These methods wrap the ModuleAction constructor method calls.

```
Public Function Add(ByVal ID As Integer, _
   ByVal Title As String, _
   ByVal CmdName As String, _
   Optional ByVal CmdArg As String = "", _
   Optional ByVal Icon As String = "", _
   Optional ByVal Url As String = "", _
   Optional ByVal UseActionEvent As Boolean = False, _
   Optional ByVal Secure As SecurityAccessLevel = SecurityAccessLevel.Anonymous, _
   Optional ByVal Visible As Boolean = True, _
   Optional ByVal NewWindow As Boolean = False) _
   As ModuleAction

Public Function Add(ByVal ID As Integer, _
    ByVal Title As String, _
    ByVal CmdName As String, _
    ByVal CmdArg As String, _
    ByVal Icon As String, _
    ByVal Url As String, _
    ByVal ClientScript As String, _
    ByVal UseActionEvent As Boolean, _
    ByVal Secure As SecurityAccessLevel, _
    ByVal Visible As Boolean, _
    ByVal NewWindow As Boolean) _
    As ModuleAction

Public Function Add(ByVal value As ModuleAction) As Integer
```

The first method in the preceding listing uses optional parameters that are not supported by C#. This method is likely to be deprecated in future versions to simplify support for C# modules and its use is not recommended.

Also note that the last method returns an integer rather than a ModuleAction and you will need to code accordingly.

The ModuleAction framework makes it easy to handle simple URL redirection from a Module Action. Just like the `Delete` and `ClearCache` actions provided by the DotNetNuke framework, your module may require the use of custom logic to determine the appropriate action to take when the menu item is clicked. To implement custom logic, the module developer must create a response to a menu click event.

In the DotNetNuke architecture, the ModuleAction menu is a child of the module container. The module is also a child of the container. Prior to DotNetNuke 5.0 both of these were children of the Skin object. Pre 5.0 the Skin object acted as the mediator. Now this section of code has been refactored, areas of responsibility have been more reasonably assigned, and these are now children of the Container object. (For a detailed description see Chapter 7, "DotNetNuke Architecture," and Figure 7.4.) In order to maintain compatibility, some of the following code still makes reference to the Skin object, but for practical purposes the Container is now the mediator between the Module and the ModuleAction menu. This architecture allows the framework to easily change out the menu implementation; however, it complicates communication between the menu and module. The menu never has a direct reference to the module and the module does not have a direct reference to the menu. This is a classic example of the Mediator design pattern. This pattern is designed to allow two classes without direct references to communicate. Figure 8-3 shows the steps involved to implement this pattern.

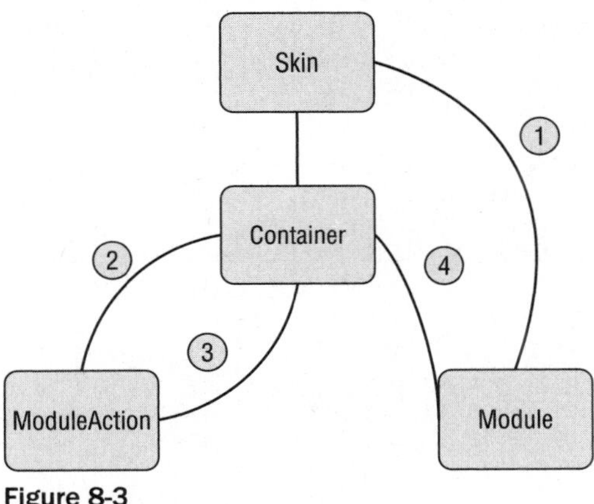

Figure 8-3

The following sections examine those steps and explore ways you can extend the framework.

Step 1: Register the Event Handler

The first step to implementing the Mediator pattern is to provide a mechanism for the module to register with the portal. The portal will use this information later when it needs to notify the module that a menu item was selected. Handling the click event is strictly optional. Your module may choose to use standard MenuActions, in which case you can skip this step. Because the module does not contain a direct reference to the page on which it is instantiated, you need to provide a registration mechanism.

The Skin class contains the `RegisterModuleActionEvent` method, which allows a module to notify the framework of the event handler for the action event (see the following Menu Action Handler Registration listing). Registration should occur in the module's `Page_Load` event to ensure that it happens before the event can be fired in the Skin class. The code that follows is from the HTML module and provides a working example of module-based event registration for the `ModuleAction` event. Although you could use another interface to define a known method to handle the event, the registration mechanism turns out to be a much more flexible design when implementing a single method.

```
'-------------------------------------------------------------------------------
'-                      Menu Action Handler Registration                       -
'-------------------------------------------------------------------------------
'This finds a reference to the containing skin
Dim ParentSkin As UI.Skins.Skin = UI.Skins.Skin.GetParentSkin(Me)

'We should always have a ParentSkin, but need to make sure
If Not ParentSkin Is Nothing Then

    'Register our EventHandler as a listener on the ParentSkin so that it may
    'tell us when a menu has been clicked.
    ParentSkin.RegisterModuleActionEvent(Me.ModuleId, AddressOf ModuleAction_Click)
End If
'-------------------------------------------------------------------------------
```

The following example shows the `ModuleAction_Click` event handler code from the Container class. With the refactoring of this to the Container class in DotNetNuke 5.0, this could be handled at the container level. To maintain compatibility with earlier version modules that may have registered their listeners on the Skin directly rather than with the helper method in PortalModuleBase, this method still checks the Skin object.

```
Private Sub ModuleAction_Click(ByVal sender As Object, ByVal e As _
            ActionEventArgs)
    'Search through the listeners
    Dim Listener As ModuleActionEventListener
    For Each Listener In ParentSkin.ActionEventListeners
        'If the associated module has registered a listener
        If e.ModuleConfiguration.ModuleID = Listener.ModuleID Then
           'Invoke the listener to handle the ModuleAction_Click event
           Listener.ActionEvent.Invoke(sender, e)
        End If
    Next
End Sub
```

The DotNetNuke framework uses a delegate (see the following code) to define the method signature for the event handler. The `RegisterModuleActionEvent` requires the address of a method with the same signature as the `ActionEventHandler` delegate.

```
Public Delegate Sub ActionEventHandler(ByVal sender As Object, _
                                       ByVal e As ActionEventArgs)
```

Step 2: Display the Menu

Now that the Container (the Mediator class) can communicate with the module, you need a mechanism to allow the menu to communicate with the Container as well. This portion of the communication chain is much easier to code. Handling the actual click event and passing it up the control tree is the responsibility of the ModuleAction rendering code.

Like much of DotNetNuke, the ModuleAction framework supports the use of custom extensions. In this case, container objects handle rendering the Module Actions. Each ModuleAction container object inherits from the DotNetNuke.UI.Containers.ActionBase class. The Container class retrieves the Module Action collection from the module by calling the `IActionable.ModuleActions` property and passes the collection to the ModuleAction container object for rendering. The ActionBase class includes the code necessary to merge the standard Module Actions with the collection provided by the Container class.

Each container object includes code in the pre-render event to convert the collection of Module Actions into an appropriate format for display using an associated server control. In the case of Actions.ascx, the server control is a menu control that is capable of fully supporting all of the features of ModuleActions including submenus and icons. Other container objects like the DropDownActions.ascx may only support a subset of the Module Action features (see Table 8-10).

Table 8-10: ModuleAction Skin Objects

Action Container Object	Menu Separator	Icons	Submenus	Client-Side JavaScript
Actions or SolPartActions	Yes	Yes	Yes	Yes
DropDownActions	Yes	No	No	Yes
LinkActions	No	No	No	No

Step 3: Notify the Portal of a Menu Item Selection

Each container object handles the click event of the associated server control. This event calls the `ProcessAction` method, which is inherited from the ActionBase class. `ProcessAction` is then responsible for handling the event as indicated by the ModuleAction properties. If you create your own ModuleAction skin object, follow this pattern.

```
Private Sub ctlActions_MenuClick(ByVal args As
              NavigationProvider.NavigationEventArgs)
              'Handles ctlActions.MenuClick
              Try
                ProcessAction(args.ID)
            Catch exc As Exception           'Module failed to load
                ProcessModuleLoadException(Me, exc)
            End Try
        End Sub
```

Step 4: Notify the Module That a Custom ModuleAction Was Clicked

If the `UseActionEvent` is set to `True`, the `ProcessAction` method calls the `OnAction` method to handle actually raising the event. This might seem like an extra method call when `ProcessAction` could just raise the event on its own. The purpose of `OnAction`, though, is to provide an opportunity for subclasses to override the default event handling behavior. Although this is not strictly necessary, it is a standard pattern in .NET and a good example to follow when developing your own event handling code. You can see this interplay in the two methods shown here:

```
Protected Sub ProcessAction(ByVal ActionID As String)
           If IsNumeric(ActionID) Then
              Dim action As ModuleAction =
```

```
                    Actions.GetActionByID(Convert.ToInt32(ActionID))
                    If action IsNot Nothing Then
                       If Not ActionManager.ProcessAction(action) Then
                          OnAction(New ActionEventArgs(action,
                                     ModuleContext.Configuration))
                       End If
                    End If
             End If
End Sub

Protected Overridable Sub OnAction(ByVal e As ActionEventArgs)
  RaiseEvent Action(Me, e)
End Sub
```

Because the container maintains a reference to the ModuleAction object, the Container class can handle the `Action` event raised by the ModuleAction object. The Container class iterates through `ActionEventListeners` to find the associated module event delegate. When a listener is found, the code invokes the event, which notifies the module that the event has occurred.

```
Public Sub ModuleAction_Click(ByVal sender As Object, ByVal e As ActionEventArgs)
  'Search through the listeners
  Dim Listener As ModuleActionEventListener
  For Each Listener In ActionEventListeners

    'If the associated module has registered a listener
    If e.ModuleConfiguration.ModuleID = Listener.ModuleID Then

      'Invoke the listener to handle the ModuleAction_Click event
      Listener.ActionEvent.Invoke(sender, e)
    End If
  Next
End Sub
```

You are now ready to take full advantage of the entire ModuleAction API to create custom menu items for your own modules, handle the associated Action event when the menu item is clicked, and create your own custom ModuleAction container objects.

IPortable

DotNetNuke provides the capability to import and export modules within the portal. Like many features in DotNetNuke, it is implemented using a combination of core code and module-specific logic. The IPortable interface defines the methods required to implement this feature on a module-by-module basis.

```
Public Interface IPortable
  Function ExportModule(ByVal ModuleID As Integer) As String

  Sub ImportModule(ByVal ModuleID As Integer, _
                   ByVal Content As String, _
                   ByVal Version As String, _
                   ByVal UserID As Integer)
End Interface
```

This interface provides a much-needed feature to DotNetNuke and is a pretty straightforward interface to implement. To support importing and exporting content, implement the interface within your module's business controller class.

As modules are being loaded by the portal for rendering a specific page, they are checked to determine whether they implement the IPortable interface. To simplify checking whether a module implements the interface, a shortcut property has been added to the ModuleInfo class. The ModuleInfo class provides a consolidated view of properties related to a module. When a module is first installed in the portal, a quick check is made to determine if the module implements the IPortable interface, and if so, the `IsPortable` flag is set on the base ModuleDefinition record. This property allows the portal to perform the interface check without unnecessarily loading the business controller class. Adding the check at the point of installation removes a requirement by previous DotNetNuke versions for a module control to implement unused stub methods. If the control implements the IPortable interface, DotNetNuke automatically adds the Import Content and Export Content menu items to your Module Action menu (see Figure 8-4).

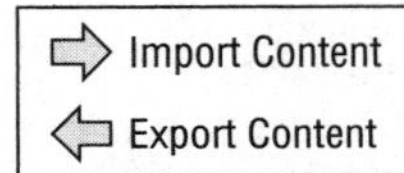

Figure 8-4

Each module should include a controller class that is identified in the `BusinessControllerClass` property of the portal's ModuleInfo class. This class is identified in the module manifest file discussed later in the book. The controller class is where you implement many of the interfaces available to modules.

Adding the IPortable interface to your module requires implementing logic for the `ExportModule` and `ImportModule` methods, respectively. Shown here are these two methods for the HTMLText module:

```
Public Function ExportModule(ByVal ModuleID As Integer) As String _
  Implements Entities.Modules.IPortable.ExportModule

  Dim strXML As String = ""

  Dim objHtmlText As HtmlTextInfo = GetHtmlText(ModuleID)
  If Not objHtmlText Is Nothing Then
    strXML += "<htmltext>"
    strXML += "<desktophtml>{0}</desktophtml>"
    strXML += "<desktopsummary>{1}</desktopsummary>"
    strXML += "</htmltext>"

    String.Format(strXML, _
              XMLEncode(objHtmlText.DeskTopHTML), _
              XMLEncode(objHtmlText.DesktopSummary))
  End If

  Return strXML

End Function
Public Sub ImportModule(ByVal ModuleID As Integer, _
                        ByVal Content As String, _
                        ByVal Version As String, _
                        ByVal UserId As Integer) _
```

```
        Implements Entities.Modules.IPortable.ImportModule

        Dim xmlHtmlText As XmlNode = GetContent(Content, "htmltext")

        Dim objText As HtmlTextInfo = New HtmlTextInfo

        objText.ModuleId = ModuleID
        objText.DeskTopHTML = xmlHtmlText.SelectSingleNode("desktophtml").InnerText
        objText.DesktopSummary = xmlHtmlText.SelectSingleNode("desktopsummary").InnerText
        objText.CreatedByUser = UserId
        AddHtmlText(objText)

      End Sub
```

The complexity of the data model for your module determines the difficulty of implementing these methods. Take a look at a simple case as implemented by the HTMLText module.

The `ExportModule` method is used to serialize the content of the module to an XML string. DotNetNuke saves the serialized string along with the module's FriendlyName and Version. The XML file is saved into the portal directory.

The `ImportModule` method reverses the process by de-serializing the XML string created by the `ExportModule` method and replacing the content of the specified module. The portal passes the version information stored during the export process along with the serialized XML string.

The IPortable interface is straightforward to implement and provides much needed functionality to the DotNetNuke framework. It is at the heart of DotNetNuke's templating capability and therefore is definitely an interface that all modules should implement.

IUpgradeable

One of DotNetNuke's greatest features is the capability to easily upgrade from one version to the next. The heart of that is the creation of script files that can be run sequentially to modify the database schema and move any existing data to the new version's schema. In later versions, DotNetNuke added a mechanism for running custom logic during the upgrade process. Unfortunately, this mechanism was not provided for modules. Therefore, third-party modules were forced to create their own mechanism for handling custom upgrade logic.

This was fixed in DotNetNuke 3.0 and updated again in 4.1. The IUpgradeable interface provides a standard upgrade capability for modules, and uses the same logic as used in the core framework. The interface includes a single method, `UpgradeModule`, which enables the module to execute custom business logic depending on the current version of the module being installed.

```
Public Interface IUpgradeable
  Function UpgradeModule(ByVal Version As String) As String
End Interface
```

`UpgradeModule` is called once for each script version included with the module. It is called only for script versions that are later than the version of the currently installed module.

Inter-Module Communication

DotNetNuke includes the capability for modules to communicate with each other through the Inter-Module Communication (IMC) framework. The IMC framework enables modules to pass objects rather than simple strings. Additionally, other properties enable a module to identify the Sender, the Target, and the Type of message. Take a look at the two main interfaces that provide this functionality to your module: IModuleCommunicator and IModuleListener.

IModuleCommunicator

The IModuleCommunicator interface defines a single event, ModuleCommunication, for your module to implement:

```
Public Interface IModuleCommunicator
  Event ModuleCommunication As ModuleCommunicationEventHandler
End Interface
```

To communicate with another module, first implement the IModuleCommunicator interface in your module. You should have an event declaration in your module, as follows:

```
Public Event ModuleCommunication(ByVal sender As Object, _
                                 ByVal e As ModuleCommunicationEventArgs) _
                                 Implements _
                                 IModuleCommunicator.ModuleCommunication
```

IModuleListener

Whereas the IModuleCommunicator is used for sending messages, the IModuleListener interface is used for receiving messages:

```
Public Interface IModuleListener
  Sub OnModuleCommunication(ByVal s As Object, _
                            ByVal e As ModuleCommunicationEventArgs)
End Interface
```

This interface defines a single method, `OnModuleCommunication`, which is called when an IModuleCommunicator on the same page raises the ModuleCommunication event. What you do in response to this event notification is totally up to you.

DotNetNuke does not filter event messages. Any module that implements the IModuleListener interface is notified when the event is raised. It is the responsibility of the module to determine whether it should take any action.

ISearchable

DotNetNuke provides a robust search API for indexing and searching content in your portal. The API is divided into three distinct parts.

1. Core search engine
2. Search data store
3. Search indexer

Like the ModuleAction framework, the search framework also implements a Mediator pattern. When combined with the Provider pattern, this framework provides lots of flexibility. In Figure 8-5, you can see the relationship between these patterns and the three parts of the search API.

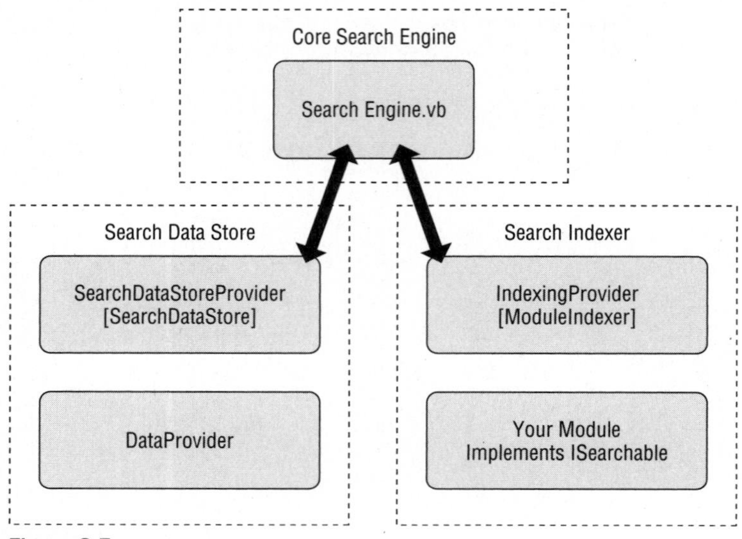

Figure 8-5

The core search engine provides a simple API for calling the IndexProvider and then storing the results using a SearchDataStoreProvider. This API is intended for use by the core framework. Future versions of the API will be extended to allow modules greater control over the indexing process.

DotNetNuke includes a default implementation of the SearchDataStoreProvider, which is meant to provide basic storage functionality, but could be replaced with a more robust search engine. As for other providers, third-party developers are implementing providers for many of the current search engines on the market. You can find links to these providers and more at `http://www.dotnetnuke.com` and in the DotNetNuke Marketplace at `http://marketplace.dotnetnuke.com`.

The IndexingProvider provides an interface between the core search engine and each module. DotNetNuke includes a default provider that indexes module content. This provider can be replaced to provide document indexing, web indexing, or even indexing legacy application content stored in another database. If you decide to replace it, keep in mind that DotNetNuke only allows for the use of a single provider of a given type. This means that if you want to index content from multiple sources, you must implement this as a single provider. Future versions of the framework may be enhanced to overcome this limitation.

When using the ModuleIndexer, you can incorporate a module's content into the search engine data store by implementing the ISearchable interface:

```
Public Interface ISearchable
  Function GetSearchItems(ByVal ModInfo As ModuleInfo) As SearchItemInfoCollection
End Interface
```

This interface is designed to allow almost any content to be indexed. By passing in a reference to the module and returning a collection of SearchItems, the modules are free to map their content to each SearchItem as they see fit. A sample implementation from the Announcements module included with DotNetNuke follows:

```
Public Function GetSearchItems(ByVal ModInfo As Entities.Modules.ModuleInfo)_
                     As Services.Search.SearchItemInfoCollection Implements _
                     Entities.Modules.ISearchable.GetSearchItems
            Dim moduleSettings As Hashtable = _
DotNetNuke.Entities.Portals.PortalSettings.GetModuleSettings(ModInfo.ModuleID)
            Dim descriptionLength As Integer = 100
            If CType(moduleSettings("descriptionLength"), String) <> "" Then
                descriptionLength = _
                Integer.Parse(CType(moduleSettings("descriptionLength"), _
                String))
                If descriptionLength < 1 Then
                    descriptionLength = 1950 'max length of description is _
                            2000 char, take a bit less to make sure it fits...
                End If
            End If

            Dim SearchItemCollection As New SearchItemInfoCollection

            Dim Announcements As ArrayList = _
                 GetCurrentAnnouncements(ModInfo.ModuleID, Null.NullDate)

            Dim objAnnouncement As Object
            For Each objAnnouncement In Announcements
                Dim SearchItem As SearchItemInfo
                With CType(objAnnouncement, AnnouncementInfo)
                    Dim strContent As String = _
                         System.Web.HttpUtility.HtmlDecode(.Title & " " _
                         & .Description)
                    Dim strDescription As String = _
HtmlUtils.Shorten(HtmlUtils.Clean(System.Web.HttpUtility.HtmlDecode(.Description),
False), descriptionLength, "...")
                    SearchItem = New SearchItemInfo(ModInfo.ModuleTitle & " _
                              - " & .Title, strDescription, .CreatedByUser, _
                                        .PublishDate, ModInfo.ModuleID, _
                                   .ItemId.ToString, strContent, "ItemId=" _
                                 & .ItemId.ToString)
                    SearchItemCollection.Add(SearchItem)
                End With
            Next

            Return SearchItemCollection
        End Function
```

In this code, you make a call to your module's Info class, just as you would when you bind to a control within your ASCX file, but in this case the results are going to populate the SearchItemInfo, which will populate the DNN index with data from the module.

The key to implementing the interface is figuring out how to map your content to a collection of SearchItemInfo objects. Table 8-11 lists the properties of the SearchItemInfo class.

Table 8-11: SearchItemInfo Properties

Property	Description
SearchItemId	An ID assigned by the search engine. It's used when deleting items from the data store.
Title	A string that is used when displaying search results.
Description	Summary of the content. It is used when displaying search results.
Author	Content author.
PubDate	Date that allows the search engine to determine the age of the content.
ModuleId	ID of the module whose content is being indexed.
SearchKey	Unique key that can be used to identify each specific search item for this module.
Content	The specific content that will be searched. The default search data store does not search on any words that are not in the content property.
GUID	Another unique identifier that is used when syndicating content in the portal.
ImageFileId	Optional property used to identify image files that accompany a search item.
HitCount	Maintained by the search engine and used to identify the number of times that a search item is returned in a search.

Now that the index is populated with data, users of your portal can search your module's information from a unified interface within DNN.

DotNetNuke 5.0 New Core Interfaces

DotNetNuke 5.0 introduces three new interfaces; IModuleControl, ISkinControl, and IActionControl. These interfaces have been abstracted from their respective base classes. The main purpose of this was to better enable testability. Each of these is implemented in a base class and if you inherit that class, you inherit the interface and the implementation of that interface. Table 8-12 lists the interface and the base class that provides the default implementation.

Table 8-12: New Core Interfaces

Interface	Base Class where Implemented
IModuleControl	PortalModuleBase
ISkinControl	SkinObjectBase
IActionControl	ActionBase

Summary

This chapter examined many of the core APIs that provide the true power behind DotNetNuke. By leveraging common APIs, you can extend the portal in almost any direction. You can replace core functions or just add a custom module — the core APIs are what make it all possible. Now that you know how to use most of the core functions, the next several chapters examine how to create your own custom modules to really take advantage of this power.

9

Member Role

In December 2004, Microsoft made available its ASP.NET v1.1 Membership Management Component Prototype. This was distributed as an SDK which, when used by a developer in a project, makes reference to an assembly named MemberRole.dll. Microsoft defines it as "a collection of classes and sample scripts that allows a developer to more easily authenticate users, authorize users, and store per-user property data in a user profile." MemberRole.dll was simply a backport of a series of classes, from the then ASP.NET 2.0 Beta 2 Framework, compiled under the 1.1 Framework. This backported version conforms to the same API as is found in ASP.NET 2.0.

Just before releasing the SDK, Microsoft informed the DotNetNuke Core Team of its intentions with this backport. The Core Team discussed the pros and cons of taking advantage of the backport and, after much debate, decided to implement it at that time, using the backport, rather than waiting eleven months to prepare for a future upgrade of DotNetNuke to the ASP.NET 2.0 Framework. When it was time to upgrade to the ASP.NET 2.0 Framework with DotNetNuke's 4.0 release, the upgrade task was made less complicated by this decision. The majority of the changes required replacing the DLL reference with a reference to the new classes within the 2.0 framework.

Other factors that weighed in this decision included what MemberRole.dll offered in addition to the easier migration path. In adapting MemberRole.dll, DotNetNuke was also preparing itself for exposure to the hosting market through Microsoft's Shared Hosting Initiative. This initiative not only placed DotNetNuke in front of a new audience, but also helped DotNetNuke form a solid relationship with Microsoft. That relationship allows DotNetNuke to work closely with Microsoft and reap additional benefits, such as the special license for MemberRole.dll usage that extends the length this DLL can remain in production use. For example, the typical MemberRole.dll license was only permitted for production usage for a period of 90 days after the release of the ASP.NET 2.0 Framework. The MemberRole.dll included in framework version 1.1 DotNetNuke releases does not contain this restriction. Another factor for the decision of using the MemberRole.dll standard functionality is that it allows other ASP.NET applications in the same database to share MemberRole information. You could have several applications and manage the user/security/profile information in one place.

Version 3.0 of the ASP.NET Framework was released by Microsoft in November of 2006. Version 3.0 was unusual in that it did not replace version 2.0, it simply added four new major components (see Figure 9-1). In fact, if you do not have the .Net Framework Version 2.0 installed, it will be installed when you install version 3.0.

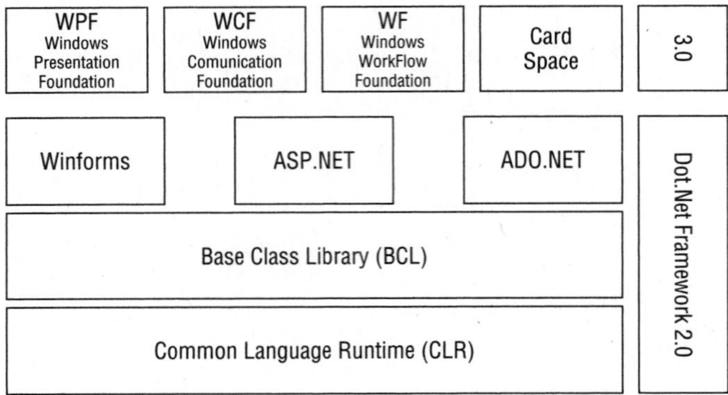

Figure 9-1

A little over a year later, version 3.5 of the framework was released. This release also added new assemblies to provide more functionality while still using the assemblies provided in versions 2.0 and 3.0 (see Figure 9-2). When Service Pack One for version 3.5 of the framework was released, it actually included Service Packs for versions 2.0 and 3.0.

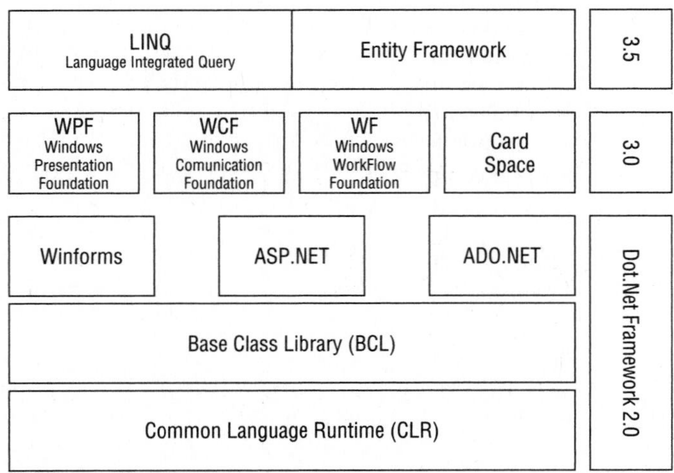

Figure 9-2

As you can see, if you have installed version 3.5 of the .NET Framework, you are actually using versions 2.0, 3.0, and 3.5. Each successive version is simply adding functionality rather than replacing previous versions.

For developers, it's important to understand that the MemberRole.dll referenced in the DotNetNuke 3.x versions, which use the ASP.NET 1.1 Framework, is now part of the ASP.NET 2.0 Framework. In DotNetNuke 4.x versions and DotNetNuke 5 versions, which use the ASP.NET 2.0/3.0/3.5 Framework, reference to the MemberRole.dll is made from the System.Web.Security namespace. With this understanding, and for the sake of simplicity, we will call it ASP.NET 3.5 for the rest of this chapter.

Before discussing the details of how DotNetNuke uses Member Role, it is first essential that you understand how security works in ASP.NET 3.5.

Security in ASP.NET 3.5

In ASP.NET 1.x, the native authentication and authorization services relied on external data stores or configuration in the web.config file. For example, in ASP.NET 1.1 an application can provide forms-based authentication. This requires the developer to create a login form and associated controls to acquire, validate, and manage user credentials. After authentication, authorization is provided through XML configurations in the web.config file.

In ASP.NET 3.5, several new security enhancements expand on these services in three distinct ways:

1. **Login and user controls**: A new suite of login and user-management controls reduces the need to rewrite standard user code for each application. You can, for example, create a set of pages for registering a new user, allowing an existing user to log in, and sending a forgotten password to a user simply by placing the appropriate controls on the page and setting a few properties.
2. **User management**: Each ASP.NET 3.5 application can be accessed through a special set of administrative pages, which enable an authorized user to create new users, assign users to roles, and store user information. If you want to write your own management tools, you can access all of the same features programmatically. Note that the ASP.NET Web Configuration can be run only in a development, non-production environment, meaning the developer has to create his own solution for the production environment.
3. **Membership/Roles Provider**: The membership feature creates a link between the front-end features (login controls and user-management site) and the persistence mechanism. A Membership Provider encapsulates all the data access code that is required to store and retrieve users and roles. Thanks to the Provider Model, this component can easily be replaced with a provider that supports your particular data source.

Together, these three components reduce the amount of code that is required to provide authentication and authorization services and persist the data to a data store. In designing these classes, Microsoft understood that it could not account for all possible use cases. Realizing this, Microsoft implemented them by using a Provider Model design pattern, the same pattern DotNetNuke uses in its own architecture throughout the application, as discussed in Chapter 7, "DotNetNuke Architecture."

In the Member Role backported version, only the Membership/Roles Provider described earlier was actually backported to the 1.1 Framework. This was not an issue for DotNetNuke because it already had its own login and user controls as well as its own user-management interface. Because the controls existed, all that was left to do was to modify the controls to use the API exposed by the Membership Provider.

The Membership/Roles Provider can actually be divided into the three distinct services: Membership, Role Management, and Profile. As a group, they are referred to as Membership Provider Services. The ASP.NET 3.5 Framework includes two Membership Providers, one using Microsoft SQL and the other using Active Directory. In DotNetNuke 5.0 the default uses Microsoft SQL. Using Active Directory is an installation option.

The Profile service hasn't been mentioned until now because it is not part of the System.Web.Security namespace. Despite this, it was part of the Member Role backported version and was utilized in the DotNetNuke implementation. Keep in mind that it is possible to implement your own concrete providers using a different data store if you so desire.

With the basics of ASP.NET 3.5 security and Membership Provider Service in mind, the following section moves on to how DotNetNuke implements these service providers.

DotNetNuke Membership Overview

Before DotNetNuke began using Member Role, it had its own data schema and services to handle membership. Because of this, when it came time to implement Member Role, there were some challenges ahead.

Portals and Applications

Among the challenges was that DotNetNuke supports running many portals from a single DotNetNuke installation. Each portal has its own users and roles that are not shared with any other portals. A portal is identified by a unique key, the PortalID. Because the default Membership/Roles Provider implementation is a generic solution, it does not natively support the concept of having multiple portals, each with their own users and roles. The default Membership/Roles Provider implementation was designed in a way that only supports a single portal site in a DotNetNuke installation. The Membership/Roles Provider refers to the DotNetNuke installation as an "application," and without customization, that application can support only a single set of users and roles (a single portal instance).

Microsoft abstracted the Membership/Roles Provider to enable a common source for validating users/roles across multiple applications. The design just didn't anticipate the kind of virtual segmentation within an application that DotNetNuke provides through portals, each with its own users and roles.

To overcome this limitation, a wrapper was needed for the Membership/Roles Providers' SQL Data Providers. This customization enables DotNetNuke to support application virtualization. The end result is that the Membership/Roles Providers, as implemented in DotNetNuke, can support multiple applications (multiple portal instances in a single DotNetNuke installation). `PortalID` in DotNetNuke was mapped to the `ApplicationName` in the Membership/Roles Provider. When a call was made to the Membership/Roles Provider, the `ApplicationName` was switched on-the-fly to match the `PortalID` of the portal instance using a concatenation of the object qualifier and the `PortalID`. The following code shows the way this is set:

```
Public Function GetApplicationName(ByVal PortalID As Integer) As String

        Dim appName As String

        'Get the Data Provider Configuration
```

```
            Dim _providerConfiguration As ProviderConfiguration = _
                 ProviderConfiguration.GetProviderConfiguration("data")

            ' Read the configuration specific information for the current Provider
             Dim objProvider As Provider = CType(_providerConfiguration.Providers _
                (_providerConfiguration.DefaultProvider), Provider)

             'Get the Object Qualifier frm the Provider Configuration
             Dim _objectQualifier As String = objProvider.Attributes("objectQualifier")
             If _objectQualifier <> "" And _objectQualifier.EndsWith("_") = False Then
                     _objectQualifier += "_"
             End If

             appName = _objectQualifier + Convert.ToString(PortalID)

             Return appName
     End Function
```

Data Model for Users and Roles

To gain the full benefit from the Membership/Roles Provider, it's important to recognize that User and Role information can be externalized from the DotNetNuke application and kept in a data store independent of the main data store. For instance, DotNetNuke may use Microsoft SQL Server as its database to store content and system settings, but the Membership/Roles Provider may use Windows authentication, LDAP, or another mechanism to handle authentication and authorization. Because security can be externalized using the Provider Model, it was essential to ensure that the implementation of the Membership/Roles Provider didn't customize any code or database tables used by the provider. The data tables used by the provider had to be independent of the other core DotNetNuke tables. Referential integrity could not be enforced between DotNetNuke data and the Membership/Roles Provider data, nor could cascade deletes or other data-level synchronization methods be used. In a nutshell, all of the magic had to happen in the business logic layer.

One of the challenges faced in implementing the Membership/Roles Provider was dealing with the fields supported by DotNetNuke but not by the provider. Ideally, a solution would have been achieved by completely replacing the DotNetNuke authentication/authorization-related tables with the tables used by the Membership/Roles Provider. This could not be accomplished because the authentication/authorization tables in DotNetNuke were already tied to so many existing and necessary features of the application. For instance, the DotNetNuke Users table has a column named UserID, which holds a unique identifier for each user. The UserID is used in nearly all core modules and third-party modules as well as the core itself. The most significant problem with UserID was that it didn't exist in the Membership/Roles Provider. Instead, the Membership/Roles Provider uses the username as the unique key for a user within an application. The challenge was that DotNetNuke needed a way to maintain the UserID to preserve the DotNetNuke functionality that depended on it. This is just one example of an attribute that cannot be handled by the default Membership/Roles Provider provided by Microsoft.

Ultimately, it was decided that DotNetNuke would need to maintain satellite tables to support the DotNetNuke attributes that could not be managed by the Membership/Roles Provider. The goal was to maintain enough information in the DotNetNuke tables so that functionality was not lost, and offload whatever data possible to the Membership/Roles Provider tables. The end result is a data model that mirrors the Membership/Roles Provider tables, as shown in Figure 9-3.

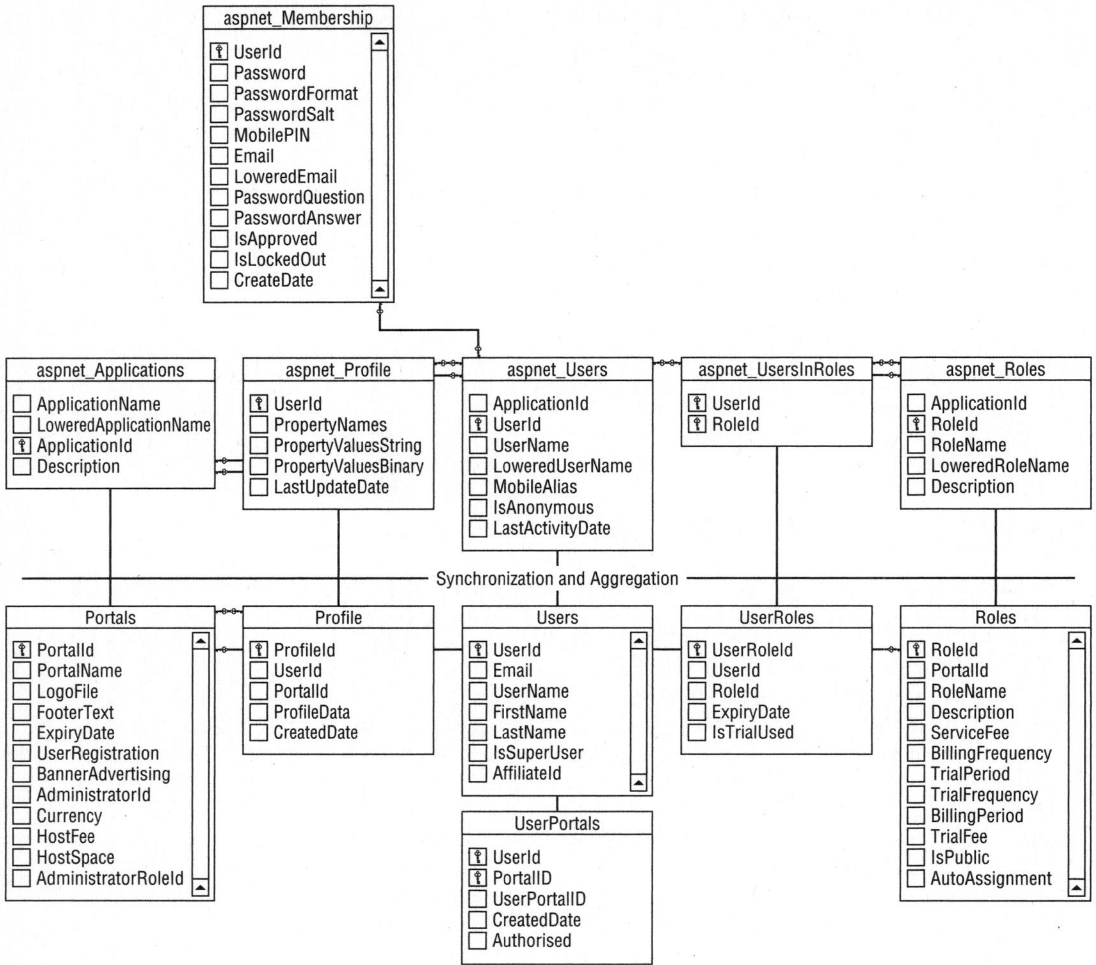

Figure 9-3

Note that none of the tables on top has database relationships to any of the tables on the bottom. The lines connecting them simply show their relationship in theory, not an actual relationship in the database.

Because the data for portals, profiles, users, and roles is stored in multiple unrelated tables, the business layer is responsible for aggregating the data. For instance, you cannot get a complete representation of a user without collecting data from both the aspnet_Users table (from the Membership/Roles Provider) and the Users table (native DotNetNuke table).

Membership, Roles, and Profile Providers

Understanding the limitations DotNetNuke had to conquer and how all three of the providers were affected is important to comprehending why the current solution works the way it does. After the original implementation of Member Role in the first official DotNetNuke 3.x release, the DotNetNuke Core

Team found its implementation of Member Role to be less extensible than it could be. To overcome the restrictions that DotNetNuke imposed on itself, the Membership, Roles, and Profile Providers have been abstracted out even further. In doing this, a new set of three concrete ASP.NET Providers was created. This opened the door and has allowed much more flexibility and choice in the implementation of each provider.

In all abstract/concrete provider implementations, the concrete public methods override the methods exposed by the abstract provider. In the concrete providers, a set of private methods and properties are used to extend and customize the concrete provider along with custom logic in the business layer. In DotNetNuke, additional logic is responsible for combining data from the data store in this layer.

DotNetNuke 5.0 by default uses the ASP.NET SqlMembershipProvider functionality located in the System.Web.Security.Membership namespace for membership information; however, it does not use it directly. It uses the AspNetMembershipProvider located in the DotNetNuke.Security.Membership namespace as a wrapper for all calls to the Microsoft-supplied provider. This also provides synchronization and aggregation between the ASP.NET tables and the DotNetNuke tables. Furthermore, because of the abstraction mentioned previously, the default Roles Provider and default Profiles Provider no longer use the ASP.NET tables but are self-contained in the DotNetNuke tables. Each of these three providers is discussed in more detail later in this chapter. For now, just note that these abstractions have segregated the code into more specific areas of responsibility. This makes it easier to replace any single section.

Because ASP SQLMembership is the current default provider, the schema shown in Figure 9-3 is still relevant today for the Membership section. The aspnet_Profile, aspnet_UsersInRoles, and aspnet_Roles tables are no longer used but are shown in Figure 9-3 for historical purposes. When creating this new set of concrete providers, extreme caution was taken to make sure the new implementation would not alter the previous one, or convert any existing data, therefore minimizing upgrade implications.

As with the previous Member Role implementation, the new ASP.NET set of providers follows the Provider Model design pattern discussed in Chapter 7. Keep in mind that it is possible to create a custom concrete Profile Provider of your own and still use the existing concrete providers. This is important because it can greatly reduce the amount of effort for your next DotNetNuke project if only one of these concrete providers does not meet your requirements.

Because these providers work so closely together, you should take special care when replacing any single one. Make sure that you do not introduce any code or data inconsistencies.

Membership Provider

The function of a Membership Provider is to interface with a data store that contains data regarding a site's registered users and to provide methods for creating and deleting users, verifying login credentials, changing passwords, and more. Within the ASP.NET 3.5 Framework System.Web.Security namespace is a MembershipUser class that defines the basic attributes of a membership user. Table 9-1 shows some of the methods and properties required by DotNetNuke to implement a custom Membership Provider. You can see a complete list by looking in the MembershipProvider Abstract class. You can find this class in the /Library/Security/Membership/MembershipProvider.vb file. If you compare this table to the Member Role table on Microsoft's site, you'll notice they are very similar.

Table 9-1: DotNetNuke Abstract Provider Membership Methods/Properties

Method/Property	Description
MinPasswordLength	Minimum length required for a password
MinNonAlphanumericCharacters	Number of non-alphanumeric characters required in a user's password
PasswordFormat	How the passwords are stored in the data store; the options are Clear, Hashed, or Encrypted
PasswordStrengthRegularExpression	A regular expression each password is passed through to verify it meets additional criteria
PasswordStrengthRegularExpression	Determines if users are required to have a question and answer for accessing their password
ChangePassword	Changes a user's password
ChangePasswordQuestionAndAnswer	Changes a user's password question and answer
CreateUser	Creates a single user
DeleteUser	Deletes a single user
GetPassword	Returns the password of a user
GetUser	Returns a single user
GetUserByUserName	Returns a single user by the username
GetUserMembership	Returns all the membership-specific information for a single user
GetUsers	Returns a list of users
GetUsersByEmail	Returns a list of users by email address
GetUsersByUserName	Returns a list of users by username
GetUsersByProfileProperty	Returns a list of users who meet criteria by various profile properties
ResetPassword	Resets a user's password
UnLockUser	Unlocks user accounts so they can login to the portal
UpdateUser	Updates a single user
UserLogin	Authenticates a single user
MaxInvalidPasswordAttempts	Property that contains the maximum number of invalid login attempts before locking user

All methods listed in the table that return more than a single row of records are set up to use record paging. All the properties listed in Table 9-1 are retrieved from the web.config file. The following XML snippet shows the set of properties for the default ASP.NET Membership Provider. This is contained in the system.web section of the web.config file. Although this listing is specific to the default ASP.NET concrete provider, having a value set for each of these for any concrete Membership Provider is required by the abstract provider within DotNetNuke.

```
<membership defaultProvider="AspNetSqlMembershipProvider"
                userIsOnlineTimeWindow="15">
  <providers>
    <clear />
    <add name="AspNetSqlMembershipProvider"
          type="System.Web.Security.SqlMembershipProvider"
          connectionStringName="SiteSqlServer"
          enablePasswordRetrieval="true"
          enablePasswordReset="true"
          requiresQuestionAndAnswer="false"
          minRequiredPasswordLength="7"
          minRequiredNonalphanumericCharacters="0"
          requiresUniqueEmail="false"
          passwordFormat="Encrypted"
          applicationName="DotNetNuke"
          description="Stores and retrieves membership data from the local
                         Microsoft SQL Server database" />
  </providers>
</membership>
```

One of the properties in this listing is `passwordFormat`. By default, its value is set to `Encrypted`. The value uses the `machinekey` property, which is also set and stored in the web.config file. This node is located within the system.web node in that file.

```
<system.web>
  <machineKey validationKey="196ED0AD77D6895D144C8C84456A70FA65533F73"
            decryptionKey="E514751408CF0DD41C67C34108100853B8F4F9076564D1D7"
            decryption="3DES" validation="SHA1" />
        ...
</system.web>
```

At installation, the validationKey and the decryptionKey are regenerated and replaced with a custom value unique to your install. Because this is what encrypts your passwords, you must be very careful to safeguard the values assigned during DotNetNuke installation. If these values are altered by someone or the entire file is overwritten, no passwords will match for any of the users who registered while the application used the old key. If none of the passwords match, nobody can log in to your install. This could become an even bigger problem if the values are changed and additional users are registered using the newest keys. You would have the previous registered users having passwords encrypted using the old key and the new users' passwords encrypted using the new key. The key set you decide to use results in one set of your users not being able to log in.

Inappropriately changing your keys will make it impossible for any users to log in, thus making the entire application unusable!

The following code shows the `CreateUser` method from the ASP.NET concrete provider code located in the AspNetMembershipProvider.vb file:

```
Public Overrides Function CreateUser(ByRef user As UserInfo) As _
UserCreateStatus
    Dim createStatus As UserCreateStatus
    Try
        ' check if username exists in database for any portal
        Dim objVerifyUser As UserInfo = GetUserByUserName(Null. _
        NullInteger, user.Membership.Username, False, False)
        If Not objVerifyUser Is Nothing Then
            If objVerifyUser.IsSuperUser Then
                ' the username belongs to an existing super user
                createStatus = UserCreateStatus.UserAlreadyRegistered
            Else
                ' the username exists so we should now verify the password
                If ValidateUser(objVerifyUser.PortalID, user. _
                Membership.Username, user.Membership.Password) Then

                    ' check if user exists for the portal specified
                    objVerifyUser = GetUserByUserName(user.PortalID, _
                    user.Membership.Username, False, False)
                    If Not objVerifyUser Is Nothing Then
                        ' the user is already registered for this portal
                        createStatus = ;
                        UserCreateStatus.UserAlreadyRegistered
                    Else
                        ' the user does not exist in this portal - add them
                        createStatus = UserCreateStatus. AddUserToPortal
                    End If
                Else
                    ' not the same person - prevent registration
                    createStatus = UserCreateStatus.UsernameAlreadyExists
                End If
            End If
        Else
            ' the user does not exist
            createStatus = UserRegistrationStatus.AddUser
        End If
        'If new user - add to aspnet membership
        If createStatus = UserRegistrationStatus.AddUser Then
            createStatus = CreateMemberhipUser(user)
        Endif

        'If asp user has been successfully created or we are adding a
        'existing user to a new portal
        If createStatus = UserCreateStatus.Success OrElse createStatus =
           UserCreateStatus.AddUserToPortal Then
            'Create the DNN User Record
            createStatus = CreateDNNUser(user)

            If createStatus = UserCreateStatus.Success Then
                'Persist the Profile to the Data Store
                ProfileController.UpdateUserProfile(user)
            End If
        End If
```

```
        Catch exc As Exception     ' an unexpected error occurred
            'LogException(exc)
            createStatus = UserCreateStatus.UnexpectedError
        End Try

        Return createStatus

    End Function
```

The method first calls the `GetUserByUserName` function, necessary in any custom concrete provider, to see whether the username is used and returns the user object if it is. If no result is returned, the `CreateStatus` variable is set to `AddUser`. If a result is returned, however, a series of steps is required to see how this should be handled:

1. A check is done to see if the `username` is a SuperUser's:
    a. If so, the `CreateStatus` variable is set to `AlreadyRegistered`.
    b. If not, the `PortalID`, `username`, and `password` are passed to the private `ValidateUser` function.
2. `ValidateUser` looks to the data store to determine if a matching username/password combination is found for this application and returns the result:
    a. If the result of the function is false, the `CreateStatus` variable is set to `UsernameAlreadyExists`.
    b. If the result is true, a check is done to see if the user exists for the specific portal by calling the function `GetUserByUserName`.
    c. Where no result is returned from `GetUserByUserName`, the `CreateStatus` variable is set to `AddUserToPortal` because the user does not exist for this specific portal. When a result is returned from `ValidateUser`, `CreateStatus` is set to `UserAlreadyRegistered`.

With the `CreateStatus` variable set, the required information is populated and the create user process can proceed. Finally, the `CreateStatus` variable is compared to the available `CreateStatus` options exposed by the `UserCreateStatus` enumerator and the proper action is taken. The `UserCreateStatus` enumerator is defined within the core in the file UserCreateStatus.vb. You can find this file and the others required to construct the abstract provider in $AppRoot\Library\Security\Membership\.

Now you know how the abstract Membership Provider uses web.config to determine what concrete provider is needed for an install of DotNetNuke to run, and how additional properties needed by the provider to function properly can be retrieved from web.config. This adds flexibility for developers and those who implement DotNetNuke because they can easily change how they want their install to function without requiring them to write a single line of code.

Roles Provider

A Roles Provider interacts with a data store that contains information mapping users to roles, and provides methods for creating and deleting roles, adding users to roles, and more. The role manager relies on the Roles Provider, given a username, to determine what role or roles the user belongs to. Table 9-2 shows the methods required by DotNetNuke to implement a custom Roles Provider.

Table 9-2: DotNetNuke Abstract Roles Provider Methods

Method	Description
CreateRole	Creates a single role.
DeleteRole	Deletes a single role.
GetRole	Returns a single role. There are two methods: one uses RoleName and the other uses RoleID.
GetRoleNames	Returns all the role names a single user belongs to.
GetRoles	Returns a list of all roles used in a single portal.
UpdateRole	Updates a single role.
AddUserToRole	Adds a single user to a role.
GetUserRole	Returns a UserRoleInfo object.
GetUserRoles	Returns a list of roles a single user belongs to. There are two methods: one uses UserID and the other uses RoleName and UserName.
GetUsersByRoleName	Returns a list of users who belong to a role.
GetuserRolesByRoleName	Returns an arraylist of UserRoleInfo objects.
RemoveUserFromRole	Removes a user from a role.
UpdateUserRole	Updates a UserRoleInfo object.
CreateRoleGroup	Creates a new Role Group.
DeleteRoleGroup	Deletes a single Role Group.
GetRoleGroup	Returns a RoleGroupInfo object.
GetRoleGroupByName	Returns a single Role Group.
GetRoleGroups	Returns all Role Groups for a given portal.
UpdateRoleGroup	Updates a Role Group.

The following code shows the default DotNetNuke Roles Provider configuration used in a standard DotNetNuke 5.0 install. It is contained in the web.config file's dotnetnuke section.

```
<roles defaultProvider="DNNRoleProvider">
  <providers>
```

```
            <clear />
            <add name="DNNRoleProvider"
                 type="DotNetNuke.Security.Membership.DNNRoleProvider,
                        DotNetNuke.Provider.DNNProvider"
                  providerPath="~\Providers\MembershipProviders\DNNMembershipProvider\"
             />
        </providers>
    </roles>
```

Again, as mentioned in the Membership Provider section, if you are creating your own concrete Roles Provider, you may need to create your own concrete Membership Provider. Of course, this depends on your implementation. What follows shows the `AddUserToRole` method from the DNN concrete provider code located in the DNNRoleProvider.vb file:

```
Public Overrides Function AddUserToRole(ByVal portalId As Integer, ;
ByVal user As UserInfo, ByVal userRole As UserRoleInfo) As Boolean
    Dim createStatus As Boolean = True

    Try
        'Add UserRole to DNN
        AddDNNUserRole(userRole)

    Catch ex As Exception
        'Clear User (duplicate User information)
        userRole = Nothing
        createStatus = False
    End Try

    Return createStatus
End Function
Private Sub AddDNNUserRole(ByVal userRole As UserRoleInfo)
    'Add UserRole to DNN
    userRole.UserRoleID = CType(dataProvider.AddUserRole(userRole.PortalID,
    userRole.UserID, userRole.RoleID, userRole.EffectiveDate,
    userRole.ExpiryDate), Integer)
End Sub
```

In this code, the private method `AddDNNUserRole` is called to add the user to DotNetNuke's UserRoles table. This is necessary because that's how DotNetNuke relates users and roles to one another throughout the entire application and is required for any custom concrete provider implementation. In earlier versions a final step was required to update the provider's data store (such as aspnet_roles). In DotNetNuke 5.0 (version 4.5.5 and later) this step is no longer required in the default implementation because DotNetNuke does not use the Microsoft's ASP Membership to manage roles. This last step may be necessary in your own custom Roles Provider if you plan to use an external data store to manage roles.

Profile Provider

A Profile Provider writes profile property values supplied by an ASP.NET application to a persistent profile data store and reads the property values back from the data store when requested by the application. Profile Providers also implement methods that enable users and administrators to manage profile data stores using specific parameters. Table 9-3 shows the methods required by DotNetNuke to implement a custom Profile Provider.

Table 9-3: DotNetNuke Abstract Profile Provider Methods

Method	Description
`GetUserProfile`	Returns a user's profile
`UpdateUserProfile`	Updates a user's profile

Previous versions required that default properties be listed in the web.config file. DotNetNuke 5.0 no longer requires this because all the information was moved to the ProfilePropertyDefinition table. Having moved the information greatly enhances the profile capabilities and usability. You can find more information on managing this in Chapter 4, ''Portal Administration.''

A Profile Provider needs to be more flexible than the other Membership Service Providers. In the Membership Service Providers already discussed, the data items are consistent one way or another. For example, the Membership Provider has a series of consistent methods that are required in your data schema in the majority of any web-facing sites. You will always need a UserName and Password set of columns using a defined data type that works for all cases. In a Roles Provider, you always need a RoleId and RoleName set of columns that are also using a defined data type that works for all its cases. Things aren't as straightforward in the Profile Provider. One install can require a list of 10 properties collected at time of registration, whereas another install may require 20 properties. Because you cannot account for the number of properties an install will require, the flexibility needs to be there to allow changes without requiring changes to the actual provider that result in schema changes or changes in the code that would require a recompile.

A Profile Provider also must supply you with the capability to add profile items from other aspects of your application. For example, you may want to add a profile item such as an avatar image for a user in a web site's membership base. If you want the avatar image to persist with the user and be accessible any time, it needs to be part of the user's profile object regardless of when it is collected from the user. This permits the avatar image in this example to be exposed to all modules used in a DotNetNuke portal and allows the module developers to know ahead of time where to access this image.

If you want to create your own concrete Profile Provider, you need to add some additional properties that are exposed throughout the DotNetNuke application and can be consumed by items plugged into the framework, such as modules. Table 9-4 shows the default and required properties, each of which has a constant assigned to it in case the concrete provider does not include these properties. (If the property is not used in the concrete provider, the value will be assigned to that of the constant.) Because DotNetNuke is no longer using Microsoft's Membership Provider to supply profile functionality, only four properties are now required with the default provider. It would still be advisable to include as many of the default properties as possible in your custom provider. This would eliminate the problems that might arise from a third-party module that depended on a specific Profile Property being there by default.

In the default DotNetNuke concrete provider, a user's profile is stored in the UserProfile table in the form of a hash table. This means that instead of having multiple columns, each with a clearly defined data type and column name, the entire set of properties is stored within a single column. This provides the flexibility to add properties to or remove properties from a profile without requiring major changes in the architecture. See the following on how a user's profile is created or updated:

```
Public Overrides Sub UpdateUserProfile(ByVal user As UserInfo)
    Dim properties As ProfilePropertyDefinitionCollection = _
                       user.Profile.ProfileProperties
    For Each profProperty As ProfilePropertyDefinition In properties
       If (Not profProperty.PropertyValue Is Nothing) AndAlso
                (profProperty.IsDirty) Then
           Dim objSecurity As New PortalSecurity
           Dim propertyValue As String =
               objSecurity.InputFilter(profProperty.PropertyValue,
               PortalSecurity.FilterFlag.NoScripting)
           dataProvider.UpdateProfileProperty(Null.NullInteger, user.UserID,_
               profProperty.PropertyDefinitionId, propertyValue, _
               profProperty.Visibility, Now())
         End If
    Next
End Sub
```

Table 9-4: DotNetNuke Concrete Profile Provider Properties

Property	Required	Description
`Prefix`	False	Users Name Prefix
`FirstName`	True	Users First Name
`MiddleName`	False	Users Middle Name
`LastName`	True	Users Last Name
`Suffix`	False	Users Name Suffix
`Unit`	False	Users Address Unit
`Street`	False	Users Address Street
`City`	False	Users Address City
`Region`	False	Users Region or State
`Country`	False	Users Country
`PostalCode`	False	Users Postal Code
`Telephone`	False	Users Telephone Number
`Cell`	False	Users Cell Phone Number

Table 9-4: *(continued)*

Property	Required	Description
`Fax`	False	Users Fax Number
`Website`	False	Users Website
`IM`	False	Users IM
`Biography`	False	Users Biography
`TimeZone`	True	Users Time Zone
`PreferredLocale`	True	Users Preferred Locale

This is a much simpler method than the versions prior to 4.5.5. Again this is due to using a pure DotNetNuke provider. It does not have to synchronize or aggregate with the Microsoft ASP Membership implementation to provide profile information. Additionally, this makes the task of creating a custom Profile Provider that uses your existing data store easier as well.

Summary

This chapter described the Member Role and how it has evolved. Simply put, it is a set of classes to be used by an ASP.NET application to handle its sites membership base and communicate with the data store. You looked at some limitations uncovered in the Member Role implementation due to DotNetNuke's multiple portals within the same application and how DotNetNuke overcame these limitations. You learned how DotNetNuke extended its abstract Membership, Roles, and Profile Providers so the concrete providers could be more flexible, and saw how a developer could create his own custom concrete providers. Now that you have an understanding of how the membership base is handled, you can move on to the next chapter where you explore some of the latest trends in web site development using DotNetNuke's Client API.

10

Client API

One of the main goals in developing a web site or a web application is to provide the best possible experience for the users. To achieve this goal, the developer must do many things, including but not limited to creating a pleasant look and feel for the site, making the application intuitive for the end users, and finally, keeping the time it takes to communicate between the client and server as limited as possible. That last item has been a challenge for web site developers for years.

When a user goes to a web site, the remote web server performs a series of events. It receives the request, processes events required by the web application, and then sends the rendered HTML to the client browser. These events are processed on the server side. What this means is the server must use valuable resources to parse each page and then send it to the client browser as HTML. This is often seen as a disadvantage. One of the major advantages of using server side is that it is browser independent. Therefore you theoretically don't have to worry about variations between browsers. Everything done by the ASP.NET framework is done on the server side.

When events are rendered on the user's machine instead of on the remote server, they are rendered on the client side. The major advantage of using client side is that each web browser uses its own resources to execute the code found on the web page, thus taking the workload away from the remote web server. The main disadvantages are that a developer cannot use client-side code to access local files, directories, or databases. In addition, various browsers may not be able to support all methods received from the server. Probably the best general example of something being done on the client side is JavaScript.

Over the years, developers have found that a combination of both client-side and server-side scripting is often best to achieve the desired results. One of the disadvantages of this combination is that it requires the developer to understand how to write code for both the server side and the client side. For example, a DotNetNuke developer would be required to understand one of the .NET languages, probably VB.NET, and JavaScript in addition to HTML. This can be difficult for a developer because a solid understanding of all three programming languages in this example would be required to achieve the best possible result.

Postbacks and View State

With the introduction of ASP.NET 1.0, an ASP.NET web page had the option of posting back to itself. Each time an ASP.NET web page is requested, a series of events that follow an ASP.NET page's life cycle fire off in a well-defined order. This is how postbacks work. Figure 10-1 outlines the life cycle of a typical ASP.NET page.

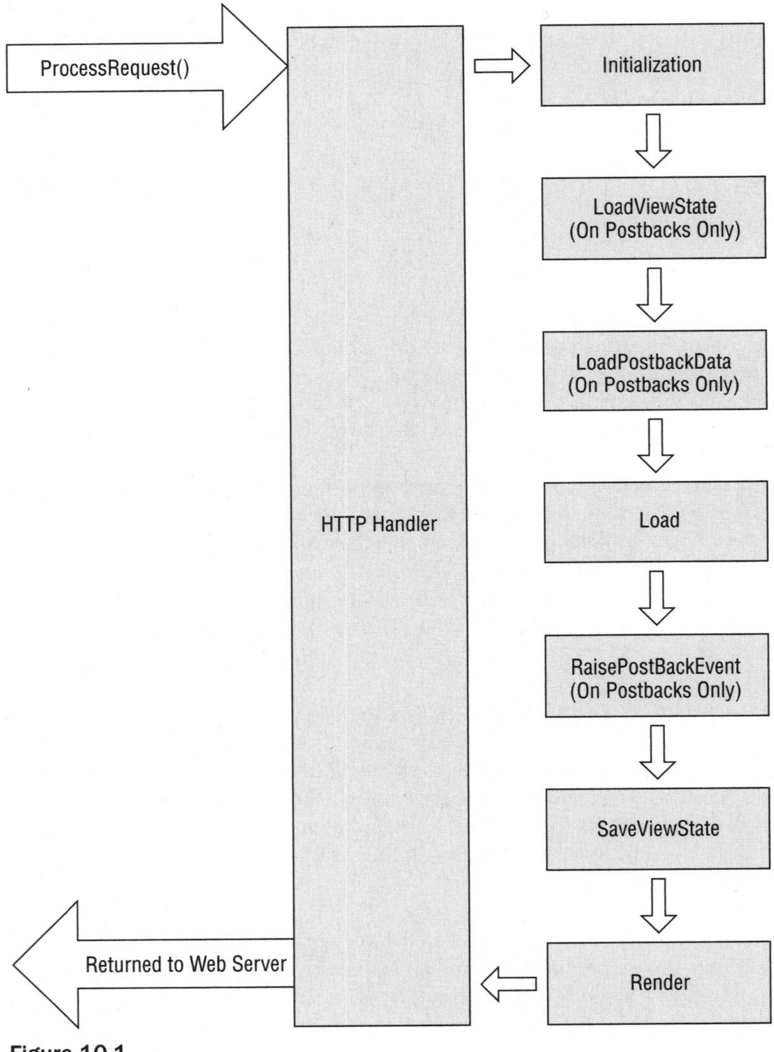

Figure 10-1

The great thing about postbacks is that they allow the developer to use view state to maintain data collected from the user on each postback to the same page. Developers can also use this data during the page's postback process as long as they do so when it is accessible, which is defined by the page life cycle. A simple example of this is when a user fills out a feedback form. When he's finished, he clicks the Submit button. The data collected from the user is then sent to the server, which may do validation on the data. If the data does not meet requirements set by the developer, a flag can be set to postback the page with the error message presented to the end user. This, with the combination of view state, allows the page to be re-rendered and the values previously collected from the user can be bound to the controls where the user already entered the data. This makes for a better end-user experience because it keeps the user from having to input all of the data a second time.

The downside of postbacks is that each time a postback is required, the entire page life cycle must be iterated through and the page reproduced. This not only increases the workload on the remote web server, but it also increases the time end users must spend for this to be processed and returned to them with the error message. In addition, it increases traffic across the network because after the users are presented the page for a second time and they make their corrections, the page must be processed on the server side a second time, plus each control exposing itself to the view state must pass the collected data to and from the server on each postback. Although this is a simple example that can be completely avoided using one of ASP.NET's built in client-side validation controls, not all situations are quite this simple.

When Microsoft introduced ASP.NET 2.0, one of the embellishments was the capability to postback to other pages and not just the same page. This allows data to be passed from one page to another without sending the data to the data store before moving to the next page, or requiring the developer to use query string parameters containing the values gathered on the first page but needed on the new page. This is accomplished using the view state embedded in a hidden input field named `__POSTBACK`, which is passed from the first page to the new page. This field is embedded only when there is an IButtonControl on the page and its `PostBackUrl` property is set to a non-null value. To access the view state of the first page, the developer can use the `PreviousPage` property on the new page.

A detailed explanation of the page life cycle and view state are far beyond the scope of this chapter. If you require more information on either of these topics, refer to the MSDN web site or Visual Studio's MSDN Library. The basics covered in this section are here to give you a briefing on these items so you can understand other sections of this chapter.

What Is the DotNetNuke Client API?

The DotNetNuke Client API was created to help ease the amount of knowledge DotNetNuke developers must have about client-side scripting, yet allow them to take full advantage of all the benefits associated with it. The DotNetNuke Client API is a combination of both server-side and client-side code that work together to enable a simple and reliable interface for developers to provide a rich client-side experience. Prior to development of the Client API, a set of goals was established that the finished project should achieve:

- Provide a means of communication between the client-side script and the server code
- Allow for the functionality to be disabled and postbacks to be used as a last resort
- Provide a uniform cross-browser API that a developer can program against to provide a rich UI
- Allow for the API to be extended and enhanced by the Core Team and third-party developers

Because most DotNetNuke developers have at least a basic understanding of one of the ASP.NET languages, the DotNetNuke Client API was written such that the majority of ASP.NET developers should be comfortable working with it. Methods and objects within the Client API are accessible using a naming convention similar to .NET's namespace structure. For example, if you wanted to use the Client API to determine the browser version the end user is using, you would call `dnn.dom.browser.version`.

Before you get into more details about the Client API, first look at some of the things that make this different from the majority of code covered in this book. For starters, the Client API is part of the DotNetNuke Web Utility project.

One thing quite different from most projects associated with DotNetNuke is that the DotNetNuke project itself depends on the DotNetNuke Web Utility project. Most DotNetNuke development requires your custom project to reference DotNetNuke. As a developer, the most important thing to know about this difference is that you could use the DotNetNuke Web Utility in other ASP.NET projects that are not DotNetNuke-related. This should give you an idea of how abstracted this project is, unlike most DotNetNuke-related projects, because the DotNetNuke project depends on the Web Utility project instead of the Web Utility project depending on the DotNetNuke project. The fact that most DotNetNuke-related projects are not as abstracted as the DotNetNuke Web Utility project should not turn you away from DotNetNuke development. The reason most projects are not this abstracted is because DotNetNuke is a web application framework that other projects should depend on and, at best, removing that dependency would require significant effort to duplicate the functionality provided by DotNetNuke.

Another project — the DotNetNuke Web Controls project — is also associated with the Client API. Neither of these projects' source code is distributed with the DotNetNuke releases available for download from the official web site. They are distributed only in their binary form with those releases. This is because these projects are official DotNetNuke projects independently developed from the core releases. That separation allows the project to develop at a more rapid pace by utilizing resources outside of the DotNetNuke Core Team and not having to adhere to the same release timelines set by the DotNetNuke Core project. If you are interested in obtaining the source code to either the DotNetNuke Web Controls project or the DotNetNuke ClientAPI project, they are available for download on the official DotNetNuke web site at:

- `http://www.dotnetnuke.com/Products/Development/Forge/ComponentWebControls/Downloads/tabid/874/Default.aspx`
- `http://www.dotnetnuke.com/Products/Development/Forge/ComponentClientAPI/Downloads/tabid/875/Default.aspx`

The DotNetNuke Web Controls project exposes a set of web controls used throughout the DotNetNuke Core project. These controls are also available for use in other DotNetNuke functionality such as modules. The Web Controls project actually references the DotNetNuke Web Utility project. This project is also architected in a manner that enables you to use it in ASP.NET applications outside of DotNetNuke.

In DotNetNuke version 4.5.0, AJAX compatibility was built into the core framework. In DotNetNuke version 5.0, the Client API was completely rewritten to utilize the Microsoft AJAX framework. This has several advantages, among which are the following:

- Allows the Microsoft AJAX JSON serializer to be utilized on both the client and server sides
- Formalizes the creation of objects such as inheritance, methods, enumerations, namespaces, and delegate creation

- New Client API ControlMethods that allow complex objects to be communicated both to and from the server
- Functionality in the Microsoft AJAX JavaScript library that is duplicated in the Client API can be removed thus promoting the use of the standardized cross-browser implementation of XmlHttp provided by Microsoft

DotNetNuke version 5.0 also added the Widget Framework. Although the Widget Framework is not part of the Client API, the JavaScript injected via a widget can make use of the Client API.

At the time of this writing, DotNetNuke Corp has just announced that DotNetNuke version 5.0 will fully support jQuery in the base DotNetNuke platform. jQuery is an Open Source JavaScript library that simplifies HTML document traversing and event handling. Over the next few releases, DotNetNuke will be migrating its current JavaScript libraries to use jQuery to do as much of the heavy lifting as possible. Although the DotNetNuke jQuery namespace is not part of the Client API namespace, it is mentioned here because it can be used to enhance client-side functionality. You can find out more about jQuery at `http://jquery.com`.

Using the DotNetNuke Client API

When using the Client API code in your application, you first want to check your .NET code to see if the client browser supports that functionality. If it does, you need to register the namespace scripts on the client.

```
If ClientAPI.BrowserSupportsFunctionality(ClientAPI.;
ClientFunctionality.DHTML) Then
      ClientAPI.RegisterClientReference(objPage, ClientAPI. ;
ClientNamespaceReferences.dnn)
End If
```

The first line, within the `If` statement, calls this function located within the ClientAPI class and passes it a value for the `ClientFunctionality` enumerator. This enumerator consists of the various client-side browser checks the class currently supports, shown in the following code. This enumerator is also located in the ClientAPI class.

```
Public Enum ClientFunctionality As Integer
   DHTML = CInt(2 ^ 0)
   XML = CInt(2 ^ 1)
   XSLT = CInt(2 ^ 2)
   Positioning = CInt(2 ^ 3)
   XMLJS = CInt(2 ^ 4)
   XMLHTTP = CInt(2 ^ 5)
   XMLHTTPJS = CInt(2 ^ 6)
   SingleCharDelimiters = CInt(2 ^ 7)
End Enum
```

The `BrowserSupportsFunctionality` function retrieves the client browser's major and minor build values. The value passed into the function is then compared to a list of supported browsers that are grouped by the enumerator names. The file containing this grouped list is named ClientAPICaps.config and it follows the basic XML version 1.0 structure, as shown in the following example. By default, ClientAPICaps.config is stored in the $Approot\Website\js\ folder. Isolating this file outside of the code was done for a good reason. There is always the possibility that a new browser or new version of an existing browser may be released to the public, and that it will support functionality contained within the current ClientAPICaps.config file. If it's a new type of browser, it won't be listed in the ClientAPICaps.config file. When a new browser or new version of a browser is released, there should be no need to require a recompile of the DotNetNuke or Web Utilities projects. The only alternative to a recompile would be for developers and users to wait for the next release of DotNetNuke to add support for client-side functionality, which the framework is already capable of providing. Keeping functionality tests in a separate configuration file that can be edited with a text editor allows changes that can be made by almost anyone instead of waiting for another release or having to edit the code and recompile. This configuration file also offers DotNetNuke developers an easy way to extend and add functionality tests of their own.

```
<?xml version="1.0" encoding="utf-8" ?>
<capabilities xmlns:xsi=http://www.w3.org/2001/XMLSchema-instance
             xmlns:xsd="http://www.w3.org/2001/XMLSchema">
    <functionality nm="DHTML" desc="Dynamic HTML">
        <supports>
            <browser nm="IE" minversion="4" />
            <browser nm="FireFox" minversion="1" />
            <browser nm="Netscape" minversion="5" />
            <browser nm="Gecko" minversion="1" />
            <browser nm="Opera" minversion="7" />
            <browser contains="Konqueror" />
            <browser contains="Safari" />
            <browser contains="Camino" />
        </supports>
        <excludes>
        </excludes>
    </functionality>
    <functionality nm="XML" desc="Client Side XML Parsing">
        <supports>
            <browser nm="IE" minversion="4" />
            <browser nm="FireFox" minversion="1" />
            <browser nm="Netscape" minversion="5" />
            <browser nm="Opera" minversion="7" />
            <browser nm="Gecko" minversion="1" />
            <browser contains="Konqueror" />
            <browser contains="Safari" />
            <browser contains="Camino" />
        </supports>
        <excludes>
            <browser contains="Mac_PowerPC)" />
        </excludes>
    </functionality>
    <functionality nm="XMLJS"
                   desc="Requires Javascript Client Side XML Parsing">
        <supports>
            <browser contains="Opera" />
            <browser contains="Konqueror" />
            <browser contains="Safari" />
        </supports>
    </functionality>
    <functionality nm="XMLHTTP" desc="Client Side HTTP Requests">
        <supports>
            <browser nm="IE" minversion="4" />
```

```
            <browser nm="FireFox" minversion="1" />
            <browser nm="Netscape" minversion="5" />
            <browser nm="Opera" minversion="7" />
            <browser nm="Gecko" minversion="1" />
            <browser contains="Camino" />
            <browser contains="Konqueror" />
            <browser contains="Safari" />
        </supports>
        <excludes>
            <browser contains="Mac_PowerPC)" />
        </excludes>
    </functionality>
    <functionality nm="XMLHTTPJS" desc="Requires Javascript HTTP Requests">
        <supports>
            <browser contains="Opera" />
            <browser contains="Konqueror" />
            <browser contains="Safari" />
        </supports>
    </functionality>
    <functionality nm="XSLT" desc="Client Side XSLT Processing">
        <supports>
            <browser nm="IE" minversion="4" />
        </supports>
        <excludes>
            <browser nm="FireFox" minversion="1" />
            <browser nm="Netscape" minversion="6" />
            <browser nm="Opera" minversion="7" />
            <browser nm="Gecko" minversion="1" />
            <browser contains="Konqueror" minversion="5" />
            <browser contains="Safari" />
            <browser contains="Mac_PowerPC)" />
            <browser contains="Camino" />
        </excludes>
    </functionality>
    <functionality nm="Positioning" desc="Dynamic Positioning of Elements">
        <supports>
            <browser nm="IE" minversion="4" />
            <browser nm="FireFox" minversion="1" />
            <browser nm="Netscape" minversion="5" />
            <browser nm="Opera" minversion="7" />
            <browser nm="Gecko" minversion="1" />
            <browser contains="Konqueror" />
            <browser contains="Safari" />
            <browser contains="Camino" />
        </supports>
        <excludes>
        </excludes>
    </functionality>
  <functionality nm="Motion" desc="Animation of elements">
    <supports>
       <browser nm="IE" minversion="4" />
       <browser nm="Netscape" minversion="5" />
       <browser nm="Opera" minversion="7" />
       <browser nm="Gecko" minversion="1" />
       <browser contains="Konqueror" />
```

```
            <browser contains="Safari" />
            <browser contains="FireFox" />
        </supports>
        <excludes>
        </excludes>
    </functionality>
    <functionality nm="SingleCharDelimiters" desc="Supports single character
delimiters (i.e. Char(18))">
        <supports>
            <browser nm="None" />
        </supports>
        <excludes>
        </excludes>
    </functionality>
    <functionality nm="UseExternalScripts" >
        <supports>
            <browser nm="*" />
        </supports>
        <excludes>
        </excludes>
    </functionality>
</capabilities>
```

As you can see, each functionality group enables you to clearly define which browsers are supported and which are excluded for each separate test. In the test shown first, the functionality being tested for is whether the client browser supports DHTML. Based on the ClientAPICaps.config file, you can see that if the user is browsing a web site using Client API with Internet Explorer version 4 or above, the user's browser is supported, and a value of `true` is returned.

After a functionality test is done, the next step is to register something on the client's browser. This can be a namespace for use on the client side or a variable or script block. When calling the `RegisterClientReference` function, you have to send it the Page object along with the `ClientNamespaceReferences` enumerator telling the function what namespace you are attempting to register. Each namespace is stored in a separate JavaScript file stored within the same folder as the ClientAPICaps.config file. When the `RegisterClientReference` function runs, it adds the corresponding file to the page so it can be downloaded by the client browser.

All of the JavaScript files in this directory have been rewritten in DotNetNuke 5.0 to better use the chaining functionality of JavaScript. It is anticipated that they will be modified over the next few releases to take advantage of Microsoft AJAX JavaScript library. The function calls themselves should not change, just the inner workings. Thus a call to `RegisterClientReference` *will continue to work as it has in the past.*

Client-Side Script Caching

Any time you are developing a web site, you want to keep the amount of data being passed from the server to the client machine minimal. That keeps the load time low for the web page so the end result improves the end-user experience. To use a large amount of client-side functionality, however, you need a large collection of JavaScript functions on the client machine. The dilemma is determining exactly how to divide up the JavaScript functions so you are sending only what you need when you need it.

There are some other factors to consider when dividing the JavaScripts. When the JavaScript files are sent to the client browser, they are locally cached by the browser based on the current URL. Each time a page is sent from the server side to the client side, the browser has to send a request to the server for each separate JavaScript file to see whether the client-side file's date is the same or older than that of the corresponding file on the server side. If the file on the server side is newer, or the client-side file does not exist yet, the server-side sends the JavaScript file to the client web browser.

Another factor that should be taken into consideration is the payload of the initial page. The more functions in a single JavaScript file, the bigger the file will be. If all client-side code were sent in a single file, that file would be rather large. The larger the file, the longer it takes to send to the client side. You never want the first page hit to your site to take so long that users have no desire to see the rest of your site. Despite the ever-increasing speed, availability, and usage of broadband connections, this is still a factor that merits your attention.

How this is handled in the DotNetNuke Client API, like many other decisions, is a compromise. The JavaScript files are grouped by functional area. These functional area groupings are similar, as is the naming of the entire Client API, to working with namespaces in ASP.NET. The JavaScript files are also structured so that all common functions are broken out into separate files. Those files make use of the functions by referring to the other JavaScript files containing that logical grouping, which is similar to working with ASP.NET namespaces.

To avoid too many requests needed on every page hit to determine if a new JavaScript file should be downloaded, the number of JavaScript files has been limited, and few will be added over time. A subsequent page hit is going to happen much more often than the initial page hit because the end user is more likely to view that page hundreds or even thousands of times again. Weighing all of this, the Core Team determined that it would be more beneficial for the end-user experience to not require a high number of requests for each page hit rather than focusing too much on the initial page hit payload. This was also one of the benefits of implementing jQuery. By using jQuery you can simplify the JavaScript files, thus reducing the payload even more. Additionally, by using a hosted version of jQuery, the likelihood of the client already having the necessary file is greatly increased.

Thus far, you have touched only on how to get files and data from the server side to the client side and how to deliver them. The next section looks at how to start communicating between the client-side code (now that you know how to check what the client-side browser supports) and the server-side code.

Client and Server Communication

There is no point to doing all these client-side tests if you are not going to do anything based on their results. Earlier, this chapter pointed out that the view state is encrypted prior to going to the client browser. Because it is encrypted, it isn't really helpful to handle things on the client side. To you, as a developer, this means you need to find a way to get items onto the client side that you can use, and then pass those back to the server side where you can also make use of them.

Starting on the Server Side

The "Using the DotNetNuke Client API" section touched on how to register a variable, namespace, or script block. This was a primer to show you how to get something over to the client side with which you can communicate. Normally this is done in one of two ways:

1. Setting the value of a hidden form field on the server side and then reading its value on the client side using the Document Object Model (DOM)
2. Setting the JavaScript variable directly on the server side by writing out a string the client side can read

With the Client API, you need to use the method `RegisterClientVariable` in your .NET code to register a variable on the server side for use on the client side. You will need to pass to this method the Page object, a variable name/value pair, and a Boolean value to determine whether the variable should be appended or overwritten. As shown in the following code, the first thing `RegisterClientVariable` does is create a dictionary object. This object will be serialized and sent down to the client via JSON. Earlier versions of the ClientAPI used a hidden HTML input control. With the full adoption of Microsoft AJAX, the JSON serializer is used.

```
Public Shared Sub RegisterClientVariable(ByVal objPage As Page, ByVal _
strVar As String, ByVal strValue As String, ByVal blnOverwrite As Boolean)
     'only add once
      Dim objDict As Generic.Dictionary(Of String, String) = _
      GetClientVariableList(objPage)
      If objDict.ContainsKey(strVar) Then
        If blnOverwrite Then
           objDict(strVar) = strValue
        Else
           'appending value
            objDict(strVar) &= strValue
        End If
      Else
        objDict.Add(strVar, strValue)
      End If
     'instead of serializing each time, do it once
      If HttpContext.Current.Items("CAPIPreRender") Is Nothing Then
        AddHandler GetDNNVariableControl(objPage).PreRender, AddressOf _
        CAPIPreRender
        HttpContext.Current.Items("CAPIPreRender") = True
      End If
     'if we are past prerender event then we need to keep serializing
      If Not HttpContext.Current.Items("CAPIPostPreRender") Is Nothing Then
         SerializeClientVariableDictionary(objPage, objDict)
      End If
End Sub
```

Calling this method will add the name/value pair to the dictionary object that will eventually be sent down to the client.

A good example of registering a variable for client-side use is in the DotNetNuke Tree control. If you look inside the DotNetNuke.WebControls\DNNTree.vb file, you will see the `DnnTree_PreRender` method.

The part of the DnnTree_PreRender method is shown where it calls the RegisterClientVariable method. This steps through the method as explained earlier and builds the dictionary object using dnn_controlid_json as the name part, and JSON data will be written out as its value part. To avoid confusion, please note that the dnn_controlid represents the ClientID variable that is generated by ASP.NET at runtime.

```
DotNetNuke.UI.Utilities.ClientAPI.RegisterClientVariable(Me.Page, Me.ClientID & _
        "_json", "{" & Me.TreeNodes.ToJSON() & "}", True))
```

Although not outlined previously, this example registers the proper JavaScript files to be sent to the client. The following code includes the RegisterClientScript method, which determines the files to send to the client side:

```
Public Sub RegisterClientScript()
   If IsDownLevel = False Then
      DotNetNuke.UI.Utilities.ClientAPI.RegisterClientReference(Me.Page, _
       DotNetNuke.UI.Utilities.ClientAPI.ClientNamespaceReferences.dnn_dom)
      If Me.PopulateNodesFromClient Then
         DotNetNuke.UI.Utilities.ClientAPI.RegisterClientReference(Me.Page, _
      DotNetNuke.UI.Utilities.ClientAPI.ClientNamespaceReferences.dnn_xmlhttp)
      End If
      RegisterSubmitComponent(Me.Page)
      RegisterClientScriptBlock(Me.Page, "dnn.controls.js")
      RegisterClientScriptBlock(Me.Page, "dnn.controls.dnntree.js")
   End If
End Sub
```

On the Client Side

All of the code discussed so far has been rendered on the server side. If you are an ASP.NET developer, everything should have seemed fairly familiar to you because it was all .NET code. Now you are about to enter client-side territory, which may be completely new to you. Because the DotNetNuke Client API took the namespace approach with its client-side script, it should help level the learning curve for those .NET developers who are working with client-side script for the first time.

In the "Starting on the Server Side" section, the DotNetNuke Tree control was used as an example. Before any values were set, the proper client-side namespaces were registered. Registering the client-side namespace sends the necessary JavaScript files and script blocks to the client. This is an important step because after the page is sent to the client, the dnn.controls.initTree function is called by the client side. dnn.controls.initTree creates a new instance of the DNNTree on the client side by creating a new XML document on the client side. The XML document retrieves its data from the controlid_json data created on the server side by calling the _loadNodes function, which in turn calls the dnn.getVar client-side function. This getVar function basically does the opposite of RegisterClientVariable and selects the matching variable on the client side, and then populates the newly created XML document with data.

```
Type.registerNamespace('dnn.controls');
dnn.extend(dnn.controls, {
   initTree: function(ctl)
   {
      if (ctl)
```

```
        {
          var tree = new dnn.controls.DNNTree(ctl);
          tree.initialize();
          return tree;
        }
    }
});
//------- Constructor -------//
dnn.controls.DNNTree = function(o)
{
    dnn.controls.DNNTree.initializeBase(this, [o]);
    this.rootNode = null;
    this.nodes = [];
    this._loadNodes();
    this.hoverTreeNode = null;
    this.selTreeNode = null;
    //--- Appearance Properties ---//
    this.css = this.getProp('css', '');
    this.cssChild = this.getProp('csschild', '');
    this.cssHover = this.getProp('csshover', '');
    this.cssSel = this.getProp('csssel', '');
    this.cssIcon = this.getProp('cssicon', '');
    this.sysImgPath = this.getProp('sysimgpath', 'images/');
    this.imageList = this.getProp('imagelist', '').split(',');
    this.expandImg = this.getProp('expimg', '');
    this.workImg = this.getProp('workimg', 'dnnanim.gif');
    this.animf = new Number(this.getProp('animf', '5'));
    this.collapseImg = this.getProp('colimg', '');
    this.indentWidth = new Number(this.getProp('indentw', '10'));
    if (this.indentWidth == 0)
        this.indentWidth = 10;
    this.checkBoxes = this.getProp('checkboxes',
'0') == '1';
    this.checkBoxMode = new Number(this.getProp('cbm', '0'));
    this.target = this.getProp('target', '');
    this.defaultJS = this.getProp('js', '');
    this.postBack = this.getProp('postback', '');
    this.callBack = this.getProp('callback', '');
    this.callBackStatFunc = this.getProp('callbackSF', '');
    if (this.callBackStatFunc.length > 0)
        this.add_handler('callBackStatus', eval(this.callBackStatFunc));
    this.expImgWidth = new Number(this.getProp('expcolimgw', '12'));
    kbCtl = this.container;
    if (this.container.tabIndex <= 0)
            this.container.tabIndex = 0;
    else {
        kbCtl = document.createElement('input');
        kbCtl.type = 'text';
        kbCtl.style.width = 0;
        kbCtl.style.height = 0;
        kbCtl.style.background = 'transparent';
        kbCtl.style.border = 0;
        kbCtl.style.positioning = 'absolute';
        kbCtl.style.left = '-999em';
        this.container.parentNode.appendChild(kbCtl);
```

```
        }
        this.addHandlers(kbCtl, { "keydown": this.keydownHandler, "focus":
                                  this.focusHandler }, this);
        this._onsubmitDelegate = Function.createDelegate(this, this._onsubmit);
        dnn.controls.submitComp.add_handler(this._onsubmitDelegate);
    }
    ... ... ...
    _loadNodes: function()
    {
        var json = dnn.evalJSON(dnn.getVar(this.ns + '_json'));
        if (json)
        {
            this.nodes = json.nodes;
            this.rootNode = {};
            this.rootNode.nodes = this.nodes;
            this.rootNode.id = this.ns;
            this.rootNode = new dnn.controls.JSONNode(this.rootNode, 'root', 0);
        }
    }
    ... ... ...
```

After the page is fully loaded and everything has been rendered on the client side, there is the possibility that a user may interact (selecting, expanding, collapsing, and so on) with the items enabled on the client side, like the DotNetNuke Tree. The entire time the user is interacting with the DotNetNuke Tree, the variable used in the example is being manipulated with each change on the client side. Assuming postbacks and callbacks are not enabled for these changes, the variable keeps getting altered until some type of state change is made. An example would be expanding a tree view until the end user sees the node he wants to select. The user then selects the node and clicks the Submit button, sending the manipulated code back to the server side for processing.

Returning to the Server Side

So far, the variables have been created on the server side and sent to the client side. When they were on the client side, these variable values were manipulated based on the actions performed by the end user. After the manipulation, the variables are sent back to the server side for processing after some type of event is thrown or a callback is done. (The details of callbacks are discussed later in this chapter.) No matter how the variable was returned, it needs to be processed on the server side. Shown here is the function called to retrieve the value of a client-side variable. This function retrieves the value of the variable and returns it so you can do something with the result.

```
Public Shared Function GetClientVariableList(ByVal objPage As Page) _
As Generic.Dictionary(Of String, String)
    Dim ctlVar As HtmlInputHidden = ClientVariableControl(objPage)
    Dim strValue As String = ""
    If Not ctlVar Is Nothing Then strValue = ctlVar.Value
    If Len(strValue) = 0 Then strValue = _
            System.Web.HttpContext.Current.Request(DNNVARIABLE_CONTROLID)
   'using request object in case we are loading before controls have values set
    If strValue Is Nothing Then strValue = ""
    Dim objDict As Generic.Dictionary(Of String, String) = _
        CType(HttpContext.Current.Items("CAPIVariableList"),  _
        Generic.Dictionary(Of String, String))
    If objDict Is Nothing Then
```

```
            objDict = MSAJAX.Deserialize(Of Generic.Dictionary(Of String, _
                      String))(strValue) 'objJSON.Deserialize(Of _
                      Generic.Dictionary(Of String, String))(strValue)
            If objDict Is Nothing Then
               objDict = New Generic.Dictionary(Of String, String)
            End If
            HttpContext.Current.Items("CAPIVariableList") = objDict
         End If
         Return objDict
      End Function
```

In the DotNetNuke Tree example, the client side manipulated the client-side data (in this case an XML document). The submit button click handler is processed and in there, assuming only single selection was permitted, you want to see what tree node the user selected. Similar to the earlier discussion regarding registering the client-side variable using the `RegisterClientVariable` function, the DotNetNuke Tree control handles the `GetClientVariable` function for you. It processes the variable, enabling you as a developer to focus on its results in your preferred ASP.NET programming language. At this point, you would write custom logic to handle the changes made on the client side with the DotNetNuke Tree and possibly send those changes to the data store.

That completes the round trip. What happens next depends on what you want your application to do. By now you should start to see that the Client API handles most of the work for you. This type of functionality has been used on the Internet for several years, but never has it been this easy to use in DotNetNuke, especially for those not familiar with client-side programming. Although not necessary in this example because it made use of the DotNetNuke Tree control, a solid understanding of the areas discussed is necessary if you want to create a custom control of your own that handles changes on the client side.

Client API's Callback

As you've seen, one of the best reasons for learning and making use of the Client API is to improve the end-user experience. Minimizing postbacks to the server was identified earlier as one of the goals that would help you achieve an improved end-user experience. Thus far, this has been accomplished by sending client-side variables to the client that can be manipulated and returned to the server-side code, in a format it can read, when a postback occurs. This helps minimize postbacks because the client side handles the client-side events — such as expanding — raised in the DotNetNuke Tree example. The control changes, the changes are saved to a variable, and the variable is processed when the client side finally communicates with the server side.

The question you are probably asking yourself now is, "What if I want to communicate with the server-side code more often without causing a postback?" Unless you are just beginning web development, you have probably heard some hype lately about AJAX. Although the buzz about AJAX is relatively new, the concept has been around since the late '90s. Most of the reason for the hype now is probably because communication between the server-side and client-side code without requiring a postback, which AJAX offers, is becoming easier to do and therefore more web sites are making use of it. The answer to the question asked at the beginning of this paragraph is asynchronous callbacks. These callbacks enable communication between the client side and server side without the need for a postback.

Life Cycle of a Client Callback

When you're working with the Client API and Client Callback, it is just as important to understand the callback life cycle as it is to understand the page life cycle when dealing with view state. The remainder of this section is broken down into the steps within the Client Callback life cycle and describes what happens at each phase. Figure 10-2 illustrates the main areas of interest in the Client Callback life cycle.

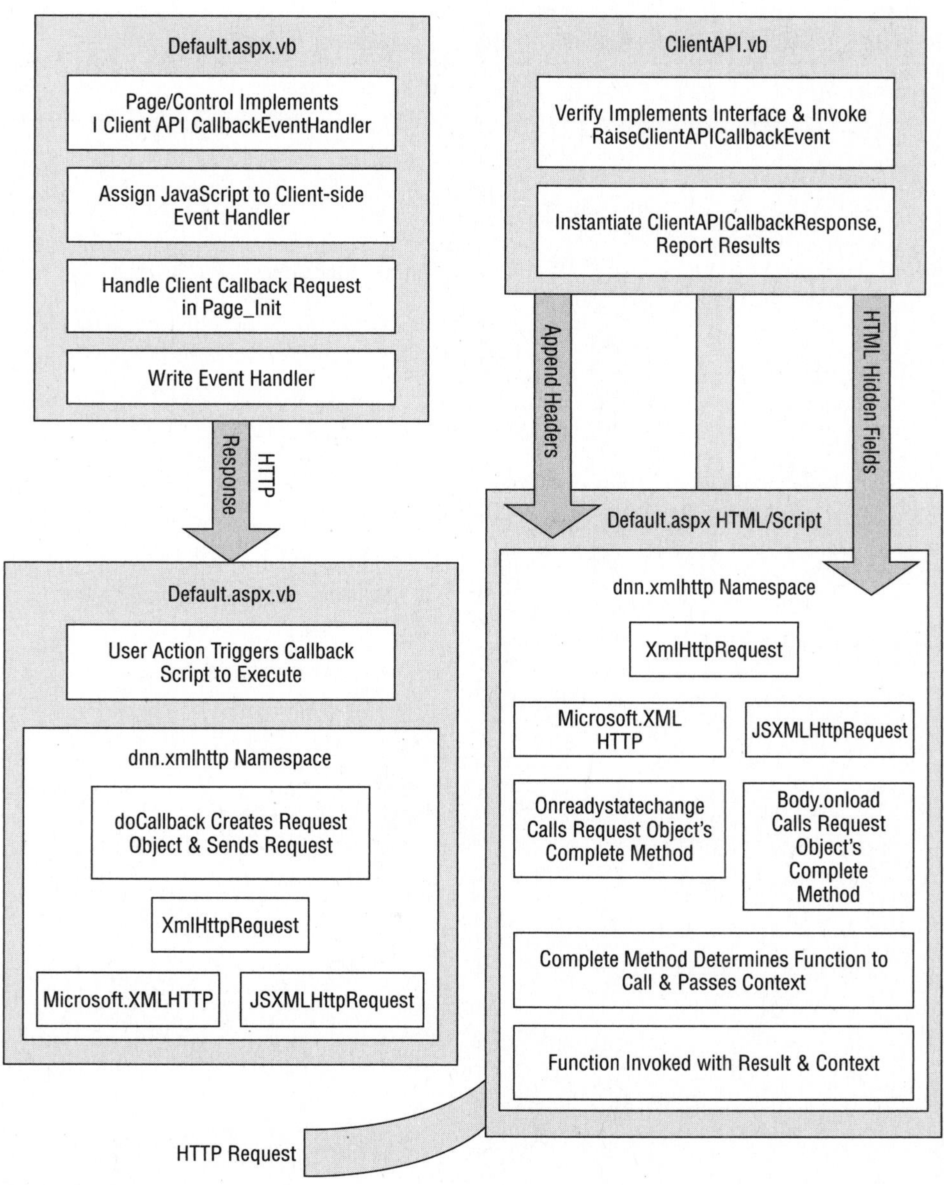

Figure 10-2

Setup and Registration

To get started using callbacks, the first thing you must do is implement IClientAPICallbackEventHandler in the page or your control. In the earlier example of the DotNetNuke Tree control, this was handled for you. After implementing the handler, you have to obtain JavaScript to invoke a callback. This is done by making a call to the `GetCallbackEventReference` method. The parameters required when calling the method are described in Table 10-1.

Table 10-1: GetCallBackEventReference Parameters

Argument	Description
`ObjControl`	The control that is responsible for handling the callback. It must implement IClientAPICallBackEventHandler.
`StrArgument`	The string is evaluated on the client side and is passed to the server-side callback handler.
`strClientCallback`	The pointer to the client-side function that is to be invoked when a callback is successful and complete.
`strContext`	The string is evaluated on the client side and passed to the client-side callback methods.
`strClientErrorCallback`	The pointer to the client-side function that is invoked when a callback errors out.
`strClientStatusCallBack`	The pointer to the client-side function that can be used to report back the progress of the asynchronous request.
`strPostChildrenOfId`	This is used to pass a client-side control Id. If an Id is passed the callback request will contain all the child input values that would have normally been included in a form post.
`eCallbackType`	This is an enumerator of the callback type. It can be `Simple`, `ProcessPage`, `CallbackMethod`, or `ProcessPageCallbackMethod`.

The `eCallbackType` parameter has four possible options as defined in the DotNetNuke.UI.Utilities .ClientAPICallBackResponse.CallBackTypeCode enumerator. Their usage is delineated in Table 10-2.

The result of the `GetCallBackEventReference` method will be JavaScript that needs to be assigned to the client-side event handler. After you have completed this, you would normally have to write logic to handle potential callbacks. This must be done early on in the page's life cycle, such as in the `Page_Init`, so that no response is written back other than the result of the callback. You handle potential callbacks by calling the `HandleClientAPICallbackEvent` method and passing it the `Page` object.

When working on a DotNetNuke project making use of callbacks, it is not necessary to write this logic because it is already handled by the code in default.aspx.vb.

```
' ClientCallback Logic
DotNetNuke.UI.Utilities.ClientAPI.HandleClientAPICallbackEvent(Me)
```

Table 10-2: CallBackTypeCode Enumerator

CallBackType Enumerator	Usage
`Simple`	This is the original callback type included in version 3.2. It supports a single string argument passed to the server and returns a string.
`ProcessPage`	This is the same as the `Simple` CallBackType except that it will execute more of the page life cycle on the server. This is necessary when the callback is executed in a control that is rendered as part of a templated control.
`CallbackMethod`	NEW to version 5.0! This allows multiple parameters of different types to be invoked and have a return type of any object.
`ProcessPageCallbackMethod`	NEW to version 5.0! This is the same as the `CallbackMethod` except that it will execute more of the page life cycle on the server.

It is assumed that prior to completing this phase in the callback life cycle, the proper namespaces and variables discussed in the "Using the DotNetNuke Client API" section have been registered. For callbacks, specifically, it requires the registering of the dnn.xmlhttp client-side namespace.

If you are making a call to the `GetCallbackEventReference` *method, the registering of the dnn.xmlhttp client-side namespace will be handled for you.*

Now, after registering the client-side namespace and setting up the server side for handling any potential callbacks, you need to implement the IClientAPICallbackEventHandler interface. When implementing an interface in your page or control, you must also implement the methods contained within it. The IClientAPICallbackEventHandler interface contains only a single method, `RaiseClientAPICallbackEvent`. This function needs to be passed the `eventArgument` variable, which is some data returned from the client side, as a string. An example of implementing the `RaiseClientAPICallbackEvent` method is shown here:

```
Public Function RaiseClientAPICallbackEvent(ByVal eventArgument As String) ;
As String Implements DotNetNuke.UI.Utilities.IClientAPICallbackEventHandler. ;
RaiseClientAPICallbackEvent
Return "Hello World! " & eventArgument
End Function
```

Essentially, this function is on the server side waiting for the client side to make a callback. When a callback is made, the function grabs the variable passed to it and returns a string as its result. What is done with the result after it's returned to the client side is up to the developer. In most situations, you will present users with some type of notification that their callback is complete and show them any necessary changes or errors that were a result of it.

If your only goal is to implement client callbacks, you need go no further. Everything required to get going has been covered. The remaining steps in the life cycle are handled via the Client API and should be reviewed for a better understanding of what is actually done by the Client API.

Client-Side Handling of the Callback

In the client-side handling of the callback, all variables are on the client side along with the necessary script files. One of the client-side namespaces that was required to be registered is the dnn.xmlhttp namespace. That's because the script contains the client-side function necessary to create a callback to the server side from the client side. The client-side code function, named `doCallBack`, is shown here:

```
doCallBack:function(sControlId,sArg,pSuccessFunc,sContext,pFailureFunc,pStatusFunc,
            bAsync,sPostChildrenId,iType)
{
    var oReq = dnn.xmlhttp.createRequestObject();
    var sURL = document.location.href;
    oReq.successFunc = pSuccessFunc;
    oReq.failureFunc = pFailureFunc;
    oReq.statusFunc = pStatusFunc;
    oReq.context = sContext;
    if(bAsync==null)
       bAsync = true;
    if(sURL.indexOf('.aspx')==-1)
       sURL += 'default.aspx';
    if(sURL.indexOf('#')!=-1)
       sURL = sURL.substring(0, sURL.indexOf('#'));
    if(sURL.indexOf('?')==-1)
       sURL += '?';
    else
        URL += '&';
    oReq.open('POST', sURL, bAsync);
    if(this.parserName=='JS')
       sArg = dnn.encode(sArg, false);
    else
       sArg = dnn.encode(sArg, true);
    if(sPostChildrenId)
       sArg += '&' + dnn.dom.getFormPostString($get(sPostChildrenId));
    if(iType!=0)
       sArg += '&__DNNCAPISCT=' + iType;
    oReq.send('__DNNCAPISCI=' + sControlId + '&__DNNCAPISCP=' + sArg);
    return oReq;
}
```

As demonstrated, the first thing this client-side function does is create a new XmlHttpRequestObject by calling the `createRequestObject` function, which is located in the same client-side namespace. `createRequestObject` is responsible for determining the callback method supported by the user's browser. After XmlHttpRequestObject is created, this method assigns the pointers to the client-side function for success and the client-side function for failure. These function names, along with other important parameters passed in to the `doCallBack` client-side function, are described in Table 10-3.

Table 10-3: Important doCallBack Parameters

Argument	Description
`sControlId`	The control that is responsible for handling the callback. It must implement IClientAPICallBackEventHandler.
`sArg`	Stores string to be passed.
`pSuccessFunc`	Stores a pointer to the function to be invoked upon a successful request.
`pFailureFunc`	Stores a pointer to the function to be invoked upon a failed request.
`sContext`	Stores the context of the request to be passed along to the success/failure function.
`pStatusFunc`	Stores a pointer to the function to be invoked by status update from the asynchronous request.
`bAsync`	Stores a Boolean to set whether the callback will be synchronous or asynchronous.
`sPostChildrenId`	Stores optional client-side control Id to pass to server.
`iType`	Stores callback type.

If the current browser type does not support the XmlHttp request, it will use the JsHttp request that is referred to as the IFRAME request. Most browsers support XmlHttp requests, but this is worth mentioning.

When the XmlHttp request object is created, the return URL for the request is set, the XmlHttp request object is opened, and communication with the server side begins using the XmlHttp request object's send function. At the end of this phase in the callback life cycle, focus is switched to the server side again.

Page_Init Handling of Callback Requests

Earlier in this chapter, you reviewed the life cycle of the page and were able to see how view state was involved at the various phases of the life cycle. This not only helps you understand the behavior of postbacks, but it also aids in clarifying things at this point in the callback life cycle.

The main reasons for handling callbacks in the `Page_Init` is that it is not possible to handle this any sooner in the life cycle of the page. Prior to this phase in the page life cycle, the controls on the page are not loaded yet. If the controls are not loaded yet, the page will not be able to use the `FindControl` method on them because prior to this phase there are no controls. On the other hand, you should not attempt to handle this later in the page life cycle than `Page_Init` because there is a chance some unwanted response text may be generated. As demonstrated earlier, the Startup and Registration phase of the callback life cycle is handled for you by DotNetNuke in its `default.aspx.vb` code.

Handle the Client API Callback Event

Part of handling the callback request is passing the request to the server-side callback event. The `HandleClientAPICallbackEvent` method, located within the ClientAPI.vb file, is now invoked and is responsible for creating a new ClientAPICallbackResponse object. With the new ClientAPICallbackResponse object created, the first order of business is to determine if certain criteria are met. The criteria are that the control must exist and be located on the server side, and the IClientAPICallbackEventHandler interface must be implemented. If those are met, the `RaiseClientAPICallbackEvent` method is called and a response and status code must be assigned.

ClientAPICallbackResponse ultimately reports back this status code and response from the server to the client side. The available status codes to return back to the client side are shown in the following code. Also handled in the ClientAPICallbackResponse, but not discussed, is how the response will be sent. This is either in the XmlHttp or JsHttp format, which is determined based on how the data was received from the client.

```
Public Enum CallBackResponseStatusCode
      OK = 200
      GenericFailure = 400
      ControlNotFound = 404
      InterfaceNotSupported = 501
End Enum
```

If the format is XmlHttp, which it normally is, the response appends the header of the page. If not, a `Response.Write` is added to the page.

Callback Response Handling

It is recommended, but not required, that callbacks be handled asynchronously.

If callbacks are not handled asynchronously, the browser won't be usable while it is checking for a callback. When that happens, it may appear to the end user that the browser is locked, which leads to confusion and lessens the end-user experience.

When a response is returned to the client side, it needs to be received by an event handler. This requires an event handler to be registered on the client side when the page is loaded. The responsibility of this client-side event handler is to determine if the callback was successful or if it failed, as shown in the following example:

```
complete:function(res)
{
    var statusCode = this.getResponseHeader('__DNNCAPISCSI');
    this.completed = true;
    if(new Number(statusCode)==dnn.xmlhttp.callbackStatus.ok)
       this.successFunc(res, this.context, this);
    else
       {
          var statusDesc = this.getResponseHeader('__DNNCAPISCSDI');
          if(this.failureFunc!=null)
             this.failureFunc(statusCode + ' - ' + statusDesc, this.context,
              this);
          else
```

```
                alert(statusCode + ' - ' + statusDesc);
            }
    }
```

Inside the complete method, the status code and status description are obtained by calling the `getResponseHeader` method. This method reads the response that was written on the server side to the header of the current page. If the JsXmlHttpRequest object was being used instead of the XmlHttpRequest object, its complete method would read the textbox's value from the IFRAME document that matches the header name.

Using either of the request object types works the same after reading the value from the server side. If the function is successful, it is passed to the success function that was assigned during the registration phase of the life cycle. If the function was anything other than successful, the client-side failure method, if one exists, is invoked.

The life cycle of a callback is now complete. You probably noticed that the majority of this is handled for you when using DotNetNuke. If you only want to use the current set of DotNetNuke Client API–enabled controls, which is discussed next, only a minimal understanding of this life cycle is required. If you want to extend the Client API or make web controls of your own, you'll need a solid understanding of the life cycle to efficiently achieve a proper end result.

Client API–Enabled DotNetNuke Controls

With DotNetNuke's focus on reusability and making the developer's experience as pleasant as possible, a series of Client API–enabled controls is included with the Core releases. In addition to the Tree control, which has been used in previous examples, all of the controls described in Table 10-4 are part of the DotNetNuke.WebControls project. These controls reside under the DotNetNuke.UI.WebControls namespace and are used in various areas of the Core framework. To make module development less of a task and also offer some nice client-side functionality, try to make use of these controls when appropriate.

Each of these controls also has its own JavaScript file, located in the js folder, which is named dnn.controls.*controlname*.js where *controlname* corresponds to the specific control's name. When using these controls in your own development, they will register the namespaces, variables, and the script blocks that they need. This makes it easier for developers to use these controls with less code. It is possible to use the controls and not be required to prepare anything for the client side; simply using one of these controls in your module will handle all of it for you.

Of course, if you would like to get fancy, you could use callbacks, as explained in the previous section. As time goes on, you will see more examples in modules and throughout the core itself using this type functionality. It is interesting to note here that both AJAX (introduced during the DotNetNuke 4.x life span) and Widgets (introduced with DotNetNuke 5.0) deal with callbacks. AJAX, as mentioned earlier, makes these callbacks easier, and Widgets offer a new way of injecting the client script to make the callbacks.

If you are looking for some examples to get started with but are not at the point of getting hands-on just yet, visit `http://webcontrols.dotnetnuke.com`. It is a live example of these controls being used in a simple ASP.NET application and not running within DotNetNuke. It enables you to view how rich the collections of controls are without requiring you to download source and install it locally. This site also displays a live version of the latest developer documentation generated at compile time. If you would like to download the example ASP.NET application utilizing these controls outside of the DotNetNuke environment, please visit the official DotNetNuke project's download page. You can also download any of the latest DotNetNuke source code discussed in this chapter as well as the project's unit tests.

Table 10-4: Client API–Enabled Controls

Control Name	Example Usage	Description
DNNLabelEdit	Module title of a container	Allows a label to be edited on the client side with no postback done. Uses callback to update the value in the data store.
DNNMenu	Core skins using solpart navigation	Allows a menu to be dynamically populated from the data store and built on the client side.
DNNTextSuggest	N/A	Allows a user to start typing in the textbox and results are immediately populated. Uses callback.
DNNTree	Core File Manager	Enables you to display hierarchical data in a tree view format.
DNNTabStrip	N/A	Allows a page to be displayed in a tabular manner.
DNNToolBar	N/A	Allows a toolbar to be attached to any control.
DNNMultiStateBox	Permissions Grid	Permits multiple states and is not required to look like a check box.

In addition to these controls, there are two series of methods used often in the core that were not covered. The first is the EnableMaxMin series of methods that enable you to show and hide a module's content all from the client side. The capability to use callbacks, if supported, is part of this series as well. The other series is the module drag-and-drop functionality exposed to site or page administrators. This is what enables you to move a module from one content pane to another and save the change to the database using callback.

Writing Custom Web Controls Using the Client API

One of the original goals outlined when the Client API was created was to allow for the API to be extended and enhanced by developers within and outside of the Core Team. It is strongly recommended that anyone attempting to create their own custom web control utilizing the Client API have a solid understanding of both the Client API and ASP.NET Web Controls. Notice that this section is about creating custom web controls, not custom DotNetNuke controls. That's because more likely than not, a custom web control developed using the Client API will be reusable outside of DotNetNuke as long as the DotNetNuke Web Utility and, in projects making use of the pre-built web controls, the DotNetNuke Web Controls projects or binaries are available as well.

The following is a brief outline of steps that should help you start creating your own custom web controls that take advantage of the Client API:

1. Create a new Web Control Library in Visual Studio.
2. Add a reference to DotNetNuke.WebUtility.dll and, if you're using the pre-built web controls, DotNetNuke.WebControls.dll.
3. Create a class and set its inheritance:
    a. Completely new web controls inherit from the .NET Framework's WebControl class.
    b. Extending an existing control inherits from the control you are extending.
4. Define properties.
5. Create your events and event handlers in the class:
    a. Use PreRender to register client-side scripts and postback handler.
    b. Handle postback using RaisePostBackEvent.
    c. Handle callbacks using RaiseClientAPICallbackEvent.
6. Create the web control's script:
    a. Initialize the control using a constructor.
    b. Declare and create methods.
    c. Create event handlers.

In addition, outline what you need to make your own design and functionality decisions, weighing the factors and determining what is best for your control. For example, an abundance of callbacks in a control ruins the end-user experience because each round trip between the client and server consumes valuable resources and Internet bandwidth. When creating a control that makes use of callbacks, you must decide on an appropriate interval that still maintains the efficiency you want.

Control Methods

As mentioned earlier in this chapter, the Client API has been rewritten to utilize the Microsoft AJAX framework. Beginning with version 5.0 of DotNetNuke, the AJAX library is a requirement. Earlier versions of DotNetNuke would allow the use of Microsoft AJAX via the update panel. Although this worked for an easy "AJAXifying" of existing modules, most of the server-side page events still had to fire, and more data was passed between the client and server than was necessary. With the new Client API, ControlMethodClasses and ControlMethods are now available. These allow the client-side scripts to call a function on the server via `dnn.xmlhttp.callControlMethod`. This short-circuits the server-side page events and sends a much smaller payload between the client and server. In order to expose your server-side methods to the client-side scripts, you must first decorate your class with the `ControlMethodClass` attribute, which will identify the class as supporting ControlMethods.

```
<ControlMethodClass("FriendlyName")> _
Partial Class MyNewClass
     Inherits PortalModuleBase
 ...
```

The `FriendlyName` parameter is normally named after a server-side namespace such as `YourCompanyName.Modules.DNNAjaxmodule.MyViewModule`. Although this naming scheme is not required, it does help keep things organized because this `FriendlyName` must be the same in this declaration as it is in the client-side script.

Additionally, you must also decorate the specific methods you wish to expose to the client-side with the `ControlMethod` attribute.

```
<ControlMethod()> _
Public Function MyNewFunction(ByVal settings as Dictionary(Of String, _ Object)) _
                               as Boolean
 ...
```

There are two very important things you should take into account when using ControlMethods. First, you should always secure your ControlMethods when interacting with sensitive data or doing data updates. For instance, if you were updating the settings of your module, you would want to make sure the current user had the rights to make those updates.

Secondly, you should note that complex objects are being passed from the client to the server. Unlike earlier versions of the ClientAPI, with the implementation of ControlMethods the new version can now pass multiple parameters of varying types!

To call the `MyNewFunction` ControlMethod from the client side you would use something like the following:

```
_onUpdate: function(src, arg)
    {
         dnn.xmlhttp.callControlMethod('FriendlyName' ,  ' MyNewFunction',
        {Settings:this._settings},
         this._delegates._updateSuccessDelegate,
         this._delegates._updateFailDelegate);
    }
```

Obviously there are other JavaScript functions that must be implemented, such as the `success` and `failure` delegates among others. These few code snippets should show you the importance of ControlMethods.

If you are interested in creating AJAX modules, you should check out the Client API section of the DotNetNuke website. Jon Henning, the Client API project lead, has provided a template for Visual Studio 2008 that will create a module with the required events and methods already wired up. This is a great place to start. He also has several excellent blogs and videos to help you get started.

Summary

This chapter introduced you to some of the common problems developers face when trying to produce a web site that offers the best possible experience for end users by utilizing a combination of server-side and client-side code. To offer this capability in a consistent manner, DotNetNuke provides the Client API for developers to limit the learning curve required for this type of functionality. When you're working with the Client API, however, there are a few major points to keep in mind:

- The Client API provides a means of communication between the client-side script and the server code yet allows the functionality to be disabled and postbacks to be used as a last resort.
- ClientAPICaps.config is a configuration file that allows browser functionality tests to be added and or extended without the need for a recompile.
- Client-side callbacks have a life cycle of their own, which is important to understand with regard to the life cycle of an ASP.NET page.
- DotNetNuke offers its own ASP.NET pre-built web controls that make use of the Client API, thus providing client-side functionality for use in custom modules.
- Developers with a minimal understanding of ASP.NET web control development can create custom web controls of their own that make use of the Client API.

11

Localization

The World Wide Web is an international network that must accommodate users from hundreds of cultures, speaking many different languages. This poses a significant challenge for every web application that is targeted at a worldwide audience. To address this challenge, DotNetNuke provides a built-in localization framework that addresses many of the issues required to make DotNetNuke usable by a global audience. This framework is built to take advantage of the ASP.NET localization features while tackling some of its shortcomings.

This chapter covers how DotNetNuke detects languages and locales, then provides instruction for using the API to implement localization in your modules. You will work with RESX files to store strings that are used to localize strings of text directly in the HTML of your modules and with method calls from code-behind. You also learn about the upgraded token replacement engine and a technique for localizing images using dynamically selected CSS style sheets.

Overview

DotNetNuke builds upon the localization API in the .NET Framework to make the functionality easier to implement and manage in core and third-party modules. At the time of writing, DotNetNuke provides localization for static text in module user interfaces and system messages, but does not provide the core modules with the ability to localize web site content stored in modules dynamically. With this limitation, multi-lingual portals are not supported using only core modules and providers. Though core modules do not implement localizable content, DotNetNuke is inherently language aware, so the functionality is there for developers to plug into to enable custom modules to provide dynamically localizable content.

A list of third-party modules that make multi-lingual portals possible is included in the summary of this chapter.

Locales in DotNetNuke

A locale is the combination of a country code and a language code. For the sake of accurate translations, it is important to use both a language code and a country code to perform localization. Many languages are spoken in more than one country, and dialects may differ from country to country. For example, a banking web site that operates in the United States and Great Britain that needs to display "check" or "cheque" changes its interface language depending upon whether the user's locale code is for English in the United States (`en-US`) or Great Britain (`en-GB`). This is the RFC 1766 standard.

Locale detection has changed very little since even the early releases of DotNetNuke version 3, but understanding the sequence of how locales are detected can help in troubleshooting and designing localization within your modules. The `OnInit` event sets the current culture of the thread using the `PageCulture` property in `DotNetNuke.Framework.PageBase` by running through a sequence of detection starting with the language parameter of the request and finishing with the default language of `en-US` as stored in the `DotNetNuke.Services.Localization.Localization.SystemLocale` constant if no other setting is found (see Figure 11-1).

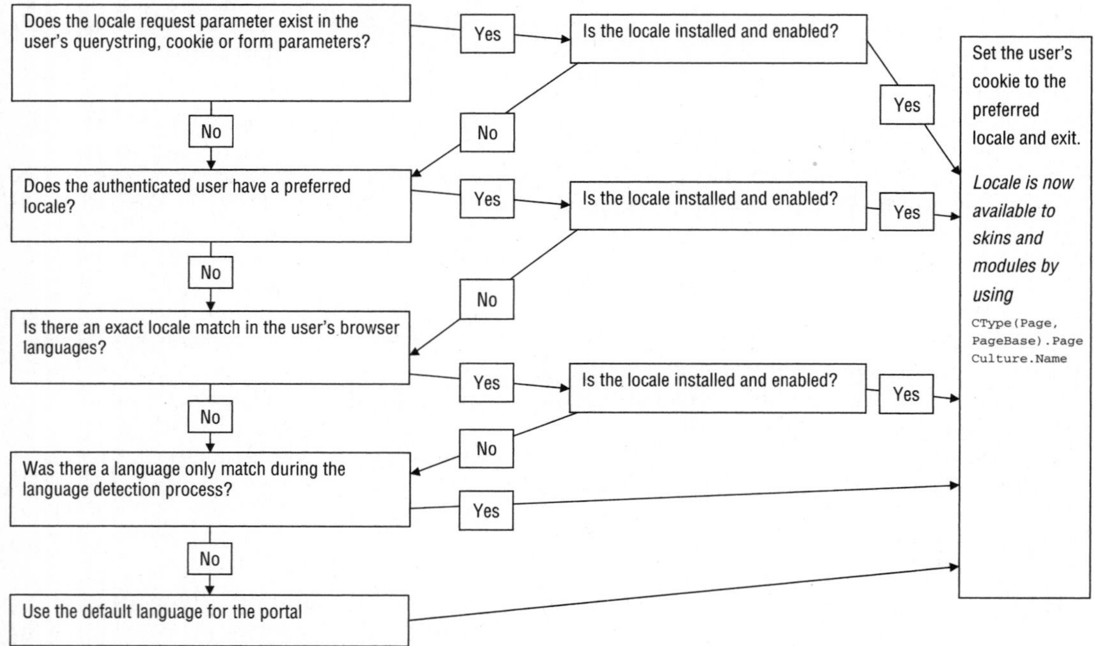

Figure 11-1

During the locale detection process, DotNetNuke will first try for an exact match of language code and country code. If an exact match is not found, it will try to find a language code match. This part is essential with languages like Spanish, a language that is spoken in many countries with slightly different dictionaries. If a portal is designed in the Spanish language for Mexico (`es-MX`), a web site visitor from Bolivia (`es-BO`) would be able to make much more sense of the Mexican Spanish dictionary than the default United States English (`en-US`).

The real utility of this process is that by the time the page begins its load process, a valid culture that is supported by the installation has been intentionally set. With DotNetNuke as a base framework, module developers can implement interface and dynamic content localization without having to manage any of the particulars of detecting and managing locales. Instead, the work is already done and developers simply use the selected locale made available to every page, module, and skin through the `CType(Page, PageBase).PageCulture.Name` call.

Resource Files

To align closely to the ASP.NET 2.0 and 3.5 localization implementation, DotNetNuke uses the Windows Resource Files (RESX) format to store translations. This file format uses XML tags to store key/value pairs of string values. Developers often use the Template.resx file in the root App_Resources directory as a starting place to create their resource files.

Here's an example format of a resource file's data elements shown with the Data Provider form fields on the Host Settings page:

```
. . .
      <data name="plDataProvider.Text">
            <value>Data Provider:</value>
      </data>
      <data name="plDataProvider.Help">
          <value>The provider name which is identified as the default data provider in
the web.config file</value>
      </data>
. . .
```

Each name attribute is referred to as a resource key. Notice that the two resource keys in this example have extensions. DotNetNuke uses a number of extensions that help identify translations more easily:

- **.Text**: Used for the text properties of controls (default if not included in resource key).
- **.Help**: Used for help text.
- **.Header**: Used for the HeaderText properties of DataGrid columns.
- **.EditText**: Used for the EditText properties of DataGrids.
- **.ErrorMessage**: Used for the ErrorMessage property of Validator controls.

Whereas `.Text` relates directly to the Text property of an ASP.NET control, the other extensions are there to instruct DotNetNuke on how to use the string for other controls. There are three types of static translations in DotNetNuke: Application Resources, Local Resources, and Global Resources. These static translations are defined in the following sections.

Application Resources

Application Resources translations are shared throughout many controls in DotNetNuke. Application Resources files are the storage area for generic translations. For example, to localize the words "True" and "False," you would store the translations in the Application Resources files. Other examples of Application Resources are Yes, No, Submit, and Continue.

Application Resources are stored in the App_GlobalResources directory, which is directly under the DotNetNuke root installation directory. The filename for the system locale (en-US) for Application Resources is SharedResources.resx. The file naming convention for other locales is SharedResources.[locale].resx. For example, the German language Application Resources file for Germany would be named `SharedResources.de-DE.resx`.

Global Resources

Global Resources translations are for localizing strings from components that do not have Local Resource files, are not necessarily shared translations, and don't fit in the first two categories. Because all Local Resources are associated with a user control or a page, there is no place to store translations for components. For this reason, there's now this other category for resource files. An example of Global Resources usage is in the component admin/Containers/ActionBase.vb, which needs to localize the word Help in the module action lists.

Global Resources are stored in the same directory as Application Resources (/App_Resources). The filename for the system default locale is /App_Resources/GlobalResources.resx. For locales other than the system default, the naming convention is as follows:

```
/App_Resources/GlobalResources.[locale].resx
```

Local Resources

Local Resources translations are unique to a user control. For example, to localize the Announcements module's user control, you would store the translations in a Local Resources file that lives in a child directory beneath the Announcements module's directory.

If the Announcements module has static translations that are generic in nature (such as True and False), the translations should be gathered from Application Resources.

Local Resources files are stored in a directory named App_LocalResources. Each directory that contains localized user controls must have a directory named App_LocalResources. The filename for the System Locale follows this naming convention:

```
[control_directory]/App_LocalResources/[user_control_file_name].resx.
```

An example for the en-US locale in the resource file for the Announcements module would be:

```
Announcements/App_LocalResources/Announcements.ascx.resx.
```

The filename for other locales follows this naming convention:

```
[control_directory]/App_LocalResources/[control_files_name].[locale].resx.
```

The API

The DotNetNuke.Services.Localization.Localization class provides the methods for localizing strings. These methods are described in Table 11-1.

Table 11-1: Localization Methods

Method	Description
`GetResourceFile`	Returns the path and filename of the resource file for a specified control.
`GetString`	Returns the localized string based on the resource key specified.
`GetLocales`	Returns the list of locales from the cache.
`GetSystemMessage`	Localizes a string and replaces system tokens with personalized strings.
`GetTimeZones`	Returns a key/value pair collection of time zones.
`LoadCultureDropDownList`	Fills a DropDownList control with the supported cultures.
`LoadTimeZoneDropDownList`	Fills a DropDownList control with the list of time zones.
`LocalizeDataGrid`	Localizes the headers in a DataGrid control.
`LocalizeGridView`	Localizes the headers in a GridView control.
`LocalizeDetailsView`	Localizes the headers in a DetailsView control.

The GetString Method

Of the methods in Table 11-1, the most widely used is `GetString`. It performs localization based on the resource key passed into it. `GetString` has eight overloaded methods, detailed here:

1. To localize a string value that has a translation in an Application Resources file, use the following method:

    ```
    Public Shared Function GetString(ByVal name As String) As String
    ```

    The resource file to be used will be selected based on the currently active locale. This automatically uses the active PortalSettings object to derive the portal's default locale.

Parameter	Type	Description
name	String	The string to be localized.

2. The following is identical to the preceding method, except you can send in a PortalSettings object to derive the portal's default locale:

```
   Public Shared Function GetString(ByVal name As String, ByVal
objPortalSettings _
   As PortalSettings) As String
```

Parameter	Type	Description
name	String	The string to be translated.
objPortalSettings	PortalSettings	The PortalSettings object for the current context. It is used to determine the default locale used for anonymous users.

3. To localize a string value in an ASCX control contained within a module that has a translation in the module's Local Resource file, use the following method:

```
Public Shared Function GetString(ByVal name As String, ByVal ctrl _
As Control) As String
```

The method locates the Local Resource file by locating the parent control in the control tree.

Parameter	Type	Description
name	String	This is the string to be translated.
ctrl	Control	This is the object representing ASCX user control and is passed as `Me` in VB.NET or `this` in C#.

4. To localize a string value that has a translation in a Local Resource file, use the following method:

```
   Public Shared Function GetString(ByVal name As String, ByVal
ResourceFileRoot _
   As String) As String
```

This method accepts an incoming parameter (`ResourceFileRoot`) from which the resource file to use is derived. It automatically uses the active PortalSettings object to derive the portal's default locale.

Parameter	Type	Description
name	String	This is the string to be translated.
ResourceFileRoot	String	The value of a module's LocalResourceFile property. It is used to derive the resource file to be used for the translation.

5. To localize a string value that has a translation in a Local Resource file with the ability to override the web.config setting to show missing localization keys, use the following method:

```
    Public Shared Function GetString(ByVal name As String, ByVal
ResourceFileRoot _
    As String, ByVal disableShowMissingKeys as Boolean) As String
```

This method accepts an incoming parameter (`ResourceFileRoot`) from which the resource file to use is derived. It automatically uses the active PortalSettings object to derive the portal's default locale.

Parameter	Type	Description
name	String	This is the string to be translated.
ResourceFileRoot	String	The value of a module's LocalResourceFile property. It is used to derive the resource file to be used for the translation.
disableShowMissingKeys	Boolean	Allows for overriding the setting to display missing localization keys.

6. The following method enables you to specify the key name to translate, and both the resource file and the user language to use for the translation:

```
    Public Shared Function GetString(ByVal name As String, ByVal
ResourceFileRoot _
    As String, ByVal strLanguage As String) As String
```

Parameter	Type	Description
name	String	The string to be translated.
ResourceFileRoot	String	The value of a module's LocalResourceFile property. It is used to derive the resource file to be used for the translation.
strLanguage	String	The name of the language used to look up the string.

7. The following method enables you to specify the key name to translate, the user language, and both the resource file and portal settings to use for the translation:

```
    Public Shared Function GetString(ByVal name As String, ByVal
ResourceFileRoot _
   As String, ByVal objPortalSettings As PortalSettings, ByVal strLanguage _
   As String) As String
```

Parameter	Type	Description
`name`	String	The string to be translated.
`ResourceFileRoot`	String	The value of a module's LocalResourceFile property. It is used to derive the resource file to be used for the translation.
`objPortalSettings`	PortalSettings	The PortalSettings object for the current context. If the localized string does not exist for the given language, the default locale specified in `objPortalSettings` is used.
`strLanguage`	String	The name of the language used to look up the string.

8. The following method is identical to the preceding method with the additional ability to override the web.config setting to show missing localization keys:

```
    Public Shared Function GetString(ByVal name As String, ByVal
ResourceFileRoot _
   As String, ByVal objPortalSettings As PortalSettings, ByVal strLanguage _
   As String, ByVal disableShowMissingKeys as Boolean) As String
```

Parameter	Type	Description
`name`	String	The string to be translated.
`ResourceFileRoot`	String	The value of a module's LocalResourceFile property. It is used to derive the resource file to be used for the translation.
`objPortalSettings`	PortalSettings	The PortalSettings object for the current context. If the localized string does not exist for the given language, the default locale specified in `objPortalSettings` is used.
`strLanguage`	String	The name of the language used to look up the string.
`disableShowMissingKeys`	Boolean	Allows for overriding the setting to display missing localization keys.

The GetSystemMessage Method

The `GetSystemMessage` method is used throughout the core code to produce localized and personalized strings. For example, it is frequently used to send email to users that register on a portal. The user registration page calls `GetSystemMessage` to retrieve the language-appropriate welcome content of the email and then replaces tokens for portal and user-specific personalization. `GetSystemMessage` gives developers a tool for localization and token replacement personalization with just one method call.

`GetSystemMessage` has nine overloaded methods, described here:

1. Use the following method if you need to localize and personalize a string when the personalization can be derived from the PortalSettings property. The translation must be stored in the Application Resources file.

```
    Public Shared Function GetSystemMessage(ByVal objPortal As
PortalSettings, _
    ByVal MessageName As String) As String
```

Parameter	Type	Description
`objPortal`	PortalSettings	The PortalSettings object for the current context. It is used to derive any personalized content within the localized system message string.
`MessageName`	String	The resource key used to get the localized system message from the resource file. Because no user information is included in this overload, "User:" MessageName types are not supported.

2. Use the following method if you need to localize and personalize a string when the personalization can be derived from either the PortalSettings or UserInfo properties. The translation must be stored in the Application Resources file.

```
    Public Shared Function GetSystemMessage(ByVal objPortal As
PortalSettings, _
    ByVal MessageName As String, ByVal objUser As UserInfo) As String
```

Parameter	Type	Description
`objPortal`	PortalSettings	The PortalSettings object for the current context. It is used to derive any personalized content within the localized system message string.
`MessageName`	String	The resource key used to get the localized system message from the resource file.
`objUser`	UserInfo	The UserInfo object for the current context. It is used to derive any personalized content within the localized system message string.

3. Use the following method if you need to localize and personalize a string when the personalization can be derived from the PortalSettings or UserInfo objects' properties. You must specify the language to use for the translation, and the translation must be stored in the Application Resources file.

```
Public Shared Function GetSystemMessage(ByVal strLanguage As String , _
ByVal objPortal As PortalSettings, ByVal MessageName As String, _
ByVal objUser As UserInfo) As String
```

Parameter	Type	Description
strLanguage	String	The name of the language used to look up the string.
objPortal	PortalSettings	The PortalSettings object for the current context. It is used to derive any personalized content within the localized system message string.
MessageName	String	The resource key used to get the localized system message from the resource file.
objUser	UserInfo	The UserInfo object to derive any personalized content within the localized system message string.

4. Use the following method if you need to localize and personalize a string when the personalization can be derived from the PortalSettings property values. You must specify the resource file to use for the translation.

```
    Public Shared Function GetSystemMessage(ByVal objPortal As
PortalSettings, _
    ByVal MessageName As String, ByVal ResourceFile As String) As String
```

Parameter	Type	Description
objPortal	PortalSettings	The PortalSettings object for the current context. It is used to derive any personalized content within the localized system message string.
MessageName	String	The resource key used to get the localized system message from the resource file.
ResourceFile	String	The resource file that the localized system message is stored in.

5. Use the following method if you need to localize and personalize a string when the personalization can be derived from either the PortalSettings or UserInfo properties. You must specify the resource file from which to retrieve the translation.

```
    Public Shared Function GetSystemMessage(ByVal objPortal As
PortalSettings, _
```

```
    ByVal MessageName As String, ByVal objUser As UserInfo, ByVal
ResourceFile _
    As String) As String
```

Parameter	Type	Description
objPortal	PortalSettings	This is the PortalSettings object for the current context. It is used to derive any personalized content within the localized system message string.
MessageName	String	This is the resource key used to get the localized system message from the resource file.
objUser	UserInfo	This is the UserInfo object to derive any personalized content within the localized system message string.
ResourceFile	String	This is the resource file that the localized system message is stored in. It is usually the value of the module's LocalResourceFile property.

6. Use the following method if you need to localize and personalize a string when the personalization can be derived from the PortalSettings object's properties and the Custom ArrayList collection items. You must specify the resource file to use for the translation.

```
    Public Shared Function GetSystemMessage(ByVal objPortal As
PortalSettings, _
    ByVal MessageName As String, ByVal ResourceFile As String, ByVal
Custom As _
    ArrayList) As String
```

Parameter	Type	Description
objPortal	PortalSettings	The PortalSettings object for the current context. It is used to derive any personalized content within the localized system message string.
MessageName	String	The resource key used to get the localized system message from the resource file.
ResourceFile	String	The resource file that the localized system message is stored in.
Custom	ArrayList	A collection of strings that can be used for personalizing the system message.

7. Use the following method if you need to localize and personalize a string when the personalization can be derived from PortalSettings, the UserInfo properties, and the Custom ArrayList collection items. You must specify the resource file from which to retrieve the translation.

```
    Public Shared Function GetSystemMessage(ByVal objPortal As
PortalSettings, _
    ByVal MessageName As String, ByVal objUser As UserInfo, ByVal
ResourceFile As _
    String, ByVal Custom As ArrayList) As String
```

Parameter	Type	Description
`objPortal`	PortalSettings	The PortalSettings object for the current context. It is used to derive any personalized content within the localized system message string.
`MessageName`	String	The resource key used to get the localized system message from the resource file.
`objUser`	UserInfo	The UserInfo object to derive any personalized content within the localized system message string.
`ResourceFile`	String	The resource file that the localized system message is stored in. It is usually the value of the module's LocalResourceFile property.
`Custom`	ArrayList	A collection of strings that can be used for personalizing the system message.

8. Use the following method if you need to localize and personalize a string when the personalization can be derived from the PortalSettings object's properties, the UserInfo object, and the Custom ArrayList collection items. Also, you must specify the resource file and the language to use for the translation.

```
Public Shared Function GetSystemMessage(ByVal strLanguage As String, _
ByVal objPortal As PortalSettings, ByVal MessageName As String, _
ByVal objUser As UserInfo, ByVal ResourceFile As String, _
ByVal Custom As ArrayList) As String
```

Parameter	Type	Description
`strLanguage`	String	The name of the language used to look up the string.
`objPortal`	PortalSettings	The PortalSettings object for the current context. It is used to derive any personalized content within the localized system message string.
`MessageName`	String	The resource key used to get the localized system message from the resource file.
`objUser`	UserInfo	The UserInfo object to derive any personalized content within the localized system message string.
`ResourceFile`	String	The resource file that the localized system message is stored in. It is usually the value of the module's LocalResourceFile property.
`Custom`	ArrayList	A collection of strings that can be used for personalizing the system message.

9. The following method is the only GetSystemMessage overload that is new in version 5. It adds the ability to override the AccessingUserID property that is used to restrict access to user profile properties during the token replacement process. By including the AccessingUserID property in the call to this method, developers can ensure the user accessing the token replacement method does not gain access to private profile properties that only administrators should be able to access.

```
Public Shared Function GetSystemMessage(ByVal strLanguage As String, _
ByVal objPortal As PortalSettings, ByVal MessageName As String, _
ByVal objUser As UserInfo, ByVal ResourceFile As String, _
ByVal Custom As ArrayList, ByVal CustomCaption As String, _
ByVal AccessingUserID As Integer) As String
```

Parameter	Type	Description
strLanguage	String	The name of the language used to look up the string.
objPortal	PortalSettings	The PortalSettings object for the current context. It is used to derive any personalized content within the localized system message string.
MessageName	String	The resource key used to get the localized system message from the resource file.
objUser	UserInfo	The UserInfo object to derive any personalized content within the localized system message string.
ResourceFile	String	The resource file that the localized system message is stored in. It is usually the value of the module's LocalResourceFile property.
Custom	ArrayList	A collection of strings that can be used for personalizing the system message.
CustomCaption	String	Property to override the default text used to access custom properties.
AccessingUserID	Integer	The User ID of the user accessing the system message — used to restrict unauthorized access to profile properties during the token replacement process.

When you use GetSystemMessage, you can specify several system tokens in the localized string. The tokens are used as keys to render property values from either the UserInfo or PortalSettings objects. Here's an example:

```
DotNetNuke.Services.Localization.Localization.GetSystemMessage(PortalSettings, _
"EMAIL_USER_REGISTRATION_PRIVATE_BODY", objNewUser, Me.LocalResourceFile)
```

This code calls the GetSystemMessage method to localize and personalize the body of an email message that is sent to a newly registered user. The code is found in the Admin/Security/Register.ascx portal module. The `MessageName` parameter value is `EMAIL_USER_REGISTRATION_PRIVATE_BODY`. It is the resource key to look up the system message in the resource file. The resource key and associated translation from the resource file /Admin/Security/App_LocalResources/Register.ascx.resx is shown in the following code:

```
<data name="EMAIL_USER_REGISTRATION_PRIVATE_BODY.Text">
    <value>
        Dear [User:DisplayName],

Thank you for registering at [Portal:PortalName]. Please read the following
information carefully and be sure to save this message in a safe location for future
reference.

Portal Website Address: [Portal:URL]
Username: [Membership:UserName]
Password: [Membership:Password]

Your account details will be reviewed by the portal Administrator and you will
receive a notification upon account activation.

Thank you, we appreciate your support...

[Portal:PortalName]

    </value>
</data>
```

`GetSystemMessage` first localizes the string within the `<value>` XML node. Then it iterates through the system tokens (enclosed in brackets), replacing the tokens with the appropriate property values. For example, in the following code example, you can see the token `[User:FullName]`. This will be replaced with the `FullName` property value of the User object. In this case, the User object is the `objUser` object passed into the `GetSystemMessage` method. The following code shows that the system message has been personalized and localized with the en-US locale:

```
Dear John Doe,

Thank you for registering at the DotNetNuke portal website. Please read the following
information carefully and be sure to save this message in a safe location for future
reference.

Portal Website Address: http://test.dotnetnuke.com

Username: jdoe1234
Password: pwdjdoe1234

Your account details will be reviewed by the portal Administrator and you will receive
a notification upon account activation.

Thank you, we appreciate your support...

DotNetNuke
```

Token Replacement Engine

New in DotNetNuke 5 is an enhanced token replacement engine that adds important new functionality to personalizing localized templates used in the `GetSystemMessage` methods and certain other modules. The new engine goes beyond simple token replacement to add formatting and analysis that allows administrators to have more control over the display of token replaced values. At the time of writing, the Text/HTML, Forms & Lists (formerly User Defined Table), Announcements, and Bulk Email modules implement the token replacement engine. Token replacement is not supported in skins.

To use tokens in system messages and the modules that implement the service, add the token to your text in the [Object:Property] format. For example, to display a user's Display Name in an email message add [User:DisplayName]. Long-time users of DotNetNuke know that this functionality has been there for a while, but the extensions now allow for new formatting and conditional replacement using the following syntax:

```
[Object :Property]
[Object :Property|Format]
[Object :Property|Format|IfEmptyReplacement]
```

Consider the following salutation from an email sent through the bulk email manager:

```
[Profile:Region|Dear {0} Resident|Dear Valued Member]
```

Users with a value stored in the `Region` property of their `Profile` framework object would be saluted as *Dear Florida Resident*, whereas users that have no value in the `Region` property would be saluted as *Dear Valued Member*.

Properties are formatted with the ability to use the same methods found in the .NET Framework for `Date`, `String`, and `Integer` types. This allows for arguments to be passed as formatting conditions. Consider the following text that can be used to show the current portal's logo with the time displayed directly beneath:

```
<img src="http://[Portal:Url][Portal:HomeDirectory][Portal:LogoFile]"
alt="[Portal:PortalName]" />
[Date:Now|MM-dd-yyy  h:mm:ss]
```

Localizing Modules

The current version of DotNetNuke supports localizing any static text within the user interface of a module. Although localizing dynamic content in the Text/HTML and other core modules is not yet supported, it is still important to localize your module so that it can be used for non–English-speaking sites. Imagine the frustration of your users if all the content for their site is written in Spanish, yet all of the static text in your module is written in English.

Though the localization API is very powerful, it would add a lot of work for module developers if it were the only mechanism for localization. To simplify the job for developers, DotNetNuke includes a localization framework that applies localization using declarative markup in the ASCX or ASPX files. This approach provides a couple of benefits:

1. It simplifies the programming model because the developer adds a single attribute/value pair to the server control markup, and the framework handles calling the appropriate localization APIs.
2. It allows localization to be applied or changed without recompiling the application.

So look at what it takes to provide localization for your module.

Table 11-2: Objects Available for Token Replacement

Object	Class/Data source	Returns
`Host`	System.Collection.Hashtable	Secure HostSettings
`Portal`	DotNetNuke.Entities.Portals.PortalSettings	Current PortalSettings
`Tab`	DotNetNuke.Entities.Tabs.TabInfo	Current TabInfo
`Module`	DotNetNuke.Entities.Modules.ModuleInfo	Current Module
`Culture`	System.Globalization.CultureInfo	Current Culture
`User`	DotNetNuke.Entities.Users.UserInfo	Current User
`Profile`	DotNetNuke.Entities.Profile	Current User.Profile
`Membership`	DotNetNuke.Entities.Users.Membership	Current User.Membership
`Date, DateTime, Time`	System.DateTime	Current DateTime
`Ticks`	System.Int64 (Long)	Current DateTime in ticks
`Row, Field`	System.Data.DataRow	Not applicable
`Custom*`	System.Collections.ArrayList	Not applicable
`User Defined Token`	Any Object by Reflection	Not applicable
`User Defined Token`	Any System.Collection.IDictionary	Not applicable

* "custom" can be replaced with custom text, passed as a separate parameter

After all of the static strings have been identified, you must determine the best approach for localizing each individual string. Each string should be categorized into one of four cases depending on how the string is used within a module:

1. Text placed directly into the HTML in the ASCX files.
2. Text declaratively set in a server control in the ASCX files.

3. Text modified or set in the source code for the module.
4. Text embedded in images.

The following sections show you how to use the localization framework and localization API to correct each of these potential problem areas.

Case 1: Handling Static Strings in the ASCX File

The key to resolving the problem of text placed directly into the HTML in the ASCX files is to understand that localization is handled programmatically. Whether it is your code or framework code, you need to have the string in an element that is easily accessed programmatically. This means that you must make sure that the code-behind file, and, therefore the DotNetNuke framework, is aware of the string's existence. This is actually quite easy to fix; just wrap the string in an HTML control. Essentially, this step transforms the problem into Case 2 and enables you to use a common approach for all strings in the ASCX file. Table 11-3 shows an example of applying this step to a simple string located in a table cell.

Table 11-3: Wrapping a String with a Web Control

Before	After

`<div class="SubHead">`
`  Title:`
`</div>`
	`<div class="SubHead">`
	`  <asp:Label id="lblTitle"`
	`runat="server">`
	`- Title:`
	`  </asp:Label>`
	`</div>`

At this point, your strings are ready to be localized.

Case 2: Handling Static Text in Server Controls

After all of your static strings are encapsulated in server controls, it is easy to tell the localization framework how to localize your strings. To localize a control, add a `resourcekey` attribute with a value that tells the framework which string resource to use for this control. Table 11-4 takes the previous example and makes this additional change.

Table 11-4: Adding a Resourcekey

Before	After

`<div class="SubHead">`
`  <asp:Label id="lblTitle"`
`runat="server"`
`   Title:`
`- </asp:Label></div>`
	`<div class="SubHead">`
	`  <asp:Label id="lblTitle"`
	`runat="server">`
	`      resourcekey="TestLabel">`
	`     Title:`
	`- </asp:Label>`

Now, the framework has all of the information it needs to find your string resources and localize this content.

As mentioned earlier in the chapter, your module should include the App_LocalResources directory with a resource file named after the user control that is being localized. When you first localize a module, it's best to leave the resource file empty. That will let you know whether you have missed localizing strings. Figure 11-2 shows the sample, the `Title: string`, before it has been localized.

Figure 11-2

To verify that you have applied the localization settings correctly, ensure that the web.config file's AppSettings section includes the following line:

```
<add key="ShowMissingKeys" value="true" />
```

If you have applied the `resourcekey` and set `ShowMissingKeys` correctly, you should see the image in Figure 11-3, the localized string with a missing value.

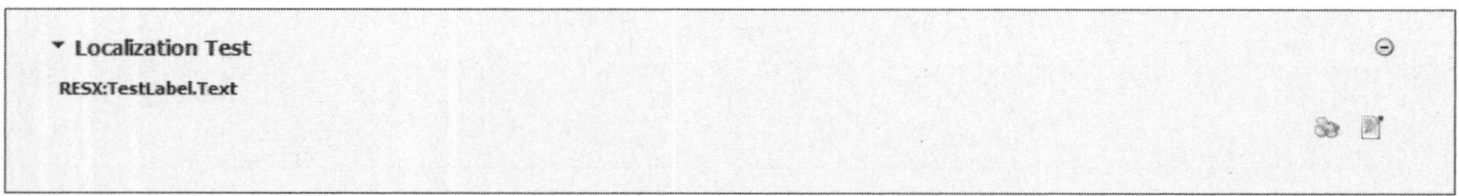

Figure 11-3

Notice that the text shows you that it is looking for `TestLabel.Text`. This makes it easy to see where you have localized a control, and where you still need to create the localized version of the string. If you were to create the `TestLabel.Text` resource string with a `Localized Title;` value in your resource file, you'd get the localized content shown in Figure 11-4.

Figure 11-4

When you localize content, keep in mind that different cultures may use different punctuation. In this example, the colon (`:`) from the original string was changed to a semicolon (`;`) when it was localized.

A Label control shows how easy it can be to localize a web control. But each control is different and contains different attributes that might need to be localized. Table 11-5 shows which attribute will be localized using the default behavior.

Table 11-5: Default Localized Attributes

Control	Type	Localized Attribute
System.Web.UI.WebControls	Label	Text
	Button	Text
	LinkButton	Text
	ImageButton	AlternateText
	Hyperlink	Text
	Image	AlternateText
	CheckBox	Text
	BaseValidator	ErrorMessage
	RadioButtonList	Items(i).Text
	DropDownList	Items(i).Text
System.Web.UI.HtmlControls	HtmlImage	Alt

If the web control you are localizing is not listed in Table 11-5, you need to localize a different attribute, or if you need to localize multiple attributes for the same control, you must use the localization techniques shown in Case 3.

Case 3: Handling Static Text Programmatically

You will find several cases where text cannot be localized using a declarative approach. This will require programmatically setting the text using the localization API. The API section outlines the most frequently used methods of the API.

Continuing with the same example, take a look at how to handle localizing the `ToolTip` attribute for the label you created. Notice that this attribute is not the default attribute for the Label control listed in Table 11-5. To localize the attribute, add the following line of code to the code-behind:

```
lblTitle.Tooltip = Localization.GetString("TestLabel.ToolTip", _
                                          Me.LocalResourceFile)
```

When the call to `Localization.GetString` *requires the* `LocalResourceFile` *parameter,* `Me.LocalResourceFile` *will not always have the location of the resource file associated with your ASCX control. If you are using an embedded user control on a module, you will need to manually set the* `LocalResourceFile` *property of your control on load for Localization to work in your modules.*

Because this is a new control, you are safe adding it to the `Page_Load` event. As you will see shortly, this is not always the appropriate spot for localizing strings. Now that you have the code, the only step left is to add the localized value to the resource file. This example uses `LocalResourceFile` because it is specific to the module. Also note that although the key is named `TestLabel.ToolTip`, you are free to use whatever key makes sense to you. Because you're using the API, you have much more control over how the keys are named.

If your key does not include a period (`.`), the framework will automatically add `.text` to your key and use that as the key for looking up the localized value. Keep this in mind when creating your keys. Assuming that you have named your key appropriately, you should see something like the localized tooltip shown in Figure 11-5 when you compile and navigate to a page with your module.

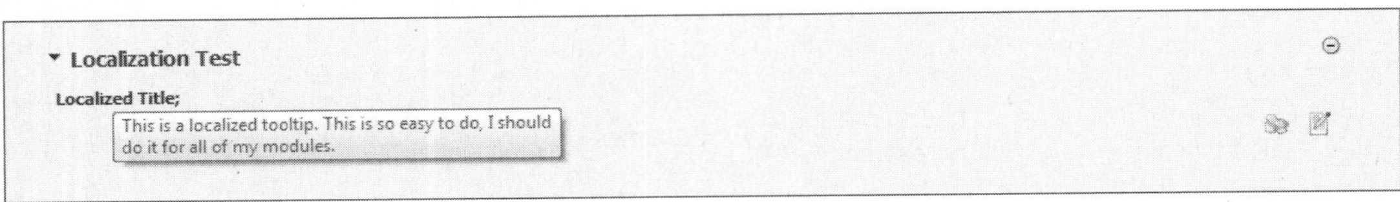

Figure 11-5

There are many instances where you might have embedded strings in your code that are changed depending on the application state. A good example of this is the Login skin object. This skin object changes between `Login` and `Logout` depending on the authentication state of the current user. To localize this control, just replace all the references to the static text with a call to one of the `GetString` methods described earlier.

The DotNetNuke localization API includes a few helper methods to simplify localizing complex controls like DataGrids, GridViews, and DetailsViews. Although you could use the standard programmatic techniques, a helper method makes it trivial to localize the `HeaderText` values. To localize column headers, include a key in the local resource file for each column in the control. This key should be the same as the `HeaderText` value for the column with `.Header` appended. For example, say your grid looks something like this:

```
<asp:datagrid id="dgSample" runat="server" >
<Columns>
<asp:TemplateColumn HeaderText="Title">
...
</asp:TemplateColumn>
</asp:datagrid>
```

In this case, your resource key would be `Title.Header`. After you have the keys defined, just add the following method call to your code:

```
Localization.LocalizeDataGrid(dgSample, LocalResourceFile)
```

This method automatically iterates through the datagrid and localizes each of the column headers.

Case 4: Localizing Images

Images are a special case. It is recommended that you never include text in your images because it complicates localization and can usually be avoided through the use of background images and CSS. If your design requires you to embed text in an image, you need to make a few changes to make it easier to localize the image. To embed text into images and switch them with CSS, override the styles from the base `module.css` style sheet in a separate style sheet and switch them dynamically using the following script directly in the HTML of your user control:

```
<link href="<%= ControlPath %>languagespecific-<% =CType(Page, PageBase).PageCulture
.Name %>.css" rel="stylesheet" type="text/css" />
```

For the links module, this would render like this with the default US English language:

```
<link href="/DesktopModules/Links/languagespecific-en-US.css" rel="stylesheet"
type="text/css" />
```

To use the same technique in a skin, simply replace `ControlPath` with `SkinPath`:

```
<link href="<%= SkinPath %>languagespecific-<% =CType(Page, PageBase).PageCulture
.Name %>.css" rel="stylesheet" type="text/css" />
```

For the default skin, this would render like this with the default US English language:

```
<link href="/Portals/_default/Skins/MinimalExtropy/languagespecific-en-US.css"
 rel="stylesheet" type="text/css" />
```

No module will ever include localized resources for every language supported by DotNetNuke. The effort to maintain the resource files would greatly exceed the cost for all other development. Most module developers will include resource files for their native language and maybe one or two other languages depending on the language skills of the module development staff. This means that many users will be forced to create the resource files for their own language. That's not usually a significant problem.

If an image file contains embedded text, though, the user is forced to re-create the image with a localized version of the text. To ease the burden for the user, include the base image without text, so that the user can easily create the text label in his language. Keep in mind that different languages have different space requirements. Just because a word or phrase is short in one language does not mean that it will be equally short in another language. That's one of the reasons for avoiding embedded text.

When your user has the image file with the localized text, he or she can use the standard `GetString` methods to set the `ImageUrl` attribute to the appropriate image filename, depending on the language they select.

Summary

In this chapter, you learned how resource strings are stored and used for the core framework and for each module. You reviewed how locale and language detection work in the DotNetNuke framework to provide a base for modules to build upon to provide localized interfaces and content. Although DotNetNuke does not support dynamically localized content with the Text/HTML and other core modules, the base is there to build upon to make custom modules dynamic.

If you need to build multi-language portals or offer them to your clients, third-party modules and add-ins are available that build upon the core localization framework to provide multi-language portal functionality. They work by creating localizable versions of the core Text/HTML and Links modules and skin objects that do not inherently support localized values like the DotNetNuke Menu. Check out `http://dnn.tiendaboliviana.com`, `http://www.apollo-software.nl` and `http://www.effority.net` for more information.

12

Beginning Module Development

This chapter begins the tour of custom module development in DotNetNuke. As you have seen in previous chapters, DotNetNuke provides a significant amount of functionality right out of the box. Nevertheless, each user will have unique business requirements that standard DotNetNuke functionality may not meet. Fortunately, DotNetNuke (DNN) provides developers and third-party independent software vendors (ISVs) the capability to extend the core framework by developing custom modules.

This chapter discusses the decision-making process surrounding the development of custom modules, and then focuses on the architecture and design setup of a sample module, the WROX.Suggestion module. Chapters 13 through 15 cover the architectural layers used for module development in more detail. You begin by setting up your module project to interact with DotNetNuke in Visual Studio 2008, exploring some configuration issues along the way.

Although the use of Visual Studio 2008 is illustrated in this book, you can still use Visual Studio 2005 to develop modules for DotNetNuke 5. The Core Team evaluated this situation extensively and made every effort to ensure the development process would be similar for developers employing either platform on .NET Framework v2.0. Because Visual Studio 2008 has multi-targeting capability on .NET Framework versions from v2.0 through v3.5, you can now use VS 2008 for development everywhere you once used VS 2005. Only the solution files are different, and both solution versions are included with the DNN sample module code. With VS 2008, of course, you can also target the new functionality available in .NET Framework 3.0 and 3.5 if your needs dictate.

Note that Visual Studio 2003 can still be used to develop DNN modules, but this environment limits you to using .NET Framework v1.1 and therefore it works only with DNN versions 2 and 3. Module development with Visual Studio 2003 is not covered in this edition of DNN 5.

Starting with the release of ASP.NET 2.0, and now through two generations of development tools, Microsoft has offered free versions of Visual Studio to the developer community. The current suite of free developer tools is known as the Visual Studio 2008 Express Editions. The Visual Web Developer 2008 Express Edition, for the purposes of DNN development, is essentially the same as the full Visual Studio 2008 development environment illustrated here and in the next three chapters of this book. You can download the Visual Web Developer 2008 Express Edition from `http://www.microsoft.com/express/vwd/`.

Understanding Your Module Project

Of course, to succeed in any project, you should plan it out before you write the first line of code. Planning includes considering the answers to any number of business questions as well as defining your requirements, readying your resources, and designing the application.

Business Considerations

You're going to have to ask yourself or your project team a few questions before beginning your application development. These questions can vary widely based on the resources and goals of the organization, but here are a few for illustration:

Q: Can the development effort justify the advantages or savings that your application will provide?

A: Many factors can come into play: skills of in-house staff, costs associated with obtaining the skills, availability of external resources, application maintenance costs, and many others that you will have to account for.

Q: Can the module be purchased from a third party?

A: DotNetNuke has grown rapidly in popularity since inception of the project, and the outlook is strong for continued growth. Many ISVs are developing modules, so increasingly there is little need to develop a module to accomplish a specific task; you can often purchase one for relatively little cost compared to developing a module. As of this writing, literally hundreds of modules are available for sale, and many more are available as free downloads. Some of these modules are written specifically for the older .NET Framework v1.1 iterations of DotNetNuke, but most commercial modules today specifically target the ASP.NET 2.0 platform and DotNetNuke versions 4 and 5. If the module developer has written the module to conform to the same standards as the DotNetNuke core modules, the module will function equally well for the DNN 4.0/5.0 versions targeting ASP.NET 2.0.

Q: Is training required for developers?

A: Module development does require some additional skills over those required for standard ASP.NET development. You develop modules in DotNetNuke using the standard tools you would use to do any ASP.NET project, but knowing how to take advantage of the available interfaces requires some understanding of the DNN framework's inner workings. In addition to this book, many resources are available for learning about DotNetNuke if you want to investigate further; simply search the web for terms such as "DotNetNuke custom module development." In the forums on the DotNetNuke.com web site, there are "Extend It!" forums dedicated to working with ASP.NET v2.0 and v3.5, each with pinned posts containing additional resources. You can find the DNN forums here: `http://www.dotnetnuke.com/tabid/795/Default.aspx`.

Q: Should I hire an outside resource to do the development?

A: Training becomes less of an issue when you have your development done by an outside resource. DotNetNuke's popularity has increased at such a phenomenal rate that many solution providers specialize in custom module development. Because DNN modules plug directly into any portal, you can leverage the use of outside resources to build compatible modules.

Q: What software development language should I use?

A: Although the DotNetNuke core code and modules are written in Visual Basic, all modules can be built as separate .NET assemblies. Because of this, you can develop custom DNN modules in any language supported by the .NET Framework, including C# and Visual Basic. For space reasons the examples in this book use only VB, but either language works as well as the other for your module development efforts. You are free to choose the language with which you are most comfortable, or that which is dictated by project or company requirements.

Q: What infrastructure issues are there?

A: How many developers are going to be working on the same code base? The more developers working on the same code, the more there is a need for source control. Scalability also may be something to consider. In addition, if you have to access resources over the web, you may need to access some of the application settings configured at a host level in DotNetNuke, such as partial trust environment setup or web farm configuration.

Q: Do I need to develop multiple data providers for the module?

A: What database are you going to use for the backend? DotNetNuke supports a Provider Model that enables developers to abstract out the physical database interaction, allowing the actual DotNetNuke core and module logic to be separate from the database logic. DotNetNuke supports SQL Server out-of-the-box, but you can develop providers for any database backend. How many physical databases you need to support will determine how many providers you need to develop. Module data provider development closely mirrors the DotNetNuke architecture. You should create a provider for each platform you want to support. If you're going to distribute your module on various DotNetNuke installations with different databases like SQL Server, Oracle, or MySQL, you need to develop a provider to support each individual database.

Q: Do I need to support different versions of DotNetNuke?

A: DotNetNuke is a mature product with many released versions. There were many major architectural changes going from version 1.x to 2.x to 3.x. DotNetNuke 4.x and 5.x use essentially the same provider model as DotNetNuke 3.x. At the time of this writing, the latest release was during the late release candidate (RC) cycles before the release of DotNetNuke 5.0. If you are developing on a later version, verify that there have not been any changes to the provider model for your version. If your module needs to be available on these various versions of DotNetNuke, you will need to manage your code base to accommodate all the required versions.

For purposes of this edition of the book, we will focus on ASP.NET 2.0 and above. Modules developed for DNN version 4.x will typically run on version 5.x unaltered because of their binary compatibility.

Q: What resources are needed for ongoing support of the module?

A: This may not be as much of an issue for modules purchased or developed by an outside party, because you may be able to obtain adequate support from the vendor. If you develop in-house, you'll need to set aside resources to provide ongoing support of the module. The type and amount of resources will depend on the environment within your organization.

Of course, this list is not all-inclusive, but these example questions should be enough to help you determine many of the relevant questions you need to ask regarding your own application.

Determine Your Module Scope

Fundamentally, there are two kinds of modules. For this discussion, we'll call them public and private. After thinking through the business requirements of building your module, the first technical decision you'll have to make is which category your module project falls into, because the answer will guide your platform and technology choices. Often, the developer has little control over the functional requirements of the module, but he or she must understand those requirements in order to define the technical needs of the module development environment.

Public modules are those you develop either to sell commercially, or those you plan to give away free within the DNN community. In the public module scenario, you'll focus on using technologies that work across the broadest possible range of target environments. For this type of module, you'll generally stick with the .NET Framework 2.0 environment, restrict your database choices to those features present in SQL Server 2000, and build your module against the DNN v4 code base. Modules developed within these bounds will usually run on any DNN 4 or 5 portal.

Private modules are generally developed by companies for internal use, or developed by a consultant under contract for a particular customer. In many cases, private modules will have a set of technical specifications that require use of new or advanced technologies. For example, you might be asked to use Language Integrated Query (LINQ) or perhaps new AJAX or jQuery features in .NET Framework 3.5 or Windows Workflow (WF) services functionality. You may need to use features specific to SQL Server 2005 or 2008. With private modules, it is likely you'll build your module against the specific version of DotNetNuke being used by your customer.

Next, you take a look at some of the decisions that you'll face in choosing the specific development environment you'll use to build your DotNetNuke custom module.

Development Environment Considerations

Now that you have decided on the type of module you will build, you need to prepare your development environment. First, you need to get an instance of DNN running; you need an operational DNN portal in which to develop your custom module. For custom module development, you'll want to use the DotNetNuke installation package that you can download from `http://www.dotnetnuke.com` (site registration is required). Depending on your circumstances, you may also need to configure separate DNN installations to test and stage deployment of your module. The portal setup process for each environment you need is the same as you saw in Chapter 2, "Installing DotNetNuke," after which you'll install or create your custom module source environment (details on this are in the next section of this chapter).

Using the DNN installation package as your module development platform versus using the DNN source package is important for a couple of reasons. First, you want your module to build and run quickly during the development process so you don't waste time with the Visual Studio overhead of handling more than thirty projects in the DNN source distribution solution. Second, you want to be sure you're always building your module against standard DNN functionality, especially if it's a public module. If you want to have a source code portal available for reference during your module development process, you should install, build, and run it in a separate portal instance from your DNN module development environment.

An important point needs to be made here: because you have the DNN sources doesn't mean that you should change them. Keep in mind that building a custom module is always preferable to modifying the DNN core code because you'll be forever on the hook for maintenance of any core changes you make. If you do have a business reason to change the DNN core code, be sure you have a full understanding of the ramifications of doing so. You will be responsible for synchronizing your custom core changes with the updated core code on any future versions you want to support, as well as handling any conflicts your custom core code may have with official core modifications through all future versions. Most importantly, whenever security vulnerabilities are fixed in the core, you will have to obtain and apply each patch and test in your own DNN version to avoid potential exploits.

Using Virtual Development Environments

A very powerful configuration strategy is to set up your development and test systems inside a virtual machine environment, such as Microsoft Virtual PC (VPC), with at least the test machine running a server operating system. Properly configured virtual machines (referred to here as VPCs) running on good hardware have little apparent overhead during the development and testing process. There are many benefits to using VPC, including being able to maintain specific environment and tool configurations for your development needs. We will not go into the specifics of using VPCs for your DNN module dev setup here, but DNN configuration inside VPC is exactly the same as on your physical development machine. Search the web, or check our blogs for development setup scenarios and discussions.

In many development environments, an extra step in the development process is introduced by placing a test (or staging) server between the development and production systems. The test server should mirror your production environment as closely as possible. Install your module to the test server and evaluate it carefully before installing the module on the production server. After the business units review the functionality and ensure it meets the requirements, publish the module to the production servers. This is another place where using VPC can help by allowing you to match closely your test and deployment environments. With VPC, you can create as many different environments as you need, and easily manage them. Whatever physical or virtual environments you choose, be sure to stay up-to-date (or match your deployment environment) with Windows, Visual Studio, and SQL Server service packs and patches in your development and test images. Doing so keeps your development environments safe from malware and potential exploits, and matching your deployment environment ensures you're testing against the same system configuration that your code will run in production.

Platform Choices

Ensure that your development environment is configured with Visual Studio 2008 (or 2005), Internet Information Server (IIS), and SQL Server 2005 Developer or Express Edition, or a different database system as your needs dictate (SQL Server 2008 also works well with DNN; it is not covered in this book because the bulk of the text was written before SQL 2008 was released). Specific choices in your development environment will likely be driven by your or your company's standards and needs, and perhaps by your customers' requirements. Note that you'll want to use IIS for development rather than the ASP.NET development web server (Cassini) because of IIS's superior stability. You want to focus your efforts on module development rather than troubleshooting platform issues, therefore IIS provides a much better module development experience overall.

An important platform choice you'll make is in the operating system (OS) to use on your development machine(s). If you choose Vista or a server OS (Server 2003 or 2008) as your development platform, you'll have the ability to create separate web sites for development of each module. If you choose Windows XP, you're limited to running every one of your module development projects in virtual directories under a single web site. Being able to create separate web sites for each of your modules provides you a high degree of isolation among them, and less chance that problems in one module will affect your other module development efforts. Using a server OS as your development platform has the advantage of mirroring your production environment. Windows Vista also works very well as a development platform, and is used as the OS for the development examples throughout this book.

Be aware that under Vista, you must run Visual Studio as an administrator in order to use IIS as your web server in local mode.

As mentioned earlier, module development using only Visual Studio 2008 is illustrated in this book. Nevertheless, solution files for both VS 2005 and VS 2008 are included in the example module code shown in the next three chapters. The source code is identical whether you're using VS 2008 or 2005, although the project files will prompt you to upgrade the first time you open the VS 2008 solution.

One of the biggest technical differentiators between .NET Framework 3.5 and earlier versions is in your ability to use LINQ in your modules. Fundamentally, you can use LINQ in two ways within your custom module development process. First is in the business logic within your module, because LINQ can provide clearer code and a quicker and more satisfying developer experience once you're used to using the LINQ syntax in your development efforts. The second use of LINQ is to replace the traditional DNN Data Access Layer (DAL) with LINQ to SQL. This is a fairly straightforward process, and is the subject of a number of tutorials and walk-throughs you can find with a web search. (Check DNN Core Team member Michael Washington's `adefwebserver.com` site in particular.) LINQ directly supports only SQL Server, so you won't be able to create providers for other database platforms if you choose to use LINQ in your DAL.

If you decide to use LINQ in your module, keep in mind that the fundamental module DAL structure has not essentially changed between DNN v3 and v5. Because of the stable architecture and a concerted effort by the Core Team not to introduce breaking changes in the core, modules in DNN have enjoyed significant portability across DNN versions. Even the migration up from a v2 module that properly uses the DAL structure is straightforward. LINQ will break this portability (because it only runs on .NET Framework 3.5), so this is an important point to consider until LINQ becomes integrated into the core DAL architecture. In either scenario, using LINQ (or other advanced .NET Framework technologies) is best done in the private module scenario, because you're no longer building for the widest reach when using Framework 3.5 features.

Besides using LINQ for your DAL code, there are other choices in Object-Relational Mapping (ORM) tools you can use to generate your data layer, such as Subsonic, NetTiers, MyGeneration, nHibernate, and others. There are many free ORM tools, and you can easily find them with a web search. Use of any tool that generates DAL code that is different from the DotNetNuke standard is best done in the private module scenario, and not where you're trying to gain the widest reach with your module.

Web Project Types

Another major consideration and technical decision point in your development process is in the type of web project you'll create within your Visual Studio development environment. There are two major styles of web development, the Web Application Project (WAP, also known as the compiled module approach) and the Web Site Project (WSP, also known as the dynamic module approach). Either may be used for custom module development, and many developers have strong personal opinions about which approach is better. This is a hotly debated topic in the DNN forums, and arguments both ways are published on many blogs. Note that if you use Visual Studio Express, you'll have to use the WSP development approach because WAP is not supported by the Express editions.

If your Visual Studio edition doesn't make the decision for you, your choice between the WAP and WSP approaches will most likely come down to the type of module you're building. In general, commercial modules are best served by the WAP model because of the ability to protect your source code through compilation, assembly distribution, and by the use of code obfuscation tools. The WSP model is often favored in private module situations because the module can be developed simply by changing your source and refreshing the page, and therefore iterated more quickly. Public modules where you distribute the source code can go either way. It may come down to your own preferences, in which case you should try both models and evaluate the tradeoffs for yourself.

Other Environment Considerations

Another consideration is the publishing process from your development environment to your production environment. Private modules are often deployed simply by copying the development assemblies, user controls, associated pages, and resource files to the production server. With public modules, you almost always create an installation package and install through the Host ➪ Module Definitions page (or the new Host ➪ Extensions page). Either way, before you compile your module for production, ensure that the build configuration in Visual Studio 2008 is set to Release, and not Debug mode.

Note that if you picked the Visual Basic Development settings when you installed Visual Studio 2008, you won't see the Configuration Manager or the build mode settings. In this case you'll need to change the configuration back to General Development Settings if you want these options to be available by using the Tools ➪ Import and Export Settings option, and choosing the Reset All Settings option. The idea behind hiding Configuration Manager in VB is that if you press F5 you'll run in Debug mode, and pressing Ctrl+F5 will run without debugging. The problem is that this doesn't work consistently, and you can be blocked from debugging your code. Also, you're never quite sure which mode (Debug or Release) is being used when you rebuild your solution.

Finally, you may want to consider installing Team Foundation Server, Visual SourceSafe, or some other source control system to ensure integrity of your project source code. Installing, configuring, and managing a source control package is beyond the scope of this book, but it is recommended that you use some sort of source control to protect your development efforts.

Starting Development

With your development decisions made, it's time to begin developing your module. This section starts by briefly discussing some of the module development approaches you might use. Next, we provide an overview of the sample module shown in this chapter and detailed in the next three. Then we show you how to install and configure the module for use. Finally, we talk about how to build your own DNN modules.

Module Development Options

As a beginning module developer, an easy way to start your development process is by reusing one of the DNN standard modules. Source code for the standard modules has been separated from the core

DNN sources, making it easy to install, inspect, and run the source code for each individual module. There is much to learn from examining the code from the experienced standard module development teams, even if you don't reuse one of the modules itself.

Alternatives to starting from an existing module are to use an empty (or template) module, or to create your module from scratch. A number of tutorials and blog posts are available on using the template approach that you can search for. Once you get some experience developing modules, you'll generally create your own empty template module and reuse it to start most of your own custom module development work.

The DotNetNuke Starter Kit is available as a separate download, and although it contains VB and C# project templates for both the compiled WAP and dynamic WSP project types, it can be a difficult starting point because it leaves you with a lot of configuration work before you can even begin your code development process. Using the SK to create a module from scratch is covered later in this chapter. The project template you create in that section is useful as a starting point for your future module work.

WROX.Suggestion Module Overview

Before diving into module development specifics, let's first take a look at how a module works by reviewing the WROX.Suggestion module. (You can download this module from the book web site.) This way, you'll have a basic understanding of its functionality when you see specific implementation pointers during code development. The WROX.Suggestion module is designed especially to illustrate a number of common module development scenarios and techniques, and it is purposely basic in function for ease of illustration. WROX.Suggestion is developed as a public module, therefore it uses features available in the .NET Framework 2.0, its database features are common to SQL Server 2000, and the module is built against DotNetNuke v4 for distribution. This chapter and the next three chapters provide an in-depth study of this module.

The WROX.Suggestion view module displays user instructions, and allows a user to input suggestion items. Those suggestion items are displayed in a second view module named DisplaySuggestions. Users in a view role for DisplaySuggestions see suggestions entered on the current page, and portal Admins see suggestions for all pages on the site. See Figure 12-1.

When you add the WROX.Suggestion module to a page, you'll normally set the Edit Module role on the module to Registered Users. This allows all users to see the module, but only those users who are logged in will be authorized to add suggestions (see Figure 12-2). You can allow anonymous users to add suggestions by setting the Edit Module role on the module to All Users. More information on setting roles is available in the "Security Roles" section of Chapter 4, "Portal Administration."

When you add the Suggestion module to a page, both the Suggestion and DisplaySuggestions user controls appear together on the page. You'll normally set the View Module role to allow specific users or security roles (groups of users) to see the entered suggestions. Create a security role for that purpose if necessary. This allows only users in that role to see suggestions on the page. Portal Admins can see all DisplaySuggestions modules on the site, and can see the suggestions entered from all Suggestion modules on the portal.

Selecting Settings from the module edit menu lets you add suggestion types. Suggestion types are unique to each Suggestion module. Users can select the desired type (or category) from a drop-down list when they're entering suggestions. On module settings, you can also change the Instructions and Thank You text by unique module instance (see Figure 12-3).

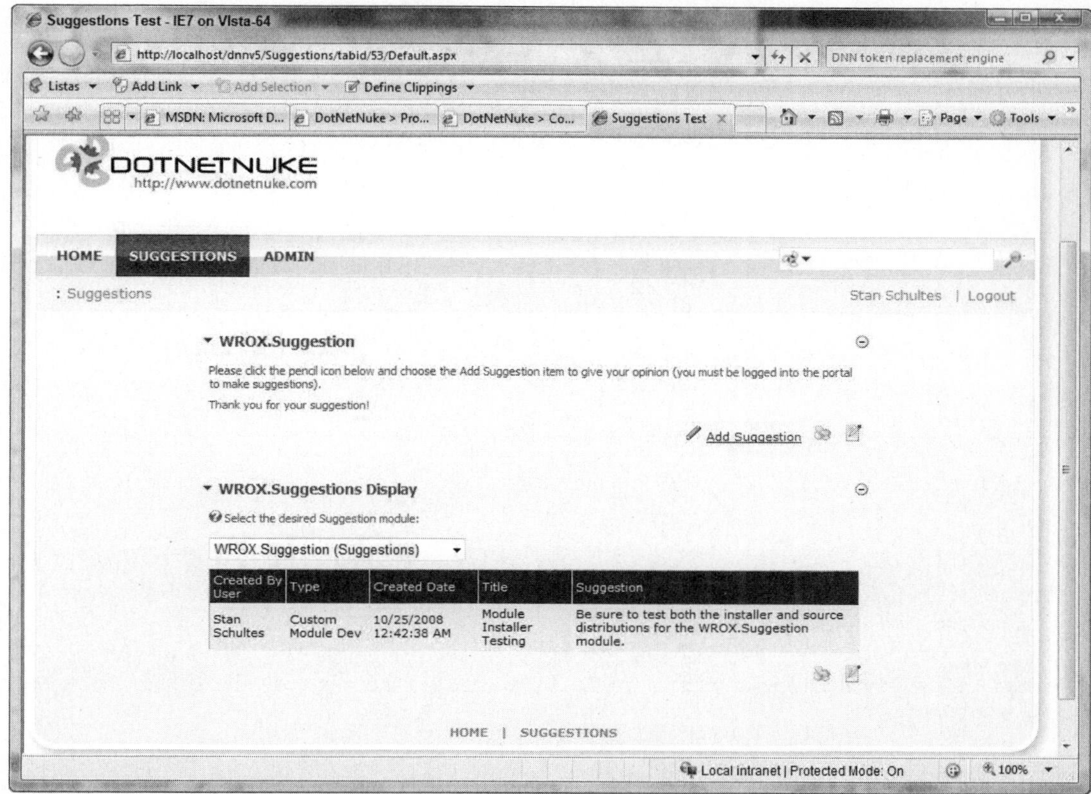

Figure 12-1

Configuring for Module Development

The first order of business is to understand how a module development project is set up, and how the module interacts with a DotNetNuke portal. In this section you walk through this process by using the WROX.Suggestion sample module. To begin, you need to have an operational DNN portal set up. As mentioned earlier, you should use the DNN Install package for this portal, and the portal setup process is the same as you saw in Chapter 2.

Module Setup

Once you have your development portal set up and running, download the WROX.Suggestion module from the book web site. Two packages are available for download — a module installer that you use when you want to install and run the WROX.Suggestion module on a new portal instance, and a source installer that can get you quickly up and running with the module source code. The source package is what you want here.

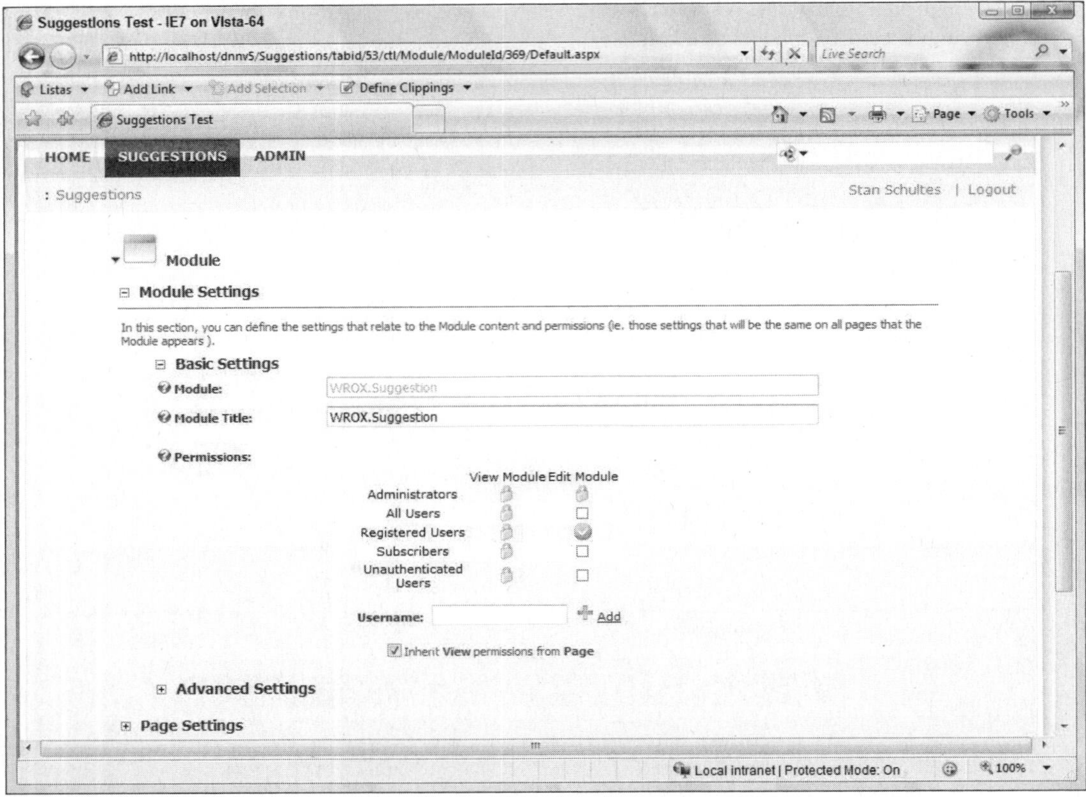

Figure 12-2

The WROX.Suggestion module is a WAP-style (compiled) module. Once you download the source package, open the zip file and examine its contents. Inside you'll find the following sets of files:

- **User Controls — Suggestion.ascx, DisplaySuggestions.ascx, EditSuggestion.ascx, and Settings.ascx**. These are the user interface elements that are dynamically injected onto the page depending on what part of the module you're looking at. The first two are known as View controls, the third is an Edit control, and the fourth is, not surprisingly, the module Settings control.
- **.NET Assemblies — WROX.Modules.Suggestion.dll, and WROX.Modules.Suggestion.SqlDataProvider.dll**. These are the compiled module assemblies that go in the portal's \bin directory. The SqlDataProvider file is specific to the SQL Server database, so if you support other database backends, you may distribute other types of data providers with your module.
- **Database Scripts — 02.00.00.SqlDataProvider and Uninstall.SqlDataProvider**. The first script creates your SQL Server database objects at module installation (tables and stored procedures), foreign key relationships, and indexes. The second script removes all objects from the database when the module is uninstalled from a portal instance.
- **Resources Zip File — WROX.Suggestion.zip**. This file contains the module source and project files in the same directory structure that should exist once the sources are properly installed in a portal instance.

- **Installation Manifest — WROX.Suggestion.dnn**. This XML file instructs the DNN module installer how to install and configure the Suggestion module for use within a portal.

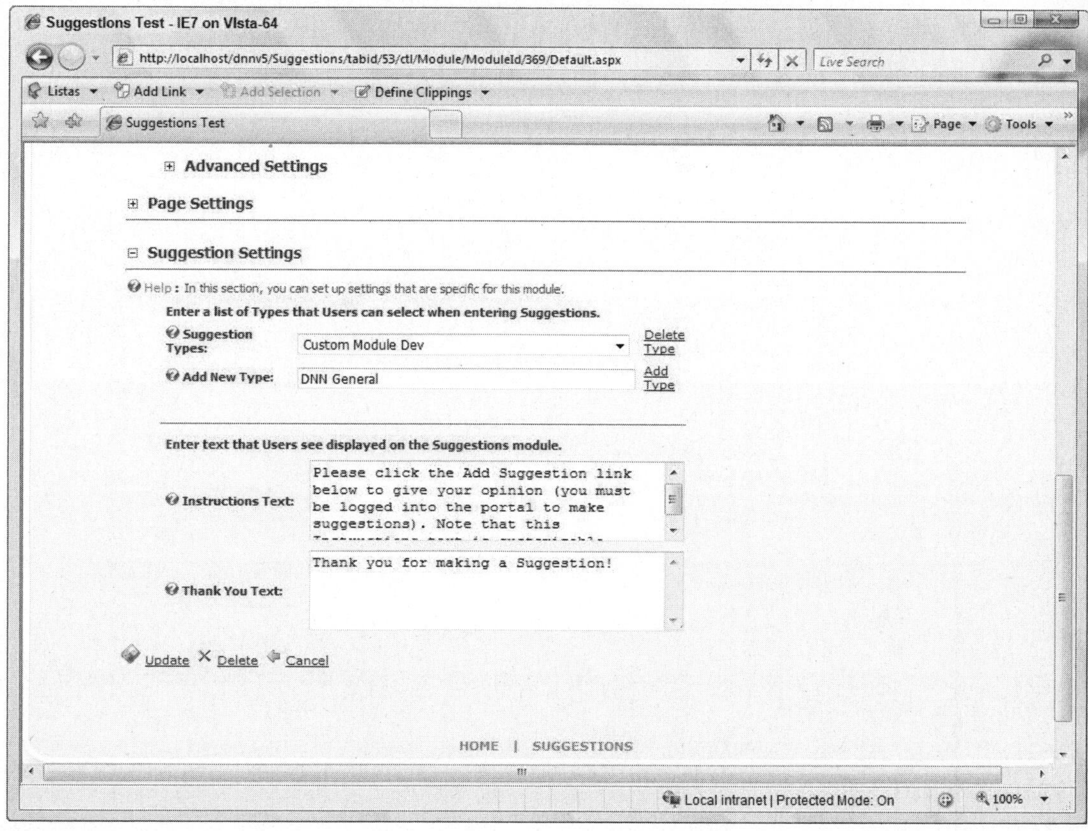

Figure 12-3

With the source installer in hand, you could simply log in to your portal with the Host account and go to the Host ➪ Module Definitions page (or use the new Host ➪ Extensions page), use the Install Module action or Install Extension Wizard, browse to your module source zip file, and DNN will walk you through a wizard and install the module, making it ready for use. Because the point of this chapter and the next three are to get an in-depth look at the module development process, let's perform the installation steps manually to see what's involved in making your module ready for development work within a DotNetNuke Portal.

Modules you develop are self-contained within the portal \DesktopModules folder. Navigate there now, and create a new directory named WROX.Suggestion. Unzip the contents of the source installer, WROX.Suggestion_Source.zip, into this directory. Move the two .dll files into the portal's \bin directory. Unzip the enclosed WROX.Suggestion.zip resource file into the current directory with the "use zip directory structure" option. The result of the two unzip actions should be a fully populated directory structure that looks like Figure 12-4.

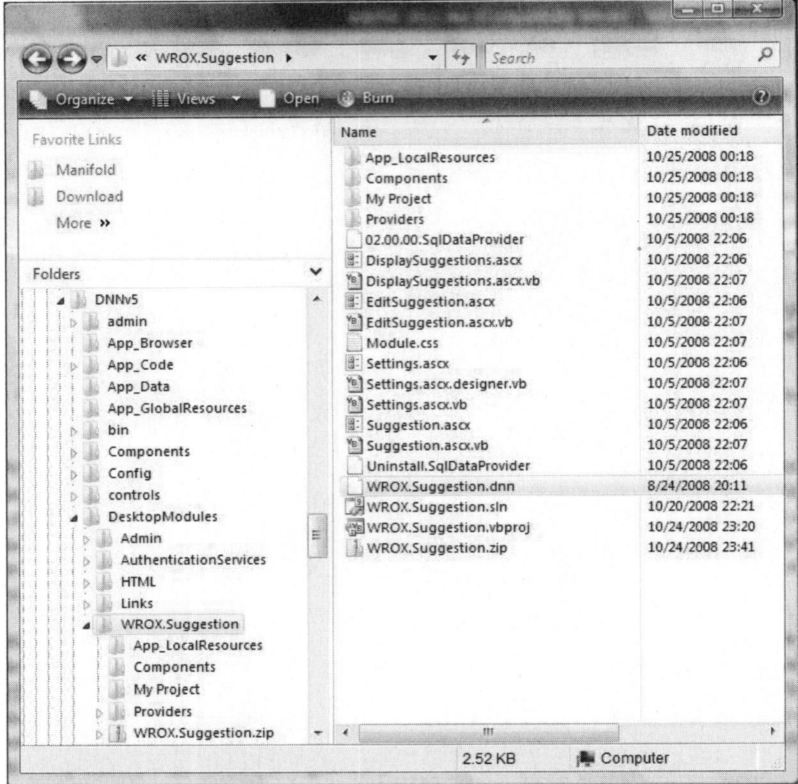

Figure 12-4

Database Setup

The directory structure is now set up correctly to run the module; next you'll set up the database and register the module within the DNN portal. Open the 02.00.00.SqlDataProvider file in the WROX.Suggestion directory in a text editor and take a quick look through the file. You'll see that it first deletes the database objects, and then adds them back into the database. A short piece of the script looks like the following:

```
CREATE PROCEDURE {databaseOwner}{objectQualifier}WROX_DeleteSuggestion
@SuggestionID INT
AS
    DELETE
    FROM    {databaseOwner}{objectQualifier}WROX_Suggestion
    WHERE   SuggestionID = @SuggestionID
GO
```

You can see that it contains special tags `{databaseOwner}` and `{objectQualifier}` in front of each database object. You can execute this script within Visual Studio or SQL Server Management Studio, but you must search and replace these tags with the appropriate setting strings, as discussed in Chapter 2 and Chapter 7, "DotNetNuke Architecture." An easier way is to execute the script directly in the portal where the DNN installer substitutes the tag values for their settings as defined in your web.config file.

Log in to your development portal with the Host account, and go to the Host ➪ SQL page. Use either the Browse button to find your 02.00.00.SqlDataProvider file and click the Load link, or open it with a text editor and copy/paste the contents into the SQL window. Next, check the Run as Script option, and click the Execute link. You should see a message saying, ''The Query completed successfully!'' (See Figure 12-5). That takes care of the database setup for the WROX.Suggestion module.

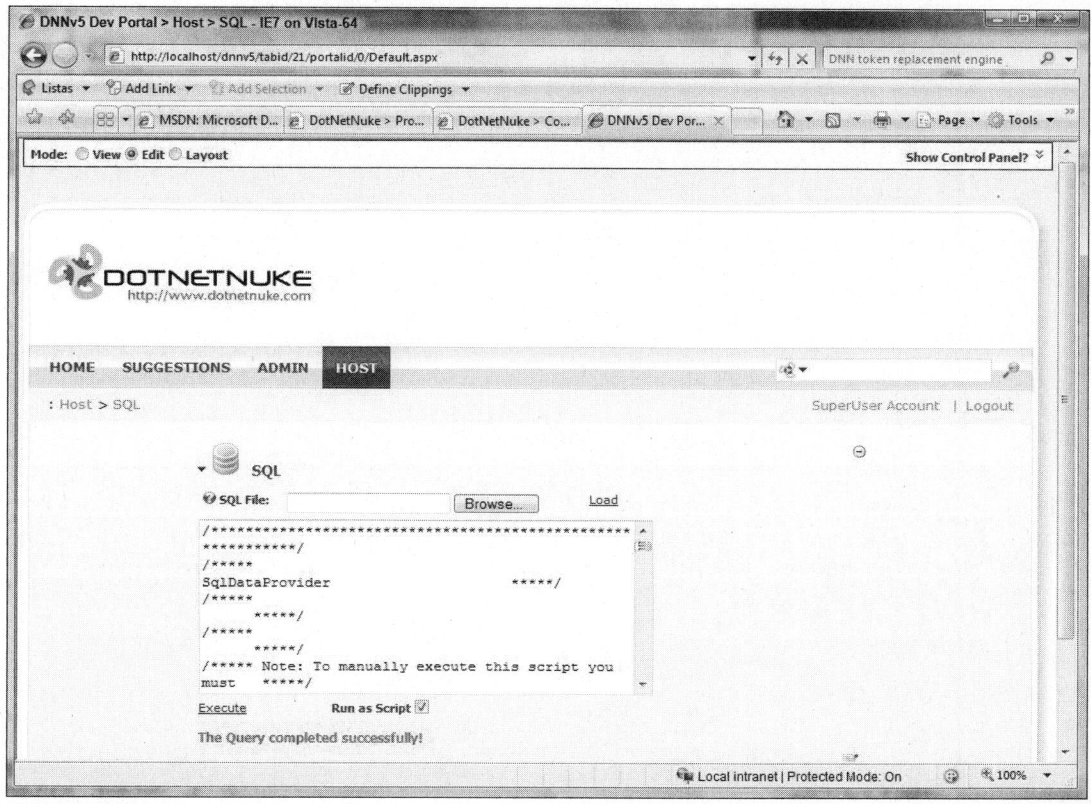

Figure 12-5

Module Registration

The last setup step before you look at the module source code is to register the module within the portal. Open the module manifest XML file named WROX.Suggestion.dnn with a text editor. Looking through the file you'll see at the top a set of nested elements, `dotnetnuke/folders/folder`, which contains a list of attributes: `<name>`, `<friendlyname>`, `<foldername>`. These are the module attributes that will be registered. Below this you find `modules/module`, and below that a list of `<control>` elements. These define the user controls registered for view, edit, and settings. So you can see this information in fact defines the structure of the module as needed for module registration within the DotNetNuke portal. You can either enter this information manually, as you will do when you create a new module, or you can import it from the manifest file for an existing module.

From the Host account, go to the Host ➪ Module Definitions page, which lists each module type currently registered in the portal. At the bottom of the page you'll find the Create New Module link for manually registering the module, which you'll use when you create a new module from scratch. Because you have the manifest file for this module, click the Import Module Definition link, open the Manifest drop-down list, and you should see the WROX.Suggestion.dnn file listed here. This bit of magic is performed by DNN simply scanning all directories below \DesktopModules and looking for .dnn files in the module directories. Choose the WROX.Suggestion.dnn file from the Manifest drop-down list and click the Import Manifest link. This will register the module and make it available for placement on a portal page. See Figure 12-6.

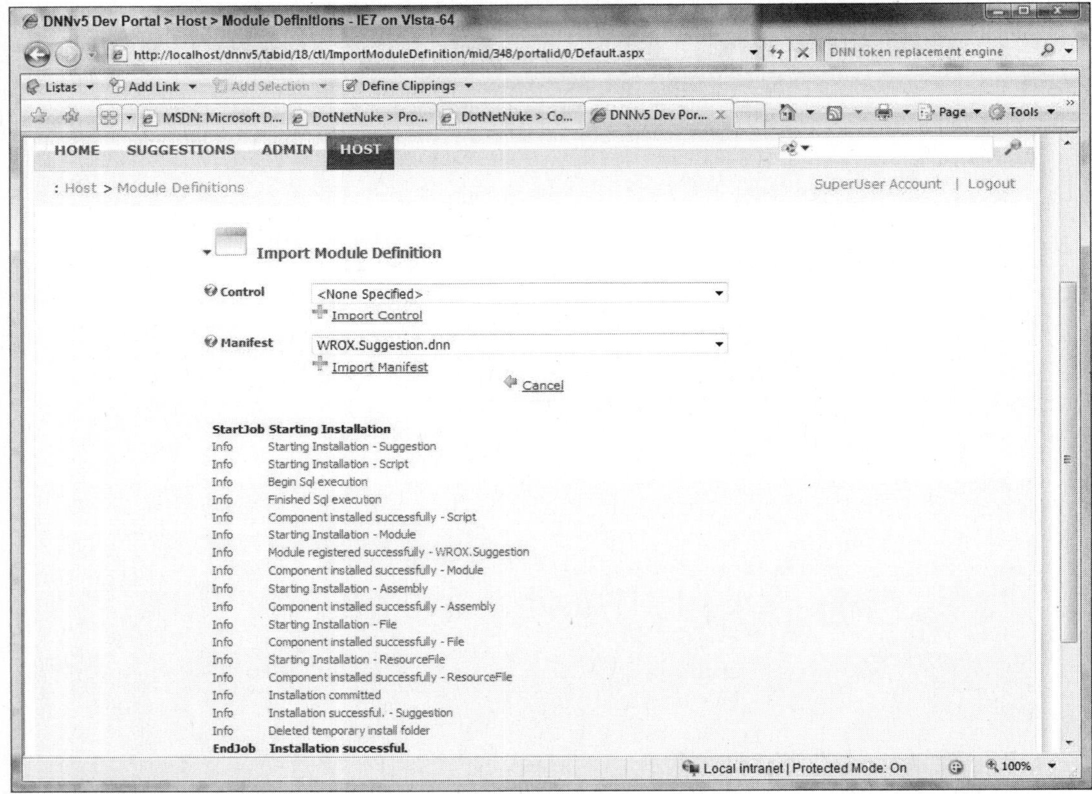

Figure 12-6

Once the module import is done, go back to the Host ➪ Module Definition page and click the edit link (pencil icon) in front of the WROX.Suggestion module. Explore the definitions created by the import to see how you might have done this manually. Note that there are two Module Definitions for the sample Suggestion module: WROX.Suggestion and WROX.SuggestionDisplay (these are the friendly, or display, names of the definitions). Each Module Definition contains a list of Module Controls that are associated with it (see Figure 12-7). Below the module controls is the Package Settings section, new to DNN 5, where you'll find a list of fields (License, Release Notes, and so on) that go into creating the DNN 5 package installation file, which you see in detail in Chapter 17, ''Distribution.''

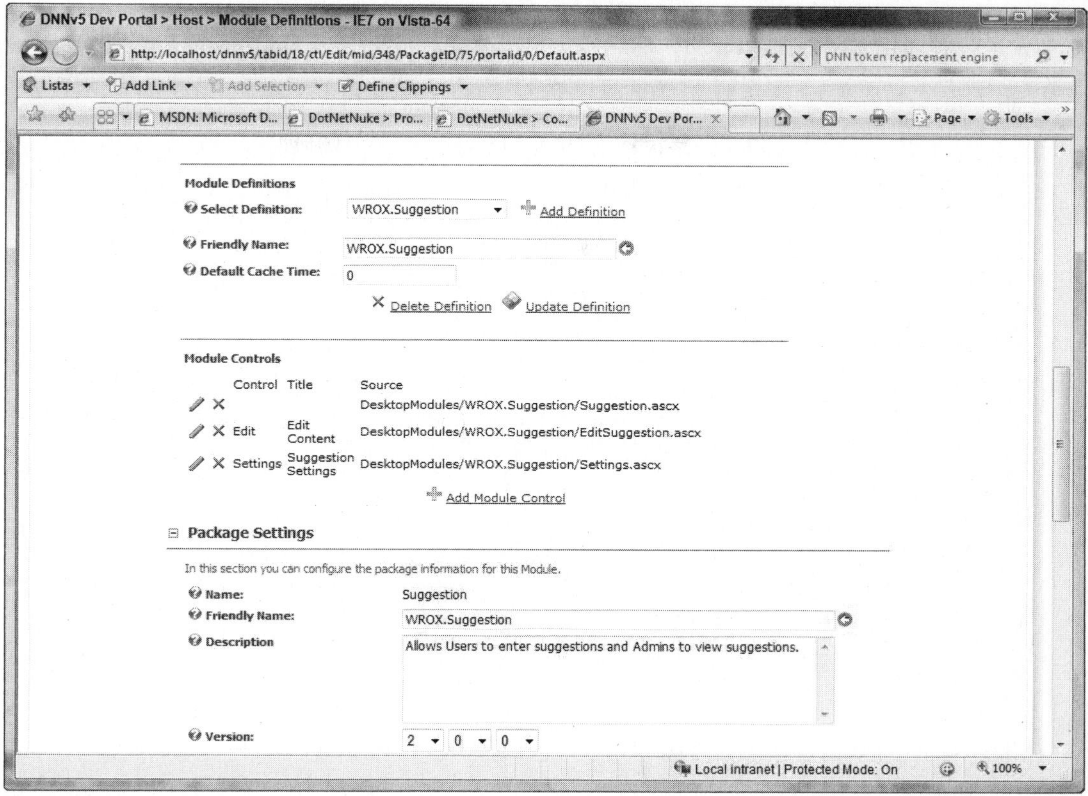

Figure 12-7

This completes the database setup and module registration process that is executed for you by the DNN installer when you install a module using its installer file. Now you should be able to add a WROX.Suggestion module to a page within your portal and try it out for yourself using the description provided in the prior section of this chapter. Remember, when you add the WROX.Suggestion module to a page, you get a view control for both the Suggestion and DisplaySuggestions module, one for each module definition. You can delete the DisplaySuggestions module anywhere you don't need it; for example, when you want to centralize display of all suggestions in your portal on an admin page.

Once you've verified that the module is properly installed and is working, you'll prepare and open the module sources in Visual Studio 2008, and run the module in debug mode.

Module Configuration in Visual Studio 2008

You have a variety of ways of setting up your development environment, each with their own advantages and tradeoffs, and many of these are covered by community blog and forum posts. The process you'll follow here is straightforward and reliable once you get it set up correctly. The following set of instructions may seem daunting to the beginning module developer, but the process is not difficult once you've been through it. You have a number of tasks to perform in preparing your module project to run in Visual Studio 2008, and following them carefully is important, otherwise you won't be able to run your project in design mode and debug the source code.

Before you can open the module solution in Visual Studio, you need to set the web site name references in the project files to match your current configuration. Within your module source directory, open the project file named WROX.Suggestion.vbproj in a text editor. Scroll nearly to the bottom of the file to the section named `<ProjectExtensions>`, and change the URL paths in two elements — `<IISUrl>` and `<IISAppRootUrl>` — to match the web site address of the development portal on your development machine. For example, if your development portal address is `http://dnnv5/`, replace the string "dotnetnuke" with "dnnv5" in both places and save the file. If you're using a virtual directory, replace "dotnetnuke" with "localhost/dnnv5" and save.

Run Visual Studio 2008 (don't forget to run as Administrator on Vista) and open the WROX .Suggestion_VS2008.sln solution file using the File ➪ Open ➪ Project/Solution menu item. Because the source code was built under DNN 4 for widest portability, you'll be prompted to upgrade the project files. The solution will open with two projects: WROX.Suggestion and WROX.Suggestion.SqlDataProvider. The sources for the latter project are found under your project directory in the \Providers\DataProviders\SqlDataProvider folder.

In the WROX.Suggestion project, double-click the My Project folder to bring up the project Properties pages. On the Application tab, make sure the root namespace is blank. On the Compile tab, set the Build Output Path to ..\..\bin\ — this will send the project's build output (the .dll) to the portal's \bin directory (which is two steps up the directory structure from the current location). Finally, on the Web tab, make sure the Use Local IIS Web Server option is selected. Set the Project Url to your project directory, for example, `http://dnnv5/DesktopModules/WROX.Suggestion`. Make sure the Override Application Root Url option check box is checked, and enter the address of your development portal here, for example, `http://dnnv5`. See Figure 12-8 for the Web tab on the project property page.

Similarly, in the WROX.Suggestion.SqlDataProvider project, double-click the My Project folder to bring up its project Properties pages. On the Application tab, again make sure the root namespace is blank. On the Compile tab, set the Build Output Path to ..\..\..\..\..\bin\. This again sends the project's build output to the portal's \bin directory (which is now five steps up the directory structure from the current location).

Next, check the References node in the WROX.Suggestion project (you may have to click the Show All Files icon in Solution Explorer). Click the DotNetNuke item and ensure that the Path in the Properties pane points to the portal's \bin folder. If necessary, remove the reference and re-add it, selecting DotNetNuke.dll in the portal's \bin folder. Under the References node in the WROX.Suggestion.SqlDataProvider project, check both the DotNetNuke reference and the reference to WROX. Suggestion.dll, which should also be found in the portal's \bin folder. Remove and re-add either reference if there is a yellow triangle showing in front of the reference, or the Path property is pointing to the wrong directory.

Set your project to Debug mode (use Build ➪ Configuration Manager to do this; see Figure 12-9), and rebuild your module solution. If all goes well, you won't have any errors at this point, but fix any that do occur and rebuild until the solution builds successfully. You may need to rebuild just the WROX.Suggestion project by itself and reset the references in the WROX.Suggestion.SqlDataProvider project before both will build successfully together. Check that your project's two .dlls in the portal \bin folder are replaced when you rebuild the solution.

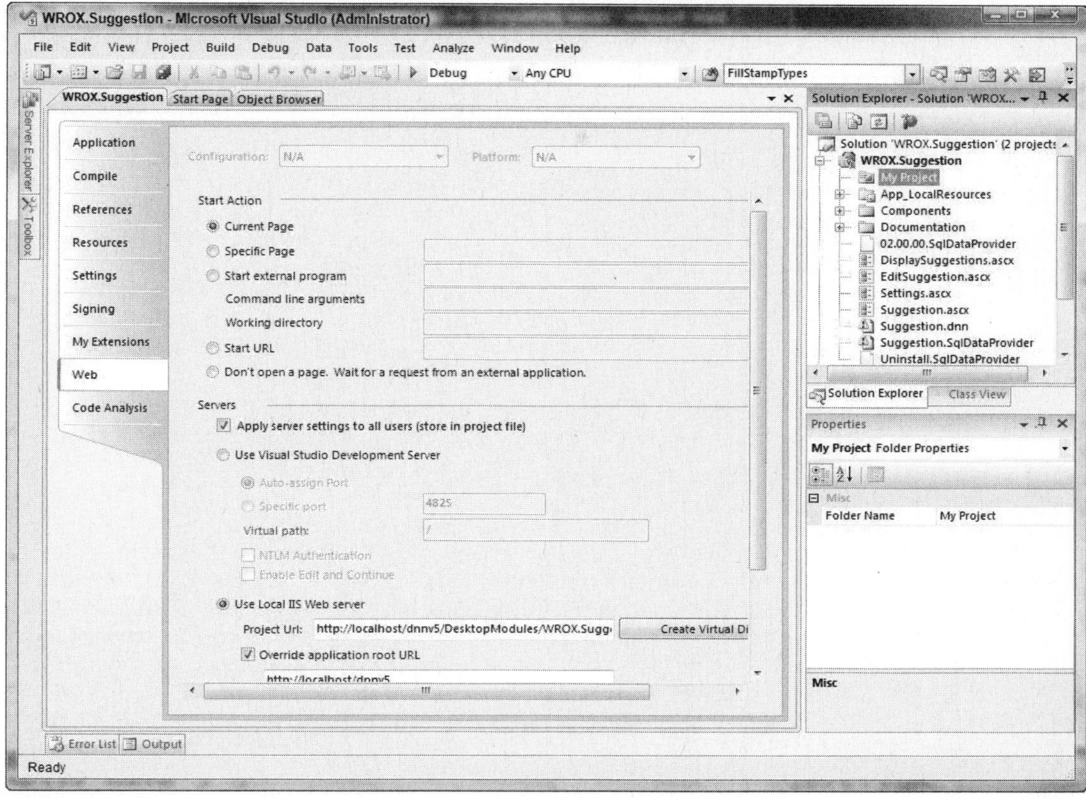

Figure 12-8

Now you're just about ready to run the project in design mode. Edit the web.config file in the portal root directory, and ensure the site debug mode is enabled as `compilation debug="true"` in the `<system.web>` section (and remember to set this value to "false" when you deploy your portal). Open the Suggestion.ascx.vb source file, and set a breakpoint on the first executable line of code in the `Page_Load` event (with the `IsPostBack` check), which is in the `Event Handlers` code region.

```
If Not Page.IsPostBack Then
```

At this point, you should already have a Suggestion module on a page, so open your development portal to the Home page in your web browser. In Visual Studio, go to the Tools ➪ Attach to Process menu item (in VS 2005, it is the Debug ➪ Attach to Process menu item). In the Available Process list, scroll down to the IIS worker process, w3wp.exe, (aspnet_wp.exe in Windows XP) item and click it, then click the Attach button. This is easiest if you only have one browser instance open to your development portal, and no other active web sites running on your machine. If the w3wp.exe (or aspnet_wp.exe) process isn't listed, it may have timed out. Simply refresh your page to reset the process, and attach to it. Now browse to the page in your site that contains an instance of the Suggestion module (or refresh the page if you're already there), and Visual Studio will stop at the breakpoint you set. When you're finished with debug, click the Stop button in Visual Studio to exit debug mode.

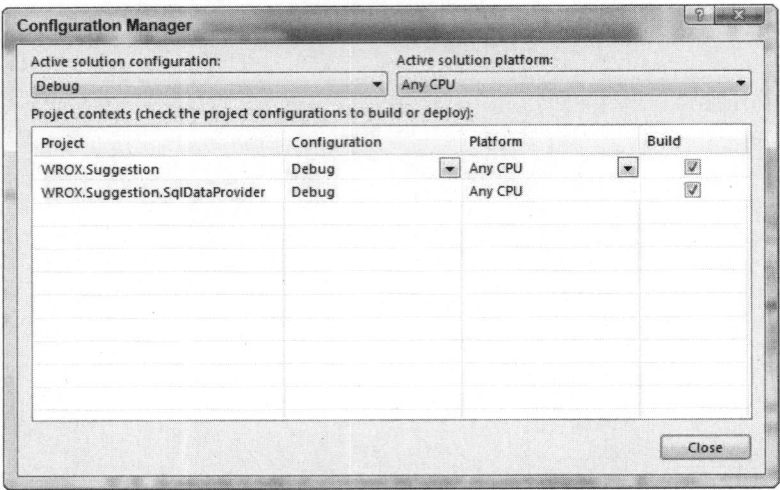

Figure 12-9

This setup process may seem quite lengthy, but once you have the environment set up for a particular project, you won't have to mess around with it. Completing the preceding configuration steps for a new module, or for another module's source project, becomes second nature once you've done it a few times and understand the kinds of things that can go wrong and how to fix them quickly and easily.

Developing with the Starter Kit

Creating a DotNetNuke module completely from scratch is not really difficult, but the process is tedious. You would create your solution, directory structure, two projects, database, user controls, and business logic, similar to what you saw in the WROX.Suggestion module example in the previous section. Wouldn't it be nice if you could start from a Visual Studio template, as the basic structure of the project is created for you, allowing you to focus on creating your module logic rather than worrying about creating the correct code structure?

Several DNN community members have created Visual Studio templates in the past, but as of this writing, those still available on the web are for Visual Studio 2003 or 2005, and therefore out of date. This is where the DotNetNuke Starter Kit (SK) comes in; the Core Team created the SK to do the basic setup and housekeeping tasks around creating a new module. This makes it much easier than starting from scratch, however, there are still a number of manual "fix-ups" you'll need to make to your solution files. Let's walk through this process in detail to see how it works.

Download the DNN 5 SK from the DotNetNuke web site downloads page (registration required); it's available as an .msi (Microsoft Installer) file. Installing it adds a pair of Visual Basic project templates that you can use to create your module project. As of this writing, the Starter Kit still generates a Visual Studio 2005 project, but it's still usable in Visual Studio 2008.

Creating the Project

Start by running Visual Studio (as Administrator in Vista), and choosing File ➪ New Project, and pick the Visual Basic ➪ Web project type (or, you can use the C# ➪ Web project type if you prefer). Choose the

DotNetNuke Compiled Module template under the My Templates section, and pick the .NET Framework version you'd like to target in the upper-right corner of the New Project dialog, as shown in Figure 12-10. Enter your project name as FirstModule, and browse to the DesktopModules folder within your DNN development portal instance. Make sure the "Create directory for solution" check box is unchecked, and click OK.

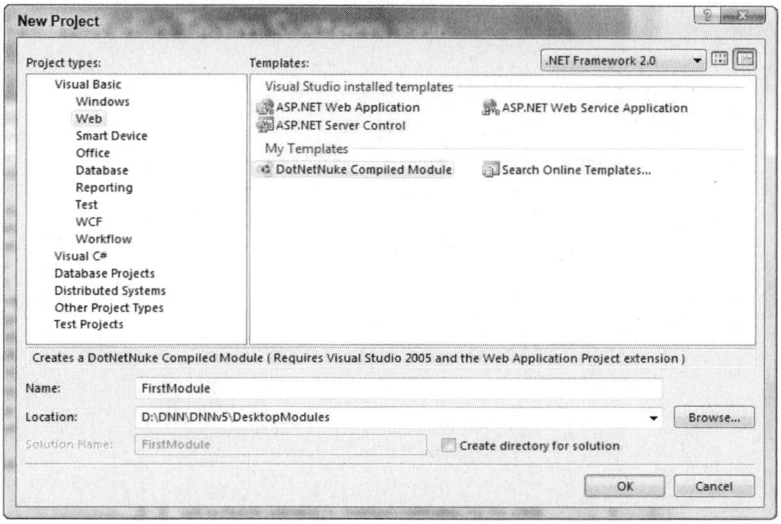

Figure 12-10

Your choice of .NET Framework version here is very important, because it defines the environment within which you can run your module. Choosing 2.0 gives you the broadest reach, but you can't use the many newer .NET technologies such as LINQ. Choosing 3.0 or 3.5 gives you access to considerably more power with the Framework, but at the cost of limiting your module to running only on those platform versions or later. This is the public versus private modules conversation all over again.

If you're developing on Vista with IIS7, you may be faced with a message box asking whether you'd like to configure a virtual directory named localhost/DotNetNuke_2 with your project path (see Figure 12-11). This is an artifact of the project template, so click Yes to continue, and the project is created by Visual Studio.

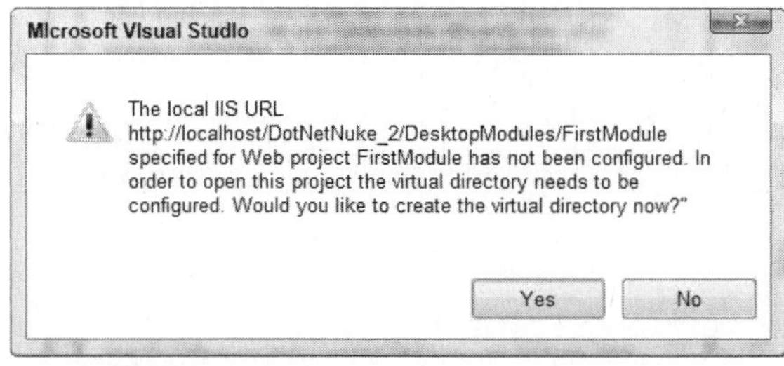

Figure 12-11

When the template is finished executing, a documentation page is displayed with some instructions that you should follow (see Figure 12-12).

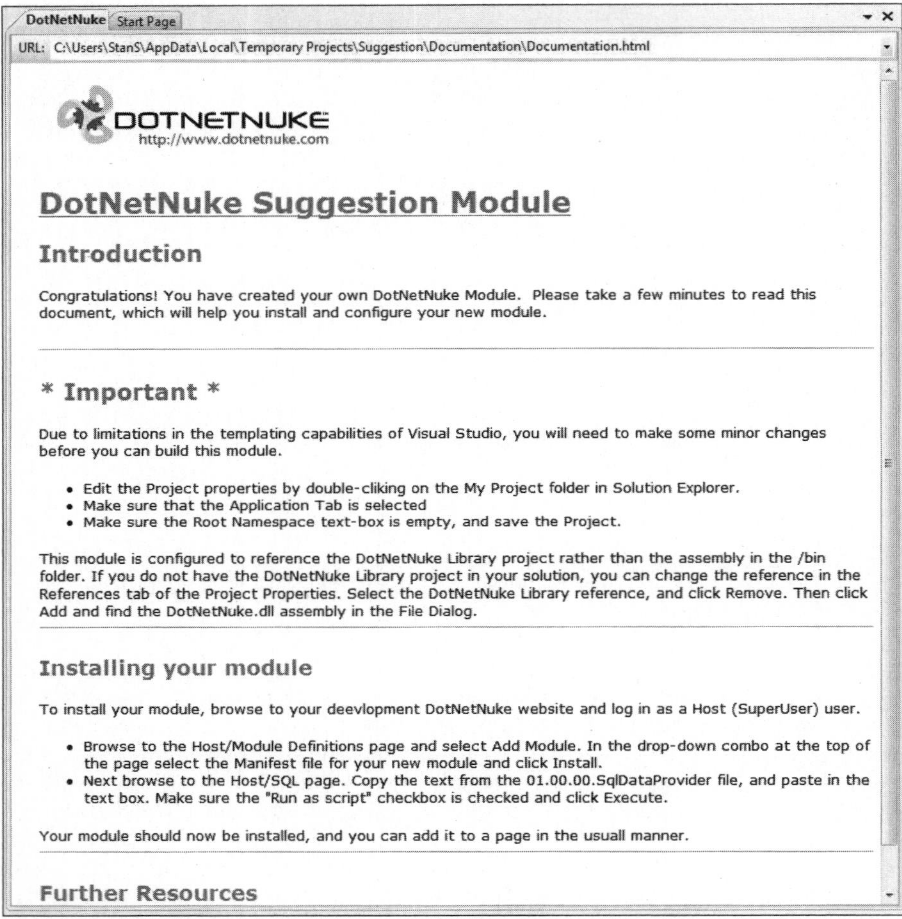

Figure 12-12

Add Your Company Name

When you create a custom module for public distribution, the convention is to name your module with your company name or acronym as a prefix, as in the WROX.Suggestion example. This avoids naming collisions with other modules that might be publicly available for portal users. As you follow along in the following instructions, replace WROX with your company name.

You created your module without your company name so the database objects are named properly, because a placeholder company name is included in the scripts, as you'll see in a moment. In Solution Explorer, right-click the FirstModule solution, click Rename, and add your company name to the solution, as in WROX.FirstModule (or you can rename your solution file outside Visual Studio). Right-click the

FirstModule project, choose Rename, and add your company name as a prefix to the project name. Also rename the manifest file as WROX.FirstModule.dnn (you may have to click the Show All Files icon in Solution Explorer to see this file). Save all changes and close the solution in Visual Studio so you can do some manual file updating.

Navigate to your project folder under your portal DesktopModules directory, and rename it with your company name (for example, WROX.FirstModule). In your project directory, create a new folder named Providers, and inside that folder create a new folder named Data Providers. This is where your data provider project will go. Next, open both the 01.00.00.SqlDataProvider and Uninstall.SqlDataProvider files, and search/replace all instances of the placeholder string YourCompany with your own company name or acronym.

Open the WROX.FirstModule.dnn manifest file and perform the same search/replace on YourCompany. Also change the instances of FirstModule found in the file to WROX.FirstModule, except in the `<businesscontrollerclass>` element, and the filenames (otherwise you will get some unwanted text replacements). Rename the FirstModule.dll file reference, and below it add another file reference to the WROX.FirstModule.SqlDataProvider.dll (you create the project for this dll shortly).

Now, open the .vbproj file in a text editor and modify the `<IISUrl>` element to point at your development portal URL (for example, `http://localhost/dnnv5/DesktopModules/WROX.FirstModule`). Finally, change the `<IISAppRootUrl>` element to reflect your development portal root URL, such as `http://localhost/dnnv5`.

Set Project Properties

Open the solution from the new folder location in Visual Studio, and now no project load errors should occur. If you have any problems, first try going back through the steps listed to make sure you haven't missed anything. If you still have trouble, search and use the DNN Forums (`http://forums.dotnetnuke.com`) for help in solving any problems you have before continuing. When good to go, reopen the documentation\Documentation.html file in Design mode, and follow the bulleted instructions in the "Important" section of the document. It will tell you to open the project properties and make sure the Root Namespace field is empty on the Application tab. Before you continue, set the Assembly Name to include your company name (for example, WROX.FirstModule) so it generates your .dll with the right name.

On the Compile tab, make sure the Build output path is set to ..\..\bin\ so the compiled .dll is directed into the portal's \bin directory at build time. On the Web tab, make sure the "Use local IIS Web server" option is selected, and fill in the Project URL with the path of your development portal and project directory (for example, `http://dnnv5/desktopmodules/WROX.FirstModule`). Although you edited the .vbproj file previously, also be sure the "Override application root URL" check box is checked, and enter the URL of your development portal (for example, `http://dnnv5`), similar to what you saw in Figure 12-6. In the References node in Solution Explorer, remove DotNetNuke.Library, and add a reference to DotNetNuke.dll in the portal's \bin folder. Be sure to set the CopyLocal property for this reference to False.

The next section of the Documentation.html file, named "Installing your module," covers database setup and registering the module. The template creation process generates starter SqlDataProvider and installation manifest files, and the setup process for these is similar to the process followed earlier for the WROX.Suggestion module. Note that these are the bare minimum data and manifest definitions. You need to fill in the details of these files according to the specific needs of your custom module. The last bit of instructions on the Documentation.html file says you can add your module to the page, but you first need to create the SqlDataProvider project in your module solution.

Data Provider Project

Because there are many potential database choices, the SK doesn't create a separate project for your SqlDataProvider assembly, so you have to do this step manually. Start by building the existing solution, and verify that the WROX.FirstModule.dll goes into the portal's \bin directory. Right-click the solution and choose Add ➪ New Project (or use the File ➪ Add New Project menu). In the Add New Project dialog, choose the Visual Basic ➪ Windows project type and select the Class Library template. Set the project name to SqlDataProvider, and the project path to \DesktopModules\WROX.FirstModule\Providers\DataProviders. Make sure that the there won't be a directory created for the solution. Click OK, and after the project is completed, delete the default Class1.vb file. Open the Components folder in the WROX.FirstModule project and drag the SqlDataProvider.vb file into the SqlDataProvider project. Finally, delete the SqlDataProvider.vb file from the WROX.FirstModule project. Your module structure should now look the same as the structure back in Figure 12-4.

Rename the project with your company name (for example, WROX.FirstModule.SqlDataProvider), and double-click the My Project item to open the project Properties page. On the Application tab, set the Assembly name to match your project name (for example, WROX.FirstModule.SqlDataProvider), and clear the Root namespace field. On the Compile tab, set the Build output path to ..\..\..\..\..\bin\, which again puts the compiled .dll into the portal's \bin directory. On the References tab, click the Add button and browse to the portal's \bin directory and pick the following three items: DotNetNuke.dll, Microsoft.ApplicationBlocks.Data, and WROX.FirstModule.dll. Click OK. Highlight all three of them in the References window. Now, in the Properties window, set Copy Local to False for all three, as shown in Figure 12-13.

Open one of the source files (for example, ViewFirstModule.aspx), and search the entire solution for the "YourCompany" placeholder, and replace it with your company name (for example, WROX). At this point, there will probably be some issues listed in the Error List. Ignore these, and rebuild the entire solution. With luck, all the errors will disappear and your module project will build. If not, you may need to close all open files before building, or even shut down Visual Studio and re-open it.

The final steps needed before you can place your new module on a page are to create the database and register the module. These steps are very similar to those covered in the "Database Setup" and "Module Registration" subsections of the "Configuring for Module Development" section earlier in the chapter. In summary, open the Host ➪ SQL page, and paste in the contents of the 01.00.00.SqlDataProvider file, check the Run as Script option, and click Execute. On the Host ➪ Module Definitions page, use the Import Module Definition link to load your new .dnn file. Now you should be able to go to your development portal and put an instance of the WROX.FirstModule module on a page. Again if something is broken, first try going back through the steps listed to make sure you haven't missed anything. If you still have trouble, search and use the DNN Forums for help in solving any problems you have before continuing.

As you can see, quite a bit of detail work goes into creating a custom module project, and this is just an empty shell of a module. At this point, save the contents of the WROX.FirstModule directory, and you can use your new empty module as a template project for any new custom modules you create. You'll have to repeat the process of renaming files, directories, script objects, and so on. This process is similar to the steps you'd follow if you were starting your module development project from any other existing module, whether a standard core module or a community module developed within the DNN ecosystem.

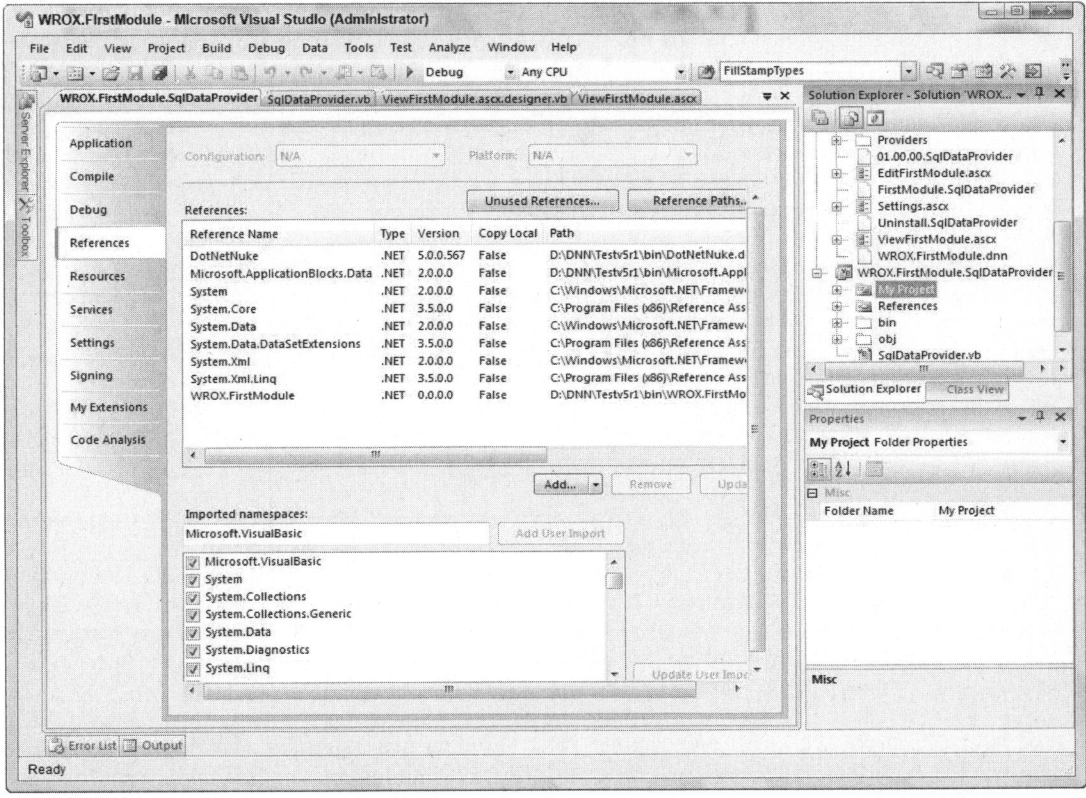

Figure 12-13

Finishing Development with the Starter Kit

You get a jump start on the module development process by using the DNN SK as outlined previously. At this point, you essentially have a "Hello World" module with a rudimentary database, data layer, and placeholders for the basic user controls. Your next steps are to create your application database, build your database layers, and construct the business logic of the application. The next three chapters walk you through the layers of an existing module so you can see and study the details involved in the overall process. You'll get a real-world view of building a custom module by example. Following are a few words about each part of the module development process as a general outline.

Constructing your database is an activity that most developers have at least a passing familiarity with, and what you need for a typical DNN module is no different than many other kinds of applications. The database creation process for DNN is exactly the same as other ASP.NET web applications. A variety of database tools are available to you, from simply working from within Visual Studio 2008 (which has very good data management capabilities), or SQL Server Management Studio (the traditional environment), to using high-end data definition and data construction applications. You can even apply new .NET technology like the Entity Framework to build your database.

Once your database is defined, you need to create your data layer. This is a very tedious process if you do it by hand, but a number of code-generation tools are available that can help you out. A wide variety of data layer code generator tools are also available. Pick your favorite search engine and search for templates to adapt your tool to DNN data layer generation. CodeSmith has been widely used in the DNN community, and several good sets of CodeSmith templates are freely available. Search for "CodeSmith DNN Templates," and you will find a variety of sources for tutorials and code generation templates that work with CodeSmith, even with the old, free 2.6 version. Most of the CodeSmith data layer generation templates were created for DNN 3 or 4, but because the DNN 5 data architecture has changed relatively little from DNN 3, many still work great in DNN 5.

Next up is building your user interface and business logic layers. Basically, you create a set of user controls that are dynamically displayed as the user interface elements of your module. You're doing this development work in the context of the DNN portal, because that's where it runs. This process is again very similar to many other kinds of web development projects, except that the plumbing is much better in DNN, and focused toward building portal and content management applications. In fact, it's relatively easy to change an existing .aspx (web page) based application to the .ascx (user control) style DNN module. In order to migrate an existing ASP.NET web application to DNN, the main challenge is to adapt it to the DNN data layer, which fortunately is fairly easy to do.

During development, you'll manually register your user controls using the Host ➪ Module Definitions page, as you saw in Figure 12-7. You may want to register the script manager in your controls to use AJAX; this is supported directly by DNN, although AJAX is not covered in the WROX.Suggestion module. See Chapter 10, "Client API," for more details on using AJAX in your module development to help make your web user interface work more smoothly. Also of note — DNN Core Team member Jon Henning has created AJAX project templates and other resources you can download from here: `http://www.codeendeavors.com/Downloads.aspx`.

You have the choice of using LINQ or other .NET Framework 3.5 features, depending on how much you want to limit the reach of your module; for private development, you definitely want to go for it! At this point in the development process, you need to start becoming quite familiar with the DotNetNuke architecture in Chapter 7, and the core APIs, Member Role, and other core technologies from Chapters 8 through 11. A lot of tutorials, blog posts, forum discussions, and other types of help are available via simple web searches as you go through the development process and come up the learning curve.

Finally, you'll develop, test, package, and deploy your module, as discussed briefly in the next section.

Building Your Module for Distribution

The best of all worlds, from choice of technologies to the module development and deployment process, is in building private modules. Here you can do anything you want, including "xCopy deployment" for DNN, where you provision portals with your module simply by copying your portal files into the runtime portal's directories. If you use the WSP style development process, you can even change your code on the fly, and the full source code is always available right there in your module. Here you can build against the latest .NET Framework version and use the latest tools, including third-party controls such as the web controls available from Telerik and ComponentOne. You have total control over your destiny.

Building public modules relegates you to the lowest common denominator, building your module to run in the widest possible scenarios. You'll build against the DNN 4 assemblies, which run in DNN 5 because there are no substantial breaking changes in the DNN APIs, only additions. If you want to support AJAX technologies in your module, DNN 4.5.5 was a very stable build, and was the earliest "dot" version (4.5) to support AJAX in the core. If you're using the `IHydratable` interface (introduced in Chapter 14) to reduce the amount of .NET Reflection used to load your business objects, you'll need to use DNN 4.6.2, the next-highest stable build. The set of DNN assemblies you should build against for broadest reach, therefore, are either 4.5.5 or 4.6.2. If you build against the DNN 5 assemblies, you can install and run your module only on DNN 5 or later portals.

The WROX.Suggestion example module used in this book has generally taken this "broadest distribution" approach, and has not done anything very fancy. It is, however, a solid starting point, even if you are building private modules.

DotNetNuke 5 Module Architecture and Directions

During the development process of the DNN 5 architecture, the Core Team has addressed several major developer challenges that continue to open the platform and make it more powerful and extensible. There are several major examples of these changes, including the introduction of a dependency injection engine, and core refactoring to support a more Test Driven Development (TDD) approach to development. Direct support for the jQuery engine, a very popular open source library, was announced late in the beta cycle for working on client-side script development. A widget framework was introduced that, as Core Team leader Joe Brinkman says, simplifies the creation and distribution of JavaScript widgets. The implementation of a sophisticated token replacement engine, and the ability to apply roles to any page (elimination of admin-only and host-only pages) rounds out the list of big architectural enhancements. The Core Team is loath to introduce breaking changes, and nothing done in DNN 5 breaks prior functionality, which has been a hallmark of the DNN portal development and release process. As of this writing, DNN 5 is still in release candidate status, and some new core features have only recently been announced (such as support for the jQuery library).

Fundamentally, changes to the DNN 5 core are mostly infrastructure related. There are very few "Wow!" portal features most users will notice, other than the nice looking new interface and page layouts. There are, however, many new knobs to turn for the portal Admin and Host. These are covered elsewhere in this book. Once it's released, DNN 5 feature development will kick into high gear; this is where the DNN ecosystem will get involved in the process. Most of the changes that will directly benefit the user community in DNN 5 will come in the "dot" versions: 5.1, 5.2, and so on, just as what happened with DNN 4. At the present time, the Core Team has committed to making the DNN 5 core run against the .NET Framework 2.0 libraries, although that doesn't restrict you from using later versions of the framework in your own modules.

As part of the DNN module developer community, we will be the source of much of the new functionality that will grow around the new architectural features in DNN 5. There is much to do in the development of content management, social networking, rich Internet application, workflow, and the web service-based web portal applications of the future. There are many more new technologies coming from Microsoft, such as the release of the Model View Controller (MVC) toolkit, and model-based development tools, where support in DNN is a very natural fit. DNN has grown and matured tremendously since the project's inception a scant six years ago, and it will continue to explode in the next decade, largely because of the quality of the people on the Core Team, in the user and developer communities, and in the services ecosystem around the DNN application itself.

Summary

This chapter discussed some of the issues you will face as you begin any module development project, walked you through the platform decision process, and demonstrated how to set up your development environment to work with an existing custom module project. You explored the creation of module projects in Visual Studio 2008, and overviewed the development process with the DotNetNuke Starter Kit. With a bit of a peek at the future of DNN, you're ready to look at the details of building a custom module on the DotNetNuke platform.

The next three chapters cover each major phase of module development — Database Layer, Business Logic Layer, and Presentation Layer — in detail using the sample WROX.Suggestion module.

13

Developing Modules: the Database Layer

Now that you understand the concept of modules and are ready to develop your own, this chapter guides you on how to begin development starting with the database layer. As in most application development, you need to build a database structure for your application. This chapter covers basic database development and how to expose your data within a DotNetNuke module.

Chapter 7, "DotNetNuke Architecture," introduced the concept of the Provider Model and how DotNetNuke uses it to abstract the business layer logic from the physical database. In this chapter, you develop your modules by modeling the three-tier architecture of DotNetNuke. In the DNN architecture, the concept of data abstraction is used to separate the business logic of your module from the specifics of data storage. A data abstraction layer defines the database operations needed by your module. You build a concrete data provider for each database backend that your module supports. You can build as many concrete providers as you need, none of which affects the business logic of your module. Please refer to Figure 7-1 for an illustration of how the data layers are constructed in DotNetNuke.

In the database layer code shown in this chapter, the stored procedures and code assume that Microsoft SQL Server is used for the backend database. Developing with SQL Server is beyond the scope of this book, but the sections on creating tables and stored procedures review basic SQL Server development concepts. From there, you learn how to expose the stored procedures through a custom Data Provider that you develop for your module. Building on the DotNetNuke architecture, you develop an abstraction layer for the module to provide a separation between the physical database and your module code.

The WROX.Suggestion module used in the example for this chapter and the next two chapters on module development is a custom module developed for the purpose of illustrating DNN module development. See Chapter 12, "Beginning Module Development," for an overview of how this module works. You can download the WROX.Suggestion module project from the book web site (`http://www.wrox.com`), both as a binary installer and as a source installer. Once installed, the *module is located in the DesktopModules folder under the root of the DotNetNuke distribution package. Refer to the discussion in Chapter 12 about how to set up your development environment to work on your custom module project.*

Database Design

This section reviews the tables and stored procedures that make up the SQL Server backend database for the WROX.Suggestion module.

The WROX.Suggestion module is a sample module that illustrates the process of custom module development for the DotNetNuke platform. The database structure consists of two tables to store suggestion information. The WROX_Suggestion table stores detail information about suggestion items, and the WROX_SuggestionType table stores types (or categories) that the user can associate with each entered suggestion item. A set of stored procedures is used to add, update, and delete suggestion and suggestion type information. In the next sections, you learn the structure of the database tables for the module and the stored procedures for performing actions on the data.

For database manipulation, you can use SQL 2005 Management Studio or Visual Studio 2008 Professional. The examples in this chapter use Visual Studio 2008 for module development and database design. SQL Server 2005 is used throughout the book because DotNetNuke natively supports SQL Server 2005 (and 2000) out of the box. The idea behind this chapter and the next two chapters on module development is to give you a comprehensive review of the module structure defined by the DNN architecture through a practical example.

As discussed in Chapter 12, keep in mind that you are not bound by the underlying physical database. You can use any database besides SQL Server as your backend for module development, and you can develop modules for whatever database your DotNetNuke install is using. The Data Provider model provides a plug-and-play mechanism that separates the business logic you write in your modules from the specific database used to store your module's data.

WROX_Suggestion Table

The WROX_Suggestion table stores your suggestion item details for the module. It is defined as shown in Figure 13-1.

For DotNetNuke integration, the most important field contained within the table structure is `ModuleID`. `ModuleID` contains an integer value that is assigned to a module by DNN when you create an instance of your module. This value identifies the specific instance of the module with which you are working. It's important because multiple instances of a module can exist on a single page or on multiple pages, and a button click on one instance of the module must not operate on data from another instance of the module. Any values you store specific to this module instance will key off the value contained in the `ModuleID` field. You will see this as you create the stored procedures. The other fields within the database are specific to the module itself, and will depend on how you structure your application.

The `SuggestionID` field is the primary key of a specific suggestion data item within your table. The main concept here is to create and fully integrate a unique instance of your module with instance items; in our case, these items are user suggestions. The combination of `SuggestionID` and `ModuleID` values provide a way of tracking suggestion items by the specific module instance they were entered into.

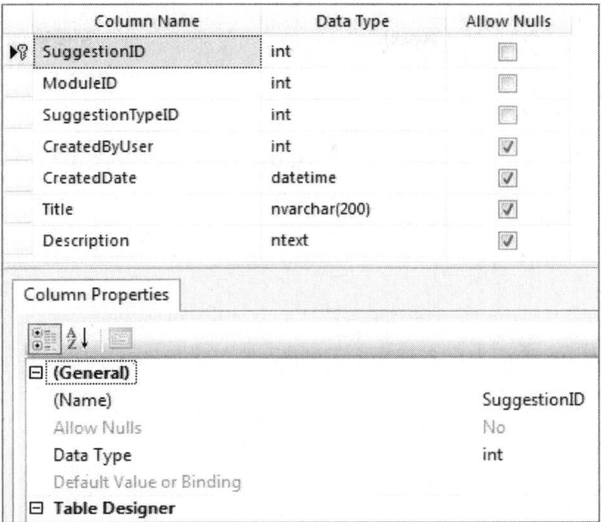

Figure 13-1

The following list describes each field in the WROX_Suggestion table:

- **SuggestionID:** The primary key of the suggestion item information within the table.
- **ModuleID:** Because DNN can contain many instances of a module, each with different information, this key consolidates suggestion items for each module instance.
- **SuggestionTypeID:** The foreign key connection to the SuggestionType table for each suggestion item. Suggestion types are categories assigned by the user for each suggestion item.
- **CreatedByUser:** Tracks the ID of the portal user that created the suggestion item.
- **CreatedDate:** When the suggestion was created.
- **Title:** The displayed title, or summary, of a suggestion item.
- **Description:** The detailed text description of the suggestion item for display.

The preceding list covers how you store the data that is entered into a suggestion module. Next, you look at the stored procedures necessary for working with the suggestion data. The T-SQL table and stored procedure definitions are found in the file named 02.00.00.SqlDataProvider in the module's project directory. You can view the contents of this file in Visual Studio or in a text editor.

WROX_AddSuggestion Stored Procedure

The first stored procedure you're going to create for this module is `WROX_AddSuggestion`. This procedure is used to add a suggestion item to the WROX_Suggestion table. This stored procedure is a basic `Insert` statement, and it accepts parameters from your database provider for populating the suggestion item.

```
create procedure {databaseOwner}{objectQualifier}WROX_AddSuggestion

@ModuleID    int,
```

```
@SuggestionTypeID  int,
@UserID       int,
@Title        nvarchar(200),
@Description ntext

as

insert into {databaseOwner}{objectQualifier}WROX_Suggestion (
  ModuleID,
  SuggestionTypeID,
  CreatedByUser,
  CreatedDate,
  Title,
  Description
)
values (
  @ModuleID,
  @SuggestionTypeID,
  @UserID,
  getdate(),
  @Title,
  @Description
)
select SCOPE_IDENTITY()
```

You'll notice two special tags in the stored procedures — `{databaseOwner}` and `{objectQualifier}`. The purpose of these is covered both in Chapter 2, "Installing DotNetNuke," and Chapter 7, "DotNetNuke Architecture." These tags are replaced at runtime by the DNN portal code when your module is installed. Note that if you want to execute these procedures manually you can paste them directly into the Host ⇨ SQL form (and check the Run as Script box), where the tags are replaced for you by the values in your portal's web.config file. You can also edit the tags to replace their values manually before executing the stored procedures through SQL Management Studio or Visual Studio.

One thing to keep in mind throughout all the stored procedures is that the `ModuleID` parameter is always passed when creating or updating a record that is associated with your module. In Chapter 14, "Developing Modules: the Business Logic Layer," you learn how to obtain the `ModuleID` for a module instance from DotNetNuke and pass it to your stored procedures.

WROX_DeleteSuggestion Stored Procedure

The `WROX_DeleteSuggestion` stored procedure deletes a suggestion item previously added to the WROX _Suggestion table.

```
create procedure {databaseOwner}{objectQualifier}WROX_DeleteSuggestion

@SuggestionID int

as

delete
from   {databaseOwner}{objectQualifier}WROX_Suggestion
where  SuggestionID = @SuggestionID
```

There is no need to pass a parameter value for ModuleID in this procedure. Because you're only concerned about performing a delete operation on a specific suggestion item, you only need to determine the primary key of the specific suggestion record you want to delete.

WROX_GetSuggestion Stored Procedure

You use the WROX_GetSuggestion stored procedure to retrieve a single suggestion item based on its primary key.

```
create procedure {databaseOwner}{objectQualifier}WROX_GetSuggestion

@SuggestionID   int

as

select SuggestionID,
      ModuleID,
       SuggestionTypeID,
       CreatedByUser,
       {databaseOwner}{objectQualifier}WROX_Suggestion.CreatedDate,
       Title,
       Description
from   {databaseOwner}{objectQualifier}WROX_Suggestion
left outer join Users on {databaseOwner}{objectQualifier}WROX_Suggestion.Created
ByUser =
       {databaseOwner}{objectQualifier}Users.UserID
where  SuggestionID = @SuggestionID
```

Here you are passing only the specific SuggestionID for the suggestion item. The CreatedByUser value is retrieved as a name for display, rather than as an ID value. Use this stored procedure for obtaining a single suggestion item for modification or display.

WROX_GetSuggestionIDs Stored Procedure

The WROX_GetSuggestionIDs stored procedure is a special-purpose procedure that gets the SuggestionID values for a specific module instance.

```
CREATE procedure {databaseOwner}{objectQualifier}WROX_GetSuggestionIDs

@ModuleID int

as

select SuggestionID
from   {databaseOwner}{objectQualifier}WROX_Suggestion
where  ModuleID = @ModuleID
```

The SuggestionID values retrieved with this procedure can each be used to get a specific suggestion item instance with the WROX_GetSuggestion stored procedure covered previously.

WROX_GetSuggestions Stored Procedure

You use the WROX_GetSuggestions stored procedure for obtaining all suggestion items for display in a specific suggestion module instance.

```
CREATE procedure {databaseOwner}{objectQualifier}WROX_GetSuggestions

@ModuleID int

as

select 'CreatedByUser' = (select FirstName + ' ' + LastName from
    {databaseOwner}{objectQualifier}Users where UserID=CreatedByUser),
       'SuggestionType' = (select SuggestionType from
    {databaseOwner}{objectQualifier}WROX_SuggestionType t where
    t.SuggestionTypeID=s.SuggestionTypeID),
       CreatedDate,
       Title,
       Description
from   {databaseOwner}{objectQualifier}WROX_Suggestion s
where  ModuleID = @ModuleID
order by SuggestionType, CreatedDate
```

The only parameter passed to this stored procedure is the ModuleID value. The CreatedByUser value is again retrieved as a name for display rather than an ID value. This procedure retrieves all suggestion items for one module instance.

WROX_UpdateSuggestion Stored Procedure

You use the WROX_UpdateSuggestion stored procedure to update a specific suggestion item.

```
CREATE procedure {databaseOwner}{objectQualifier}WROX_UpdateSuggestion

@SuggestionID      int,
@SuggestionTypeID  int,
@UserID      int,
@Title       nvarchar(200),
@Description nvarchar(2000)

as

update {databaseOwner}{objectQualifier}WROX_Suggestion
set    SuggestionTypeID = @SuggestionTypeID,
       CreatedByUser = @UserID,
       CreatedDate   = GetDate(),
       Title         = @Title,
       Description   = @Description
where  SuggestionID = @SuggestionID
```

Here you can see the CreatedDate field is updated to the current date and time when a suggestion item is updated. The ModuleID field is not passed into this routine, because it does not change during a suggestion item update (and indeed, should not be allowed to change, or else the item will switch which module it's associated with). Note that the module user interface doesn't implement the logic required to update a suggestion item; this stored procedure is provided for completeness.

WROX_GetSuggestionModulesAllTabs Stored Procedure

The WROX_GetSuggestionModulesAllTabs stored procedure is a special-purpose procedure that gets a list of the suggestion modules in the entire portal. The list of modules is displayed to an Admin user in a drop-down list on the DisplaySuggestions form.

```
CREATE PROCEDURE {databaseOwner}{objectQualifier}WROX_GetSuggestionModulesAllTabs

as

declare @SuggestionModuleDefID int

set @SuggestionModuleDefID = (select ModuleDefID from
{databaseOwner}{objectQualifier}ModuleDefinitions where FriendlyName
='WROX.Suggestion')

select m.ModuleID,
       'ModuleTitle' = m.ModuleTitle + ' (' + t.TabName + ')'
from   {databaseOwner}{objectQualifier}Modules m inner join
 {databaseOwner}{objectQualifier}TabModules tm on m.ModuleID = tm.ModuleID inner join
 {databaseOwner}{objectQualifier}Tabs t on tm.TabID=t.TabID
where  m.ModuleDefID = @SuggestionModuleDefID
  and  t.IsDeleted = 0
order by t.TabID, m.ModuleTitle
```

Here, the ModuleTitle field is returned with a combination of each suggestion module's title, and the page name on which it's displayed; for example, Energy Saving Ideas (Production). This procedure returns a module list that may span multiple pages, so this procedure aids the Admin user in identifying which module instance he wants to view in a DisplaySuggestions user control.

WROX_GetSuggestionModulesThisTab Stored Procedure

The WROX_GetSuggestionModulesThisTab stored procedure is a special-purpose procedure that gets a list of the suggestion modules on the current page only, for display in a drop-down list to a user with view permissions on the DisplaySuggestions form.

```
CREATE PROCEDURE {databaseOwner}{objectQualifier}WROX_GetSuggestionModulesThisTab

@TabID int

as

declare @SuggestionModuleDefID int

set @SuggestionModuleDefID = (select ModuleDefID from
{databaseOwner}{objectQualifier}ModuleDefinitions where FriendlyName
='WROX.Suggestion')

select m.ModuleID,
       m.ModuleTitle
```

```
from   {databaseOwner}{objectQualifier}Modules m Inner Join
{databaseOwner}{objectQualifier}TabModules tm on m.ModuleID = tm.ModuleID
where  m.ModuleDefID = @SuggestionModuleDefID
  and  tm.TabID = @TabID
order by ModuleTitle
```

Unlike in the previous procedure, the `ModuleTitle` field does not include the current page name because the list of modules to be displayed in the drop-down list on the DisplaySuggestions form are from the current page.

That's it for the WROX_Suggestion table database procedures. The next section covers the WROX_SuggestionType table and its stored procedures.

WROX_SuggestionType Table

The WROX_SuggestionType table stores suggestion type, or category, values that can be associated by the user at entry time with each suggestion item. A list of suggestion type values can be created by a module Admin using the suggestion module settings page. If a type list hasn't been created when a user enters a suggestion, the type value defaults to "General." The suggestion type table is defined as shown in Figure 13-2.

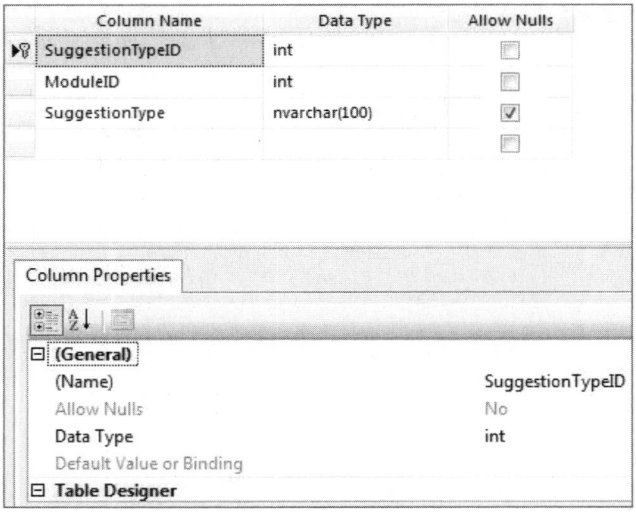

Column Name	Data Type	Allow Nulls
SuggestionTypeID	int	☐
ModuleID	int	☐
SuggestionType	nvarchar(100)	☑
		☐

Column Properties

(General)

(Name)	SuggestionTypeID
Allow Nulls	No
Data Type	int
Default Value or Binding	

Table Designer

Figure 13-2

This table again contains a `ModuleID` field, which identifies the specific instance of the module with which you are working. The `SuggestionTypeID` field is the primary key of the table, and in combination with `ModuleID`, provides a way to associate suggestion type values with unique instances of the module.

The following list describes each item in the WROX_SuggestionType table:

- **SuggestionTypeID:** The primary key of the suggestion type within the table.
- **ModuleID:** The link to a specific module instance.
- **SuggestionType:** The type (or category) users will assign to each suggestion item they enter.

The preceding list covered how you store the type data that is entered into the module by a module Admin through the module's settings page. Next, you look at the stored procedures necessary for working with the suggestion type data.

WROX_AddSuggestionType Stored Procedure

The first stored procedure you're going to create for this table is `WROX_AddSuggestionType`. This procedure is used to add a suggestion type to the WROX_SuggestionType table.

```
CREATE procedure {databaseOwner}{objectQualifier}WROX_AddSuggestionType

@ModuleID  int,
@SuggestionType  nvarchar(100)

as

insert {databaseOwner}{objectQualifier}WROX_SuggestionType (
  ModuleID,
  SuggestionType
)
values (
  @ModuleID,
  @SuggestionType
)
select SCOPE_IDENTITY()
```

As with other Add and Update stored procedures, the `ModuleID` parameter is used to associate suggestion types with a specific suggestion module instance.

WROX_DeleteSuggestionType Stored Procedure

The `WROX_DeleteSuggestionType` stored procedure is for deleting a suggestion type previously added to the WROX_SuggestionType table.

```
CREATE PROCEDURE {databaseOwner}{objectQualifier}WROX_DeleteSuggestionType

@SuggestionTypeID int,
@ModuleID int

as

delete
from   {databaseOwner}{objectQualifier}WROX_SuggestionType
```

```
where  SuggestionTypeID = @SuggestionTypeID
and ModuleID = @ModuleID
```

The sample module doesn't implement the logic required to delete a suggestion type item. This procedure is only included for completeness.

WROX_GetSuggestionTypes Stored Procedure

You use the `WROX_GetSuggestionTypes` stored procedure for obtaining all the suggestion type values for a specific module instance to display in a drop-down list to the user.

```
CREATE procedure {databaseOwner}{objectQualifier}WROX_GetSuggestionTypes

@ModuleID int

as

select SuggestionTypeId,
       SuggestionType
from   {databaseOwner}{objectQualifier}WROX_SuggestionType
where  ModuleID=@ModuleID
order by SuggestionType
```

WROX_UpdateSuggestionType Stored Procedure

The final stored procedure for the WROX.Suggestion module is the `WROX_UpdateSuggestionType` procedure. This enables you to update an existing suggestion type value.

```
CREATE PROCEDURE {databaseOwner}{objectQualifier}WROX_UpdateSuggestionType

@SuggestionTypeID int,
@ModuleID int,
@SuggestionType     nvarchar(100)

as

update {databaseOwner}{objectQualifier}WROX_SuggestionType
set    SuggestionType = @SuggestionType
where  SuggestionTypeID = @SuggestionTypeID
and ModuleID = @ModuleID
```

Note that the sample module doesn't implement the logic required to update a suggestion type item. This procedure is only included for completeness.

That's it for the tables and database procedures. The next section covers how to wrap this up and create your own physical database provider for your module.

Concrete Data Provider

Module development closely mirrors the DotNetNuke architecture, and so each module should provide its own abstraction to the underlying database. This enables you to change physical databases without having to change or recompile the underlying code of your module, or of DotNetNuke. Remember, if you want to support multiple databases with your module, you need to create a concrete (or physical) provider for each database you want to support. For example, if your DotNetNuke implementation is using the Oracle database, you need to create a provider for your module to support Oracle using the appropriate underlying database language.

The only direct interaction with the stored procedures shown in the previous sections is done in the concrete data provider project. Even in the DotNetNuke core modules, all modules have a corresponding project for a SQL Data Provider. In the current example, the main module project called WROX .Suggestion is located in the DesktopModules folder. Within a Providers subfolder structure, you also have a project named WROX.Suggestion.SqlDataProvider. This data provider project contains the class and methods necessary to interact with the stored procedures covered earlier in this chapter. If you were also supporting the Oracle database, in addition to creating Oracle database procedures, you would also supply a WROX.Suggestion.OracleDataProvider project to interact with the Oracle database.

The following sections cover the data provider class and the methods it contains to implement a concrete provider for this module. The SqlDataProvider class for any DNN module within the DesktopModules folder closely mirrors the structure of the DotNetNuke core architecture. Therefore, you will see very similar methods contained in the WROX.Suggestion project as you would see in any of the DotNetNuke core module projects that you can download and examine separately.

This section breaks down the structure of the data provider class for the WROX.Suggestion module. The SqlDataProvider.vb file, which implements the SQL Server concrete data provider, is located within the WROX.Suggestion.SqlDataProvider project. The file is physically located within the Providers subfolder of the WROX.Suggestion project. The SqlDataProvider.vb source file starts out with namespace imports needed for the concrete data provider.

```
Imports Microsoft.ApplicationBlocks.Data    'for SqlHelper

Imports DotNetNuke.Common.Utilities         'for Config object
Imports DotNetNuke.Framework.Providers      'for ProviderConfiguration

Imports WROX.Modules.Suggestion
```

Because this assembly connects to the physical database, you need to use specific classes for connecting to and manipulating the database. The Microsoft.ApplicationBlocks.Data import provides an assembly from the Microsoft Enterprise Library, which helps to reduce the code required for creating SQL commands and calling stored procedures in the SQL Server database.

> *You can find more information on the Microsoft Enterprise Library and Application Blocks in the "Patterns and Practices" section within the Microsoft Developer Network (MSDN) site at* `http://msdn.microsoft.com/en-us/practices/default.aspx`.

Next is your module namespace declaration:

```
Namespace WROX.Modules.Suggestion
```

When you develop your own custom modules for DotNetNuke, you should create your own unique namespace in the form of `CompanyName.Modules.ModuleName`. This ensures that your namespace is unique and does not conflict with other third-party modules installed within a single DotNetNuke portal framework.

From here you have your standard class name, and because you're creating a concrete data provider class, you'll also inherit from the module's DataProvider class. Each concrete data provider class must implement the methods contained in its abstract DataProvider class, which are overridden for each physical database type (as you'll see later in this chapter).

```
Public Class SqlDataProvider
        Inherits WROX.Modules.Suggestion.DataProvider
```

Each of the following sections of code for the data provider class is broken down by code region. Code regions are used in DotNetNuke development projects to organize code and make it more readable.

The first region in the class is named `Private Members`. In this region, you declare the variables for your provider, which are defined within your portal's web.config file, as follows:

```
#Region " Private Members "

    Private Const ProviderType As String = "data"
    Private Const ModuleQualifier As String = "WROX_"

    Private _providerConfiguration As ProviderConfiguration = _
      ProviderConfiguration.GetProviderConfiguration(ProviderType)
    Private _connectionString As String
    Private _providerPath As String
    Private _objectQualifier As String
    Private _databaseOwner As String

#End Region
```

As in the overall DotNetNuke architecture, the code refers to the provider configuration within the data section of web.config. In this section, you define the values for properties in the SqlDataProvider class. These properties are loaded from the web.config file in the class constructor when your module is loaded.

```
    <data defaultProvider="SqlDataProvider">
      <providers>
        <clear />
        <add name="SqlDataProvider"
             type="DotNetNuke.Data.SqlDataProvider, DotNetNuke.SqlDataProvider"
             connectionStringName="SiteSqlServer"
             upgradeConnectionString=""
             providerPath="~\Providers\DataProviders\SqlDataProvider\"
             objectQualifier=""
             databaseOwner="dbo" />
      </providers>
    </data>
```

Next is the Constructors region, where you read the web.config settings to populate the values from the data section to the private members within your class.

```
#Region " Constructors "

    Public Sub New()
```

```
            ' Read the configuration specific information for this provider
            Dim objProvider As Provider = CType(_providerConfiguration.Providers _
              (_providerConfiguration.DefaultProvider), Provider)

            'Get Connection string from web.config
            _connectionString = Config.GetConnectionString()

            If _connectionString = "" Then
                ' Use connection string specified in provider
                _connectionString = objProvider.Attributes("connectionString")
            End If

            _providerPath = objProvider.Attributes("providerPath")

            _objectQualifier = objProvider.Attributes("objectQualifier")
            If _objectQualifier <> "" And _objectQualifier.EndsWith("_") = False Then
                _objectQualifier += "_"
            End If

            _databaseOwner = objProvider.Attributes("databaseOwner")
            If _databaseOwner <> "" And _databaseOwner.EndsWith(".") = False Then
                _databaseOwner += "."
            End If

        End Sub

    #End Region
```

After populating the private members with values from the data provider section in the web.config file, you then expose public properties for your class. These properties are read-only and contain the values from web.config.

```
    #Region " Properties "

        Public ReadOnly Property ConnectionString() As String
            Get
                Return _connectionString
            End Get
        End Property

        Public ReadOnly Property ProviderPath() As String
            Get
                Return _providerPath
            End Get
        End Property

        Public ReadOnly Property ObjectQualifier() As String
            Get
                Return _objectQualifier
            End Get
        End Property

        Public ReadOnly Property DatabaseOwner() As String
            Get
```

```
            Return _databaseOwner
        End Get
    End Property

#End Region
```

Next are some private methods used within the SqlDataProvider class, and these are listed in the `Private Methods` region.

```
#Region " Private Methods "

    Private Function GetFullyQualifiedName(ByVal name As String) As String
        Return DatabaseOwner & ObjectQualifier & ModuleQualifier & name
    End Function

    Private Function GetNull(ByVal Field As Object) As Object
        Return DotNetNuke.Common.Utilities.Null.GetNull(Field, DBNull.Value)
    End Function

#End Region
```

The `GetFullyQualifiedName` method returns the full name of a stored procedure in the database, given just the base name of the procedure as a string value. The `GetNull` method wraps a DNN utility routine that prevents exceptions from occurring within your code due to any null values that may exist in your data fields in the database.

The database operations of your SqlDataProvider class are contained within the `Public Methods` region. The public methods expose the database stored procedures covered earlier to your module so you can perform your add, update, and delete operations, as well as obtain the data so it can be displayed in your module.

```
#Region " Public Methods "

    Public Overrides Function AddSuggestion(ByVal ModuleId As Integer, _
      ByVal SuggestionTypeID As Integer, UserID As Integer, _
      ByVal Title As String, ByVal Description As String) As Integer

        Return CType(SqlHelper.ExecuteScalar(ConnectionString, _
          GetFullyQualifiedName("AddSuggestion"), ModuleId, SuggestionTypeID, _
          GetNull(UserID), GetNull(Title), GetNull(Description)), Integer)

    End Function

    Public Overrides Sub DeleteSuggestion(ByVal SuggestionID As Integer)

        SqlHelper.ExecuteNonQuery(ConnectionString, _
          GetFullyQualifiedName("DeleteSuggestion"), SuggestionID)

    End Sub

    Public Overrides Function GetSuggestions(ByVal ModuleId As Integer) _
      As IDataReader
```

```
        Return CType(SqlHelper.ExecuteReader(ConnectionString, _
          GetFullyQualifiedName("GetSuggestions"), ModuleId), IDataReader)

    End Function

    Public Overrides Function GetSuggestion(ByVal SuggestionID As Integer) _
      As IDataReader

        Return CType(SqlHelper.ExecuteReader(ConnectionString, _
          GetFullyQualifiedName("GetSuggestion"), SuggestionID), IDataReader)

    End Function

    Public Overrides Function GetSuggestionIDs(ByVal ModuleId As Integer) _
      As IDataReader

        Return CType(SqlHelper.ExecuteReader(ConnectionString, _
          GetFullyQualifiedName("GetSuggestionIDs"), ModuleId), IDataReader)

    End Function

    Public Overrides Sub UpdateSuggestion(ByVal SuggestionID As Integer, _
      ByVal SuggestionTypeID As Integer, UserID As Integer, _
      ByVal Title As String, ByVal Description As String)

        SqlHelper.ExecuteNonQuery(ConnectionString, _
        GetFullyQualifiedName("UpdateSuggestion"), SuggestionID, _
        SuggestionTypeID, UserID, GetNull(Title), _
        GetNull(Description))

    End Sub

    Public Overrides Function AddSuggestionType(ByVal ModuleID As Integer, _
      ByVal SuggestionType As String) As Integer

        Return CType(SqlHelper.ExecuteScalar(ConnectionString, _
          GetFullyQualifiedName("AddSuggestionType"), ModuleID, _
          GetNull(SuggestionType)), Integer)

    End Function

    Public Overrides Sub DeleteSuggestionType(ByVal SuggestionTypeID As Integer, _
      ByVal ModuleID As Integer)

        SqlHelper.ExecuteNonQuery(ConnectionString, _
          GetFullyQualifiedName("DeleteSuggestionType"), SuggestionTypeID, _
          ModuleID)

    End Sub

    Public Overrides Function GetSuggestionTypes(ByVal ModuleID As Integer) _
      As IDataReader

        Return CType(SqlHelper.ExecuteReader(ConnectionString, _
          GetFullyQualifiedName("GetSuggestionTypes"), ModuleID), IDataReader)
```

```
    End Function

    Public Overrides Sub UpdateSuggestionType(ByVal SuggestionTypeID As Integer, _
      ByVal ModuleID As Integer, ByVal SuggestionType As String)

        SqlHelper.ExecuteNonQuery(ConnectionString, _
          GetFullyQualifiedName("UpdateSuggestionType"), SuggestionTypeID, _
          ModuleID, GetNull(SuggestionType))

    End Sub

    Public Overrides Function GetSuggestionModulesAllTabs() As IDataReader

        Return CType(SqlHelper.ExecuteReader(ConnectionString, _
          GetFullyQualifiedName("GetSuggestionModulesAllTabs")), IDataReader)

    End Function

    Public Overrides Function GetSuggestionModulesThisTab(ByVal TabID As Integer) _
      As IDataReader

        Return CType(SqlHelper.ExecuteReader(ConnectionString, _
          GetFullyQualifiedName("GetSuggestionModulesThisTab"), TabID), _
          IDataReader)

    End Function

#End Region
```

You can see that there is a one-to-one relationship between the methods in this class and the stored procedures within your SQL database. This data interface implementation is known as a concrete data layer because of its dependence on SQL Server–specific database routines. Following is a breakdown of what is happening within the concrete data provider layer.

Each routine in the preceding `Public Methods` code is a public method that overrides a corresponding method within the abstract base class (DataProvider), which you inherited in the beginning of the class. So not only do you have a corresponding method in this class for each stored procedure, but you also have a corresponding method in the DataProvider class, which is located in the main module project. The method within the base class is an abstracted method that your module implements, which enables you to separate the physical database interactions from your module assembly.

All parameters accepted by the underlying stored procedure are passed through your methods as well. In addition, you execute the SQL command and pass database connection information such as the connection string, database owner account, object qualifier, and the name of the stored procedure using the `GetFullyQualifiedName` function.

The `GetSuggestions` method, as an example, returns an `IDataReader` containing the result set from the database using the `SQLHelper.ExecuteReader` method provided by the Microsoft Data Access Application Block you referenced at the beginning of the class.

Finally, to handle null values returned from the database, DotNetNuke provides the `GetNull` method. When you create a method for your database, as was done in `AddSuggestion` and `UpdateSuggestion`, you should wrap any parameters that can contain a null value with the GetNull method. This prevents errors from being raised in your Data Provider due to any null values that may exist in your data.

That's it for the concrete data provider class. Remember this layer is compiled into its own assembly DLL separate from the module's main assembly. By maintaining this separation, you can easily plug in providers for other databases. In addition, you don't need to recompile your base class when changing database operations or when replacing physical database providers.

Data Abstraction Layer

The next part of the module for data operations is the creation of the data abstraction class. In the concrete data provider section, you created methods that overrode the base DataProvider class. Now you'll see how to provide the data abstraction layer for the WROX.Suggestion module.

In the WROX.Suggestion main module project, you have a class file called DataProvider.vb within the Components folder. The class contains nothing but abstract, overridable methods that contain no code themselves. You overrode these methods within your concrete data provider class in the previous section, providing an implementation for each.

The first thing you'll do in the source code is to define your class. You use the MustInherit keyword within your class to specify that it can be used only as a base class, as you saw in the SqlDataProvider class earlier.

```
Namespace WROX.Modules.Suggestion

  Public MustInherit Class DataProvider
```

Next is the Shared/Static Methods region within the class. When the class is instantiated, you call the CreateProvider method.

```
#Region " Shared/Static Methods "

    ' singleton reference to the instantiated object
    Private Shared objProvider As DataProvider = Nothing

    ' constructor
    Shared Sub New()
        CreateProvider()
    End Sub

    ' dynamically create provider
    Private Shared Sub CreateProvider()
        objProvider = CType(Framework.Reflection.CreateObject("data", _
          "WROX.Modules.Suggestion", ""), DataProvider)
    End Sub

    ' return the provider instance
    Public Shared Shadows Function Instance() As DataProvider
        Return objProvider
    End Function

#End Region
```

Finally, within the DataProvider class you have what provides the data operations abstraction: the abstract methods themselves. Each method contained in this base class has a corresponding implementation method within your concrete data provider class. You'll notice each abstract method in the following code uses the `MustOverride` keyword to specify that each will be overridden by the class inheriting it.

```
#Region " Abstract methods "

    Public MustOverride Function AddSuggestion(ByVal ModuleId As Integer, _
      ByVal SuggestionTypeID As Integer, UserID As Integer, _
      ByVal Title As String, ByVal Description As String) As Integer
    Public MustOverride Sub DeleteSuggestion(ByVal SuggestionID As Integer)
    Public MustOverride Function GetSuggestions(ByVal ModuleId As Integer) _
      As IDataReader
    Public MustOverride Function GetSuggestion(ByVal SuggestionID As Integer) _
      As IDataReader
    Public MustOverride Function GetSuggestionIDs(ByVal ModuleId As Integer) _
      As IDataReader
    Public MustOverride Sub UpdateSuggestion(ByVal SuggestionID As Integer, _
      ByVal SuggestionTypeID As Integer, UserID As Integer, _
      ByVal Title As String, ByVal Description As String)
    Public MustOverride Function AddSuggestionType(ByVal ModuleID As Integer, _
      ByVal SuggestionType As String) As Integer
    Public MustOverride Sub DeleteSuggestionType(ByVal SuggestionTypeID _
      As Integer, ByVal ModuleID As Integer)
    Public MustOverride Function GetSuggestionTypes(ByVal ModuleID As Integer) _
      As IDataReader
    Public MustOverride Sub UpdateSuggestionType(ByVal SuggestionTypeID _
      As Integer, ByVal ModuleID As Integer, ByVal SuggestionType As String)
    Public MustOverride Function GetSuggestionModulesAllTabs() As IDataReader
    Public MustOverride Function GetSuggestionModulesThisTab(ByVal TabID _
      As Integer) As IDataReader

#End Region
```

This completes the abstraction of your module's data routines from the physical database. All portions of your module code remain the same if you change the underlying database by switching the concrete provider. Only the concrete data provider class itself is changed by replacing the data provider assembly DLL and updating the web.config file, as seen in the previous example.

Module development closely mirrors DotNetNuke architecture: all aspects of the application are totally separated from the underlying physical database.

Summary

This chapter covers the physical database creation, data access layer, and the data abstraction class contained in your module project. Here are the main points to remember when developing the database and data classes for your module:

- In addition to a primary key for module records, add a `ModuleID` field, because each module instance is assigned a unique `ModuleID` by the DotNetNuke framework.

- Each database stored procedure will have a corresponding method contained within the concrete data provider.
- Each physical database provider will be created in its own assembly project with the same namespace as the module.
- Each abstraction base class will contain duplicate method names in the concrete data provider that must be overridden.

That's it for the database layer. The next chapter covers the business logic layer (BLL), in which you take the data from your database and create objects that you later bind to your user controls for display.

14

Developing Modules: The Business Logic Layer

The previous chapter covered how to create a physical database provider for your module, and how all the methods contained in the provider directly correlate to stored procedures within the database. After the provider was completed, you created an abstraction class that defines the methods contained in the provider that will be used by the Business Logic Layer (BLL).

In this chapter, you transform the `DataReader` returned from the database by the data provider into a collection of business objects provided by the Business Logic Layer within your module. This chapter continues with concepts that were introduced in Chapter 7, "DotNetNuke Architecture," because module architecture mirrors the architecture provided by DNN.

The idea is to separate totally the physical database from the module or application logic that you create. Separating the two enables plug-and-play extensibility when you or the user of your module wants to change the database provider. Because the provider is abstracted from the actual business logic, you can use the same code, but a different data store. Because they're separate assemblies, there is no need to rebuild the application to change the database provider.

You will now extend this provider architecture to the business logic of the application. Here you create a collection of objects with specific properties that will be exposed to your presentation layer, which is covered in Chapter 15, "Developing Modules: the Presentation Layer."

Developing the Business Logic Layer

Start by opening the sample WROX.Suggestion module project located in your DesktopModules folder off the root of the DotNetNuke 5 distribution package. Remember to run Visual Studio 2008 as Administrator in Vista to view and work with the module projects; specifically, the WROX.Suggestion and WROX.Suggestion.SqlDataProvider module projects you were working with in the previous chapter. Running VS 2008 as Administrator is required to use IIS.

As you'll recall, the DataProvider.vb class within the WROX.Suggestion project is the abstraction class, and it uses the `MustOverride` keyword for each method contained in the physical provider class. Now you take these abstract methods and wrap them with additional classes to populate an array of business objects with specific properties.

The files in the Business Logic Layer are located within the WROX.Suggestion project's Components folder. Here, you'll find pairs of files, an Info class and a Controller class, defined for each business object in your project. The Info class is the business object itself, consisting of a set of properties for the related data, namely each column in the database table. The Controller class contains the CRUD methods that call into the DataProvider.vb abstraction methods to create, retrieve, update, and delete data in the related tables, based on the data in the related Info class.

In a DotNetNuke module project, you'll typically define a separate business object for each major data element, or set of related data in the project. These data elements are used as a unit, for example, to access related data, or to bind to view controls on a web form. The Info class often contains data from a single database table, but you can also join data from multiple tables or transform fields if your business objects require it.

In the WROX.Suggestion project are four business object classes — `SuggestionInfo`, `SuggestionTypeInfo`, `SuggestionIdInfo`, and `SuggestionsDisplayInfo` — each having a corresponding Controller class. `SuggestionInfo` contains the fields related to a specific suggestion item, `SuggestionTypeInfo` contains the fields for a specific type (or category) of suggestion, `SuggestionIdInfo` is a special-purpose class that returns the IDs for suggestion items by module instance, and `SuggestionsDisplayInfo` contains the fields that are bound to a data grid in the `SuggestionsDisplay` module that shows a list of suggestions by module instance.

Defining Properties for the Info Classes

This section covers the `SuggestionInfo`, `SuggestionTypeInfo`, `SuggestionIdInfo`, and `SuggestionsDisplayInfo` classes contained in the project's Components folder. These classes make up the business objects for data that are going to or returned from the database in the WROX.Suggestion module.

SuggestionInfo Business Object

At the top of the `SuggestionInfo` class file are the `Imports` statements as shown in the following code:

```
Imports DotNetNuke.Entities.Modules     'for IHydratable
```

Next is the `Namespace` declaration, which is of the form `CompanyName.Modules.ModuleName`:

```
Namespace WROX.Modules.Suggestion
```

The following example shows the `Private Members` region at the top of the class. Here you define private variables and their types. These variables will be used to store the values in each property for your class. The `Implements IHydratable` declaration is covered later in the "Optional Interface for the Business Layer Info Classes" section.

```
    Public Class SuggestionInfo
        Implements IHydratable

#Region " Private Members "

        'class member declarations
        Private _SuggestionID As Integer
        Private _ModuleID As Integer
        Private _SuggestionTypeID As Integer
        Private _CreatedByUser As Integer
        Private _CreatedDate As Date
        Private _Title As String
        Private _Description As String
        Private _ModuleTitle As String

#End Region
```

Below the `Private Members` region is the `Constructors` region. In object-oriented programming, the constructor is a special method for a class that must be present for the object to be instantiated. In the WROX.Suggestion module with Visual Basic, the constructor method is `New`. If you need to write any initialization code for the `SuggestionInfo` class, you would do so here to ensure the code is executed when the class is created.

```
#Region " Constructors "

    Public Sub New()
    End Sub

#End Region
```

Next are the public properties of the `SuggestionInfo` class, which are used to define your business object. For example, a suggestion has a `SuggestionID`, `ModuleID`, `CreatedDate`, `Description`, and other properties. These correspond to the fields contained within the database for this module (see Chapter 13, "Developing Modules: the Database Layer").

```
#Region " Properties "

    Public Property SuggestionID() As Integer
        Get
            Return _SuggestionID
        End Get
        Set(ByVal Value As Integer)
            _SuggestionID = Value
        End Set
    End Property

    Public Property ModuleID() As Integer
        Get
            Return _ModuleID
        End Get
        Set(ByVal Value As Integer)
            _ModuleID = Value
        End Set
    End Property
```

```
        Public Property SuggestionTypeID() As Integer
            Get
                Return _SuggestionTypeID
            End Get
            Set(ByVal Value As Integer)
                _SuggestionTypeID = Value
            End Set
        End Property

        Public Property CreatedByUser() As Integer
            Get
                Return _CreatedByUser
            End Get
            Set(ByVal Value As Integer)
                _CreatedByUser = Value
            End Set
        End Property

        Public Property CreatedDate() As Date
            Get
                Return _CreatedDate
            End Get
            Set(ByVal Value As Date)
                _CreatedDate = Value
            End Set
        End Property

        Public Property Title() As String
            Get
                Return _Title
            End Get
            Set(ByVal Value As String)
                _Title = Value
            End Set
        End Property

        Public Property Description() As String
            Get
                Return _Description
            End Get
            Set(ByVal Value As String)
                _Description = Value
            End Set
        End Property

        Public Property ModuleTitle() As String
            Get
                Return _ModuleTitle
            End Get
            Set(ByVal Value As String)
                _ModuleTitle = Value
            End Set
        End Property

    #End Region
```

Notice that each property you expose for your object corresponds to a field name in the WROX_Suggestion table in the database except for `ModuleTitle`, which comes from the title field of the module displaying the suggestion item. The `ModuleTitle` property is used to display a drop-down list of modules available for viewing in the `SuggestionsDisplay` module.

This illustrates a useful practice — that of reusing an individual Info object for multiple purposes to avoid defining special-purpose business objects for each specific use. More is said on this subject shortly.

SuggestionTypeInfo Business Object

Each property exposed in the `SuggestionTypeInfo` object corresponds to a field name in the `WROX_SuggestionType` table in the database. At the top of the `SuggestionTypeInfo` class file are the `Imports` statements and the `Namespace` declaration:

```
Imports DotNetNuke.Entities.Modules    'for IHydratable

Namespace WROX.Modules.Suggestion
```

The following example shows the `Private Members` region at the top of the class. Here you define private variables and their types. These variables will be used to store the values for each property in the class.

```
Public Class SuggestionTypeInfo
      Implements IHydratable

#Region " Private Members "

    'class member declarations
    Private _SuggestionTypeID As Integer
    Private _ModuleID As Integer
    Private _SuggestionType As String

#End Region
```

Below the `Private Members` region is the `Constructors` region:

```
#Region " Constructors "

    Public Sub New()
    End Sub

#End Region
```

Next are the public properties of the `SuggestionTypeInfo` class, which define your business object:

```
#Region " Properties "

    Public Property SuggestionTypeID() As Integer
        Get
            Return _SuggestionTypeID
        End Get
        Set(ByVal Value As Integer)
            _SuggestionTypeID = Value
        End Set
```

```
        End Property

        Public Property ModuleID() As Integer
            Get
                Return _ModuleID
            End Get
            Set(ByVal Value As Integer)
                _ModuleID = Value
            End Set
        End Property

        Public Property SuggestionType() As String
            Get
                Return _SuggestionType
            End Get
            Set(ByVal Value As String)
                _SuggestionType = Value
            End Set
        End Property

    #End Region
```

SuggestionIdInfo Business Object

The `SuggestionIdInfo` business object is a special-purpose class used to retrieve `SuggestionID` values for all suggestions entered on a particular Suggestion module. `SuggestionIdInfo` is used in conjunction with the `GetSuggestion` method to return details of each suggestion item when the search index is constructed for a WROX.Suggestion module. This is discussed in more detail in the "`ISearchable` Interface" section later in the chapter.

At the top of the `SuggestionIdInfo` class file is the `Namespace` declaration, which looks similar to the `SuggestionInfo` class discussed earlier, except there is no `Implements IHydratable` declaration.

```
Namespace WROX.Modules.Suggestion
```

The following example shows the class declaration and the `Private Members` region at the top of the class. Here you define private variables and their types. These variables will be used to store the values for each property in the class.

```
    Public Class SuggestionIdInfo

    #Region " Private Members "

            'class member declarations
            Private _SuggestionID As Integer

    #End Region
```

Below the `Private Members` region is the `Constructors` region:

```
    #Region " Constructors "

        Public Sub New()
```

```
        End Sub

    #End Region
```

Next are the public properties of the `SuggestionIdInfo` class, which are used to define the object:

```
    #Region " Properties "

        Public Property SuggestionID() As Integer
            Get
                Return _SuggestionID
            End Get
            Set(ByVal Value As Integer)
                _SuggestionID = Value
            End Set
        End Property

    #End Region
```

SuggestionsDisplayInfo Business Object

The `SuggestionsDisplayInfo` business object is made up of fields retrieved from the WROX _Suggestion table in the database, and is used specifically for data binding to the data grid on the `SuggestionsDisplay` user control. It is similar to the `SuggestionInfo` class, but note that the `SuggestionInfo` class is not reused for this purpose because only the fields bound to the data grid are present in `SuggestionsDisplayInfo`.

At the top of the `SuggestionsDisplayInfo` class file is the `Namespace` and class declaration, which again has no `Implements IHydratable` declaration:

```
    Namespace WROX.Modules.Suggestion

    Public Class SuggestionsDisplayInfo
```

The following example shows the `Private Members` region at the top of the class. Here you define private variables and their types. These variables will be used to store the values for each property in the class.

```
    #Region " Private Members "

            'class member declarations
            Private _CreatedByUser As String
            Private _SuggestionType As String
            Private _CreatedDate As Date
            Private _Title As String
            Private _Description As String

    #End Region
```

Below the `Private Members` region is the `Constructors` region:

```
    #Region " Constructors "

        Public Sub New()
```

```
        End Sub

    #End Region
```

Next are the public properties of the `SuggestionsDisplayInfo` class, which are used to define your object:

```
    #Region " Properties "

        Public Property CreatedByUser() As String
            Get
                Return _CreatedByUser
            End Get
            Set(ByVal Value As String)
                _CreatedByUser = Value
            End Set
        End Property

        Public Property SuggestionType() As String
            Get
                Return _SuggestionType
            End Get
            Set(ByVal Value As String)
                _SuggestionType = Value
            End Set
        End Property

        Public Property CreatedDate() As Date
            Get
                Return _CreatedDate
            End Get
            Set(ByVal Value As Date)
                _CreatedDate = Value
            End Set
        End Property

        Public Property Title() As String
            Get
                Return _Title
            End Get
            Set(ByVal Value As String)
                _Title = Value
            End Set
        End Property

        Public Property Description() As String
            Get
                Return _Description
            End Get
            Set(ByVal Value As String)
                _Description = Value
            End Set
        End Property

    #End Region
```

Custom Business Object Helper Class

In the architecture discussion in Chapter 7, you learned about the Custom Business Object (CBO) helper class. CBO makes it very easy to write the code to hydrate (or fill) your Info classes from the underlying data store by writing a single line of code. Using the CBO comes at a steep price however, because .NET Reflection is used to match incoming database field names with the Info object properties to fill the properties automatically. This CBO class is located in the `DotNetNuke.Common.Utilities` namespace within DNN.

The CBO class provides several methods, but for this area of concern, you want to focus on two:

- `FillObject`: Creates an object with one item as in the case with the `GetSuggestion` method.
- `FillCollection`: Creates an `ArrayList` or generic `List(of T)` from matching records returned from the database.

Optional Interface for the Business Layer Info Classes

One of the major objectives in DotNetNuke v4.4 was optimization of portal performance by the DNN core team. At that time, the realization was made that the CBOs were one of the more expensive parts of the data architecture, in terms of how long it took to transfer data out of the database and into business objects via the CBOs using Reflection. Therefore, in DNN v4.6 was born the `IHydratable` interface.

IHydratable Interface

Implementing `Entities.Modules.IHydratable` in your business layer Info objects is optional. You write your CBO hydrator code in your Controller classes the same way as always. Under the covers, the CBO hydrator determines if you've provided an implementation for `IHydratable`. If you have, the hydrator will call your `IHydratable.Fill` method, in which you manually copy the data fields into your Info class properties. Because .NET Reflection calls are avoided by using `IHydratable` in the CBO classes, this can result in significant performance improvements. The amount of improvement you'll get depends on the number of fields in your Info objects, and the number of times the CBO hydrator gets called to copy the data.

The `IHydratable` interface is made up of a `Fill` method and a `KeyID` property. The `Fill` method is straightforward, because you simply copy the incoming data fields into your Info class properties. The `KeyID` property wraps the primary key field for the data being retrieved. An important restriction in using `IHydratable` is that your key must be an `Integer` value.

For efficient data caching, the CBO hydrator can use the method `FillDictionary(of T as IHydratable)` to store your data. This dictionary is a generic collection in which your data is stored by a key value. The `KeyID` is simply a known property name CBO uses to insert and retrieve your data in the dictionary.

The following example shows the `Fill` method and `KeyID` property for the `SuggestionInfo` class. Here, the data fields are transferred one at a time into their corresponding properties. Besides performance, there are two other key advantages to using `IHydratable` to transfer your data into the business objects. First, the database fields don't need to have the exact same names as the properties they go into, as the CBO requires. Second, you can perform transformations on the data as it moves between data layers using this technique.

```
#Region " IHydratable Implementation "
```

```
    Public Sub Fill(ByVal dr As IDataReader) Implements IHydratable.Fill
        Select Case dr.FieldCount
            Case 2      'ModuleID and ModuleTitle
                ModuleID = Convert.ToInt32(Null.SetNull(dr.Item("ModuleID"), _
                  ModuleID))
                ModuleTitle = Convert.ToString(Null.SetNull(dr.Item _
                  ("ModuleTitle"), ModuleTitle))
            Case Else   'all fields except ModuleTitle
                ModuleID = Convert.ToInt32(Null.SetNull(dr.Item("ModuleID"), _
                  ModuleID))
                SuggestionID = Convert.ToInt32(Null.SetNull(dr.Item _
                  ("SuggestionID"), SuggestionID))
                SuggestionTypeID = Convert.ToInt32(Null.SetNull(dr.Item _
                  ("SuggestionTypeID"), SuggestionTypeID))
                CreatedByUser = Convert.ToInt32(Null.SetNull(dr.Item _
                 ("CreatedByUser"), CreatedByUser))
                CreatedDate = Convert.ToDateTime(Null.SetNull(dr.Item _
                  ("CreatedDate"), CreatedDate))
                Title = Convert.ToString(Null.SetNull(dr.Item("Title"), Title))
                Description = Convert.ToString(Null.SetNull _
                  (dr.Item("Description"), Description))
        End Select
    End Sub

    Public Property KeyID() As Integer _
      Implements Entities.Modules.IHydratable.KeyID
        Get
            Return SuggestionID
        End Get
        Set(ByVal value As Integer)
            SuggestionID = value
        End Set
    End Property

#End Region
```

In the preceding `Fill` method, a `Select Case` statement splits the data copy task into two separate operations. This is because the `SuggestionInfo` class is used for two purposes — one to store all fields (except `ModuleTitle`) when working with suggestions in the database (using the `Add`, `Get`, and `UpdateSuggestions` methods in `SuggestionController`). This sharing technique is not required, and is illustrated here as an alternative to creating separate business objects and controllers for each unique use.

The other purpose is to retrieve just the `ModuleID` and `ModuleTitle` fields for use in populating the module selection drop-down on the `SuggestionsDisplay` module (using the `GetSuggestionModulesAllTabs` and `GetSuggestionModulesThisTab` methods). Also note that this object sharing can occur because the two data retrieval mechanisms share the same primary key value (`ModuleID`), and hence the same `IHydratable KeyID` property.

The following example shows the `IHydratable` implementation for the `SuggestionTypeInfo` class. Note in the `Fill` method that the `ModuleID` property is omitted because `ModuleID` is only used in the `Add` and `UpdateSuggestionType` methods that store `SuggestionType` values into the database, which don't use the CBO hydrator. The ModuleID field is not loaded in the GetSuggestionTypes method, so it's not needed here.

```
#Region " IHydratable Implementation "

    Public Sub Fill(ByVal dr As IDataReader) Implements IHydratable.Fill
        SuggestionTypeID = Convert.ToInt32(Null.SetNull(dr.Item _
          ("SuggestionTypeID"), SuggestionTypeID))
        SuggestionType = Convert.ToString(Null.SetNull(dr.Item("SuggestionType"), _
          SuggestionType))
    End Sub

    Public Property KeyID() As Integer _
      Implements Entities.Modules.IHydratable.KeyID
        Get
            Return SuggestionTypeID
        End Get
        Set(ByVal value As Integer)
            SuggestionTypeID = value
        End Set
    End Property

#End Region
```

Neither of the other two Info classes, SuggestionIdInfo or SuggestionsDisplayInfo, have IHydratable implementations in the WROX.Suggestions module. In the case of SuggestionIdInfo it's because there is only one property, and that's also the primary key field. For SuggestionsDisplayInfo, there is no Integer primary key in the class properties (the KeyID field requires one), so IHydratable cannot be used for this data. In both cases, the default CBO hydration using .NET Reflection loads the data fields. In SuggestionIdInfo, very little advantage is gained by manually loading a single field, so it doesn't matter. In SuggestionDisplayInfo, there's no Integer key present in the structure because these fields are bound to a grid for user display, so there's no choice about using IHydratable.

Creating Business Objects Using the Controller Classes

This section covers the SuggestionController, SuggestionTypeController, SuggestionIdController, and SuggestionsDisplayController classes contained in the project's Components folder. Controller classes are paired with the Info classes you looked at in the previous section, and each Controller calls into the DataProvider class to populate the business objects with data that is returned from the database in the WROX.Suggestion module.

There are two optional interfaces that you can implement in your controller classes: Entities.Modules.ISearchable and Entities.Modules.IPortable. The ISearchable interface provides your module with the capability to tie into the DNN search mechanism. The IPortable interface allows you to export data from your module and import it into another instance of your module, whether on the same portal or a different portal instance. Where and how you implement these interfaces is up to you, depending on the needs of your business objects. In the WROX.Suggestion module, only the SuggestionController class implements these interfaces. The ISearchable and IPortable interface implementations are covered in more detail later in this chapter.

SuggestionController Class

The `SuggestionController` class is responsible for loading data into the `SuggestionInfo` business object from the underlying data store. At the top of the file are the `Imports` statements needed by the controller:

```
Imports System.Xml    'for XmlWriter

Imports DotNetNuke.Services.Search    'for SearchItemInfo
```

Following this you specify your `Namespace`:

```
Namespace WROX.Modules.Suggestion
```

Next is the class declaration, where you declare any optional interfaces needed by your class. In this module, you implement the `Entities.Modules.ISearchable` and `Entities.Modules.IPortable` interfaces:

```
Public Class SuggestionController
    Implements Entities.Modules.ISearchable
    Implements Entities.Modules.IPortable
```

The following code shows the public methods within the Controller class that are used to populate the `SuggestionInfo` business object from the `DataReader` received from the `DataProvider` abstraction class:

```
#Region " Public Methods "

    Public Function AddSuggestion(ByVal Suggestion As SuggestionInfo) As Integer
        Return CType(DataProvider.Instance().AddSuggestion _
          (Suggestion.ModuleID, Suggestion.SuggestionTypeID, _
          Suggestion.CreatedByUser, Suggestion.Title, _
          Suggestion.Description), Integer)
    End Function

    Public Sub DeleteSuggestion(ByVal SuggestionID As Integer)
        DataProvider.Instance.DeleteSuggestion(SuggestionID)
    End Sub

    Public Function GetSuggestion(ByVal SuggestionID As Integer) _
      As SuggestionInfo
        Return CType(CBO.FillObject(DataProvider.Instance().GetSuggestion _
          (SuggestionID), GetType(SuggestionInfo)), SuggestionInfo)
    End Function

    Public Function GetSuggestionModulesAllTabs() As ArrayList
        Return CBO.FillCollection(DataProvider.Instance() _
          .GetSuggestionModulesAllTabs(), GetType(SuggestionInfo))
    End Function

    Public Function GetSuggestionModulesThisTab(ByVal TabID As Integer) _
      As ArrayList
        Return CBO.FillCollection(DataProvider.Instance() _
          .GetSuggestionModulesThisTab(TabID), GetType(SuggestionInfo))
```

```
        End Function

        Public Sub UpdateSuggestion(ByVal Suggestion As SuggestionInfo)
            DataProvider.Instance().UpdateSuggestion(Suggestion.SuggestionID, _
              Suggestion.SuggestionTypeID, Suggestion.CreatedByUser, _
              Suggestion.Title, Suggestion.Description)
        End Sub

    #End Region
```

Notice that each method corresponds to a method in the data abstraction class (DataProvider.vb). Each method creates an instance of the `DataProvider` class, and calls its corresponding abstraction method. Recall from Chapter 13 that each method in the abstraction class also has a corresponding method in the physical provider (the SqlDataProvider project) as a wrapper to the stored procedures contained in the SQL Server database.

Each controller method accepts values that correspond to parameters in the underlying stored procedure. For example, the `DeleteSuggestion` stored procedure contains a parameter of `SuggestionID` for specifying the primary key of the item contained in the WROX_Suggestion table that is to be deleted. As such, the `DeleteSuggestion` method in the Controller class accepts a `SuggestionID` of type `Integer`.

The `SuggestionInfo` object is used for multiple purposes by the `SuggestionController` class. All properties except `ModuleTitle` are used by the `Add`, `Get`, and `UpdateSuggestion` controller methods. Only the `ModuleID` and `ModuleTitle` properties are used by the `GetSuggestionModulesAllTabs` and `GetSuggestionModulesThisTab` methods. As mentioned earlier, doing this avoids the creation of special business objects when existing objects can be reused.

Be aware that when extra properties exist in the Info class passed to a controller method, the extra properties are ignored and result in a value of `Nothing`. You have to be aware of this fact and write your module code accordingly if you share Info objects between multiple uses. Do not reference the extra properties in your code, say to assign their values to some other variables, because you'll generate an exception trying to assign a value of `Nothing`.

SuggestionTypeController Class

The `SuggestionTypeController` class is responsible for loading data into the `SuggestionType` business object from the underlying data store. At the top of the file is the `Namespace` definition needed by the controller:

```
Namespace WROX.Modules.Suggestion
```

The class definition is next, and neither of the optional interface declarations, `ISearchable` or `IPortable`, is needed here. This is because there is no need to search SuggestionType items, and the SuggestionType data is exported and imported with the suggestion items themselves.

```
Public Class SuggestionTypeController
```

`SuggestionType` data is maintained in the `EditSuggestion` form, which you look at in the next chapter. You'll see how the `SuggestionTypeInfo` is exported and imported with the `IPortable` interface in the "Optional Interfaces for the SuggestionController Class" section later in this chapter.

The following example shows the public methods within the Controller class that are used to populate the `SuggestionTypeInfo` business object from the `DataReader` received from the abstraction class:

```
#Region " Public Methods "

    Public Function AddSuggestionType(ByVal SuggestionType As SuggestionTypeInfo) _
      As Integer
        Return CType(DataProvider.Instance().AddSuggestionType(SuggestionType _
          .ModuleID, SuggestionType.Type), Integer)
    End Function

    Public Sub DeleteSuggestionType(ByVal SuggestionTypeID As Integer, _
      ByVal ModuleID As Integer)
        DataProvider.Instance().DeleteSuggestionType(SuggestionTypeID, ModuleID)
    End Sub

    Public Function GetSuggestionTypes(ByVal ModuleID As Integer) As ArrayList
        Return CBO.FillCollection(DataProvider.Instance().GetSuggestionTypes _
          (ModuleID), GetType(SuggestionTypeInfo))
    End Function

    Public Sub UpdateSuggestionType(ByVal SuggestionType As SuggestionTypeInfo)
        DataProvider.Instance().UpdateSuggestionType(SuggestionType _
          .SuggestionTypeID, SuggestionType.ModuleID, SuggestionType.SuggestionType)
    End Sub

#End Region
```

Notice that each method corresponds to a method in the data abstraction class (DataProvider.vb). Each method creates an instance of the `DataProvider` class and calls its corresponding abstraction method, in this case, the ones related to retrieving `SuggestionTypeInfo` data.

SuggestionIdController Class

The `SuggestionIDController` class is responsible for loading data into the `SuggestionIDInfo` business object from the underlying data store. At the top of the file is the `Namespace` definition needed by the controller:

```
Namespace WROX.Modules.Suggestion
```

The class definition comes next; again notice that optional interfaces `ISearchable` and `IPortable` are not defined here. Because `SuggestionIdInfo` data is not searchable, and is only used to retrieve `SuggestionIDs` when the DNN Search Index is created, no additional import or export of this data is required.

```
Public Class SuggestionIdController
```

The following example shows the public methods within the Controller class that are used to populate the `SuggestionIdInfo` business object from the `DataReader` received from the abstraction class:

```
#Region " Public Methods "
```

```
        Public Function GetSuggestionIDs(ByVal ModuleID As Integer) As ArrayList
            Return CBO.FillCollection(DataProvider.Instance().GetSuggestionIDs _
              (ModuleID), GetType(SuggestionIdInfo))
        End Function

    #End Region
```

Notice that each method corresponds to a method in the Data Abstraction class (DataProvider.vb). Each method creates an instance of the `DataProvider` class and calls its corresponding method, in this case, the ones related to retrieving `SuggestionIdInfo` data.

SuggestionsDisplayController Class

The `SuggestionsDisplayController` class is responsible for loading data into the `SuggestionsDisplayInfo` business object from the underlying data store. At the top of the file is the `Namespace` definition needed by the controller:

```
    Namespace WROX.Modules.Suggestion
```

The class definition comes next, again notice the optional interfaces `ISearchable` and `IPortable` are not defined here. Because this module is simply displaying the suggestion data in another format, there is nothing new to search, and import and export of all suggestion data is handled in the `SuggestionController` class.

```
    Public Class SuggestionsDisplayController
```

The following example shows the public methods within the Controller class that are used to populate the `SuggestionsDisplayInfo` business object from the `DataReader` received from the abstraction class:

```
    #Region " Public Methods "

        Public Function GetSuggestions(ByVal ModuleID As Integer) As ArrayList
            Return CBO.FillCollection(DataProvider.Instance().GetSuggestions _
              (ModuleID), GetType(SuggestionsDisplayInfo))
        End Function

    #End Region
```

Notice that each method corresponds to a method in the data abstraction class (DataProvider.vb). Each method creates an instance of the `DataProvider` class, and calls its corresponding abstraction method, in this case, the ones related to retrieving `SuggestionsDisplayInfo` data.

Optional Interfaces for the SuggestionController Class

The last code region in the `SuggestionController` class is `Optional Interfaces`. Contained in this region are methods for implementing the `ISearchable` and `IPortable` interfaces provided by DotNetNuke. You do not have to use these methods, but it is recommended to provide a fully functional module that is capable of exposing all the features of DNN.

ISearchable Interface

Implementing the DNN `ISearchable` interface in your module is optional, but doing so allows your module to contribute its own search index data, and participate in portal-wide full-text searching. Implementing the `ISearchable` interface in your module only requires that you provide a method named `GetSearchItems`, which returns a `SearchItemInfoCollection`. How you supply search index data to DNN is up to you. Typically this is dependent upon the functionality of your module, and also upon what kind of data your module stores.

The DNN search indexer runs on a schedule, or the Host user can request a re-index of the portal by clicking the Re-index Content link on the Host ➪ Search Admin page. When re-indexing content, the search indexer calls the `GetSearchItems` method on each module in the portal that supports the `ISearchable` interface. It then uses the returned `SearchItemInfoCollection` to populate the portal search index. You can learn more about the ISearchable interface in Chapter 8, "Core DotNetNuke APIs."

The method in the following example from the `SuggestionController` class defines properties from the individual suggestion items from your module to be placed in the catalog of the DotNetNuke search index:

```
Public Function GetSearchItems(ByVal ModInfo As Entities.Modules.ModuleInfo) _
  As DotNetNuke.Services.Search.SearchItemInfoCollection _
  Implements Entities.Modules.ISearchable.GetSearchItems
    Dim SearchItem As SearchItemInfo
    Dim SearchItemCollection As New SearchItemInfoCollection
    Dim sc As New SuggestionController
    Dim sic As New SuggestionIdController
    Dim SuggestionIDs As ArrayList = sic.GetSuggestionIDs(ModInfo.ModuleID)

    For Each sii As SuggestionIdInfo In SuggestionIDs
        Dim suggestion As SuggestionInfo = sc.GetSuggestion(sii.SuggestionID)

        With suggestion
            SearchItem = New SearchItemInfo(ModInfo.ModuleTitle & " - " _
              & .Title, .Description, .CreatedByUser, .CreatedDate, _
              ModInfo.ModuleID, .SuggestionID.ToString, .Description, _
              "SuggestionId=" & .SuggestionID.ToString)
            SearchItemCollection.Add(SearchItem)
        End With
    Next

    Return SearchItemCollection
End Function
```

The `GetSearchItems` method shown here reads through the suggestion items in its module instance, and returns a `SearchItemInfoCollection` that the DNN search provider uses to populate the portal search index. You first call the special-purpose `GetSuggestionIDs` method to return the ID of each suggestion item in the module instance. Then you loop through the `SuggestionIDs` returned and call the `GetSuggestion` method on each ID to return its suggestion data, and create a new `SearchItemInfo` object for each one. Finally, each `SearchItemInfo` object is added to the `SearchItemCollection` that's returned to the DNN search indexer.

A number of parameters are passed to the `SearchItemInfo` constructor for each suggestion data item that's found. The parameters and what is passed in for Suggestion items are listed here:

- `Title` — Made up of the title of the suggestion module, a hyphen, and the title of the suggestion.
- `Description` — The body of the suggestion item.
- `Author` — UserID of the portal user who created the suggestion item.
- `PubDate` — The date the suggestion item was created.
- `ModuleID` — The ID of the suggestion module this suggestion item came from.
- `SearchKey` — The suggestion item ID value from the suggestion table.
- `Content` — The body of the suggestion item. Note this same info is put into the `Description` field.
- `Guid` — A unique identifier for the item in the portal search index, made up of the string "`SearchID="` with the suggestion item ID from the suggestion table.

The process is done this way because the `SuggestionID` values for each suggestion item are needed by the `SearchItemInfo` object so that items returned from a search can link back to their matching suggestion items in the database, each by its `SuggestionID`. If you do not want to make your module items searchable in the portal, do not implement the interface and exclude the `GetSearchItems` function.

IPortable Interface

The WROX.Suggestion module also implements the optional DotNetNuke `IPortable` interface. This interface provides your module with the capability to export the data contained in a module instance to an XML file. Your module also has the capability of importing the XML file so that you can populate another module instance with the same data, whether the importing module instance is on the same portal or a completely different portal. You can learn more about the IPortable interface in Chapter 8.

The ability to export and import data from modules is useful for a number of reasons. It lets you make a backup of data contained in a module. You can move the module instance from one page to another page, or even to a page on a different site. For example, you may want to develop the content of a module on a staging portal, and move the new content to a module on a production portal once you're satisfied with the staging results. The Export Portal function found on the Host ➪ Portals page also uses the module Export function for each module on the portal that supports the `IPortable` interface.

The following example from the `SuggestionController` class looks at how you export data from a module instance when the Export menu item is selected on the module:

```
Public Function ExportModule(ByVal ModuleID As Integer) As String _
  Implements Entities.Modules.IPortable.ExportModule
    Dim strXML As New StringBuilder()
    Dim settings As New XmlWriterSettings()
    settings.Indent = True
    settings.OmitXmlDeclaration = True
    settings.ConformanceLevel = ConformanceLevel.Fragment
    Dim Writer As XmlWriter = XmlWriter.Create(strXML, settings)
    'write the root XML element
    Writer.WriteStartElement("suggestiondata")
    'list the SuggestionTypes this module uses (only the names)
    Dim stc As New SuggestionTypeController
    Dim arrTypes As ArrayList = stc.GetSuggestionTypes(ModuleID)
    If arrTypes.Count > 0 Then
```

```
                Writer.WriteStartElement("suggestiontypes")
                Dim objType As SuggestionTypeInfo
                For Each objType In arrTypes
                    Writer.WriteElementString("suggestiontype", objType.SuggestionType)
                Next
                Writer.WriteEndElement()    '</suggestiontypes>
            End If
            'save a list of the Suggestion entries.
            Dim sdc As New SuggestionsDisplayController
            Dim arrSuggestions As ArrayList = sdc.GetSuggestions(ModuleID)
            If arrSuggestions.Count > 0 Then
                Writer.WriteStartElement("suggestions")
                Dim objSuggestion As SuggestionsDisplayInfo
                For Each objSuggestion In arrSuggestions
                    Writer.WriteStartElement("suggestion")
                    Writer.WriteElementString("title", objSuggestion.Title)
                    Writer.WriteElementString("description", objSuggestion.Description)
                    Writer.WriteElementString("suggestiontype", _
                      objSuggestion.SuggestionType)
                    Writer.WriteElementString("createddate", objSuggestion.CreatedDate)
                    Writer.WriteElementString("createdbyuser", _
                      objSuggestion.CreatedByUser)
                    Writer.WriteEndElement()    '</suggestion>
                Next
                Writer.WriteEndElement()    '</suggestions>
            End If
            Writer.WriteEndElement()    '</suggestiondata>
            Writer.Close()
            Return strXML.ToString
        End Function
```

The `ExportModule` method shown here uses an `XmlWriter` object to create the export file because it can easily generate formatted XML, and its process flow is easy to follow. The `XmlWriter` constructor takes a `StringBuilder` variable and an `XmlWriterSettings` object. The `StringBuilder` provides an efficient mechanism for building up a long string value, such as the content of an XML file. The `XmlWriterSettings` lets you control the output format of the generated XML data. `XmlWriter` works by creating the opening and closing tags for an element using the `WriteStartElement` and `WriteEndElement` methods. For individual elements containing a single string value, the `WriteElementString` method writes out the whole element including the start tag, string content, and the end tag.

In this case, two sets of data are saved by the `ExportModule` function: the list of types that suggestion items can be assigned to, and the suggestions items themselves. You call the `GetSuggestionTypes` method to obtain the suggestion type values, and the `GetSuggestions` method to obtain all suggestions for this particular instance of the module. You then loop through the results using an `XmlWriter` to generate formatted XML output in a format specific to your module. The complete XML output describing the suggestion types and items from your module instance is returned as a string by the method.

The following example shows an XML file resulting from the export of a WROX.Suggestion module that has two type values defined, and two suggestion items:

```
<?xml version="1.0" encoding="utf-8" ?>
<content type="WROXSuggestion" version="2.0.0"><suggestiondata>
  <suggestiontypes>
```

```
    <suggestiontype>Build</suggestiontype>
    <suggestiontype>Buy</suggestiontype>
  </suggestiontypes>
  <suggestions>
    <suggestion>
      <title>Events Planning</title>
      <description>We need an Events Planning module.</description>
      <suggestiontype>Build</suggestiontype>
      <createddate>12/8/2008 12:02:33 PM</createddate>
      <createdbyuser>Stan Schultes</createdbyuser>
    </suggestion>
    <suggestion>
      <title>eCommerce</title>
      <description>We should buy an eCommerce module.</description>
      <suggestiontype>Buy</suggestiontype>
      <createddate>12/8/2008 12:04:15 PM</createddate>
      <createdbyuser>Stan Schultes</createdbyuser>
    </suggestion>
  </suggestions>
</suggestiondata></content>
```

In this example, the first line is the XML definition line. The `content` element is provided by DNN as a wrapper element for your data. The root element written by the `ExportModule` method is `suggestiondata`, which in turn contains `suggestiontypes` and `suggestions` elements. Within the `suggestiontypes` element is a list of `suggestiontype` elements, one for each suggestion type defined by this module instance. Finally, within the `suggestions` element is the list of suggestion items, each with a title field, description, and so on.

The following `ImportModule` example from the `SuggestionController` class shows how you import module data from the previously generated XML output:

```
Public Sub ImportModule(ByVal ModuleID As Integer, ByVal Content As String, _
  ByVal Version As String, ByVal UserId As Integer) _
  Implements Entities.Modules.IPortable.ImportModule
    Dim xmlType As XmlNode
    Dim xmlData As XmlNode = GetContent(Content, "suggestiondata")
    Dim xmlTypes As XmlNode = xmlData.FirstChild()  'suggestiontypes
    Dim stc As New SuggestionTypeController
    Dim iTypeID As Integer
    Dim htTypes As New Hashtable
    For Each xmlType In xmlTypes.SelectNodes("suggestiontype")
        Dim objType As New SuggestionTypeInfo
        objType.ModuleID = ModuleID
        objType.SuggestionType = xmlType.InnerText
        iTypeID = stc.AddSuggestionType(objType)
        'store returned SuggestionTypeID in Hashtable by name
        htTypes.Add(objType.Type, iTypeID)
    Next

    Dim xmlSuggestion As XmlNode
    For Each xmlSuggestion In xmlData.SelectNodes("suggestions/suggestion")
        Dim objSuggestion As New SuggestionInfo
        objSuggestion.ModuleID = ModuleID
        objSuggestion.Title = xmlSuggestion.Item("title").InnerText
```

```
            objSuggestion.Description = xmlSuggestion.Item("description").InnerText
            'obtain SuggestionTypeID from Hashtable by name
            If htTypes.ContainsKey(xmlSuggestion.Item("suggestiontype") _
              .InnerText) Then
                objSuggestion.SuggestionTypeID = htTypes(xmlSuggestion.Item _
                  ("suggestiontype").InnerText)
            Else
                'use default type if not found
                objSuggestion.SuggestionTypeID = htTypes("General")
            End If
            'gets the importing User's ID
            objSuggestion.CreatedByUser = UserId
            AddSuggestion(objSuggestion)
        Next

    End Sub
```

As you can see, the XML generated by the `ExportModule` method in the previous example is processed by the `ImportModule` method. For each `SuggestionType` found, you call the `AddSuggestionType` method of the `SuggestionTypeController`. This populates the suggestion type in the database for the current module instance for each type element in the XML file. You also save the type in a `Hashtable` by type name so each can be associated with suggestion items in the second loop.

For each suggestion item found in the XML file, you call the `AddSuggestion` method of the `SuggestionController` class to populate the suggestion items in the database for the current module instance. Note that the `UserID` assigned to each item is the user who is running the import, because there is no way of knowing if the user who submitted the suggestion exists on the portal where the data is imported. This is simply a shortcut in the sample code. In a production module, you could check for existence of the user by username in the database, and store the actual `UserID` if that user is found to exist.

Implementing optional interfaces should sound very familiar after getting to this point in the book, because module development closely mirrors the architecture of DotNetNuke. Not only does the core application support abstraction classes and the Provider Model extensively, but you should also duplicate this methodology in your own development. This ensures your development is consistent with other modules contained in DNN and also eases the task of upgrading to future versions of the portal.

Summary

This chapter completes a description of the process of obtaining data from your database. In Chapter 13, you learned how to write a provider for a physical database. In this chapter, you learned the following:

- You converted the data to collections of business objects that are either used in your module logic or get bound to user controls in your modules.
- In building the Business Logic Layer for your modules, you can take advantage of three interfaces provided by the DotNetNuke core code:
    - `IHydratable` — Provides your modules with the capability to use custom logic to hydrate your business objects from the database through the Custom Business Object (CBO), avoiding the overhead of .NET Reflection. In the `IHydratable.Fill` method, you can also

perform field mapping and data transformation tasks that the standard CBO object doesn't allow.

- `ISearchable` — Enables your modules to take advantage of the full-text indexing capabilities native to DotNetNuke, and allows your module to be included in the portal search mechanism.
- `IPortable` — Provides your modules with the capability to export the data and settings of one module instance over to another module instance within your portal, or to another portal altogether.

Next, Chapter 15 covers the user interface of the module. Here you'll take the collections of business objects created by the Business Logic Layer and bind them to controls on your module's web forms so that your module's users can add suggestion items, types, and display entered suggestion values.

15

Developing Modules: The Presentation Layer

In previous chapters, you have learned how to pull data from the database via an abstraction layer, and how to transform the data to a collection of business objects from your Controller classes. Now you're at a point where you can create the presentation layer for your custom module. This chapter provides you with an overview of how to display, modify, and work with the various user controls that make up your custom module in DotNetNuke (DNN).

The examples in this chapter show you how to define the set of user controls that your module's users will interact with while using your module. First, you see how to create the View controls that handle display of suggestion data, then how to create a Settings control to define settings that are specific to the module instance, and finally an Edit control that lets your users enter suggestions items in your module.

From there, the chapter moves on to the various built-in user controls and interfaces that you can use to your advantage in your module development.

Module User Controls

Chapter 12, ''Beginning Module Development,'' introduced you to the structure of a custom module, and explained how to manually create references to user controls to define your module. Each module consists of several user controls that enable the user to interface with your application logic. These user controls provide a means to view and modify the data contained in the database supporting the module. DotNetNuke provides you with the ability to define these controls and register them in the DNN portal using a module definition.

Table 15-1 lists the files that make up an example module, their keys (see Chapter 12), and their functions. The examples in this chapter continue with the WROX.Suggestion module shown in previous chapters.

Table 15-1: Module Definitions for the WROX.Suggestion Module

Type	Filename	Key	Description
`View`	DesktopModules\WROX.Suggestion\Suggestion.ascx		The main View control, which in this case simply displays instructions to the user for entering suggestion items, and a thank you message after an item is entered.
`View`	DesktopModules\WROX.Suggestion\DisplaySuggestions.ascx		The secondary View control, which in this case displays a list of suggestion items. Permission to view this module is normally set so that only authorized users can view suggestions entered by users.
`Edit`	DesktopModules\WROX.Suggestion\EditSuggestion.ascx	Edit	Used to add suggestion items. A module can implement several Edit controls based on the complexity of the module. Security for edit permissions is normally set at the module level.
`Settings`	DesktopModules\WROX.Suggestion\Settings.ascx	Settings	Used to enter module-specific settings. In this module, a user with Edit permission can add suggestion types, and change the user instructions and thank you message.

As you can see from this table, several controls are involved in the implementation of the WROX.Suggestion module. For module development, there may be data that you want to allow only certain users to access through portal roles. For example, if the module manipulates the application settings or file system, you would want to restrict that functionality to the host who has control over the overall application instance. Your module may also modify settings configured at a portal level, like the banner ad management system, in which case you could restrict the control to just administrators within a portal. See Chapter 9, ''Member Role,'' for more information on using roles within your DNN portal.

You can use many different control configurations when doing module development, depending on the needs of your module. For now, the focus is to continue with the WROX.Suggestion module covered in the previous two chapters as an example of how you can configure the user controls in your own module development work.

The preceding table covered the controls specific to the WROX.Suggestion module. This module consists of four primary user controls for displaying and manipulating data:

- **View (DesktopModules\WROX.Suggestion\Suggestion.ascx):** Used to provide instructions to the user for entering suggestion items.

- **View (DesktopModules\WROX.Suggestion\DisplaySuggestions.ascx):** Used to view the suggestions entered by users. A drop-down list of Suggestion modules on the current page is displayed to users with Edit permission on the module, and a data grid shows all suggestions from the module selected in the drop-down list. For the portal Admin, the drop-down list shows all Suggestion modules in the portal, and the data grid again shows all suggestions from the module selected in the drop-down list.
- **Settings (DesktopModules\WROX.Suggestion\Settings.ascx):** Used to configure module-specific settings like suggestion types, and strings for instructions and a thank you message that's displayed after a user enters a suggestion item.
- **Edit (DesktopModules\WROX.Suggestion\EditSuggestion.ascx):** Used to add suggestion items to the database.

The next few sections describe each user control definition, the styles and localization resources associated with the control, and the code that edits or displays data from the collections that were defined in the Business Logic Layer covered in Chapter 14, ''Developing Modules: the Business Logic Layer.''

View Control

In the WROX.Suggestion module, there are two View controls — a default Suggestions view, and the DisplaySuggestions view for listing user-entered suggestions (covered in the next section). The default View control is located in the DesktopModules\WROX.Suggestion directory and is named Suggestion.ascx. Open the WROX.Suggestion project and open the user interface designer to see the controls it contains (see Figure 15-1).

Within this user control are two primary controls, both ASP.NET labels. The `lblInstructions` label provides the users with instructions for entering suggestion items. The `lblThankYou` label is shown to the users after they enter a suggestion item. Visibility of the thank you label is controlled with an ASP.NET Session variable, as you'll see later. Listing 15-1 reviews the layout of the Suggestion.ascx file.

Listing 15-1: Suggestion.ascx User Control

```
<%@ Control language="vb" Inherits="WROX.Modules.Suggestion.Suggestion"
CodeBehind="Suggestion.ascx.vb" AutoEventWireup="false" Explicit="True" %>
<table cellspacing="0" cellpadding="4" border="0">
  <tr>
    <td>
      <asp:label id="lblInstructions" resourcekey="lblInstructions" runat="server"
CssClass="Normal">Please click the pencil icon below and choose the Add Suggestion
item to give your opinion (you must be logged into the portal to make
suggestions).</asp:label>
    </td>
  </tr>
  <tr>
    <td>
      <asp:label id="lblThankYou" resourcekey="lblThankYou" Runat="server"
CssClass="Normal" visible="False">Thank you for your suggestion!</asp:label>
    </td>
  </tr>
</table>
```

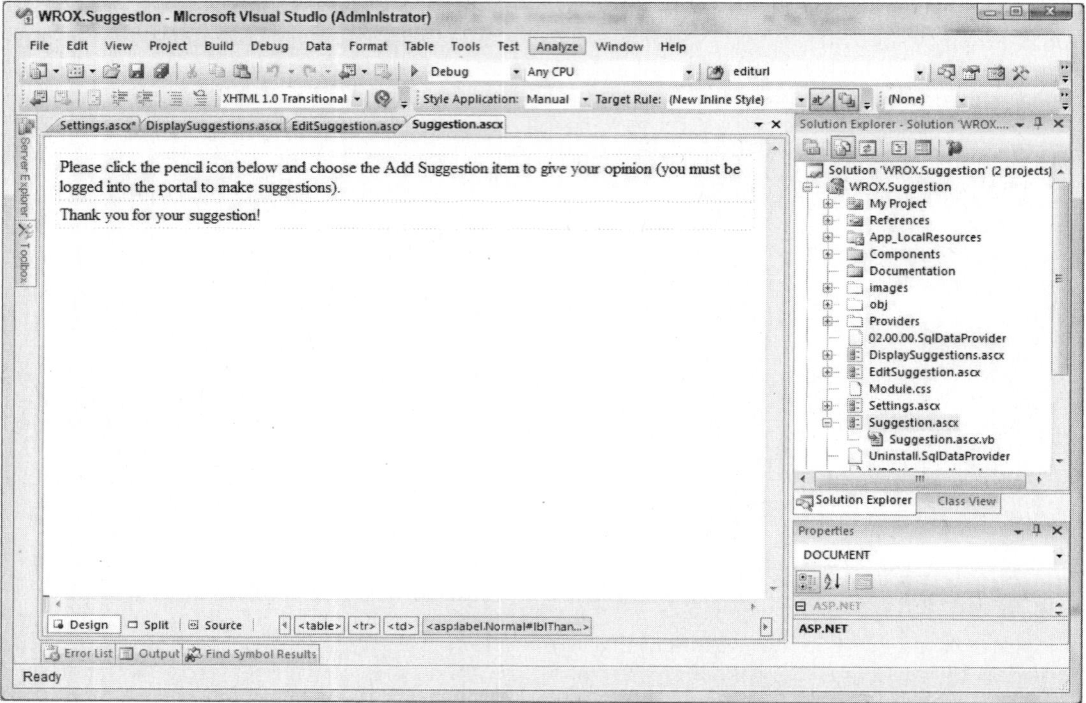

Figure 15-1

The strings displayed in both labels can be customized by a user with Edit permission on the module (on the module settings page). If the label strings are customized by the user, they're stored in module settings. Otherwise, the default localized values come from the local resource file, as you see later in the "Module Localization and Resource Files" section.

CSS Styling within User Controls

Setting the CSS style of controls on a form allows the visual display of the controls to change by simply updating the style's definition in a `.css` file, and not by changing the code within the user control itself. Therefore, changing a style is easily done by a portal host or admin user without involving a programmer.

In Listing 15-1, notice the CSS attributes listed in each `asp:label` control, where they're declared as `CssClass="Normal"`. You will likely use several common CSS class definitions within DNN on the user controls making up your modules:

- `Normal` — Use this style for general text displayed in your user controls.
- `SubHead` — Use this style as section heads or paragraph and label titles on forms.
- `Head` — Use this style as the equivalent of an `<h1>` HTML tag for main headers.
- `CommandButton` — Use this style for links and linkbutton controls.

The DNN label control is an exception because it doesn't allow you to specify a style class directly in the markup. In this case, you must apply the class definition to the enclosing or parent element as shown in the following code snippet, where the <td> element has the style definition:

```
<td class="SubHead">
  <dnn:label id="dlSuggestionTypes" resourcekey="dlSuggestionTypes"
text="Suggestion Types:" controlname="cboTypesOption" runat="server" />
</td>
```

Note that if you're using tables, DataGrids, GridViews, or DataLists, you should add the `class` attribute to the <table> element containing the control to keep the control from picking up extraneous styles. This holds true even if you have a <span> or <div> tag around your table with the `Normal` or `SubHead` class assigned to it.

Using the common class styles in the preceding bulleted list (and a host of others that weren't listed) allows you to redefine the look of an entire site very easily by changing the definitions within a variety of `.css` files in your portal directories. Here is the hierarchy of CSS style files, with the weakest on the top (in other words, a style found in a file closer to the bottom of the list overrides styles in files above it):

- (Modules)/DesktopModules/WROX.Suggestion/module.css
- (Default)/Portals/_default/default.css
- (Skins)/Portals/_default/Skins/MinimalExtropy/skin.css
- (Containers)/Portals/_default/Containers/MinimalExtropy/container.css
- (Containers)/Portals/_default/Containers/MinimalExtropy/title_grey.css
- (Portal)/Portals/0/portal.css

If you define styles for your module, you should include them in the module.css file in your module folder, to make it easier for designers to find your custom styles. You should define your own styles only if there isn't a related style in the file hierarchy, and only for specific items that need to have their look changed at design time.

Module Localization and Resource Files

As you can see in Listing 15-1, English text strings are provided as the default values for the label controls. This works fine as long as your module is used only on English-language sites. Though portal admins on a non–English-language site could edit the `.ascx` files to provide their own language translation, doing so would support only their default language. DotNetNuke, via ASP.NET, uses resource files as a way of localizing your module so it can support a variety of languages by default.

Each user control in a module has at least one associated resource file. Each resource file contains a set of name-value pairs where the name is tied (by naming convention) as a key to controls in your `.ascx` file and the value is the localized string for that key name and the language of the file. The default Suggestion.ascx resource file is located in `<approot>\DesktopModules\WROX.Suggestion\App_LocalResources\` and is named Suggestion.ascx.resx.

Portal admins can support additional languages in your module by putting additional resource files in your module's `App.LocalResources` directory. For example, a file named Suggestion.ascx.de-DE.resx supports the German language in Germany. If the portal admin switches the portal language to German, or the portal user sets German as his preferred language in his profile, this resource file will be used to look up the strings for your module instead of the default file. See Chapter 11, ''Localization,'' for more details of how resource files enable support of multiple languages.

View Control Resources

Listing 15-2 shows the string content of the Suggestion.ascx.resx file as name-value pairs. This file provides the default language strings by name for each control displayed on your user control's form. In a site with alternate language resource files, any named tag not specified in a language-specific resource file will display the default language string from the following file. For example, if there was a Suggestion.ascs.de-DE.resx file in the `\App_LocalResources` folder, but it was missing the German language translation for the `AddContent.Action` key, the string value `"Add Suggestion"` would be obtained from the default string file, as shown in the listing.

Listing 15-2: Suggestion.ascx.resx Resource File

```
<data name="AddContent.Action" xml:space="preserve">
  <value>Add Suggestion</value>
</data>
<data name="lblInstructions.Text" xml:space="preserve">
  <value>Please click the pencil icon below and choose the Add Suggestion item to
give your opinion (you must be logged into the portal to make suggestions).</value>
</data>
<data name="lblThankYou.Text" xml:space="preserve">
  <value>Thank you for your suggestion!</value>
</data>
<data name="ModuleHelp.Text" xml:space="preserve">
  <value>&lt;h1&gt;WROX.Suggestions Module&lt;/h1&gt;&lt;p&gt;The Suggestion module
allows users to enter suggestions and Admins to view suggestions. Page Admins see
Suggestions modules listed in a SuggestionsDisplay module on the current page. Site
Admins see Suggestions listed for all pages in a SuggestionsDisplay
module.&lt;/p&gt;

&lt;p&gt;When you add a Suggestions module to a page (as an admin for that page),
you'll normally set the View Module permission to All Users and the Edit Module
permission to Registered Users. This allows all users to see the module, but only
those users who are logged in to add suggestions. You can allow anonymous users to
add suggestions by setting the Edit Module permission to All Users.&lt;/p&gt;

&lt;p&gt;Selecting module Settings from the edit menu (the pencil icon) lets you
add Suggestion Types. Suggestion Types are unique to each Suggestion Module, and
the user can select the type from a dropdown list when they're entering
suggestions.&lt;/p&gt;

&lt;p&gt;On module Settings, you can also change the Instructions and ThankYou text
by Suggestion Module. These strings are text displayed in the body of the
Suggestion module. Instructions are displayed before entering a suggestion, and
ThankYou text is displayed after a user enters a suggestion.&lt;/p&gt;</value>
</data>
```

The first name-value pair in Listing 15-2 is `AddContent.Action` with the value `"Add Suggestion"`. The part of the name after the dot is the called the tag, and in this case, associates the value with the `ModuleActionType.AddContent` menu setup that you see later in Listing 15-3. The menu resources use a special pairing of the action type (AddContent) with an Action tag, rather than the web control name with the property name as the tag as you'll see for most other resource names.

The next two names, lblInstructions.Text and lblThankYou.Text, both have tags of Text, indicating that they're bound to the Text properties of the two label controls. Earlier, in Listing 15-1, you saw how the label controls in the Suggestion.ascx file had resourcekey="lblInstruction" and resourcekey="lblThankYou", respectively; these attributes create the association between each of the label controls' Text property and the resource string in the Suggestion.ascx.resx file.

The last name-value pair in Listing 15-2 is ModuleHelp.Text with a long encoded HTML string as the value. This special-purpose tag associates itself with the Help control on the module itself, as the text of the module's drop-down Help menu item. Users who have edit permission on the module see this drop-down menu next to the module name on the default skins, and can find on that menu the Edit, Import, Export, Move, Help, and other optional commands that you associate with the module. Note that the location of the drop-down menu is dependent on how the skin designer positioned the module elements. The menu skin token can actually be loaded anywhere within the module container.

As you create resource associations between your controls with the resource name-value pairs, you also need to be aware of which strings are global to the portal (for example, "Submit" and "Cancel"), and which are local to your module. In addition to the module-specific resource files you create in App.LocalResources, Application and Global resource files are also available that you should use to share common strings across modules in the portal. In this way, a portal admin has to make a minimum number of changes to resource files to support additional languages. See Chapter 11 for more details of how the name-value pairs are associated by tag between your resource files and the individual controls in your module .ascx files, and also the concepts of local, application, and global resources.

View Control Code-Behind Class

Now that you have your controls on the form and have them declared with styles and localization tags, you need some code in your control to pull the parts together. Often in your View control you need to bind module-specific data to your controls for display. In the case of the WROX.Suggestion module, the default View control is very simple, because it only provides some instruction for the user on how to enter a suggestion, and displays a thank you message once the suggestion is entered.

At the top of your class in the Suggestion.ascx.vb file, you first need to import references, declare your namespace, and define your class:

```
Imports System.Web.UI.WebControls          'for Label
Imports DotNetNuke.Services.Localization   'for Localization
Imports DotNetNuke.Services.Exceptions     'for ProcessModuleLoadException

Namespace WROX.Modules.Suggestion

    Public MustInherit Class Suggestion
        Inherits Entities.Modules.PortalModuleBase
```

PortalModuleBase Class

In custom module development, your user controls always inherit from the Entities.Modules .PortalModuleBase class. The PortalModuleBase class file is located in the DotNetNuke.Library project in the <sourcedir>\Library\Entities\Modules\PortalModuleBase.vb file. In addition to inheriting from the UserControlBase class, which in turn inherits from the UserControl class of ASP.NET, this class is central to your module development efforts. It provides several important methods and properties for your module (see Table 15-2).

DotNetNuke Optional Interfaces

Right below your class declaration, you have the option to implement the IActionable interface:

```
Implements Entities.Modules.IActionable
```

This interface provides you with the ability to tie into the Menu control for your module. As covered previously in this book, each module contains a menu with a list of action items. To add items to the menus you need to implement the IActionable interface. See Chapter 8, "Core DotNetNuke APIs," and Chapter 14 for more information on this interface and how to use it in your modules.

As previously mentioned, the IActionable interface is optional, but if you don't implement it, you won't be able to expose menu items for your module. At the bottom of the Suggestion.ascx.vb class file, you'll find the Optional Interfaces code region. Within this region is the code showing you how to implement IActionable (see Listing 15-3) for this module via the ModuleActions property.

Listing 15-3: Optional Interfaces Region of the WROX.Suggestion Module

```
#Region " Optional Interfaces "
    Public ReadOnly Property ModuleActions() As _
      Entities.Modules.Actions.ModuleActionCollection _
      Implements Entities.Modules.IActionable.ModuleActions
        Get
            Dim Actions As New Entities.Modules.Actions.ModuleActionCollection
            Actions.Add(GetNextActionID, Localization.GetString _
              (Entities.Modules.Actions.ModuleActionType.AddContent, _
              LocalResourceFile), Entities.Modules.Actions.ModuleActionType. _
              AddContent, "", "", EditUrl(), False, DotNetNuke.Security. _
              SecurityAccessLevel.Edit, True, False)
            Return Actions
        End Get
    End Property
#End Region
```

In Listing 15-3, the ModuleActions property implements the IActionable interface to add items into the menu for the module. The menu is made up of a collection of menu items, each with an accompanying action. As in this example, you add a single menu item using the Actions.Add method. You can see that instead of passing a hard-coded string value for the menu listing, you're providing a localized string with the Localization.GetString method. By using the localization interface provided by DotNetNuke (see Chapters 8 and 11), you will have menu items displayed in the language of the current user's profile. Because the AddContent action controls editing of module items, you pass EditURL as the action property for this item. This will load your Edit control when the user selects the Add Content option from the module menu.

Table 15-2: PortalModuleBase Class — Exposed Methods and Properties

Property	Type	Description

`IsEditable`	Boolean	Can be used as a reference to check and see if the current user has permissions to edit the module. For example:
		`If IsEditable Then`
		`    txtEditField.Visible = True`
		`End If`

`LocalResourceFile`	String	Contains the path to the resource file that is being used for the module, which enables you to support localization for your modules. This is covered in more detail in Chapter 11.
`HelpURL`	String	Contains the value for a help URL to an external help file for your module.
`ModuleConfiguration`	ModuleInfo	Provides information about your module instance, such as `ModuleID`, `TabID` (the page your module is on), and `Permissions`.
`PortalId`	Integer	ID of the portal that the current web request is for. This is generated by DotNetNuke when the Host user creates the portal.
`TabId`	Integer	ID of the page that the current web request is going to. This is generated by DotNetNuke when an Admin user creates a new page within the portal.
`TabModuleId`	Integer	Contains the index value of your module within a page (tab). Multiple instances of a module can point to the same `ModuleID`, allowing each to point to the same data. This allows you to display the same content within multiple modules in a portal.
`ModuleId`	Integer	Returns the ID of the current module instance. This is generated by DotNetNuke when a user with proper permissions adds a new instance of a module into a page.
`UserId`	Integer	Returns the ID of the user that is currently logged on.
`UserInfo`	UserInfo	Contains information for all portal users that are logged on. These fields include the `UserID`, `Roles`, and a link to the user's `Profile`.
`PortalAlias`	PortalAliasInfo	Each portal in a DNN installation has the capability of answering to one or more unique web URLs. This is a key feature of DotNetNuke, and through `PortalAlias`, exposes a list of all the `HTTPAlias` values assigned to the current portal instance.

Continued

Table 15-2: PortalModuleBase Class — Exposed Methods and Properties *(continued)*

Property	Type	Description

`Settings`	HashTable	The Settings hashtable is very important to module development, and is probably one of the most common tools you'll use. Consider it analogous to the registry in Windows. You can use the Settings hash to store and retrieve key/value pairs specific to your module instance. For example, to retrieve the `mykey` value from the Settings hash:
		`Dim myVar As String =`
		`Settings("mykey").ToString`
		To set the `mykey` setting to the value of the `myVar` variable:
		`Dim objModules As New`
		`Entities.Modules.ModuleController`
		`objModules.UpdateTabModuleSetting`
		`(TabModuleId, "mykey", myVar)`

`ContainerControl`	Control	Provides a reference to the module container that wraps your module instance (see Chapter 6, "Modules," to learn about what a container is).
`HasModulePermission`	Boolean	Checks permissions for a specific module instance, such as Edit and View, so the portal knows whether to display the module to the currently logged-on user, and whether the user can edit the module. Note: this is actually a property and not a method of `PortalModuleBase`, but is included here for completeness.

In addition to the localized menu text and the control-to-load properties, the two empty parameters represent a command-argument list, and the path to an icon if you care to supply either value. The first `False` parameter is the optional `UseActionEvent` parameter, where an event can be generated when your menu item is activated. Next, by specifying the security type as `SecurityAccessLevel.Edit` for the item display, you can restrict the functionality to specific roles configured within your portal. The final `True` and `False` parameters indicate whether the module should be visible when the page is displayed, and whether a new window should be opened at display time.

Code-Behind Regions

To organize your code, break your class into several regions. DotNetNuke makes use of named regions throughout the code for better readability. The first of these regions are the `Controls` and `Private Members` regions. As in any ASP.NET development project, you need to declare your web controls to expose the actions, properties, and methods that they contain. In addition, for this specific example there are some private members — string constants to use as keys for module settings and a session variable name (see Listing 15-4).

Listing 15-4: Controls and Private Members Regions of the WROX.Suggestion Default View Module

```
#Region " Controls "
    Protected WithEvents lblInstructions As Label
    Protected WithEvents lblThankYou As Label
#End Region

#Region " Private Members "
    Private Const ksSetInstructions As String = "Instructions"
    Private Const ksSetThankYou As String = "ThankYou"
    Private Const ksThankYouFlag As String = "ThankYouFlag_"
#End Region
```

Following these two regions is your View control code. The default View control for the WROX.Suggestion module doesn't display any data from the database; it's simply a placeholder for user instructions, a thank you message that's displayed to the user once a suggestion item is entered, and the Edit Suggestion link.

The only other code in the WROX.Suggestion module is in the `Event Handlers` region. As you know from ASP.NET programming, event handlers are methods that respond to a certain action, be it an action performed by a user, such as a click event, or a system action such as the page loading. The `Page_Load` event in your module is usually where you determine the initial state of your user control. For example, you may check to see if the request is a postback, which means the user clicked a link or form button to call into the module again. Listing 15-5 looks at the code in the `Event Handlers` region to see how the `Page_Load` event is handled in this module.

Listing 15-5: Event Handlers Region in the WROX.Suggestion Default View Module

```
#Region " Event Handlers "
    Private Sub Page_Load(ByVal sender As System.Object, _
      ByVal e As System.EventArgs) Handles MyBase.Load
        Try
            If Not Page.IsPostBack Then
                Dim sInstructions As String = CType(Settings(ksSetInstructions), _
                  String)
                If Not IsNothing(sInstructions) AndAlso sInstructions.Length > 0 _
                  Then
                    lblInstructions.Text = sInstructions
                End If

                Dim sTY As String = CType(Session(ksThankYouFlag & _
                  ModuleId.ToString), String)
                Dim bTY As Boolean = IIf(IsNothing(sTY), False, _
                  IIf(sTY = "1", True, False))
                Dim sThankYou As String = CType(Settings(ksSetThankYou), String)
                If Not IsNothing(sThankYou) AndAlso sThankYou.Length > 0 Then
                    lblThankYou.Text = sThankYou
                End If
                lblThankYou.Visible = bTY
            End If
```

```
            Catch exc As Exception    'Module failed to load
                ProcessModuleLoadException(Me, exc)
            End Try
        End Sub
    #End Region
```

In the `Page_Load` event, one of the first things you do is check values contained within the Settings hash. Remember from Table 15-2 that the Settings hash is similar to the Windows registry where you can store module settings as key/value pairs. In this case, you check to see whether user instructions and a thank you message have been stored:

```
Dim sInstructions As String = CType(Settings(ksSetInstructions), String)
Dim sThankYou As String = CType(Settings(ksSetThankYou), String)
```

These are checked for a value, and the labels on the form are updated if the setting exists, otherwise the default value from the local resource file is used (when the value of the `If` statement is false):

```
If Not IsNothing(sInstructions) AndAlso sInstructions.Length > 0 Then
    lblInstructions.Text = sInstructions
End If
```

This is the purpose of the Settings hash — it enables you to have unique values for each instance of a module on a page. In the WROX.Suggestion module, you can specify different sets of instructions and thank you text for each module instance. The use of module settings can be applied to any module to provide maximum flexibility for your application.

Another feature of the WROX.Suggestion default View module is that when a user enters a suggestion, a thank you message is displayed. A flag value controlling the display of this message is stored in an ASP.NET Session variable:

```
Dim sTY As String = CType(Session(ksThankYouFlag & ModuleId.ToString), String)
```

Here, you can see that the `ModuleID` is appended to a string constant so the session variable name is unique for this instance of the module.

Finally, in the exception `Catch` block, there's a call to `ProcessModuleLoadException`. The DotNetNuke framework provides this method for error trapping, which is discussed near the end of this chapter. Because this is a very simple module, that's all there is to the default View control for the WROX.Suggestion module.

This section explored the basic structure of a simple View control for a DesktopModule. Many modules will have only a single View control, but you can have as many as you need to complete the functionality of your module. In the case of the WROX.Suggestion module, there is a second View control, which is used to view the lists of suggestion items entered by users on your portal. This second View control is covered in the next section.

Secondary View Control

In the WROX.Suggestion module, there are two View modules: the default Suggestions view (covered in the preceding section), and the DisplaySuggestions view for listing user-entered suggestions, which is the subject of this section. The secondary View control is located in the DesktopModules\WROX.Suggestion directory and is named DisplaySuggestions.ascx. Open the WROX.Suggestion project and look at the user interface to see the controls it contains (see Figure 15-2).

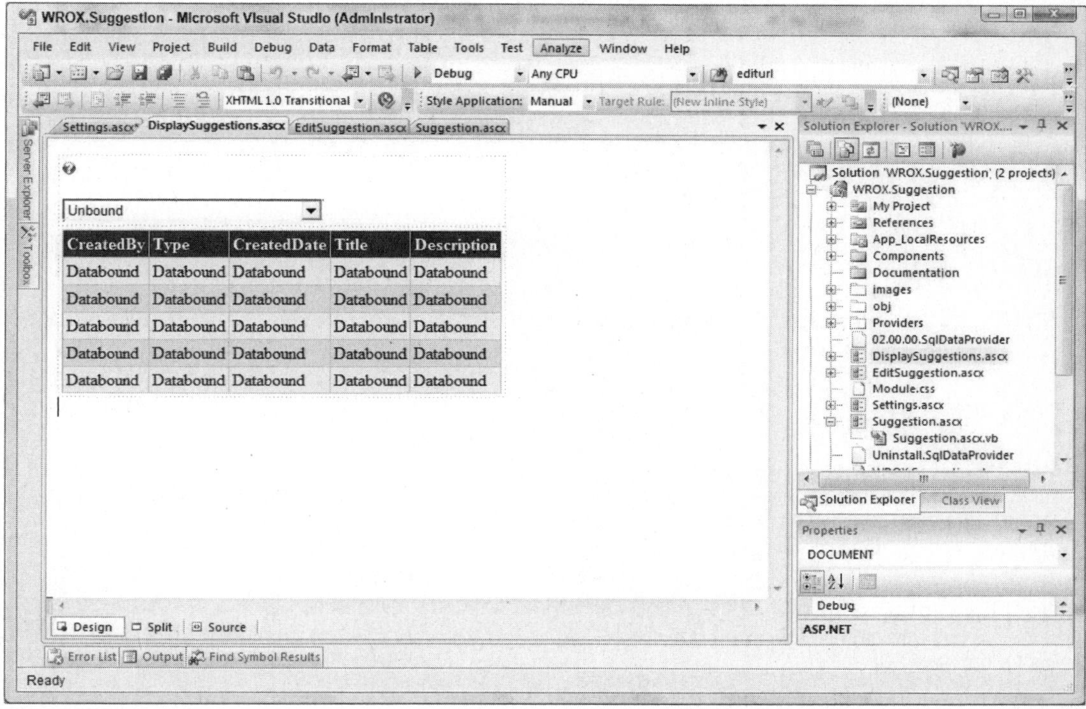

Figure 15-2

Three primary controls are within the DisplaySuggestions user control: a DNN Label (named `dlSelect`), an ASP.NET DropDownList control (named `cboSuggestionModules`), and an ASP.NET DataGrid (named `dgrSuggestions`). The `dlSelect` control's label provides the user with instructions for entering suggestion items, and is a DNN Label control rather than an ASP.NET label because there is additional help text available along with the DNN label control. The `cboSuggestionModules` drop-down allows an authorized user to choose a specific Suggestion module instance to display its suggestion items. The `dgrSuggestions` grid is for displaying user suggestions for the module chosen in the drop-down.

Listing 15-6 reviews the controls in the DisplaySuggestions.ascx file.

Listing 15-6: Controls in the DisplaySuggestions.ascx User Control

```
<%@ Control language="vb" Inherits="WROX.Modules.Suggestion.DisplaySuggestions"
CodeBehind="DisplaySuggestions.ascx.vb" AutoEventWireup="false" Explicit="True" %>
<%@ Register TagPrefix="dnn" TagName="label" Src="~/controls/LabelControl.ascx" %>
<table cellspacing="0" cellpadding="4" border="0">
  <tr>
    <td class="Normal"><dnn:label id="dlSelect" resourcekey="dlSelect" text="Select
the desired Suggestion module:" controlname="cboSuggestionModules" runat="server"
/>
```

```
        <br /><asp:DropDownList id="cboSuggestionModules" runat="server" Width="241px"
DataTextField="ModuleTitle" DataValueField="ModuleID"
AutoPostBack="True"></asp:DropDownList></td>
    </tr>
    <tr>
      <td>
        <asp:DataGrid id="dgrSuggestions" runat="server" CssClass="Normal"
BorderColor="#999999" BorderStyle="None" BorderWidth="1px" BackColor="White"
CellPadding="3" GridLines="Vertical" AutoGenerateColumns="false">
          <SelectedItemStyle Font-Bold="True" ForeColor="White"
BackColor="#008A8C"></SelectedItemStyle>
          <AlternatingItemStyle BackColor="#DCDCDC"></AlternatingItemStyle>
          <ItemStyle ForeColor="Black" BackColor="#EEEEEE"></ItemStyle>
          <HeaderStyle Font-Bold="True" ForeColor="White"
BackColor="#000084"></HeaderStyle>
          <FooterStyle ForeColor="Black" BackColor="#CCCCCC"></FooterStyle>
          <PagerStyle HorizontalAlign="Center" ForeColor="Black" BackColor="#999999"
Mode="NumericPages"></PagerStyle>
          <Columns>
            <asp:BoundColumn DataField="CreatedByUser" HeaderText="CreatedBy"
HeaderStyle-ForeColor="White"></asp:BoundColumn>
            <asp:BoundColumn DataField="Type" HeaderText="Type" HeaderStyle-
ForeColor="White"></asp:BoundColumn>
            <asp:BoundColumn DataField="CreatedDate" HeaderText="CreatedDate"
HeaderStyle-ForeColor="White"></asp:BoundColumn>
            <asp:BoundColumn DataField="Title" HeaderText="Title" HeaderStyle-
ForeColor="White"></asp:BoundColumn>
            <asp:BoundColumn DataField="Description" HeaderText="Description"
HeaderStyle-ForeColor="White"></asp:BoundColumn>
          </Columns>
        </asp:DataGrid></td>
    </tr>
</table>
```

In the preceding control definition, note the use of the DNN Label control. As mentioned briefly, the DNN Label control has both text and help strings associated with it. The help string is an additional piece of info the users can refer to if they're unsure about use of the field in question. By using DotNetNuke intrinsic controls, such as the DNN Label, you can take advantage of extra functionality as well as built-in localization capability within your modules.

Module Styling

In Listing 15-6, the styling picture is quite simple. The DNN Label and ASP.NET DropDown controls are wrapped in a table data element `<td class="Normal">`, which applies the `Normal` CSS class definition to both controls (remember, you must set the DNN Label control's style this way). The DataGrid is itself defined with a number of styles, with most of the style definitions applying to the grid's appearance. The attribute `CSSClass="Normal"` in the DataGrid definition element applies to the text displayed within the grid body, and any other text not explicitly defined by one of the grid style attributes.

Notice in the DataGrid definition element, the attribute value `AutoGenerateColumns="false"`. This keeps the grid from showing the database field names of the columns as the column headings. A columns collection is defined starting in the middle of Listing 15-6. Each column is declared as an `asp:BoundColumn` with attributes defined for which `DataField` in the bound data is to be displayed, and for the column's `HeaderText`. This pulls the localized header string from the control's resource file, as you see in the next section.

Secondary View Control Resources

Listing 15-7 shows the name-value pair content of the DisplaySuggestions.ascx.resx resource file. This is the default-language definition for this user control in your module.

Listing 15-7: DisplaySuggestions.ascx.resx Resource File

```
<data name="dlSelect.Help" xml:space="preserve">
  <value>Choose the Suggestion module whose contents you want to display from the
dropdown list</value>
</data>
<data name="dlSelect.Text" xml:space="preserve">
  <value>Select the desired Suggestion module:</value>
</data>
<data name="ModuleHelp.Text" xml:space="preserve">
  <value>&lt;h1&gt;SuggestionsDisplay Module&lt;/h1&gt;&lt;p&gt;The WROX.Suggestion
module allows users to enter suggestions and Admins to view suggestions. Page
Admins see Suggestions modules listed in a SuggestionsDisplay module on the current
page. Site Admins see Suggestions listed for all pages in a SuggestionsDisplay
module.&lt;/p&gt;&lt;p&gt;When you add a DisplaySuggestions module to a page (as
Site admin), you'll normally set the View Module permission to an administrator
role for the page (create a role for that purpose if necessary). This allows only
the page admin to see suggestions on that page.&lt;/p&gt;&lt;p&gt;Site admins can
see all DisplaySuggestions modules on the portal. They can also see the suggestions
entered from all Suggestions modules on the portal in any DisplaySuggestions
module.&lt;/p&gt;</value>
</data>
<data name="CreatedBy.Header" xml:space="preserve">
  <value>Created By User</value>
</data>
<data name="CreatedDate.Header" xml:space="preserve">
  <value>Created Date</value>
</data>
<data name="Description.Header" xml:space="preserve">
  <value>Suggestion</value>
</data>
<data name="Title.Header" xml:space="preserve">
  <value>Title</value>
</data>
<data name="Type.Header" xml:space="preserve">
  <value>Type</value>
</data>
```

The first two name-value pairs in Listing 15-7 are related to the same DNN Label control. The first is `dlSelect.Help`, and the second is `dlSelect.Text`. As you've seen, the `Text` tag is used by the label to display its text value. The `Help` tag is displayed when the user clicks the Help icon next to the label.

The next name-value pair is `ModuleHelp.Text` with a long encoded HTML string as the value. The content of this tag is displayed when the Help item on the module action menu is clicked by a user with Edit permission on the module. See Figure 15-3 for what the module Help text looks like when it's displayed in the module.

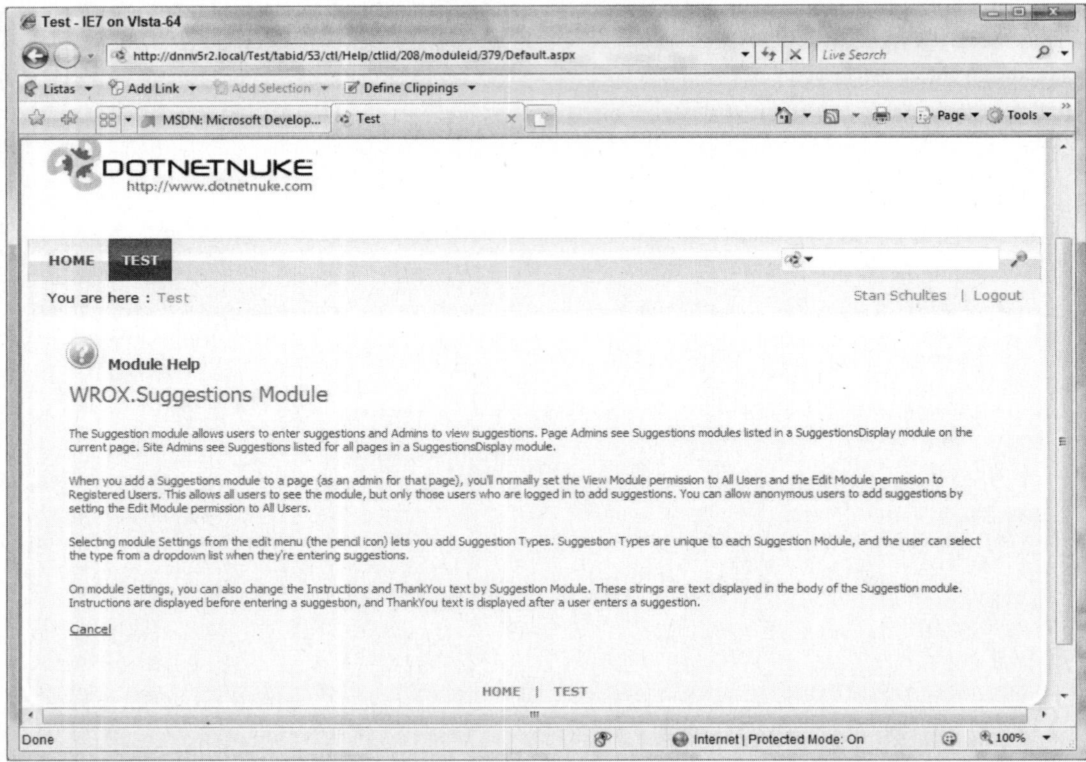

Figure 15-3

The final five name-value pairs are Header tags, which are associated to the column header text strings by the `HeaderText` attributes of the DataGrid columns in Listing 15-7. This association is detailed in Chapter 11.

Secondary View Control Code-Behind Class

Now take a look at the code-behind class for the DisplaySuggestions.ascx file. At the top of your class, you first need to import references, declare your namespace, and define your class:

```
Imports DotNetNuke.Services.Exceptions      'for ProcessModuleLoadException
Imports DotNetNuke.Services.Localization    'for Localization

Namespace WROX.Modules.Suggestion

    Public MustInherit Class DisplaySuggestions
        Inherits Entities.Modules.PortalModuleBase
```

Code-Behind Regions

Listing 15-8 shows the `Controls` region, which defines all the web controls used on the DisplaySuggestions.ascx control.

Listing 15-8: Controls Region of the DisplaySuggestions View Module

```
#Region " Controls "
    Protected WithEvents cboSuggestionModules As _
      System.Web.UI.WebControls.DropDownList
    Protected WithEvents dgrSuggestions As System.Web.UI.WebControls.DataGrid
#End Region
```

Here you have declared only a DropDownList and a DataGrid as the user interface for this control, as shown in Figure 15-2. The drop-down list allows the user to select an instance of a Suggestion module, and that module's suggestion item contents are listed in the DataGrid. As mentioned earlier, a user with View permission on the DisplaySuggestions module can see a list of the Suggestion modules only on the current page. A user who is a portal Admin can see a list of all Suggestion modules from any page on the site.

Listing 15-9 looks at the code in the `Event Handlers` section to see how the `Page_Load` event is handled in this module.

Listing 15-9: Event Handlers Region in the WROX.DisplaySuggestions View Module

```
#Region " Event Handlers "
    Private Sub Page_Load(ByVal sender As System.Object, _
      ByVal e As System.EventArgs) Handles MyBase.Load
        Dim Suggestions As New SuggestionController
        Dim SuggestionsDisplay As New SuggestionsDisplayController
        Try
            If Not Page.IsPostBack Then
                If DotNetNuke.Security.PortalSecurity.IsInRoles _
                  (PortalSettings.AdministratorRoleName.ToString) Then
                    'list all Suggestion modules for a site admin
                    cboSuggestionModules.DataSource = _
                      Suggestions.GetSuggestionModulesAllTabs
                    cboSuggestionModules.DataBind()
                Else
                    'list only modules on this tab for other users
                    cboSuggestionModules.DataSource = _
                      Suggestions.GetSuggestionModulesThisTab(TabId)
                    cboSuggestionModules.DataBind()
                End If
            End If

            'localize grid header
            Localization.LocalizeDataGrid(dgrSuggestions, Me.LocalResourceFile)
            'fill grid from item selected or first item listed in combo
            If cboSuggestionModules.SelectedIndex >= 0 Then
                dgrSuggestions.DataSource = SuggestionsDisplay.GetSuggestions _
                  (cboSuggestionModules.SelectedItem.Value)
                dgrSuggestions.DataBind()
            End If
        Catch exc As Exception    'Module failed to load
            ProcessModuleLoadException(Me, exc)
```

```
            End Try
        End Sub
    #End Region
```

In the `Page_Load` event, the permissions of the current user are checked against the portal administrator role. If the user is a portal administrator, the `GetSuggestionModulesAllTabs` method of the `SuggestionController` is called to retrieve the names of all Suggestion modules on the portal. Otherwise, the `GetSuggestionModulesThisTab` method of the `SuggestionController` is called to retrieve the names of only the Suggestion modules on the current page. This scheme assumes that the DisplaySuggestions module is visible only to users who are authorized by role to see the suggestion items entered on the page.

This is a good example of user permissions checking using the built-in DNN roles and security mechanisms. A good resource in the DNN source distribution to research permissions checking is in the <sourcedir>\Library\Security\PortalSecurity.vb file.

The previous sections covered the View controls in the WROX.Suggestion module. The next two sections cover the Settings and Edit controls. The Settings control is where authorized users can change definitions of module data, and the Edit control is where users actually enter suggestion items.

Settings Control

Now you need to create a control that enables you to customize your module. Open the WROX.Suggestion project and look at the user interface to see the controls it contains (see Figure 15-4).

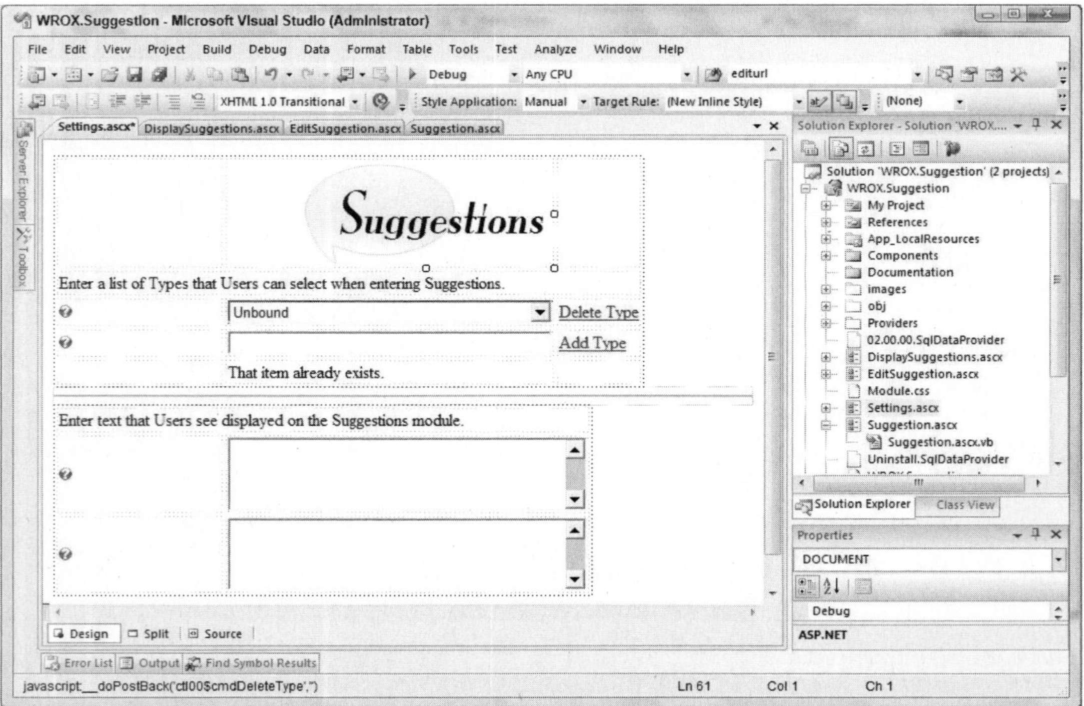

Figure 15-4

In the WROX.Suggestion module, two sets of data are maintained for the module. First is a list of suggestion types, or categories, which the users assign whenever they enter a suggestion item. Second is a pair of values stored in the Settings hashtable by module instance — instructions to the user, and a thank you message displayed to the user once a suggestion item is entered.

Listing 15-10 reviews the Settings user control in the WROX.Suggestion module. This file is located in the WROX.Suggestion project folder, and is named Settings.ascx.

Listing 15-10: Settings User Control for the WROX.Suggestion Module

```
<%@ Control language="vb" CodeBehind="Settings.ascx.vb" AutoEventWireup="false"
Explicit="True" Inherits="WROX.Modules.Suggestion.Settings" %>
<%@ Register TagPrefix="dnn" TagName="Label" Src="~/controls/LabelControl.ascx" %>
<table cellspacing="3" cellpadding="2" border="0">
  <tr>
    <td class="SubHead" colspan="3"><asp:label id="lblSuggestionTypes"
resourcekey="lblSuggestionTypes" runat="server">Enter a list of Types that Users
can select when entering Suggestions.</asp:label></td>
  </tr>
  <tr>
    <td class="SubHead" valign="middle" width="150"><dnn:label
id="dlSuggestionTypes" resourcekey="dlSuggestionTypes" text="Suggestion Types:"
controlname="cboTypesOption" runat="server" />
    </td>
    <td class="SubHead" valign="bottom" width="300"><asp:DropDownList
id="cboTypesOption" Runat="server" DataTextField="Type"
DataValueField="SuggestionTypeID" width="300"
CssClass="NormalTextBox"></asp:DropDownList></td>
    <td class="SubHead"><asp:LinkButton class="CommandButton" id="cmdDeleteType"
resourcekey="cmdDeleteType" runat="server" CausesValidation="False"
BorderStyle="none" Text="Delete Type"></asp:LinkButton></td>
  </tr>
  <tr>
    <td class="SubHead" valign="middle" width="150"><dnn:label id="dlAddNewType"
resourcekey="dlAddNewType" text="Add New Type:" controlname="txtNewType"
runat="server" />
    </td>
    <td class="SubHead" valign="bottom" width="300"><asp:TextBox id="txtNewType"
runat="server" width="300" CssClass="NormalTextBox" maxlength="100"
Columns="30"></asp:TextBox></td>
    <td class="SubHead"><asp:LinkButton class="CommandButton" id="cmdAddType"
resourcekey="cmdAddType" runat="server" CausesValidation="False"
BorderStyle="none" Text="Add Type"></asp:LinkButton></td>
  </tr>
  <tr>
    <td class="SubHead" valign="middle" width="150"> </td>
    <td class="SubHead" valign="bottom" width="300"><asp:label id="lblDuplicate"
resourcekey="lblDuplicate" runat="server" Visible="False" CssClass="NormalRed">
That item already exists.</asp:label></td>
    <td> </td>
  </tr>
</table>
<hr />
<table cellspacing="3" cellpadding="2" border="0">
  <tr>
```

```
    <td class="SubHead" colspan="2"><asp:label id="lblSuggestionText"
resourcekey="lblSuggestionText" runat="server">Enter text that Users see displayed
on the Suggestions module.</asp:label></td>
  </tr>
  <tr>
    <td class="SubHead" valign="middle" width="150"><dnn:label
id="dlInstructionsText" resourcekey="dlInstructionsText" text="Instructions Text:"
controlname="txtInstructions" runat="server" />
    </td>
    <td valign="bottom" width="264"><asp:TextBox id="txtInstructions"
runat="server" Visible="False" TextMode="MultiLine" Width="333px"
Height="69px"></asp:TextBox></td>
  </tr>
  <tr>
    <td class="SubHead" valign="middle" width="150"><dnn:label id="dlThankYouText"
resourcekey="dlThankYouText" text="Thank You Text:" controlname="txtThankYou"
runat="server" />
    </td>
    <td valign="bottom" width="264"><asp:TextBox id="txtThankYou" runat="server"
Visible="False" TextMode="MultiLine" Width="333px"
Height="69px"></asp:TextBox></td>
  </tr>
</table>
```

In the preceding code, a wider variety of controls than you've seen before in an `.ascx` file are used: ASP.NET label, DNN Label, DropDownList, TextBox, and LinkButton.

Module Styling

Notice the <td class="SubHead"> CSS attribute definitions listed in many of the table data elements in Listing 15-10. Using the `SubHead` class value in displayed strings, such as in the <dnn:label> controls, makes these strings stand out in a larger font as a form label. See Figure 15-5, where you can see the drop-down list and textbox labels appear in the `SubHead` style.

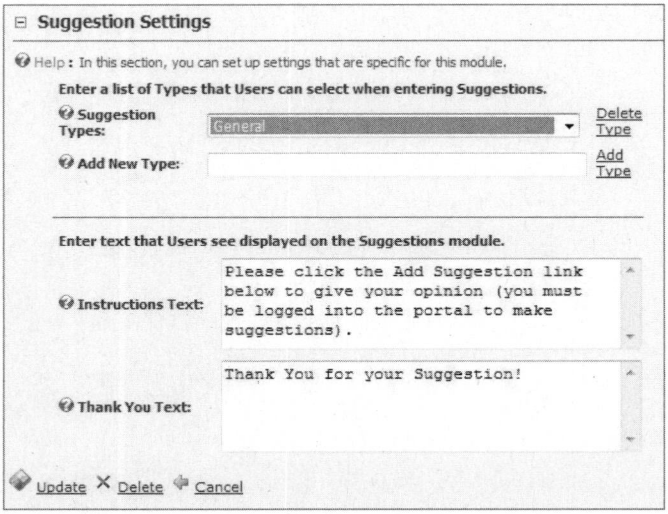

Figure 15-5

You can also see other common styling elements in use: `NormalTextBox`, `CommandButton`, and `NormalRed` (which are similar to those discussed earlier, in Portal.css). In your modules, you want to be sure that you reuse common styles provided by the DNN framework before you create your own styles (which would go into the module.css file in your `DesktopModules\WROX.Suggestion` folder if you were to create them).

Setting Control Resources

Listing 15-11 shows the name-value pair content of the Settings.ascx.resx resource file.

Listing 15-11: Settings.ascx.resx Resource File

```
<data name="lblTemplate.Text" xml:space="preserve">
  <value>Template</value>
</data>
<data name="lblTemplate.Help" xml:space="preserve">
  <value>Allows you to provide a custom template for displaying the items. Use
parameters for dynamic substitution ( ie. [CONTENT] [CREATEDDATE] [CREATEDBYUSER]
[CREATEDBYUSERNAME] )</value>
</data>
<data name="ControlTitle_settings.Text" xml:space="preserve">
  <value>Suggestion Settings</value>
</data>
<data name="ModuleHelp.Text" xml:space="preserve">
  <value>&lt;h1&gt;Suggestion Settings&lt;/h1&gt;&lt;p&gt;A list of Suggestion
Types can be created and viewed in the top section. Click the Suggestion Types
dropdown to see a list of current types. Click the Delete Type link to remove an
entry from the list. Enter a new value in the Add New Type box and click the Add
Type link to enter a new value in the Type list&lt;/p&gt;&lt;p&gt;Change the
instructions text displayed in the Suggestion module by updating the text in the
Instructions Text list box. Change the Thank You message displayed after a user
enters a suggestion by updating the text in the Thank You Text list box. When
finished changing settings, click the Update link at the bottom of the
page.&lt;/p&gt;</value>
</data>
<data name="cmdAddType.Text" xml:space="preserve">
  <value>Add Type</value>
</data>
<data name="cmdDeleteType.Text" xml:space="preserve">
  <value>Delete Type</value>
</data>
<data name="dlAddNewType.Help" xml:space="preserve">
  <value>Enter a unique type name to add to the list</value>
</data>
<data name="dlAddNewType.Text" xml:space="preserve">
  <value>Add New Type:</value>
</data>
<data name="dlInstructionsText.Help" xml:space="preserve">
  <value>These instructions will be displayed on the Suggestion module before the
user enters a Suggestion</value>
</data>
<data name="dlInstructionsText.Text" xml:space="preserve">
  <value>Instructions Text:</value>
</data>
```

```
<data name="dlSuggestionTypes.Help" xml:space="preserve">
  <value>Types (categories) that users can assign their Suggestions to</value>
</data>
<data name="dlSuggestionTypes.Text" xml:space="preserve">
  <value>Suggestion Types:</value>
</data>
<data name="dlThankYouText.Help" xml:space="preserve">
  <value>This text will be displayed on the Suggestion module after the user enters
a Suggestion</value>
</data>
<data name="dlThankYouText.Text" xml:space="preserve">
  <value>Thank You Text:</value>
</data>
<data name="lblDuplicate.Text" xml:space="preserve">
  <value>That item already exists.</value>
</data>
<data name="lblSuggestionText.Text" xml:space="preserve">
  <value>Enter text that Users see displayed on the Suggestions module.</value>
</data>
<data name="lblSuggestionTypes.Text" xml:space="preserve">
  <value>Enter a list of Types that Users can select when entering
Suggestions.</value>
</data>
<data name="txtInstructions.Default" xml:space="preserve">
  <value>Please click the Add Suggestion link below to give your opinion (you must
be logged into the portal to make suggestions).</value>
</data>
<data name="txtThankYou.Default" xml:space="preserve">
  <value>Thank You for your Suggestion!</value>
</data>
```

The resource name-value pairs in Listing 15-11 are similar to those seen in previous controls. The DNN Label has `Text` and `Help` tag pairs, whereas the label and text controls only have the `Text` tag. `ModuleHelp.Text` contains encoded HTML and is displayed by the Help menu item on the control action menu.

There are two additional items that you haven't seen yet. First, `ControlTitle_settings.Text`, which is a special tag. Each of your user controls that are shown as a particular view in your module has a `Title` string that's injected by DNN as part of the module control. You can put values in these special tags if you can find where they are.

The trick to doing this was covered in Chapter 11. You change a web.config setting in the `<appSettings>` section:

```
<add key="ShowMissingKeys" value="true" />
```

The result of this is that all localization tags are highlighted, including special tags like `ControlTitle_settings.Text`, that you can localize if you want. If you leave these tags' localized values blank, the text simply won't show on the form. See Figure 15-6 for an example of the Settings.ascx page showing the key values.

In the figure, all displayed text items that come from a resources file are prefixed with the string `[L]`. If there is no matching key, the resource string name shows up in the form, as with the special

RESX:Breadcrumb.Text tag, which is just under the main menu at the left edge of the screen. This is a candidate tag that you can associate a resource string with by adding a string value with Breadcrumb.Text as the resource key name to the default resource file.

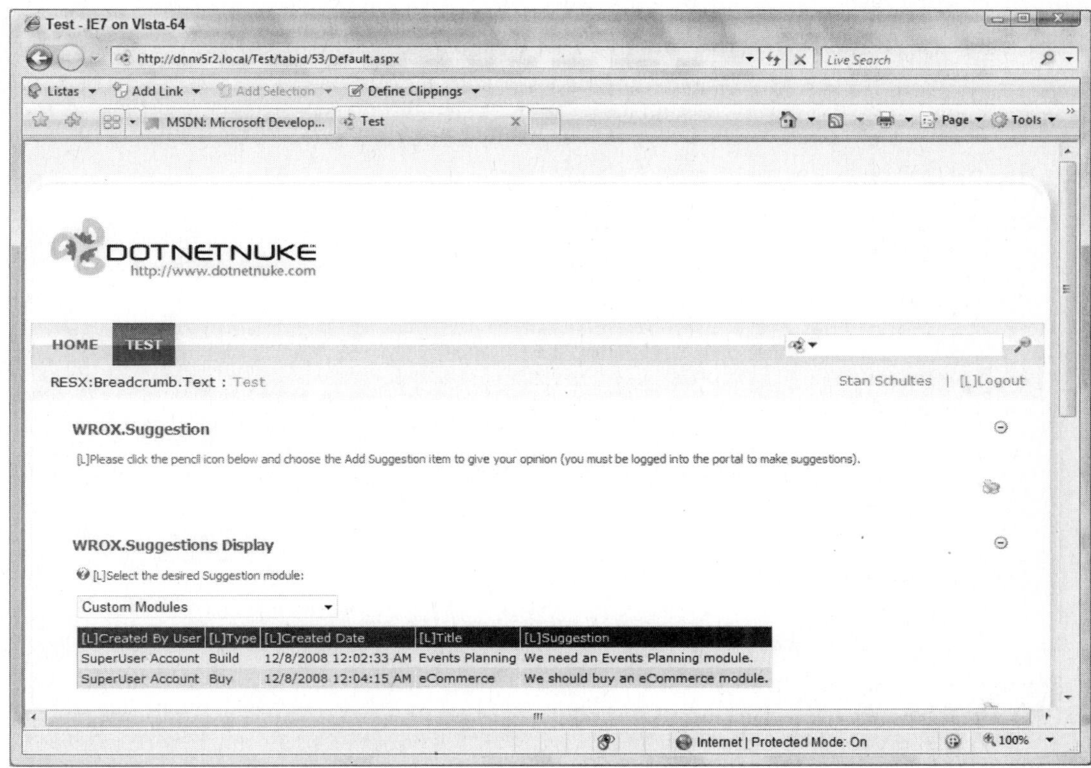

Figure 15-6

The second set of tags that are new in Listing 15-11 are the Default tag values. These are custom localization tags, also covered in Chapter 11. You see how to load these custom values using the Localization.GetString function in the following code-behind section.

Settings Control Code-Behind Class

If you look through the code-behind, you'll notice this file is about the same size as the code-behind for both View controls. This is because the View controls are very simple in WROX.Suggestion, but there are several settings that define how you want the module to look, along with the code for managing those settings. Listing 15-12 shows the reference imports, namespace, and the class definition in the Settings.ascx.vb file.

Listing 15-12: Defining the Settings Control for the WROX.Suggestion Module

```
Imports DotNetNuke.Services.Localization    'for Localization
Imports DotNetNuke.Services.Exceptions      'for ProcessModuleLoadException
```

```
Namespace WROX.Modules.Suggestion

    Public Class Settings
        Inherits Entities.Modules.ModuleSettingsBase
```

You can see here that you inherit the `Entities.Modules.ModuleSettingsBase` class. This class is provided by DotNetNuke and inherits `PortalModuleBase` as discussed earlier in the chapter, but it extends the `PortalModuleBase` to include some additional properties. The `ModuleSettingsBase` class provides methods and properties specific to configuring setting values for the module instance. Table 15.3 reviews what this class provides for your module development, in addition to the `PortalModuleBase` properties detailed in Table 15-2.

Table 15-3: ModuleSettingsBase Class

Name	Type	Description
`ModuleSettings`	Hashtable	Configuration options that affect all instances of a module.
`Settings`	Hashtable	This hashtable is loaded with the key/value pairs of all ModuleSettings and TabModuleSettings when the module is loaded. This simply provides easy access to the module settings. For example: `Dim sThankYou As String = CType(Settings("ThankYou"), String)`
`TabModuleSettings`	Hashtable	Affects only a specific instance of a module. This enables you to display the same information for a module, but in a different way.

One item to clarify here is the difference between the two hashtables (`ModuleSettings` and `TabModuleSettings`). This is provided so you can apply the same data in the same or two different module instances. So, for example, if you want to update the event view for all instances of the same type of module, you would do so as follows:

```
Dim objModules As New Entities.Modules.ModuleController
objModules.UpdateModuleSetting(ModuleId, "eventview", optView.SelectedItem.Value)
```

On the other hand, if you want to update the event view for only the current instance of the module, you would do so as follows:

```
Dim objModules As New Entities.Modules.ModuleController
objModules.UpdateTabModuleSetting(TabModuleId, "eventview",
  optView.SelectedItem.Value)
```

In the next section, you update the specific instance using the `UpdateTabModuleSettings` method. This updates the view of all module containers pointing to the same data for a specific module, which is identified by its `ModuleID`.

Code-Behind Regions

Next in the Settings class, the various code sections are broken down into code regions.

You'll notice that throughout DotNetNuke, certain standards are applied for coding conventions. As a module developer, you should strive to emulate the DotNetNuke coding style for easier readability and management.

Listing 15-13 shows the `Controls` region, which defines all the web controls used on the Settings.ascx user control.

Listing 15-13: Controls Region of the Settings Module

```
#Region " Settings Controls "ystem.Web.UI.WebControls.DropDownList
    Protected WithEvents cmdAddType As System.Web.UI.WebControls.LinkButton
    Protected WithEvents txtNewType As System.Web.UI.WebControls.TextBox
    Protected WithEvents cmdDeleteType As System.Web.UI.WebControls.LinkButton
    Protected WithEvents txtTitle As System.Web.UI.WebControls.TextBox
    Protected WithEvents valTitle As _
      System.Web.UI.WebControls.RequiredFieldValidator
    Protected WithEvents lblDuplicate As System.Web.UI.WebControls.Label
    Protected WithEvents txtInstructions As System.Web.UI.WebControls.TextBox
    Protected WithEvents txtThankYou As System.Web.UI.WebControls.TextBox
#End Region
```

These are all common controls from ASP.NET, including a `RequiredFieldValidator` that notifies the user if a required field is not filled out.

Following this in Listing 15-14 is the `Local Strings` region, which defines string values used internal to the Settings.ascx control.

Listing 15-14: Local Strings Region of the Settings Module

```
#Region " Local Strings "
    Private Const ksSetInstructions As String = "Instructions"
    Private Const ksDefaultInstructions As String = "txtInstructions.Default"
    Private Const ksSetThankYou As String = "ThankYou"
    Private Const ksDefaultThankYou As String = "txtThankYou.Default"
#End Region
```

Here you can see where two custom tag names are defined, each using the `Default` tag extension. You see how to load these custom tags in the next code listing, using the `Localization.GetString` method.

Next is the `Base Method Implementations` region (see Listing 15-15). Here you have two methods implemented from the `ModuleSettingsBase` class: `LoadSettings` to load settings from your hashtable, and `UpdateSettings` to update the settings values in the hashtable when the user changes them.

Listing 15-15: Base Method Implementations in Settings.ascx.vb for the WROX.Suggestion Module

```
#Region " Base Method Implementations "
    Public Overrides Sub LoadSettings()
        Try
            If (Page.IsPostBack = False) Then
                txtInstructions.Visible = True
                txtThankYou.Visible = True
                If CType(TabModuleSettings(ksSetInstructions), String) <> "" Then
                    txtInstructions.Text = CType(Settings(ksSetInstructions), _
                      String)
                Else
                    txtInstructions.Text = Localization.GetString _
                      (ksDefaultInstructions, LocalResourceFile)
                End If

                If CType(TabModuleSettings(ksSetThankYou), String) <> "" Then
                    txtThankYou.Text = CType(Settings(ksSetThankYou), String)
                Else
                    txtThankYou.Text = Localization.GetString(ksDefaultThankYou, _
                      LocalResourceFile)
                End If
                'display suggestion types dropdown
                DisplaySuggestionTypesOption()
            End If
        Catch exc As Exception    'Module failed to load
            ProcessModuleLoadException(Me, exc)
        End Try
    End Sub

    Public Overrides Sub UpdateSettings()
        Try
            Dim objModules As New Entities.Modules.ModuleController

            'update prompt & Thank You message if new text is specified
            If txtInstructions.Text.Length > 0 Then
                objModules.UpdateTabModuleSetting(TabModuleId, ksSetInstructions, _
                  txtInstructions.Text)
            End If
            If txtThankYou.Text.Length > 0 Then
                objModules.UpdateTabModuleSetting(TabModuleId, ksSetThankYou, _
                  txtThankYou.Text)
            End If

        Catch exc As Exception    'Module failed to load
            ProcessModuleLoadException(Me, exc)
        End Try
    End Sub
#End Region
```

Listing 15-16 shows the `Class Events` region, containing the event-handling routines for the Settings.ascx control.

Listing 15-16: Class Events Region of the Settings Module

```
#Region " Class Events "
    Private Sub cmdAddType_Click(ByVal sender As Object, ByVal e As EventArgs) _
      Handles cmdAddType.Click
        Dim Suggestions As New SuggestionTypeController 'SuggestionsDB
        Dim sti As New SuggestionTypeInfo
        ' Add new Type in the SuggestionTypes table if it isn't already in the list
        If txtNewType.Text.Length > 0 Then
            If (cboTypesOption.Items.FindByText(txtNewType.Text)) Is Nothing Then
                sti.ModuleID = ModuleId
                sti.Type = txtNewType.Text
                Suggestions.AddSuggestionType(sti)
                txtNewType.Text = String.Empty
                ' re-bind SuggestionTypes to dropdown list
                DisplaySuggestionTypesOption()
                lblDuplicate.Visible = False
            Else
                lblDuplicate.Visible = True
            End If
        End If
    End Sub

    Private Sub cmdDeleteType_Click(ByVal sender As Object, ByVal e As EventArgs) _
      Handles cmdDeleteType.Click
        Dim Suggestions As New SuggestionTypeController 'SuggestionsDB
        ' Delete the Suggestion Type within the SuggestionTypes table
        If cboTypesOption.SelectedIndex >= 0 Then
            Suggestions.DeleteSuggestionType(cboTypesOption.SelectedItem.Value, _
              ModuleId)
            ' re-bind SuggestionTypes to dropdown list
            DisplaySuggestionTypesOption()
        End If
        lblDuplicate.Visible = False
    End Sub
#End Region
```

These routines handle command button clicks in the top section of the settings control, where the user can add and delete suggestion types. Users categorize their suggestion entry by selecting a suggestion type when submitting a new suggestion.

Finally in Listing 15-17 is the `Private Methods` region, which contains methods local to the operation of the Settings.ascx control. Normally, your `Private Methods` will obtain your data and bind to your controls.

Listing 15-17: Private Methods Region of the Settings Module

```
#Region " Private Methods "
    Private Function DisplaySuggestionTypesOption() As Boolean
        ' load the SuggestionTypes dropdown in the Module Options edit area
        Try
            Dim Suggestions As New SuggestionTypeController
```

```
            Dim st As ArrayList = Suggestions.GetSuggestionTypes(ModuleId)
            If st.Count > 0 Then
                cboTypesOption.DataSource = st
                cboTypesOption.DataBind()
                Return True
            Else
                Return False
            End If
        Catch exc As Exception    'Module failed to load
            ProcessModuleLoadException(Me, exc)
        End Try
    End Function
#End Region
```

In this example, there is one method called `GetSuggestionTypes`, which accepts a `ModuleID` for obtaining the suggestion types list from your database (see Listing 15-17). Chapter 13, ''Developing Modules: the Database Layer,'' covered the various stored procedures for this module, and this method uses the process of obtaining a collection from the Business Logic Layer (BLL) by calling the `GetSuggestionTypes` method. The BLL calls the abstraction layer, which contains a method that is overridden by the physical provider class, which then calls the SQL stored procedure `GetSuggestionTypes`. The stored procedure returns the fields matching the query to the physical provider, which finally is converted by DotNetNuke's Custom Business Object helper class to a collection type you define in the BLL. This returned `ArrayList` is bound to a control that was placed on the page, in this case a `DropDownList` control.

That's what it takes to configure the settings for your module. The next section covers the Edit control that users of your module use to enter suggestion items.

Edit Control

The WROX.Suggestion module is designed to allow users to enter and categorize suggestion items. Open the EditSuggestion.ascx control contained in the WROX.Suggestion module project to look at the user interface for adding your suggestion items (see Figure 15-7).

The Edit control is where your users will actually add their suggestion items, so it's displayed to the user when the Add Suggestion link is clicked on the primary view control. Once the user enters the suggestion data and clicks the submit command button, you're going to make a call to your Business Logic Layer to pass an insert SQL command to your physical provider. Take a look at Listing 15-18 to see how the code-behind and control registrations within the EditSuggestion.ascx file are structured.

Listing 15-18: Registering Controls for the EditSuggestion.ascx Control

```
<%@ Control language="vb" CodeBehind="EditSuggestion.ascx.vb"
AutoEventWireup="false" Explicit="True"
Inherits="WROX.Modules.Suggestion.EditSuggestion" %>
<%@ Register TagPrefix="dnn" TagName="Label" Src="~/controls/LabelControl.ascx" %>
```

Here again you're registering the DotNetNuke intrinsic `Label` control, as you did in your other user controls involved in the WROX.Suggestion module. A number of reusable common controls are provided by DotNetNuke that you can use in your own modules. Table 15.4 lists the DNN common controls and explains their purpose.

Table 15-4: DotNetNuke Reusable User Controls

Control	Location	Description
`Label`	<approot>\controls\LabelControl.ascx	Supports display of localized text strings.
`URL`	<approot>\controls\URLControl.ascx	Supports display of information for stored URLs in your user control.
`Audit`	<approot>\controls\ModuleAuditControl.ascx	Displays information on which the user created an entered item, and the date of creation.
`Text Editor`	<approot>\controls\TextEditor.ascx	Provides both a text-based and WYSIWYG environment for editing text and HTML in your module.
`Address`	<approot>\controls\Address.ascx	Provides a view of address information entered for a user of the portal.
`Dual List`	<approot>\controls\DualListControl.ascx	Provides two lists for passing values from one list to the other. An example of this control is implemented in the security settings for a module or page.
`Help`	<approot>\controls\Help.ascx	Provides localized, in-line help for your module.
`Section Head`	<approot>\controls\SectionHeadControl.ascx	Provides expandable areas for sections of your module. This control is implemented throughout DotNetNuke.
`Skin`	<approot>\controls\SkinControl.ascx	Provides a drop-down list of skins installed for a portal.
`Skin Thumbnail`	<approot>\controls\SkinThumbnailControl.ascx	Generates a thumbnail image of the skin. You can view the functionality of this module in the DotNetNuke skins section under the Admin menu.
`URL Tracking`	<approot>\controls\URLTrackingControl.ascx	Supports URL link click tracking within your module.

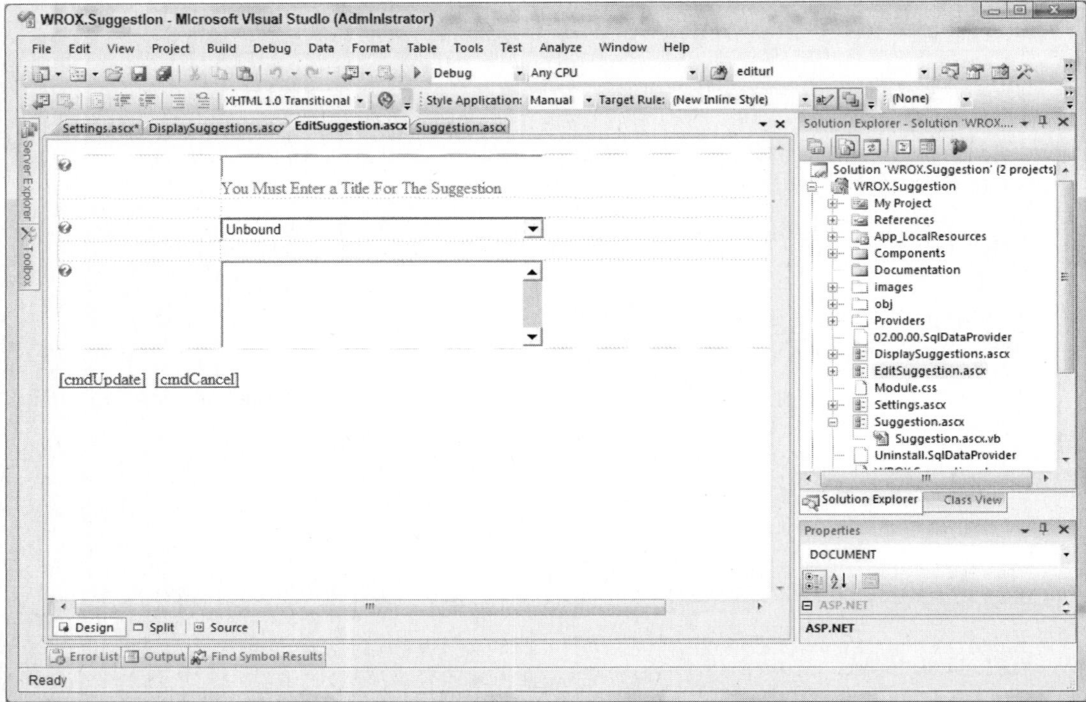

Figure 15-7

As you can see from this table, DotNetNuke provides a number of controls, all of which you can use in your own development efforts. Because DotNetNuke is open source, you can easily open any of the pages of code to find the implementation of these controls so you can modify, extend, or reuse them.

Back to the Edit control in the WROX.Suggestion module. Now that the control has been registered in the page and your code-behind declared, you can continue with the rest of the user control definition (see Listing 15-19).

Listing 15-19: EditSuggestion.ascx Control

```
<table cellspacing="0" cellpadding="0" width="750" border="0">
  <tr>
    <td class="SubHead" valign="top" width="150"><dnn:label id="dlTitle"
resourcekey="dlTitle" text="Title:" controlname="txtTitle" runat="server" />
    </td>
    <td><asp:textbox id="txtTitle" CssClass="NormalTextBox" width="300"
runat="server" Columns="30" maxlength="100"></asp:textbox><br />
    <asp:requiredfieldvalidator id="valTitle" resourcekey="valTitle"
CssClass="NormalRed" runat="server" Display="Static" ErrorMessage="You Must Enter a
Title For The Suggestion" ControlToValidate="txtTitle">
</asp:requiredfieldvalidator></td>
```

```
    </tr>
    <tr>
      <td class="SubHead" valign="top" width="150"> 
      </td>
      <td> </td>
    </tr>
    <tr>
      <td class="SubHead" valign="top" width="150"><dnn:label id="dlType"
  resourcekey="dlType" text="Type:" controlname="cboTypes" runat="server" />
      </td>
      <td><asp:dropdownlist id="cboTypes" CssClass="NormalTextBox" width="300"
  DataValueField="SuggestionTypeId" DataTextField="Type"
  Runat="server"></asp:dropdownlist></td>
    </tr>
    <tr>
      <td class="SubHead" valign="top" width="150"> </td>
      <td> 
      </td>
    </tr>
    <tr>
      <td class="SubHead" valign="top" width="150"><dnn:label id="dlSuggestion"
  resourcekey="dlSuggestion" text="Suggestion:" controlname="txtDescription"
  runat="server" />
      </td>
      <td><asp:textbox id="txtDescription" CssClass="NormalTextBox" width="300"
  runat="server" Columns="30" maxlength="4000" TextMode="MultiLine"
  Rows="5"></asp:textbox></td>
    </tr>
  </table>
  <p><asp:linkbutton id="cmdUpdate" CssClass="CommandButton" ResourceKey="cmdUpdate"
  BorderStyle="none" runat="server"></asp:linkbutton> 
  <asp:linkbutton id="cmdCancel" CssClass="CommandButton" ResourceKey="cmdCancel"
  BorderStyle="none" CausesValidation="False" runat="server"></asp:linkbutton> 
  </p>
```

As you can see in Listing 15-19, the EditSuggestion user control consists of the usual set of web controls.

Module Styling

Listing 15-19 uses the following styling elements: `SubHead`, `NormalTextBox`, `CommandButton`, and `NormalRed`. There are no new style elements, so there should not be any surprises here.

Setting Control Resources

Listing 15-20 shows the name-value pair content of the EditSuggestion.ascx.resx resource file.

Listing 15-20: EditSuggestion.ascx.resx Resource File

```
  <data name="lblContent.Text" xml:space="preserve">
    <value>Sample Suggestion</value>
```

```
</data>
<data name="lblContent.Help" xml:space="preserve">
  <value>Enter a Suggestion</value>
</data>
<data name="valTitle.ErrorMessage" xml:space="preserve">
  <value>You Must Enter a Title For The Suggestion</value>
</data>
<data name="ModuleHelp.Text" xml:space="preserve">
  <value>&lt;h1&gt;Add a Suggestion&lt;/h1&gt;&lt;p&gt;Enter the suggestion title
and body in the text boxes labeled 'Title' and 'Suggesion'. Pick a suggestion type
from the 'Type' dropdown. When finished, click the Update link. New types can be
added by a page admin who has permission to edit the settings of the Suggestion
module.&lt;/p&gt;</value>
</data>
<data name="ControlTitle_edit.Text" xml:space="preserve">
  <value>Edit Suggestion</value>
</data>
<data name="dlSuggestion.Help" xml:space="preserve">
  <value>Enter the Suggestion text</value>
</data>
<data name="dlSuggestion.Text" xml:space="preserve">
  <value>Suggestion:</value>
</data>
<data name="dlTitle.Help" xml:space="preserve">
  <value>This is the title field of the Suggestion you enter</value>
</data>
<data name="dlTitle.Text" xml:space="preserve">
  <value>Title:</value>
</data>
<data name="dlType.Help" xml:space="preserve">
  <value>Select a Type (category) for your Suggestion</value>
</data>
<data name="dlType.Text" xml:space="preserve">
  <value>Type:</value>
</data>
<data name="SuggestionType.Default" xml:space="preserve">
  <value>General</value>
</data>
```

The resource name-value pairs in Listing 15-20 are similar to those seen in the previous user controls. The DNN Label has `Text` and `Help` tag pairs, whereas the label and text controls only have the `Text` tag. `ModuleHelp.Text` contains encoded HTML that displays in the Help menu item on the control. The `ControlTitle_edit.Text` tag provides `Title` text. New here is `valTitle.ErrorMessage`, which provides the `valTitle` validator control its error text.

The `SuggestionType.Default` tag is another `Default` custom tag control defined here, which you load with the `Localization.GetString` method as before. This allows you to provide a default value for the SuggestionType if the user hasn't entered any types before entering the first suggestion item. There must be at least one type defined for a suggestion item, and this is the default type string used for that.

Now check out the code-behind to see how to work with the data and the controls. So far, you've dealt with displaying data from the BLL. Next you're going to be adding information, so you'll need to pass parameters to your stored procedures in SQL. Refer to Chapters 13 and 14 to see how this all comes together.

EditSuggestion.ascx.vb Code-Behind Class

Now that you've seen the front-end controls that the user interacts with, take a look at the code-behind file and see how the class is structured. As before, you import the references, declare your namespace, and define the class:

```
Imports DotNetNuke.Services.Localization    'for Localization
Imports DotNetNuke.Services.Exceptions      'for ProcessModuleLoadException

Namespace WROX.Modules.Suggestion

    Public Class EditSuggestion
        Inherits Entities.Modules.PortalModuleBase
```

Because this control is used for adding data specific to your application, you inherit from the `PortalModuleBase` class as you did in the View control. Just to be clear on the difference between this control and the Settings control, which inherits from the `ModuleSettingsBase` class of DotNetNuke, the Settings control is specific to the operation of the module, not the item data that is entered in tables that you create. The Settings data is stored within internal tables native to DotNetNuke, so there you need to inherit from the `ModuleSettingsBase` class, which is focused on the settings task. An Edit control is specific to your application so it inherits from `PortalModuleBase`.

EditSuggestion Code Regions

Again, each section in the class is broken down into code regions for readability and organization. Here you review the regions specific to the EditSuggestion.ascx.vb file.

The first region is the `Controls` region, where you declare the web controls you created in your EditSuggestion.ascx user control (see Listing 15-21).

Listing 15-21: Controls Region of the EditSuggestion.ascx.vb File

```
#Region " Edit Controls "
    Protected WithEvents txtTitle As System.Web.UI.WebControls.TextBox
    Protected WithEvents valTitle As System.Web.UI.WebControls _
      .RequiredFieldValidator
    Protected WithEvents txtDescription As System.Web.UI.WebControls.TextBox
    Protected WithEvents cboTypes As System.Web.UI.WebControls.DropDownList
    Protected WithEvents cmdUpdate As System.Web.UI.WebControls.LinkButton
    Protected WithEvents cmdCancel As System.Web.UI.WebControls.LinkButton
#End Region
```

These are all common, previously covered ASP.NET controls.

The next region is `Local Strings` for declaring string values used in the module (see Listing 15-22).

Listing 15-22: Local Strings Region of the Edit Control

```
#Region " Local Strings "
    Private Const ksThankYouFlag As String = "ThankYouFlag_"  'uses ModuleID suffix
    Private Const ksDefaultType As String = "SuggestionType.Default"  '"General"
#End Region
```

You can see here the string definition for your Default custom localization tag name, `SuggestionType.Default`.

The next region is the `Class Events` region for handling events as they occur in the control (see Listing 15-23).

Listing 15-23: Class Events Region of the Edit Control

```
#Region " Class Events "
    Private Sub Page_Load(ByVal sender As System.Object, _
      ByVal e As System.EventArgs) Handles MyBase.Load
        Try
            If Not Page.IsPostBack Then
                ' fill combo boxes on the edit panel
                If Not DisplaySuggestionTypes() Then
                    'add a default SuggestionType if the list is empty
                    Dim Suggestions As New SuggestionTypeController
                    Dim sti As New SuggestionTypeInfo
                    sti.ModuleID = ModuleId
                    sti.Type = Localization.GetString(ksDefaultType, _
                      LocalResourceFile)
                    Suggestions.AddSuggestionType(sti)
                    DisplaySuggestionTypes()
                End If
            End If
        Catch exc As Exception    'Module failed to load
            ProcessModuleLoadException(Me, exc)
        End Try
    End Sub

    Private Sub cmdUpdate_Click(ByVal sender As Object, ByVal e As EventArgs) _
      Handles cmdUpdate.Click
        Try
            Dim SuggestionTypeID As Integer = cboTypes.SelectedItem.Value
            If Page.IsValid = True Then
                ' Create an instance of the Suggestion DB component
                Dim Suggestions As New SuggestionController
                Dim si As New SuggestionInfo
                si.ModuleID = ModuleId
                si.SuggestionTypeID = SuggestionTypeID
                si.CreatedByUser = UserInfo.UserID.ToString
                si.Title = txtTitle.Text
                si.Description = txtDescription.Text
                ' Add the Suggestion to the Suggestions table
                Suggestions.AddSuggestion(si)
                Session(ksThankYouFlag & ModuleId.ToString) = "1"
                ' Redirect back to the calling page
                Response.Redirect(NavigateURL(), True)
            End If
        Catch exc As Exception    'Module failed to load
            ProcessModuleLoadException(Me, exc)
        End Try
    End Sub
```

```
    Private Sub cmdCancel_Click(ByVal sender As Object, ByVal e As EventArgs) _
      Handles cmdCancel.Click
        Try
            Session(ksThankYouFlag & ModuleId.ToString) = String.Empty
            ' Redirect back to the calling page
            Response.Redirect(NavigateURL(), True)
        Catch exc As Exception    'Module failed to load
            ProcessModuleLoadException(Me, exc)
        End Try
    End Sub
#End Region
```

The first event handled is `Page_Load`. This event simply loads the drop-down box with Suggestion Types. If no type exists yet, it adds one by calling the `Localization.GetString` method with a local string constant containing the value `SuggestionType.Default`, to pick this up from the resource file. This is a custom resource tag type, which you can create for any use in your own modules.

Next is the `cmdUpdate_Click` event. This event handler contains a little more code than the previous methods. Initially you create an instance of the `SuggestionController` class and populate the properties for a `SuggestionInfo` object. These values are passed from the user controls contained in the web form on the web control. You're adding a suggestion, so you call the `AddSuggestion` method of the `SuggestionController` class. You set an ASP.NET Session value to display a thank you message based on the `ModuleID`. Finally, you use the `NavigateURL` function and redirect back to the default View control of the module.

One thing you'll notice is the use of `NavigateURL`, which is a function that returns a string for your module's view page. `NavigateURL` is provided by the DotNetNuke framework to provide navigation through your module logic to load the appropriate controls based on the module's key that you defined when you first configured DotNetNuke to interface with the module (see Chapter 12). Another key feature to the navigation methods provided by DotNetNuke is the support of friendly URLs (which you learn about near the end of this chapter), which eliminates query strings being passed in the URL and instead uses a directory-like URL structure for passing parameters.

The last event you're handling in Listing 15-23 is `cmdCancel_Click`. Basically all you want to do is reset the thank you Session variable and redirect the users back to their starting point, which is the default view of the module.

The last region is `Private Methods`, containing routines used internally to the control (see Listing 15-24). Normally, your private methods will obtain your data and bind to your controls.

Listing 15-24: Private Methods Region of the EditSuggestion Control

```
#Region " Private Methods "
    Private Function DisplaySuggestionTypes () As Boolean
        ' load the SuggestionTypes dropdown in the suggestions area
        Try
            Dim Suggestions As New SuggestionTypeController
            Dim st As ArrayList = Suggestions.GetSuggestionTypes(ModuleId)
            If st.Count > 0 Then
                cboTypes.DataSource = st
```

```
                cboTypes.DataBind()
                Return True
            Else
                Return False
            End If
        Catch exc As Exception    'Module failed to load
            ProcessModuleLoadException(Me, exc)
        End Try
    End Function
#End Region
```

This method retrieves all Suggestion Type values as a list for this ModuleID, and databinds the list to a DropDownList control.

That completes the architectural review of a DotNetNuke module.

DotNetNuke Helper Functions

In the previous code samples, you may have noticed several functions provided by the DotNetNuke core framework to ease your module development. These helper functions consist of error handling and URL navigation. This section provides some quick examples on what these functions do and how to use them in your own modules. More detail is provided in Chapter 8, but this section reviews common methods that were used in the examples in this chapter.

Exception Handling

If you've been developing with ASP.NET for any length of time, you've probably seen the yellow exception dump on a web page when something goes wrong. This isn't a very nice sight for your users to see, and occasionally it displays a little more information about your application than you would like. Sometimes you don't even realize there is a problem. You could write your own exception-handling routines, but with DotNetNuke you don't have to.

The core framework provides module developers with the ability to check a logged-on user's security level, and display an appropriate user-friendly error message based on who is logged on. For example, an administrator can be presented with a little bit more detail about what specifically caused the exception, and average users can just be presented with a friendly error message informing them that something is wrong. In addition, with the Logging Provider in DotNetNuke, you can view a log of the errors that occurred within a time frame. This ensures you can see what has been happening with your portal and any errors your modules may have raised.

In this chapter, the code examples call the `ProcessModuleLoadException` method when an exception is thrown. For example:

```
Try
    'some logic
Catch exc As Exception
    ProcessModuleLoadException(Me, exc)
End Try
```

By using this method, you raise the exception to the DotNetNuke built-in exception-handling subsystem, and the amount of information displayed on the exception screen is automatically dependent on the user's permissions. Portal Admins are shown more technical detail than a user without extra portal permissions. To view portal exceptions, log on using an Admin or Host-level account and select the Admin ➪ Event Viewer menu item (see Figure 15-8). This brings up the Event Viewer screen. Errors are presented with a red entry by default. Just click an entry to view the error information.

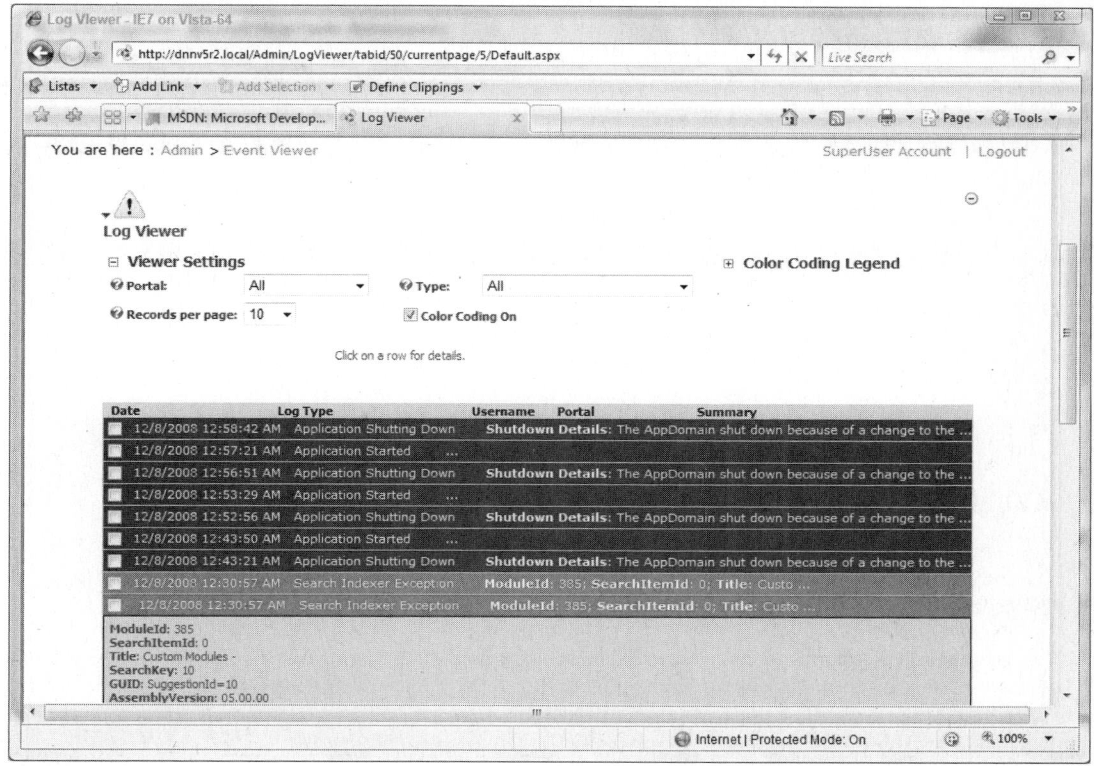

Figure 15-8

Navigation URLs

Also covered in the sample code was the use of `NavigateURL` and `EditURL`. These provide two major functions: to load the appropriate control based on the module key being passed to the function, and to provide support for friendly URLs in your module. Friendly URLs eliminate the need for your module to pass query strings in the URL. By using friendly URLs, you make it easier for spiders to search your site, and it is easier to display and remember the URLs linking to various pages in your site. For example, instead of using something like `http://www.dotnetnuke.com/default.aspx?tabid=233` to navigate to a page within a portal, friendly URLs would provide you with `http://www.dotnetnuke.com/tabid/233/default.aspx` as a path to the page. You can find out more about the friendly URLs interface in Chapter 8.

`NavigateURL` provides you with the ability to navigate to the appropriate user control. This function is provided by `DotNetNuke.Common.Globals.NavigateURL`, located within the Globals.vb file in the <approot>\library\common\directory in the DotNetNuke source solution. This method accepts a `TabID`, which is the unique identifier of a page in your portal; `ControlKey`, which is the unique key you defined when you configured your module definition and identifies which user control to load for the module; and `AdditionalParameters`, which is for adding any additional parameters. The additional parameters are a string array of the query string parameters you may need to pass in the URL. By using `AdditionalParameters`, you can easily implement friendly URLs for your module because DotNetNuke converts the string array to a directory-like structure to be displayed in the portal URLs.

For example, the following code snippet redirects back to the calling page using the `DotNetNuke.Common.Globals.NavigateURL` method (the `True` parameter ends the current ASP.NET Response stream). This is commonly used in the Cancel command event routine of your user controls:

```
Response.Redirect(NavigateURL(), True)
```

The ID of the currently active page is passed to the URL, and the control you want to load is the control with the `Edit` key. In addition, you pass several parameters for the control such as the `ModuleID` and current `UserID`.

In addition to the features provided by the `NavigateURL` method, `EditURL` is another function for building navigation for your module. It is provided by `PortalModuleBase`. This method does not accept a `TabID` value because it assumes it is being used for the current module instance, and it simply returns the URL to the page displaying the `Edit` user control of your module. The only place that `EditUrl` is used in the WROX.Suggestion module is in the `ModuleActions` property in Suggestion.ascx.vb where the `Edit` menu item is defined.

Summary

This completes the chapter series on module development and architecture. In Chapter 13, you developed your physical provider class, which provides methods to expose your stored procedures in the database. From there, you moved on to creating an abstraction class, and finally exposing the result set of records as a collection of objects from your Business Logic Layer (see Chapter 14).

In this chapter, you did the following:

- You combined your work with those classes from the previous two chapters and then bound them to your module controls. Modules consist of several types of controls. The more common ones are as follows:
  - The View control for the initial view of a module, and you can have multiple View controls, as in the WROX.Suggestion module example
  - The Settings control, for configuring properties of a module instance
  - The Edit control, for editing information specific to your business logic for the module application
- You learned about styling your user controls with CSS definitions.

- You learned about localizing the strings displayed by your module.
- You learned about reusable DNN controls, such as the DNN Label control, that you can use in your projects to reduce development time and easily improve the functionality of your modules.
- You learned of various helper functions that you can use in your own projects to reduce the amount of custom code.

This should provide you with enough information to begin developing your own module for DotNetNuke. In Chapter 17, ''Distribution,'' you learn how to package these modules for distribution to other DotNetNuke portals. But first, in Chapter 16, ''Skinning DotNetNuke,'' you explore skinning the DotNetNuke application and how to provide a unique look for your portal installation.

16

Skinning DotNetNuke

DotNetNuke 5 is an exciting time for skin developers. Enhancements to existing functionality, like the new format for Skinobjects, make existing features easier to use. New layout features like super stylesheets add layout templates to make CSS-based layouts simpler to implement and more consistent across all skins. The client-side widget framework opens up a whole new area for designers and developers to collaborate to add interactive and dynamic features to DotNetNuke skins. With these new tools and the emerging focus on standards compliance, skin developers and designers will be able create more dynamic, interactive, and accessible designs in less time. This chapter covers using HTML and CSS to create skins and containers to change the look and feel of DotNetNuke web sites. This chapter demonstrates skinning using XHTML- and CSS-based layouts. You learn the basics of how to build a skin and container from scratch, use CSS to create advanced layouts, and use Skinobjects and widgets to add functionality to your designs.

DotNetNuke uses templates to accomplish skinning because they provide for the separation of the presentation and layout attributes from the application logic required to display content to the user. The Core Team studied various approaches to enable this functionality and have created a solution that will give both developers and designers independence when implementing DotNetNuke sites. This results in faster deployment times and, more importantly, reduced expense with getting your portal functional and performing its intended purpose.

The abstraction of the user interface elements from a page can be accomplished using different methodologies. The method chosen includes some degree of parsing to merge the presentation with the business logic. Therefore, defining where, when, and how this parsing will take place becomes critical to the success of the entire solution.

The use of tokens or identifiers in the user interface files to represent dynamic functionality is a popular technique employed in many skinning solutions. DotNetNuke uses this approach in its skinning engine solution: as the page is processed, the token is replaced to the proper Skinobject or control for the function the token identifies. Some of these tokens serve as what are referred to as *Content Panes*. Content Panes, simply put, are areas of HTML where dynamic content will be populated at runtime. The dynamic content is populated by the use of modules. The details of how this is accomplished are discussed later.

DotNetNuke enables you to create skins using your favorite editor, which gives you as a skin developer a good amount of flexibility — you only need to follow the rules for creating a skin; the tool you use to create it is up to you. You can create either an ASCX or HTML skin. The type you create depends on your choice of editor and the set of rules you choose to follow. Offering designers the ability to create the skins in HTML or ASP.NET was a conscious choice made to allow for the most flexibility with creating these skins and to help bridge the gap between designers and developers. The Core Team realized there are still more HTML developers in the world than ASP.NET developers, so allowing skins to be created in HTML enables many more individuals to use this functionality without having to learn new skills — other than how to place the tokens within the skin design. Now that you have a little history of why the engine was created, the following section looks at why it is still being used despite the introduction of Master Pages.

ASP.NET 2.0 Master Pages Versus Skinning

The goal behind this section is to offer a minimal understanding of ASP.NET 2.0 Master Pages so there is a basis for comparison between them and the DotNetNuke skinning engine. This section is not a definitive guide on how to get started using Master Pages.

A Brief Introduction to Master Pages

With ASP.NET 2.0 a new concept of Master Pages was introduced. For those who have done HTML design work in the past with Dreamweaver, this concept is similar to Dreamweaver HTML templates that have a file extension of `.dwt`. The idea behind Master Pages is a pretty simple one: create a page template that allows for a consistent look and feel throughout an ASP.NET application while also allowing for various content areas to be replaced at runtime. Each Master Page template uses the `.master` file extension and can be created and used when you're working within Microsoft's Visual Web Developer.

One of the things that makes Master Pages different from normal HTML design templates is that they use a ContentPlaceHolder that allows for content to be merged from Content Pages at runtime. These content placeholders are represented by `<asp:contentplaceholder>` controls in the HTML code view of the Master Page template. As a developer or designer, you have the ability to use more than one ContentPlaceHolder within a single Master Page as long as you give each one its own unique ID within that page. Each ContentPlaceHolder on a Master Page is replaced with a Content Page at runtime. This means that for each ContentPlaceHolder you want to have replaced at runtime, you must create a Content Page for it. If you do not have a Content Page for every ContentPlaceHolder, default content will be loaded into the ContentPlaceHolders with no corresponding Content Pages. These Content Pages are linked to the Master Page using the @ Page directive at the top of the page, and the actual content area is enclosed within the `<asp:content>` tag and its corresponding closing tag. Because the Content Page is linked to the Master Page, and will get injected into that Master Page at runtime, the normal `HTML`, `BODY`, `HEAD`, and `FORM` markup tags are not necessary. In fact, using one of these HTML markup tags outside of the Content control throws the following error at time of compilation: "Only Content controls are allowed directly in a Content Page that contains Content control."

Master Pages are definitely a step in the right direction for Microsoft and the `.NET` platform. They allow for the separation of content from the page and provide an easier way to get a consistent look and feel throughout the entire application.

Why DotNetNuke Still Uses Its Skinning Engine

Considering all the advancements that were made for developers and designers with the introduction of Master Pages, you are probably asking yourself, "Why is DotNetNuke still using its proprietary skinning engine rather than taking advantage of Master Pages?" Even with the flexibility introduced with Master Pages, they are not without restrictions of their own.

One restriction of Master Pages is the lack of complete separation between the developer and the designer. It's great that with Master Pages a developer can isolate the content area and then ask the designer to work on that specific area. Although this isolates the designer to a specific area, many designers are not comfortable working within the Visual Studio environment despite the IDE used in Visual Studio, which shows the Master Page with the Content Page loaded into it at design time. For designers to be as productive as possible, they must be able to use the tools they feel most comfortable with. One thing that should not be overlooked is that many designers use an Apple operating system, which will not run Visual Studio, therefore making the concept of Master Pages useless to these designers unless they work in a text editor. Why should HTML design be limited to a designer using a Microsoft Windows operating system?

This is one of the great benefits of the DotNetNuke skinning engine. It removes these restrictions placed on the designers. They are free to design on whatever operating system using whatever tools they choose, thus allowing them to be more productive.

Another restriction of Master Pages is that even though the designer is limited to a specific content area, there is still `.NET` code throughout that area. If designers open a Content Page in Visual Studio or their favorite HTML editor, they will see the @ Page directive and server control tags. If the designer has little or no experience working with ASP.NET applications, he could easily, and possibly unknowingly, alter one of these lines of code. If this happens, it means the developer has to spend time tracking down the problem. Because DotNetNuke completely isolates the design from the code by using the skins in combination with modules and skin objects, this situation is less likely to occur. Not only do the chances of a designer altering a developer's work decrease exponentially, it also allows them to work completely independent of one another. The developers can now spend their time developing modules, and the designers can spend their time creating skins and containers. With this complete separation between the two, both designers and developers can be working on the same site simultaneously instead of one waiting for the other.

As you can see, there are several good reasons why DotNetNuke still uses its own proprietary skinning engine instead of implementing Master Pages. One thing that was not addressed is the amount of development effort it would have taken to implement the Master Pages model. Just because a new feature was introduced to the ASP.NET framework, it is not necessarily better than one that was designed to fill a void left by the previous version of the ASP.NET framework. Using the DotNetNuke skinning engine, designers can work more efficiently and produce a better design without having to be concerned with altering the developer's code. The decision to still use the DotNetNuke skinning engine instead of Master Pages was not one that held DotNetNuke back, but one that kept it a step ahead.

File Organization

A skin package must meet certain conditions before it will install into the application. After the requirements are met, you can upload a compressed zip file containing your skin using the extensions manager, and the application will convert your files for use as a portal skin. Then, after the portal skins are successfully installed, they can be applied at several levels within the application — you can define a skin to be Host-, portal-, or page-level, depending on your needs.

Though skins can be applied at three separate levels, they can be stored in one of two separate places on the file system. Where these files actually reside depends on from where and on what portal they are installed.

When the skin is installed from the Host's Extensions menu item — something that is only possible if you are logged in as a SuperUser — it is placed in the Portals_default\Skins directory. During the skin install process, a folder is created in this directory matching the name of your zip file minus the `.zip` extension. This folder will contain the contents of your installed zip file, retaining the directory structure it had within this zip file. Please note that the legacy method of having a zip file of one name that contains a skins.zip file, which during the install process is stored in a folder with the same name as the zip file you uploaded, is still supported. A skin package made in this way often has a master zip file such as skinpackage.zip that contains a skins.zip, so that the skin package can also contain a containers.zip, which includes all containers designed for the skin package. This installs the containers.zip following the same rules with the exception that it places the files in the Portals_default\Containers folder instead.

If a skin is installed from the Admin's Extensions menu item, the resulting folder will be placed in the Portals\PortalId\Skins directory. PortalId varies, depending on which portal you installed this on. If you are running only one portal on a DotNetNuke install, for example, this normally is named 0. Depending on your Host Settings, it may only be possible for a SuperUser to install skins at the portal level. This chapter's examples use the _default Host-level folder. Anywhere in the remainder of this chapter that you see Portals_default\Skins, assume that you could also substitute PortalId for _default and accomplish the same thing, except the skin will be available at the portal level.

In DotNetNuke 5, skins are treated as extensions just like modules, providers, and any other extension that you can add into your DotNetNuke installation. New features come with the ability to treat skins as extensions including licensing agreements, release notes, and an uninstall feature for skins. The new features in the deployment and packaging of skins are covered in Chapter 17, "Distribution."

Skin Parsing

In order to create DotNetNuke skins from graphic designers' files you'll need to convert the design files to HTML and decorate the HTML with tokens using the new HTML object format or ASCX user controls to let the DotNetNuke skinning engine know where to inject the functionality required to run the DotNetNuke site. The process of converting graphic design files (often from Adobe Photoshop or Illustrator files) to HTML formatted as DotNetNuke skins and containers is often called the *production* phase of skinning.

The DotNetNuke skinning engine has a parser built into it that converts *.HTM and *.HTML into the correct file type so that HTML developers can use the tools they are most comfortable with and then convert the files once they are ready to use them in their portal. For DotNetNuke to be able to use a skin or container, it must be an ASP.NET ASCX user control. Though it is a simple step, many developers choose to work directly in the ASCX format so that they can see changes to their skins and containers without having to convert the HTML files to the ASP.NET format. Figure 16-1 shows the folder where the default skin is stored in the \portals_default\Skins\MinimalExtropy\ folder. Use the following steps to convert the HTML files into the ASCX file format that DotNetNuke uses for skins.

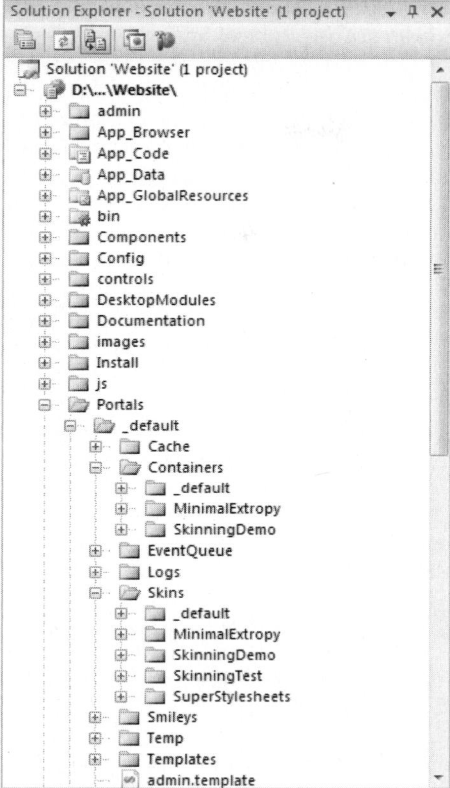

Figure 16-1

1. Make a copy of the MinimalExtropy folder and name it SkinningTest.
2. Navigate to the Extensions page under the Admin menu. Select the Manage Skins link from the hover menu for the module.
3. Change the drop-down to SkinningTest to bring up the skin package you just copied.
4. Notice that there is one skin available for this package named Index. Delete Index.ascx from the SkinningTest folder, then refresh the skinning administration in the browser. Notice that it now says "No Skin Files Exist in Folder."
5. Click the Parse Skin Package link. There should now be a file called Index.ascx in the SkinningTest folder and a skin named Index available in the skin package.

By clicking the Parse Skin Package link, you told DotNetNuke to search the folder and convert any *.HTM and *.HTML files to the ASP.NET ASCX user control format that DotNetNuke uses for skins. Because there was a file named Index.html, DotNetNuke converted it to Index.ascx to make it available as a DotNetNuke skin.

For the most part, whether to design in HTML or directly in the ASP.NET ASCX User Control format is a matter of preference. HTML developers who are more familiar with the tools created for HTML designers like Adobe Dreamweaver or Microsoft Expression will feel most comfortable using those tools to create DotNetNuke skins in the HTML format and using the skin parser to convert them to ASCX user controls. Developers who are accustomed to using Visual Studio or Visual Web Developer, the free version of Visual Studio, will most likely work directly in the ASCX format. There are two main benefits to working in the native ASCX format: IntelliSense for Skinobject controls (see Figure 16-2) and the ability to test changes to your skin without having to reparse it after every change. To address those two shortcomings of the HTML skinning method, the Core Team has promised future enhancements to allow WYSIWYG editing for the skins in HTML format and Dreamweaver extensions to enable IntelliSense for DotNetNuke skin objects, but at the time of writing these are not yet available.

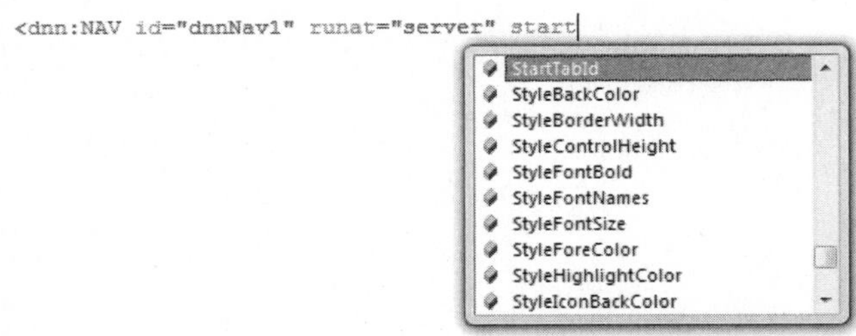

Figure 16-2

Building DotNetNuke Skins

To create a skin, a few elements must be included within your skin. First, you'll need a `<div>`, `<span>`, or table cell `<td>` that is named `ContentPane`. `ContentPane` is the default Pane to which DotNetNuke adds modules for display. Second, you'll need a menu so that you can navigate the public and administration pages in your site. Third, you'll need the login and user profile controls to be able to log in, log out, and edit your profile. Use the following walkthrough to try creating a basic skin from scratch.

To begin, create a folder named SkinningDemo within \portals_default\Skins\, and add a file within the folder named skin.css with the following styles (modified from the menu.css stylesheet in the default MinimalExtropy skin):

```
/*--------- dnn menu style ----------*/
/* main menu td */
.main_dnnmenu_bar
{
 cursor:pointer;
 font-size: 11px;
 background-color:transparent;
}

/*  Main Menu Normal  */
.main_dnnmenu_rootitem
{
 color: #43494D;
 font-size: 13px;
 font-weight:bold;
 text-align:center;
 line-height:40px;
 padding:12px 12px 12px 12px;
```

```
 text-transform:uppercase; margin-right:1px;
}

/*  Main menu hover  */
.main_dnnmenu_rootitem_hover
{
 color:#CE0D0D;
 font-size: 13px;
 font-weight:bold;
 text-align:center;
 line-height:40px;
 padding:12px 12px 12px 12px;
 text-transform:uppercase; margin-right:1px;
}

/*  Main menu selected  */
.main_dnnmenu_rootitem_selected
{
 color:#CE0D0D;
 font-weight:bold;
 text-align:center;
 font-size: 13px;
 line-height:40px;
 padding:12px 12px 12px 12px;
 text-transform:uppercase; margin-right:1px;
}

/*  SUB Menu Normal */
.main_dnnmenu_submenu
{
 border:1px solid #C0D6E5;
}

.main_dnnmenu_submenu td
{
 background-color:#E1E8ED;
 z-index: 1000;
 font-size: 11px;
 font-weight:bold;
 text-align:left;
 color:#000000;
 line-height:2em;
 padding: 0px 5px;
 margin:0px;
}

/*  SUB Menu hover & selected */
.main_dnnmenu_itemhover td,.main_dnnmenu_itemselected td
{
 font-size: 11px;
 background: #CE0D0D;
 color:#ffffff;
 font-weight:bold;
 text-align:left;
 line-height:2em;
```

```
  z-index: 1000;
  padding: 0px 5px;
  margin:0px;
}
```

To demonstrate how to make skins using the HTML skinning method, this section starts with a standard HTML page and adds in the Skinobjects to manage the skin. To begin, add a new HTML file in the \portals_default\Skins\SkinningDemo folder named HTMLMethod.html with the text that follows:

```
<!DOCTYPE html PUBLIC "-//W3C//DTD XHTML 1.0 Transitional//EN"
"http://www.w3.org/TR/xhtml1/DTD/xhtml1-transitional.dtd">
<html xmlns="http://www.w3.org/1999/xhtml">
<head>
<link id="skin_css" href="skin.css" type="text/css" rel="stylesheet" />
    <title></title>
</head>
<body>
</body>
</html>
```

Within the BODY tag, add the four required skin objects:

```
<!-- Menu Skinobject -->
<div id="Menu">
 <object id="dnnNAV" codetype="dotnetnuke/server" codebase="NAV" >
  <param name="ProviderName" value="DNNMenuNavigationProvider" />
  <param name="ControlOrientation" value="Horizontal" />
  <param name="CSSNodeRoot" value="main_dnnmenu_rootitem" />
  <param name="CSSNodeHoverRoot" value="main_dnnmenu_rootitem_hover" />
  <param name="CSSNodeSelectedRoot" value="main_dnnmenu_rootitem_selected" />
  <param name="CSSBreadCrumbRoot" value="main_dnnmenu_rootitem_selected" />
  <param name="CSSContainerSub" value="main_dnnmenu_submenu" />
  <param name="CSSNodeHoverSub" value="main_dnnmenu_itemhover" />
  <param name="CSSNodeSelectedSub" value="main_dnnmenu_itemselected" />
  <param name="CSSContainerRoot" value="main_dnnmenu_container" />
  <param name="CSSControl" value="main_dnnmenu_bar" />
  <param name="CSSBreak" value="main_dnnmenu_break" />
 </object>
</div>


<!-- User and Login Skinobjects -->
<div id="User">
<object id="dnnUSER" codetype="dotnetnuke/server" codebase="USER" ></object>
  |  
<object id="dnnLOGIN" codetype="dotnetnuke/server" codebase="LOGIN" ></object>
</div>


<!-- ContentPane Skinobject -->
<object id="ContentPane" codetype="dotnetnuke/server" codebase="CONTENTPANE">
</object>
```

Now that you have the base requirements for a skin, use the Parse Skin Package link on the Manage Skins screen on the Admin, Extensions page to convert your HTMLMethod.html to a DotNetNuke skin. There should now be a file in the folder name HTMLMethod.ascx, which is shown in the following code:

```
<%@ Control language="vb" AutoEventWireup="false" Explicit="True"
Inherits="DotNetNuke.UI.Skins.Skin" %>
<%@ Register TagPrefix="dnn" TagName="NAV" Src="~/Admin/Skins/Nav.ascx" %>
<%@ Register TagPrefix="dnn" TagName="USER" Src="~/Admin/Skins/User.ascx" %>
<%@ Register TagPrefix="dnn" TagName="LOGIN" Src="~/Admin/Skins/Login.ascx" %>


<!-- Menu Skinobject -->
<div id="Menu">
 <dnn:NAV runat="server" id="dnnNAV"  ProviderName="DNNMenuNavigationProvider"
ControlOrientation="Horizontal" CSSNodeRoot="main_dnnmenu_rootitem"
CSSNodeHoverRoot="main_dnnmenu_rootitem_hover"
CSSNodeSelectedRoot="main_dnnmenu_rootitem_selected"
CSSBreadCrumbRoot="main_dnnmenu_rootitem_selected"
CSSContainerSub="main_dnnmenu_submenu" CSSNodeHoverSub="main_dnnmenu_itemhover"
CSSNodeSelectedSub="main_dnnmenu_itemselected"
CSSContainerRoot="main_dnnmenu_container" CSSControl="main_dnnmenu_bar"
CSSBreak="main_dnnmenu_break" />
</div>


<!-- User and Login Skinobjects -->
<div id="User">
<dnn:USER runat="server" id="dnnUSER" />
  |  
<dnn:LOGIN runat="server" id="dnnLOGIN" />
</div>


<!-- ContentPane Skinobject -->
<div runat="server" id="ContentPane" ></div>
```

Developers and designers familiar with ASP.NET will recognize that the resulting skin file is made up of ASCX user controls. A couple of things were removed, though, from the original HTML. First, everything outside the `BODY` tag was removed from the final skin. This removed the `doctype` declaration that defined the HTML file as XHTML, and the stylesheet reference was removed because that was in the head tag. DotNetNuke has a convention for naming stylesheets that accounts for this, so by naming your stylesheet skin.css, the link tag with the reference to your stylesheet is automatically created by DotNetNuke. The `doctype`, though, was not automatically added. To set the `doctype`, create a file called `[SKINNAME].doctype.xml`. For the HTMLMethod skin to be set as XHTML Transitional as was set in the original HTML file, add the filename `HTMLMethod.doctype.xml` to your SkinningDemo folder with the following code:

```
<SkinDocType>
 <![CDATA[<!DOCTYPE html PUBLIC "-//W3C//DTD XHTML 1.0 Transitional//EN"
"http://www.w3.org/TR/xhtml1/DTD/xhtml1-transitional.dtd">]]>
</SkinDocType>
```

ASCX Skinning Method

Many developers would see the conversion process as an unnecessary extra step in the production phase of skinning and would rather start with the ASP.NET user controls so that they are able to make changes directly to the skin files and see the results without having to parse the skin package every time a change is made. To design a skin in ASCX format, you'll need to add a couple of extra steps to the beginning of your skinning process. First, in order to tell ASP.NET what kind of control the skin file is, add the following directive to the very top of the ASCX skin:

```
<%@ Control language="vb" AutoEventWireup="false" Explicit="True"
Inherits="DotNetNuke.UI.Skins.Skin" %>
```

With the ASCX method, adding Skinobjects to a skin is done by adding the control declaration to the top of the skin, and then placing the Skinobject anywhere within the HTML of the skin. Continuing with the code, the following example has the control declaration for the login control at the top, then the login within a `<div>` with the ID "User" for controlling layout and style from the stylesheet. Also, add in a `<div>` with the ID attribute set to `ContentPane` and the `runat="server"` attribute and your skin will be ready to be used.

```
<%@ Control language="vb" AutoEventWireup="false" Explicit="True"
Inherits="DotNetNuke.UI.Skins.Skin" %>
<%@ Register TagPrefix="dnn" TagName="LOGIN" Src="~/Admin/Skins/Login.ascx" %>

<!-- Login Skinobject -->
<div id="User">
 <dnn:LOGIN runat="server" id="dnnLOGIN" />
</div>

<!-- ContentPane Skinobject -->
<div runat="server" id="ContentPane" ></div>
```

To complete your skin, copy the `User` and `Nav` user controls resulting from the HTML conversion process and you will have covered the basics to have a functional skin.

Controlling Layout with Panes and Stylesheets

The preceding section covered the basics of how to use the Skinobjects required to create a skin, but the result was anything but pretty. This section explores layout options with Panes and controlling layout with CSS stylesheets. As you learned earlier in the chapter, DotNetNuke skins have dynamic content regions called Panes. Pane layouts create the structure through which modules can be added to DotNet-Nuke pages. In a DotNetNuke skin, three HTML elements can be made into a Pane: the `<div>`, table cell `<td>`, and `<span>`. By allowing any of these three elements to be turned into a Pane, the DotNetNuke skinning engine enables designers to use any number of layout combinations that they could use in a static HTML page.

Earlier in this chapter you used the Skinobject with codebase set to `CONTENTPANE`. You may have noticed that after parsing the skin, the `CONTENTPANE` Skinobject was simply turned into a `<div>` with special `runat="server"` attributes added to it. Because Panes are simply HTML elements with a special attribute, most HTML method developers will skip the `CONTENTPANE` Skinobject in favor of having a WYSIWYG experience of seeing the Panes as they are being developed. To use one of the three possible HTML elements as a Pane, simply add a unique id and the attribute `runat="server"` and the

DotNetNuke skinning engine will treat the element as a Pane. The following example shows three ways to create a layout Pane in your DotNetNuke skins:

```
<table>
    <tr>
        <td id="ContentPane" runat="server"  class="ContentPane"></>
        </td>
    </tr>
</table>
<div runat="server" id="DivPane" class="DivPane"></></div>
<span runat="server" id="SpanPane" class="SpanPane"></></span>
```

Even though the `runat="server"` attribute is an ASP.NET attribute, the attribute will be ignored by browsers when viewing the file as a standard HTML page before the skin parsing process. This gives designers using popular HTML development tools like Adobe Dreamweaver or Expression a better WYSIWYG experience than using the `CONTENTPANE` Skinobject, because they will be able to see the results of the layout and CSS changes as they make edits.

IDs and Classes

Taking the time to understand the HTML that is rendered on the final page will help HTML developers spend less time revising and troubleshooting their markup. Using the `<div>` example, the `ID` is set to `ContentPane` in the source HTML. After the page is rendered as a DotNetNuke page, ASP.NET changes the `ID`:

```
<div id="dnn_DivPane" class="DivPane"></div>
```

Though this is not a drastic change in how the content is rendered, it does bring up the point that a Pane's layout should not be controlled in CSS with the `ID`. For this reason, the examples make use of a class attribute, which can be used to control the layout.

Handling Empty Panes

The Pane layout system affords designers the ability to create multiple Pane layouts within the same skin. Designers can create multiple layout options in a single skin and the layout option that is not used can be set to collapse. For instance, a web site may have several different layouts used for different sections of the site. A product details section may need a left Pane with a smaller content area, where the catalog section may show a grid where the content takes up the full area. With DotNetNuke, designers can make one skin that handles these two layout options by collapsing the section that is not used. When a Pane does not have any modules added to it, the Pane will have a class added to it to indicate that it is an empty Pane:

```
<div runat="server" id="ContentPane" class="ContentPane"></div>
```

When the Pane in this example is rendered, it will appear in the final HTML as shown in the following code example:

```
<div id="dnn_ContentPane" class="ContentPane DNNEmptyPane"></div>
```

DotNetNuke automatically adds an additional class to the Pane to indicate that the Pane is empty. Though this is useful because it provides the ability to control the element or even hide it by using the `display:none` CSS rule, there is still an extra HTML element in the rendered skin that may affect the layout of the page. Because adding the `runat="server"` attribute makes the Pane an ASP.NET control, there is another way to hide the element. By adding `visible="false"`, DotNetNuke will only render the HTML element for the Pane on the page if the Pane has module contents. The following code will be removed and never rendered to the DotNetNuke page if it contains no module contents:

```
<div runat="server" id="ContentPane" class="ContentPane" visible="false"></div>
```

HTML developers who still use tables for layout should not use the `visible="false"` technique because it results in invalid HTML. The following example shows the result of empty Panes in a table layout system that uses `visible="false"` to hide empty Panes:

```
<table>
<tr>
 <td id="TopPane" runat="server" visible="false"></td>
</tr>
<tr>
 <td id="LeftPane" runat="server" visible="false"></td>
 <td id="ContentPane" runat="server" visible="false"></td>
 <td id="RighPane" runat="server" visible="false"></td>
</tr>
</table>
<table>
<tr>

</tr>
<tr>



</tr>
</table>
```

For developers who use tables for layout, there is also a client-side widget for handling empty Panes covered later in this chapter.

Using CSS and divs to Create Valid Layouts

By using CSS layout, HTML developers can create skins that are more standards-compliant, faster to load, and easier to maintain. Although an explanation of CSS layout and its techniques are outside of the scope of this book, the following example shows how to achieve the same layout behavior without the extra markup required to use the table layout method:

```
<div id="wrapper">
<div id="wrapper-inner">

<!-- ContentPane Skinobject -->
<div id="OneCol">
 <div class="OneColFull" runat="server" id="ContentPane" visible="false"></div>
</div><!-- End One Col -->

<div id="TwoColR">
 <div class="TwoColThird" id="RightThird" runat="server" visible="false"></div>
 <div class="TwoColFull" id="RightFull" runat="server" visible="false"></div>
</div><!-- End Two Col Right -->
```

```
<div id="TwoColL">
 <div class="TwoColFull" id="LeftFull" runat="server" visible="false"></div>
 <div class="TwoColThird" id="LeftThird" runat="server" visible="false"></div>
</div><!-- End Two Col Left -->

<div id="ThreeCol">
 <div class="ThreeColLeft" id="ThreeColLeft" runat="server" visible="false"></div>
 <div class="ThreeColCenter" id="ThreeColCenter" runat="server" visible="false">
</div>
 <div class="ThreeColRight" id="ThreeColRight" runat="server" visible="false">
</div>
</div><!-- End Three Col -->

</div><!-- End Wrapper Inner -->
</div><!-- End Wrapper -->
```

To make the preceding example function correctly, the following styles should be added to the skin's skin.css file:

```
#wrapper{text-align: center;}
#wrapper-inner{
 clear:both;
 margin: 0 auto;
 width: 974px;
 text-align:left;
}
#TwoColR, #TwoColL, #OneCol, #ThreeCol{clear:both;}

.OneColFull{width:100%;}
.TwoColThird{float:left;width:33%;}
.TwoColFull{float:left;width:67%;}
.ThreeColLeft{float:left;width:25%;}
.ThreeColCenter{float:left;width:50%;}
.ThreeColRight{float:left;width:25%;}
```

This layout provides ultimate flexibility because a page manager can choose from any of the three layouts on a single skin by simply adding content to the Pane layout they choose. Whichever layout is not used will be collapsed.

One problem with this setup is that, in Layout mode, DotNetNuke places an inline style to add a border around each Pane. In Mozilla browsers, that will break the `float` effect of the `divs` acting as Panes and result in a poor WYSIWYG experience for page managers. The problem is caused by how Mozilla browsers add the border to the outside of the element, which means that the width of Panes in layouts that add up to 100% width end up with 100% width plus 1px of dotted border on each line. That causes the `float` rule to wrap the Pane to the next line, like in Figure 16-3.

To get around this problem, you can add the class NoPaneBorder to each Pane div and add the following CSS rules to your skin.css to hide the border and make the Pane title label appear as a header (see Figure 16-4):

```
<div class="OneColFull NoPaneBorder" runat="server" id="ContentPane"
visible="false"></div>
.NoPaneBorder{border:0px !important;}
```

```
.NoPaneBorder span.SubHead center{background-color:#efefef;border: 2px solid
#e9e9e9;color:#000000;margin:1px;padding:2px;}
```

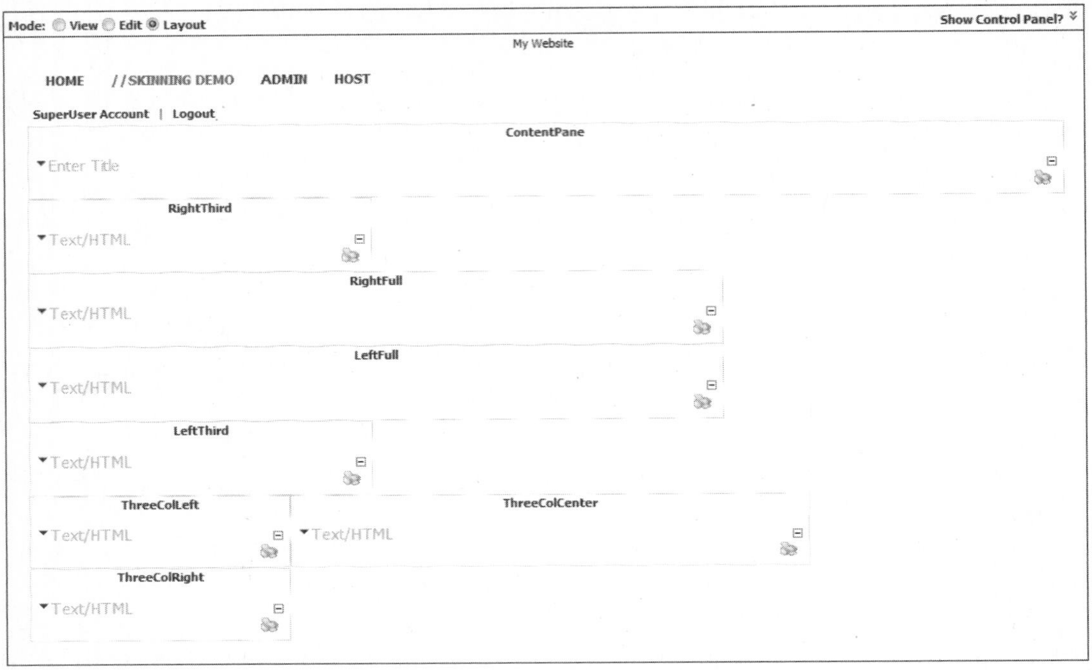

Figure 16-3

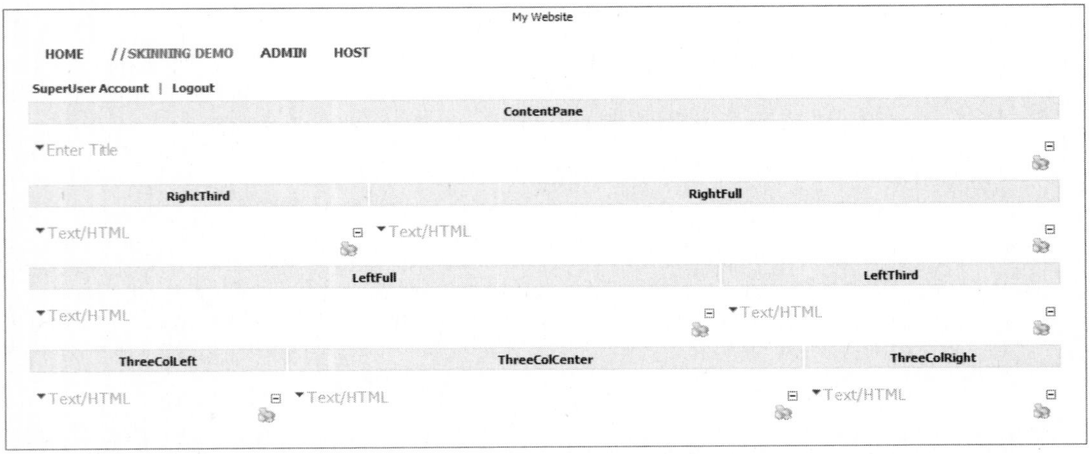

Figure 16-4

Creating a Basic Container

As explained in the beginning of the chapter, a container is the HTML markup that decorates a module on a DotNetNuke page. Like a skin, a container has Skinobjects to place functionality within the HTML template to give the designer complete control over how the DotNetNuke pages and modules should lay out. Like skins, there are a few elements that must be included within your container. First, you'll need a `<div>`, `<span>`, or table cell `<td>` that is named `ContentPane`. `ContentPane` is the Pane in which DotNetNuke injects module content for display. Second, you'll need to add the controls that enable management of the module.

To begin, create a folder named SkinningDemo within \portals_default\Containers\, and add a file within the folder named container.css. Next, create a new HTML file named HTMLContainer.html in your new SkinningDemo folder and add links to the skin.css and container.css files to test against the existing skins:

```
<!DOCTYPE html PUBLIC "-//W3C//DTD XHTML 1.0 Transitional//EN"
"http://www.w3.org/TR/xhtml1/DTD/xhtml1-transitional.dtd">

<html xmlns="http://www.w3.org/1999/xhtml">
<head>
<link id="skin_css" href="../../Skins/SkinningDemo/skin.css" type="text/css"
rel="stylesheet" />
<link id="container_css" href="container.css" type="text/css" rel="stylesheet" />
    <title></title>
</head>
<body>

</body>
</html>
```

The two controls that are required to be in the container for the container to work are the `ContentPane` and the `ACTIONS` menu. Like in skins, the `ContentPane` in the container is the placeholder in which content is rendered. In this case, the module contents are displayed within the `ContentPane`. The `ACTIONS` Skinobject places the drop-down menu that gives access to the Settings interface, Move menu, and other module-specific actions. Add the object tag and the `ContentPane` to your container.

```
<div id="ContentPane" class="Demo_Content Normal" runat="server"></div>
<object id="ModuleMenu" codetype="dotnetnuke/server" codebase="ACTIONS" >
 <param name="ProviderName" value="DNNMenuNavigationProvider" />
 <param name="ExpandDepth" value="1" />
 <param name="PopulateNodesFromClient" value="True" />
</object>
```

With these two Skinobjects, the basic requirements of a container are fulfilled, but like the basic skin created in the beginning of the "Building DotNetNuke Skins" section, the layout is not yet usable. To begin, wrap the container's contents with a `<div>` that controls the margin around the module content. By including the margin within the module's contents, the problem that was run into in the preceding section with the border around Panes being included in the calculation of width for a layout is not introduced. The margin is then applied to the module contents, and whether Mozilla applies the margin to the outside of the width of the Pane or Internet Explorer applies it inside the Pane is inconsequential because the div expands to fill the Pane in the skin in which it is placed. The other Skinobjects that are important regardless of whether they are required are the `TITLE` object, the management action objects, and the user interface action objects. The following code example shows the Layout and Skinobjects included, with the `Body` and `Head` sections of the HTML document removed for brevity:

```
<div class="PaneMargin">
<div class="Demo_Header">
```

```
<object id="ModuleMenu" codetype="dotnetnuke/server" codebase="ACTIONS" >
 <param name="ProviderName" value="DNNMenuNavigationProvider" />
 <param name="ExpandDepth" value="1" />
 <param name="PopulateNodesFromClient" value="True" />
</object>

<div class="Demo_Visibility">
 <object id="Visibility" codetype="dotnetnuke/server"
codebase="VISIBILITY"></object>
</div><!--Visibility-->

 <h2>
 <object id="Title" codetype="dotnetnuke/server" codebase="TITLE" >
  <param name="cssclass" value="Demo_TitleLabel" />
 </object>
 </h2><!--Title-->

</div><!-- Header -->

<div id="ContentPane" class="Demo_Content Normal" runat="server"></div>

<div class="Demo_Footer">
<object id="AddContent" codetype="dotnetnuke/server" codebase="ACTIONBUTTON" >
 <param name="CommandName" value="AddContent.Action" />
 <param name="DisplayIcon" value="True" />
 <param name="DisplayLink" value="True" />
</object><!-- Add Action -->

<object id="Settings" codetype="dotnetnuke/server" codebase="ACTIONBUTTON" >
 <param name="CommandName" value="ModuleSettings.Action" />
 <param name="DisplayIcon" value="True" />
 <param name="DisplayLink" value="True" />
</object><!-- Module Settings Action -->

<object id="Syndicate" codetype="dotnetnuke/server" codebase="ACTIONBUTTON" >
 <param name="CommandName" value="SyndicateModule.Action" />
 <param name="DisplayIcon" value="True" />
 <param name="DisplayLink" value="False" />
</object><!-- RSS Syndication Action -->

<object id="Print" codetype="dotnetnuke/server" codebase="ACTIONBUTTON" >
 <param name="CommandName" value="PrintModule.Action" />
 <param name="DisplayIcon" value="True" />
 <param name="DisplayLink" value="False" />
</object><!-- Print Module Action -->

</div><!-- Footer -->

</div><!-- Pane Margin -->
```

Now, in the container.css stylesheet, add the following rules to control the layout of the module contents:

```
.Demo_Content{clear:both;}
.Demo_Footer{text-align:right;}
.Demo_Visibility{float:right;}
.Demo_Header span.ModuleTitle_MenuBar{float:left;}
.Demo_TitleLabel{color:GrayText;font-size:15px;}
```

To test the container, use the Parse Skin Package link on the manage skins interface of the extensions page in the Admin menu of your portal. The resulting HTML will appear consistently in up-level browsers and collapse footer regions that are not needed due to empty contents. HTML developers with their XHTML compliance hat on, however, will notice that the three divs that are included for layout do not include an ID attribute. This is done purposefully because the container can be used many times on a page and that will result in duplicate `IDs` for each of those elements every time it is used for a module. There is a way to handle this with server-side code injected into the module. You can see how the div associated with the class `demo_footer` could be updated to use the unique `ModuleID` that is wraps to provide a unique ID for the `div`:

```
div id="dnn_<%= ModuleConfiguration.ModuleID %>_Footer"  class="Demo_Footer">
<div id="dnn_372_Footer"  class="Demo_Footer">
```

Styles Guide — Stylesheet Inheritance and Core DotNetNuke Classes

One of the challenging aspects of DotNetNuke skinning is finding all of the base classes and overriding them. Most skin developers that use the HTML method of skinning have gotten their layout to look and work perfectly in their WYSIWYG editor only to upload the skin into DotNetNuke and see their design fall apart. The reason this happens is that stylesheets required to control the default look and management of DotNetNuke are applied before a custom skin is applied. These stylesheets can create default styles that are different from browser defaults, which will change the way a skin looks and behaves once it is part of DotNetNuke. Table 16-1 shows the hierarchy of stylesheet inheritance listed from highest to lowest priority using the example from earlier in the chapter for stylesheet names.

Developers who use the ASCX method of skinning will be able to see the effects of the stylesheets that cause the most trouble, like default.css and portal.css, because they are applied while the design process is taking place. HTML developers, on the other hand, can sometimes be surprised the first time they install their skin into DotNetNuke. This can add hours of troubleshooting and rework that can be avoided with a few simple additions to the base skin during the design process. Using the HTMLMethod.html skin from earlier in this chapter, add the stylesheet links to your skin, shown here. Note that the order is important because this will apply the stylesheets in the same order they will be applied in DotNetNuke.

```
<head>
<link id="default_css" href="../../default.css" type="text/css" rel="Stylesheet" />
<link id="skin_css" href="skin.css" type="text/css" rel="Stylesheet" />
<link id="portal_css" href="../../../0/portal.css" type="text/css" rel="
Stylesheet" /> </head>
```

Beyond overriding the default styles in DotNetNuke, skin designers need to include a handful of rules in their stylesheet to make sure that DotNetNuke controls and Skinobjects match the design they create. Table 16-2 lists the styles that should be included in every skin's stylesheet.

Table 16-1: Stylesheet Hierarchy in DotNetNuke Skins

File	Description
Portal.css	Stored in the root of the current portal at `/portals/PortalId/portal.css` where `PortalId` is replaced by the actual portal number. This file can be edited using the stylesheet editor on the Admin, Site Settings page.
HTMLContainer.css	Container-specific style. Whereas Container.css is the common stylesheet for all containers in a skin package, this can be used to apply styles specific to one container in the package. This is commonly used to create different color versions of the same container.
Container.css	Common stylesheet for all containers in a skin package.
HTMLMethod.css	Skin-specific style. Whereas Skin.css is the common stylesheet for all skins in a skin package, this can be used to apply styles specific to one skin in the package. This is commonly used to apply section-specific skin variations in a web site.
Skin.css	Common stylesheet for all skins in a skin package.
Default.css	This is the stylesheet used to define styles that are common to all portals in an installation. It contains default definitions for controls like the control panel, file manager, and wizard controls. This can cause problems with some styles because it defines styles for the H1, H2, a, UL, and other common HTML elements.
Module.css	Each module can have a custom stylesheet named module.css included with it. The styles included in this stylesheet define how that module should lay out. HTML designers should familiarize themselves with the classes defined in modules they need to style by reviewing the module.css stylesheet in the associated desktopmodules folder.

Add Functionality with Skinobjects

The newest version of DotNetNuke has enhanced the existing skinning engine with a new format for tokens using the native HTML `OBJECT` element. With this enhancement, HTML designers have complete control over the elements and attributes of the DotNetNuke skin objects without having to include an XML package within their skin package to format the tokens any longer.

Consider the following example:

```
<object id="dnnBREADCRUMB" codetype="dotnetnuke/server" codebase="BREADCRUMB" >
<param name="CssClass" value="Breadcrumb" />
<param name="RootLevel" value="0" />
<param name="Separator" value=" // " />
</object>
```

Table 16-2: Core DotNetNuke Style Classes

Class Name	Description
`Normal`, `NormalDisabled`	This class is used for general text throughout the site and controls. Developers apply this style to the text within tables, datagrids, gridviews, and datalists.
`NormalRed`	This class is used to style error messages in modules.
`NormalBold`	This class is used to style general text that is bold. This style is less common than `Normal` and `NormalRed`.
`NormalTextBox`	This class is used to style input textboxes.
`SubHead`	This class is used as section heads or paragraph titles and label titles on forms.
`SubSubHead`	This class is used to style third-level section headers and is used much less frequently than `SubHead`.
`Head`	This is the equivalent of an H1 tag. It is the default style for module titles and developers use it throughout their modules to signify main headings or section titles.
`SkinObjectSkinobject`	This class is used to define the Skinobject controls like the login, date, user, and breadcrumb controls. Because this can be used on links, make sure to define the a.SkinObjectSkinobject, a.SkinObjectSkinobject:link, and other link styles as well.
`CommandButton`	This style is used for links and linkbuttons.

The object tag is used to describe the DotNetNuke breadcrumb control. To include the same breadcrumb control in an ASCX skin, you have to register the tag at the beginning of the skin, and then you can add the user control anywhere within the skin.

```
<%@ Register TagPrefix="dnn" TagName="BREADCRUMB" Src="~/Admin/Skins
/BreadCrumb.ascx" %>

<dnn:BREADCRUMB runat="server" id="dnnBREADCRUMB"  CssClass="Breadcrumb"
RootLevel="0" Separator=" // " />
```

Skinobjects Reference

As explained in the beginning of the chapter, Skinobjects follow the common practice of using tokens to place server-side functionality into the templates used to format the CMS. This section is a reference for the available Skinobjects for DotNetNuke skins at the time of writing.

BANNER SKINOBJECT

Displays a random banner ad.

HTML Codebase Attribute BANNER

ASCX Register Code `<%@ Register TagPrefix="dnn" TagName="BANNER" Src="~/Admin/Skins/Banner.ascx" %>`

ASCX Control Usage `<dnn:BANNER runat="server" id="dnnBANNER" />`

BANNER SKINOBJECT PARAMETERS

Name	Description	Possible Values
GroupName	The groupname of the banner. Multiple banners in the same group can be displayed together or alternate between each other	
BannerTypeId	Defines the type of the banner: 1=Banner, 2=MicroButton, 3=Button, 4=Block, 5=Skyscraper, 6=Text, 7=Script	1,2,3,4,5,6,7
BannerCount	The number of banners to display at once	
Width	The width of the banners	
Orientation	Defines whether to display the banners Horizontally or Vertically	H,V
BorderWidth	The width of the border	
BorderColor	The color of the border	All HTML color names

BREADCRUMB SKINOBJECT

Displays the path to the currently selected tab in the form of PageName1 > PageName2 > PageName3.

HTML Codebase Attribute BREADCRUMB

ASCX Register Code `<%@ Register TagPrefix="dnn" TagName="BREADCRUMB" Src="~\Admin\Skins\BREADCRUMB.ascx" %>`

ASCX Control Usage `<dnn:BREADCRUMB runat="server" id="dnnBREADCRUMB" />`

BREADCRUMB SKINOBJECT PARAMETERS

Name	Description	Possible Values
CssClass	Sets the CSS class used to render this skin object	
Separator	Defines the separator to be used in between links	
RootLevel	Defines from which level in the page hierarchy the breadcrumb should render Same,Child,Parent,Root	
UseTitle	Defines whether to use the page name or the page title	True,False

COPYRIGHT SKINOBJECT

Displays the copyright notice for the portal.

HTML Codebase Attribute `COPYRIGHT`

ASCX Register Code
```
<%@ Register TagPrefix="dnn" TagName="COPYRIGHT"
Src="~\Admin\Skins\COPYRIGHT.ascx" %>
```

ASCX Control Usage
```
<dnn:COPYRIGHT runat="server" id="dnnCOPYRIGHT" />
```

COPYRIGHT SKINOBJECT PARAMETERS

Name	Description
CssClass	Sets the CSS class used to render this skin object

CURRENTDATE SKINOBJECT

Displays the current date according to the time on the server.

HTML Codebase Attribute `CURRENTDATE`

ASCX Register Code
```
<%@ Register TagPrefix="dnn" TagName="CURRENTDATE"
Src="~\Admin\Skins\CURRENTDATE.ascx" %>
```

ASCX Control Usage
```
<dnn:CURRENTDATE runat="server" id="dnnCURRENTDATE" />
```

CURRENTDATE SKINOBJECT PARAMETERS

Name	Description
CssClass	Sets the CSS class used to render this skin object
DateFormat	Sets the date format used to render the date

DOTNETNUKE SKINOBJECT

Displays the copyright notice for DotNetNuke.

HTML Codebase Attribute `DOTNETNUKE`

ASCX Register Code `<%@ Register TagPrefix="dnn" TagName="DOTNETNUKE" Src="~\Admin\Skins\DOTNETNUKE.ascx" %>`

ASCX Control Usage `<dnn:DOTNETNUKE runat="server" id="dnnDOTNETNUKE" />`

DOTNETNUKE SKINOBJECT PARAMETERS

Name	Description
CssClass	Sets the CSS class used to render this skin object

HELP SKINOBJECT

Displays a link for help, which will launch the user's email client and send mail to the portal administrator.

HTML Codebase Attribute `HELP`

ASCX Register Code `<%@ Register TagPrefix="dnn" TagName="HELP" Src="~\Admin\Skins\HELP.ascx" %>`

ASCX Control Usage `<dnn:HELP runat="server" id="dnnHELP" />`

HELP SKINOBJECT PARAMETERS

Name	Description
CssClass	Sets the CSS class used to render this skin object

HOSTNAME SKINOBJECT

Displays the host title linked to the host URL.

HTML Codebase Attribute `HOSTNAME`

ASCX Register Code `<%@ Register TagPrefix="dnn" TagName="HOSTNAME" Src="~\Admin\Skins\HOSTNAME.ascx" %>`

ASCX Control Usage `<dnn:HOSTNAME runat="server" id="dnnHOSTNAME" />`

HOSTNAME SKINOBJECT PARAMETERS

Name	Description
CssClass	Sets the CSS class used to render this skin object

LANGUAGE SKINOBJECT

Displays a selector to change the current language as a drop-down or a list of flags for each supported language.

HTML Codebase Attribute `LANGUAGE`

ASCX Register Code `<%@ Register TagPrefix="dnn" TagName="LANGUAGE" Src="~\Admin\Skins\LANGUAGE.ascx" %>`

ASCX Control Usage `<dnn:LANGUAGE runat="server" id="dnnLANGUAGE" />`

LANGUAGE SKINOBJECT PARAMETERS

Name	Description	Possible Values
CssClass	Sets the CSS class used to render the language menu when not in Links mode	
ItemTemplate	The item template to be used for displaying languages	
HeaderTemplate	The Header template to be used for displaying languages	
FooterTemplate	The Footer template to be used for displaying languages	

Name	Description	Possible Values
AlternateTemplate	The Alternate Template to be used for displaying language selections	
SeparatorTemplate	The Separator Template to be used for displaying language selections	
CommonHeaderTemplate	The Common Header Template to be used for displaying language selections	
CommonFooterTemplate	The Common Footer Template to be used for displaying language selections	
ShowMenu	Defines whether to display the language drop-down menu	True,False
ShowLinks	Defines whether to display the language links repeater	True,False

LINKS SKINOBJECT

Displays a flat menu of links related to the current tab level and parent node. This is useful for search engine spiders and robots.

HTML Codebase Attribute `LINKS`

ASCX Register Code `<%@ Register TagPrefix="dnn" TagName="LINKS" Src="~\Admin\Skins\LINKS.ascx" %>`

ASCX Control Usage `<dnn:LINKS runat="server" id="dnnLINKS" />`

LINKS SKINOBJECT PARAMETERS

Name	Description	Possible Values
CssClass	Sets the CSS class used to render this skin object	
Separator	Defines the separator to be used between links	
Level	Defines from where in the page tree links should be rendered	Same,Child, Parent,Root
Alignment	Defines whether the links will be rendered horizontally or vertically	Horizontal, Vertical
ShowDisabled	Sets whether disabled pages are displayed, defaults to False	True,False
ForceLinks	Sets if the links will be rendered with `Level="Same"` if there are not links in the current level	True,False

LOGIN SKINOBJECT

Displays the sign-in control for providing your username and password.

HTML Codebase Attribute `LOGIN`

ASCX Register Code `<%@ Register TagPrefix="dnn" TagName="LOGIN" Src="~\Admin\Skins\LOGIN.ascx" %>`

ASCX Control Usage `<dnn:LOGIN runat="server" id="dnnLOGIN" />`

LOGIN SKINOBJECT PARAMETERS

Name	Description
CssClass	Sets the CSS class used to render this skin object
Text	Overrides the default text for "Login"
LogoffText	Overrides the default text for "Logout"

LOGO SKINOBJECT

Displays the logo for the portal from the site settings page.

HTML Codebase Attribute `LOGO`

ASCX Register Code `<%@ Register TagPrefix="dnn" TagName="LOGO" Src="~\Admin\Skins\LOGO.ascx" %>`

ASCX Control Usage `<dnn:LOGO runat="server" id="dnnLOGO" />`

LOGO SKINOBJECT PARAMETERS

Name	Description
CssClass	Sets the CSS class used to render this skin object

NAV SKINOBJECT

Displays a hierarchical navigation menu constructed from the pages in the current portal. In the most recent version, this replaces the SolPartMenu Skinobject. It supports the provider model of menus to use different types of menus depending upon the designer's choice. The parameters listed are those that apply to the default menu provider DNNMenuNavigationProvider.

HTML Codebase Attribute NAV

ASCX Register Code `<%@ Register TagPrefix="dnn" TagName="NAV" Src="~\Admin\Skins\NAV.ascx" %>`

ASCX Control Usage `<dnn:NAV runat="server" id="dnnNAV" />`

NAV SKINOBJECT PARAMETERS

Name	Description	Possible Values
ControlOrientation	The orientation of the menu, default is Horizontal, usage depends on the provider used	Horizontal, Vertical
ExpandDepth	Sets the depth of the menu. Needs to be set at least to 1 in order for the menu to render	
ForceCrawlerDisplay	Defines whether to force rendering for crawlers	True,False
ForceDownLevel	Defines whether to force rendering for old (downlevel) browsers	True,False
IndicateChild-ImageRoot	Path to the root folder where the image is stored that is prepended to the image location	
IndicateChildImageSub	Path to an image to be used to indicate sub submenu items are present	
IndicateChildren	Whether to display an indicator to show that there are child menu items	True,False
Level	Defines which level needs to be used to render the menu, default value is "root"	Root, Child, Parent, Same
NodeLeftHTML-BreadCrumbRoot	Text to prepend to each menu item in the root level of the menu when the active page is a submenu item of that parent	
NodeLeftHTML-BreadCrumbSub	Text to prepend to each submenu item of the menu when the active page is a submenu item of that parent	
NodeLeftHTMLRoot	Text to prepend to each menu item in the root level of the menu	
NodeLeftHTMLSub	Text to prepend to each submenu item in the root level of the menu	
NodeRightHTML-BreadCrumbRoot	Text to append to each menu item in the root level of the menu when the active page is a submenu item of that parent	
NodeRightHTML BreadCrumbSub	Text to append to each submenu item of the menu when the active page is a submenu item of that parent	

Name	Description	Possible Values
NodeRightHTMLRoot	Text to append to each menu item in the root level of the menu	
NodeRightHTMLSub	Text to append to each submenu item in the root level of the menu	
PathSystemScript	Optional override location for the scripts that drive the menu	
PopulateNodes FromClient	Sets whether to use AJAX to render the menu	True,False
ProviderName	Sets the menu provider used to render the menu, defaults to SolpartMenuNavigationProvider	SolpartMenu-NavigationProvider, DNNMenuNavigationProvider, DNNTree-NavigationProvider, DNNDropDown-NavigationProvider, ASP2Menu-NavigationProvider
SeparatorHTML	Text to use as a separator for root menu items	
SeparatorLeftHTML	Text to use as a left-only separator for root menu items that are not the first item in the menu	
SeparatorLeftHTML-Active	Text to use as a left-only separator for root menu items that are not the first item in the menu and are active	
SeparatorLeftHTML-BreadCrumb	Text to use as a left-only separator for root menu items that are not the first item in the menu where any of its children are active	
SeparatorRightHTML	Text to use as a right-only separator for root menu items that are not the first item in the menu	
SeparatorRightHTML-Active	Text to use as a right-only separator for root menu items that are not the first item in the menu and are active	
SeparatorRightHTML-BreadCrumb	Text to use as a right-only separator for root menu items that are not the first item in the menu where any of its children are active	
StartTabId	Defines which TabId uses as root menu item, default value is -1	
ToolTip	Defines which value to use for tooltips. Default value is "none"	none, name, title, description

PRIVACY SKINOBJECT

Displays a link to the privacy policy for the portal.

HTML Codebase Attribute `PRIVACY`

ASCX Register Code `<%@ Register TagPrefix="dnn" TagName="PRIVACY" Src="~\Admin\Skins\PRIVACY.ascx" %>`

ASCX Control Usage `<dnn:PRIVACY runat="server" id="dnnPRIVACY" />`

PRIVACY SKINOBJECT PARAMETERS

Name	Description
CssClass	Sets the CSS class used to render this skin object
Text	Overrides the default text for the Privacy link

SEARCH SKINOBJECT

Displays a search box for searching the portal or searching the web.

HTML Codebase Attribute `SEARCH`

ASCX Register Code `<%@ Register TagPrefix="dnn" TagName="SEARCH" Src="~\Admin\Skins\SEARCH.ascx" %>`

ASCX Control Usage `<dnn:SEARCH runat="server" id="dnnSEARCH" />`

SEARCH SKINOBJECT PARAMETERS

Name	Description	Possible Values
Submit	Overrides the Text for the Search link	
CssClass	Overrides the CSS class used to render the Search link	
ShowSite	Instructs the Search control to display an internal Site search option	True,False
ShowWeb	Instructs the Search control to display an external Web search option	True,False
UseWebForSite	Instructs the Search control to use the external Web search feature for the internal Site search	True,False

STYLES SKINOBJECT

Dynamically selects stylesheets based upon the browser.

HTML Codebase Attribute STYLES

ASCX Register Code

```
<%@ Register TagPrefix="dnn" TagName="STYLES"
Src="~\Admin\Skins\STYLES.ascx" %>
```

ASCX Control Usage

```
<dnn:STYLES runat="server" ID="StylesIE6" Name="IE6Minus"
StyleSheet="ie6skin.css" Condition="LT IE 7" UseSkinPath="true"/>
```

STYLES SKINOBJECT PARAMETERS

Name	Description
Condition	Defines the conditional logic to apply whether to include the stylesheet using the Internet Explorer conditional comments format
Name	Defines the Id that should be used for the HTML link element
StyleSheet	Sets the location of the stylesheet to be included if the condition is true
UseSkinPath	Defines whether to prepend the skinpath to the stylesheet location. If false, include the location, relative to the root, of the stylesheet

TERMS SKINOBJECT

Displays a link to the terms of use for the web site.

HTML Codebase Attribute TERMS

ASCX Register Code

```
<%@ Register TagPrefix="dnn" TagName="TERMS"
Src="~\Admin\Skins\TERMS.ascx" %>
```

ASCX Control Usage

```
<dnn:TERMS runat="server" id="dnnTERMS" />
```

TERMS SKINOBJECT PARAMETERS

Name	Description
CssClass	Sets the CSS class used to render this skin object
Text	Overrides the default text for the Terms link

TEXT SKINOBJECT

The text Skinobject displays localizable text. It also supports the token replacement engine for full access to user's profile properties and portal information with conditional logic inline. See Chapter 11 for a full discussion of what is possible with the token replacement engine.

HTML Codebase Attribute `TEXT`

ASCX Register Code `<%@ Register TagPrefix="dnn" TagName="TEXT" Src="~\Admin\Skins\TEXT.ascx" %>`

ASCX Control Usage `<dnn:TEXT runat="server" id="dnnTEXT" Text="[Portal:PortalName]" ReplaceTokens="true" />`

TEXT SKINOBJECT PARAMETERS

Name	Description
CssClass	Sets the CSS class used to render this skin object
ReplaceTokens	Boolean parameter, sets whether to use the token replacement engine
ResourceKey	The key to localized text from the local, shared, or global resources. Overrides the text parameter
Text	Text to be rendered by the control

USER SKINOBJECT

Displays a link to the user profile to authenticated users and a link to register for unauthenticated users.

HTML Codebase Attribute `USER`

ASCX Register Code `<%@ Register TagPrefix="dnn" TagName="USER" Src="~\Admin\Skins\USER.ascx" %>`

ASCX Control Usage `<dnn:USER runat="server" id="dnnUSER" />`

USER SKINOBJECT PARAMETERS

Name	Description
Text	Overrides the default text for the User link
URL	URL of login page

ACTIONBUTTON SKINOBJECT

Generic control to add action links for the actions available from a module.

HTML Codebase Attribute `ACTIONBUTTON`

ASCX Register Code `<%@ Register TagPrefix="dnn" TagName="ACTIONBUTTON" Src="~\Admin\Containers\ACTIONBUTTON.ascx" %>`

ASCX Control Usage `<dnn:ACTIONBUTTON runat="server" id="dnnACTIONBUTTON" />`

ACTIONBUTTON SKINOBJECT PARAMETERS

Name	Description	Possible Values
CssClass	Sets the CSS class used to render this skin object, defaults to "CommandButton"	
CommandName	Sets the Command Name, maps to ModuleActionType in DotNetNuke.Entities.Modules.Actions	
DisplayLink	Sets whether the link is displayed, defaults to True	True,False
DisplayIcom	Sets whether the icon is displayed, defaults to True	True,False
IconFile	Sets the Icon used, defaults to the icon defined in Action	
ButtonSeparator	Sets the Separator between Buttons, defaults to two non-breaking spaces	

ACTIONS SKINOBJECT

Displays the hover menu to display all core and custom actions for a module.

HTML Codebase Attribute `ACTIONS`

ASCX Register Code `<%@ Register TagPrefix="dnn" TagName="ACTIONS" Src="~\Admin\Containers\SolPartActions.ascx" %>`

ASCX Control Usage `<dnn:ACTIONS runat="server" id="dnnACTIONS" />`

ACTIONS SKINOBJECT PARAMETERS

Name	Description	Possible Values
ProviderName	Sets the menu provider used to render the action menu, defaults to SolpartMenuNavigationProvider	SolpartMenu-NavigationProvider, DNN-MenuNavigationProvider, DNNDropDownNavigation-Provider, ASP2Menu-NavigationProvider
PopulateNodes-FromClient	Sets whether to use AJAX to render the action menu	True,False
ExpandDepth	Sets the depth of the menu. Needs to be set at least to 1 in order for the menu to render.	
PathSystemScript	Optional override location for the scripts that drive the menu	

ICON SKINOBJECT

Displays the icon controlled in the module settings.

HTML Codebase Attribute `ICON`

ASCX Register Code `<%@ Register TagPrefix="dnn" TagName="ICON" Src="~\Admin\Containers\ICON.ascx" %>`

ASCX Control Usage `<dnn:ICON runat="server" id="dnnICON" />`

ICON SKINOBJECT PARAMETERS

Name	Description
BorderWidth	Sets the border width of the icon

LINKACTIONS SKINOBJECT

The module actions listed as links that are exposed to users with the appropriate permissions.

HTML Codebase Attribute `LINKACTIONS`

ASCX Register Code <%@ Register TagPrefix="dnn" TagName="LINKACTIONS" Src="~\Admin\Containers\LINKACTIONS.ascx" %>

ASCX Control Usage <dnn:LINKACTIONS runat="server" id="dnnLINKACTIONS" />

LINKACTIONS SKINOBJECT PARAMETERS

Name	Description
BorderWidth	Sets the border width of the icon

PRINTMODULE SKINOBJECT

Displays the print icon to launch print view for a module.

HTML Codebase Attribute PRINTMODULE

ASCX Register Code <%@ Register TagPrefix="dnn" TagName="PRINTMODULE" Src="~\Admin\Containers\PRINTMODULE.ascx" %>

ASCX Control Usage <dnn:PRINTMODULE runat="server" id="dnnPRINTMODULE" />

PRINTMODULE SKINOBJECT PARAMETERS

Name	Description
PrintIcon	Overrides the default image to be used for the print icon

VISIBILITY SKINOBJECT

Displays the min/max icon for a module.

HTML Codebase Attribute VISIBILITY

ASCX Register Code <%@ Register TagPrefix="dnn" TagName="VISIBILITY" Src="~\Admin\Containers\VISIBILITY.ascx" %>

ASCX Control Usage <dnn:VISIBILITY runat="server" id="dnnVISIBILITY" />

VISIBILITY SKINOBJECT PARAMETERS

Name	Description	Possible Values
BorderWidth	Sets the border width of the icon	
MinIcon	Override image for the default minimize icon. The expected folder of the image is the folder the container file resides in.	
MaxIcon	Override image for the default maximize icon. The expected folder of the image is the folder the container file resides in.	
AnimationFrames	Number of frames to use when animating the opening and closing of the container. The default number is 5.	

TITLE SKINOBJECT

Displays the title for the module.

HTML Codebase Attribute `TITLE`

ASCX Register Code `<%@ Register TagPrefix="dnn" TagName="TITLE" Src="~\Admin\Containers\TITLE.ascx" %>`

ASCX Control Usage `<dnn:TITLE runat="server" id="dnnTITLE" />`

TITLE SKINOBJECT PARAMETERS

Name	Description
CssClass	Sets the CSS class used to render this skin object

Client-Side Widget Framework

Client-side widgets are pluggable pieces of functionality that can be included in skins to deliver JavaScript functionality that runs in the browser instead of on the server like a Skinobject or DotNetNuke module. Client-side widgets are generally targeted at Web 2.0–style interactivity or DOM manipulation as an enhancement to the skinning engine. The best application of this technology is to develop and distribute JavaScript mini-applications that can be used for enhancing the user experience. The widget framework uses the ASP.NET AJAX Library so the only limits to functionality are the developer's imagination and JavaScript skills.

The syntax for using a client-side widget is almost identical to the new Skinobject format that is based upon the HTML `OBJECT` element with `PARAM`s included for configuration options. The only difference between the Skinobject and the client-side widget object format is that the codetype attribute is `dotnetnuke\client` for a widget, whereas it is `dotnetnuke\server` for a Skinobject.

Widgets are stored in the \Resources\Widgets folder. DotNetNuke widgets are all stored in the DNN subfolder, whereas custom widgets each have their own folder in the User subfolder (see Figure 16-5).

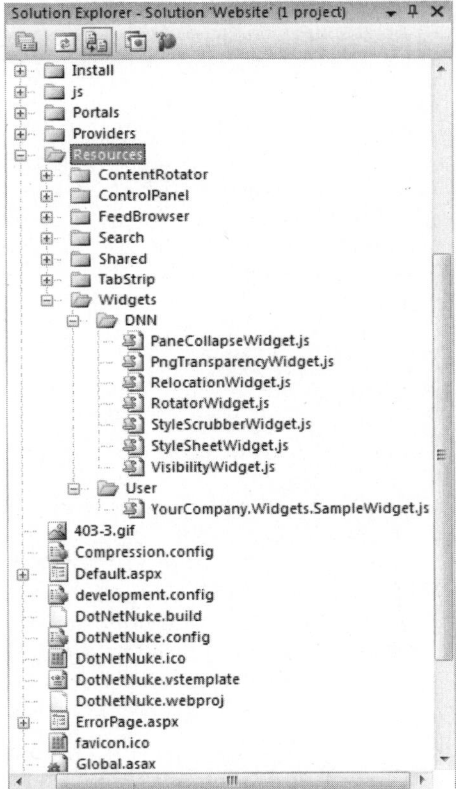

Figure 16-5

This section covers the widgets that are included with DotNetNuke 5 at the time of writing and explains how to use the included template to create a basic custom widget. Packaging and distributing widgets are explained in Chapter 17. Most of the widgets included with DotNetNuke 5 are used in the `Extropy` skin. For a good working example on how the widgets can be used together for a dynamic user experience, make sure to install the `Extropy` skin.

Rotator Widget

The Rotator Widget allows skin designers to supply a list of images that should be rotated using one of a couple of different animations for the transition between them. The following example shows a Rotator Widget:

```
<object id="Rotator" codetype="dotnetnuke/client" codebase="RotatorWidget">
    <param name="height" value="60" />
    <param name="width" value="120" />
    <param name="imageUrl" value="<%= SkinPath %>/rotator/" />
    <param name="imageCount" value="4" />
    <param name="imageTemplate" value="pic_number_{INDEX}.gif" />
    <param name="interval" value="3000" />
    <param name="direction" value="left" />
    <param name="transition" value="snap" />
</object>
```

The `imageUrl` parameter sets the path to the folder that contains the images to be rotated and the `imageTemplate` parameter creates a template to construct the filename of the image to be rotated. If the preceding example was included within the HTMLMethod skin package earlier in the chapter, the script would rotate four images from the \portals_default\skins\SkinningDemo\rotator\ folder with the names `pic_number_1.gif`, `pic_number_2.gif`, `pic_number_3.gif`, and `pic_number_4.gif`. `Interval` sets the time in milliseconds between changing images. Values for `direction` include `left`, `right`, `up`, `down`, and `blend`. Valid `transition` values are `slide` and `snap`.

Pane Collapse Widget

The Pane Collapse Widget gives another way to manage empty Panes in a skin. The Widget checks to see whether one or more HTML elements are empty by checking to see if there are any child elements. If all of the supplied elements are empty, the Widget applies a class to the specified element. There is one parameter in the Pane Collapse Widget called `Rule`. To supply a `Rule`, break the `Rule` into three parts separated by a colon. Part one is the element that should be modified if all Panes are empty. Part two defines one or more Panes that need to be empty for the widget to execute separated by a plus sign. Part three is the name of the class to be applied to the element in part one. Look for the parameter format to change in this widget for future versions to make it less complicated. You can see how to use the Pane Collapse Widget to apply a style to a table to hide it when all of the Panes contained within it are empty using the following example:

```
<table class="Layout-Table" id="tblMainLayout">
<tr>
    <td id="LeftPane" class="Layout-SidePane" runat="server">
    </td>
    <td id="ContentPane" class="Layout-ContentPane" runat="server">
    </td>
    <td id="RightPane" class="Layout-SidePane" runat="server">
    </td>
</tr>
</table>
<object id="PaneCollapse" codetype="dotnetnuke/client" codebase="
PaneCollapseWidget" declare="declare">
<param name="Rule" value=" tblMainLayout:dnn_LeftPane+dnn_ContentPane+dnn_
```

```
RightPane:clsDisplayNone" />
</object>
```

In this example, if the LeftPane, ContentPane, and RightPane are all empty, the Widget will apply the clsDisplayNone class. Then, by defining the clsDisplayNone class in your stylesheet you could set the display:none; rule to hide the layout table if it is has no modules in any of its Panes.

PNG Transparency Widget

The Transparency Widget is a simple Widget that runs only on Internet Explorer 6 and below. When the page loads, it will iterate through all <div> and <span> elements on a page to check for a PNG format background image. If a PNG background image is found, the Widget will apply the Internet Explorer transparency filter to make Internet Explorer display transparent PNGs correctly. At the time of writing, the PNG Transparency Widget only works on <div> and <span> elements with the background-image rule applied as an inline style, and does not work on backgrounds set in CSS stylesheets.

```
<object id="PNGFix" codetype="dotnetnuke/client" codebase=
"PngTransparencyWidget" declare="declare">
</object>
```

Relocation Widget

The Relocation Widget is a simple but powerful SEO widget that runs when the page loads to move the HTML element with the ID supplied in the sourceId parameter to be a child element of the targeted parameter. This allows skin designers to put their most relevant content at the top of the page for search engines and inject it into the appropriate parent element for meaningful display to the end user.

```
<object id="RelocationWidget" codetype="dotnetnuke/client" codebase=
"RelocationWidget" declare="declare">
 <param name="sourceId" value="dvMainContent" />
 <param name="targetId" value="dvTarget" />
</object>
```

Style Scrubber Widget

The Style Scrubber Widget is a very clever module that runs at load to remove all inline styles from HTML elements with the one or more supplied classes. If recursive is set to true, it will also remove any inline styles from child elements of the HTML elements that are applicable. If you are using the Style Sheet Widget to change stylesheets dynamically, this is especially useful to ensure that there are not conflicting inline styles that interfere with the CSS rules. The following example shows how to use the Style Scrubber Widget with three HTML elements whose inline styles would be removed by the Widget:

```
<object id="StyleScrubber" codetype="dotnetnuke/client" codebase=
"StyleScrubberWidget" declare="declare">
 <param name="classNames" value="ServerSkinWidget;OtherClassName" />
 <param name="removeAttribute" value="style" />
 <param name="recursive" value="True" />
</object>
<div id="dvOne" class="ServerSkinWidget" style="background-color:Lime;">  
 <div id="dvtwo" style="background-color:Fuchsia;">  </div>
```

```
</div>
<div id="dvThree" class="OtherClassName" style="background-color:Purple;">
 </div>
```

In this example, `dvOne` and `dvThree` both have their style attribute removed because their class names are in the list of classes to which the widget should be applied. `dvTwo`'s styles are removed because the `recursive` parameter is set to `true` and its parent element met the class name condition.

Stylesheet Widget

The Stylesheet Widget enables skin designers to create dynamic stylesheet switching with JavaScript. The following example from the `Extropy` skin that is included with DotNetNuke 5 shows how the Widget can allow users to set the size of the layout by clicking a button to change the stylesheet. Figure 16-6 shows how the buttons in the template are rendered on the page. The user selection is also remembered the next time the user visits the page.

```
<object id="TextSizeWidget" codetype="dotnetnuke/client" codebase=
"StyleSheetWidget" declare="declare">
 <param name="baseUrl" value="<%= SkinPath %>stylesheets/textsizes/" />
 <param name="template" value="&lt;input type='button' title='{TEXT}' value=" {ID}
{CLASS} /&gt; " />
 <param name="default" value="textsize-small" />
 <param name="Small Text" value="textsize-small" />
 <param name="Medium Text" value="textsize-medium" />
 <param name="Large Text" value="textsize-large" />
</object>
```

The best example of how this can be leveraged is in the Extropy skin that is included in the DotNetNuke 5 installation. Be sure that you do not confuse this with the Minimal Extropy *skin that is installed by default. The skin is not installed by default, so make sure to install the skin using the Host Extensions page.*

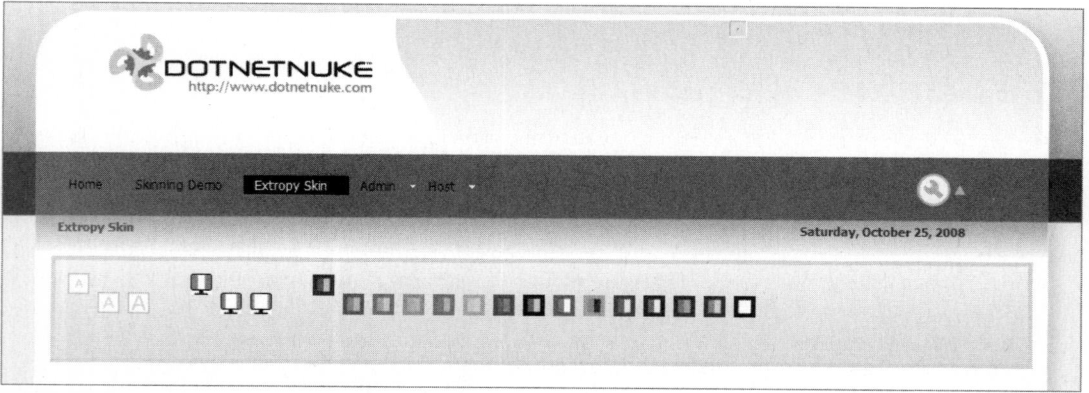

Figure 16-6

Visibility Widget

The Visibility Widget controls visibility of a supplied HTML element anywhere on the page. The `OBJECT` renders an HTML button where the `OBJECT` is declared with an `onclick` JavaScript event to toggle visibility of the `targetElementId`. When the button is clicked, the class attribute of the button is also switched between the values supplied in the `expandClassName` and `collapseClassName` parameter to allow for an open and closed icon as a background to the button.

```
<object id="Toolbox" codetype="dotnetnuke/client" codebase=
"VisibilityWidget" declare="declare">
 <param name="expandClassName" value="Layout-Masthead-InfoBar-ToolBoxIcon-
Expanded" />
 <param name="collapseClassName" value="Layout-Masthead-InfoBar-
ToolBoxIcon-Collapsed" />
 <param name="targetElementId" value="Layout-ToolBox" />
 <param name="title" value="Toolbox" />
</object>
```

Custom Widgets

Custom Widgets are stored in the \Resources\Widgets\User folder. Creating custom Widgets in DotNetNuke is remarkably easy. This section walks through using the sample widget to create a custom widget.

1. Create a folder in the User folder named FictitiousCompany.SampleWidget.
2. Copy the `YourCompany.Widgets.SampleWidget.js` file from the `User` folder into your newly created folder.
3. Rename the file `FictitiousCompany.Widgets.SampleWidget.js`.
4. Replace all instances of `YourCompany` with `FictitiousCompany` in the JavaScript file.
5. Add the following code to your DotNetNuke skin and the sample widget will render in the browser:

```
<object id="SampleWidget" codetype="dotnetnuke/client"
codebase="FictitiousCompany.Widgets.SampleWidget" declare="declare">
 <param name="widgetFolder" value="FictitiousCompany.SampleWidget" />
 <param name="text" value="Click Here to See the ID of this Object." />
</object>
```

In order to use a custom widget, you'll need to supply the `widgetFolder` parameter to let the JavaScript that loads the custom Widget know where the file is stored. The Widget loader uses the codebase attribute to instantiate the Widget code and add the JavaScript file that contains the definition to the page. By convention, then, the **JavaScript filename must be identical to the fully qualified name of the JavaScript prototype** to be loaded by the widget `OBJECT` for the script to load correctly.

Super Stylesheets

Another exciting new feature in the DotNetNuke 5 version of the skinning engine is super stylesheets. Super stylesheets offer base layout features for skin designers using CSS-driven layouts. The DotNetNuke Core Team chose to include the Yahoo! YUI library into DotNetNuke's shared resources to give skin designers a toolkit upon which to base CSS layouts. By using Yahoo!'s YUI library, designers can implement custom layouts in CSS with very little customization necessary and the result is a lean, well-tested layout with accessibility considerations built in. The YUI library provides layout templates and a global reset for all browser styles so that HTML behaves consistently across all browsers. This section also covers the dnnlayouts.css stylesheet that provides template layouts for designers to implement and the rounded corner stylesheet to provide the common design effect of rounded corners and drop shadow background images around layout elements.

Yahoo!'s YUI Grids, Fonts, and Reset Libraries

YUI Grids allow skin designers to use common stylesheets for base functionality for CSS-driven layouts. Because this is a paradigm shift for most designers that are used to setting the width of all elements in a skin, an example will give the best picture of the benefit of using the YUI library in DotNetNuke skins. To use the YUI Reset, simply import the stylesheet from the DotNetNuke resources folder:

```
@import url("../../../../resources/shared/stylesheets/yui/reset-fonts-grids.css");
```

Importing this stylesheet from the shared resources folder imports the YUI Reset, YUI Fonts, and YUI Grids libraries into one common stylesheet. The YUI Reset provides base CSS rules that remove default behaviors from HTML elements to make the UI interpretation consistent across all browsers. The YUI Fonts library adds to the reset by making fonts sizes, line-spacing, and font degradation paths behave consistently cross-browser and cross-platform. The Fonts library also makes typography use em-based sizing, which enhances accessibility by allowing web site users to change the size of their text with browser settings. The YUI Grids library that is included in this stylesheet creates the base layouts discussed earlier in this chapter. The power of the YUI Grids system is demonstrated in the following code by using nine lines of HTML to create a center-aligned, two-column, CSS-based layout:

```
<div id="doc4" class="yui-t6">
 <div id="yui-main">
  <div class="yui-b">
  <div id="ContentPane" runat="server"></div>
  </div>
 </div>
 <div class="yui-b">
  <div id="RightPane" runat="server"></div>
 </div>
</div>
```

This example gave a 974px width, center-aligned layout with a 300px right Pane and a 1em gutter between the main content area and the right rail. Figure 16-7 shows the layout using mockup text. The Text/HTML modules placed in the `ContentPane` and `RightPane` have their containers hidden to demonstrate that the margins are managed from the stylesheet and not in the containers as in examples earlier in the chapter.

In using the YUI Grids, the outermost `<div>`'s `ID` and `class` set the width of the site and the layout template to be used as a two-column layout. Table 16-3 shows the different options for the `ID` and the associated sizes. Table 16-4 shows the different layout templates that can be set with the main layout's class attribute.

Mode: View Edit Layout   Show Control Panel?

Lorem ipsum dolor sit amet, consectetuer adipiscing elit. Cras ligula. Curabitur et nisi. Quisque mollis neque vel leo. Praesent semper. Class aptent taciti sociosqu ad litora torquent per conubia nostra, per inceptos himenaeos. Vivamus sed libero eget sapien dictum mollis. Nunc eget neque. Nam id eros. Sed luctus. In sollicitudin magna vitae est. Sed porta leo in lorem.
Fusce accumsan, ipsum a congue facilisis, mi nisl scelerisque augue, et adipiscing lorem leo a odio. Morbi in augue. Donec non nibh in massa pharetra facilisis. Suspendisse et purus. Ut augue sapien, porttitor eget, posuere in, malesuada quis, arcu. Nulla venenatis, arcu et euismod mattis, justo ligula pellentesque tellus, quis feugiat erat metus in ipsum. Nullam elit. Nullam tristique neque eu mauris. Donec mi augue, mollis dignissim, commodo tincidunt, volutpat lacinia, tellus. Sed a nibh. Curabitur lectus ipsum, auctor et, sodales sit amet, auctor nec, pede. Praesent vel purus sit amet nibh varius tempor. Donec lectus ipsum, porttitor malesuada, consectetuer condimentum, aliquet sed, risus. Nunc tincidunt semper purus.
Vestibulum ante ipsum primis in faucibus orci luctus et ultrices posuere cubilia Curae; Quisque sed risus ac velit vehicula condimentum. Suspendisse non augue ut justo ultricies egestas. Class aptent taciti sociosqu ad litora torquent per conubia nostra, per inceptos himenaeos. Quisque risus tellus, ornare commodo, dapibus quis, hendrerit nec, elit. Pellentesque sodales dui ac dolor gravida mattis. Maecenas odio eros, vestibulum eget, tristique sit amet, varius at, enim. Sed erat tellus, adipiscing non, imperdiet et, venenatis congue, elit. Suspendisse potenti. Sed auctor dolor a quam. In augue ante, iaculis sed, suscipit ac, rhoncus sed, leo. Aliquam erat volutpat. Suspendisse potenti. Maecenas vestibulum nibh a turpis fermentum porttitor. Pellentesque dignissim condimentum magna. Nam fringilla est nec nisl. Pellentesque sit amet est. Nulla faucibus, massa sit amet bibendum congue, sem odio porta diam, sit amet porttitor neque arcu sit amet lectus. Nullam pulvinar, tellus ut faucibus facilisis, elit tortor posuere neque, ac semper lorem est sit amet ante. Etiam non massa non sapien porttitor posuere.

Lorem ipsum dolor sit amet, consectetuer adipiscing elit. Cras ligula. Curabitur et nisi. Quisque mollis neque vel leo. Praesent semper. Class aptent taciti sociosqu ad litora torquent per conubia nostra, per inceptos himenaeos. Vivamus sed libero eget sapien dictum mollis. Nunc eget neque. Nam id eros. Sed luctus. In sollicitudin magna vitae est. Sed porta leo in lorem.
Fusce accumsan, ipsum a congue facilisis, mi nisl scelerisque augue, et adipiscing lorem leo a odio. Morbi in augue. Donec non nibh in massa pharetra facilisis. Suspendisse et purus. Ut augue sapien, porttitor eget, posuere in, malesuada quis, arcu. Nulla venenatis, arcu et euismod mattis, justo ligula pellentesque tellus, quis feugiat erat metus in ipsum. Nullam elit. Nullam tristique neque eu mauris. Donec mi augue, mollis dignissim, commodo tincidunt, volutpat lacinia, tellus. Sed a nibh. Curabitur lectus ipsum, auctor et, sodales sit amet, auctor nec, pede. Praesent vel purus sit amet nibh varius tempor. Donec lectus ipsum, porttitor malesuada, consectetuer condimentum, aliquet sed, risus. Nunc tincidunt semper purus.

Figure 16-7

Table 16-3: Layout Size Id Options

Id	Layout Width
doc	750px width, center-aligned
doc2	950px width, center-aligned
doc3	100% width, fluid layout
doc4	974px width, center-aligned

Table 16-4: Two-Column Template Class Options

Class	Template
`yui-t1`	160 Left
`yui-t2`	180 Left
`yui-t3`	300 Left
`yui-t4`	160 Right
`yui-t5`	180 Right
`yui-t6`	300 Right

YUI's library refers to `<div>`s intended to hold content as blocks, so the class `yui-b` is used to designate a block. In this two-column scenario, designers should add two blocks within the main layout `<div>` with the class set to `yui-b`, then wrap a `<div>` with the id set to `yui-main` around the block that is the main block. The `<div>` that is not wrapped with `yui-main` will inherit the width according to the templates listed in Table 16-4. Ordering within the main div is not important, so designers can put their most important content at the top and advertisements in the side rail at the bottom regardless of the layout template they choose. Beyond these six layout templates, the YUI Grids system supports nested layouts that can create more than 600 different layout combinations. Because this is a book on DotNetNuke skinning and not the YUI Grids system, this chapter does not discuss advanced layouts with YUI grids. For excellent videos and tutorials on the YUI libraries, visit the web site at `http://developer.yahoo.com/yui`.

DNN Layouts

The dnnlayouts.css is another super stylesheet within the shared resources folder at \resources\shared\stylesheets that adds layout templates for CSS-driven skins in DotNetNuke. Like the YUI Grids library, the DNN Layouts stylesheet creates CSS layout templates that can be applied to DotNetNuke skins using special class attributes. The advantage this layout system has over the YUI Grids is that it supports the three-column layout much better because it allows skin developers to create variable or equal width three-column layouts. The four layouts supported at the time of writing are listed in Table 16-5.

Table 16-5: DNN Layouts

Class Name	Description
threecol-portal	Three-column layout with two side Panes and a center Pane that expands to fill the space not taken by the sides
threecol-blog	Three-column layout with both side panels on the right-hand side and a center Pane that expands to fill the space not taken by the sides
twocol-contentL	Two-column layout with the main content on the left
twocol-contentR	Two-column layout with the main content on the right

The following example shows a three-column layout using the DotNetNuke super stylesheets:

```
<div id="em16" class="em16">
<div id="Layout-Content-ThreeCol" class="threecol-portal">
 <div class="dnn-mid">
  <div class="dnn-side">
  <div class="dnn-main">
    <div class="dnn-a" id="ContentPane" runat="server"></div>
  </div>
    <div class="dnn-b" id="LeftPane" runat="server"></div>
    <div class="dnn-c" id="RightPane" runat="server"></div>
  </div>
 </div>
```

```
</div>
<div id="Layout-Content-Blog" class="threecol-blog">
 <div class="dnn-mid">
  <div class="dnn-side">
  <div class="dnn-main">
    <div class="dnn-a" id="ContentPane" runat="server"></div>
  </div>
    <div class="dnn-b" id="LeftPane" runat="server"></div>
    <div class="dnn-c" id="RightPane" runat="server"></div>
  </div>
 </div>
</div>
<div id="Layout-Content-TwoColL" class="twocol-contentL">
 <div class="dnn-mid">
  <div class="dnn-side">
  <div class="dnn-main">
    <div class="dnn-a" id="ContentPane" runat="server"></div>
  </div>
    <div class="dnn-b"></div>
    <div class="dnn-c" id="LeftPane" runat="server"></div>
  </div>
 </div>
</div>
<div id="Layout-Content-TwoColR" class="twocol-contentR">
 <div class="dnn-mid">
  <div class="dnn-side">
  <div class="dnn-main">
    <div class="dnn-a" id="ContentPane" runat="server"></div>
  </div>
    <div class="dnn-b" id="LeftPane" runat="server"></div>
    <div class="dnn-c" ></div>
  </div>
 </div>
</div>
</div>
```

The DNN Layout system is based upon em width units rather than hard-coded pixels. Using ems instead of pixels allows content to grow proportionally for users who have accessibility needs and change their browser text size. The scalable nature supports mobile browsers through wide format monitors. DotNetNuke Layouts support changing the size of the side-columns to be one of the three widths shown in Table 16-6.

Table 16-6: Supported Sizes

Class	Side-Column Size
em14	182px
em16	208px
em18	234px

This example shows how to use a parent <div> to set the size of the side columns according to the information in Table 16-6:

```
<div class="em14">
<div id="Layout-Content-TwoColL" class="twocol-contentL">
 <div class="dnn-mid">
  <div class="dnn-side">
  <div class="dnn-main">
    <div class="dnn-a" id="ContentPane" runat="server"></div>
  </div>
    <div class="dnn-b"></div>
    <div class="dnn-c" id="LeftPane" runat="server"></div>
  </div>
 </div>
</div>
</div>
```

Rounded Corners

The last stylesheet covered in this chapter is dnnroundedcorners.css, located in the \resources\shared\stylesheets folder. The purpose of the rounded corners stylesheet is to address the common need to wrap rounded corner background images around an expandable content area. This super stylesheet template can work well for a skin, container, or for a content within a module. Figure 16-8 shows the pieces that make up a rounded corners implementation and the code examples show the HTML and CSS to use the template within your skins and containers.

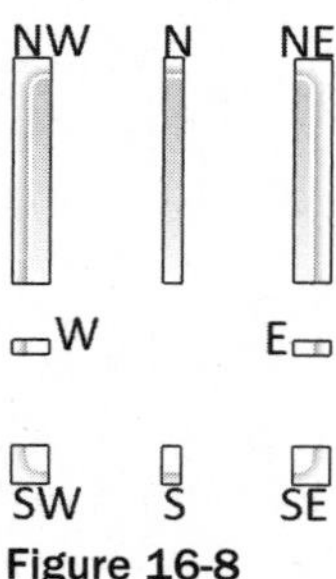

Figure 16-8

```
<div class="RoundedCorners">
<div class="W">
    <div class="E">
        <div class="N">
            <div class="NW">
                <div class="NE">
                    Your content goes here...
                </div><!-- NE -->
            </div><!-- NW -->
        </div><!-- N -->
        <div class="S">
            <div class="SW">
```

```
                <div class="SE">
                    Your optional footer goes here.
                </div><!-- SE -->
            </div><!-- SW -->
        </div><!-- S -->
    </div><!-- E -->
</div><!-- W -->
</div><!-- RoundedCorners -->
```

The following CSS should be included in your skin.css to set the images for the regions of the rounded corner layout:

```
@import url("../../../../resources/shared/stylesheets/dnn-roundedcorners.css");

.RoundedCorners .NW{    background-image: url("images/layout_nw.png");}
.RoundedCorners .N{    background-image: url("images/layout_n.png");}
.RoundedCorners .NE{    background-image: url("images/layout_ne.png");}
.RoundedCorners .W{    background-image: url("images/layout_w.png");}
.RoundedCorners .E{    background-image: url("images/layout_e.png");}
.RoundedCorners .SW{    background-image: url("images/layout_sw.png");}
.RoundedCorners .S{    background-image: url("images/layout_s.png");}
.RoundedCorners .SE{    background-image: url("images/layout_se.png");}
```

Creating a Skin Preview Image

After you have the skin created, you need to create an image so that you will be able to display the skin in the preview gallery. To do this, you need to create a high-quality image file with a `.jpg` extension that must be named the same as your skin file. For example, if your skin is named `mySkin.ascx`, then your image file must be named `mySkin.jpg`. At the time of upload, a thumbnail image will be generated for each properly named `.jpg`. This same concept is also true of container files you have created as part of your skin design. The skin preview images are displayed on the same page as the HTMLMethod.htm link discussed previously in this chapter and shown in Figure 16-9.

Deploying Your Skin

The last step in skin creation is to package the skin for deployment. The method described here will be called the legacy method of packaging skins in DotNetNuke 5. The new method of packaging skins gives new abilities including the ability to uninstall a skin and include license agreements and release notes to enhance the install process. Although these are important enhancements, many developers will stick to the legacy method because the added benefits are not applicable to their business needs. The new skin packaging method treats skins as extensions and is covered in Chapter 17.

To create a legacy skin package, you must put the correctly named files in a specific structure, the method commonly referred to as *convention over configuration*. The compressed file must be a *.zip file. You can use any number of third-party compression utilities, such as WinZip or the Windows built-in utility. One thing to watch out for when zipping your package is to ensure there are no buried folders between your skin files and the first-level compressed folder. This is a common mistake that causes the upload process to fail.

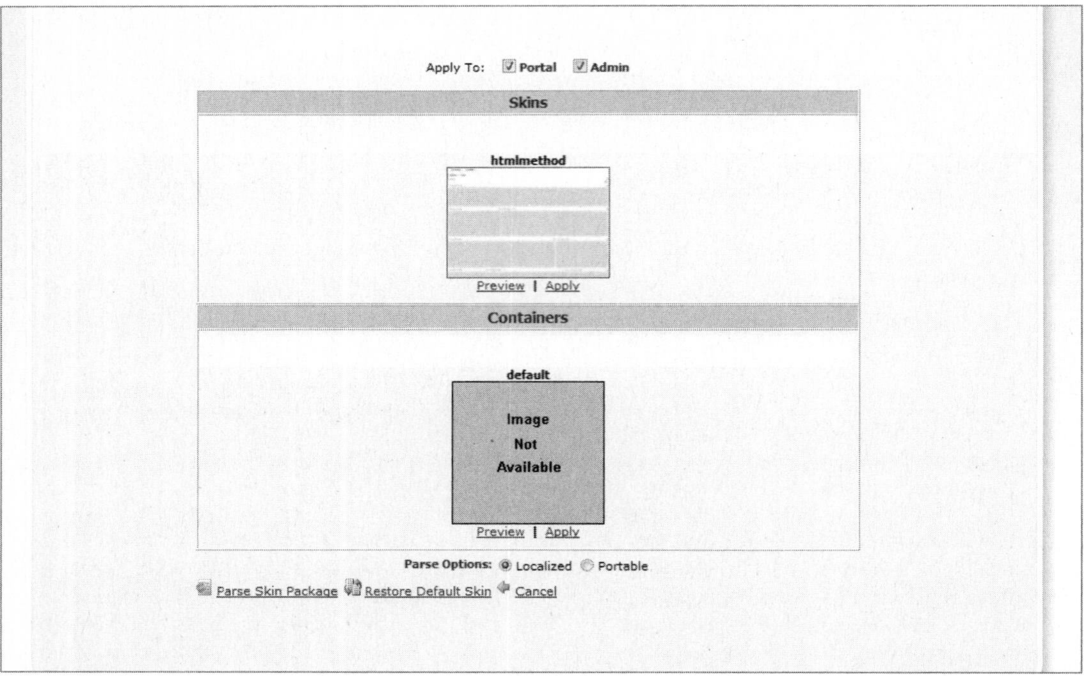

Figure 16-9

In many cases, you will want to package a complementary set of skin files and container files in one distribution file. To do this, package your container files in a compressed *.zip file named containers.zip. Similarly, package your skin files in a compressed *.zip file named skins.zip, which was mentioned at the beginning of this chapter. Then, package these two files into a single *.zip file that is named after your skin. This allows people to install the full skin package (skins and containers) by uploading a single file through the Skin Uploader.

Summary

This chapter explored DotNetNuke 5's new features to make skins easier to design, implement, and extend. This chapter gave an overview of creating skins from the ground up and how to implement CSS layouts from scratch or with super stylesheets. You learned to use core and custom client-side widgets to add JavaScript functionality to skins, as well as Skinobjects to include server-based functionality within your skin. Skinning is a fluid topic and small changes are introduced with each release, so make sure to check the author's blog at `http://www.dotnetnukeconsulting.wordpress.com` for updates to features and techniques related to DotNetNuke skinning.

17

Distribution

DotNetNuke's commercial and free module market has been instrumental in the success of the platform. The ability to do a quick search on the Internet and find free or relatively inexpensive modules that fulfill a need significantly reduces the cost to operate a web site when compared to a custom web site and other commercially available platforms. With the wide potential customer base, it's no wonder that developers have filled the void with low- to medium-cost solutions to countless business needs. This market is no accident. The modular nature of DotNetNuke and the extensibility and distribution model have created an environment from which developers can easily share the modules they create and designers can easily share the skins they design. This chapter explains the extensions model for packaging and distributing modules, skins, language packs, and all other application extensions available to DotNetNuke developers and designers.

The New Extensions Model

In previous versions of DotNetNuke, installing modules, skins, languages, and other extensions was achieved using a different process for each type of add-on. Skins were packaged using convention over configuration, meaning that if you put the correct files with the correct filename in the correct structure, it would install correctly. Modules were installed through the Module Definitions interface using a DotNetNuke manifest file that instructed the installer where and how to install modules. In version 4.6, a new installer was introduced to handle authentication system installations. All of these different models created more code to maintain, and was an inconsistent experience for developers that had to learn a different way to package each type of extension they wanted to distribute.

In version 5, the Core Team has consolidated all of these installation models into a unified model called *extensions*. This new model provides developers and administrators a single place through which all add-ons to the core are managed. By using a common interface, module developers can reuse the same skills for distributing modules, providers, authentication systems, skins, and even custom extension types. The new model also adds license agreements, release notes, and an uninstall process — features that were previously unavailable for skins and language packs.

Extensions can be managed by Host- and Administrator-level users to varying degrees. The extensions page under the admin menu for a portal allows portal administrators to control which modules are available to users with edit permissions based upon role. With this new feature in DotNetNuke 5, Host Administrators have more granular control over the types of content that page editors and Administrators can add to pages they have access to edit. For more information on managing the modules available to users with edit permissions, see Chapter 4, "Portal Administration." Authentication systems and skins can also be managed from the admin extensions page. The Host extensions page gives complete control to SuperUsers to manage authentication systems, containers, language packs, libraries, modules, providers, skins, and skinobjects. The Host extensions page is also where the interface for installing and uninstalling extensions is located.

Creating New Extensions

To add custom extensions to your installation, you will need to begin by making DotNetNuke aware of the extension. For developers, this is generally one of the first steps taken to start developing and testing modules and providers, once the file and folder structure is ready. Although it is possible to create a package configuration file from scratch and build the extension package to install into your portal, the simpler way in most cases to build your extension package is through the extensions management interface from the Host menu. Once you have created your package, you can manage the controls and files for the package and even export an installable extension package using the wizard. This section explains how to use the extensions management interface to create and distribute extensions packages.

To begin the process of creating your extension, log in with your Host account and navigate to the extensions page in the Host menu. As an example, you will create an extension for the `SkinningDemo` skin from Chapter 16, "Skinning DotNetNuke." Begin by clicking the Create New Extension link at the bottom of the Host extensions page. The first screen in the New Extension Wizard gathers basic information about your extension. For the example skin package, change the extension type to `Skin`, set the name to `SkinningDemo`, the Friendly Name to `Skinning Demo XHTML Skin`, enter a short description, and set the version to `1.0.0`. When your inputs match Figure 17-1, click Next to go to the next step in the wizard.

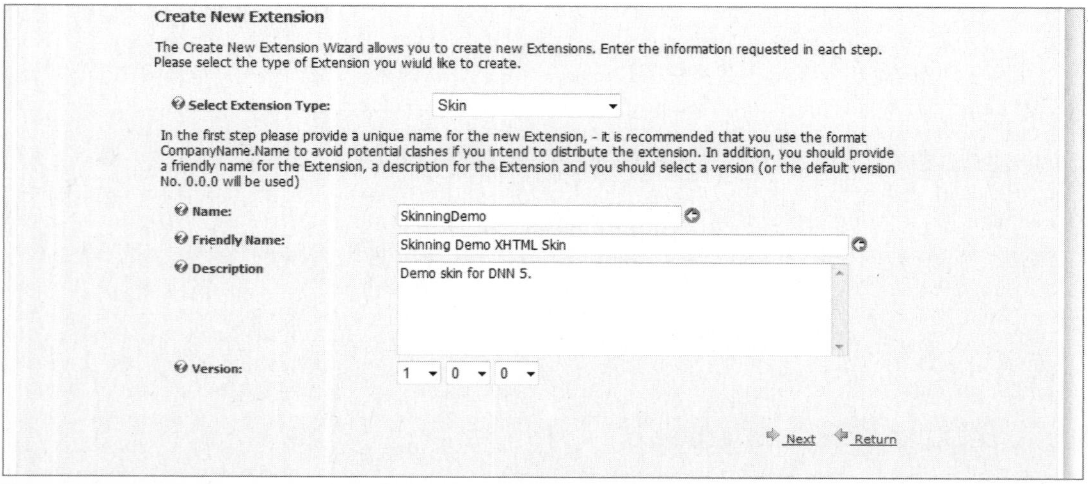

Figure 17-1

The Owner Details screen is the last step in the New Extension Wizard for skins. Figure 17-2 shows a typical Owner Details screen content. Once your input matches Figure 17-2, click Next to add your extension to the DotNetNuke installation.

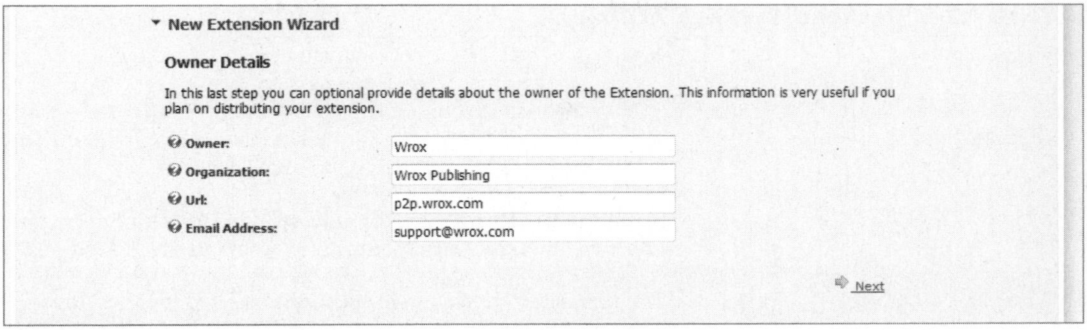

Figure 17-2

Now that DotNetNuke knows about your extension, you can edit the details of your extension from the Host extensions page. Change the drop-down on the extensions page to `Skin` to filter the list and display only skin extensions. Click the pencil next to the `Skinning Demo` skin to enter edit mode for the extension. This common page allows you to manage the details of your extension. Regardless of the type of extension you are creating, there are common attributes associated with all package types that are managed in the Package Settings section on the details page for an extension. Table 17-1 explains each of the attributes in the Package Settings.

Extension Configuration

Each extension type has different configuration options that instruct DotNetNuke how to use the extension that are managed in the Extensions Settings section at the top of each extension detail page. Each extension type can have very detailed configuration that is necessary to use the extension, like the module extension type. Other extension types, like the library extension, have no configuration outside of the common package settings. This section explains the configuration options available to each extension type.

Skin and Container Extension Configuration

The skin and container extensions are managed using the same interface and available options. Once you have created your base skin or container extension, the only other configuration options are to change the package name and make the extension aware of the skin and container files. Figure 17-3 shows the `Skinning Demo` example skin. With skin and container extensions, making DotNetNuke aware of the skins or containers in the extension is unnecessary because skins are made available through the convention of having them in the correct folder under your Host- or portal-specific Skins or Containers folder. For more information on the folder structure of skins and containers, see Chapter 16.

Module Extension Configuration

A DotNetNuke module has to be configured correctly before it can be added to a page and used in a portal. The Extension Settings for a module is broken up into two sections. The first section is where Host administrators can manage the folder name, business controller class, and whether the module should be available only to specified portals. Table 17-2 explains the configuration options in the first section for module extensions.

Table 17-1: Package Settings Attributes

Setting	Purpose
Name	This name must be unique because it is used in portal and page templates to refer to modules and extensions.
Type	Setting that instructs DotNetNuke whether to treat the extension as a `module`, `skin`, `provider`, or any other custom extension type.
Friendly Name	The setting for display to end users. It is used in drop-downs, lists, and the control panel for modules.
Description	Setting to display a short description of the extension in the list of extensions on the Host and admin extensions pages.
Version	The version of the extension.
License	A description of the terms of use for the extension.
Release Notes	Notes about the current version of the extension.
Owner	The owner of the package.
Organization	The name of the company that owns the package.
URL	The web site address for the owner of the extension.
Email Address	The package owner's support or contact email address.

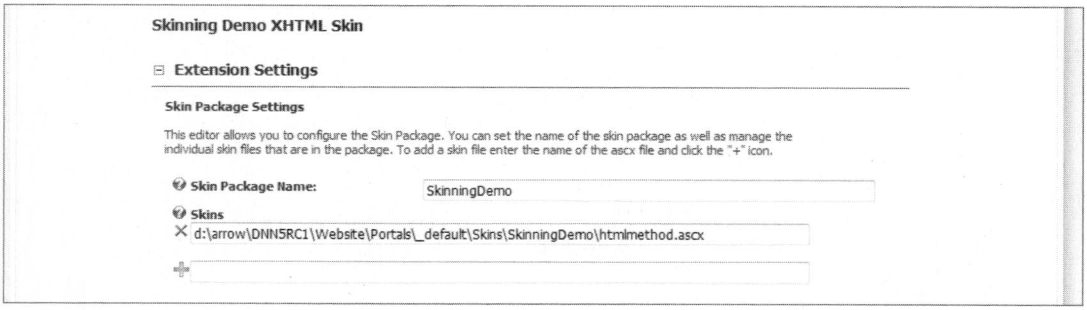

Skinning Demo XHTML Skin

Extension Settings

Skin Package Settings

This editor allows you to configure the Skin Package. You can set the name of the skin package as well as manage the individual skin files that are in the package. To add a skin file enter the name of the ascx file and click the "+" icon.

Skin Package Name: SkinningDemo

Skins

d:\arrow\DNN5RC1\Website\Portals_default\Skins\SkinningDemo\htmlmethod.ascx

Figure 17-3

Table 17-2: Configuration Options for Module Extensions

Attribute	Purpose
Module Name	Used within page and portal templates to specify the module type. Must be unique.
Folder Name	The name of the folder within the `DesktopModules` folder where the module's controls are stored.
Business Controller Class	The fully qualified namespace and assembly name where the methods that implement the `IPortable` and `ISearchable` interfaces for making data available to core DotNetNuke APIs.
IsPortable	Read-only setting that indicates whether the module exposes import/export functionality through implementing the `IPortable` interface.
IsSearchable	Read-only setting that indicates whether the module implements the `ISearchable` interface necessary to expose information to the DotNetNuke search index engine.
IsUpgradable	Read-only setting that indicates whether the module supports the `IUpgradable` interface allowing it to run custom code when upgraded.
IsPremium	Sets whether, on portal creation, a module should automatically be available to be used by administrators of that portal.
Portal Assignment Box	Sets which portals have access to premium modules.

The second section for configuration is for managing Module Definitions. Most modules will have a single Module Definition for each module extension. A Module Definition is the parent entity for controls to be used to add functionality with a DotNetNuke module. If your module needs to have more than one control added to the page for the module to function correctly, you can achieve this through adding multiple Module Definitions. When a module with multiple Module Definitions is added to a page, a module instance is added for each definition. The best example of this is the blog module. When the blog module is added to a page, it actually adds five module controls to the page: the blog entry viewer, the blog list, blog management, blog search, and the blog archive. Figure 17-4 shows a page that has had the blog module added to it.

By adding multiple Module Definitions, you can split functionality that is necessary into different control parts that can be laid out with container and security settings that are independent of each other. For the blog module example, this hides the complexity of having to add five modules to the page to have the module behave correctly and allows portal administrators to place the archive, search, and blog list in whichever order meets the needs and design requirements of the organization.

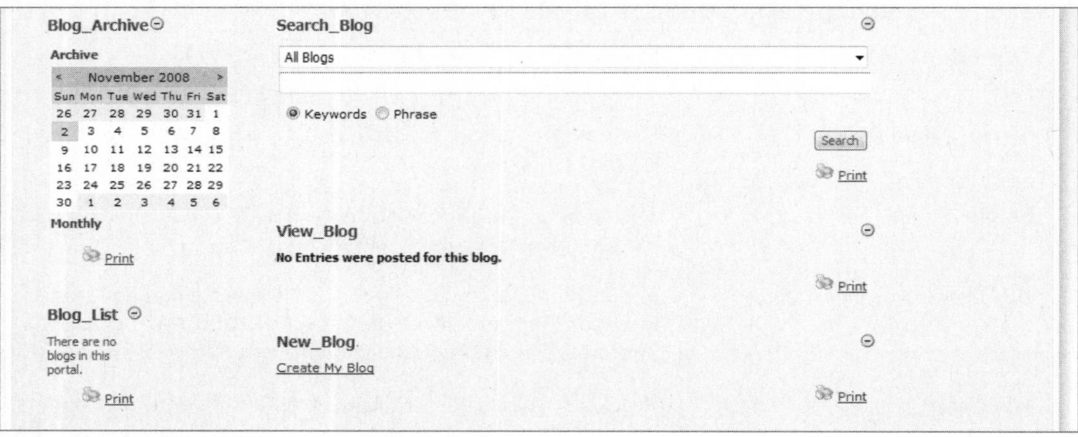

Figure 17-4

Once you have created a Module Definition for your module, you will need to add controls to it. Using controls, module developers add the default `view`, `settings`, and `edit` controls, then any other custom controls the module needs. Follow these steps to set up the `Wrox.Suggestions` module from the module development chapters earlier in the book:

1. Click the Create New Extension link on the Host extensions page.
2. Select Module from the drop-down list.
3. Enter **Wrox.Suggestion** for the Name.
4. Enter **Suggestions Module** for the Friendly Name.
5. Enter **The Suggestions demo module** for the Description.
6. Set the Version to 2.0.0.
7. Once your screen matches Figure 17-5, click Next.
8. On the next screen, enter **Wrox.Suggestion** for the Folder Name to let the extensions management know where to find the module controls.
9. Enter **WROX.Modules.Suggestion.SuggestionController, WROX.Modules.Suggestion** for the Business Controller Class.
10. Click Next.
11. Leave the owner details blank and click Next again to complete the Module Extension Creation Wizard.

Now that your Module extension is created, click the pencil icon to edit the details for that module. The next step is to create the Module Definitions for the Suggestions module. Click Add Definition, then type **Wrox.Suggestion** in the Friendly Name textbox and click Create Definition to create the management Module Definition. Once you have created the Module Definition, a new interface is available below the definition area for managing module controls as shown in Figure 17-6.

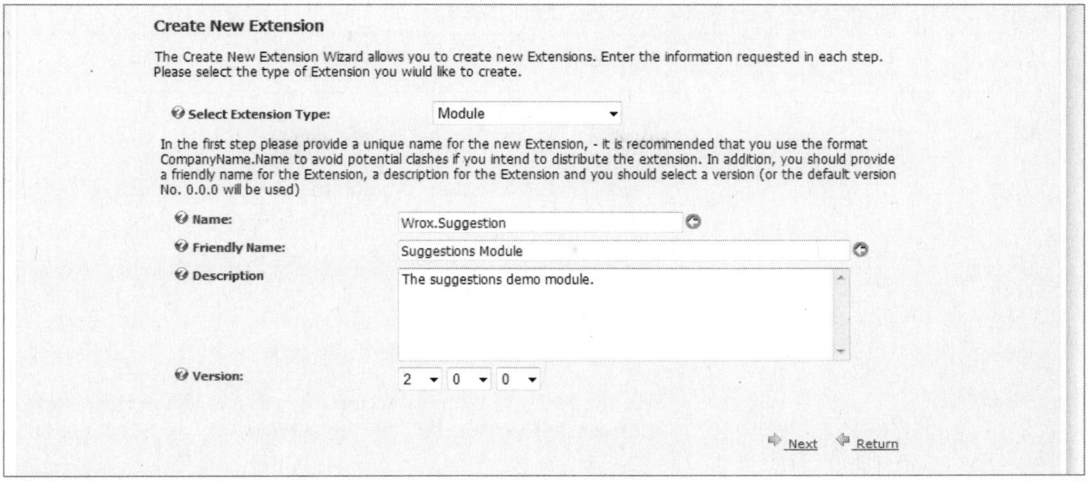

Create New Extension

The Create New Extension Wizard allows you to create new Extensions. Enter the information requested in each step. Please select the type of Extension you wiuld like to create.

Select Extension Type: Module

In the first step please provide a unique name for the new Extension, - it is recommended that you use the format CompanyName.Name to avoid potential clashes if you intend to distribute the extension. In addition, you should provide a friendly name for the Extension, a description for the Extension and you should select a version (or the default version No. 0.0.0 will be used)

Name: Wrox.Suggestion

Friendly Name: Suggestions Module

Description: The suggestions demo module.

Version: 2 0 0

Next Return

Figure 17-5

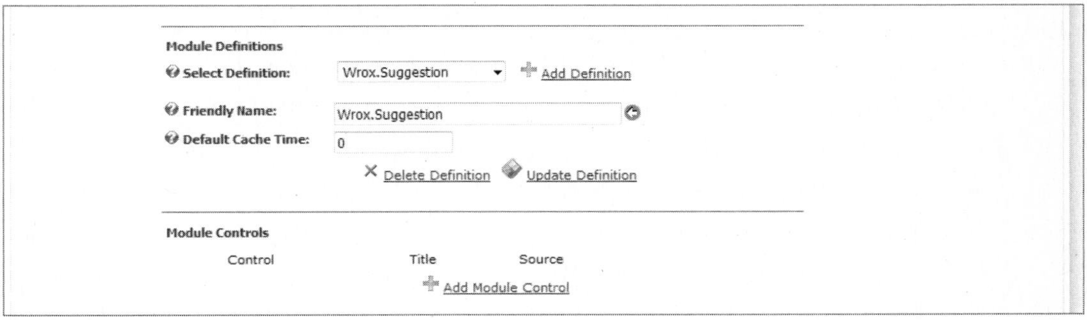

Module Definitions

Select Definition: Wrox.Suggestion Add Definition

Friendly Name: Wrox.Suggestion

Default Cache Time: 0

Delete Definition Update Definition

Module Controls

Control Title Source

Add Module Control

Figure 17-6

Click the Add Module Control link to add a new control to the Module Definition. The Edit Module Control screen allows developers to define the controls to operate the module. Table 17-3 explains what each field does.

To continue building the suggestions Module Definition, add the three controls according to Table 17-4.

To finish setting up the Suggestions module, add a second Module Definition named Wrox.Suggestion .Display with a single view control pointing to `DesktopModules/WROX.Suggestion/DisplaySuggestions.ascx`. Click Update Extensions to save your changes to the extension.

Skinobject Configuration

The Skinobject extension type is used to extend the DotNetNuke skinning engine by adding ASCX user controls that can be added to skins using tokens and the new Skinobject format described in Chapter 16. The Skinobject configuration attributes are explained in Table 17-5.

Table 17-3: Module Control Definition Attributes

Name	Purpose
Key	Sets the URL parameter to load the control.
Title	For controls other than the default view control, this will display as the module title when the control loads.
Source	The ASCX user control to use for displaying the interface to the user.
Type	Sets the security level type of the control.
View Order	Sets the order in which the control is displayed in the list of controls on the Module Definition page.
Icon	Sets the icon to be displayed with the module title when the control is loaded. Like the Module Title, this is only used when loaded as a control other than the default view control.
Help URL	The URL that should be used for the help link in the module actions menu. If this is left blank, it will use the context-sensitive Online Help at the DotNetNuke web site.
Supports Partial Rendering	This tells DotNetNuke to wrap the user control in an ASP.NET AJAX Update Panel control.

Table 17-4: Wrox.Suggestion Module Definitions Module Controls

Key	Control Source	Title	Type
Blank	DesktopModules/WROX .Suggestion/Suggestion.ascx	Blank	View
Edit	DesktopModules/WROX .Suggestion/EditSuggestion.ascx	Edit Content	Edit
Settings	DesktopModules/WROX .Suggestion/Settings.ascx	Suggestion Settings	Edit

Provider Extension Configuration

Providers are pluggable pieces of functionality used to perform base behaviors and framework building blocks for DotNetNuke. Providers have no custom configuration interface. All management for providers is handled through the package configuration file.

Table 17-5: Configuration Options for Skinobject Extensions

Setting	Purpose
Control Key	The unique key used to refer to the Skinobject from HTML-based skins. This is the value used in the codebase parameter for Skinobjects.
Control Src	The location of the ASCX user control that the Skinobject should use to render the control on the page.
Supports Partial Rendering	This tells DotNetNuke to wrap the user control in an ASP.NET AJAX Update Panel control to intercept postbacks.

Authentication System Configuration

The Authentication System extension type is a special type of provider that controls authentication and authorization for resources belonging to a portal. The options available for configuration to the Authentication System extension type are listed in Table 17-6.

Table 17-6: Configuration Options for Authentication System Extensions

Setting	Purpose
Authentication Type	This is the unique key to set the name of the authentication system.
Login Control Source	This is the ASCX user control that should process a login.
Logoff Control Source	This is the ASCX user control that should process a logoff.
Settings Control Source	This is the ASCX user control that manages the configuration options for an authentication provider.
Enabled	Sets whether this authentication provider should be available.

Core Language Pack Extensions Configuration

The Core Language Pack extension allows Host administrators to install and manage sets of local resource files containing strings to translate interface text for different languages that are supported. The New Extension Wizard requires you to choose the language that the language pack should be associated with and the fallback language to use if the language pack does not have a requested resource. The extension configuration can be updated to change the fallback language, but once the language is associated with a language pack it cannot be changed.

Extensions Language Pack Extensions Configuration

The Extensions Language Pack extension type creates a way to distribute language packs for modules, providers, and other extension types. The New Extension Wizard asks for the language and package with which to associate the Language Pack. Once configured, neither the language nor the package can be changed.

Using the Wizard to Create Packages

DotNetNuke 5's enhancements to the Package Creation Wizard have dramatically simplified the process of packaging extensions for distribution. The Package Creation Wizard takes an existing extension and creates the properly formatted package definition file and zips the selected files to create the distributable package. To create a package, click the Create Package link at the bottom of the extension details page. Once you click the Create Package link, you will start the Create Package Wizard. The following lists the steps in the Package Creation Wizard:

1. Review Package Information

   The first step in the Create Package Wizard is a simple review of the extension from which you have chosen to create a package. The two options on this screen are Use Existing Manifest and Review Manifest. The Use Existing option bypasses the step to create a package manifest. The Review Manifest option tells the wizard to display an editable version of the package manifest before the package is created.

2. Choose Files to Include

   Most packages include the second step to allow you to select files to include in the extension package. Select the folder to scan and click Refresh File List to populate a list of all files and subfolders' files. To exclude a file that was selected, simply delete the line from the textbox.

3. Choose Assemblies to Include

   Packages that include server-side functionality, like modules, providers, and authentication systems, will show the third possible step in the wizard for including assemblies. To include an assembly, simply add a line for each dll to include. The wizard assumes that the root folder for assemblies is the `bin` folder in the root of the web site, so there is no need to add the folder name to the beginning of the filename. Figure 17-7 shows the assemblies entry for the `Wrox.Suggestion` module example from this and earlier chapters.

4. Create Manifest

   All extension types require a manifest file. The Create Manifest step in the wizard allows you to review the manifest file created by the wizard before it is included in the package in the last step of the wizard. The manifest is displayed in an editable textbox so that you can edit any elements in the manifest before creating your package.

5. Create Package

   The final step tells the wizard what to name the manifest file and where to save the package. Manifest files should have the extension `.dnn` and the archive filename should use the `.zip` extension because it is a compressed zip folder. Regardless of whether you choose to create the manifest or create the archive, the package will be added to the database and the manifest will be saved to the package archive. All packages that are created will be placed in the `\portals\_default` folder in the DotNetNuke instance.

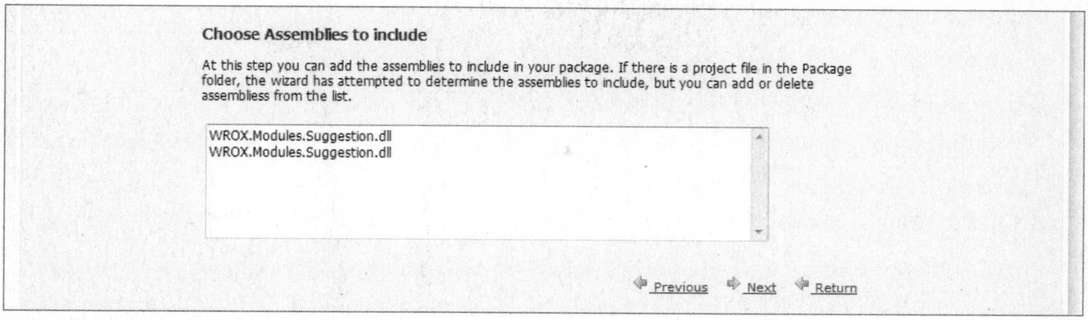

Choose Assemblies to include

At this step you can add the assemblies to include in your package. If there is a project file in the Package folder, the wizard has attempted to determine the assemblies to include, but you can add or delete assembliess from the list.

WROX.Modules.Suggestion.dll
WROX.Modules.Suggestion.dll

Previous Next Return

Figure 17-7

Building Packages with Manifest Files

In the previous section of this chapter, you learned that the new Package Creation Wizard in DotNetNuke 5 is a simple way to package skins, modules, and other extensions for distribution. Though the wizard simplifies the process of packaging and creating the manifest for packages to be distributed, there will always be times that you'll need to modify the package and the manifest manually to get the exact behavior you require for your installation process. This section explains version 5 of the DotNetNuke manifest file format and provides examples for common tasks using the manifest file.

Manifest Packages

Packaging an extension without using the package wizard is done by adding the files from your extension into a compressed zip folder and telling the installer how to use the files with an XML-based manifest file. An installable extension is referred to in the manifest as a *package*. The architecture of the DotNetNuke installer provides for installing multiple packages into a single installation by adding multiple packages under the packages node. This could allow a developer to distribute an install package with libraries, skins, modules, and a provider in a single install. The package information begins at the `dotnetnuke/packages/package` element within the XML structure. Table 17-7 explains the general package elements and attributes.

Table 17-7: Package Elements and Attributes

Name	Path	Purpose
Package Name	`dotnetnuke/packages/package/@name`	This name must be unique because it is used in portal and page templates to refer to modules and extensions.
Type	`dotnetnuke/packages/package/@type`	Setting that instructs DotNetNuke whether to treat the extension as a module, skin, provider, or any other custom extension type.

Continued

Table 17-7: *(continued)*

Name	Path	Purpose
Version	`dotnetnuke/packages/package/@version`	Version number for the package.
Friendly Name	`dotnetnuke/packages/package/friendlyName`	This setting is for the name to display to end users. It is used in drop-downs, lists, and the control panel for modules.
Description	`dotnetnuke/packages/package/description`	Setting to display a short description of the extension in the list of extensions on the Host and admin extensions pages.
Owner Name	`dotnetnuke/packages/package/owner/name`	The owner of the package.
Organization	`dotnetnuke/packages/package/owner/organization`	The name of the company that owns the package.
URL	`dotnetnuke/packages/package/owner/url`	The web site address for the owner of the extension.
Email Address	`dotnetnuke/packages/package/owner/email`	The package owner's support or contact email address.
License	`dotnetnuke/packages/package/license`	The version of the extension.
License Source	`dotnetnuke/packages/package/license/@src`	Optional parameter to use a `.txt` file with the license information.
Release Notes	`dotnetnuke/packages/package/releaseNotes`	Notes about the current version of the extension.
Source	`dotnetnuke/packages/package/releaseNotes/@src`	Optional parameter to use a `.txt` file with the release notes information.

Continuing with the example from earlier in this chapter, the following code shows the package description part of the manifest file for the `Wrox.Suggestion` module:

```
<dotnetnuke type="Package" version="5.0">
  <packages>
    <package name="Wrox.Suggestion" type="Module" version="2.0.0">
      <friendlyName>Suggestions Demo Module</friendlyName>
      <description>The suggestions demo module.</description>
      <owner>
```

```
        <name>Wrox</name>
        <organization>Wiley and Sons Publishing</organization>
        <url>http://p2p.wrox.com</url>
        <email>support@wrox.com</email>
      </owner>
      <license>Suggestions is provided as a demonstration module for DotNetNuke as
part of the Professional DotNetNuke 5 book from Wrox. It may not be redistributed or
sold. </license>
      <releaseNotes>Version 2.0 is dependant upon DotNetNuke 5.
Any questions can be submitted through p2p.wrox.com. </releaseNotes>
      <components>
              ...
      </components>
    </package>
  </packages>
</dotnetnuke>
```

Package Components

The building blocks of an extension manifest file are the components that are included in the package. A component is a logical grouping of a part of the package to be installed. For most package types, there is a component type that matches the package type. For example, a skin package type will have a skin component type and a module package type will include a module component type. The real advancement in the package manifest file is that common installation types like SQL scripts, assemblies, and generic files have been broken out so that they can be used across all package types.

File Components

The File component is a common component type that adds files to the DotNetNuke installation. This component type can be used in all package types. The addition of the File component type is an advancement over previous versions of DotNetNuke because it allows developers to install files into other parts of the web site than the `DesktopModules` folder. Using the File component type, set the `basePath` attribute to set where the group of files should be installed and include a list of files to install with the package. The following example shows a File component:

```
<component type="File">
<files>
 <basePath>DesktopModules\Wrox.Suggestion</basePath>
 <file>
  <path>app_localresources</path>
  <name>suggestion.ascx.resx</name>
 </file>
 <file>
  <name>displaysuggestions.ascx</name>
 </file>
</files>
</component>
```

In the example, you can see that the `basePath` node sets the folder into which all listed files are relative. Within the `files` node, each file has a name and optional path that is relative to the `basePath` root folder.

Assembly Components

The Assembly component is used for installing DLLs into the `bin` folder in your DotNetNuke installation. The Assembly component is very similar in structure to the File component. Set the `basePath` to `bin` and list the assemblies using the `assembly` node type.

```
<component type="Assembly">
<assemblies>
  <basePath>bin</basePath>
  <assembly>
    <name>WROX.Modules.Suggestion.dll</name>
  </assembly>
  <assembly>
    <name>WROX.Modules.Suggestion.SqlDataProvider.dll</name>
  </assembly>
</assemblies>
</component>
```

Script Components

The Script component is used for executing install and uninstall SQL scripts to configure the database storage and methods needed to support the extension in the package. SQL script filenames should follow the convention `[version number].SQLDataProvider` or `XX.XX.XX.SQLDataProvider`. In previous versions of the installer, versioning was managed using the convention of the filename. In this version of the installer, the `version` node in the script element should correspond to the version number of the package being installed. The `version` node tells DotNetNuke when to run the script. By versioning your SQLDataProvider files consistently with the version number of the package, the DotNetNuke installer will run the SQL scripts as database upgrade scripts depending upon the currently installed version. When installing a newer version of an existing package, the installer will only run scripts with version numbers after the current version. For example, if you have version `01.00.00` of a module installed and you install an upgrade for version `01.00.01`, if the package includes scripts with the version set to `01.00.00` and `01.00.01`, the DotNetNuke installer would only run the second SQL script. If the package has never been installed, then all scripts will be executed in order of version number. This functionality protects existing tables from accidentally being deleted or cleared with the initial creation scripts and ensures that table update scripts run only once. The following example shows the Script component type from the `Wrox.Suggesion` module:

```
<component type="Script">
<scripts>
  <basePath>DesktopModules\Wrox.Suggestion</basePath>
  <script type="Install">
    <name>02.00.00.sqldataprovider</name>
    <version>02.00.00</version>
  </script>
  <script type="UnInstall">
    <name>uninstall.sqldataprovider</name>
    <version>2.0.0</version>
  </script>
</scripts>
</component>
```

Cleanup Components

The Cleanup component provides a mechanism for deleting files and assemblies that are no longer needed for a version of a package. In previous versions of the installer, developers could instruct DotNetNuke to remove a list of files by providing a file with the naming convention `[version number].txt` or `XX.XX.XX.txt` that included a list of files to delete when installing that version. For instance, if developers wanted to delete an image file that was no longer used in the `01.00.02` version of their module, they would include a file named `01.00.02.txt` in the package and DotNetNuke would delete the legacy files. Like the SQLDataProvider scripts, the installer would run all files between the current version of the module and the version being installed.

Because the installer for DotNetNuke 5 is based upon configuration over convention, developers are required to declare explicitly the files to be removed in the manifest file. Files can be listed within the Cleanup component or referred to through a `src` attribute. The version must be set within the `version` attribute of the Cleanup component for the installer to know which cleanup tasks should be performed to upgrade an installed version to a current version of the package. The following examples show how to mark files for deletion:

```
<component type="Cleanup" version="02.00.00">
<files>
<file>
 <path>DesktopModules\WROX.Suggestion\images</path>
 <name>oldImage.jpg</name>
</file>
</files>
</component>
```

Alternatively, you can point your Cleanup element to a file included in your package like in the following example:

```
<component type="Cleanup" version="02.00.00" src="02.00.00.txt" />
02.00.00.txt Contents
DesktopModules\WROX.Suggestion\images\oldImage.jpg
```

Config Components

The Config component gives developers the ability to manage changes to the `web.config` files from the install process. This feature can save users without experience from having to edit the web.config file when it is necessary for a package to be installed. It also protects commercial developers from the support calls and emails that will inevitably come from those inexperienced users breaking their web.config when they incorrectly make the changes necessary for the package.

The Config component has an `install` and an `uninstall` section to provide instructions on how to make the changes to the web.config when the package is installed and how to remove or revert the configuration to its state before the configuration was changed. The following code shows how the Config component could be used to add an `appSetting` key to the `configuration` section of the web.config and remove the same key when the package is uninstalled:

```
<component type="Config">
<config>
```

```
<configFile>web.config</configFile>
<install>
<configuration>
  <nodes>
  <node path="/configuration/appSettings" action="add" key="key" collision=
"overwrite">
   <add key="WROX.Suggest.Type" value="Module"/>
  </node>
  </nodes>
</configuration>
</install>
<uninstall>
<configuration>
  <nodes>
    <node path="/configuration/appSettings/add[@key='WROX.Suggest.Type']" action=
"remove" />
  </nodes>
</configuration>
</uninstall>
</config>
</component>
```

Each node in the nodes element defines an action to be performed on the config file. Using the path, the section of the `.config` file to be modified is selected using an xpath expression. Table 17-8 lists the actions for the `node` element and how it is used to manage the web.config.

Table 17-8: Node Action Types

Action Type	Purpose
`add`	Adds the content within the node element to the location selected in the path.
`insertbefore`	Inserts the supplied content before the selected node in the path.
`insertafter`	Inserts the supplied content after the selected node.
`remove`	Removes the node selected in the path.
`removeattribute`	Removes the attribute selected in the path.
`update`	Updates the node selected in the path with the supplied content.
`updateattribute`	Updates the selected attribute.

Besides `path` and `action`, two other node attributes control how the node action is performed on the selected node. The `key` attribute instructs DotNetNuke which attribute in the XML node to use to compare nodes to look for duplicates. In the earlier example, the `key` was set to `key` to let the installer know that `appSettings` that have the same `key` attribute are duplicates. In the provider config type, you would change the `key` to `name`. The last attribute for the `node` element is `collision`. `Collision` tells the installer how to handle duplicates that it finds using the key attribute. You can supply save to have the installer save a commented-out version of the old node or you can supply overwrite to replace the old node with the one you supply.

Module Components

The Module component is used to install modules as part of a package. The Module component is built with a serialized XML DesktopModule object type. The layout of the Module component type should look very familiar if you have worked through the Create Package Wizard for building a module package. Using the desktopModule node, the storage location, Module Definitions, and controls are defined in XML.

```
<component type="Module">
<desktopModule>
<moduleName>Wrox.Suggestion</moduleName>
<foldername>Wrox.Suggestion</foldername>
<businessControllerClass>WROX.Modules.Suggestion.SuggestionController,
WROX.Modules.Suggestion</businessControllerClass>
 <supportedFeatures>
  <supportedFeature type="Portable" />
  <supportedFeature type="Searchable" />
 </supportedFeatures>
<moduleDefinitions>
<moduleDefinition>
<friendlyName>Wrox.Suggestion</friendlyName>
<defaultCacheTime>0</defaultCacheTime>
<moduleControls>
  <moduleControl>
  <controlKey />
<controlSrc>DesktopModules/WROX.Suggestion/Suggestion.ascx</controlSrc>
    <supportsPartialRendering>False</supportsPartialRendering>
    <controlTitle />
    <controlType>View</controlType>
    <iconFile />
    <helpUrl />
  </moduleControl>
  </moduleControls>
</moduleDefinition>
</moduleDefinitions>
</desktopModule>
</component>
```

Developers who use the web site project model for developing modules and have business logic included in the App_Code folder can include the .cs or .vb files in their installation packages with the Files component explained earlier in the chapter.

IUpgradeable Interface and the eventMessage Section

The version control and management within the Scripts and Cleanup components of the extension manifest provides a rich API for developers to provide upgrade paths to consumers of their modules, but there are times when these tools are no substitute for access to the full .NET Framework. The DotNetNuke extensions manifest accounts for the need to execute ASP.NET code to execute upgrade operations that are not covered with file copy, file delete, or T-SQL scripts with the eventMessage section within the `Module` component. When the module install process runs, the last action that the installer performs is installing dll assemblies into the `bin` folder of the web site. Because adding assemblies to the `bin` of an ASP.NET web site always causes the application to restart, access to the current thread is lost with that application restart and no more server-side code can be run until the ASP.NET re-JITs and starts the worker process. The problem that this presents for server-side upgrade code is that the upgrade code is included in the new assembly, which cannot be run until the application restarts, at which point the upgrade process is no longer running. To address this problem, DotNetNuke uses the `eventMessage` process of storing an upgrade action to be run on `Application_Start` event. The following example shows a sample `eventMessage` section:

```
<component type="Module">
<desktopModule>
<moduleName>WROX.Modules.UpgradeApp</moduleName>
<foldername>WROX.Modules.UpgradeApp</foldername>
<businessControllerClass>WROX.Modules.UpgradeApp.WroxBusinessController,
WROX.Modules.UpgradeApp</businessControllerClass>          <supportedFeatures />
<moduleDefinitions />
</desktopModule>
<eventMessage>
<processorType>DotNetNuke.Entities.Modules.EventMessageProcessor,
DotNetNuke</processorType>
<processorCommand>UpgradeModule</processorCommand>
<attributes>
 <businessControllerClass>WROX.Modules.UpgradeApp.WroxBusinessController,
WROX.Modules.UpgradeApp</businessControllerClass>
 <desktopModuleID>[DESKTOPMODULEID]</desktopModuleID>
 <upgradeVersionsList>01.00.00,01.00.01,02.00.01</upgradeVersionsList>
</attributes>
</eventMessage>
</component>
```

When the module is upgraded, DotNetNuke uses the `eventMessage` section of the `Module` node to store an event in the `EventMessage` table to run the next time the application starts. When the `EventMessage` is run, the business controller's `UpgradeModule` event will be run once for every version listed in the `upgradeVersionsList` node. The method is executed in the order in which it is listed, regardless of the version that is currently installed or the version to which it is being upgraded. That means that the upgrade process runs differently than the `Scripts` upgrade process in that it does not keep track of the version it is upgrading to or from. Within the `UpgradeModule` event, the logic will have to account for the version number being passed to it and execute the appropriate upgrade operations based upon that. Following is an example `UpgradeModule` using a `switch` statement to execute code specific to the version that is being upgraded:

```
namespace WROX.Modules.UpgradeApp
{
public class WroxBusinessController: DotNetNuke.Entities.Modules.IUpgradeable
{
#region IUpgradeable Members
public string UpgradeModule(string Version)
{
switch (Version)
{
case "01.00.00":
    //Upgrade from 01.00.00
```

```
        return (string.Format("Successfully upgraded from version {0}", Version));
    case "01.00.01":
        //Upgrade from 01.00.01
        return (string.Format("Successfully upgraded from version {0}", Version));
    case "02.00.01":
        //Upgrade from 02.00.01
        return (string.Format("Successfully upgraded from version {0}", Version));
    default:
        return (string.Format("Version {0} upgrade not supported.", Version));
    }
    }
    #endregion
    }
    }
```

The returned string is saved to a log entry for each upgrade event that is viewable on the Event Viewer page in the admin menu.

Skin and Container Components

Skins and containers are created easily and efficiently with the Create Package Wizard. Designers and developers should not generally need to create a manifest file from scratch for skins and containers. All files in the skin or container package are listed under the respective `skinFiles` or `containerFiles` node. The following code shows example skin and container component types:

```
<component type="Skin">
<skinFiles>
  <skinName>SkinningDemo</skinName>
  <basePath>Portals\_default\Skins\SkinningDemo</basePath>
  <skinFile>
    <name>htmlmethod.ascx</name>
  </skinFile>
  <skinFile>
    <name>htmlmethod.jpg</name>
  </skinFile>
  <skinFile>
    <name>htmlmethod.css</name>
  </skinFile>
  <skinFile>
    <name>htmlmethod.doctype.xml</name>
  </skinFile>
</skinFiles>
</component>
<component type="Container">
<containerFiles>
  <containerName>MinimalExtropy</containerName>
  <basePath>Portals\_default\Containers\MinimalExtropy</basePath>
  <containerFile>
    <path>images</path>
    <name>dnn-plus.png</name>
  </containerFile>
  <containerFile>
    <name>container.css</name>
  </containerFile>
```

```
    <containerFile>
      <name>title_blue.ascx</name>
    </containerFile>
    <containerFile>
      <name>title_blue.css</name>
    </containerFile>
    <containerFile>
      <name>title_blue.jpg</name>
    </containerFile>
  </containerFiles>
  </component>
```

Skinobject Components

The Skinobject component tells DotNetNuke how to use the files included in the package to create the token for use in DotNetNuke skins using the same configuration from the Create Extension Wizard. The Skinobject component does not include the actual ASCX files that are used for the Skinobject; it only maps the token to the user control used to render the Skinobject. You should also include a File component type to include the ASCX files and any other supporting images or files needed to render the Skinobject.

```
<component type="SkinObject">
 <moduleControl>
 <controlKey>ACTIONBUTTON</controlKey>
 <controlSrc>Admin/Containers/ActionButton.ascx</controlSrc>
 <supportsPartialRendering>False</supportsPartialRendering>
 </moduleControl>
</component>
```

Language Pack Components

In order to instruct the DotNetNuke installer how to use your language pack, you will provide a group of `languageFiles` elements for each language that is in the install package. Like the create wizard shown earlier in the chapter, you will set the language code, display name, and fallback language. The remainder of the component type is filled with `languageFile` elements. `LanguageFile` elements should all have a `path` element and a `name` element for each `RESX` file like in the following code example. The Extension Language package should be created with the same structure as the `CoreLanguage` element except with `ExtensionLanguage` as the component type key.

```
<component type="CoreLanguage">
 <languageFiles>
<code>en-US</code>
 <displayName>English (United States)</displayName>
 <fallback />
 <languageFile>
 <path>admin\controlpanel\app_localresources</path>
<name>classic.ascx.resx</name>
 </languageFile>
 </languageFiles>
</component>
```

Authentication System Components

The Authentication System component type is a serialization of the inputs from the Create New Extension Wizard to control the login, logoff, and settings control sources. The Authentication System settings and

Assembly component types can be mostly generated using the wizard, but web.config changes will have to be created manually using the config component type explained earlier in this chapter. The following code shows an example Authentication System component:

```
<component type="AuthenticationSystem">
<authenticationService>
  <type>LiveID</type>  <settingsControlSrc>DesktopModules/AuthenticationServices/
LiveID/Settings.ascx</settingsControlSrc>  <loginControlSrc>DesktopModules/
AuthenticationServices/LiveID/Login.ascx</loginControlSrc>  <logoffControlSrc>
DesktopModules/AuthenticationServices/LiveID/Logoff.ascx</logoffControlSrc>
</authenticationService>
</component>
```

Provider Packages

Provider packages do not have their own component types. Instead, components are made up of the Assembly, Config, and optionally the Script and File component types.

Library Packages

The Library Package extension is created to manage generic package types. Like the Provider package type, the Library Package does not have a component type. Using the Assembly, File, Script, and Config components, developers can install any kind of files or groups of files into a DotNetNuke installation. The library package type can be used to install and manage custom widgets, portal templates, common DLLs, icon libraries, and anything else developers can think of to install.

Summary

In this chapter you learned how to create and package extensions to the DotNetNuke platform. You learned how to use the wizard to create install packages for the extensions that have an automated Package Creation Wizard. Lastly, you learned how to use the new DotNetNuke manifest file format to install and manage extensions and providers for your installation.

18

DotNetNuke's Commercial Evolution

The concept of open source has revolutionized the technology industry. Over the past 10 to 15 years, open source has established itself as an economic movement — an economic movement that has leveraged both the distributive and collaborative power of the Internet; an economic movement that is based on free and fair markets; and is driven by the needs of the end user or customer.

The Fundamentals

Now — as much as some people would like you to believe — this isn't an ideology or a fad. It isn't a communal experiment either. At its most fundamental level, open source is an economic movement. It is a new way of doing things that is rooting out inefficiencies in the software sector — inefficiencies that have become ingrained in the sector for decades. In that sense, open source is the philosophical essence of capitalism in action.

Software Industry Today — Inefficiency Spirals Costs

The best way to get an understanding of the economic movement of open source is to compare the hardware sector with software. In 1996, a computer with a 486 CPU, 8 MB of RAM, and a 500 MB hard drive cost $3000. In contrast, today a mere $300 will buy you a Celeron/Pentium processor, 512 MB of RAM, and 80 GB of hard disk space. In essence, in a matter of 12 short years, we get hundreds of times the computing power — at just a tenth of the price. That is price/performance improvement of thousands.

How Has That Been Made Possible?

The remarkable price/performance improvement has largely been possible due to technological advances in design, manufacturing, and distribution driven by massive market demand. Massive

---

Shaun Walker gratefully acknowledges DotNetNuke Corporation CEO Navin Nagiah for his assistance writing this chapter

market demand results in commoditization, and commoditization drives prices down. This is the story of any product — business or consumer — especially in the technology industry. Think of cell phones, stereos, telecommunications, servers, computers — the story of "improvement in performance" and "drop in price" is strikingly similar.

Nevertheless, there seems to be one exception; that is business software. Here, prices have for the most part either remained static or have decreased marginally. For all the supposed "openness" of the J2EE framework, truth be said — J2EE-based business software products have been two to four times more expensive than products based on the Microsoft platform. It was only when open source–based JBOSS challenged the application server market that BEA and IBM dropped their Application Server prices — and dropped them dramatically at that. Likewise for MySQL and Oracle. We saw a similar story earlier with Linux-based high-powered PCs and SUN Servers.

At the risk of sounding repetitive, history has shown us, time and time again, that open source isn't about being "right" or "wrong" — it isn't an ideology — it is very simply about rooting out inefficiencies so that the "value derived per dollar invested" for the customer increases.

Why Has the Cost and Therefore the Price of Business Software Been High?

One reason for the high cost has been the substantial expense it took to develop the software. This high cost of software has been primarily determined by the traditional (and now defunct) nature of software development — a tendency to develop monolithic instead of modular software — a tendency to layer software one layer over the other instead of making it flexible, open, and extensible. The best example of this, just a few years ago, was that it turned out to be much easier, less time consuming, and less expensive to write an entire operating system from the ground up than to rewrite portions of an existing OS to make it better.

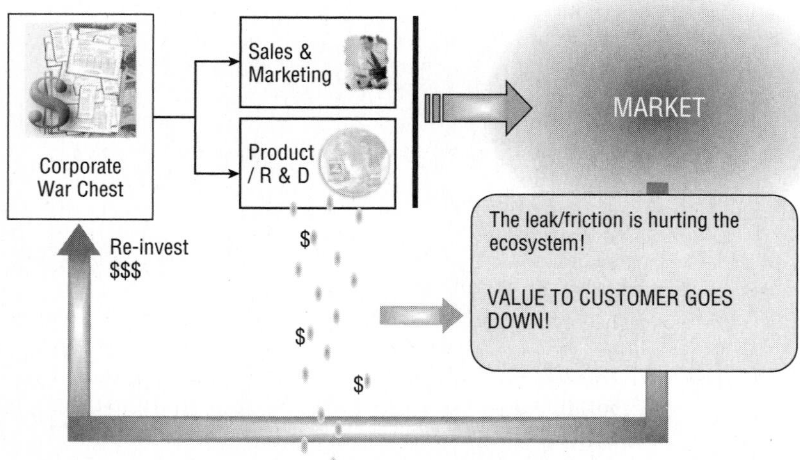

Figure 18-1

Another factor that increases the cost of software development has been the tendency of software companies to use the "closed" model of development — to build proprietary software and file for patents either as an offense or defense mechanism. This process takes time, effort, and money — the total cost of which is passed on to the end user or customer.

In addition to the traditional high cost of software development, the cost of selling and distributing the developed software has also been high. When the software product itself isn't difficult to mimic or reproduce, companies invest large amounts of money in positioning, branding, and marketing strategies and in highly paid sales resources in an effort to sell their product and gain (or retain) market share. One 2004 Goldman Sachs report estimates that 76% of the licensing revenue of the typical business software company is spent on sales and marketing.

Needless to say, the (unnecessary) cost incurred in both software development and sales/distribution is being passed on to the end user or customer. The ecosystem has a frictional cost — the brunt of which is being felt by the small and mid-sized organizations (the large ones are typically able to "afford" high-priced business software).

Open source has made (some) software products just as affordable and accessible to the small and mid-sized organizations as they are to large organizations. Examples of this include Linux-based servers, databases such as MySQL, application servers like JBOSS, and web application frameworks such as DotNetNuke and Drupal.

In essence, open source is rooting out the inefficiencies in the software sector, commoditizing the products (by making them available to the masses), and thereby leveling the playing field.

DotNetNuke is proud to be one of the leaders in such a movement — the largest open source–based web application framework and the largest open source project on the Microsoft platform.

DotNetNuke — Our Time Is Now!

The open source movement has been a bottom-up movement in three key aspects — technology, organizational size, and people. The open source technology revolution originated at the "bottom of the stack" with the Linux operating system, which now has greater than 35% of the server market in the enterprise. The rise of Linux resulted in a drop in server prices; it also resulted in small and mid-sized organizations being able to afford servers based on Linux for email, for networking, for managing their web properties, and for other uses. One step up is the database layer — MySQL (now acquired by SUN) with greater than 10 million downloads is now the third largest database in the world; this also resulted in the drop in prices of databases. The next layer in the technology stack is application servers — JBOSS's success in this segment resulted in the drop in prices of both BEA and IBM application servers. In each of these instances, an open source player caused a "power shift" in the marketplace thereby forcing the proprietary incumbents to drop their prices or risk being obliterated.

The open source company in each of these instances managed to drop prices by keeping the cost of software development low (collaborative development based on a modular, flexible, and open architecture); the cost of software distribution low (the Internet was the medium of distribution); and by keeping the process transparent and open — that is, by having users continuously involved in the iterative development cycles.

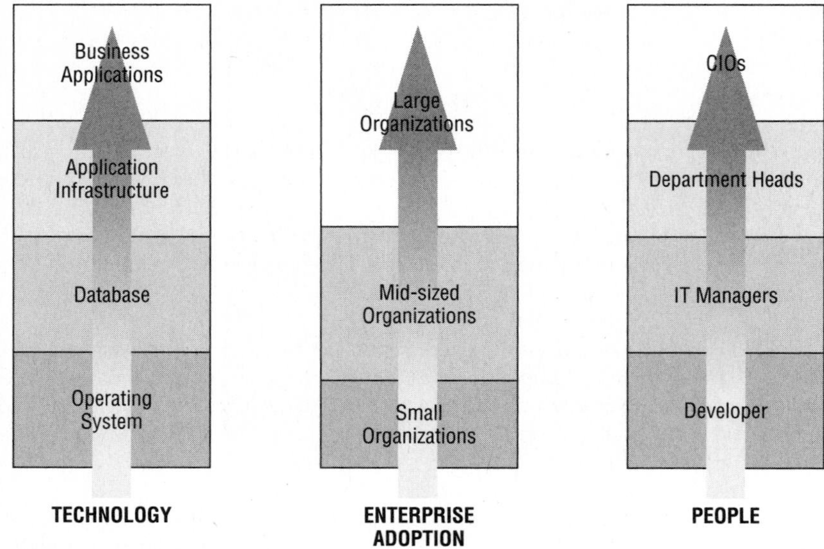

Figure 18-2

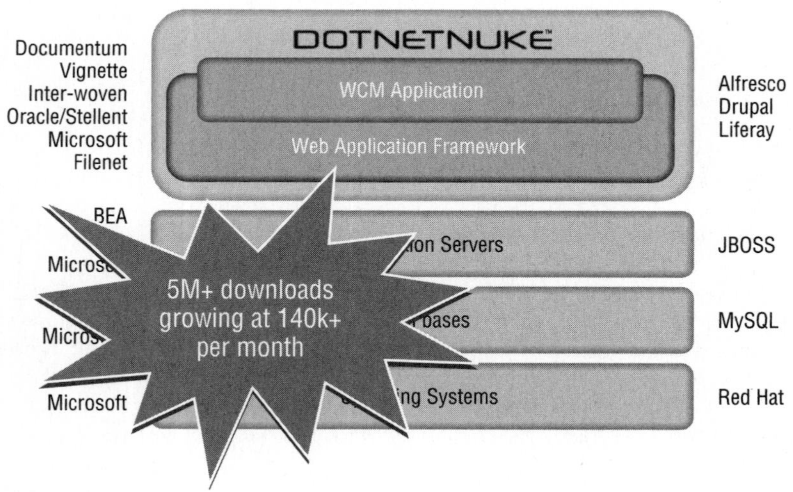

Figure 18-3

DotNetNuke is a web application framework that sits in-between the application server and the Applications layer of the technology stack. We have used a collaborative development model coupled with open and customer/user led iterative development cycles to create one of the most well-developed and robust web application frameworks in the market today. In addition, we have used the web to distribute this framework at no cost, resulting in millions of downloads of our product and hundreds of thousands of live production instances. Numerous companies (module vendors, web designers, and systems integrators) make all or a substantial portion of their livelihood on this framework.

We are proud of the product we have created. We are proud of the users we have attracted to our product. We are proud of the commercial ecosystem that has come around this product. To us, this is but the beginning of a "paradigm shift" that we are beginning to effect in the domain of web applications. We will effect this "paradigm shift" by continuing to do the following:

- Lower the cost and complexity of building web applications
- Make it affordable and accessible to all companies (small and large) to build web applications using our framework
- Ensure that our web application framework remains the most powerful in the world

Open source has traditionally been a bottom-up movement in that it has been the small organizations that have adopted it before the mid-sized, and the mid-sized organizations have adopted it before the large. Likewise, it has typically been developers and IT Managers who have introduced open source products to organizations, which has attracted the attention of the department heads and CIOs over time. Our experience with DotNetNuke has been no different; it has been a bottom-up movement all three fronts: technology, company adoption, and people.

DotNetNuke — Philosophy, Vision, Mission, and Values

Our philosophy as people and as a business is that "community" and "commerce" are both essential for the success of an open source project. They essentially form the *yin* and *yang* of DotNetNuke. These aren't opposing forces; these forces are essential to and feed off of each other. The two forces together strengthen the ecosystem that is DotNetNuke. All our actions as an organization will endeavor to maintain the delicate balance that is required if we are to reach our potential as a company and as an ecosystem.

Our vision as an organization is to make DotNetNuke the most deployed, most valuable, and most cost-effective web application platform in the world. We would like every application in the world to be built on DotNetNuke. In addition, we intend to continue to lead and become the standard bearer for all open source projects in the Microsoft ecosystem.

We intend to realize our vision by making it cost-, time-, and resource-effective for organizations (small and large) to build and deploy web applications, and by supporting, nurturing, and growing the DotNetNuke ecosystem; the "ecosystem" here refers to module vendors, systems integrators, web designers, customers, users, and hosting providers.

As an organization, we will live by the following values, and will actively promote this same set of values in our ecosystem:

Customer First — Our every action will be determined and defined by what is best for our customer. In our definition, "customer" includes both "commercial customers" and "end users" of our platform.

Create Opportunities — "Modularity" and "extensibility" has been the cornerstone of how we have designed and built this platform. This approach hasn't just been superior technology for technology's sake, but to provide an abundance of opportunities to designers and developers to push the limits of the application, and create innovative solutions for business and technical problems.

Spread Entrepreneurship — We intend to spread entrepreneurship by ensuring that the platform allows entrepreneurial individuals and organizations to create and market ancillary products and services.

To the World — Our project, brand, and company transcends geographical, racial, cultural, and political borders. We are affiliated to no country, to no region, and to no culture. Individuals and organizations anywhere in the world, and with any affiliations can participate in the active development community and in the ecosystem.

Superior — We will endeavor to take steps to ensure that our web application platform continues to be superior to every other web application platform in the world, irrespective of technology.

Commercial Ecosystem — We are and will be proud supporters and promoters of a commercial ecosystem. Trade and commerce have been essential to man's survival and progress since time immemorial. We aren't here to change the natural order and philosophy of the world. We are here to be consistent with that natural order.

Directness, Integrity, and Transparency — We will do the right things and endeavor to be seen doing the right things by all our stakeholders: users, customers, vendors, systems integrators, hosting providers, partners, and community members.

The Commercialization of DotNetNuke

First and foremost, in the past six years you have seen us put in ardent efforts to take care of both the platform and the community (users and active participants). That will continue unabated. However, even as we do that, if we don't add a strong commercial element to our organization at this juncture; we will be remiss in our responsibilities toward the community and the ecosystem that is DotNetNuke.

In business and in life, you are either going up or you are going down ... there is no provision for standing still.

DotNetNuke has grown enormously and at a very rapid pace over the past 5 to 6 years. It has grown in terms of the functionality of the platform; the number of downloads; the number of deployed production instances; the number of vendors and systems integrators in the ecosystem; the number of commercial modules available; the number of hosting providers offering hosting services; the number of registered members; the number of proficient developers; the number of posts on our discussion forums ... by almost any single parameter, our growth has been phenomenal.

This has been achieved with limited resources. As a team we have strained every sinew in our system to get to this point. Nevertheless, what we have done to-date isn't sufficient for this product, and for this ecosystem, to become self-sustaining. As stewards of this ecosystem, it is our responsibility to ensure its continued sustenance, and more importantly, growth. The next step in our evolution and growth is for DotNetNuke to become a core and required element of an organization's (both small and large) software infrastructure. We have to become a mission-critical piece of an organization's IT strategy. We have to become the platform or engine that helps them design, build, and deploy their entire web strategy — both applications and content. It isn't difficult to do this without adding the "commercial" element. It is impossible.

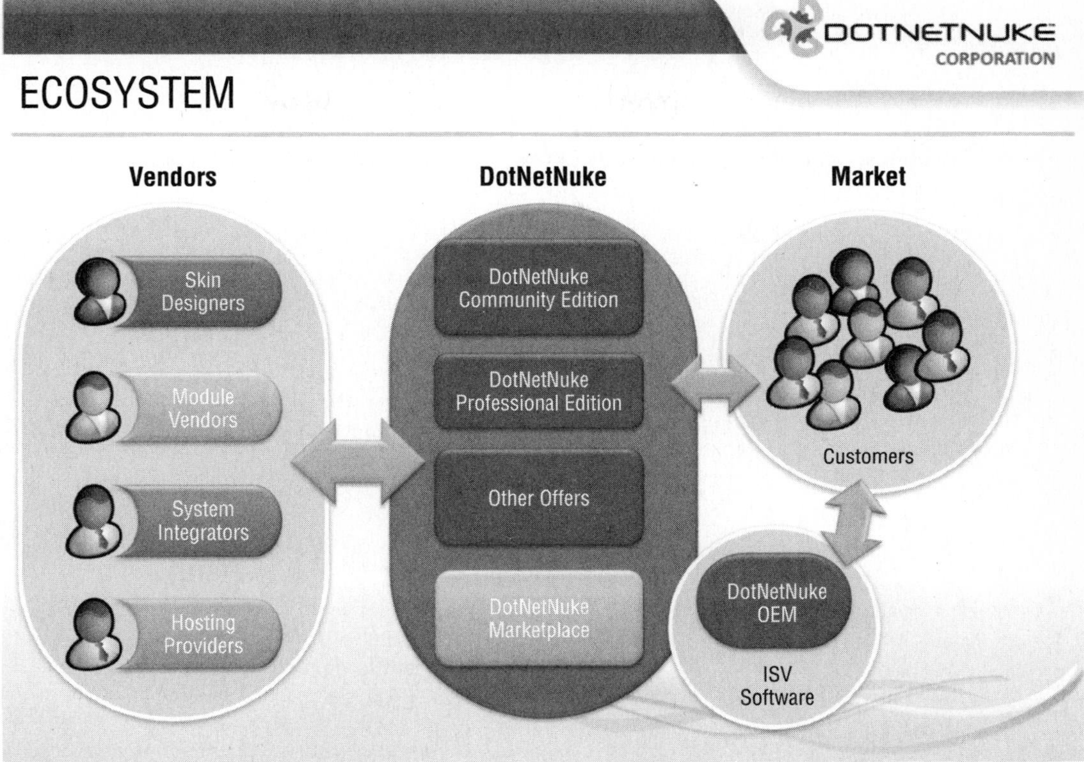

Figure 18-4

If we can make DotNetNuke "central," "core," or "mission critical" to an organization's web strategy or plan, and if we do this in a way that the cost of DotNetNuke continues to be affordable to organizations both large and small, we would have served the community in the following respects:

a. Software that becomes "core," "central," and "mission critical" to an organization will gain sustenance — it will not just survive but prosper as a productivity tool in the business ecosystem. As a result, by assuring its sustenance and growth, we would have ensured the business sustenance of both the platform and the numerous stakeholders (systems integrators, module vendors, web designers, hosting providers, customers, and users) associated with this platform.

b. We will have increased commercial opportunities for the participants of our ecosystem: Systems integrators, and so on. "When the ocean rises, all the boats rise with it."

c. We will have provided customers with a world-class web application platform and a rich ecosystem that not only supports the platform but also provides numerous solutions and a wide variety of services.

Community feeds commerce. Commerce feeds community. We intend to strike the optimal balance between the two to accomplish the preceding goals. We aren't saying this is easy, but, we are saying that this is possible and required if we have to take our platform and ecosystem to that next cycle of growth. We are saying that this isn't a choice, but a necessity. We intend to take the required steps in the weeks, months, and years to come. In that process, we will:

a. Embrace key community stakeholders and work with them in both defining and refining our commercial plans.

b. Increase the value proposition of the community edition of the platform. Commercialization can't and won't be at the expense of the community. Commercialization will benefit the community.

c. Work to provide opportunities to the different commercial entities in our ecosystem to benefit from the process of commercialization.

As we begin this journey with you, we don't expect to get everything right from the get-go. We intend to go on this journey *with* you; we intend to work *with* you . . . to make this the most successful and vibrant open source ecosystem in the world. We look forward to the journey together.

Resources

Numerous effective resources are available that bring value to the development or business aspects of using DotNetNuke. Table A-1 describes a number of great developer tools, many of which are used by the DotNetNuke community and Core Team members. Some of these developer tools are free and others have fees.

Table A-2 describes several useful custom third-party modules. As of the date of the publication of this book, several of these modules are free. Because DotNetNuke 5 is a relatively new release, there aren't many DotNetNuke 5.0-only modules on the market yet, but the Core Team went to great lengths to ensure that modules developed for the DotNetNuke 4.x versions still function on the new 5.0 version.

Projects are the newest addition to the DotNetNuke offerings, and all of the core modules have now been broken out into their own subprojects. This allows the module projects to release new versions of the modules as they are ready, without needing to wait for a core framework release. You can read the latest news on the various module projects and download the latest releases from the DotNetNuke web site.

Table A-1: Developer Tools

Tool	Description
Beyond Compare by Scooter Software `www.scootersoftware.com`	Helpful for comparing files and folders to identify changes in code and to keep directories in sync.
Windows PowerShell `http://www.microsoft.com/windowsserver2003/technologies/management/powershell/default.mspx`	Microsoft Windows PowerShell command line shell and scripting language helps IT professionals achieve greater control and productivity. Using a new admin-focused scripting language, more than 130 standard command line tools, and consistent syntax and utilities, Windows PowerShell allows IT professionals to more easily control system administration and accelerate automation. Windows PowerShell is easy to adopt, learn, and use, because it works with your existing IT infrastructure and existing script investments, and because it runs on Windows XP, Windows Vista, and Windows Server 2003. Windows PowerShell is now included as part of Windows Server 2008 and can be evaluated in Windows Server 2008 Beta 3. Exchange Server 2007, System Center Operations Manager 2007, System Center Data Protection Manager V2, and System Center Virtual Machine Manager also leverage Windows PowerShell to improve administrator control, efficiency, and productivity.
.NET Reflector by Red Gate (formerly Reflector for .NET by Lutz Roeder) `http://www.red-gate.com/products/reflector/`	A class browser for .NET assemblies. It includes code viewers for IL, Visual Basic, Delphi, and C#, dependency trees, and accepts plug-ins for many more features.
NUnit by Jamie Cansdale, Gary Feldman, James W. Newkirk, Michael C. Two, Alexei A. Vorontsov, Philip A. Craig, and Charlie Poole `www.nunit.org`	A powerful unit-testing framework for all .NET languages. It is a port of the Unit Java utility.
SQL Backup by Red-Gate `www.red-gate.com`	Creates compressed, encrypted, and secured backups of SQL Server databases on user-defined schedules.
SQL Compare by Red-Gate `www.red-gate.com`	Compares the structures of Microsoft SQL Server databases and generates scripts to synchronize the databases objects.
SQL Data Compare by Red-Gate `www.red-gate.com`	Compares the data in Microsoft SQL Server databases and generates scripts to synchronize the data.
ANTS Profiler by Red-Gate `www.red-gate.com`	A code and memory profiler for applications written in any .NET language.
ANTS Load by Red-Gate `www.red-gate.com`	Load tests web sites and web services.

Continued

Table A-1: Developer Tools *(continued)*

Tool	Description
FileZilla by Tim Kosse http://sourceforge.net/projects/filezilla	A great open-source FTP client.
CodeSmith by Eric J. Smith www.codesmithtools.com	A commercial template-based code generator. It can generate code for any ASCII-based language, including.NET.
ATGen SDK for DotNetNuke by AppTheory http://projects.apptheory.com	This SDK, based on the commercial code generator MyGeneration, enables developers to create modules and the associated data access layers. It generates the DAL, UI, Business Logic Layer, and installation items required for any module.
FXCop by Microsoft http://msdn.microsoft.com/en-us/library/bb429476.aspx	Analyzes .NET-managed code assemblies to verify that they conform to the Microsoft .NET Framework Design Guidelines.
SnagIt by TechSmith www.techsmith.com	A terrific tool for taking screenshots. It can even take screen captures of scrolling windows (like long web pages).
Araxis Merge by Araxis LTD www.araxis.com	An advanced file comparison and merging tool with integrated folder comparison and synchronization. It allows for two-way or three-way comparisons.
SourceGear Vault by SourceGear LLC www.sourcegear.com	Vault is the source control tool used by the DotNetNuke Core Team. It is a fantastic source control tool for a distributed development team.
Draco.NET by Chive Software Limited http://draconet.sourceforge.net	A Windows service application that facilitates continuous integration. It monitors your source code repository, rebuilds your project, and emails the results automatically.
CruiseControl .NET by ThoughtWorks, Inc. http://ccnet.thoughtworks.com	A powerful open source Automated Continuous Integration server, implemented using the Microsoft.NET Framework.
Gemini by CounterSoft Limited www.countersoft.com	Comprehensive issue, task, and defect management tracking for multiple projects. Generous support of open-source, non-profit, and academic use.
Camtasia Studio by TechSmith www.techsmith.com	A robust application for easily creating compelling training and presentations videos for Web and CD-ROM delivery.

Table A-2: Modules

Module	Description
Snapsis PageBlaster www.snapsis.com	You don't get a second chance to make a first impression, so one important thing is that your web pages load fast to keep your customers from leaving your site. PageBlaster automatically makes a copy of your dynamically built pages and stores them in memory and on disk with optional compression for super-fast delivery.
Aggregator – Tabbed Modules by DNNStuff www.dnnstuff.com	Acts as a tabbed container for one or more modules. This is a great module to effectively manage page real estate.
Enterprise Forms by Ethuongmai www.ethuongmai.com	Designed to enable an average DNN user to create and manage forms and content without any knowledge of HTML or DNN custom-module development.
DNN Photo Gallery by Dave Wilson www.dnnphotogallery.com	Highly configurable professional photo gallery that offers a "lite" version as well as a free trial download.
Active Forums by Active Modules www.activemodules.com	Feature-packed forum module that provides a built-in conversion utility for the DNN Core forum.
Module Wrapper by ZLDNN www.zldnn.com	Enables you to combine multiple modules into a single container using a table format that permits row and column spanning, and many more advanced options.
SQLView by DNNStuff www.dnnstuff.com	Displays the results from any SQL query in tabular format.
Speerio File Manager Pro v3.0 by Speerio, Inc. www.speerio.net	Provides enhanced file-management capabilities for DotNetNuke portals, including multi-server file management, customizable metadata, WebDAV and photo/audio/video content, and metadata management.
Speerio Community Studio v1.0 by Speerio, Inc. www.speerio.net	Integrated solution for community-centric DotNetNuke portals, providing collaborative file and media sharing, blogging, calendar, forum, chat, and an advanced folksonomy engine that helps users quickly and easily locate information.
Private Messages by Scott McCulloch www.ventrian.com	A module that enables you to send private messages to other users of a portal.
Simple Gallery by Scott McCulloch www.ventrian.com	Allows photos to be uploaded and displayed, including dynamically generated thumbnails. Advanced functionality includes approval of photos, albums, bulk upload, search integration, and syndication via RSS.

Continued

Table A-2: Modules *(continued)*

Module	Description
SwirlChat by Swirlhost `www.swirlhost.com`	Simple but fast, customizable chat room client based on AJAX technology.
InfoMap by Vicenç Masanas `http://dnnjungle.vmasanas.net`	Dynamically displays information on a picture. It can position user contact lists on a map. InfoMap presents a clickable map with "hot" areas where some information has been entered. When you click in any given area, the list of contacts for this area is displayed.
TemplatePrint, PagePrint by Vicenç Masanas `http://dnnjungle.vmasanas.net`	Skin objects to enhance the printing capabilities of DNN. You can define skins and containers for the printing.
Podcaster by Arrow Consulting & Design, Inc. `www.arrownuke.com`	Publish single or multiple episode podcasts optimized for iTunes. RSS 2.0 compliant.
Help Desk by DnnToolset `www.dnntoolset.com`	Powerful, easy-to-use system for the management and tracking of help system tickets.
Email Management by MAKI Software `http://makisoftware.com/dnn`	Open source email and newsletter management module that can perform scheduled mailing and logging.
MMLinks by Locopon's DNN `http://dnn.tiendaboliviana.com`	Template-based links module with extensive support for localization, role-based access, custom CSS, and JavaScript effects.
HrefExchanger by Anthony Glenright `www.inventua.com`	Automatically swaps outgoing DotNetNuke URLs for friendly URLs, and incoming friendly URLs for DotNetNuke URLs (requires IIS configuration).
XMod by Kelly Ford `www.dnndev.com`	Highly configurable and extensible form builder that can be leveraged to create applications without the use of traditional programming. It can take the place of several modules.
ListX by R2integrated (R2i) `www.bi4ce.com`	Powerful presentation/reporting engine that builds fully functional, hierarchical views of data. ListX modules can interact with one another, each configured to perform complex display logic and runtime actions.
Custom Page Options by DNNSpired `www.dnnspired.com`	Custom Page Options allows you to custom define unlimited options for your DNN page, including social bookmarks. You can use your icons and configure your email page option to email the WYSIWYG page or just a hyperlink.

System Message Tokens

System tokens were introduced in Chapter 4, ''Portal Administration,'' in the context of customizing portal email templates (although they are also used for other purposes). The tables in this appendix identify and briefly describe the properties of each token. Recall that token properties may be referenced in email templates using the pattern `[Token:Property]`.

Table B-1 describes the `HostSettings` properties that are available for the token `Host` (such as `[Host:ControlPanel]`).

The `PortalSettings` properties are available for the token `Portal` (such as `[Portal:PortalId]`). Table B-2 describes them.

Table B-3 describes the `UserInfo` properties available for the token `User` (such as `[User:UserID]`).

Table B-4 describes the `UserMembership` properties available for the token `Membership` (such as `[Membership:Password]`).

Table B-5 describes the `UserProfile` properties available for the `Profile` token (such as `[Profile:FirstName]`).

Table B-1: Standard HostSettings Properties

Property Name	Description
`AutoAccountUnlock`	Number of minutes after which an account that has been locked due to successive failed login attempts will reset.
`ControlPanel`	Shows whether the new 3.0+ Control Panel is displayed or version 2.0.
`Copyright`	Shows whether the copyright information is displayed in the Page Title. (Y/N)
`DemoPeriod`	Number of days that a demo portal will be active.
`DemoSignup`	Shows whether users are allowed to sign up for a demo portal. (Y/N)
`DisableUsersOnline`	Shows whether the UsersOnline scheduler tasks are disabled. (Y/N)
`EnableModuleOnlineHelp`	Shows whether the online help option for modules is enabled. (Y/N)
`EventLogBuffer`	Shows whether buffering of event log entries is enabled. (Y/N)
`FileExtensions`	List of acceptable file extensions that can be uploaded to the site using any of the file upload mechanisms.
`HelpURL`	URL for online help.
`HostCurrency`	Default currency used when making payments for host services.
`HostEmail`	Email address of the portal host.
`HostFee`	The base fee for site hosting.
`HostPortalId`	ID of the default portal.
`HostSpace`	Amount of file space allowed for an account in megabytes.
`HostTitle`	Name of the hosting account. This name is used throughout the site for identifying the host.
`HostURL`	URL for the host web site.
`ModuleCaching`	Module caching method, either memory or disk (M/D).
`PaymentProcessor`	Payment processing gateway used for handling payments from client sites.

Continued

Table B-1: *(continued)*

Property Name	Description
`PerformanceSetting`	Determines the optimization level (1–4) for site performance versus memory consumption.
`ProxyPort`	Port number of the proxy server.
`ProxyServer`	Proxy server used for web requests.
`SchedulePollingRate`	Shows the interval between scheduled task execution cycles.
`SchedulerMode`	Shows which method will execute scheduled tasks in the scheduling provider.
`SiteLogBuffer`	How many items to hold in the SiteLog before purging the log to disk.
`SiteLogHistory`	Number of days of activity to keep in the SiteLog.
`SiteLogStorage`	Identifies storage location for the SiteLog (`File` or `Database`).
`SkinUpload`	Shows whether skins can be uploaded by portal administrators.
`SMTPAuthentication`	SMTP authentication method: `Anonymous`, `Basic`, or `NTLM`.
`SMTPServer`	URL of the SMTP server used for sending email messages.
`SMTPUsername`	Name of user account used for sending messages.
`UseCustomErrorMessages`	Shows whether the portal displays the standard DotNetNuke custom error messages or whether raw ASP.NET errors are shown.
`UseFriendlyUrls`	Enables or disables the URL rewriter used for implementing FriendlyURLs.
`UsersOnlineTime`	Length of the user's online buffer in minutes. If a user is inactive for this period of time, he or she will be marked as offline.

Table B-2: Standard PortalSettings Properties

Property Name	Description
`PortalId`	ID of the current portal.
`PortalName`	Name of the current portal. This name is used for branding the portal.

Continued

Table B-2: *(continued)*

Property Name	Description
`HomeDirectory`	Folder name associated with the current portal. The name is a relative path to the portal root directory.
`LogoFile`	Graphic file used for displaying the portal logo.
`FooterText`	Information displayed in the copyright skin object.
`ExpiryDate`	Date that the hosting contract for the portal expires.
`UserRegistration`	Shows whether user registration is required and whether the registration is private (accounts created by the portal administrator), public (users can register for their own account and gain immediate access), or verified (users can register their own account but only get access after verification of email address).
`BannerAdvertising`	Enables or disables use of default banner ads.
`Currency`	Default currency used for portal services.
`AdministratorId`	ID of the primary portal administrator.
`Email`	Email address for the portal administrator (this is generally set to a support email address).
`HostFee`	Monthly charge the portal pays for hosting services.
`HostSpace`	Maximum amount of disk space allocated to this web site.
`AdministratorRoleId`	RoleId of the administrator's role for the portal.
`AdministratorRoleName`	RoleName of the administrator's role for the portal.
`RegisteredRoleId`	RoleId of the registered user's role for the portal.
`RegisteredRoleName`	RoleName of the registered user's role for the portal.
`Description`	Web site description. This information will be included in the meta tags used by search engines.
`KeyWords`	Specific meta tag keywords.
`BackgroundFile`	Graphic file used for the portal background.
`SiteLogHistory`	How many days to keep the SiteLog history for the portal.

Continued

Table B-2: *(continued)*

Property Name	Description
`AdminTabId`	Page ID of the Admin page (`PageId` is the DotNetNuke 3 equivalent of `TabID`). This is the parent page for all portal administration pages.
`SuperTabId`	Page ID of the Host page. This is the parent page for all host administration pages.
`SplashTabId`	Page ID to use when no page is specified in the URL.
`HomeTabId`	Page ID to use as the portal home page. If no `SplashTabId` is designated, the `HomeTabId` is used.
`LoginTabId`	Page ID to use when the user selects the login link. This page should include the Login module.
`UserTabId`	Page ID to use when registering users or editing user profiles.
`DefaultLanguage`	Default locale of the web site. This will determine the language used when anonymous users visit the site.
`TimeZoneOffset`	Time zone where the web server is located.
`Version`	Build number for the current portal application.

Table B-3: Standard UserInfo Properties

Property Name	Description
`UserID`	Unique identifier for a specific portal user.
`Username`	Logon name of the specific user.
`FirstName`	User's first name.
`LastName`	User's last name.
`FullName`	First name and last name with a single space between.
`PortalID`	`PortalID` to which this user belongs.
`IsSuperUser`	Does the user have `Host` permissions?
`AffiliateID`	Identifies the link used to navigate to the portal. When a user follows an affiliate link and registers on the portal, a unique `AffiliateID` is then associated with the user.

Table B-4: Standard UserMembership Properties

Property Name	Description
`Password` (There are obvious security issues surrounding sending passwords in email)	User's password if available.
`Email`	Email address of the user.
`Username`	Login name of the user.
`LastLoginDate`	Last date/time the user logged in to the portal.
`CreatedDate`	Date/time when the user account was created.
`Approved`	If the user's account has been approved for access to the web site.
`LockedOut`	If the user's account has been locked due to potential security issues.

Table B-5: Standard UserProfile Properties

Property Name	Description
`FirstName`	User's first name.
`LastName`	User's last name.
`Street`	Street address.
`City`	City.
`Region`	State, province, or region for the user. Primarily used for U.S. and Canada.
`PostalCode`	Postal code for the user's mailing address.
`Country`	Country where the user lives.
`Unit`	Apartment, post office box, or suite for the user's address.
`Telephone`	Telephone number for the user.

Continued

Table B-5: *(continued)*

Property Name	Description
`Cell`	Mobile phone number.
`Fax`	Fax number.
`Website`	Personal or corporate web site for the user.
`IM`	Instant messenger contact ID.
`TimeZone`	User's default time zone. This is used for translating times from the SiteLog.
`PreferredLocale`	User's preferred locale. This determines the language used for all static content on the portal.

Index

A

B

C

E

J

K

L

X

Y

Z

oks24x7
CSS
PHP6
VB.NET 2003
VB.NET Databases
VBScript
Professional
Oracle Programming
Beginning
Visual C++ 6
Beginning
Web Programming with HTML, XHTML, and CSS
Web Standards
VBScript
2nd Edition
Beginning
XML
3rd Edition
Professional
XML Development with Apache Tools
XPath 2.0
Wrox